book

FOURTH EDITION

Other titles available from Law Society Publishing:

Age Discrimination
A Guide to the New Law
General Editor: Shaman Kapoor

Discrimination in Employment
Law and Practice
General Editor: Jenny Mulvaney

Employment Tribunals (2nd Edn)
A Practical Guide
Isabel Manley and Elaine Heslop

All books from Law Society Publishing can be ordered from all good bookshops or direct (telephone 0870 850 1422, email **lawsociety@prolog.uk.com** or visit our online shop at **www.lawsociety.org.uk/bookshop**).

EMPLOYMENT LAW HANDBOOK

FOURTH EDITION

Henry Scrope and Daniel Barnett

The Law Society

All rights reserved. No part of this publication may be reproduced in any material form, whether by photocopying, scanning, downloading onto computer or otherwise without the written permission of the Law Society and the authors except in accordance with the provisions of the Copyright, Designs and Patents Act 1988. Applications should be addressed in the first instance, in writing, to Law Society Publishing. Any unauthorised or restricted act in relation to this publication may result in civil proceedings and/or criminal prosecution.

Whilst all reasonable care has been taken in the preparation of this publication, neither the publisher nor the authors can accept any responsibility for any loss occasioned to any person acting or refraining from action as a result of relying upon its contents.

The views expressed in this publication should be taken as those of the authors only unless it is specifically indicated that the Law Society has given its endorsement.

The authors have asserted the right, under the Copyright, Designs and Patents Act 1988, to be identified as author of this work.

Crown copyright material is reproduced with the permission of the Controller of HMSO.

© Henry Scrope and Daniel Barnett 2008

ISBN 978-1-85328-674-2

First edition published in 2002
Second edition published in 2004
Third edition published in 2006
This fourth edition published in 2008 by the Law Society
113 Chancery Lane, London WC2A 1PL

Typeset by IDSUK (DataConnection) Ltd
Printed by MPG Books Ltd, Bodmin, Cornwall

PEFC
PEFC/16-33-111
CATG-PEFC-052
www.pefc.org

Text printed on PEFC accredited material

Contents

Preface xi
Abbreviations xiv
Table of cases xvi
Table of statutes xliv
Table of statutory instruments liii
Table of European legislation lxviii

1 Background and overview 1

   1.1   Brief outline history of modern British employment law   1
   1.2   Codes of practice   13
   1.3   Unfair dismissal and wrongful dismissal   15

2 Categories of worker 20

   2.1   Why it matters   20
   2.2   Contracts of employment   23
   2.3   Specific types of workers: how they fit in   26
   2.4   The future   34

3 Contracts of employment 35

   3.1   General information   35
   3.2   Where do contract terms come from?   36
   3.3   Common contractual terms   40
   3.4   Duties of fidelity   46
   3.5   Restrictive covenants   47
   3.6   Varying contract terms   50

4 Problems during employment 54

   4.1   General information   54
   4.2   The right to be accompanied   55

CONTENTS

	4.3	Disciplinary procedures	56
	4.4	Written statement of reasons for dismissal	58
5	**Small employers**		**60**
	5.1	General information	60
	5.2	Specific provisions	61
6	**Trade unions**		**66**
	6.1	General information	66
	6.2	Individual employment rights	69
	6.3	Miscellaneous	76
	6.4	Problem areas	77
7	**Working time and time off work**		**79**
	7.1	General information	79
	7.2	The Working Time Regulations	80
	7.3	Time off work	98
8	**Health and safety at work**		**124**
	8.1	General information	124
	8.2	Common law duties	124
	8.3	Statutory duties	125
	8.4	Specific examples	128
9	**Miscellaneous matters**		**135**
	9.1	Bank and public holidays	135
	9.2	Bullying at work	136
	9.3	Company directors	137
	9.4	Consultation	138
	9.5	Data protection	142
	9.6	Deductions from wages	143
	9.7	Diplomatic immunity	145
	9.8	Employment agencies	146
	9.9	Employers' liability insurance	148
	9.10	Flexible working	149
	9.11	Freedom of movement	150
	9.12	Guarantee payments	152

9.13	Insolvency guarantees		152
9.14	Itemised pay statements		153
9.15	Job advertisements (anti-discrimination rules)		153
9.16	Lay off and short time		154
9.17	Minimum wage		155
9.18	Notice periods		159
9.19	Overseas employment		160
9.20	Patents and inventions		162
9.21	Right not to work		163
9.22	Right to work		163
9.23	Smoking at work		164
9.24	Sunday trading		166
9.25	Whistleblowing		167
9.26	Written statement of particulars of employment		168

10 Termination of employment — 171

10.1	General information	171
10.2	Unambiguous dismissals and resignations	172
10.3	Ambiguous and heat of the moment dismissals	172
10.4	Ambiguous and heat of the moment resignations	173
10.5	Pressured resignation and ultimatums to resign	173
10.6	Constructive dismissal	174
10.7	Termination by mutual agreement	181
10.8	Frustration	182
10.9	Death and insolvency	184

11 Unfair dismissal — 187

11.1	General information	187
11.2	Qualifications	187
11.3	Exceptions	190
11.4	Capability or qualifications	199
11.5	Conduct	206
11.6	Retirement	212
11.7	Redundancy	212
11.8	Contravention of a statutory duty	212
11.9	Dismissal for some other substantial reason	213
11.10	Reasonableness of disciplinary sanctions	216
11.11	Automatically unfair dismissals	218

CONTENTS

12 Redundancy — 230

12.1	General information	230
12.2	When is an employee redundant?	230
12.3	Who argues redundancy?	232
12.4	Qualifying for a statutory redundancy payment	233
12.5	Challenging the fairness of redundancies	233
12.6	Automatically unfair reasons for redundancy	234
12.7	Unreasonable method of selection	234
12.8	Consultation	236
12.9	Establishing the pool of redundancy candidates	241
12.10	The selection process	242
12.11	Suitable alternative employment	245
12.12	Bumping	248
12.13	Time off work	249
12.14	Appeals	249

13 Transfer of undertakings — 250

13.1	Introduction	250
13.2	Differences between TUPE 1981 and TUPE 2006	252
13.3	Continuity of employment	253
13.4	Information and consultation (employees)	254
13.5	Information and consultation (between employers)	256
13.6	Changes to terms of employment on transfer of ownership	257
13.7	Dismissal connected with a TUPE transfer	258
13.8	What undertakings and transfers are covered?	259
13.9	What rights and obligations are transferred?	263
13.10	Who can benefit?	264
13.11	Opting out	265
13.12	Pensions	265
13.13	Insolvent companies	266
13.14	Public sector	267

14 Sex and race discrimination — 270

14.1	General information	270
14.2	Qualifications for bringing a claim	273
14.3	Direct discrimination	278
14.4	Indirect discrimination	285
14.5	Harassment	291
14.6	Questionnaires	292

14.7	Defences and exemptions	293
14.8	Positive discrimination	298
14.9	Vicarious responsibility	298
14.10	Part-time workers	300

15 Disability discrimination — 301

15.1	General information	301
15.2	What is a 'disability'?	303
15.3	What is discrimination under DDA 1995?	310
15.4	Who is protected?	311
15.5	What are they protected against?	312
15.6	Reasonable adjustments	313
15.7	Defence of justification	316
15.8	Comparators	317
15.9	Time limits	320
15.10	Vicarious liability	320
15.11	Victimisation	321
15.12	Remedies	321
15.13	Advertisements	322

16 Other categories of discrimination — 324

16.1	Age discrimination	324
16.2	Discrimination on grounds of religion or belief	334
16.3	Discrimination on grounds of sexual orientation	340
16.4	Fixed-term employees	345
16.5	Part-time workers	346

17 Equal pay and terms of employment — 350

17.1	Background	350
17.2	Recent importance of the Equal Pay Act	352
17.3	Equal Pay Act basics	354
17.4	Comparators	355
17.5	Extended meaning of 'pay'	356
17.6	Defences	359
17.7	What is 'like work'?	361
17.8	Procedure and time limits	361
17.9	Wrongful deduction from wages claims	365
17.10	And finally...	367

CONTENTS

18	**Wrongful dismissal**		**368**
	18.1	General information	368
	18.2	Remedies	373
	18.3	Time limits	378
	18.4	Mitigation of loss	379

19	**Remedies and compensation**		**383**
	19.1	Introduction	383
	19.2	Unfair dismissal	383
	19.3	Discrimination	400

20	**Time limits, procedure and settlement**		**405**
	20.1	General information	405
	20.2	Time limits	405
	20.3	Tribunal procedures	413
	20.4	Compromise of claims	421

	Appendices		**426**
	A	Employment tribunal addresses	426
	B	Legislative changes in progress	433
	C	Main employment law related Bills before Parliament	436
	D	Postscript: important developments between 1 July 2008 and 1 October 2008	439

Index	449

x

Preface

The previous (third) edition of this book was based on law at 1 September 2005. This latest (fourth) edition is based on law at 1 July 2008, with an addendum of further developments known at 1 October 2008 (see **Appendices C** and **D**). However, employment law is a fast moving subject and care should be taken to check that any particular comment is still current.

In addition to developments in the law which have made it necessary to update this book, it is probably fair to say that the single biggest change since the last edition is the increased use of the Internet by lawyers generally. As a general rule we have now caught up with, and sometimes even overtaken, at least our younger children in computer use. The Internet, and intranets, have now developed into normal mainstream tools for lawyers wishing to access source material and other information.

It would be hard to overemphasise the significance of the Statute Law Database (SLD). The Ministry of Justice made this available online for public use on 20 December 2006. From the point of view of a user wishing to consult Acts of Parliament the main differences between the SLD and the OPSI (Office of Public Sector Information) website is that the SLD provides the updated text of most statutes from the middle ages to date whereas the OPSI site generally provides only the wording as at the date of enactment. Unimportant, but demonstrating that the SLD is not yet fully comprehensive, is the fact that the 1563 Statute of Artificers, which provided legal protection for apprentices in the reign of Elizabeth I, is not there. Much more important is that users should be aware that, as at 1 July 2008, the SLD version of the Employment Rights Act 1996 was not up to date. However, the updating process is ongoing. No doubt relatively minor errors and omissions will gradually be sorted and this enormous and very valuable project is clearly destined to become one of the ordinary day-to-day tools used by British lawyers.

Other important IT developments include the advance of BAILII (the British and Irish Legal Information Institute), now wholly independent of its original parent, AUSTLII, the Australian Legal Information Institute. The collection of full text judgments on BAILII, sourced from a wide variety of courts and tribunals, is growing all the time and is now huge. For employment lawyers, even though the Employment Appeal Tribunal revamped its website

PREFACE

in Spring 2008, it seems to us that the copies of EAT judgments provided on the BAILII website are easier to use than the EAT's own versions. In addition, BAILII also provides a mass of other source material including full text judgments of decisions from major courts such as the European Court of Justice (ECJ) and the European Court of Human Rights (ECHR) as well as British courts.

As the Internet has developed into a mainstream tool for lawyers so locating relevant source and other material without being swamped by irrelevant items has become a major problem – a search using an Internet search engine such as Google for a general term such as 'employment law' will produce over 15 million results and even a search for a technical phrase such as 'compulsory maternity leave' or 'protective award' provides several thousand results. We believe that another important development for employment lawyers is the recent introduction of an Internet search engine designed specifically for those who wish to find British employment law information from the web. This is the ELISE search tool provided on the **www.emplaw.co.uk** website (with which one of the authors of this book, who must declare an interest, is closely associated).

This book presents employment law in a practical format which we hope is easy to follow. At the same time it provides precise references. Our hope is that this format will help general practitioners who require an overview of the subject and provide pointers for further research. At the same time we hope it will serve as a simple aide mémoire for specialist practitioners whose prime need is to locate source material quickly and easily. While self-contained and free standing this book is one of a series of practical handbooks published by the Law Society (see page ii for more information).

Employment law embraces both collective labour law (for example, trade union rights) and individual employment law (for example, dismissal, discrimination and maternity rights). This book is primarily concerned with individual employment law although consideration is given to aspects of collective labour law which overlap with individual employment law or have a direct effect on individuals (see in particular **Chapter 6**). However, this is not a book on trade union law or the law of industrial relations.

This book is concerned with employment law in England and Wales. While it does not cover the position in Scotland or Northern Ireland as a general rule employment law in those countries is the same as in England and Wales although there are important differences, notably in relation to law enforcement. Reference is occasionally made to the more obvious differences but we do not attempt, and are not competent, to deal with those aspects of UK employment law which are exclusively Scottish or Northern Irish. It should be noted that since October 2004 the same rules of procedure have applied to employment tribunals in both England and Wales on the one hand and Scotland on the other (Employment Tribunals (Constitution and Rules of Procedure) Regulations 2004, SI 2004/1861).

For those wishing to have a comprehensive insight into the differences between employment law in England and Wales on the one hand and Scotland on the other, we would recommend downloading a copy of a paper presented by Brian Napier QC to the Glasgow Conference of the Council of Employment Tribunal Chairmen on 19 April 2008 entitled 'British Employment Law – does it exist' (available for download from **www.emplaw.co.uk/lshandbook**). According to Peter Grant-Hutchison, a Scottish advocate practising employment law, the differences between the two jurisdictions nowadays are as much cultural as substantive. In particular he has pointed out that Scottish tribunals have been more cautious than those in England in the matter of costs/expenses but suggests that increased involvement of English solicitors north of the border, either directly or through the instruction of Scottish counsel, is leading to increased harmonisation in this area.

As noted above, the law in this book is stated as at 1 July 2008 with an addendum of further developments as at 1 October 2008 at **Appendix D**.

Henry Scrope
Daniel Barnett
1 July 2008

Abbreviations

Acas	Advisory, Conciliation and Arbitration Service
AML	additional maternity leave
CAC	Central Arbitration Committee
DDA 1995	Disability Discrimination Act 1995
EAT	Employment Appeal Tribunal
ECHR	European Court of Human Rights
ECJ	European Court of Justice
EDT	effective date of termination
EE(RB)R 2003	Employment Equality (Religion or Belief) Regulations 2003, SI 2003/1660
EE(SO)R 2003	Employment Equality (Sexual Orientation) Regulations 2003, SI 2003/1661
EHRC	Equality and Human Rights Commission
EqPA 1970	Equal Pay Act 1970
ERA 1996	Employment Rights Act 1996
ET(CRP)R 2004	Employment Tribunal (Constitution and Rules of Procedure) Regulations 2004, SI 2004/1861
ETO	economic, technical or organisational
FTER 2002	Fixed-Term Employees (Prevention of Less Favourable Treatment) Regulations 2002, SI 2002/2034
HMRC	HM Revenue & Customs
HSWA 1974	Health and Safety at Work etc. Act 1974
MHSWR 1999	Management of Health and Safety at Work Regulations 1999, SI 1999/3242
NI	national insurance
NMW	national minimum wage
OML	ordinary maternity leave
OPSI	Office of Public Sector Information
PAL 2002	Paternity and Adoption Leave Regulations 2002, SI 2002/2788

PTWR 2000	Part-Time Workers (Prevention of Less Favourable Treatment) Regulations 2000, SI 2000/1551
RRA 1976	Race Relations Act 1976
SAP	Statutory adoption pay
SDA 1975	Sex Discrimination Act 1975
SLD	Statute Law Database
SMP	statutory maternity pay
TULRCA 1992	Trade Union and Labour Relations (Consolidation) Act 1992
TUPE 1981	Transfer of Undertakings (Protection of Employment) Regulations 1981, SI 1981/1794
TUPE 2006	Transfer of Undertakings (Protection of Employment) Regulations 2006, SI 2006/246
WTR 1998	Working Time Regulations 1998, SI 1998/1833

Table of cases

A v. B [2003] IRLR 405, EAT 57
Abadeh v. British Telecom plc [2001] ICR 156, EAT 307
Abbey Cars (West Horndon) Ltd v. Ford, unreported, 23 May 2008, EAT 180
ABC News Intercontinental Inc. v. Gizbert, unreported,
    21 August 2006, EAT 223
Abler v. Sodexho Catering Gesellschaft mbH [2004] IRLR 168, ECJ 260
Abrahams v. Performing Rights Society Ltd [1995] ICR 1028, CA 380
Ackinclose v. Gateshead Council [2005] IRLR 79, EAT 39
Adamson v. B & L Cleaning Services Ltd [1995] IRLR 193, EAT 210
Addis v. Gramophone Co. Ltd [1909] AC 488, HL 374
Addison v. Babcock FATA Ltd [1987] ICR 805, CA 381, 392
Addison (t/a Brayton News) v. Ashby [2003] ICR 667 94
ADI (UK) Ltd v. Willer [2001] IRLR 542, CA 261
Afzal v. Europackaging Ltd, unreported, 25 October 2006, EAT 75
Agrico UK Ltd v. Amanda Ireland, unreported, 10 August 2005, EAT 408
Air Canada v. Lee [1978] IRLR 392 181
Airbus UK Ltd v. Webb [2008] ICR 561, CA 218
Airbus UK Ltd v. Wilson, unreported, 25 April 2006, EAT 373
AirFix Footwear Ltd v. Cope [1978] ICR 1210 24
Alabaster v. Barclays Bank plc and Secretary of State for Social
    Security [2005] EWCA Civ 508; [2005] ICR 1246 .... 144, 365
Alabaster v. Woolwich plc [2005] ICR 1246, CA 356
Alamo Group v. Tucker [2003] ICR 829, EAT 255
Albion Automotive v. Walker [2002] EWCA Civ 946 233
Alexander v. Home Office [1988] IRLR 396; [1988] ICR 685, CA 322, 402
Alexander v. Standard Telephones and Cables Ltd (No. 2) [1991]
    IRLR 286, HC 38, 67
Ali v. Christian Salvesen Food Services Ltd [1997] ICR 25, CA 40
Allan Janes LLP v. Johal [2006] ICR 742, ChD 49
Allders Department Stores (in administration), Re [2005] ICR 87, ChD 185
Allen v. Amalgamated Construction Co. Ltd [2000] ICR 436, ECJ 251
Allen v. GMB [2008] EWCA Civ 810, [2008] IRLR 690,
    CA 448
Allen v. Robles [1969] 1 WLR 1193 181
Alliance & Leicester plc v. Kidd, unreported, 13 April 2007, EAT 409
Alliance Paper Group v. Prestwich [1996] IRLR 25, HC 48

TABLE OF CASES

Allonby v. Accrington & Rossendale College [2001] ICR 1189, CA 355
Alstom Traction Ltd v. Birkenhead, unreported, 17 June 2002, EAT 249
Alvis Vickers Ltd v. Lloyd, unreported, 5 August 2005, EAT 248, 249
American Cyanamid Co. v. Ethicon Ltd [1975] AC 396, HL 163, 374
Amicus v. GBS Tooling Ltd [2005] IRLR 683 399
Amicus v. Nissan Motor Manufacturing (UK) Ltd, unreported,
    26 July 2005, EAT 239
Anderson v. George S Hall Ltd, unreported, 3 March 2006, EAT 410
Anderson v. Jarvis Hotels plc, unreported, 30 May 2006, EAT 83, 157
Angestelltenbetriebsrat der Wiener Gebietskrankenkasse v. Wiener
    Gebietskrankenkasse (Case C-309/97) [2000] ICR 1134, ECJ 361
Aniagwu v. Hackney LBC [1999] IRLR 303 410
Annandale Engineering v. Samson [1994] IRLR 59, EAT 196
Anya v. University of Oxford [2001] ICR 847, CA 284
AON Training Ltd v. Dore [2005] EWCA Civ 411 392
Apex Masonry Contractors Ltd v. Everitt, unreported, 26 September 2005, EAT 90
Appiah v. Bishop Douglass RC High School [2007] IRLR 264, CA 284
Appleyard v. Smith (Hull) Ltd [1972] IRLR 19 212
Application for Judicial Review by the Christian Institute [2008]
    IRLR 36, NIQB 340
Aptuit (Edinburgh) Ltd v. Kennedy, unreported, 4 July 2007, EAT 389
Archibald v. Fife Council [2004] ICR 954, HL 246, 315
Argyll Training Ltd v. Sinclair; and Argyll and The Islands
    Enterprise Ltd [2000] IRLR 630, EAT 261
Arqiva Ltd v. Sagoo, unreported, 22 March 2007, EAT 58
Asda Stores Ltd v. Kauser, unreported, 28 September 2007, EAT 408
Asda Stores Ltd v. Malyn, unreported, 6 March 2001, EAT 218
Ashcroft v. Haberdashers Aske's Boys School [2008] IRLR 375, EAT 409
Asif v. Key People Ltd, unreported, 7 March 2008, EAT 144
ASLEF v. United Kingdom [2007] IRLR 361, ECHR 67, 70, 438
Aspden v. Webbs Poultry & Meat Group (Holdings) Ltd [1996] IRLR 521 .....99, 182
Astle v. Cheshire CC [2004] IRLR 12 261
Atabo v. Kings College London [2007] EWCA Civ 324 284
Atkins v. Coyle Personnel plc [2008] IRLR 420, EAT 110, 172–3, 226
Atos Origin IT Services UK Ltd v. Haddock [2005] ICR 277, EAT 403
Attorney General v. Blake [2001] IRLR 36, HL 376
Attridge Law v. Coleman [2007] IRLR 88, EAT *see also* Coleman v.
    Attridge Law 312
Auguste Noel v. Curtis [1990] IRLR 326, EAT 218
Awotona v. South Tyneside Healthcare NHS Trust [2005] ICR 958, CA 386
Aylward v. Glamorgan Holiday Hotels, unreported, 5 February 2003, EAT 231
Aziz v. Republic of Yemen [2005] ICR 1391, CA 146
Azmi v. Kirlees MBC [2007] ICR 1154, EAT 290, 339
B v. A, unreported, 9 January 2007, EAT 279
B v. A, unreported, 3 April 2007, EAT (Scotland) 208, 216
B v. BAA plc [2005] ICR 1530; [2005] IRLR 927, EAT 215
Babula v. Waltham Forest College [2007] ICR 1026, CA 168, 213
Bainbridge v. Westinghouse Brake & Signal Co. Ltd [1966] 1 ITR 55 246

xvii

TABLE OF CASES

Bakersfield Entertainment Ltd v. Church and Stuart, unreported,
    4 November 2005, EAT 194
Balamoody v. UK Central Council for Nursing, Midwifery and Health
    Visiting [2002] IRLR 288, CA 278
Baldwin v. Brighton and Hove City Council [2007] IRLR 232, EAT 41
Balfour Kilpatrick Ltd v. Acheson [2003] IRLR 683, EAT 223
Bamgbose v. Royal Star and Garter Home, unreported,
    26 November 1996, EAT 194
Bamsey v. Albon Engineering Ltd [2004] EWCA Civ 359 89
Banks v. Ablex Ltd [2005] IRLR 357, CA 137
Barber v. Guardian Royal Exchange Assurance Group [1990] ICR 616, ECJ 357
Barber v. RJB Mining (UK) Ltd [1999] ICR 679, QBD 37, 80, 97
Barber v. Somerset CC [2004] ICR 457, HL 125, 133
Barber v. Staffordshire CC [1996] ICR 379, CA 408
Barclays Bank v. Kapur [1991] ICR 208, HL 409
Bari v. Hashi, unreported, 27 February 2004, EAT 334
Barke v. SEETEC Business Technology Centre Ltd [2005] IRLR 633, CA 3
Barke v. SEETEC Business Technology Centre Ltd, unreported,
    13 January 2006, EAT 42, 179, 369
Barker v. Corus (UK) plc [2006] ICR 809 ....128, 129
Barker v. Westbridge International, unreported, 8 June 2000, EAT 309
Barlow v. Broxbourne BC [2003] EWHC 50 QB 133
Barry v. Midland Bank plc [1999] IRLR 581, HL 290
Bartholomew v. Hackney LBC [1999] IRLR 246, CA 43
Barton v. Investec Henderson Crosthwaite Securities Ltd [2003] IRLR 332 283
Bass v. Travis Perkins Trading Co. Ltd, unreported, 15 December 2005, EAT 181
Bass Leisure Ltd v. Thomas [1994] IRLR 104 245
Bateman v. British Leyland (UK) Ltd [1974] ICR 403, NIRC 384
Bauman v. Hulton Press Ltd [1952] 2 All ER 1121 163
Bayoomi v. British Railways Board [1981] IRLR 431 290
BBC v. Beckett [1983] IRLR 43, EAT 43
BBC Scotland v. Souster [2001] IRLR 150 276
BCCI v. Ali [1999] IRLR 226, HC 41
Beales v. Secretary of State for Work and Pensions, unreported,
    18 September 2006, EAT 305
Beart v. HM Prison Service (No. 2) [2005] IRLR 568, CA 313
Beasley v. National Grid [2008] EWCA Civ 742 406
Beauvale Furnishings Ltd v. Chapman [2001] Emp LR 501 195
Beckmann v. Dynamco Whicheloe MacFarlane Ltd [2003] ICR 50, ECJ 265, 266
Beedell v. West Ferry Printers [2000] IRLR 650, EAT 211
Beevor v. Humberside Fire Brigade, unreported, 19 November 2003, EAT 174
Bell v. Governing Body of Grampian Primary School, unreported,
    24 August 2007, EAT 395
Bell v. Lever Brothers [1932] AC 161, HL 41
Benton v. Sanderson Kayser Ltd [1989] IRLR 19, CA 247
Bentwood Bros (Manchester) Ltd v. Shepherd [2003] IRLR 364, CA 391, 392
Bernadone v. Pall Mall Services Group Ltd [2001] ICR 197, CA 263
BG plc v. O'Brien [2001] IRLR 496, EAT 178

TABLE OF CASES

Biggs v. Somerset CC [1996] ICR 364, CA 407, 408
Bilka-Kaufhaus GmbH v. Weber von Hartz [1987] ICR 110, ECJ 358
Birch & Humber v. University of Liverpool [1985] IRLR 165, CA 181
Birmingham City Council v. Jaddoo, unreported, 28 October 2004, EAT 391
Blake Envelopes v. Cromie [2005] IRLR 535 415
Bland v. Sparkes (1999) *The Times*, 17 December 211
Bleuse v. MBT Transport Ltd [2008] IRLR 264, EAT 161, 408
Bloxham v. Freshfields Bruckhaus Deringer, unreported, 9 October 2007,
 London Central ET 329
Blue Star Ship Management Ltd v. Williams [1979] IRLR 16 200
Bombardier Aerospace-Shorts Brothers plc v. McConnell [2008] IRLR 51,
 CA (NI) 398
Bouchaala v. Trusthouse Forte Hotels Ltd [1980] IRLR 382, EAT 213
Boulting v. ACTAT [1963] 1 All ER 716 69
Boyo v. Lambeth LBC [1994] ICR 727, CA 374
Boys & Girls Welfare v. McDonald [1997] ICR 693, EAT 210
Bracebridge Engineering v. Darby [1990] IRLR 3, EAT 41
Bradburn v. Great Western Rail Co. (1874) LR 10 Ex 1 375
Bradford Hospitals NHS Trust v. Al-Shabib [2003] IRLR 4, EAT 276
Brandon and Goold v. Murphy Bros [1983] IRLR 54 210
Breach v. Epsylon Industries Ltd [1976] ICR 316, EAT 164
Brett v. University of Reading [2007] EWCA Civ 88 129
Bridges v. Industrial Rubber plc, unreported, 21 September 2004, EAT 29, 157
Brigden v. American Express Bank Ltd [2000] IRLR 94 ....23, 37
Briggs v. Oates [1990] IRLR 473 184
British Aerospace plc v. Green [1995] IRLR 433, CA 244
British Airways (European Operations at Gatwick) v. Moore and
 Botterill [2000] ICR 678, EAT 360
British Coal Corp. v. Smith [1996] ICR 515, HL 363
British Gas Services Ltd v. McCaull [2001] IRLR 60, EAT 314
British Home Stores v. Burchell [1980] ICR 303, EAT 206, 207
British Steel plc's Patent, Re [1992] RPC 117 162
British Steel plc v. Simmons [2004] ICR 585, HL 402, 403
British Sugar plc v. Kirker [1998] IRLR 624, EAT 322
British Telecommunications plc v. Pousson, unreported,
 5 August 2005, EAT 305
British Telecommunications plc v. Roberts [1996] IRLR 601, EAT 286
British Transport Commission v. Gourley [1955] 3 All ER 796, HL 376
British Westinghouse Electric and Manufacturing Co. Ltd v. Underground
 Electric Railways Co. of London Ltd [1912] AC 673, HL 380
Britool v. Roberts [1993] IRLR 481 118
Brodie v. Ward (t/a First Steps Nursery), unreported, 7 February 2008, EAT 176
Brookes v. Borough Care Services [1998] ICR 1198, EAT 251
Brooks v. Olyslager OMS (UK) Ltd [1998] IRLR 590, CA 46
Brown v. Croydon LBC [2007] ICR 909, CA 284
Brown v. Rentokil Ltd (Case C-394/96) [1998] IRLR 445, ECJ 282
Buck v. Nottinghamshire Healthcare NHS Trust [2006] EWCA Civ 1576 ....44, 125
Budgen & Co. v. Thomas [1976] IRLR 174, EAT 57

xix

TABLE OF CASES

Bull v. Nottinghamshire and City of Nottingham Fire and Rescue
  Authority [2007] ICR 1631, CA 45
Bullock v. Alice Ottley School [1993] ICR 138, CA 290, 325
Bunce v. Postworth Ltd (t/a Skyblue) [2005] IRLR 557, CA 23, 25, 44, 146
Bunning v. GT Bunning & Sons Ltd [2005] EWCA Civ 983 ....174, 180, 369
Burke v. British Council; ADT Fire & Security plc v. Speyer; Cameron v.
  Navy, Army and Air Force Institutes, unreported,
  14 December 2006, EAT 198, 199
Burton v. Glycosynth Ltd, unreported, 11 February 2005 173
Burton & Rhule v. De Vere Hotels [1997] ICR 1, EAT 299
Butlins Skyline Ltd and Smith v. Beynon [2007] ICR 121, EAT 414
Byrne Brothers (Formwork) Ltd v. Baird [2002] IRLR 96; [2002]
  ICR 667, EAT 23, 25, 81
CAB Automotive Ltd v. Blake and Singh, unreported, 12 February 2008, EAT 221
Cable & Wireless plc v. Muscat [2006] IRLR 354, CA 26, 28
Cairns v. Visteon UK Ltd [2007] IRLR 175, EAT 27, 146
Calder & Ciakowsky v. Rowntree Mackintosh Confectionery Ltd [1993]
  ICR 811, CA 360
Cambridge & District Co-operative Society Ltd v. Ruse [1993] IRLR 156, EAT 245
Camden & Islington Mental Health and Social Care Trust v. Atkinson,
  unreported, 20 August 2007, EAT 155
Camden LBC v. Price-Job, unreported, 4 July 2007, EAT 314
Campbell v. Frisbee [2003] ICR 141, CA 47
Campbell v. Union Carbide Ltd [2002] Emp LR 1267, EAT 176
Campbell and Cosans v. United Kingdom (1982) 4 EHRR 293, ECHR 336
Cantor Fitzgerald International v. Bird [2002] IRLR 867, HC 41
Cape Industrial Services Ltd v. Ambler [2002] EWCA Civ 1264 ....175, 370
Capek v. Lincolnshire CC [2000] ICR 878, CA 379
Capita Health Solutions v. BBC and McLean [2008] IRLR 595, EAT 265
Capital Foods Retail v. Corrigan [1993] IRLR 430, EAT 409
Carden v. Pickerings Europe Ltd [2005] IRLR 720, EAT 307
Carmarthen & Pumsaint Farmers Ltd v. Evans, unreported,
  12 October 2007, EAT 408
Carmichael v. National Power plc [2000] IRLR 43; [1999] ICR 1226, HL 20, 23
Cast v. Croydon College [1998] ICR 500, CA 409
Catamaran Cruisers Ltd v. Williams [1994] IRLR 386 ....26, 214
Caulfield v. Hanson Clay Products Ltd (formerly Marshalls Clay
  Products Ltd) [2006] IRLR 386 91
Cave v. Goodwin [2001] EWCA Civ 391, CA 307
Celtec Ltd v. Astley [2006] ICR 992, HL 253, 420
Centrum voor Gelijkheid van Kansen en voor Racismebestrijding v. Firma Feryn
  NV (Case C54107) ECJ 154
Cerberus Software Ltd v. Rowley [2001] ICR 376, CA 381
CH Giles & Co. Ltd v. Morris [1972] 1 All ER 960 163
Chacón Navas v. Eurest Colectividades SA (Case C-13/05)
  [2007] ICR 1, ECJ 303
Chandlers (Farm Equipment) Ltd v. Rainthorpe, unreported,
  8 February 2005, EAT 215

Charles Robertson v. White [1995] ICR 349, EAT 395
Cheesman v. Brewer Contracts [2001] IRLR 144, EAT 260
Chief Constable of Avon and Somerset v. Chew [2001] All ER 101; [2002]
  Emp LR 370 ....286, 287
Chief Constable of Bedfordshire Police v. Liversidge [2002] EWCA Civ 894 299
Chief Constable of Greater Manchester Police v. Hope [1999] ICR 338, EAT 280
Chief Constable of Lincolnshire Police v. Stubbs [1999] IRLR 81, EAT 292, 299
Chief Constable of Lincolnshire Police v. Weaver, unreported,
  12 March 2008, EAT 314
Chief Constable of Norfolk v. Arthurton, unreported, 6 December 2006, EAT 273
Chief Constable of West Yorkshire Police v. Khan [2001] IRLR 830, HL 272
Chief Constable of West Yorkshire Police v. Vento [2001] IRLR 124, EAT 279, 310
Chohan v. Derby Law Centre [2004] IRLR 685, EAT 410
Christie v. DCA [2007] ICR 1553, EAT 348
Chronos Richardson Ltd v. Watson, unreported, 27 March 2001, EAT 240
Church v. West Lancashire NHS Trust [1998] IRLR 4, EAT 248
Clamp v. Aerial Systems, unreported, 6 October 2004, EAT 85
Clancy v. Cannock Chase Technical College [2001] IRLR 331, EAT 384
Clapson v. British Airways [2001] IRLR 184, EAT 3
Clark v. Clark Construction Initiatives Ltd [2008] IRLR 364, EAT 33, 137
Clark v. Nomura International plc [2000] IRLR 766, QBD 377
Clark v. Novacold [1999] ICR 951, CA 318, 319
Clark Tokeley Ltd (t/a Spell Brook Ltd) v. Oakes [1999] ICR 276, CA 253
Clarke v. Arriva Kent Thameside Ltd, unreported, 25 July 2001, EAT 417
Clarke v. Frank Staddon Ltd (Case C-257/04), ECJ 91
Clarke v. Frank Staddon Ltd [2006] EWCA Civ 1470 92
Clarks of Hove Ltd v. Bakers Union [1978] ICR 1076, CA 237
Coales v. John Wood & Co. [1986] ICR 71, EAT 153
Cobley v. Forward Technology Industries plc [2003] ICR 1050, CA 215
Coca-Cola Enterprises Ltd v. Shergill, unreported, 2 September 2002, EAT 303
Coker & Osamor v. Lord Chancellor [2002] ICR 321, CA 154
Cold Drawn Tubes Ltd v. Middleton [192] ICR 318, EAT 384
Colegio de Ingenieros de Caminos, Canales y Puertos v. Administracion del
  Estado (Case C-330/03), ECJ 151
Coleman v. Attridge Law (Case C-303/06) [2008] IRLR 722, ECJ 441
Coleman v. S & W Baldwin [1977] IRLR 342 176
Colen v. Cebrian (UK) Ltd [2004] ICR 568, CA 36, 196
Colley v. Corkindale [1995] ICR 964, EAT 30
Collidge v. Freeport plc [2008] EWCA Civ 485 423
Collier v. Sunday Referee Publishing Co Ltd [1940] 2 KB 647 44
Collino v. Telecom Italia SpA (Case C-343/98) [2000] IRLR 788, ECJ 258
Collins v. Royal National Theatre Board Ltd [2004] IRLR 395, CA 317
Collins & Ashbourne v. Department of Constitutional Affairs, unreported,
  12 October 2007, EAT 161, 328
Collison v. BBC [1998] IRLR 238, EAT 386
Commerzbank AG v. Keen [2007] IRLR 132, CA 37, 42
Commission v. United Kingdom (Case 61/81) [1982] ICR 578, ECJ 297, 352
Commission v. United Kingdom (Case C-484/04) [2006] IRLR 888, ECJ 84, 93

TABLE OF CASES

Commission for Racial Equality v. Dutton [1989] IRLR 8, CA 277
Commotion Ltd v. Rutty [2006] IRLR 171, EAT 150
Computershare Investor Services plc v. Jackson [2008] IRLR 70, CA 253
Conn v. Sunderland City Council [2007] EWCA Civ 1492 137
Consignia plc v. Sealy [2002] IRLR 624 ....406, 409
Consistent Group Ltd v. Kalwak [2008] IRLR 505, CA; [2007] IRLR 560, EAT 27
Converfoam (Darwen) Ltd v. Bell [1981] IRLR 193, EAT 204
Cook v. Thomas Linnell & Sons Ltd [1977] IRLR 132 201
Cooper v. Isle of Wight College [2008] IRLR 124, QBD....................144
Coors Brewers v. Adcock [2007] ICR 983, CA............................372
Copsey v. WWB Devon Clays Ltd [2005] IRLR 811; [2005] ICR 1789, CA 216, 335
Cortest Ltd v. O'Toole, unreported, 7 November 2007, EAT 116
Corus & Regal Hotels plc v. Wilkinson, unreported, 28 June 2004, EAT 231
Corus Hotels plc v. Williams, unreported, 28 June 2006, EAT 246
Corus UK Ltd v. AM Mainwaring, unreported, 22 June 2007, EAT 212
Cosgrove v. Caesar & Howie [2001] IRLR 653, EAT 310
Costain Building & Engineering v. Smith [2000] ICR 215 26
Courtaulds Northern Spinning Ltd v. Sibson & TGWU [1988] IRLR 305 177
Coutts & Co. plc v. Cure & Fraser [2005] ICR 1098, EAT 346
Cow v. Surrey and Berkshire Newspapers Ltd, unreported, 7 March 2003, EAT 181
Cowen v. Rentokil Initial Facility Services (UK) Ltd (t/a Initial Transport
  Services), unreported, 6 March 2008, EAT........................382, 393
Cowley v. Manson Timber Ltd [1995] IRLR 153, CA......................383
Cox v. Post Office, unreported, IT/1301162/97...........................304
Cox v. Sun Alliance [2001] IRLR 448, CA................................43
Crampton v. Dacorum Motors Ltd [1975] IRLR 168 205
Cranswick Country Foods plc v. Beall [2007] ICR 691, EAT 399
Crawford v. Swinton Insurance Brokers Ltd [1990] IRLR 42, EAT 53
Credit Suisse First Boston (Europe) Ltd v. Lister [1999] ICR 794, CA 258
Cresswell v. Inland Revenue [1984] ICR 508, HC......................45, 370
Croal v. Network Rail Infrastructure Ltd, unreported, 28 February 2008, EAT 309
Croft v. Royal Mail Group plc [2003] EWCA Civ 1045 275
Croke v. Hydro Aluminium Worcester Ltd [2007] ICR 1303, EAT 168
Crossley v. Faithful and Gould Holdings [2004] ICR 1615, CA 42
Crown Suppliers (PSA) Ltd v. Dawkins [1993] ICR 517, CA 277
Cruickshank v. VAW Motorcast Ltd [2002] ICR 729, EAT 309
Crystal Palace FC (2000) Ltd v. Dowie [2007] IRLR 682, QBD 423
Cumbria CC v. Carlisle-Morgan [2007] IRLR 314, EAT 300
Curr v. Marks & Spencer [2003] IRLR 74 188
Dacas v. Brook Street Bureau (UK) Ltd [2004] IRLR 358; [2004]
  ICR 1437, CA 27, 146
Dal v. Orr [1980] IRLR 413 39
Danlardy v. Southwark Race Equalities Council, unreported,
  19 May 2006, EAT 220
Darling v. ME Ilic Haulage [2004] ICR 1176, EAT 386
Dashwood v. Dashwood [1927] WN 276 425
Dattani v. Chief Constable of West Mercia Police [2005] IRLR 327, EAT 293
Davidson v. Ministry of Defence, unreported, 17 June 1999, EAT 410

TABLE OF CASES

Davies v. MJ Wyatt Decorators Ltd [2000] IRLR 759, EAT 52
Davies v. Presbyterian Church of Wales [1986] ICR 280, HL 20
Dawes Cycles Ltd v. Sedgley, unreported, 12 March 1998, EAT 382, 393
Dawnay Day & Co. Ltd v. De Braconier D'Alphen [1997] IRLR 442, CA 48
Daymond v. Enterprise South Devon, unreported, 6 June 2007, EAT 195
De Grasse v. Stockwell Ltd [1992] IRLR 269, EAT 61, 241
Deadman v. Bristol City Council [2007] EWCA Civ 822 41
Deane v. Ealing LBC [1993] ICR 329, EAT 322, 402
Debtor, Re (Nos. 2021 & 2022), unreported, 20 November 1995, ChD 406
Dedman v. British Building & Engineering Appliances Ltd [1974] ICR 53, CA 408
Defrenne v. SABENA [1976] ICR 547, ECJ 353
Delabole Slate Ltd v. Berriman [1985] IRLR 305, CA 53
Delaney v. Staples [1992] ICR 483, HL 144, 371
Dench v. Flynn & Partners [1998] IRLR 653, CA 382, 393
Denco Ltd v. Joinson [1991] ICR 172, EAT 210
Dentmaster (UK) Ltd v. Kent [1997] IRLR 636, CA 49
Department for Constitutional Affairs v. Jones [2008] IRLR 128 320
Department for Environment, Food and Rural Affairs v. Robertson [2005]
    ICR 750 356
Department of Trade and Industry v. Walden [2000] IRLR 168 186
Department for Work and Pensions v. Macklin, unreported,
    28 February 2008, EAT 313–314
Department for Work and Pensions v. Webley [2005] IRLR 288, CA 345
Derby City Council v. Marshall [1979] IRLR 261 177
Devonald v. Rosser & Sons [1906] 2 KB 728 .... 40, 163
Dickie v. Cathay Pacific Airways Ltd [2004] ICR 1733, EAT 373
Digital Equipment Co. Ltd v. Clements (No. 2) [1998] ICR 258, CA;
    reversing [1997] IRLR 140, EAT 389, 393, 397
Diocese of Hallam Trustee v. Connaughton [1996] ICR 860, EAT 356
Diocese of Southwark v. Coker [1998] ICR 140, CA 31
Dixon v. Automobile Association, unreported, 20 April 2004, EAT 248, 315
DJM International Ltd v. Nicholas [1996] IRLR 76, EAT 263
Dobie v. Burns International Security Services (UK) Ltd [1984]
    ICR 812, CA 215, 216
Doherty v. British Midland Airways [2006] IRLR 90, EAT 176
Douce v. F Bond & Sons Ltd [1966] 1 ITR 365 245
Dowling & Rutter v. Abacus Frozen Foods (No. 2) 2002 SLT 491 36
Drake International (t/a Drake Ports Distribution Services) v. O'Hare,
    unreported, 2 September 2003, EAT 235
Driskel v. Peninsula Business Services Ltd [2000] IRLR 151 292
Dryden v. Greater Glasgow Health Board [1992] IRLR 469, EAT 39
D'Silva v. NATFHE (University and College Union) [2008] IRLR 412, EAT 293
Duffy v. Yeomans & Partners Ltd [1994] IRLR 642, CA 245
Duncan v. Marconi Command & Control Systems Ltd, unreported, 1988, EAT 244
Dunham v. Ashford Windows [2005] IRLR 608, EAT 305
Dunnachie v. Kingston upon Hull City Council [2004]
    IRLR 727; [2004] ICR 1052, HL 134, 136, 374, 389, 394
Dunnachie v. Kingston upon Hull City Council (No. 3) [2003] IRLR 843 391

TABLE OF CASES

Dunning & Sons (Shop Fitters) v. Jacomb [1973] IRLR 206 201
Durant v. Financial Services Authority [2003] EWCA Civ 1746 143
Dynamex Friction Ltd & Ferotec Realty v. Amicus [2008] IRLR 515 264
Earl of Bradford v. Jowet (No. 2) [1978] IRLR 16 241
East Berkshire HA v. Matadeen [1992] ICR 724, EAT 210
East Lancashire Coachbuilders v. Hilton, unreported, 24 August 2006, EAT 208
East Lindsey DC v. Daubney [1977] IRLR 181 205
East Sussex CC v. Walker (1972) 7 ITR 280 174
Eastwood v. Magnox Electric plc; McCabe v. Cornwall CC [2004]
   UKHL 35; [2004] ICR 1064 .... 19, 372
Eaton v. King [1995] IRLR 75, EAT 244
Eaton Ltd v. Nuttall [1977] ICR 272, EAT 361
EB v. BA [2006] IRLR 471, CA 284, 285
ECM (Vehicle Delivery Services) Ltd v. Cox [1999] IRLR 559, CA 260
Edmonds v. Lawson [2000] ICR 567, CA 32
Edmund Nuttall Ltd v. Butterfield [2006] ICR 77; [2005] IRLR 751, EAT 304
Edwards v. Governors of Hanson School [2001] IRLR 733, EAT 204
Edwards v. Mid Suffolk DC [2001] IRLR 190, EAT 313
EFTA Surveillance Authority v. Kingdom of Norway [2003] IRLR 318 298
Egg Stores v. Leibovici [1976] IRLR 376 182
Ekpe v. Metropolitan Police Commissioner [2001] ICR 1084, EAT 306, 309
Elkouil v. Coney Island Ltd [2002] IRLR 174, EAT 239
Elliott v. Pertemps Recruitment Partnership Ltd, unreported,
   5 March 2003, EAT 308
Elliott v. Richard Stump Ltd [1987] IRLR 215 247
Elliott Turbomachinery Ltd v. Bates [1981] ICR 218 248
Ely v. YKK Fasteners Ltd [1994] ICR 164, CA 215
EMI Group Electronics Ltd v. Coldicott (HMIT) [1999] IRLR 630, CA 376
Empire Meat Co. Ltd v. Patrick [1939] 2 All ER 85, CA 49
Enderby v. Frenchay HA [1993] IRLR 591, ECJ 290
Enderby v. Frenchay HA (No. 2) [2000] ICR 612, CA 355, 363
Endres v. T-Systems International GmbH, Federal Labour Court,
   Germany 263, 264
Enessy Co. SA v. Minoprio [1978] IRLR 489 384
Enfield Technical Services Ltd v. Payne; Grace v. BF Components Ltd
   [2008] EWCA Civ 393; [2007] IRLR 840, EAT 36, 195
English v. Kwik-Save, unreported, December 2003, IT 305
English v. Thomas Sanderson Blinds Ltd [2008] IRLR 342 345
Enterprise Liverpool plc v. Bauress, unreported, 30 January 2006, EAT 209
Equal Opportunities Commission v. DTI [2007] IRLR 327, QBD 102
Essa v. Laing Ltd [2003] IRLR 346 401
Evans v. George Galloway & Co. [1974] IRLR 167 203
Evans v. Malley Organisation Ltd (t/a First Business Support) [2003]
   IRLR 156 89
Evans, Motture & Hutchins v. Permacell Finesse Ltd (in administration),
   unreported, 23 October 2007, EAT 152, 186, 399
Express & Echo Publications v. Tanton [1999] ICR 693, CA 24, 25
Eyres v. Atkinsons Kitchens and Bedrooms Ltd [2007] EWCA Civ 365 97–98

TABLE OF CASES

Ezsias v. Welsh Ministers [2007] All ER (D) 65 143
F & C Asset Management plc v. Switalski, unreported, 23 May 2008, EAT 404
Faccenda Chicken v. Fowler [1986] IRLR 69, CA 46
Fahrenheit 451 (Communications) Ltd v. Clark [2000] All ER 849, EAT 159
Fairchild v. Glenhaven Funeral Services Ltd [2002] UKHL 22 128
Fairmile Kindergarten v. Macdonald, unreported, 20 January 2006, EAT 58
Farnsworth (FW) Ltd v. McCoid [1999] ICR 1047, CA 74
Faulkner v. Hampshire Constabulary, unreported, 2 March 2007, EAT 287
FC Gardner Ltd v. Beresford [1978] IRLR 63, EAT 41, 177
FC Shepherd v. Jerrom [1986] IRLR 358, CA 182
Fearn v. Tayford Motor Co. Ltd [1975] IRLR 336 212
Federatie Nederlandse Vakbeweging v. Staat der Nederlanden (Case
    C-124/05) 6 April 2006, ECJ 90
Ferguson v. Prestwick Circuits [1992] IRLR 266 238
Ferrotech Ltd, Re [2006] ICR 205, CA 153, 185
First West Yorkshire (t/a First Leeds) v. Haigh [2008] IRLR 182, EAT 205
Fisher v. Hoopoe Finance Ltd, unreported, 13 April 2005, EAT 246
Fitzpatrick v. British Railways Board [1992] ICR 221, CA 76
Fletcher v. Clay Cross (Quarry Services) Ltd [1979] ICR 1, CA 359
Flett v. Matheson [2006] IRLR 277, CA 32
Foley v. Post Office *See* Post Office v. Foley
Ford Motor Car Co. Ltd v. Nawaz [1987] IRLR 163......................206
Foreningen v. Daddy's Dance Hall AS [1988] ECR 739, ECJ 258
Forest Mere Lodges Ltd v. Watt & Cameron, unreported, 6 February 2007, EAT 24
Forshaw v. Archcraft Ltd [2005] IRLR 600, EAT 52, 216
Forster v. Cartwright Black [2004] IRLR 781, EAT 115
Foster Bryant Surveying Ltd v. Bryant [2007] IRLR 425, CA..............47, 138
Four Seasons Healthcare Ltd v. Maughan [2005] IRLR 324, EAT 183, 203
Frames Snooker Centre v. Boyce [1992] IRLR 472, EAT 208
Frank v. Reuters Ltd [2003] IRLR 423, CA 27
Frankling v. BPS Public Sector Ltd [1999] ICR 347, EAT 266
Fraser v. HLMAD Ltd [2006] IRLR 687, CA 17, 35, 372
French v. Barclay's Bank plc [1998] IRLR 646, CA 42
FTATU v. Modgill [1980] IRLR 142, EAT 278
Fulton v. RMC Russell plc, unreported, 17 December 2003, EAT 381
Futty v. D & D Brekkes Ltd [1974] IRLR 130 172
GAB Robins (UK) Ltd v. Triggs [2008] ICR 529, CA; [2007]
    ICR 1424, EAR 42, 179, 369
Gaca v. Pirelli General plc [2004] EWCA Civ 373 375
Gallagher v. Alpha Catering Services Ltd (t/a Alpha Flight Services) [2005]
    ICR 673, CA 92
Gallier v. Lothian Buses plc, unreported, 26 August 2003, EAT (Scotland) 308
Galt and ors v. National Starch and Chemical Ltd, unreported,
    14 July 2008, ET 446
GAP Personnel Franchises Ltd v. Robinson, unreported,
    16 October 2007, EAT 52
Gardiner-Hill v. Roland Berger Technics Ltd [1982] IRLR 498 392
Garland v. British Rail Engineering [1982] ICR 420, HL 351, 357

TABLE OF CASES

Garrett Electrical Ltd v. Cotton, unreported, 15 November 2005, EAT 156
General Billposting Co. Ltd v. Atkinson [1909] AC 118, HL 47, 371
Gerster v. Freistaat Bayern [1998] ICR 327, ECJ 290
GF Sharp v. McMillan [1998] IRLR 632 182
Gibson v. British Transport Docks Board [1982] IRLR 228 395
Gibson v. East Riding of Yorkshire Council [2000] IRLR 598; [2000]
 ICR 890, CA 80, 97
Gibson (t/a Blandford House Surgery) v. Hughes, unreported,
 13 September 2006, EAT 180, 369
Gillespie v. Northern Health and SS Board [1996] ICR 498, CA 357
Gillies v. Richard Daniels & Co. Ltd [1979] IRLR 457 179
Glasgow City Council v. McNab [2007] IRLR 476, EAT 339
Glasgow City Council v. Marshall [2000] ICR 196, HL 352, 359
Glendale Managed Services Ltd v. Graham [2003] EWCA Civ 773 178
Glennie v. Independent Magazines (UK) Ltd [1999] IRLR 719, CA 420
Gloystarne & Co. Ltd v. Martin [2001] IRLR 15, EAT 423
GMB v. Allen [2007] IRLR 752, EAT see also Allen v. GMB 73, 290, 367
GMB & Amicus v. Beloit Walmsley Ltd [2003] ICR 1396, EAT 51
GMB Union v. Brown, unreported, 16 October 2007, EAT 42
Gogay v. Hertfordshire CC [2000] IRLR 703, CA 374
Goodeve v. Gilsons [1985] ICR 401, CA 197
Goodwin v. Patent Office [1999] ICR 302, EAT 306
Goodwin v. United Kingdom, 3 July 2002, ECHR 295
Gould v. Governors of Haileybury and Imperial Service College, unreported,
 19 July 2003, EAT 390
Gover v. Property Care Ltd [2006] ICR 1073, CA 421
Governing Body of Addey and Stanhope School v. Vakante [2003]
 ICR 290, EAT 274
Graham v. ABF Ltd [1986] IRLR 90 242
Graham v. Chief Constable of Bedfordshire Constabulary [2002]
 IRLR 239, EAT 275
Graham Oxley Tool Steels Ltd v. Firth [1980] IRLR 135, EAT 125, 369
Grant v. Ampex (Great Britain) Ltd [1980] IRLR 461 202
Grant v. BSS Group plc, unreported, 13 March 2003, EAT 238
Grant v. In 2 Focus Sales Development Services Ltd, unreported,
 30 January 2007, EAT 414
Grant v. South-West Trains Ltd [1998] IRLR 188, HC 39
Grant v. United Kingdom (Case 32570/03), ECHR 275
Gravell v. Bexley LBC, unreported, 2 March 2007, EAT 299
Greater Glasgow Health Board v. Carey [1987] IRLR 484, EAT 290
Greater Manchester Police Authority v. Lea [1990] IRLR 372, EAT 288
Green v. DB Group Services (UK) Ltd [2006] EWHC 1898, QB; [2006]
 IRLR 764, HC 133
Green v. Elan Care, unreported, 4 March 2002, EAT 53
Green & Son (Castings) Ltd v. ASTMS [1984] ICR 352 236
Greenhof v. Barnsley MBC [2006] IRLR 98, EAT 41
Greenwood v. Whiteghyll Plastics Ltd, unreported, 6 August 2007, EAT 216
Greig v. Initial Security, unreported, 19 October 2005, EAT 401

TABLE OF CASES

Grieg v. Community Industry [1979] ICR 356, EAT 294
Griffiths v. Perco Engineering Services, unreported, 14 March 2006, EAT 219
Griffiths v. Reading University Students Union, unreported,
    24 October 1996, EAT 276
Griffiths v. Secretary of State for Social Services [1974] QB 468 185
Grimmer v. KLM Cityhopper [2005] IRLR 596 414
Grootcon (UK) Ltd v. Keld [1984] IRLR 302 215
Gryf-Lowczowski v. Hinchingbooke Healthcare NHS Trust [2006]
    IRLR 100, QBD 164, 183
Guernina v. Thames Valley University, unreported, 21 December 2006, EAT 217
Gunton v. Richmond-upon-Thames BC [1980] ICR 755, CA 374
GUS Home Shopping Ltd v. Green & McLaughli [2001] IRLR 75, EAT 282
GW Stephens & Son v. Fish [1989] ICR 324 181
Hachette Filipacchi UK Ltd v. Johnson, unreported,
    14 December 2005, EAT 231, 237
Hackney LBC v. Adams [2003] IRLR 402 74
Hackney LBC v. Benn [1997] IRLR 157, CA............................200
Hadjioannou v. Coral Casinos Ltd [1981] IRLR 352 209
Halfpenny v. IGE Medical Systems Ltd [2001] IRLR 96, HL 219
Hall v. Woolston Hall Leisure Co. [2001] ICR 99, CA 26, 36, 195, 273
Hallett & Want v. MAT Transport Ltd [1976] IRLR 5 210
Halliday v. Archdiocese of Southwark, unreported, 5 March 2001, EAT........232
Hamilton v. Arriva Trains Northern Ltd, unreported, 4 August 2004, EAT 117
Hamling v. Coxlease School Ltd [2007] IRLR 8, EAT 414
Hammersmith & Fulham LBC v. Farnsworth [2000] IRLR 691, EAT 302, 309
Hampton v. Lord Chancellor and MoJ [2008] IRLR 258 ....191, 329
Hancill v. Marcon Engineering Ltd [1990] ICR 103, EAT 60
Handels-og v. Dansk Ag (Hertz case) [1992] ICR 332, ECJ 282
Hardman v. Mallon (t/a Orchard Lodge Nursing Home) [2002]
    IRLR 516, EAT 107, 282
Hardy v. Polk (Leeds) Ltd [2004] IRLR 420; [2005] ICR 557, EAT 393, 394
Hardys & Hansons plc v. Lax [2005] EWCA Civ 846 105
Harford v. DTI, unreported, 12 February 2008, EAT 399
Harris v. NKL Automotive and Matrix Consultancy UK Ltd, unreported,
    3 October 2007, EAT 336
Harris v. Richard Lawson Autologistics [2002] IRLR 476, CA 38
Harrison v. Kent CC [1995] ICR 434, EAT 76
Hart v. Bolton Hospitals NHS Trust, unreported, 9 March 2005, EAT 302
Hartman v. South Essex Mental Health and Community Care NHS
    Trust [2005] IRLR 293, CA 133
Harvest Town Circle v. Rutherford [2001] IRLR 599 288
Hasley v. Fair Employment Agency [1989] IRLR 106, CA 60
Haughton v. Olau Line (UK) Ltd [1985] ICR 711, EAT 161
Hauxwell v. Secretary of State for Trade and Industry, unreported,
    19 June 2002, EAT 33
Havering Primary Care Trust v. Bidwell, unreported, 22 April 2008 EAT 395
Health & Safety Executive v. Cadman [2006] ICR 1623, ECJ 359
Health Development Agency v. Parish, unreported, 24 October 2003, EAT 59

xxvii

TABLE OF CASES

Healy v. Corp. of London, unreported, 24 June 1999, EAT 67
Heatherwood & Wrexham Park Hospitals Trust v. Beer, unreported,
    14 June 2006, EAT 308
Heathrow Express Operating Co. Ltd v. Jenkins, unreported,
    9 February 2007, EAT 307, 317
Henderson v. Henderson (1843) 3 Hare 100 372
Henderson v. Masson Scott Thrissel Engineering Ltd [1974] IRLR 98 203
Hendricks v. Metropolitan Police Commissioner [2003] IRLR 96, CA 410
Hendrickson Europe Ltd v. Pipe, unreported, 15 April 2003, EAT 244
Hendy Banks City Print Ltd v. Fairbrother, unreported,
    21 December 2004, EAT 241
Hennessy v. Craigmyle & Co. Ltd [1986] ICR 461 421
Henry v. London General Transport Services Ltd [2002] IRLR 472; [2002]
    ICR 910, CA 38, 144
Hepworth Heating Ltd v. Akers, unreported, 21 January 2003, EAT 50
Herbert Clayton and Jack Waller Ltd v. Oliver [1930] AC 209, HL 44, 163
Herbert Morris Ltd v. Saxelby [1916] 1 AC 688, HL 48
Hewcastle Catering Ltd v. Ahmed & Elkamah [1992] ICR 626, CA 196
Hewett v. Motorola Ltd [2004] IRLR 545, EAT 304
Hewison v. Meridian Shipping Services Pte Ltd [2003] ICR 766, CA 378
Hewlett Packard v. O'Murphy [2002] IRLR 4 26
Hicks v. Allied Glass Containers Ltd, unreported, 25 March 2003, EAT 208
High Quality Lifestyles Ltd v. Watts [2006] IRLR 850 EAT 317
Hill v. CA Parsons [1972] Ch 305 172
Hill v. Chapell [2003] IRLR 19, EAT 90, 144
Hillingdon LBC v. Thomas (2002) *The Times*, October 4 211
Hilton International Hotels v. Protopapa [1990] IRLR 316, EAT 41, 177
Hinton v. University of East London [2005] ICR 1260, CA 422
Hivac Ltd v. Park Royal Scientific Instruments [1946] All ER 350 47
HM Prison Service v. Beart (No. 2) [2005] ICR 1206 402
HM Prison Service v. Ibimidun, unreported, 2 April 2006, EAT 272
HM Prison Service v. Potter, unreported, 14 November 2006, EAT 286
HM Prison Service v. Salmon [2001] IRLR 425, EAT 401, 402
HM Revenue and Customs v. Annabels (Berkley Square) Ltd (1)
    George (Mount Street) Ltd (2) Harry's Bar (3) [2008]
    ICR 1076, EAT 446
HM Revenue and Customs v. Rinaldi-Tranter, unreported,
    13 September 2007, EAT 156
Hodes v. Marks & Spencer, unreported, 1 November 2001. EAT 375
Hogg v. Dover College [1990] ICR 39, EAT 51
Holis Metal Industries Ltd v. GMB & Newell Ltd [2008] IRLR 187, EAT 251
Hollis & Co. v. Stocks [2000] IRLR 712, CA 49
Holmes v. Bolton MBC, unreported, December 1988, IT 305
Home Office v. Bailey [2005] EWCA Civ 327 356
Home Office v. Collins [2005] EWCA Civ 598, CA 305
Home Office v. Evans & Laidlaw [2008] IRLR 59, CA 39
Hopkins v. Norcros plc [1994] ICR 11, CA 375, 393
Hopper v. Feedex Ltd [1974] IRLR 99 201

Horkulak v. Cantor Fitzgerald International [2005] ICR 402, CA;
  [2004] ICR 697, QBD 42, 177
Horrigan v. Lewisham LBC [1978] ICR 15, EAT 211
Howard v. Millrise Ltd (t/a Colourflow) (In Liquidation); Howard v. SG
  Printers (t/a Colourflow) [2005] IRLR 84; [2005] ICR 435, EAT 140, 255, 400
Hulland v. Sanders [1945] KB 78, CA 67
Humphries v. Chevler Packaging Ltd, unreported, 15 June 2006, EAT 315, 320
Hunt v. Power Resources Ltd, unreported, 10 February 2005, EAT 195
Hunt v. Storm Communications Ltd, unreported, 1 June 2007, EAT 263
Hutchings v. Coinseed Ltd [1998] IRLR 190 179
Hutchinson v. Enfield Rolling Mills Ltd [1981] IRLR 318, EAT 210
Hutchison 3G UK Ltd v. Mason, unreported, 16 July 2003, EAT 304
Iceland Frozen Foods Ltd v. Jones [1982] IRLR 439; [1983] ICR 17, EAT ...207, 217
ICTS (UK) Ltd v. Tchoula [2000] IRLR 642, EAT 322
Igbo v. Johnson Matthey Chemicals [1986] IRLR 215, CA 181
Igen Ltd v. Wong [2005] ICR 931, CA 284
Imperial Group Pension Trust Ltd v. Imperial Tobacco Ltd [1991] IRLR 66 177
Industrial Rubber Products v. Gillon [1977] IRLR 389 176
Ingram v. Foxon [1985] IRLR 5 386
Initial Electronic Security Systems Ltd v. Avdic [2005] IRLR 671, EAT 406
Inner London Education Authority v. Gravett [1988] IRLR 497 384
Inner London Education Authority v. Lloyd [1981] IRLR 394, CA 202
Intel Corp. (UK) Ltd v. Daw [2007] IRLR 346, CA 133
International Sports Co. Ltd v. Thompson [1980] IRLR 340 205
IPCS v. Secretary of State for Defence [1987] IRLR 373 254
Iske v. P & O European Ferries (Dover) Ltd [1997] IRLR 401, EAT 106
Islington LBC v. Brown, unreported, 24 June 2008, EAT 409
Item Software (UK) Ltd v. Fassihi [2005] ICR 450, HC 47
J & J Stern v. Simpson [1983] IRLR 52 173
J Sainsbury Ltd v. Hitt [2002] EWCA Civ 1588; [2003] ICR 111; [2003]
  IRLR 23 ....207, 217
J Sainsbury Ltd v. Savage [1981] ICR 1, CA 155
JA Mont (UK) Ltd v. Mills [1993] IRLR 172, CA 50
James v. Greenwich LBC [2008] IRLR 302, CA 27, 146, 147
James v. Redcats (Brands) Ltd [2007] IRLR, 296, EAT 23, 29, 30, 156, 157
James v. Waltham Holy Cross UDC [1973] IRLR 202 202
James W Cook & Co. (Wivenhoe) Ltd v. Tipper [1990] IRLR 386, CA 234, 391
Jamie v. Management Solution Partners Ltd, unreported,
  31 January 2006, EAT 370
Janata Bank v. Ahmed [1981] IRLR 47, CA 45
Janda v. Foyle & Co. Ltd, unreported, 16 November 1999, CA 303
Jeffery v. Secretary of State for Education [2006] ICR 1062, EAT 362, 411
Jenkins v. Hugh James Solicitors, unreported, 3 March 2005, EAT 306
Jepson v. Labour Party [1996] IRLR 116 298
JH Walker Ltd v. Hussain [1996] IRLR 11, EAT 277, 335
John Brown Engineering Ltd v. Brown [1997] IRLR 90, EAT 244
John Lewis plc v. Coyne [2001] IRLR 139, EAT 211
Johns v. Solent SD Ltd [2008] EWCA Civ 790 ....330, 407

TABLE OF CASES

Johnson v. Nottinghamshire Combined Police Authority [1974] ICR 170, CA ... .232
Johnson v. Queen Elizabeth Hospital NHS Trust, unreported,
    11 September 2003, EAT 282
Johnson v. Unisys Ltd [2001] IRLR 279, HL 374
Johnston v. NEI International Combustion Ltd; Rothwell v. Chemical &
    Insulating Co. Ltd [2007] ICR 1745, HL 129, 401
Johnstone v. Bloomsbury HA [1991] IRLR 118; [1991] ICR 269 ....79, 125
Jones v. F Sirl & Son (Furnishers) Ltd [1997] IRLR 493 180
Jones v. Friction Dynamics Ltd, unreported, 28 March 2007, EAT 183, 203
Jones v. GEC Elliott Automation Ltd [1972] IRLR 111 202
Jones v. Governing Body of Burdett Coutts School [1999] ICR 38, CA 420
Jones v. Gwent CC [1992] IRLR 521 374
Jones v. London Co-operative Society [1975] IRLR 110 202
Jones v. MEM Marketing Retail Services, unreported, 19 October 2007, EAT ...245
Jones v. Post Office [2001] ICR 805, CA 317
Jones v. Sirl & Son (Furnishers) Ltd [1997] IRLR 493 370
Jones v. Tower Boot Co. Ltd [1997] IRLR 168; [1997] ICR 254, CA 299, 321
Joshi v. Manchester CC, unreported, 30 January 2008, EAT 407
Jouini v. Princess Personal Service GmbH [2007] IRLR 1005, ECJ 261
JP Ticktum & Shranks Solicitors v. Bannister, unreported, 5 July 2007, EAT 420
Judge v. Crown Leisure Ltd [2005] IRLR 823, CA 178, 369
Junk v. Wolfgang Kuhnel (Case C-188/03) [2005] IRLR 310, ECJ 139, 239
Jurkowska v. Hlmad Ltd [2008] EWCA Civ 231 413
Kanapathiar v. Harrow LBC [2003] IRLR 571 413
Kapfunde v. Abbey National [1999] ICR 1, CA 20
Katsikas v. Konstantinidis [1993] IRLR 179, ECJ 265
Keeley v. Fosroc International Ltd [2006] IRLR 961, CA 39
Keisner v. Terrus Group Ltd [2006] EWHC 2765, ChD 47, 138
Kent CC v. Mingo [2000] IRLR 90, EAT 199, 314
Kerry Foods Ltd v. Lynch [2005] IRLR 680, EAT 371
Kettle Produce Ltd v. Ward, unreported, 8 November 2006, EAT 279
Khan v. Home Office, unreported, 17 November 2006, EAT 442
Khan v. Kirklees MBC [2007] EWCA Civ 1342 419
Khan v. Royal Mail plc [2006] EWCA Civ 2 420
Khan (Mohammed Sajwal), Re, unreported, 14 January 2005, Leeds ET 338
Kidd v. DRG (UK) Ltd [1985] IRLR 190 288
King v. Eaton [1996] IRLR 199, CS 240
Kircher v. Hillingdon Primary Care Trust [2006] EWHC 21, QB 164, 374
Kirker v. British Sugar plc [2003] ICT 867, HL 311
Kirton v. Tetrosyl Ltd [2003] IRLR 352, CA 307
Klusova v. Hounslow LBC [2008] ICR 396, CA 213
Kotecha v. Insurety plc (t/a Capita Health Care), unreported, 14 April 2008, EAT 4
Kraus v. Penna plc [2004] IRLR 260, EAT 168
Kumchyk v. Derby City Council [1978] ICR 116, EAT 420
Kuzel v. Roche Products Ltd [2008] IRLR 530, CA 283
Kvaerner Oil and Gas Ltd v. Parker, unreported, 28 January 2003, EAT 241
Kwik-Fit (GB) Ltd v. Lineham [1992] IRLR 156 173
Kyndal Spirits v. Burns, unreported, 27 June 2002, EAT 393

TABLE OF CASES

Ladbrokes Betting & Gaming Ltd v. Ally, unreported, 11 May 2006, EAT 155
Laing v. Manchester City Council [2006] IRLR 748, EAT 284
Lamb v. 186K Ltd [2004] EWCA Civ 1045 240
Land Brandenburg v. Sass (Case C-284/02) [2005] IRLR 147, ECJ 107
Land Securities Trillium Ltd v. Thornley [2005] IRLR 765, EAT 44, 164
Landeshaupstadt Kiel v. Jaeger (Case C-151/02) [2003] IRLR 805, ECJ 83
Landsorganisationen i Danmark v. Ny Molle Kro [1989] ICR 330, ECJ 260
Langley v. Burlo [2007] ICR 390, CA 17, 380, 394
Langston v. Amalgamated Union of Engineering Workers [1974]
    IRLR 15, EAT 44
Lansing Linde Ltd v. Kerr [1991] 1 All ER 418, CA 46
Latchman v. Reed Business Information Ltd [2002] ICR 1453, EAT 308
Lavarack v. Woods of Colchester Ltd [1966] 3 All ER 683 377
Law Society v. Kamlesh Bahl [2003] IRLR 640, EAT 278
Lawrence v. Regent Office Care Ltd [2003] ICR 1092, ECJ 355
Lawson v. Serco [2006] IRLR 289; [2006] ICR 250, HL 160, 161, 198, 312, 328
Lee v. Chung [1990] IRLR 236 20
Lee v. GEC Plessey Telecommunications [1993] IRLR 383, HC 38, 51, 67
Leeds Rhino Club v. Sterling, unreported, 9 September 2002, EAT 402
Leeds United Association Football Club Ltd, Re [2007] ICR 1688, HC 185
Leicestershire CC v. Unison [2005] IRLR 920, EAT 239
Leicestershire CC v. Unison [2006] EWCA Civ 825, CA 420
Leisure Leagues UK Ltd v. Maconnachie [2002] IRLR 600, EAT 90
Lesney Products & Co. Ltd v. Nolan [1977] IRLR 77 231
Levenes Solicitors v. Dalley, unreported, 23 November 2006, EAT 209
Levez v. TH Jennings (Harlow Pools) Ltd (Case C-326/96), ECJ 7, 353
Levez v. TH Jennings (Harlow Pools) Ltd [2000] ICR 58, EAT 353, 411
Levy v. Dudley Bower Facilities Management Ltd, unreported,
    22 May 2002, EAT 364
Lewis v. Motorworld Garages Ltd [1985] IRLR 465 179
Lewis Shops Group v. Wiggins [1973] IRLR 205 199
Lewisham & Guy's Mental Health NHS Trust v. Andrews [2000] ICR 707, CA 184
Lincolnshire CC v. Hopper [2002] ICR 1301, EAT 192
Linfood Cash & Carry Ltd v. Thomson [1989] IRLR 235, EAT 58
Lionel Levanthal Ltd v. North, unreported, 27 October 2004, EAT 248
Lipkin Gorman (a firm) v. Karpnale Ltd [1992] 4 All ER 512 145
Lipscombe v. Forestry Commission, unreported, 28 September 2006, EAT 420
List Design Group Ltd v. Douglas [2002] ICR 686, EAT 92
Lister v. Hesley Hall [2001] IRLR 472, HL 299
Litster v. Forth Dry Dock and Engineering Co. Ltd [1989] ICR 341, HL 264
Lloyd v. Taylor Woodrow Construction [1999] IRLR 782 249
Lodwick v. Southwark LBC [2004] ICR 884, CA 419
Logan v. Customs & Excise Commissioners [2003] EWCA Civ 1068 180
London Fire & Civil Defence Authority v. Betty [1994] IRLR 384 204
London International College Ltd v. Sen [1993] IRLR 333 ....408, 409
London Metropolitan University v. Dr Sackur & Ors, unreported,
    17 August 2006, EAT 257
London Probation Board v. Kirkpatrick [2005] ICR 965, EAT 386

xxxi

TABLE OF CASES

London Underground Ltd *v.* Edwards (No. 2) [1998] IRLR 364, CA 286
London Underground Ltd *v.* Ferenc-Batchelor; Harding *v.* London
   Underground Ltd [2003] IRLR 252, EAT 56
Look Ahead Housing & Care Ltd *v.* Odili and Mendes, unreported,
   28 January 2008, EAT 235, 242
Loxley *v.* BAE Systems Land Systems (Munitions & Ordnance) Ltd,
   unreported, 28 July 2008, EAT 447
LTI Ltd *v.* Radford, unreported, 19 July 2001, EAT 38
Luce *v.* Bexley LBC [1990] ICR 591, EAT 117
Luke *v.* Stoke on Trent City Council [2007] IRLR 305, EAT 45
Lunt *v.* Merseyside TEC Ltd [1999] ICR 17, EAT 422
Lustig-Prean & Beckett *v.* United Kingdom; Smith & Grady *v.*
   United Kingdom [1999] IRLR 734, ECHR 214
Mabirizi *v.* National Hospital for Nervous Diseases [1990] IRLR 133 ......385, 386
McAdie *v.* Royal Bank of Scotland [2007] EWCA Civ 806; [2007]
   IRLR 895 ....183, 204
Macartney *v.* Oversley House Management [2006] ICR 510; [2006]
   IRLR 514, EAT 83, 157
McCarthy Ltd *v.* Wendy Smith (Case 127/79), ECJ 356
McClintock *v.* DCA [2008] IRLR 29, EAT 336
MacCulloch *v.* Imperial Chemical Industries plc, unreported,
   22 July 2008, EAT 446
MacDonald *v.* Advocate General for Scotland; Pearce *v.* Governing
   Body of Mayfield Secondary School [2003] IRLR 512 ....275, 292
MacFarlane *v.* Glasgow City Council [2001] IRLR 7, EAT 25
McGowan *v.* Scottish Water [2005] IRLR 167, EAT 211
McClory *v.* Post Office [1993] IRLR 159, HC 43
McLean *v.* Rainbow Homeloans Ltd [2007] IRLR 14, EAT (Scotland) 221
McMeechan *v.* Secretary of State for Employment [1997] IRLR 353, CA 20
McMenemey *v.* Capita Business Services Ltd [2007] IRLR 400, CS 88, 347, 348
Madani *v.* Spirit SSR Ltd, unreported, 18 November 2003, EAT 158
Madarassy *v.* Nomura International plc [2007] ICR 867, CA 284
Magorrian and Cunningham *v.* Eastern HSS Board (Case C-246/96), ECJ 353
Majrowski *v.* Guy's & St Thomas's NHS Trust [2000] IRLR 695, HL 137
Malik *v.* BCCI (in liquidation) [1997] IRLR 462; [1997] ICR 606, HL 40, 376
Mandla *v.* Dowell Lee [1983] IRLR 209; [1983] ICR 385, HL 276, 277,
   289, 290
Mangold *v.* Helm (Case C-144/04), ECJ 324
Marcan Shipping *v.* Kefalas [2007] EWCA Civ 463 416
Marks & Spencer *v.* Williams-Ryan [2005] IRLR 562 ....408, 409
Marley *v.* Forward Trust Group [1986] IRLR 369, CA 38
Marley (UK) Ltd *v.* Anderson [1996] ICR 728, CA 409
Marshall *v.* Harland & Wolff Ltd [1972] ICR 101, NIRC 183
Marshall *v.* Industrial Systems [1992] IRLR 294, EAT 47
Marshall *v.* Southampton and SW Hampshire HA (No. 1) [1986]
   ICR 335, ECJ..325, 357
Marshall Specialist Vehicles Ltd *v.* Osborne [2003] IRLR 672, EAT 44, 79, 125
Martin *v.* Lancashire CC [2001] ICR 197, CA 263

Martland v. Co-operative Insurance Society Ltd, unreported,
    10 April 2008, EAT 38
Maruko v. Versorgungsanstalt der deutschen Bühnen (Case C-267/06)
    [2008] IRLR 450 344
Massey v. Crown Life [1978] 2 All ER 576, CA 26
Massey v. Unifi [2007] IRLR 912, CA 72
Matthews v. Kent and Medway Towns Fire Authority [2006] ICR 365, HL 349
Matthews (t/a Anton Motors) v. Smith [2002] EWCA Civ 1722 221
May Gurney Ltd v. Adshead, unreported, 3 July 2006, EAT 89
Mayor and Burgesses of Lewisham LBC v. Malcolm
    [2008] UKHL 43 ....302, 318, 319
Mayr v. Backerei und Konditorei Gerhard Flockner OHG [2008] IRLR 387 ...282
Melhuish v. Redbridge Citizens Advice Bureau [2005] IRLR 419, EAT 23
Melia v. Magna Kansei Ltd [2005] ICR 874 390
Memco-Med Ltd's Patenet, Re [1992] RPC 403 162
Mennell v. Newell & Wright [1997] IRLR 519, CA 220
Merino Gómez v. Continental Industrias del Caucho SA (Case
    C-342/01) [2004] IRLR 407, ECJ 101
Mersey Steel & Iron Co. v. Naylor Benzon & Co. (1884) 9 App Cas 434 ...369
Merseyside & North Wales Electricity Board v. Taylor [1975] IRLR 60 ...206
Metropolitan Police Commissioner v. Lowrey-Mesbit [1999] ICR 401, EAT .196
Meyer Dunmore International Ltd v. Rogers [1978] IRLR 167, EAT 218
Mezey v. South West London and St George's Mental Health NHS
    Trust [2007] IRLR 244, CA 44, 164, 374
Mid-Staffordshire General Hospital NHS Trust v. Cambridge [2003]
    IRLR 566, EAT 316
Middlesbrough BC v. Surtees (No. 1) [2007] IRLR 869, EAT 359
Middlesbrough BC v. Surtees (No. 2) [2008] ICR 349, EAT *see also* Redcar
    and Cleveland BC v. Bainbridge; Surtees and ors v. Middlesbrough BC ...363
Midland Bank plc v. Madden [2002] 2 All ER 741 207
Midland Counties Bank v. Attwood [1905] 1 Ch 357 185
Miles v. Gilbank [2006] ICR 1297, CA 401
Miles v. Linkage Community Trust Ltd, unreported, 10 March 2008, EAT ...83, 97
Millbrook Proving Ground Ltd v. Jefferson, unreported, 11 March 2008, EAT ...208
Miller v. Community Links Trust, unreported, 29 October 2007, EAT 406
Miller Bros & FP Butler Ltd v. Johnston [2002] IRLR 386 35
Ministry of Defence v. Jeremiah [1980] ICR 13 74
Mirror Group Newspapers Ltd v. Gunning [1986] IRLR 27 273
Mitchell v. Arkwood Plastics (Engineering) Ltd [1993] ICR 471 205
Mohmed v. West Coast Trains Ltd, unreported, 30 August 2006, EAT 339
Monie v. Coral Racing Ltd [1980] IRLR 464, CA 208
Moon v. Homeworthy Furniture (Northern) Ltd [1976] IRLR 298 234
Moore v. C & A Modes [1981] IRLR 71 210
Morgan v. Glamorgan CC [1995] IRLR 68 145
Morgan v. Staffordshire University [2002] IRLR 190, EAT 133, 305
Morgans v. Alpha Plus Security Ltd [2005] ICR 525, EAT 393, 394
Morris v. John Grose Group Ltd [1998] IRLR 499, EAT 221
Morrish v. Henlys (Folkestone) Ltd [1973] IRLR 61, EAT 45, 210, 395

TABLE OF CASES

Morrish v. NTL Group Ltd [2007] CSIH 56 160
Morris Angel & Son Ltd v. Hollande [1993] ICR 71, CA 50
Morrison v. ODS Business Services Ltd, unreported, 21 June 2007, EAT 33
Morrison & Poole v. Cramic Engineering Co. Ltd [1966] 1 ITR 404 246
Morrow v. Safeway Stores plc [2002] IRLR 9, EAT 41, 176, 179
Mowat-Brown v. University of Surrey [2002] IRLR 235, EAT 307
MSF v. Refuge Assurance plc [2002] IRLR 324 239
Mugford v. Midland Bank [1997] IRLR 208; [1997] ICR 399, EAT 237, 238
Murray v. Foyle Meats Ltd [1999] ICR 827, HL 232, 248
Murray v. Newham CAB [2003] ICR 643, EAT 304
Nagy v. Metropolitan Police Commissioner, unreported,
   22 September 2004, EAT 416
National Grid Co. plc v. Virdee [1992] IRLR 555, EAT 416
Nelson v. Carillion Services Ltd [2003] IRLR 428, CA 360
Nerva v. Paradiso E Inferno Wine Bar [2002] IRLR 815, ECHR 159
Nesbitt v. Department of Trade and Industry [2007] IRLR 847, EAT 33, 137
Nethermere Ltd v. Taverna [1984] IRLR 240, CA 29
Neufeld v. A & N Communication in Print Ltd, unreported,
   11 April 2008, EAT 34, 138
New ISG Ltd v. Vernon [2008] IRLR 115, ChD 50, 140, 265
New Testament Church of God v. Stewart [2008] IRLR 134 31
Newland v. Simons & Willer (Hairdressers) Ltd [1981] IRLR 359 194
Nikoloudi v. Organismos Tilepikinonion Ellados (Case C-196/02), ECJ 286
Ninni-Orasche v. Bundesminister für Wissenschaft, Verkehr und Kunst
   (Case C-413/01), ECJ 151
Nkengfack v. Southwark LBC [2002] EWCA Civ 711 217
Noel v. London Underground Ltd [1999] IRLR 621 408
Nokes v. Doncaster Amalgamated Collieries Ltd [1940] 3 All ER 549 250
North East London Strategic Health Authority v. Nassir-Deen,
   unreported, 18 December 2006, EAT 64
North Yorkshire CC v. Fay [1985] IRLR 247, CA 194
Northumberland CC v. Thompson, unreported, 14 September 2007, EAT 408
Norton Tool Co Ltd v. Tewson [1972] ICR 501, NIRC 16, 380
Norwest Holst Group Administration Ltd v. Harrison [1984] IRLR 419 180
Nothman v. Barnet LBC (No. 2) [1980] IRLR 54 384
Nottingham University v. Fishel [2000] ICR 1462, QBD 47
Nottinghamshire CC v. Meikle [2005] ICR 1, CA 315
NTL Group Ltd v. Difolco, unreported, 27 January 2006, EAT 243
O'Brien v. Associated Fire Alarms Ltd [1969] 1 All ER 93 45
O'Connor v. Montrose Canned Foods Ltd [1966] 1 ITR 171 246
O'Donoghue v. Elmbridge Housing Trust [2004] EWCA Civ 939 204
Office Angels Ltd v. Rainer-Thomas [1991] IRLR 214, CA 49
O'Flynn v. Airlinks the Airport Coach Co. Ltd [2002] Emp LR 1217 217
Ogilvie v. Neyrfor-Weir Ltd, unreported, 15 May 2003, EAT 177
O'Grady v. Saper [1940] 3 All ER 527 45
O'Hanlon v. HM Revenue & Customs [2007] ICR 1359, CA 310, 315
O'Hara v. Reality (White Arrow Express) Ltd, unreported,
   18 November 2003, EAT 247

TABLE OF CASES

Ojinaka v. Sheffield College, unreported, 18 May 2001, EAT 282
O'Kelly v. Trusthouse Forte [1983] IRLR 369, CA 23
Okonu v. G4S Security Services (UK) Ltd [2008] ICR 598, EAT ...64, 283, 290, 292
Omilaju v. Waltham Forest LBC [2005] ICR 481, CA 42, 369
O'Neill v. Governors of St Thomas More RC School [1997] ICR 33, EAT 282
O'Neill v. Symm & Co. Ltd [1998] ICR 481, EAT 305, 314
Optare Group Ltd v. TGWU [2007] IRLR 931, EAT 139, 236
Optical Express v. Williams [2008] ICR 1, EAT 247
Optikinetics Ltd v. Whooley [1999] ICR 984, EAT 210
Oriental Bank Corp., Re (1886) 32 Ch D 366 185
Orthet Ltd v. Vince-Cain [2005] ICR 374 392
O'Shea v. Coventry City Council, unreported, 15 February 2005, EAT 175
Österreichischer Gewerkschaftsbund, Gewerkschaft der Privatangestellten v.
    Wirtschaftskammer Österreich (Case C-220/02), ECJ 355
Ottoman Bank v. Chakarian [1930] AC 277 45
Oyarce v. Cheshire CC [2008] EWCA Civ 434 285
P & O Trans European Ltd v. Initial Transport Services Ltd [2003]
    IRLR 128, EAT 260
Paal Wilson & Co. A/S v. Parfenreederei Hannah Blumenthal (The Hannah
    Blumenthal) [1983] 1 AC 854, HL 183
Paggetti v. Cobb [2002] IRLR 861 387
Palacios de la Villa v. Cortefiel Servicios SA (Case C-411/05) [2007]
    IRLR 989, ECJ 191
Palihakkara v. British Telecommunications plc, unreported,
    9 October 2006, EAT 423
Palmanor Ltd v. Cedron [1978] IRLR 303; [1978] ICR 1008, EAT 41, 177
Panama v. Hackney LBC [2003] IRLR 278, CA 211, 391
Panesar v. Nestlé Co Ltd [1980] ICR 144, CA 290
Parker v. Northumbrian Water, unreported, 12 May 2008, EAT 169
Parkins v. Sodexho Ltd [2002] IRLR 109, EAT 167
Parliamentary Commission for Administration v. Fernandez [2004]
    ICR 123, EAT 359
Parry v. Cleaver [1970] 1 AC 1, HL 375, 393
Parry v. National Westminster Bank plc [2005] ICR 396, CA 386
Patel v. General Medical Council [2003] IRLR 316, PC 209
Paterson v. Metropolitan Police Commissioner [2007] ICR 1522, EAT 306, 309
Peara v. Enderlin [1979] ICR 804, EAT 381
Pearce v. Governing Body of Mayfield Secondary School; MacDonald v.
    Advocate General for Scotland [2003] IRLR 512; [2003] ICR 937, HL 299, 341
Pearce and Pearce v. Dyer, unreported, 20 October 2004, EAT 145
Pearson v. United Kingdom, 22 August 2006, ECHR 325
Peninsula Business Services Ltd v. Sweeney [2004] IRLR 49, EAT 37
Percy v. Church of Scotland Board of National Mission [2006] IRLR 195, HL ...31
Perera v. Civil Service Commission [1983] IRLR 166, CA 288
Perkin v. St Georges Healthcare NHS Trust [2005] IRLR 934, CA 395
Pestle & Mortar, The v. Turner, unreported, 9 December 2005, EAT 415
Peterson v. Hewlett-Packard, USA Ct of Appeals, 9th Circuit 340
Petrie v. MacFisheries Ltd [1940] 1 KB 258 39

TABLE OF CASES

Pickford v. ICI plc [1998] IRLR 435, HL 125
Polkey v. AE Dayton Services Ltd [1988] AC 344; [1987] IRLR 504;
  [1988] ICR 142, HL 202, 236, 245, 391, 394, 396, 437, 438
Poly Lina v. Finch [1995] FSR 751 49
Port of London Authority v. Payne [1994] ICR 555, CA 75
Port of Sheerness Ltd v. Brachers [1997] IRLR 214 231
Porter v. HMRC [2005] UKSPC SPC00501, 7 September 2005 376
Porter v. Oakbank School [2004] SC 603, IH (Ex Div) 208
Post Office v. Fennell [1981] IRLR 221, CA 217
Post Office v. Foley [2000] ICR 1283; [2000] IRLR 827, CA 207, 217
Post Office v. Moore [1981] ICR 621 406
Post Office v. Roberts [1980] IRLR 347, EAT 18
Povey v. Dorset CC, unreported, 10 October 2002, EAT 219
Powdrill v. Watson [1995] ICR 1100, HL 185
Powell v. Brent LBC [1988] ICR 176, CA 163, 374
Practice Direction 2004, EAT 3, 412
Practice Direction, 15 November 2007, ET 31–32
Practice Direction, 22 May 2008, EAT 412, 413, 421
Premier Mortgage Connections Ltd v. Miller, unreported, 14 September
  2007, EAT 168
Preston v. Wolverhampton Healthcare NHS Trust [2001] IRLR 237, HL 411
Price v. Civil Service Commission [1977] IRLR 291; [1978] ICR 27, EAT ... 286, 325
Property Guards Ltd v. Taylor and Kershaw [1982] IRLR 175, EAT 227
Prospect Care Services v. Curtis, unreported, 6 November 2001, EAT 284
Pudney v. Network Rail Ltd, unreported, 22 March 2006, EAT 217
Pugh v. National Assembly for Wales, unreported, 26 September
  2006, EAT 320, 410
Puglia v. C James & Sons [1996] ICR 301 393
Purves v. Joydisc Ltd [2003] IRLR 420 401
Qua v. John Ford Morrison Solicitors [2003] IRLR 184, EAT 116
Queen Elizabeth Hospital NHS Trust v. Ogunlana, unreported, 6 October
  2006, EAT 208
Quinn v. Schwarzkopf Ltd [2002] IRLR 602, Ct Sess 306
R v. A [2001] UKHL 25 214
R v. Attorney General for Northern Ireland, ex parte Burns [1999] IRLR 315 95
R v. British Coal Corp., ex parte Price (No. 3) [1994] IRLR 72 240
R v. British Coal Corp., ex parte Vardy [1993] ICR 720, QBD 241
R v. Countryside Alliance, ex parte Attorney General [2006] EWCA Civ 817 164
R v. Lord Chancellor's Department, ex parte Nangle [1991] ICR 743 31
R v. Rogers [2007] UKHL 8 277
R v. Secretary of State for Employment, ex parte EOC and Day [1994]
  ICR 317, HL 357
R v. Secretary of State for Employment, ex parte Seymour-Smith [1995]
  IRLR 464, CA 290
R v. Secretary of State for Employment, ex parte Seymour-Smith [1999]
  ICR 447, ECJ 357
R v. Secretary of State for the Home Department, ex parte Benwell [1984]
  ICR 723, QBD 196

… TABLE OF CASES

R v. Securities & Futures Authority Ltd, ex parte Fleurose [2002] IRLR 297,
    CA 56
R (on the application of Amicus, NATFHE, Unison, NASUWT, Public &
    Commercial Services Union, NURMTW and NUT) v. Secretary of State for
    Trade and Industry [2004] IRLR 430 344
R (on the application of Begum) v. Headteacher & Governors of Denbigh
    High School [2006] UKHL 15 335
R (on the application of Playfoot (a minor)) v. Millais School [2007] EWHC
    Admin 1698 339
R (on the application of Trustees of the National Council on Ageing (Age
    Concern England)) v. Department for BERR (Case C-388/07), ECJ 330
Radford v. De Froberville [1977] 1 WLR 1262 375
Ralton v. Havering College [2001] IRLR 738, EAT 53
Raspin v. United New Shops Ltd [1999] IRLR 9, EAT 160, 377, 378
RDF Media Group plc v. Clements [2008] IRLR 207, QBD 371
Read v. Members of Llanyrafon Community, unreported, 9 February 2006, EAT 419
Ready Mixed Concrete v. Minister of Pensions [1968] 2 QB 497 24
Reaney v. Hereford Diocesan Board of Finance, unreported, 17 July 2007,
    Cardiff ET 340, 343
Redcar & Cleveland BC v. Bainbridge [2007] IRLR 984, CA 351
Redcar & Cleveland BC v. Bainbridge; Surtees v. Middlesbrough Borough
    Council [2008] EWCA Civ 885, [2008] IRLR 776, CA 442
Redcar & Cleveland BC v. Degnan [2005] IRLR 615, CA 358
Redrow Homes (Yorkshire) Ltd v. Wright [2004] ICR 1126, CA 81
Regent Security Services v. Power [2008] IRLR 66; [2008] ICR 442, CA 53, 257
Reid v. Explosives Co. Ltd (1887) 19 QBD 264 185
Relaxion Group plc v. Rhys-Harper [2003] IRLR 484, HL 272
Retarded Children's Aid Society v. Day [1978] IRLR 128, CA 202, 218
Retirement Care Group Ltd v. Greener, unreported, 22 May 2002, EAT 210
Richards v. Secretary of State for Work and Pensions (Case C-423/04), ECJ 275
Richardson v. U Mole Ltd [2005] IRLR 668 414
Richardson (Inspector of Taxes) v. Delaney [2001] IRLR 663 ....376, 397
Richmond Adult Community College v. McDougall [2008] IRLR 227, CA 309
Ridgway v. JP Morgan Chase Bank National Association [2007]
    EWHC 1325 (QB) 42
Rihal v. Ealing LBC [2004] IRLR 642 284
Riley-Williams v. Argos, unreported, 29 May 2003, EAT 119
RKS Services v. Palen, unreported, 2 November 2006, EAT 169
RNLI v. Bushaway [2005] IRLR 674 27
Robertson v. Bexley Community Centre [2003] IRLR 434 410
Robinson v. City of London Territorial and Auxiliary Forces Association
    [1967] 2 ITR 652 31
Robinson v. Crompton Parkinson Ltd [1978] IRLR 61, EAT 41
Robinson v. Harman (1848) 1 Exch 850 375
Robinson v. Oddbins, unreported, 19 June 1996, EAT 286
Robinson v. Tescom Corp. [2008] IRLR 408, EAT 51
Robinson v. Ulster Carpet Mills [1991] IRLR 348 249
Robinson-Steele v. RD Retail Services Ltd (Case C-131/04) 91

TABLE OF CASES

Rock Refrigeration Ltd v. Jones [1997] ICR 938, CA 47, 371
Rockfon AS v. Nielson [1996] ICR 673, ECJ 237
Rodway v. South Central Trains Ltd [2005] IRLR 583, CA 113
Rolls-Royce Motors Ltd v. Dewhurst [1985] IRLR 184, EAT 235
Rolls-Royce Motors Ltd v. Price [1993] IRLR 203 238
Rose v. Dodd [2005] EWCA Civ 957 184
Rossiter v. Pendragon plc [2002] EWCA Civ 745; [2002] IRLR 483; [2002]
    ICR 1063, CA; [2001] ICR 1265, EAT 18, 53, 175, 179, 258, 373
Rowell v. Hubbard Group Services Ltd [1995] IRLR 195, EAT 139, 240
Royal Bank of Scotland plc v. McAdie, unreported, 29 November 2006, EAT ...204
Royal Bank of Scotland plc v. Theobald, unreported, 10 January 2007, EAT 408
Royal Mail Group v. Lynch, unreported, 2 September 2002, EAT 347
Royal National Orthopaedic Hospital Trust v. Howard [2002] IRLR 849 422
Rubel Bronze & Metal Co. Ltd and Vos Arbitration, Re [1918] 1 KB 315 369
Rubenstein v. McGloughlin [1997] ICR 318 393
Rugamer v. Sony Music Entertainment UK Ltd [2001] IRLR 644, EAT 179
Rutter v. Abacus Frozen Foods (No. 1) (2000) *The Times*, 26 April 36
S v. Floyd and Equality and Human Rights Commission [2008] EWCA Civ 201 319
Saggar v. Ministry of Defence [2005] ICR 1073, CA 161
St Helens MBC v. Mrs J Derbyshire [2007] IRLR 540, HL 273
Sajid v. Chowdhury [2002] IRLR 113, CA 36, 372
Salvesen v. Simons [1994] ICR 409, EAT 195
Samuel v. Lewisham LBC, unreported, 29 November 2001, EAT 15, 368
Sandhu v. Department of Education and Science [1978] IRLR 208, EAT 213
Sarieddine v. Abou Zaki Holding Co. [2008] EWCA Civ 453 385
Sarker v. South Tees Acute Hospitals NHS Trust [1997] ICR 673, EAT 379
Sartor v. P&O European Ferries (Felixstowe) Ltd [1992] IRLR 271, CA 57
Saunders v. Edwards [1987] 1 WLR 1116 196
Saunders v. Scottish National Camps Association Ltd [1980] IRLR 174 214
Savoia v. Chiltern Herb Farms Ltd [1982] IRLR 166 175
Sayers v. Loganair Ltd, unreported, 17 May 2005, EAT 200
SBJ Stephenson v. Mandy [2000] IRLR 233, QBD 46
Schmidt v. Austicks Bookshop [1978] ICR 85, EAT 280
Schmidt v. Spar und Leikhasse of Bordesholm [1995] ICR 237, ECJ 262
Schultz-Hoff v. Deutsche Rentenversicherung Bund (Case C-350/06), ECJ 90, 99
Scott & Co. v. Richardson, unreported, 26 April 2005, EAT 214
Scott Packing & Warehouse Co. Ltd v. Paterson [1978] IRLR 166 215
Scottish Co-operative Wholesale Society Ltd v. Lloyd [1973] IRLR 93 202
Scully UK Ltd v. Lee [1998] IRLR 259, CA 49
Secretary of State for Defence v. Elias [2006] IRLR 934, CA 286
Secretary of State for Employment v. ASLEF [1972] 2 QB 455 39
Secretary of State for Employment v. Banks [1983] ICR 48, EAT 406
Secretary of State for Scotland v. Taylor [1999] IRLR 362, CS 39
Secretary of State for Trade and Industry v. Bottrill [1999] ICR 592, CA 33, 137
Secretary of State for Trade and Industry v. Rutherford [2003] IRLR 858 288
Secretary of State for Trade and Industry v. Slater [2008] ICR 54; [2007]
    IRLR 928, EAT 267
Seide v. Gillette Industries Ltd [1980] IRLR 427, EAT 277

Seldon v. Clarkson Wright & Jakes, unreported, 4 December 2007, Ashford (Kent) ET 191, 329
Seligman v. Crown Leisure Ltd [21979] IRLR 130 178
Sellars Arenascene Ltd v. Connolly [2001] ICR 760, CA 137
Selvarajan v. Wilmot & ors [2008] IRLR 824, CA 442
Serco Ltd v. Redfearn [2006] ICR 1367, CA 276
Serco Ltd (t/a Bardford) v. Quarshie, unreported, 17 January 2006, EAT 285
Seymour v. British Airways Board [1983] IRLR 55 302
Shamoon v. Chief Constable of Royal Ulster Constabulary [2003] IRLR 285, HL 278
Sharma v. Ealing LBC, unreported, 5 January 2006, EAT 419
Shaw v. CCL Ltd [2008] IRLR 284, EAT 105, 177
Shepherds Investments Ltd v. Walters [2007] IRLR 110, ChD 47, 138
Sheridan v. Prospects, unreported, May 2008, Abergele ET 339
Sheriff v. Klyne Tugs (Lowestoft) Ltd [1999] IRLR 481; [1999] ICR 1170, CA 322, 372, 403, 423
Shiner Ltd v. Hilton [2001] IRLR 727, EAT 41
Shove v. Downs Surgical plc [1984] ICR 532 397
Showboat Entertainment Centre Ltd v. Owens [1984] IRLR 7 279
Sian v. Abbey National plc [2004] ICR 55, EAT 412
Sibun v. Modern Telephones Ltd [1976] IRLR 81 203
Sigurour A Sigurjonsson v. Iceland (1993) EHRR 462, ECHR 71
SIMAP v. Conselleria de Sanidad y Consumo de la Generalidad Valenciana [2000] IRLR 845, ECJ 85, 95, 96
Sime v. Imperial College London, unreported, 20 April 2005, EAT 41
Simmons v. British Steel plc *See* British Steel plc v. Simmons
Sims Ltd v. McKee, unreported, 16 March 2006, EAT 419
Sinclair v. Wandsworth LBC, unreported, 4 October 2007, EAT 395
Sindicato Medicos Publica v. Valenciana (Case C-303/98) [2001] ICR 1116, ECJ 83
Singh v. British Rail Engineering Ltd [1986] ICR 22, EAT 290
Sita UK Ltd v. Hope, unreported, 8 March 2005, EAT 361
Sivanandan v. Enfield LBC [2005] EWCA Civ 10 372
Skiggs v. South West Trains Ltd [2005] IRLR 459, EAT 117
Skyrail Oceanic (t/a Goodmos Tours) v. Coleman [1981] ICR 864, CA 215
Smith v. Giraud UK Ltd [2000] IRLR 763, EAT 381
Smith v. Safeway plc [1996] ICR 868, CA 280
Software 2000 Ltd v. Andrews, Trinder, Prowse and Lawrence [2007] ICR 825; [2008] IRLR 568, EAT 57
Solectron Scotland Ltd v. Roper [2004] IRLR 4, EAT 53
Soros & Soros v. Davison & Davison [1994] ICR 590, EAT 396
Soteriou v. Ultrachem [2004] IRLR 870, QBD 195
Sothern v. Franks Charlesly [1981] IRLR 278, CA 173
South Ayrshire Council v. Morton [2002] ICR 956, CS 355
South Tyneside MBC v. Anderson [2007] IRLR 715, CA 360
South West Trains Ltd v. McDonnell, unreported, 7 August 2003, EAT 75
Southampton City College v. Randall [2006] IRLR 18, EAT 314
Southwark LBC v. Whillier [2001] ICR 1016, CA 74

TABLE OF CASES

Sovereign Business Integration plc v. Trybus, unreported, 15 June
    2007, EAT 442
Sovereign House Security Services Ltd v. Savage [1989] IRLR 115 173
Spackman v. London Metropolitan University [2007] IRLR 744,
    Shoreditch CC 368
Spence v. British Railways Board [2001] ICR 232, EAT 197
Spencer v. Marchington [1988] IRLR 392, HC 49
Spencer v. Paragon Wallpapers Ltd [1976] IRLR 373, EAT 204
Spring v. Guardian Assurance [1994] IRLR 460, HL 43
Staffordshire CC v. Donovan [1981] IRLR 108 174
Stages v. Jackson & Canter, unreported, 31 March 2008, EAT 314
Stanley Cole (Wainfleet) Ltd v. Sheridan [2003] IRLR 885, CA; [2003]
    IRLR 52 .... 43, 178, 217
Steel Stockholders (Birmingham) Ltd v. Kirkwood [1993] IRLR 515 391
Stephenson Jordan & Harrison Ltd v. Macdonald and Evans (1952) 69 RPC 10 24
Sterling Engineering Co. Ltd v. Patchett [1955] 1 All ER 369 162
Stevedoring & Haulage Services v. Fuller [2001] IRLR 627, CA 23
Stevenson v. JM Skinner & Co., unreported, 6 March 2008, EAT 107
Stewart v. The Moray Council [2006] IRLR 168, CAC 39
Stolt Offshore Ltd v. Fraser, unreported, 26 February 2003, EAT 203
Strathclyde RC v. Wallace [1998] ICR 205, HL 359
Street v. Derbyshire Unemployed Workers Centre [2005] ICR 97, CA 168
Stringer, Thwaites, Ainsworth and Khan v. HMRC (Case C-520/06), ECJ 90, 92, 99
Strouthos v. London Underground Ltd [2004] IRLR 636, CA 211
Susie Radin Ltd v. GMB [2004] ICR 893 399
Sutcliffe & Eaton v. Pinney [1977] IRLR 349, EAT 213
Sutherland v. Hatton [2002] EWCA Civ 76 133
Sutton v. The Ranch Ltd [2006] ICR 1170, EAT 419
Sutton & Gates (Luton) v. Boxall [1979] ICR 67, EAT 200
Süzen v. Zehnacker Gebaudereiningung GmbH Krankenhausservice [1997]
    ICR 662, ECJ 260
Swainston v. Hetton Victory Club Ltd [1983] ICR 341 406
Sweeney v. Chief Constable of Ministry of Defence, unreported, 28 May
    2001, EAT 197
Sweetin v. Coral Racing [2006] IRLR 252, EAT 255, 400
Swift v. Chief Constable of Wiltshire Constabulary [2004] IRLR 540, EAT 308
Sybron Corp. v. Rochem [1983] 2 All ER 706 41
Taff Vale Railway Co v. Amalgamated Society of Railway Servants [1901]
    AC 426, HL 10, 11, 68
Tarbuck v. Sainsbury's Supermarkets Ltd [2006] IRLR 664, EAT 316
Tasci v. Pekalp of London Ltd [2001] ICR 633, CA 125
Taylor v. Alidair Ltd [1978] IRLR 82, CA 201, 202
Taylor v. East Midlands Offender Employment [2000] IRLR 760 90
Taylor v. Kent CC [1969] 2 QB 560 245
Taylor v. Secretary of State for Scotland [2000] ICR 595, HL 325
Taylor Gordon & Co Ltd v. Timmons [2004] IRLR 180 144
Tayside Regional Council v. McIntosh [1982] IRLR 272 200
Tele Danmark A/S v. Handels [2001] IRLR 853, ECJ 282

TABLE OF CASES

Ten Oever v. Stichting Bedrijfspensioenfonds voor het Glazenwassers en
    Schoonmaakbedrijf (Case C-109/91) [1995] ICR 74, ECJ 357
Terry v. East Sussex CC [1976] ICR 536, EAT 194
Tesco Stores Ltd v. Pook [2004] IRLR 618, HC 41, 47
Tesco Stores Ltd v. Pryke, unreported, 10 May 2006, EAT 207
TFS Derivatives Ltd v. Morgan [2005] IRLR 246, HC 44, 49
TGWU v. Brauer Coley Ltd (in administration) [2007] ICR 226; [2007]
    IRLR 207, EAT 399
TGWU v. Swissport (UK) Ltd (in administration) & Aer Lingus Ltd [2007]
    ICR 1593, EAT 260
Thanet DC v. Websper, unreported, 30 September 2002, EAT 44, 178
Thomas v. Farr plc [2007] ICR 932, CA 49
Thomas v. On Reflection Ltd, unreported, 1 February 2006, EAT 261
Thomas v. Robinson [2003] IRLR 7, EAT 280
Thompson v. DWP (Job Centre Plus) [2004] IRLR 348 280
Thompson v. SCS Consulting Ltd [2001] IRLR 801, EAT 264
Thorpe v. Dul [2003] ICR 1556 32
Tice v. Cartwright [1999] ICR 769, EAT 61
Tisson v. Telewest Communications Group Ltd, unreported, 19 February
    2008, EAT 3
Titchener v. DTI [2002] IRLR 195, EAT 186
TNT Express Worldwide (UK) Ltd v. Brown [2001] ICR 192, CA 273
Torgeir Langeland v. Norske Fabricom A/S (Case E-3/95) [1997[2
    CMLR 966, EFTA Court 258
Torith Ltd v. Flynn [2003] All ER 45 81
Tracey v. Crosville Wales Ltd [1997] ICR 862, HL 396
Tradition Securities & Futures SA v. Mouradian, unreported, 14 December 2007,
    EAT 145
Trafford Housing v. Hughes and Burke, unreported, 8 August 2007, EAT 395
Transco (formerly BG plc) v. O'Brien [2003] IRLR 441; [2002] ICR 721, CA 18, 42
Triangle Cars v. Hook, unreported, 1 July 1999, EAT 215
Truelove v. Safeway Stores plc [2005] ICR 589, EAT 116
TSC Europe (UK) Ltd v. Massey [1999] IRLR 22, HC 50
Tudor v. Spen Corner Veterinary Centre, unreported, 11 May 2006, EAT 310
Turner v. Commonwealth & British Minerals Ltd [2000] IRLR 114, CA 50
Turner Coulston v. Janko, unreported, 3 September 2001, EAT 18, 42
Unison v. United Kingdom [2002] IRLR 497, ECHR 67
United Arab Emirates v. Adbelghafar [1995] ICR 65, EAT 413
United Bank v. Akhtar [1989] IRLR 507, EAT 211
United Kingdom v. EU Council [1997] IRLR 30, ECJ 80
United Kingdom Coal Mining Ltd v. NUM & British Association of
    Colliery Management [2008] IRLR 4, EAT 140, 241
United Kingdom Coal Mining Ltd v. Raby, unreported, 30 January 2003, EAT 209
University of Oxford v. Humphreys [2000] ICR 405, CA 265
Vakante v. Addey and Stanhope School [2004] EWCA Civ 1065 195
Vakante v. Addey and Stanhope School (No. 2) [2005] ICR 231, CA 26, 36
Vauxhall Motors Ltd v. TGWU [2006] IRLR 674, EAT 240
Vento v. Chief Constable of West Yorkshire (No. 2) [2003] IRLR 102 401

TABLE OF CASES

Vicary v. British Telecom plc [1999] IRLR 680, EAT 307
Viggosdottir v. Islandspostur HF (Case E-3/01) [2002] IRLR 425,
    EFTA Court 53, 258
Villella v. MFI Furniture Centres [1999] IRLR 468 183
Virdi v. Metropolitan Police Commissioner and Central Police Training
    & Development [2007] IRLR 24, EAT 303, 308, 410, 411
Virgin Net Ltd v. Harper [2004] EWCA Civ 271; [2005] ICR 921; [2003]
    IRLR 831 ....160, 189, 377, 378
Virgo Fidelis Senior School v. Boyle [2004] IRLR 268, EAT 168
Voith Turbo Ltd v. Stowe [2005] ICR 543, EAT.......................393, 394
W Brooks & Son v. Skinner [1984] IRLR 379, EAT 218
W Devis & Sons v. Atkins [1977] IRLR 314, HL...........................396
W Gimber & Sons Ltd v. Spurrett (1967) 2 ITR 308 248
WA Goold (Pearmak) Ltd v. McConnell [1995] IRLR 516, EAT 43
Walker v. Heathrow Refuelling Services, unreported, 6 October 2004, EAT 418
Walker v. Hussain [1996] IRLR 11 277
Walker v. Northumberland CC [1995] IRLR 35; [1995] ICR 702 ....125, 132
Wallace Bogan & Co. Ltd v. Cove [1997] IRLR 453, CA 48
Walls Meat Co. v. Selby [1989] ICR 601, CA 238
Walton v. Independent Living Organisation Ltd [2003] ICR 688, CA 157
Walton Centre for Neurology and Neurosurgery NHS Trust v. Bewdley [2008]
    IRLR 588, EAT 356
Waltons & Morse v. Dorrington [1997] IRLR 488 ....178, 370
Warburton v. Taff Vale Railway Co. (1902) 18 TLR 420 177
Ward v. Cambridgeshire CC, unreported, 26 July 2001, EAT 182
Warner v. Adnet Ltd [1998] ICR 1056, CA 245
Waters v. Metropolitan Police Commissioner [2000] ICR 1064, HL 136
Way & IntroCate Chemicals v. Crouch [2005] IRLR 603 401
Weathersfield Ltd v. Sargent [1999] IRLR 94, CA 180
Webb v. Emo Air Cargo (UK) Ltd [1995] ICR 1021; [1995]
    IRLR 645, HL 107, 289, 356
Webb v. Emo Air Cargo (UK) Ltd (Case C-32/93) [1994] ICR 770, ECJ 279, 282, 283
West Midlands Co-operative Society Ltd v. Tipton [1986] ICR 192, HL 43
Western Excavating (ECC) Ltd v. Sharp [1977] IRLR 25; [1978]
    ICR 221, CA 18, 176
Wetherill v. Birmingham City Council [2007] IRLR 781, CA 368
Wheeler v. Durham CC [2001] EWCA Civ 844 284
Wheeler v. Quality Deep Ltd [2005] ICR 265 36
Whelan (Cheers Off Licence) v. Richardson [1998] ICR 318, EAT 382, 392
White v. Reflecting Road Studs Ltd [1991] IRLR 331; [1991] ICR 733, EAT 18, 179
Whitehead v. Governors of Corley School and Coventry City Council,
    unreported, 13 March 2007, EAT 420
Whitehouse v. Blatchford & Sons Ltd [2000] ICR 542, CA 259
Whitewater Leisure Management Ltd v. Barnes [2000] IRLR 456, EAT 260
Whittle v. Parity Training, unreported, 1 July 2003, EAT 246
Wigan BC v. Davies [1979] IRLR 127; [1979] ICR 411, EAT 41, 136
Wilding v. British Telecommunications plc [2002] EWCA Civ 349; [2002]
    ICR 1079 ....380, 393

William Hill Organisation Ltd v. Tucker [1999] ICR 291, CA 44, 164
Williams v. Compair Maxam Ltd [1982] IRLR 83, EAT 235, 236
Williams v. Cowell [2000] ICR 85, CA 276
Williams v. J Walter Thompson Group Ltd [2005] IRLR 376, CA 317
Williams v. University of Nottingham [2007] IRLR 660, EAT 161, 312, 328
Williams-Drabble v. Pathway Care Soultions Ltd, ET/2601718/04 339
Willow Oak Developments Ltd (t/a Windsor Recruitment) v.
    Silverwood [2006] IRLR 607; [2006] ICR 1552, CA 49, 52, 216
Wilson v. Racher [1974] ICR 428, CA 210
Wilson & Sanders v. St Helens BC [1998] ICR 1141, HL 258
Wilson (Inspector of Taxes) v. Clayton [2005] IRLR 108, CA 397
Wilsons and Clyde Coal Co. Ltd v. English [1938] AC 57, HL 125
Wincanton Ltd v. Cranny [2000] IRLR 716, CA 50
Wincanton Trans European Ltd v. Whiteford, unreported, 28 August 2003,
    EAT (Scotland) 382
Winterhalter Gastranom Ltd v. Webb [1973] IRLR 120; [1973] ICR 245 ....202, 203
Wippel v. Peek & Cloppenburg GmbH [2005] IRLR 211 347
Wise Group v. Mitchell [2005] ICR 896, EAT 160, 189, 378, 390
Witley & District Men's Club v. McKay [2001] IRLR 595, EAT 91
Withers v. Perry Chain Co Ltd [1961] 3 All ER 676 44
Wolesley Centres Ltd v. Simmons [1994] ICR 503, EAT 394
Wolff v. Kingston upon Hull City Council, unreported, 7 June 2007, EAT 4, 418
Wood v. William Ball Ltd [2000] ICR 277, EAT 364
Woodfine v. British Telecommunications plc, unreported, 10 December
    2003, EAT 164
Woodrup v. Southwark LBC [2003] IRLR 111, CA 306
Woods v. Olympic Aluminium Co. Ltd [1975] IRLR 356 201
Woods v. WM Car Services (Peterborough) Ltd [1982] IRLR 413; [1982]
    ICR 693, CA 41, 369, 370
Wylie v. Dee & Co. (Menswear) Ltd [1978] IRLR 103 295
Yarrow v. Edwards Chartered Accountants, unreported, 8 June 2007, EAT 90
Yearwood v. Metropolitan Police Commissioner [2004] ICR 1660, EAT 416
Yeboah v. Crofton [2002] IRLR 634 300
Yemen v. Aziz [2005] ICR 1391, CA 193
Yorke (t/a Yorkes of Dundee) v. Moonlight, unreported, 19 January
    2007, EAT 176, 370
Yorkshire Blood Transfusion Service v. Plaskitt [1994] ICR 74, EAT 360
Yorkshire Housing Ltd v. Swanson [2008] IRLR 607, EAT 442
Young v. John D Wood & Co., unreported, 29 September 1999, EAT 370
Young, James and Webster v. United Kingdom [1981] ECHR 4 71
Zaiwalla & Co. v. Walia [2002] IRLR 697 402
Zepbrook Ltd v. Magnus, unreported, 18 October 2006, EAT 16, 380

Table of statutes

Agriculture (Safety, Health and Welfare Provisions) Act 1956
   s.7 130
Asylum and Immigration Act 1996 . . .36
Bank Holidays Act 1871 135
Banking Act 1971
   s.1(2) 136
Banking and Financial Dealing Act 1971 135
Betting, Gaming and Lotteries Act 1963
   s.21 130
Children Act 1972
   s.1 131
Children and Young Persons Act 1933
   s.18 131
      (1) 131
         (b) 132
         (j) .95
      (2)(a)(ii) 132
   s.23 131
Children and Young Persons Act 1963
   s.34 131
   s.37(3)(a), (b) 131
Children and Young Persons (Scotland) Act 1937 . . . . .95, 131
Christmas Day (Trading) Act 2004 . . .166
Chronically Sick and Disabled Persons Act 1970 302
Civil Jurisdiction and Judgments Act 1982
   ss.24, 25 397
Civil Partnership Act 2004 344
   s.251 275
   Sched.27, para.151 116
Companies Act 2006
   s.217 378

   s.220 378
   ss.382, 465 60
Company Directors Disqualification Act 1986
   ss.6, 8 138
Compensation Act 2006
   s.3 129
Consular Relations Act 1968 . . .145, 193
Contracts of Employment Act 1963 . . . . .1, 6
Contracts (Rights of Third Parties) Act 1999 268
Corporate Manslaughter and Corporate Homicide Act 2007 126
Crime and Disorder Act 1998 277
Criminal Justice and Immigration Act 2008 69
Criminal Justice and Public Order Act 1994 . . . . .136, 196
Damages (Scotland) Act 1976 129
Data Protection Act 1984 142
Data Protection Act 1998 . . . . .142, 365
   s.7 143
   s.8(2)(a) 143
   Sched.2, para.3 365
Deregulation and Contracting Out Act 1994
   s.36 242
Diplomatic Privileges Act 1964 . . . . .145, 193
Disability Discrimination Act 1995 . . . . .33, 41, 62, 98, 154, 199, 203, 243, 270, 301, 302, 309, 318, 319, 364

s.1 ....302, 303, 304, 307	Sched.1, para.2..............308
s.2........................303	(2) 308
s.3(3) 303	para.6(1) 306
s.3A....................310, 317	(3) 305
(1)..................316	paras.6A, 8 307
(2)................310, 313	Sched.2, para.5..............308
(3)................316, 317	Sched.3, para.3 ....409, 410
(4)....................310	(1)–(3) 320
(5) 310, 312, 316, 441	Sched.3A, Pt 1, para.1(3) 302
s.3B.......................311	Disability Discrimination
s.4(1) 312	Act 2005 ....301, 307, 362
(2).....................313	s.10 154
(6) 161	s.18(2) 304
ss.4A–14D 311	Education Act 1996
s.4A...................302, 313	ss.8, 558 130
(3) 314	Education Act 1997 130
s.4B.......................311	Education (Scotland) Act 1980
s.6 313	s.31 130
s.7 302	Emergency Workers (Obstruction) Act
ss.7A–7D 312	2006 136
s.8 400	Employers' Liability (Compulsory
(2)(c) 403	Insurance) Act 1969 ....62, 149
(4) 401	Employment Act 1982..............11
s.9 421	Employment Act 1988 ....11, 71
s.11 322	Employment Act 1989 ....11, 360
ss.13–15 73	s.12 297
s.14A......................317	Employment Act 2002 ......7, 68, 110,
s.16A......................311	389, 394
s.16B 153, 322	s.1 107
(2A), (5) 323	ss.29–33 ....4, 396, 437
s.17A......................321	s.30 ....42, 43
(1C) 311	s.31 ....395, 396
(2) 404	s.32 174
(3) 321	s.37 169
(4) 322	s.38 ....35, 169
(5) 404	s.42 ....364, 365
s.18(2) 305	s.43 118
s.18A......................315	s.47 105
s.18B......................315	Scheds.2–4 ....4, 437
s.55 ....302, 321	Sched.2 55
(2)(b) 321	para.12 42
(4) 321	Employment Agencies
ss.57, 58 321	Act 1973 ....7, 146, 437
s.59 316	s.3A 148
s.64 311	Employment of Children
(2), (3), (7) 312	Act 1973.....................131
s.68 ....311, 312	Employment of Women, Young
(1).....................21	Persons and Children Act 1920 ...130

xlv

TABLE OF STATUTES

Employment Protection
 (Consolidation) Act 1978 .....6, 438
Employment Relations
 Act 1999 ....6, 7, 11, 65,
                             66, 68, 198
   s.10 ....55, 221
    (4), (5) 56
    (6) 121
   s.11 ....55, 56
   s.12 ....55, 121, 222, 398
   s.13 ....55, 56, 57, 221
   s.14 55
   s.15 55
   s.18 193
   s.23 ....30, 34
   s.32(3) 160
   s.33 ....77, 219
   s.34(1) 16
    (4) 372
   s.40 122
   Sched.1 69
   Sched.2, para.2 73
   Sched.9 160
Employment Relations
 Act 2004 ....1, 7, 9, 12,
                             68, 75, 78
   ss.22, 25 68
   s.26 12
   s.29 74
   ss.30, 31 73
   s.33 71
   s.34 ....71, 72
    (3) 70
   s.35 76
   s.41 ....150, 223
   s.57 72
   Sched.1, para.6 72
Employment Rights
 Act 1996 ....xi, 6, 7, 9, 31,
                          32, 79, 92, 196,
                          236, 301, 438
   Pt II 45
   ss.1–3 35
   s.1 ....168, 169, 256
   s.3(1) 57
   s.4 ....52, 169
   ss.7A, 7B 169
   s.8 153

s.11 ....35, 169
ss.13–27 ....13, 144
s.13 ....365, 366
  (1)(a), (b) 145
s.14(1), (5) 145
s.23 157
ss.28–35 152
ss.36–43 166
s.36(6) 167
s.40 167
  (3)(b) 167
s.41 167
s.42 167
  (1) 167
ss.43A–43L 167
s.43KA 33
s.44(1) 127
s.45 ....166, 335
s.45A 85, 97
s.46 120
s.47A 109, 113, 120
s.47B(2) 390
s.47C 105, 115
s.47E 150
s.48 ....105, 115
s.49 ....105, 115
  (2) 390
s.50 119
  (1), (3), (4) 119
ss.52, 53 ....121, 249
s.54 121
s.55(1)–(3) 99
s.56 99
s.57A 116, 228
  (1) 115
  (2)–(5) 116
ss.58, 59 119
s.60 120
s.63A 120
  (4) 120
ss.63B, 63C 120
s.64 118
  (2) 190
  (4) 118
s.65 118
s.66(1) 106
s.68 107
ss.71–80 113

xlvi

TABLE OF STATUTES

s.71 100	(4) 220, 221, 229
(5)(b) 444	(c) 117, 118,
ss.72, 73 100	145, 228, 229
ss.80F–80I 150	s.104A 225
s.80F 223	s.104B 227
(1)(a) 150	s.104C 150, 223
s.80G(1)(b) 150	s.105 ....218, 227, 234
s.86 ....159, 172, 189	(1)(b) 227
s.92 ....58, 170	s.106 ....106, 197, 215
s.95 ....32, 171, 193	s.108 ....188, 227, 232
(1)(b) 182	(2) 190
(c) 174, 368	(3) 189
s.97 172	(aa) 224
(1) 379	(c) 127
(4) 189	(dd) 221
s.98 ....204, 208, 219,	s.109 190
232, 259, 283	s.110 193
(1) 197, 231	s.111 ....407, 409
(b) 213, 216	(2), (3) 407
(2) 213	s.112(2)–(4) 383
(a) 199	(5), (6) 385
(b) 206	s.113 386
(ba) 212, 330, 333	s.114 386
(c) 232, 233	(2) 385, 386
(d) 36, 212	(a) 384
(3) 200	s.115 386
(3A) 212	(2) 385
(4) 61, 206, 209,	(a) 383
212, 213, 234	(d) 384
s.98A 394, 437	s.116 384
(1) 385, 388	(5), (6) 384
s.98B 122, 190, 224	s.117(2), (2A) 385
s.98ZA 212, 330, 333	(3)(b) 385, 399
s.98ZC, 98ZD, 98ZE 333	(4) 386
s.98ZG 212, 330,	s.119 ....334, 387
331, 333	s.120 ....219, 388
ss.99–104 218	(1A) 388
s.99 ....105, 115, 225	s.121 388
(2) 104	s.122(1) 388
(3)(d) 228	(2) 387, 388
s.100 ....127, 197, 223	(3A), (4) 388
s.101 ....166, 227, 335	s.123 180
s.101A 97, 229	(1) 388
s.102 120	(2)(b) 390
(1) 226	(4) 392, 394
s.103 222	(5) 396
s.103A 229, 390	(6) 210, 389, 395, 396
s.104(3) 220	(7), (8) 396

xlvii

TABLE OF STATUTES

Employment Rights Act 1996 (*cont.*)
  s.124 397
    (1) 388
    (1A) 388, 397
    (4) 386
  s.124A 395, 396
  s.128(1)(b) 398
    (2) 398
  s.133(1) 184
  s.135(1)(b) 233
  s.136 .... 171, 193
    (1)(b) 182
    (c) 174, 368
    (5)(b) 184
  s.138 .... 184, 245
    (6) 247
  s.139 .... 182, 230, 231
    (1)(b) 231, 232
  s.141 245
  ss.147, 148 233
  s.155 .... 232, 233
  s.156 233
  s.159 411
  s.162 334
  s.163(2) 232
  s.164 411
  s.174 184
  ss.182–190 152
  s.184(1)(a) 152
  s.186 .... 186, 399
  s.191 31
    (5) 123
  s.192 .... 123, 192
    (4) 192
  s.193 192
  s.196 .... 160, 161, 198
  s.199(2) 122, 123, 197
  s.200 197
    (1) 123
  s.203 .... 23, 37, 181, 421, 422
    (2)(e) 424
  s.205(1) 371
  s.206 184
  s.210(5) 188
  s.212 188
    (3)(c) 386
  s.215 161
  s.216 188

  s.218 .... 188, 253
    (2) 253
  ss.220–229 387
  s.227 ...... 90, 186, 255, 334, 400
    (1)(b) 385
  s.230 .... 33, 187, 188, 251
    (1) 21
    (2) 21, 32
    (3) 21
  s.231 60
  s.232 .... 166, 167
  s.233 167
  Sched.2, para.16 ...... 123, 192
Employment Rights (Dispute
  Resolution) Act 1998 3
  s.7 4
Employment Tribunals Act
  1996 .... 6, 438
  s.4(5) 365
  s.10 192
  s.18 .... 421, 423, 424
  s.21 420
  s.37(1) 421
Enterprise Act 2002
  s.248 185
  Sched.16 185
Equal Pay Act 1970 ..... 7, 8, 144, 272,
               350, 359, 360,
            363, 364, 406, 421
  s.1 .... 37, 161, 356, 365
    (1) 354, 362
    (2) 357
    (a) 350, 355
    (b) 350, 351, 355, 443
    (c) 350, 351, 355,
               362, 443
    (4) 361
    (6)(a) 355
  s.2(1), (3) 362
    (4) 411
    (6A), (6D) 358
  s.2A(1) 352, 363
  s.2ZA(4) 361, 362
    (5) 361
    (6) 362
  s.2ZB 353, 354, 411
  s.2ZC 353, 411
  s.6 360

TABLE OF STATUTES

s.7B 364
  (4) 365
s.11(2A) 362
s.78 366
Equality Act 2006 .... 271, 302
  s.14 14
  s.42(3) 14
  s.77 .... 335, 336
  Sched.3, paras.8, 23, 42 154
European Union (Accessions)
  Act 2006 151
Finance Act 2000
  Sched.20 60
Gangmasters (Licensing)
  Act 2004 15
Gender Recognition Act 2004 295
  Sched.5 275
Health Act 2006
  s.1(2)(b) 165
  s.2 .... 164, 165
Health and Safety at Work etc.
  Act 1974 .... 62, 125
  s.2(3) 126
  s.16 106
Human Rights Act 1998 .... 211, 277, 335
  ss.3, 4 214
  s.6 .... 67, 214, 436
  Sched.1 67
Hunting Act 2004 164
Immigration, Asylum and
  Nationality Act 2006 36
Income and Corporation
  Taxes Act 1988
  s.148 .... 376, 397
  s.188 .... 376, 397
  (4) 381
Income Tax (Earnings and Pensions)
  Act 2003
  s.401 397
  s.403 376
Industrial Relations Act 1971 ..... 2, 6
Industrial Training Act 1964 2
Insolvency Act 1986
  s.14(5) 185
  s.19(5) 185
  s.44(1)(a) 185
  (2) 185
  Sched.B1, para.99 185

Insolvency Act 2000 138
International Organisations
  Act 1968 .... 145, 193
Interpretation Act 1978
  s.6 219
  Sched.1 153
Law Reform (Miscellaneous Provisions)
  Act 1934
  s.1 184
Learning and Skills Act 2000 32
Licensing Act 1964
  s.170(1A) 130
Limitation Act 1980 ...... 353, 378, 406
  s.5 .... 378, 412
  s.32 378
Local Government Act 2003
  ss.101, 102 268
Merchant Shipping Act 1970
  s.51 130
National Minimum Wage
  Act 1998 13
  s.10 158
  s.25 225
  s.31(5)(b) 158
  s.34 156
  s.35 .... 29, 157
  s.49 421
  s.54(3) 22
Offices, Shops and Railway Premises
  Act 1963
  s.8 130
Partnership Act 1890
  s.1 34
Patents Act 1977
  s.40 162
Patents Act 2004
  s.10 162
Pension Schemes Act 1993
  s.11(5) 140
  s.113 140
Pensions Act 1995 360
  ss.62, 63, 126 358
  Sched.4, Pt 1 358
Pensions Act 2004 153
  s.257 266
  s.258 266
  (6) 266
  s.259 266

xlix

TABLE OF STATUTES

Police Act 1996
    ss.50, 85 196
    s.91 69
Police Reform Act 2002
    s.37 ....33, 168
Prisons Act 1952 196
Protection from Harassment
    Act 1997....................136
    ss.1, 3, 7 137
Public Interest Disclosure
    Act 1998 ....46, 167
    s.5 229
Public Order Act 1986 136
Race Relations Act 1976 ....20, 136, 154,
                     270, 272, 273,
                     277, 285, 287,
                     334, 364
    s.1(1)(a) 278
        (1A) 271, 289
            (a) 288
            (b)(ii) 289
            (c) 286, 289
        (2) 278
    s.2 ....272, 297
        (2) 272
    s.3(1) 276
        (4) 279
    s.3A 299
        (1) 291, 292
        (2) 292
    s.4 ....161, 272
        (2)(a) 272
        (2A) 280
        (3) 297
    s.4A 293, 294
    s.5 ....293, 294
        (2)(a), (b) 294
            (c) 295
            (d) 294
        (4) 294
    s.7 274
    s.10 ....34, 64, 274
    s.11 73
    s.19B 300
    ss.26A, 26B 274
    s.27A(2) 272
    s.29 153
    s.32(1) 299

    (3) 300
    s.33(2) 299
    ss.37, 38 298
    s.41 296
    s.54A 64, 283, 284, 285
    s.56 400
        (1), (4) 404
    s.57 400
        (4) 401
    s.65 ....292, 293
    s.68 ....409, 410
    s.72 ....421, 422
    s.76A 33
    s.78 21
        (1) 273
Racial and Religious Hatred
    Act 2006 335
Redundancy Payments Act 1965 ....1, 6
Registration Services Act 1953
    s.6(4) 192
Regulation of Investigatory Powers
    Act 2000 15
Rehabilitation of Offenders Act 1974
    s.4(3) 227
Reserve Forces Act 1996 122
    s.122(3) 122
Reserve Forces (Safeguard of
    Employment) Act 1985
    ss.3, 17 122
Rights of Relatives to Damages
    (Mesothelioma) (Scotland)
    Act 2007 129
St Andrew's Day Bank Holiday
    (Scotland) Act 2007 136
School Education (Amendment)
    (Scotland) Act 2002 130
School Standards and Framework
    Act 1998
    s.69 340
Scotland Act 1998 129
    Sched.5, Pt II, A3 136
Sex Discrimination Act 1975 ....7, 8, 20,
                    31, 34, 107,
                  136, 154, 225,
                  270, 272, 285,
                  287, 294, 310,
                  316, 350, 351,
                  356, 357, 364

s.1(1)(a) 274, 278	(3) 298
(b) 325	s.48 298
(iii) 271	s.51 296
(2) 271	s.63A 283, 284
(b)(i) 288	s.65 400
(ii) 289	(1), (3) 404
(iii) 286, 289	s.66 400
s.2 274	(4) 401
s.2A 274, 341	s.74 ....292, 293
s.3 275	s.76 ....409, 410
s.3A 279, 280	s.77 ....421, 422
s.4 ....272, 366	s.79(3), (4) 355
s.4A 291	s.82 21
s.5(3) 279	(1) 273
s.6 ....161, 272	Sex Discrimination
(2A) 280	Act 1986 ....297, 325, 357
s.6A 101, 102, 281	Sex Discrimination (Election
s.7 ....293, 294, 295	Candidates) Act 2002 ....296, 298
(1A) 300	Sex Disqualification (Removal)
(2)(a) 294, 295	Act 1919 351
(b), (ba) 295	Shops (Early Closing Days)
(c), (d) 296	Act 1965 135
(e) 294	s.3 167
(g), (h) 296	Smoking, Health and Social
(4) 294	Care (Scotland) Act 2005 166
s.7A(4) 295	Social Security Act 1989
s.7B(3) 295	Sched.5, para.5 444
s.8 352	Social Security Contributions
(1) 354, 355	and Benefits Act 1992
s.9 274	Pt XI 98
s.10(1) 161	ss.164–171 101
s.11 ....34, 274	s.164(2)(a) 101, 102
s.12 73	s.166(4) 101
s.17 33	s.171ZA–171ZK 108
(3) 297	Standards in Scotland's Schools
s.18 297	etc. Act 2000 130
s.19 ....31, 343	State Immunity Act 1978 145
(1) 296	s.1 145
s.20A 272	s.2 146
ss.35A, 35B 274	s.4 ....145, 193
s.35C....................272	s.16 145
s.38 153	Statute of Artificers 1563 xi
s.41(3) 300	Sunday Trading Act 1994 166
s.42(1), (2) 299	Sunday Working (Scotland)
(3) 300	Act 2003 166
s.42A....................296	Tax Credits Act 1999
s.44 297	ss.6, 18 227
s.47 298	Sched.3 227

TABLE OF STATUTES

Teaching and Higher Education
Act 1998
    ss.32, 33 120
Trade Disputes Act 1906 .....11, 12, 68, 77
Trade Union and Labour Relations
    (Consolidation) Act 1992 .....67, 68
    Pt V 11
    s.18(6) 240
    s.24 76
    ss.27–30 77
    s.64(1), (2) 71
    s.65(2), (5) 72
    s.67 72
        (8A) 72
    s.68 76
    s.69 71
    s.82(1)(c)(ii) 72
        (d) 72
    s.137 ....75, 229
    s.142 71
    ss.145A–145F 74
    s.146 ....73, 74, 117
    s.148(3) 74
    ss.149, 150 74
    s.152 ....75, 76, 118,
                   218, 228, 398
        (1)(c) 71, 75
    s.153 ....75, 218, 228
    s.154 ....218, 228
        (1) 189
    s.156 ....76, 219
    s.160 ....71, 77
    s.164 386
    s.168 117
    s.168A 118, 228
    s.169 ....117, 118
    s.170 ....117, 118
    s.174 ....67, 69, 438
        (4A), (4B) 70
    s.176(6), (6A), (6B) 71
    s.178 67
    s.179 ....37, 67
    s.181 141
    s.188 ....51, 139, 236, 239

        (1) 62
        (1A) 139, 239
        (4), (6) 240
    s.188A 237
    s.189 399
        (1) 399
        (1B)(a) 399
    s.190(4) 399
    ss.193, 194 239
    s.195(1) 236
    s.207A 5, 171, 437
    s.219 ....68, 75
    ss.222–225 68
    s.226 ....11, 68
    s.226A 12, 68, 78
        (2)(c) 11
    s.234 69
    s.234A 11, 68
    s.236 163
    s.237(1) 197
        (2) 224
    s.238 197
    s.238A 75, 197
        (2), (3) 224
    s.239(2) 407
    s.274(1) 123
    ss.280, 284 123
    s.285 122
    s.288 421
    s.297 60
    Sched.A1 69
        para. 7(1) 65
Trade Union Reform and
    Employment Rights Act 1993 68
    s.33 260
Tribunals, Courts and Enforcement
    Act 2007 3
Truck Act 1896 ....12, 13
Unfair Contract Terms
    Act 1977 ....23, 37
    s.3 37
Wages Act 1986
    Pt II 13
Work and Families Act 2006 100

Table of statutory instruments

Accession (Immigration and Worker Authorisation) Regulations 2006,
  SI 2006/3317 151
Armed Forces Act 2006 (Commencement No.3) Order 2008,
  SI 2008/1650 440
Children (Protection at Work) Regulations 1998, SI 1998/276 131
  reg.2(2)(a) 130
Children (Protection at Work) (Scotland) Regulations 2000, SI 2000/149 95
Children (Protection at Work) (Scotland) Regulations 2006, SI 2006/140 95
Civil Aviation (Working Time) Regulations 2004, SI 2004/756 ....80, 84, 89, 94
Civil Procedure Rules 3, 405
  rule 44.3(2) 3
Civil Service Order in Council 1995 ....31, 32
Collective Redundancies (Amendment) Regulations 2006, SI 2006/2387 239
Collective Redundancies and Transfer of Undertakings (Protection of
  Employment) (Amendment) Regulations 1995, SI 1995/2587 ....62, 254, 255
  reg.14 222
Collective Redundancies and Transfer of Undertakings (Protection of
  Employment) (Amendment) Regulations 1999, SI 1999/1925 ......139, 237, 254, 255
  reg.13 222
Companies Act 2006 (Commencement No. 6, Saving and Commencement
  Nos. 3 and 5 (Amendment)) Order 2008, SI 2008/674 440
Compensation Act 2006 (Contribution for Mesothelioma Claims)
  Regulations 2006, SI 2006/3259 129
Conduct of Employment Agencies and Employment Businesses
  (Amendment) Regulations 2007, SI 2007/3575 ....28, 147, 148
Conduct of Employment Agencies and Employment Business Regulations
  2003, SI 2003/3319 ....147, 148
    regs.5, 6, 10 148
    regs.13, 14 ....28, 148
    reg.15 148
      (1) 28
    regs.16, 17, 18–22, 24, 28 148
Construction (Design and Management) Regulations 2007, SI 2007/320 126
Control of Asbestos at Work Regulations 2002, SI 2002/2675 128
  reg.4 128
Control of Asbestos Regulations 2006, SI 2006/2739 ....125, 128

TABLE OF STATUTORY INSTRUMENTS

Control of Lead at Work Regulations 1998, SI 1998/543 118
Control of Noise at Work Regulations 2005, SI 2005/1643 125
Control of Substances Hazardous to Health Regulations 1999, SI 1999/437 118
Control of Vibration at Work Regulations 2005, SI 2005/1093 125
Data Protection (Subject Access) (Fees and Miscellaneous Provisions)
    Regulations 2000, SI 2000/191 142
Deregulation (Deduction from Pay of Union Subscriptions) Order 1998, SI
    1998/1529. 76
Disability Discrimination Act 1995 (Amendment) Regulations 2003,
    SI 2003/1673 . . . . .62, 301, 302, 313, 322
    reg.4(2) 310, 311
    reg.15 311
    reg.25 33
Disability Discrimination Act 1995 (Pensions) Regulations 2003,
    SI 2003/2770 301
Disability Discrimination (Blind and Partially Sighted Persons) Regulations
    2003, SI 2003/712 305
Disability Discrimination (Employment Field) (Leasehold Premises)
    Regulations 2004, SI 2004/153 315
Disability Discrimination (Guidance on the Definition of Disability)
    Appointed Day Order 2006, SI 2006/1005 303
Disability Discrimination (Meaning of Disability) Regulations 1996,
    SI 1996/1455 304
Disability Discrimination (Questions and Replies) Order 2004, SI 2004/1168
    art.4 320
Employers' Health and Safety Policy Statements (Exemptions) Regulations 1975, SI
    1975/1584. 126
Employers' Liability (Compulsory Insurance) (Amendment) Regulations
    2004, SI 2004/2882 . . . . .62, 149
Employers' Liability (Compulsory Insurance) regulations 1998, SI 1998/2573 149
Employers' Policy Statements (Exceptions) Regulations 1975, SI 1975/1584 62
Employment Act 2002 (Dispute Resolution) Regulations 2004,
    SI 2004/752 . . . . .4, 5, 14, 54, 171,
                                                                   256, 327, 331, 407
    reg.15 . . . . .406, 407, 410
    Sched.8, para.64 327
Employment Appeal Tribunal (Amendment) Rules 2001, SI 2001/1128 . . . . .413, 418
Employment Appeal Tribunal (Amendment) Rules 2004, SI 2004/2526 418
    para.3 405
    para.4 413
Employment Appeal Tribunal Rules 1993, SI 1993/2854
    rule 3 418
        (2) 412
        (3)(a) 413
Employment Equality (Age) (Amendment No. 2) Regulations 2006, SI 2006/293 327
Employment Equality (Age) (Amendment) Regulations 2006, SI 2006/2408 327
Employment Equality (Age) Regulations 2006, SI 2006/1031 . . . . .1, 153, 190, 191,
                                                                    212, 242, 324, 325, 325, 329

reg.1(2) 334
reg.2 ....21, 327
reg.3 ....328, 333
    (1) 330
        (a), (b) 326
regs.4, 5 327
reg.6 326
reg.7 327
reg.8 332
reg.9 ....327, 328
reg.10 161
reg.11 ....327, 328
reg.12 ....192, 327
regs.13–16 327
reg.17 ....34, 191, 327
reg.18 ....73, 328
reg.19–21, 23 328
reg.24 328
reg.25 333
reg.26 328
reg.27 332
    (1) 256
regs.28, 29 332
reg.30 ....34, 191, 331
    (2) 190, 330
reg.31 332
reg.32(2) 332
reg.33 ....332, 446
reg.34 332
regs.36, 37 327
regs.38–40 400
reg.38 404
    (3) 404
reg.41(4) 327
reg.42 327
regs.44–46 328
Sched.2 327
Sched.3 327
Sched.5, Pt 1 421
Sched.6 330
    para.2(3) 331
    paras.5–9 331
    para.11(3), (5) 331
    para.13(5) 222
Sched.8 233
    paras.21–33 334
    paras.21, 22 ....333, 334
    para.64 331

TABLE OF STATUTORY INSTRUMENTS

Employment Equality (Age) Regulations (Northern Ireland) 2006,
SR 2006/261 333
Employment Equality (Religion or Belief) (Amendment) Regulations 2003,
SI 2003/2828 335
Employment Equality (Religion or Belief) (Amendment) Regulations 2004,
SI 2004/437 337
Employment Equality (Religion or Belief) Regulations 2003,
SI 2003/1660 .... 153, 276, 277, 334, 335, 339–40
    reg.2(1) 335
    reg.3 336
        (1)(b) 336
    regs.4, 5 336
    reg.6 .... 161, 337
    reg.7 338
    regs.8, 10–14 337
    reg.15 .... 73, 338
    regs.16–18, 20–23 337
    regs.24, 25 38
    reg.26 .... 337, 338
    regs.27–32 338
    reg.29 339
    reg.30 .... 400, 404
        (1)(b) 338
    reg.31 400
    regs.33, 34, 35 338
    reg.38 337
    Sched.2 338
    Sched.3 338
    Sched.4 338
        Pt 1 421
Employment Equality (Sex Discrimination) Regulations 2005,
SI 2005/2467 .... 270, 271, 274, 280,
                                                         281, 285, 286, 291
    reg.3 271
    reg.32 293
Employment Equality (Sexual Orientation) (Amendment)
Regulations 2003, SI 2003/2827 342
Employment Equality (Sexual Orientation) Regulations 2003,
SI 2003/1661 .... 214, 275, 339,
                                                         340, 341, 344, 345
    reg.3(1)(a), (b) 342
    regs.6–21 341
    reg.6 .... 161, 342
    reg.7 343
        (3) 343
    regs.8, 10–14 342
    reg.15 .... 73, 342
    regs.16–18, 20, 22 342

TABLE OF STATUTORY INSTRUMENTS

regs.24, 25 343
reg.26 344
reg.30 ....400, 404
reg.31 400
reg.36 342
Sched.2 342
Sched.3 342
Sched.4 342
    Pt 1 421
Employment Equality (Sexual Orientation) (Religion or Belief)
(Amendment) Regulations 2007, SI 2007/2269 ....328, 337, 342
Employment Liability (Compulsory Insurance) (Amendment)
Regulations 2008, SI 2008/1765 440
Employment Protection Code of Practice (Time Off) Order 1998, SI 1998/46 117
Employment Protection (Continuity of Employment) Regulations 1996,
SI 1996/3147 386
Employment Protection (Recoupment of Jobseeker's Allowance and
Income Support) Regulations 1996, SI 1996/2349 ....393, 425
Employment Relations Act 1999 (Commencement No. 8) Order 2001,
SI 2001/1187 192
Employment Relations Act 2004 (Commencement No. 4 and Transitional
Provisions) Order 2005, SI 2005/2419 69
Employment Rights (Increase of Limits) Order 2007, SI 2007/3570 ...16, 71, 76, 77,
                                                                                                                     186, 219, 397
Employment Tribunals (Constitution and Rules of Procedure) (Amendment)
Regulations 2004, SI 2004/2351 363
Employment Tribunals (Constitution and Rules of Procedure)
Regulations 2004, SI 2004/1861 ....xii, 413, 423
    reg.3 ....3, 405, 415
    reg.40(3) 4
    Sched.1, rule 1(4)(b) 414
        rule 2(2) 414
        rule 3(1) 414
        rule 4 ....414, 415
            (3) 414
        rule 7(1) 414
        rule 8 ....415, 417
            (5), (6) 415
        rule 9 ....415, 417
        rule 10 ....408, 416
        rule 13(1) 416
        rule 14(2) 417
        rule 20 416
        rule 30(3) 417
        rule 33 415
        rule 36 420
        rule 38 419
            (4), (10) 419

TABLE OF STATUTORY INSTRUMENTS

Employment Tribunals (Constitution and Rules of Procedure)
Regulations 2004, SI 2004/1861 (*cont.*)
    rule 39 418
    rule 40(1), (3) 418
    rule 41 419
        (2) 418
    rule 42 418
    rule 45(3), (4) 418
    rule 48 419
    Sched.6 363
    rule 4(3)(b), (g) 363
Employment Tribunals Extension of Jurisdiction (England and Wales)
Order 1994, SI 1994/1623 ....17, 371
    art.3(c) 35, 412
    art.7 ....379, 412
    art.8 379
Employment Tribunals Extension of Jurisdiction (Scotland) Order 1994,
SI 1994/1624 ....17, 371
Employment Tribunals (Interest on Awards in Discrimination Cases)
Regulations 1996, SI 1996/2803 ....322, 364, 403
Employment Tribunals (Interest) Order 1990, SI 1990/479
    art.2(1) 364
Equal Opportunities (Employment Legislation) (Territorial Limits)
Regulations 1999, SI 1999/3163 312
    reg.2(2) 161
Equal Pay Act 1970 (Amendment) Regulations 2003, SI 2003/1656 ....7, 353
    reg.4 362
    reg.5 411
Equal Pay Act 1970 (Amendment) Regulations 2004, SI 2004/2352 363
    reg.2 364
Equal Pay (Questions and Replies) Order 2003, SI 2003/722 ....364, 366
    arts.3, 4 364
Equality Act (Sexual Orientation) Regulations 2007, SI 2007/1263 ....153, 341
    reg.30 341
European Communities (Recognition of Professional Qualifications)
(First General System) Regulations 2005, SI 2005/18 151
European Communities (Recognition of Professional Qualifications)
Regulations 2007, SI 2007/2781 151
European Co-operative Society (Involvement of Employees) Regulations 2006,
SI 2006/2059
    reg.31 229
European Public Limited-Liability Company Regulations 2004,
SI 2004/2326 ....120, 224, 229
    reg.42 222
European Qualifications (Health and Social Care Professions)
Regulations 2007, SI 2007/3101 151
Finance Act 2000, Sched.20 (Definition of Small and Medium-Sized
Enterprises) Order 2004, SI 2004/3267 60

TABLE OF STATUTORY INSTRUMENTS

Fire Precautions (Workplace) Regulations 1997, SI 1997/1840 126
Fishing Vessels (Working Time: Sea-fishermen) Regulations 2004,
   SI 2004/1713 .... 84, 94
Fixed Term Employees (Prevention of Less Favourable Treatment)
   Regulations 2002, SI 2002/2034 .... 161, 198, 223, 233,
                                                                                                                     328, 345, 346
      reg.1 21
         (2) 345
      reg.2 345
      reg.3 345
         (1)(b) 345
      reg.5 345
      reg.8 .... 182, 194, 345
      regs.18–20 345
      Sched.2, para.3 345
Flexible Working (Eligibility, Complaints and Remedies) (Amendment)
   Regulations 2006, SI 2006/3314
      reg.5 149
Flexible Working (Eligibility, Complaints and Remedies) Regulations 2002,
   SI 2002/3236 21
      reg.3(1)(a) 149
Flexible Working (Procedural Requirements) Regulations 2002, SI 2002/3207
      reg.3, 12 150
Health and Safety (Consultation with Employees) Regulations 1996,
   SI 1996/1513 .... 116, 141, 223
      regs.3, 4 127
      reg.7 116
Health and Safety (Enforcing Authority) Regulations 1998, SI 1998/494 97
Health and Safety Information for Employees (Modifications and Repeals)
   Regulations 1995, SI 1995/2923 126
Health and Safety Information for Employees Regulations 1989, SI 1989/682 ... 126
Immigration (European Economic Area) Regulations 2006, SI 2006/1003 151
Immigration (Notices) (Amendment) Regulations 2006, SI 2006/2168 151
Immigration (Restrictions on Employment) Order 2007, SI 2007/3290 36
Income Tax (Employments) (Amendment) Regulations 2000, SI 2000/1152 63
Income Tax (Pay As You Earn) Regulations 2003, SI 2003/2682
      regs.191, 199, 205, 206 64
Independent Schools (Employment of Teachers in Schools with a Religious
   Character) Regulations 2003, SI 2003/2037 340
Industrial Training Levy (Construction Industry Training Board) Order 2008,
   SI 2008/534 62
Industrial Training Levy (Engineering Construction Industry Training Board)
   Order 2008, SI 2008/535 63
Information and Consultation of Employees (Amendment) Regulations 2006,
   SI 2006/514 142
Information and Consultation of Employees Regulations 2004,
   SI 2004/3426 .... 51, 61, 120, 141, 222, 229, 237
      reg.30 224

TABLE OF STATUTORY INSTRUMENTS

Ionising Radiations Regulations 1999, SI 1999/3232 118
Legislative Reform (Health and Safety Executive) Order 2008, SI 2008/960 124
Local Government Superannuation (Equality and Maternity Absence)
    Regulations 1995, SI 1995/901 358
Management of Health and Safety at Work (Amendment) Regulations 2006,
    SI 2006/438 126
Management of Health and Safety at Work Regulations 1992, SI 1992/2051 127
Management of Health and Safety at Work Regulations 1999,
    SI 1999/3242 . . . . .125, 126, 130, 282
        reg.3 126
        regs.16–19 106
Management of Health and Safety at Work and Fire Precautions (Workplace)
    (Amendment) Regulations 2003, SI 2003/2457 126
Maternity and Parental Leave (Amendment) Regulations 2001, SI 2001/4010 113
Maternity and Parental Leave (Amendment) Regulations 2002,
    SI 2002/2789 . . . . .106, 113
Maternity and Parental Leave etc. and Paternity and Adoption
    Leave (Amendment) Regulations 2006, SI 2006/2014 . . . . . . .63, 100, 112, 225, 247
        reg.6 100
        reg.9 102
        reg.10 104
        reg.11 104
            (b) 105
Maternity and Parental Leave etc. and Paternity and Adoption Leave
    (Amendment) Regulations 2008, SI 2008/1966 444
        reg.4 444
            (1)(f) 444
Maternity and Parental Leave etc. Regulations 1999,
    SI 1999/3312 . . . . .32, 102, 111, 113, 246
        reg.2 21
        reg.4 . . . . .100, 103
            (3), (4), (6) 103
        reg.6 100
            (3) 100
        reg.7 104
            (4) 100
            (6), (7) 106
        reg. 8 100
        reg.9 444
            (4) 444
        reg.10 . . . . .104, 105
        reg.11 104
        reg.12A 102
        reg.13 114
        reg.15 113
        reg.16 114
        reg.18 114
            (2) 104, 115

(3) 115
(4) 104, 115
(5) 115
reg.18A 104, 114
reg.19 .... 104, 115
reg.20 .... 104, 105, 115
  (3) 104, 106, 225
    (e)(ii) 226
        (iii) 228
    (ee) 106
  (6) 247
  (7) 225
Sched.2, paras.2, 3, 4, 6 114
  para.7 113
Merchant Shipping and Fishing Vessels (Health and Safety at Work)
  (Carcinogens and Mutagens) Regulations 2007, SI 2007/3100 22
Merchant Shipping (Hours of Work) Regulations 2002, SI 2002/2125 ..... 80, 84, 89
Merchant Shipping (Working Time: Inland Waterways) Regulations
  2003, SI 2003/3049 .... 80, 84, 93
Mesothelioma Lump Sum Payments (Claims and Reconsiderations)
  Regulations 2008, SI 2008/1595 440
Mesothelioma Lump Sum Payments (Conditions and Amounts)
  Regulations 2008, SI 2008/1963 440
Metropolitan Police Authority Regulations 2008, SI 2008/631 440
National Minimum Wage Act 1998 (Amendment) Regulations 2007,
  SI 2007/2042 156
National Minimum Wage Regulations 1999 (Amendment) Regulations 2001,
  SI 2001/1108 158
National Minimum Wage Regulations 1999 (Amendment) Regulations 2004,
  SI 2004/1161 157
National Minimum Wage Regulations 1999 (Amendment) Regulations 2008,
  SI 2008/1894 440
National Minimum Wage Regulations 1999, SI 1999/584 .... 13, 325
  reg.2(3), (4) 158
  reg.3 156
  reg.4 157
  reg.6 156
  reg.12(2) 156
  reg.31(1)(e) 158–9
Occupational and Personal Pension Schemes (Consultation by Employers
  and Miscellaneous Amendments) Regulations 2006, SI 2006/349 141
  Sched.5 .... 120, 226
Occupational and Personal Pension Schemes (Disclosure of Information)
  Regulations 1996, SI 1996/1655
  regs.4, 5 141
Occupational Pension Schemes (Equal Treatment) (Amendment)
  Regulations 2005, SI 2005/1923 358
  reg.5(2), (6) 362

TABLE OF STATUTORY INSTRUMENTS

Occupational Pension Schemes (Equal Treatment) Regulations 1995,
SI 1995/3183 358
 regs.5, 10 362
Occupational Pension Schemes (Transfer Values) (Amendment)
Regulations 2008, SI 2008/1050 440
Part-Time Workers (Prevention of Less Favourable Treatment)
(Amendment) Regulations 2002, SI 2002/2035 347
Part-Time Workers (Prevention of Less Favourable Treatment)
Regulations 2000, SI 2000/1551 ....88, 226, 243,
                288, 300, 346
 reg.1 ....21, 22
 reg.2(1)–(4) 347
 reg.5 ....347, 348
 regs.7, 17 348
Patents Rules 2007, SI 2007/3291 162
 r.91 162
Paternity and Adoption Leave (Amendment) Regulations 2004,
SI 2004/923 ....112, 113
Paternity and Adoption Leave Regulations 2002, SI 2002/2788 ....102, 107, 111, 247
 regs.4–14 108
 reg.5(1) 109
 reg.6 109
  (3) 109
 reg.10 109
  (3) 109
 reg.12 111
 reg.13(1), (3) 109
 reg.15 110
 reg.17 112
  (3)(b) 112
 reg.18 111
 regs.22, 23, 25, 26 112
 reg.27(1)(b) 113
 reg.29 ....109, 110, 113, 220, 226
  (5) 225
Personal and Occupational Pension Schemes (Amendment) Regulations
2008, SI 2008/1979 440
Police Authorities (Selection Panel) Regulations 1994, SI 1994/2023 440
Police Authority Regulations 2008, SI 2008/630 440
Privacy and Electronic Communications (EC Directive) Regulations
2003, SI 2003/2426 143
Provision and Use of Work Equipment Regulations 1998, SI 1998/2306 125
Public Interest Disclosure (Prescribed Persons (Amendment) Order 2004,
SI 2004/3265 ....33, 168
Public Interest Disclosure (Prescribed Persons) Order 1999,
SI 1999/1549 168
Race Relations Act 1976 (Amendment) Regulations 2003,
SI 2003/1626 ....270, 283, 285, 286, 291, 292, 293

TABLE OF STATUTORY INSTRUMENTS

reg.3 .... .64
reg.6(2)(b) .... .297
Race Relations (Questions and Replies) Order 1977, SI 1977/842 .... .292
Regulatory Reform (Fire Safety) Order 2005, SI 2005/1541 .... .62
Rehabilitation of Offenders Act 1974 (Exceptions) (Amendment) (England
  and Wales) Order 2007, SI 2007/2149 .... .227
Rehabilitation of Offenders Act 1974 (Exceptions) (Amendment) Order 1975,
  SI 1975/1023 .... .227
Religious Character of Schools (Designation Procedure) (Independent
  Schools) (England) Regulations 2003, SI 2003/2314 .... .340
Religious Character of Schools (Designation Procedure) Regulations 1998,
  SI 1998/2535 .... .340
Reporting of Injuries, Diseases and Dangerous Occurrences Regulations 1995,
  SI 1995/3163 .... .128
Reserve Forces (Call-out and Recall) (Financial Assistance) Regulations 2005,
  SI 2005/859 .... .122
Right to Time Off for Study or Training Regulations 2001, SI 2001/2801 ...... .120
Road Transport (Working Time) Regulations 2005, SI 2005/639 .... .80, 84, 94
Safety Representatives and Safety Committee Regulations 1977,
  SI 1977/500 .... .116, 127, 141
  reg.4 .... .116
  reg.9(1) .... .127
Sex Discrimination Act 1975 (Amendment) Regulations 2008,
  SI 2008/656 .... .102, 103, 271, 279, 281,
                                                       291, 299, 434, 440
  reg.1(3), (5) .... .445
  reg.5 .... .281
Sex Discrimination and Equal Pay (Miscellaneous Amendments)
  Regulations 1996, SI 1996/438 .... .352, 363
Sex Discrimination (Burden of Proof) Regulations 2001, SI 2001/2660 .... .283
Sex Discrimination (Gender Reassignment) Regulations 1999,
  SI 1999/1102 .... .274, 341
Sex Discrimination (Indirect Discrimination and Burden of Proof)
  Regulations 2001, SI 2001/2660 .... .289
Sex Discrimination (Questions and Replies) Order 1975, SI 1975/2048 .... .292
Smoke-free (Exemptions and Vehicles) Regulations 2007, SI 2007/765 .... .166
Smoke-free (Penalties and Discounted Amounts) Regulations 2007,
  SI 2007/764 .... .166
Smoke-free (Premises and Enforcement) Regulations 2006, SI 2006/3368 .... .165
Smoke-free Premises etc. (Wales) Regulations 2007, SI 2007/787 W.68 .... .166
Smoke-free (Signs) Regulations 2007, SI 2007/923 .... .166
Smoke-free (Vehicle Operators and Penalty Notices) Regulations 2007,
  SI 2007/760 .... .165
Smoking (Northern Ireland) Order 2006, SI 2006/2957 NI 20 .... .166
Smoking (2006 Order) (Commencement) Order (Northern Ireland) 2007,
  SR 2007/118 .... .166
Social Security (Contributions) (Amendment No. 5) Regulations 2000,
  SI 2000/1149 .... .63

TABLE OF STATUTORY INSTRUMENTS

Social Security Benefits Up-rating Order 2008, SI 2008/632 108
   art.10 102
Social Security (Maternity Allowance) (Earnings) Regulations 2000,
   SI 2000/688 102
Social Security (Miscellaneous Amendments) (No.3) Regulations 2008,
   SI 2008/2365 440
Social Security (Recovery of Benefits) (Lump Sum Payments) Regulations
   2008, SI 2008/1596 440
Stakeholder Pension Schemes Regulations 2000, SI 2000/1403
   reg.22(1) 64
Statutory Maternity Pay (Compensation of Employers) Amendment
   Regulations 2002, SI 2002/225 101
Statutory Maternity Pay (Compensation of Employers) Amendment
   Regulations 2004, SI 2004/698 ....63, 101
Statutory Maternity Pay (Compensation of Employers) and Miscellaneous
   Amendment Regulations 1994, SI 1994/1882
      reg.1(4) 63
      reg.2(2) 63
Statutory Maternity Pay (General) and Statutory Paternity Pay and Statutory
   Adoption Pay (General) (Amendment) Regulations 2005, SI 2005/358 ...102, 108,
  109, 387
Statutory Maternity Pay (General) Regulation 1986, SI 1986/1960 101
Statutory Maternity Pay, Social Security (Maternity Allowance) and Social Security
   (Overlapping Benefits) (Amendment) Regulations 2006, SI 2006/2379
      reg.3 101
Statutory Paternity Pay and Statutory Adoption Pay (Administration)
   Regulations 2002, SI 2002/2820
      reg.3(b) 63
Statutory Paternity Pay and Statutory Adoption Pay (General) and the Statutory
   Paternity Pay Statutory Adoption Pay (Weekly Rates) (Amendment)
   Regulations 2006, SI 2006/2236 111
Statutory Paternity Pay and Statutory Adoption Pay (General) Regulations
   2002, SI 2002/2822 108
Statutory Paternity Pay and Statutory Adoption Rates (Weekly Rate)
   Regulations 2002, SI 2002/2818
      reg.2 108
Statutory Sick Pay (Medical Evidence) Regulations 1985, SI 1985/1604 98
Suspension from Work on Maternity Grounds (Merchant Shipping and
   Fishing Vessels) Order 1998, SI 1998/587 106
Suspension from Work on Maternity Grounds Order 1994, SI 1994/2930 106
Transfer of Employment (Pension Protection) Regulations 2005,
   SI 2005/649 ....252, 263, 265, 266
      reg.3 266
Transfer of Undertakings (Protection of Employment) Regulations
   1981, SI 1981/1794 ....8, 53, 178, 250, 252, 253,
                                                                                                                                                           254, 255, 258, 259, 261
      reg.2 251
      reg.3(1) 251

reg.5 .... 250, 251
reg.8 251
Transfer of Undertakings (Protection of Employment) Regulations 2006,
    SI 2006/246 .... 8, 18, 32, 39, 53,
                                                                     179, 220, 260, 268,
                                                                              373, 386
    reg.2 251
        (1) 21
    reg.3(1)(a) 251, 259
        (b) 251, 252, 259, 261, 262
        (3)(a) 259
    reg.4 .... 250, 251, 255, 266
        (1), (2) 263
        (3) 264
        (4) 257
        (5) 178
        (6) 263
        (7) 140, 263, 265
        (9) 53, 253, 258
        (11) 257
    reg.5 256
    reg.7 .... 221, 251, 259, 264, 266
        (1) 53, 190, 264
        (3) 259
            (b) 214
        (6) 190, 221
    reg.8 .... 253, 266
        (6) 267
        (7) 266
    reg.9 .... 253, 267
        (7) 267
    reg.10 .... 252, 265
    reg.11 252
        (1), (4)–(6) 256
    reg.12 252
        (4)–(6) 257
    reg.13–16 .... 140, 253, 399
    reg.13 254
        (2) 254
        (3) 255
        (6) 254
        (9) 256
        (11) 255
    reg.14 255
    reg.15 255
        (9) 255
    reg.16(3), (4) 255, 400
    regs.20, 21 250

TABLE OF STATUTORY INSTRUMENTS

Transnational Information and Consultation of Employees Regulations
1999, SI 1999/3323 .... 120, 141
    reg.28 229
Unfair Dismissal and Statement of Reasons for Dismissal (Variation of
Qualifying Period) Order 1999, SI 1999/1436 .... 59, 188
Work at Height (Amendment) Regulations 2007, SI 2007/114 125
Work at Height Regulations 2005, SI 2005/735 125
Working Time (Amendment) (No. 2) Regulations 206, SI 2006/2389 84
Working Time (Amendment) Regulations 2001, SI 2001/3256 .... 80, 87
Working Time (Amendment) Regulations 2002, SI 2002/3128 .... 80, 94, 132
    regs.6, 8, 17 94
Working Time (Amendment) Regulations 2003, SI 2003/1684 .... 80, 84, 85
Working Time (Amendment) Regulations 2006, SI 2006/99 84
Working Time (Amendment) Regulations 2007, SI 2007/2079 .... 80, 86, 88, 89, 434
Working Time Regulations 1998, SI 1998/1833 .... 25, 80, 83, 85, 86, 135,
144, 157, 161, 189, 220,
221, 325, 398
    reg.2 21
        (1) 80, 81, 92, 95, 130
            (b) 81
    reg.4(1) 82, 85
        (2) 83
        (3)–(7) 82
    reg.5 .... 84, 85
        (2)(b) 85
    reg.5A 84, 94, 132
    reg.6(1), (2) 95
        (7), (8) 96
    reg.6A 94
    reg.7 96
        (6) 96
    reg.8 93
    reg.9 .... 83, 96
    reg.10(1), (2) 93
    reg.11(1), (2) 93
        (3) 93, 132
    reg.12 93
    reg.13 86
        (6) 89
        (9)(b) 90
    reg.13A 86, 87
        (3) 87
        (6), (7) 88
        (8) 89
    reg.14 90
        (4) 90
    reg.15(1) 89
        (2)(a) 89

TABLE OF STATUTORY INSTRUMENTS

    (4)(a), (b) 89
  reg.16 ....89, 91
  reg.18(2) 84
  reg.19 ....84, 94
  reg.20 ....84, 94
    (2) 84
  reg.21 ....82, 92
  reg.23(b) 82
  reg.24 92
  reg.25A 84
  reg.26A 89
  reg.27A 94
  regs.28, 29 97
  reg.30 ....92, 97
  reg.32 229
  reg.35 421
  Sched.1, para.1(b), (e) 97
    (d) 96
    para.3 96
Working Time Regulations 1998 (Amendment) Order 2005, SI 2005/2241 80
Working Time Regulations 1998 (Amendment) Regulations 2004, SI 2004/2516 ...80
Working Time Regulations 1999, SI 1999/3372 80
Workplace (Health, Safety and Welfare) Regulations 1992, SI 1992/3004 122

Table of European legislation

EC Treaty (Treaty of Rome) 80
    Art.141 (ex Art.119) 270, 351, 352, 353, 354, 356, 357
Maastricht Treaty 1992 358
Directive 75/117/EC Equal Pay Directive 351, 352, 353, 356
Directive 76/207/EEC Equal Treatment Directive 270, 280, 281–2, 285, 351
    Art.2(3) 107, 360
Directive 77/187/EEC Acquired Rights Directive 8, 250, 251
    Art.3(1) 253
    (3) 266
Directive 79/7/EEC
    Art.7 .... 325, 358
Directive 80/987/EEC
    Art.3 152
Directive 83/477/EEC 128
Directive 89/391/EEC 223
Directive 91/553/EEC Written Particulars Directive 169
Directive 92/85/EC Pregnant Workers' Directive 282, 445
Directive 93/104/EC Working Time Directive 80, 81, 83
    Art.2 97
Directive 94/45/EC Works Council Directive 141
Directive 98/50/EC 251
Directive 98/59/EC Collective Redundancies Directive 139, 239
Directive 1999/70/EC Fixed Term Contracts 345
Directive 2000/43/EC Race Directive 270
Directive 2000/78/EC Equal Treatment Framework Directive 62, 190, 191, 301,
303, 312, 324, 330,
334, 341, 344, 441
    Art.2 .... 310, 316
        (2)(a), (b) 326
        (3) 326
    Art.6 .... 328, 329
Directive 2001/23/EC Acquired Rights Directive 251, 261
Directive 2002/14/EC National Information and Consultation
    Directive 61, 142, 237
Directive 2002/73/EC Equal Treatment Directive 102, 270, 291, 298, 351
Directive 2002/74/EC 152

TABLE OF EUROPEAN LEGISLATION

Directive 2003/18/EC
    Art.8 128
Directive 2003/88/EC Consolidated Working Time Directive 88, 90, 93
    Art.7 91
    Art.22 85
Directive 2004/38/EC 151
Directive 2006/123 Services Directive 434
Regulation 1612/68
    Art.8 73
Regulation 3820/85 Community Drivers' Hours 94
Regulation 2157/2001 222
European Convention on Human Rights 164, 213, 341, 438
    Art.6 56
    Art.8 275
        (1) 214
    Art.9 335
        (2) 335
    Art.10 67
    Art.11 . . . . .67, 71
    Art.14 325

CHAPTER 1
Background and overview

This introductory chapter offers a short overview of three general subjects which permeate individual employment law: first, a brief historical outline; secondly, a brief consideration of the relevance of various Codes of Practice; and finally the perceived trend towards a blurring of the distinction between unfair dismissal and wrongful dismissal. A fourth all-permeating topic, the gradual lessening in practical importance of the distinction between an 'employee' and a 'worker', is covered in **Chapter 2**. Current practice is generally to extend statutory rights to workers rather than just to employees, a practice exemplified by the Employment Relations Act 2004 which specifically extends to 'workers' the statutory right to be protected against suffering a detriment by reason of membership of a trade union, a right which was previously available only to 'employees'. On the other hand the Employment Equality (Age) Regulations 2006 apply only to employees and job applicants, thus demonstrating that the distinction in employment law between 'workers' and 'employees' is still of fundamental importance.

1.1 BRIEF OUTLINE HISTORY OF MODERN BRITISH EMPLOYMENT LAW

1.1.1 Individual employment rights

A major law textbook published in 1963 stated with no trace of irony that 'it may be correct to regard the importance of the law in relation to employment as minimal' (G.H. Fridman, *The Modern Law of Employment* (Stevens & Sons, 1963)). The book went on for over 1,000 pages, so the comment may have already been dated, but that short extract indicates the enormity of the change which has taken place in recent years.

Only a few months after publication of Professor Fridman's book, the first 'modern' employment law statute, the Contracts of Employment Act 1963, was passed and within a short space of time what started as a trickle of employment legislation had grown into a flood. The 1963 Act gave employees a statutory right to a minimum period of notice of dismissal and to be provided with written particulars of their main terms of employment. Two years later the Redundancy Payments Act 1965 introduced a right to statutory redundancy pay, and then a torrent of employment protection and anti-discrimination legislation followed, much of it required by European Directives, which continues to flow until this day.

Unfair dismissal

Of particular importance was the introduction in 1971 by Edward Heath's (Conservative) government of the right not to be unfairly dismissed. In 1964 a previous government had accepted the International Labour Organisation (ILO) Recommendation 119 on 'Termination of Employment' and set up an employment/industrial relations commission under Lord Donovan. While its main recommendations concerned industrial relations generally, the Donovan Commission report (Cmnd 3623 of 1968) included a recommendation for a law of unfair dismissal based on ILO Recommendation 119.

Following the Donovan Commission report, Barbara Castle, as responsible Minister in Harold Wilson's (Labour) government, produced a famous paper ('In Place of Strife', Cmnd 3888, January 1969) proposing new industrial relations legislation. The unions would have none of it and at the 1970 general election the Wilson government was defeated. One of the first acts of the incoming Conservative government was to pass the Industrial Relations Act 1971. Although mainly concerned with general industrial relations matters, derived from the Conservative party's 1968 Fair Deal at Work document, the 1971 Industrial Relations Act also introduced unfair dismissal.

The essential feature of unfair dismissal was, and almost 40 years later still is, that it is purely a statutory right. It is based entirely on Acts of Parliament and is wholly independent of breach of contract. Indeed, there are circumstances in which an individual can claim that he has been unfairly dismissed even though in ordinary parlance the event which triggered his claim was neither 'unfair' nor 'dismissal', for example, the coming to an end of a fixed-term employment contract without renewal.

It is also important to note that it is not only dismissal for an unfair reason which gives an employee the right to claim unfair dismissal. Even if the reason is perfectly fair, for example, because an employee has taken an unreasonable amount of time off work without permission a dismissal can and will be an unfair dismissal if the manner in which it was handled was unfair (for example, if the employee was not consulted or given an adequate chance to mend his ways).

Industrial tribunals/employment tribunals

Another main feature of the unfair dismissal system proposed in 1971 was that the procedure would be non-legalistic, informal and inexpensive. A new system of operation for industrial tribunals (originally established under the Industrial Training Act 1964) would be managed by non-lawyer members with a legally qualified chairman. These tribunals would be given exclusive jurisdiction, and the courts would not be involved in unfair dismissal cases except where there was an appeal on a point of law. In practice these tribunals, renamed employment tribunals by the Employment Tribunals Act 1996, have found it difficult to combine fairness with informality and in particular it has been difficult for legally qualified chairmen with years of experience as advocates in the courts to operate with the degree of non-legalistic informality which the original proposers of the system intended.

The difficulty was compounded by the new rules of procedure introduced in October 2004. While on the one hand the 2004 rules are far more detailed, extensive and precise than the rules they replaced, thus arguably narrowing the ability of tribunals to exercise discretion, on the other hand, unlike their simpler predecessors before 2001, the 2004 rules are specifically stated to be subject to the broadening overriding objective of ensuring that cases are dealt with 'justly' (Employment Tribunals (Constitution and Rules of Procedure) Regulations 2004, SI 2004/1861, reg.3).

Whilst the rules of procedure do give tribunals wide discretionary powers, in practice it is tempting for chairmen with wide experience of advocacy in the normal courts to err on the side of caution and excess formality. There is a tendency to apply formal court rules and employment tribunals have become more 'court-like' over the years. Thus, for example, under the Tribunals, Courts and Enforcement Act 2007, employment tribunal chairmen became officially known as 'Employment Judges' with effect from 1 December 2007. However the trend goes deeper than just names. Thus in *Clapson* v. *British Airways* [2001] IRLR 184, EAT, an employment tribunal refused even to consider whether its wide discretionary powers were adequate to allow a person to cross-examine his own witness, a procedure which would not be allowed in court. More recently, in the context of considering the matters which an employment tribunal should take into account if it is asked to review a striking out order, the Employment Appeal Tribunal (EAT) specifically ruled that the principles 'enunciated in [the Civil Procedure Rules] should be applied by analogy' (see *Tisson* v. *Telewest Communications Group Ltd* (unreported, EAT, 19 February 2008) at para.19).

The lessening of differences between the way the courts and employment tribunals work can also lead to desirable results – for example, in 2005 the Court of Appeal confirmed that the sensible procedure adopted by the courts under which an appellate court can ask a lower court to provide adequate reasons for a decision if inadequate reasons had been given applies also for the EAT and employment tribunals (*Barke* v. *SEETEC Business Technology Centre Ltd* [2005] IRLR 633, CA and EAT Practice Direction 2004, para.2.3).

Traditionally there is one area in which proceedings in employment tribunals have been substantially different from those in courts: costs. In the civil courts the general rule, subject to the court's discretion, is that the unsuccessful party is ordered to pay the costs of the successful party (Civil Procedure Rules, r.44.3(2)). In employment tribunals the general rule is that costs are not awarded. However, even that difference has been eroded. It used to be that employment tribunals could award costs only in exceptional cases involving 'frivolous or vexatious' behaviour by a party but they now also have power, which they regularly exercise, to award costs if a party acted 'unreasonably' in bringing proceedings or if he or his representative acted 'unreasonably' in conducting the proceedings or if the bringing or conducting of the proceedings was 'misconceived' (Employment Tribunals (Constitution and Rules of Procedure) Regulations 2004, reg.40(3)). It remains true that in employment tribunals an award of costs is related to the conduct of the parties, whereas in the courts it is related to whether they win or lose. One of the consequences is that it is not particularly unusual for an employment tribunal to award costs against a winning party if that party has behaved unreasonably, something which would only be done in very exceptional circumstances by a court (see, for example, *Wolff* v. *Kingston upon Hull City Council & anor* (unreported, EAT, 7 June 2007) and *Kotecha* v. *Insurety Plc (t/a Capita Health Care) & ors* (unreported, EAT, 14 April 2008)).

The unintended formality of tribunal proceedings which has developed over the years has probably been an influential factor leading the government to look for alternatives. Two which have been put forward in recent years have proved unsuccessful.

The first was a voluntary arbitration scheme for settling unfair dismissal and flexible working disputes, run by the Advisory, Conciliation and Arbitration Service (Acas) (see Employment Rights (Dispute Resolution) Act 1998, s.7). Although the Acas arbitration scheme was generally cheaper, simpler and less legalistic than recourse to an employment tribunal, it has not proved attractive and in practice has been little used.

The second was much more significant: the introduction of compulsory dispute and grievance resolution procedural rules under Employment Act 2002, ss.29–33 and Scheds. 2–4 supplemented by the Employment Act 2002 (Dispute Resolution) Regulations 2004, SI 2004/752. These rules came into force on 1 October 2004. The main impetus behind the 2004 Dispute Resolution regulations was to achieve cost savings by reducing by some 30 per cent the number of applications made to employment tribunals – which had risen from 43,243 in 1990 to some 115,000 in the year to 31 March 2003. Another beneficial result should have been a reduction in formality as it was hoped that the new rules would encourage private settlement of many disputes. The well-intentioned idea was to ensure that the parties to an employment dispute would not be able to present a claim to an employment tribunal unless they had first made a serious attempt at resolving their differences 'out of court'. If that could not be shown, an employment tribunal would not have jurisdiction. However, in practice this involved prescribing detailed compulsory rules. Compulsory rules inevitably give rise to disputes as to whether they apply and if so whether they have been complied with. Disputes about the rules were themselves matters for employment tribunals so rather than reducing the number of claims being made, the new rules instead gave rise to a completely new type of dispute – arguments about whether the new rules applied and if so whether they had been properly observed. In addition, far from adding to 'fairness', the new rules had the undesirable side effect of increasing the likelihood that a dismissal would be found to be unfair for procedural rather than substantial reasons.

By late 2006, a little more than two years after the 2004 Dispute Resolution Regulations had come into force, it had become obvious that they were not having the effect which the government had intended. The DTI commissioned a review of 'options for simplifying and improving all aspects of employment dispute resolution' in December 2006. The headline recommendation of the resulting Gibbons 'Review of employment dispute resolution in Great Britain' (March 2007) was 'complete repeal of the statutory dispute resolution procedures set out in the 2004 Dispute Resolution Regulations', a recommendation which the government has accepted. Accordingly the Employment Bill introduced in the House of Lords in December 2007 repeals the statutory dispute resolution procedure provisions noted above. They are to be replaced with less prescriptive measures. In particular the Acas Code of Practice on Disciplinary and Grievance procedures is to be reviewed and given teeth. The normal position is that employment tribunals do little more than take note of official Codes of Practice but the new rules will provide that if an employer has failed to follow various Codes of Practice, including the Acas Code, there will be specific power for an employment tribunal to increase compensation by up to 25 per cent if it considers it just and equitable to do so (the Employment Bill, cl.3 provides for a new s.207A to be inserted into the Trade Union and Labour Relations (Consolidation) Act 1992 (TULRCA 1992) to implement this proposal).

The Employment Bill thus effectively introduces a third attempt to balance the unintended formality of tribunal proceedings by providing for Acas, which is perhaps best known for its involvement in settling large-scale industrial disputes, to play an increasingly important role in helping to settle individual disputes. The government announced on 1 April 2008 that:

> Legislative measures which aim to simplify and improve employment dispute resolution are included within the Employment Bill. Additionally, the Government are making up to £37 million available over the next three years which will allow ACAS to boost its helpline and advice services and enable it to facilitate informal resolutions at any stage of a dispute. A full account of the changes to employment dispute resolution which the Government propose will be included in the Government's response to the consultation 'Resolving disputes in the workplace', which will be published in due course.

It is expected that the new system will be in place in April 2009 and that the current rules will continue in place until then. Even so the new provisions have already had some effect. One of the details in the proposals is abolition of the fixed periods for Acas conciliation in many types of dispute introduced in 2004. Although Acas still had power to provide conciliation after expiry of a fixed period it did so only rarely, but in the light of the proposals Acas has said that from 1 April 2008 it will exercise its power to conciliate in all cases, irrespective of whether the fixed period for conciliation has expired.

Along with the increased involvement of Acas conciliation in helping to settle individual employment disputes it is likely that there will be increasing official encouragement for use of mediation. There is an important difference between 'conciliation' and 'mediation'. The most basic difference is the practical one that a mediator and the parties usually fix a time and place where they will all be together (usually not in the same room) whereas conciliation is more typically a telephone arrangement. In general a conciliator will talk through the issues with both parties, explain the legal issues and look for settlement possibilities but will take a less pro-active role than a mediator. A mediator will generally shuttle backwards and forwards between rooms where the parties are seated, seeking to help them find a solution to their dispute. It should be noted that there is an even more important difference between the skills of a mediator and/or conciliator and those of a lawyer/advocate or those of a judge. Indeed, the combative training and natural mindset of lawyers and the judgmental mindset of judges may in some ways make it more difficult for them to be effective as mediators/conciliators. Even someone as eminent as Sir Henry Brooke, who retired as a senior judge in late 2007 and then became a mediator, has seen fit to write an article entitled 'My place at the mediation table: What I needed to "unlearn"' (January 2008).

Rejection of the 1971 Act

The complications of the tribunal system were of course not known in 1971 and so did not form any part of the unions' rejection of the Industrial Relations Act 1971. Union hostility to the Act came to a head with the 1974 miners' strike. Edward Heath called a general election on a 'who governs the country, unions or government?' theme – and lost. Although the new (1974) Labour government immediately repealed the Industrial Relations Act 1971 it re-enacted the unfair dismissal part, with minor amendments.

Consolidation Acts

In 1978 unfair dismissal law was consolidated with the 1963 Contracts of Employment Act and the 1965 Redundancy Payments Act becoming part of the comprehensive Employment Protection (Consolidation) Act 1978. This itself was repealed and replaced with effect from 22 August 1996 by the Employment Rights Act 1996 (ERA 1996) and the Employment Tribunals Act 1996, commonly known as the '1996 Consolidation Acts'.

In 1999 the Labour government's employment law flagship legislation was enacted as the Employment Relations Act 1999, dealing with trade union rights, 'family friendly policies', individual employment rights and miscellaneous matters such as rights for employment agency workers and those with fixed-term contracts. From the point of view of individual employment law, the 1999 Act worked mainly by amending ERA 1996 which, along with anti-discrimination legislation, continues in extensively amended form as the main current source of individual statutory employment rights. In July 2002, the Employment Act 2002 paved the way for further extensive amendments, especially in regard to family friendly policies and dispute resolution procedures, starting from April 2003. The Employment Relations Act 2004 made further changes, mainly for the benefit of trade unions and their members. The Employment Bill 2007/2008 was originally to be called the Employment Simplification Bill, but in light of its content the name has sensibly been changed. As noted above it will bring to an end the ill-fated 2004 compulsory dispute resolution. It also provides for improved national minimum wage enforcement powers, for strengthening of the Employment Agencies Act 1973 and, following a 2007 ruling by the European Court of Human Rights in February 2007, enables trade unions to refuse membership, and exclude individuals, on the grounds of membership of a political party.

Following the 1 October 2007 merger of the Equal Opportunities Commission, the Commission for Racial Equality and the Disability Rights Commission, a consolidation of anti-discrimination law is understood to be more than a glimmer in the eye but clearly will be an enormous and difficult undertaking. Apart from that, so far as we are aware there is no current proposal for another employment law consolidation Act. However, it would not be surprising if one were to come in the fairly near future as there has been more employment law legislation, including secondary legislation, in the 12 years since the 1996 consolidation than there was in the 18 years since the previous consolidation in 1978.

Anti-discrimination law

The introduction of specific rules outlawing discrimination against workers on various grounds has been an important and developing feature of modern employment law. The first modern anti-discrimination statute was the Equal Pay Act 1970 (EqPA 1970) which in its current form is designed to ensure that men and women receive the same pay for the same work, work of equal value or work rated as equivalent. Although enacted in 1970, it was five years later that it came into force, along with the Sex Discrimination Act, at the end of 1975. Even then it proved so complicated that it was little used until the present century. However, at the end of 1999 the ECJ ruled that an important provision in the Act which restricted back-pay claims to two years was contrary to EC law and so was not enforceable (*Levez* v. *T.H. Jennings (Harlow Pools) Ltd*, ECJ Case C-326/96). This two-year period noted above was increased to (normally) six years with effect from 19 July 2003 (Equal Pay Act 1970 (Amendment) Regulations 2003, SI 2003/1656) and the floodgates opened.

Soon enormous claims were being put forward on behalf of large numbers of female local authority workers, and local councils are still being bailed out by central government. The Act is considered further at **Chapter 17**.

In addition to discrimination outlawed by EqPA 1970 and SDA 1975, anti-discrimination law in the employment field now covers race, nationality and colour (1976), disability (1995), whistleblowing (1998), part-time work (2000), fixed-term work (2002), sexual orientation (2003), religion or philosophical belief (2003) and, most recently, discrimination on grounds of age (2006). The rules are considered in more detail later in this book although it is worth mentioning here that as a general rule discrimination rights have three features in common which make them different from many other 'employment law' rights. First, they apply to all 'workers' not just to 'employees'; secondly, the rights normally accrue without any qualification period of employment being required; and, thirdly, there are in general no statutory limits to the amount of compensation which an employment tribunal can award where an employer is found 'guilty' of unlawful discrimination.

Transfer of undertakings

Another landmark was the introduction in 1981 of regulations protecting employees in the event of a transfer of ownership of an employing business. The old common law position was based on the idea that employment contracts are fundamentally personal contracts and therefore do not transfer if either party changes. The Transfer of Undertakings (Protection of Employment) Regulations 1981, SI 1981/1794 (TUPE 1981) (made to implement in the UK the EC Acquired Rights Directive 77/187/EEC) overrode this common law position and provided instead that contracts of employment and most employment rights of employees engaged in an undertaking or business immediately before a transfer of ownership of that business are automatically transferred (i.e. are novated) to the new proprietor, who automatically becomes their employer. In September 2001 the British government published proposals for reform of some important details of the TUPE regulations and eventually in March 2005 a set of new draft regulations were published. The finished version came into force in April 2006 as the Transfer of Undertakings (Protection of Employment) Regulations 2006, SI 2006/246 (TUPE 2006). We look at employment law relating to transfer of undertakings in **Chapter 13**.

Changing patterns of work

When Professor Fridman wrote the 1963 textbook mentioned at the start of this section, there was no such thing as an 'employment lawyer' and employment law was not a subject in its own right. Collective industrial rights existed for the benefit of trade unions and their members but the legal rights and obligations of individual employees and employers had not yet crystallised into anything which could be regarded as a body of 'employment law' and so far as we can see the word 'discrimination' does not even appear in the book. It is no coincidence that what we now call 'employment tribunals' were called 'industrial tribunals' from inception until the 1990s and that the two leading sets of employment law reports, both started in the 1970s, were, and still are, named the Industrial Cases Reports and the Industrial Relations Law Reports. Similarly, the names of the two leading employment lawyers groups reflect this evolution – the Industrial Law Society was founded in 1967 and the Employment Lawyers Association was founded 25 years later in 1992.

While of course there are still many hangovers from the past, for practical purposes 'employment law' as such came into existence only during and after the second half of the 1960s and, within just a few years of making it, Professor Fridman would have been unlikely to repeat his minimalist view of the importance of the law in relation to employment.

What can we expect next? Already, 40 years on, there are signs that employment law as a discrete subject may not last much longer. We suggest this for two main reasons. First, the traditional employer/employee relationship as a normal pattern for work has already disappeared in many organisations and this trend is certain to continue. Even where the traditional employer/employee relationship is still normal, as in the public sector, the idea of a job for life is now old hat. The sociological reasons for these ongoing changes are outside the scope of this book but the fact is that they are happening and new work methods such as homeworking, tele-work, flexitime, job-share, annualised hours, staggered hours, term-time work, part-time and casual work along with self-employment and contract and agency work are proliferating. The changes have official encouragement in the shape of 'family friendly' policies, exemplified by the 'flexible working' provisions inserted into the Employment Rights Act 1996 with effect from April 2003.

Notwithstanding this general trend away from traditional forms of employment, progress in this direction is not consistently one way. Figures from the official Economic and Labour Market Review for August–October 2007, show an increase of 693,000 in the number of full-time employees since the equivalent period in 2004 and of 121,000 in the numbers of part-time employees.

One consequence of this change in work patterns is that recent employment protection legislation generally benefits 'workers' rather than the more narrowly defined 'employees' who were generally the beneficiaries of pre-1990s employment statutes. A recent example is provided by the Employment Relations Act 2004 which extends the rules providing protection to trade union members against detriment on account of their union membership to cover members who count as 'workers'. Previously this protection was only available to 'employees'.

The subject of employment status generally was subject to a DTI review which started in July 2002 (URN 02/1058). This was followed by an official 'summary of responses' in March 2006 (URN 06/1050) but there was no recommendation to change the current categorisation system.

A second reason for thinking that employment law as a discrete subject may be on the way out is that distinctions between employment law and general law, especially the general law of tort, are being progressively whittled away as employment law matures and develops into part of the mainstream law of the land. Employment tribunals are now frequently released from any restrictions on the amount of compensation they can award. One of the authors of this book can remember when the statutory limit on compensation that a tribunal could award for unfair dismissal was £5,200 but even in unfair dismissal since February 2008 that limit has been increased to £63,000 and there is no statutory limit at all on the amount that a tribunal can award in discrimination cases (statutory limits on compensation in sex and race discrimination cases were entirely removed in 1993 and 1994 respectively and, while not routine, tribunal awards can now reach several hundred thousand pounds). Oddly, the limit of £25,000 on compensation in a breach of contract (wrongful dismissal) case has never been raised since 1994 when industrial tribunals were given jurisdiction to hear such cases – itself another indication of how the tribunals have progressively become more like 'courts'.

The development by the courts and tribunals of the doctrine of the implied contractual term in an employment context and the need to develop systems of purposive construction of statutes to facilitate compliance with European Directives demonstrate how important it is for those concerned with employment law to be aware of developments in other branches of the law. Indeed, the overlap between personal injury law and employment law is now so extensive that any lawyer practising in either field will almost certainly wish to have more than a passing knowledge of the other. The Law Society's *Personal Injury Handbook* (Law Society, 2005) which comes complete with a CD-rom of documents, questionnaires and contact links, is recommended.

1.1.2 Collective labour law

The brief historical outline above, while no more than a basic and simplistic overview is, we hope, nevertheless a broadly accurate description of the position in so far as individual employment law rights are concerned. However, it does not cover the significant developments which have taken place since the beginning of the 20th century in the field of collective labour law. Whilst this book is not directly concerned with collective labour law, some aspects of it are of particular importance to individuals and an even briefer overview may therefore be of value.

Trade disputes

Modern collective labour law started in 1901. That was the year of the *Taff Vale* case in which the House of Lords held, contrary to general belief, that a trade union could be sued even though it was an unincorporated association (*Taff Vale Railway Co* v. *Amalgamated Society of Railway Servants* [1901] AC 426, HL). A few years later a new (Liberal) government, elected with support from the embryo Labour Party, passed the Trade Disputes Act 1906. The 1906 Act did not override *Taff Vale* but granted trade unions and their members immunity from most civil actions arising from trade disputes.

This blanket immunity from actions in tort was a major stimulus to the development of union power and lasted some 75 years. Whilst this power was generally exercised responsibly, by the late 1970s organised industrial action had sometimes got out of control and a correction was considered necessary. The basic method used was to introduce a new narrow definition of what constituted a 'trade dispute' for the purposes of trade union immunity from civil actions (Employment Act 1982, now consolidated as, in the main, TULRCA 1992, Part V). In particular under the new definition a dispute only counts as a trade dispute if it is 'between workers and their employer' thereby ensuring that industrial action taken in contemplation or furtherance of a dispute between 'workers and workers' would no longer entitle the unions involved to immunity from being sued. Important procedural requirements which a union must satisfy to qualify for immunity were also introduced. These currently include requirements to conduct a ballot of members before taking industrial action (TULRCA 1992, s.226), to notify the employer of the intention to hold a ballot, describing the employees who will be entitled to vote (TULRCA 1992, s.226A(2)(c)) and to give at least seven days' notice to the employer before promoting the industrial action (TULRCA 1992, s.234A).

Closed shop

Union-related industrial problems often resulted from 'closed shop' arrangements under which an employer and a trade union sometimes agreed that only members of that union would be employed. Closed shop agreements, formally known as 'union membership agreements', were not and still are not unlawful. However, the cost to both employers and trade unions of enforcing them was made impossibly high by the Employment Acts 1988 and 1989. Under the present law an individual who loses his job, or cannot get a job, because of a closed shop agreement will be entitled to substantial compensation.

Collective bargaining and trade union recognition

More recently, compulsory recognition of trade unions by employers for collective bargaining purposes, a fundamental plank of the Labour Party's 1997 election manifesto, was implemented by the Employment Relations Act 1999 with effect from 6 June 2000. The essential feature is to provide a process for compulsory recognition of a trade union which wishes to be recognised by an employer who, together with any associated employer, employs at least 21 workers. Although the main aim is to encourage voluntary recognition, this is achieved by setting up compulsory recognition arrangements if negotiations for voluntary recognition fail. The old Central Arbitration Committee (CAC), an organisation which traces its origins to an early industrial court created immediately after the First World War but which had ceased over the years to have any great significance, was revived. In 2000 the CAC was given a senior High Court judge as chairman, a semi-judicial role in resolving recognition disputes, and new premises and staff. Among the powers it now has there is one under which, in appropriate circumstances, it can arrange for the holding of secret ballots of workers to ascertain whether they want a particular union (or unions) to conduct collective bargaining on their behalf.

The Employment Relations Act 2004 (mainly in force by April 2005) made changes to the law on strike ballots and notices. The 2004 Act extended from 8 to 12 weeks the period of protected industrial action during which dismissal of a striker is normally automatically unfair dismissal and provided that any lock-out days are to be disregarded in calculating the 12-week period (Employment Relations Act 2004, s.26). Also the practice of offering inducements or bribes to individual trade union members to persuade them to forego union rights, was made unlawful by repeal of what is often colloquially referred to as the 'Ullswater amendment'.

A short eight-clause 'Trade Union Rights and Freedoms Bill' was introduced in the House of Commons with TUC support in 2006. This was partly to mark the centenary of the 1906 Trade Disputes Act noted above, but if enacted it would have made significant changes in trade union law, including legitimisation of secondary industrial action and repeal of the provision noted above which requires trade unions to give employers seven days' notice of industrial action ballots (TULRCA 1992, s.226A). The Bill failed to become law in the session of Parliament which ended in November 2007 and as at the time of writing has not been reintroduced.

Since Tony Blair stood down as Prime Minister in summer 2007 the Labour party has clearly depended more than previously on funding from trade unions. At the time of writing there is only a month or so to go until the next formal round of 'Warwick Two' agreement talks between unions and the Labour party set for July 2008. Gordon Brown is on record as saying that he will not give in to demands from the unions who want new rights but financial pressure may mean that this, like the promise to allow employment law to settle down after a few years of almost frenetic Parliamentary activity, will turn out to be more aspiration than attainable reality.

1.1.3 Wages

Finally, in this brief historical overview, mention should be made of wage regulation. The 1896 Truck Act made it illegal for an employer to make any deduction from wages (e.g. to cover breakages or as a crude form of discipline) unless the worker had agreed in writing and it was fair and reasonable for the deduction to be made. The Truck Acts were repealed and replaced by Part II of the Wages Act 1986 which in turn was replaced in 1996 by ERA 1996, ss.13–27.

As to minimum levels of wages, collective bargaining over the years had ensured that employers could not impose unreasonably low terms of remuneration on workers who had the back-up of trade union muscle. However, this was no direct help to workers without trade union or organised representation. Wages Councils, starting in 1909 as Trade Boards, were therefore established to set minimum levels of remuneration in specific industries in which collective bargaining did not operate. Indirect methods were also used to protect workers from unfair exploitation by employers. Thus during the First World War the first Rent Acts were enacted to prevent Glasgow shipyard owners, who frequently also owned the houses in which their workers lived, from increasing rents as a way of recouping additional wages which they had to pay workers for hurried repairs to naval ships after the battle of Scapa Flow. Back in the mainstream, with the exception of the Agricultural Wages Board, which still continues to set minimum wage levels for agricultural workers, Wages Councils were abolished in 1993. At that time, 26 Wages Councils were still operating, ranging from the Aerated Waters Wages Council, the Boot and Shoe Repairing Wages Council and the Button Manufacturing Wages Council to the Sack and Bag Wages Council, the Toy Manufacturing Wages Council and the Unlicensed Places of Refreshment Wages Council. For a while after 1993 the UK was the only EU Member State to have no general minimum wage-setting machinery, but since April 1999 the National Minimum Wage Act 1998 and the accompanying National Minimum Wage Regulations 1999 have ensured that all workers are entitled to at least a 'national minimum wage' (NMW) fixed from time to time by the government. In addition to entitling workers to arrears of pay, the Act includes criminal provisions. Prosecution has proved difficult (in the 10 years to April 2008 there were only two criminal prosecutions, both successful) and as a result the 2007/2008 Employment Bill provides for substantial increases in possible penalties and fines and for enhancement of the powers of HM Revenue & Customs (HMRC) to ensure compliance with the NMW rules.

1.2 CODES OF PRACTICE

Codes of Practice are made under statute by various organisations such as Acas, the Health and Safety Commission and, importantly, by the Secretary of State at the Department for Business, Enterprise & Regulatory Reform (BERR). For practical purposes they are essential reading where relevant and are often also useful as guides to official (albeit not necessarily always absolutely correct) understanding of the law in the areas to which they relate.

EMPLOYMENT LAW HANDBOOK

Failure to act in accordance with a Code of Practice does not of itself render a person liable to any proceedings. However, in most cases such failure is admissible in evidence and is an important, but not conclusive, consideration which a tribunal must take into account in deciding any relevant question, such as whether a particular dismissal is 'fair' or 'unfair'. Further, a significant element in arrangements noted above to replace the 2004 Dispute Resolution Regulations is a proposal (in clause 3 of the 2007/2008 Employment Bill) to give employment tribunals power to increase by up to 25 per cent the amount of any awards they make in cases where a Code of Practice applies and has not been complied with.

The Equal Opportunities Commission, the Commission for Racial Equality and the Disability Rights Commission were merged into a single Equality and Human Rights Commission (EHRC) with effect from 1 October 2007 but Codes of Practice they have issued continue to have effect until specifically revoked, with the new EHRC being given power to amend them and to issue new Codes (by Equality Act 2006, ss.14 and 42(3)).

Some of the main current Codes of Practice are noted in the list below.

1. Acas Codes of Practice:

    (a) CoP 1 – Disciplinary and Grievance Procedures (a draft revised version of this CoP was issued in May 2008);
    (b) CoP 2 – Disclosure of Information to Trade Unions for Collective Bargaining Purposes;
    (c) CoP 3 – Time Off for Trade Union Duties and Activities.

2. BERR (formerly DTI) CoP on Industrial Action Ballots and Notice to Employers.
3. BERR (formerly DTI) CoP on Access and Unfair Practices during Recognition and Derecognition Ballots.
4. BERR (formerly DTI) CoP on Picketing.
5. EHRC (ex-EoC) CoP on Sex Discrimination.
6. EHRC (ex-EoC) CoP on Equal Pay.
7. EHRC (ex-CRE) Code of Practice on Racial Equality in Employment.
8. EHRC (ex-DRC) CoP on Disability Discrimination 'Employment and Occupation'.
9. EHRC (ex-DRC) CoP on Disability Discrimination 'Duties of Trade Organisations to their Disabled Members and Applicants'.
10. EC Recommendation 92/131/EEC with annexed Code of Practice is entitled 'on the protection of the dignity of women and men at work' (sexual harassment).
11. Age Diversity at Work Code of Practice, issued by 'Age Positive', an agency of the DWP.
12. Health and Safety Commission Codes of Practice: Safety Representatives and Safety Committees, Time Off for Training of Safety Representatives,

Practice on First Aid at Work, Management of Asbestos in Non-Domestic Premises and over 50 other Health and Safety Codes of Practice.
13. Data Protection in the Employment Field (in four parts, consolidated version issued June 2005 by the Information Commissioner).
14. Code of Practice covering interception of communications under the Regulation of Investigatory Powers Act 2000.
15. A Code of Practice: Workforce Matters in Local Authority Service Contracts applies to all local authority contracts advertised from 13 March 2003. As from 18 March 2005 it was extended to cover not only local government but also the wider public sector, including the Civil Service, NHS and maintained schools. This Code, along with the Statement of Practice on Staff Transfers in the Public Sector issued by the Cabinet Office in January 2000, effectively 'gold-plates' the TUPE regulations in relation to public sector transfers and are sometimes known together as the 'TUPE plus' provisions.
16. A Gangmasters' Code of Practice for the agriculture and the fresh produce trades issued in November 2004, complementing the Gangmasters (Licensing) Act 2004.

There are many other non-statutory codes of practice issued by various authorities. Examples include two Codes of Practice issued by HMRC in connection with enforcement of the NMW, entitled 'Information for Employers' and 'Complaints by Workers'.

1.3 UNFAIR DISMISSAL AND WRONGFUL DISMISSAL

Unfair dismissal and wrongful dismissal are totally separate concepts. A dismissal may be unfair or wrongful, or both, or neither.

Wrongful dismissal is a common law concept. It is simply another name for a dismissal in breach of contract (typically, failure to give employees the contractual notice to which they are entitled when the circumstances do not justify instant dismissal).

On the other hand, unfair dismissal is entirely a creature of statute. As noted above, it is wholly independent of breach of contract to such an extent that there are circumstances in which an individual can be entitled to claim that he has been unfairly dismissed even though in ordinary parlance the event which triggered his claim may be neither 'unfair' nor 'dismissal'.

In 2001 the EAT reconfirmed that there is no logical inconsistency in finding that a wrongful dismissal is not unfair dismissal 'nor indeed the other way about'. The EAT rejected an argument that where an 'appellant was wrongfully dismissed at common law it must follow that the appellant was unfairly dismissed' (*Samuel* v. *London Borough of Lewisham* (unreported, EAT, 29 November 2001)).

Nevertheless it is possible to discern a trend towards the two concepts coming together if not in legal theory at least in so far as day-to-day practice is concerned. Four examples of this trend follow.

1.3.1 Compensation

Leaving aside the basic award (which currently has a theoretical maximum of £9,900 but is calculated according to a formula and only rarely reaches that amount), until 25 October 1999 the maximum an employment tribunal could award in an unfair dismissal case was £12,000. In October 1999 this was increased to £50,000.

Under Employment Relations Act 1999, s.34(1) the Secretary of State is required to make annual orders to index link the maximum compensatory award which employment tribunals can order by reference to percentage changes in RPI (Retail Prices Index), up or down, for the 12 months to the previous September. Inflation measured by the RPI is consistently at a greater rate than as measured by the government's generally preferred CPI (Consumer Prices Index) measure so increases in the statutory cap on compensatory award are significant. At the date of writing the maximum limit to a compensatory award is £63,000 (Employment Rights (Increase of Limits) Order 2007, SI 2007/3570, which came into effect on 1 February 2008).

Clearly the increase from £12,000 in 1999 to £63,000 in 2008 in the amount a tribunal can award has meant that since 1999 there have been many more cases in which there is no longer a practical difference between unfair and wrongful dismissal, at least so far as the financial rewards and costs to employee and employer are concerned. There is, of course, no statutory limit to the amount of damages which a court can award for wrongful dismissal.

1.3.2 Compensation offset

A second aspect of the coming together of unfair and wrongful dismissal concerns offset of monies received against compensation for dismissal. There is a long-established rule in unfair dismissal cases that a person who has been dismissed without notice should not be required to offset any wages he earns during what would have been the notice period against compensation/damages (*Norton Tool Co Ltd* v. *Tewson* [1972] ICR 501, NIRC). This is a special rule which applies in unfair dismissal cases only and does NOT apply in wrongful dismissal cases. In wrongful dismissal cases the normal common law rule applies to the effect that a claimant is under a duty to mitigate his loss and so must bring into account by way of offset against damages to which he is entitled for not being given proper notice any monies he has earned during what should have been the period of notice (see, for example, *Zepbrook Ltd* v. *Magnus* (unreported, EAT, 18 October 2006)).

The Court of Appeal has suggested that the time may have come to bring the unfair dismissal position in this respect into line with the common law, wrongful dismissal, position (see *Langley & anor* v. *Burlo* [2007] ICR 390, CA).

1.3.3 Legal process

Since 12 July 1994 tribunals have been given jurisdiction to hear wrongful dismissal claims as well as unfair dismissal claims (Employment Tribunals Extension of Jurisdiction (England and Wales) Order 1994, SI 1994/1623, or SI 1994/1624 for Scotland). Again, therefore, so far as employee and employer are concerned the difference between unfair and wrongful dismissal is of less importance than formerly, although in this instance it is still important as there is a cash limit on the amount of compensation that a tribunal can award for wrongful dismissal. Oddly, this cash limit has never been raised from the £25,000 figure set in 1994.

Although an ex-employee who includes a wrongful dismissal claim in his application to an employment tribunal may be able to apply to withdraw his claim so that he can pursue it in the High Court where the £25,000 limit noted above does not apply this is not a recommended practice. In *Fraser* v. *HLMAD Ltd* [2006] IRLR 687 the Court of Appeal (Mummery LJ) said that:

> ... claimants and their legal advisers would be well advised to confine claims in employment tribunal proceedings to unfair dismissal, unless they are sure that the claimant is willing to limit the total damages claimed for wrongful dismissal to £25,000 or less. If the claimant wishes to recover over £25,000, the wrongful dismissal claim should only be made in High Court proceedings.
>
> *Fraser* v. *HLMAD Ltd* [2006] IRLR 687, CA, para 31

1.3.4 Implied terms

The fourth example of the blurring of the traditional distinction between unfair and wrongful dismissal is more subtle but is rapidly assuming greater long-term significance. In recent years the courts have developed the theory of the 'implied contractual term of trust and confidence' in employment contracts. Because an implied term is just as much a contractual term as an express one, an employee may in some circumstances be able to claim that dismissal was wrongful dismissal even though the employer was not in breach of any of the written terms of the employment contract. One of the consequences is that the employee can then bring a claim in the courts, with no statutory limit on the amount of damages, rather than being restricted to bringing a claim in an employment tribunal with the limitations on possible compensation which would follow.

This situation is especially likely to arise where an employee resigns in reaction to unacceptable conduct by the employer and claims 'constructive dismissal'. It is well-established law that as a general rule constructive dismissal can only occur if the employer has committed a breach of contract (*Western Excavating (ECC) Ltd* v. *Sharp* [1978] ICR 221, CA). Thus, traditionally, it has not been possible for employees to claim constructive unfair dismissal unless they can establish that the constructive dismissal was also wrongful dismissal. This can lead not only to confusion but also to unsatisfactory consequences. The EAT found one way out of the problem when it held that the traditional rule did not apply in circumstances in which a constructive dismissal was automatically also unfair dismissal by virtue of the 1981 TUPE regulations (*Rossiter* v. *Pendragon plc* [2001] ICR 1265, EAT). Another more general way out of the problem may be for tribunals to look for a breach of the 'implied contractual term of trust and confidence' as a way of allowing constructive unfair dismissal claims which might previously have been excluded on the basis of the *Western Excavating* case.

Employees are also finding that employment tribunals are now receptive to the argument in appropriate cases that unequal treatment by an employer of different employees can amount to a breach of the implied term of trust and confidence. Although it is well-established law that there is no implied term, as such, that an employer will treat an employee reasonably (see, for example, *Post Office* v. *Roberts* [1980] IRLR 347 and *White* v. *Reflecting Road Studs Ltd* [1991] ICR 733, EAT) this principle has been weakened by use of arguments based on breach by an employer of the implied term of trust and confidence. Thus in one case British Gas offered different redundancy terms to different categories of employee, and an employee who complained that he had been unfairly treated as a result won his case (see *Transco (formerly BG plc)* v. *O'Brien* [2002] ICR 721, CA). In another case, the EAT held that a solicitor's secretary had been unfairly constructively dismissed when she resigned because her workload was increased but that of other secretaries was not (*Turner Coulston* v. *Janko* (unreported, EAT, 3 September 2001)).

The implications and effects of the implied term of trust and confidence, and the possible resulting overlap between the jurisdiction of employment tribunals and of the ordinary courts, are still being worked out at the highest judicial level. One example is a problem which has arisen in recent years in connection with the interaction between claims for breach of the implied term of trust and confidence and unfair dismissal claims. Employment tribunals, which have exclusive jurisdiction to hear unfair dismissal claims, are (unlike a county court or the High Court) bound by the statutory limit to the amount of compensation which they can award in non-discrimination dismissal cases. In appropriate situations, some dismissed employees have therefore attempted to bring court proceedings for breach of the implied term of trust and confidence, seeking damages of hundreds of thousands of pounds, as well as bringing unfair dismissal claims in the tribunals where the maximum compensatory award they could win is capped at £63,000 by statute. It was held by the House of Lords in July 2004 that this 'two pronged' approach is permissible provided that the facts are such that it can be shown that the breach of the implied term occurred quite separately from the dismissal (*Eastwood & anor v. Magnox Electric plc* and *McCabe v. Cornwall County Council* [2004] UKHL 35). Recognition by courts and tribunals of this implied contract term is thus eroding not only the practical importance but also the theoretical basis of the distinction between wrongful and unfair dismissal.

A dedicated website at **www.emplaw.co.uk/lshandbook** provides links to judgments and other source material referred to in this chapter.

CHAPTER 2
Categories of worker

2.1 WHY IT MATTERS

2.1.1 Background

When employment law began to emerge as a discrete subject in the early 1970s, employment protection applied to 'employees' only. Individuals who were not employees in the traditional sense of master and servant, were not entitled to statutory rights such as redundancy payments and the right to claim unfair dismissal.

Successive governments made subtle extensions to the definition of 'employee' in legislation. Thus the Sex Discrimination Act 1975 (SDA 1975) and Race Relations Act 1976 (RRA 1976) extended the protected category of employee to somebody who has entered into 'a contract personally to execute any work or labour'.

Recent legislation tends to use the concept of a worker rather than an employee. Depending on the precise definition used, 'worker' normally covers all people who work for a company, other than the genuinely self-employed; so casual workers, agency workers or miscellaneous categories of workers might be included.

When advising a client, it is important to check the exact definition of 'employee' or 'worker' within the relevant legislation in order to ensure that the client qualifies for protection. For ease of reference, the most commonly used definitions are set out below.

The question of employment status is regarded as one of fact, not law, so there can generally be no appeal from an employment tribunal's finding (*Lee* v. *Chung* [1990] IRLR 236; *Kapfunde* v. *Abbey National* [1999] ICR 1, CA). Of course if the question turns on proper construction of a contract or other document the position will be different – questions of construction are questions of law and so leave to appeal can be granted in such cases (*Davies* v. *Presbyterian Church of Wales* [1986] ICR 280, HL; *McMeechan* v. *Secretary of State for Employment* [1997] IRLR 353, CA and *Carmichael & anor* v. *National Power plc* [2000] IRLR 43, HL).

2.1.2 The statutory definitions

The main statutory definitions are:
Employee:

- 'an individual who has entered into or works under (or, where the employment has ceased, worked under) a contract of employment'
  - ERA 1996, s.230 (1);
  - Maternity and Parental Leave etc. Regulations 1999, reg.2;
  - Part-Time Workers (Prevention etc.) Regulations 2000, reg.1;
  - Flexible Working (Eligibility, Complaints and Remedies) Regulations 2002;
  - Fixed Term Employees etc. Regulations 2002, reg.1.
- 'contract of employment means a contract of service or apprenticeship, whether express or implied, and (if it is express) whether oral or in writing'
  - ERA 1996, s.230(2);
- 'employment means ... employment under a contract of service or apprenticeship or a contract personally to execute any work or labour'
  - SDA 1975, s.82; RRA 1976, s.78;
- 'employment means ... employment under a contract of service or of apprenticeship or a contract personally to do any work'
  - Disability Discrimination Act 1995, s.68(1);
  - Employment Equality (Age) Regulations 2006, reg.2;
- 'any individual who works for another person whether under a contract of service or apprenticeship or otherwise, but does not include anyone who provides services under a contract for services'
  - TUPE 2006, reg.2(1);

Worker:

- 'an individual who has entered into or works under ...
  (a) a contract of employment; or,
  (b) any other contract, whether express or implied and (if it is express) whether oral or in writing, whereby the individual undertakes to do or perform personally any work or services for another party to the contract whose status is not by virtue of the contract that of a client or customer of any profession or business undertaking carried on by the individual.'
  - ERA 1996, s.230 (3);
  - Working Time Regulations 1998, reg.2;

- National Minimum Wage Act 1998, s.54(3);
- Part-Time Workers (Prevention etc.) Regulations 2000, reg.1.

A similar (but not identical) definition of 'worker' is used in other, less mainstream, regulations such as the Merchant Shipping and Fishing Vessels (Health and Safety at Work) (Carcinogens and Mutagens) Regulations 2007, SI 2007/3100

Thus it can be seen that the definition of 'worker' excludes somebody in business on their own account such as a plumber, but might include subcontractors who work predominantly for one principal.

2.1.3 When it matters

A brief summary of the main legislative rights appears below:

	Employee	Workers
Unfair dismissal rights	✓	✗
Redundancy rights (including right to consultation)	✓	✗
Right to minimum period of notice	✓	✗
Right to SMP and SSP	✓	✗
Employer vicariously liable	✓	✗
Implied contract terms (e.g. mutual trust and confidence)	✓	✗
Protected under a TUPE transfer	✓	✗
Discrimination (fixed-term employees)	✓	✗
Discrimination (sex, race, disability, religion or belief, sexual orientation or age)	✓	✗ (although it does apply to contract workers)
Discrimination (part-time workers)	✓	✓
National minimum wage	✓	✓
Maximum 48-hour week	✓	✓
Right to rest breaks and minimum annual holiday under WTR	✓	✓
Whistleblowing legislation	✓	✓
Right to be accompanied at a disciplinary or grievance hearing	✓	✓

2.1.4 Mutuality of obligation

For a contract (whether a contract of employment or a contract for services) to exist at all, there must be mutuality of obligation between the parties. In other words, both parties must have agreed to render performance personally under the contract and the agreement must be for valuable consideration so a volunteer at a Citizens Advice Bureau, who neither received nor had any entitlement to remuneration, could not be an employee (*Melhuish* v. *Redbridge Citizens Advice Bureau* [2005] IRLR 419, EAT).

In practice what this means is that on the one side there must be an obligation to provide some work and on the other an obligation to personally undertake the work (*O'Kelly* v. *Trusthouse Forte* [1983] IRLR 369, CA; *Carmichael* v. *National Power* [1999] ICR 1226, HL; *Stevedoring & Haulage Services* v. *Fuller* [2001] IRLR 627, CA; *Bunce* v. *Postworth Ltd* [2005] IRLR 557, CA). However, the fact that there may be occasional acts of delegation is not inconsistent with agreement to perform work personally (*Byrne Brothers (Formwork) Ltd* v. *Baird & Ors* [2002] IRLR 96, EAT).

In the *Fuller* case, the employer inserted a specific clause into the contract denying mutuality of obligation, and this was held to be conclusive. However, the Court of Appeal did not permit argument (because the point had not been raised before the employment tribunal) on the question of whether a contractual clause denying mutuality of obligation is an attempt to contract out of the rights otherwise conferred by the contract, and thus void under ERA 1996, s.203. Another challenge to such a clause might be that it falls foul of the test of reasonableness under the Unfair Contract Terms Act 1977 (*Brigden* v. *American Express Bank Ltd* [2000] IRLR 94).

The EAT has held that the fact that there is no mutuality of obligation when work is not being performed is of little significance in determining the status of the relationship when a person is actually at work. It is simply one of the factors to take into account in deciding whether the person is a worker, an employee or self-employed (*James* v. *Redcats (Brands) Ltd* [2007] IRLR 296).

2.2　CONTRACTS OF EMPLOYMENT

2.2.1　Background

As seen above, many of the main employment rights (including unfair dismissal and the right to redundancy payments) are only available to people employed under a contract of employment (or apprenticeship). They are not available to other categories of worker, such as agency workers, casual workers or the genuinely self-employed.

Many of the cases on the distinction between employees and the self-employed adopt dated terminology such as 'master and servant', or 'contract of service' (employee) and 'contract for services' (self-employed).

2.2.2 The test for employment status

The courts have toyed with various tests to decide whether an individual was employed or self-employed. These include the 'control test' (was the individual subject to the employer's control?), the 'integration test' (was the individual fully integrated into the employer's business?) and the 'economic reality test' (was the individual in business on his own account?).

The modern law on employment status is set out in *Ready Mixed Concrete* v. *Minister of Pensions* [1968] 2 QB 497, 515C. In that case, McKenna J. held:

> A contract of service exists if these three conditions are fulfilled:
>
> (i) The servant agrees that, in consideration of a wage or other remuneration, he will provide his own work and skill in the performance of some service for his master.
> (ii) He agrees, expressly or impliedly, that in the performance of that service he will be subject to the other's control in a sufficient degree to make that other master.
> (iii) The other provisions of the contract are consistent with its being a contract of service.

It is usually obvious whether a particular contract is a contract of employment (i.e. one for service) or a contract for services (i.e. with an independent contractor/self-employed person). A simple and straightforward example is the contrast between the jobs of chauffeur and taxi-driver referred to in *Stephenson Jordan & Harrison Ltd* v. *Macdonald and Evans* [1952] 69 RPC 10). Recognising the relevance of what is sometimes called the 'elephant test' (you can recognise something you cannot describe or define) the EAT will not lightly overrule a decision by an employment tribunal that a particular individual is or is not an employee or is or is not self-employed (see, for example, *Forest Mere Lodges Ltd.* v. *Watt & Cameron* (unreported, EAT, 6 February 2007)).

2.2.3 The big decision – employee or self-employed?

Tribunals will look at a number of factors to determine whether somebody is an employee. These include general indicators and specific pointers.

General indicators:

- What the job advertisement said.
- What any written contract or job offer letter says.
- The tax status of the worker – Schedule E is a strong indicator of employment; Schedule D of self-employment. Note that this is not determinative: *AirFix Footwear Ltd* v. *Cope* [1978] ICR 1210, where a person treated as self-employed by the Inland Revenue was treated as an employee by the employment tribunal, or *Express & Echo Publications* v. *Tanton* [1999] ICR 693, CA where the opposite was the case.
- Whether there are other workers doing similar duties for the employer, and whether they are employed or self-employed.

CATEGORIES OF WORKER

- The extent of control exercised by the employer over the worker.
- Who arranges a replacement if the worker cannot attend work. If the employer arranges a replacement, this will normally indicate employee status. If the worker can arrange his own replacement, this will normally indicate self-employed status. However, whilst often conclusive (*Express & Echo Publications* v. *Tanton* [1999] ICR 693, CA; *Bunce* v. *Postworth Ltd* [2005] IRLR 557, CA), it is not necessarily so (*MacFarlane* v. *Glasgow City Council* [2001] IRLR 7, EAT; *Byrne Brothers (Formwork) Ltd* v. *Baird* [2002] IRLR 96).
- Who provides the equipment.
- Who pays for any professional insurance.

Specific pointers towards employee status:

- The existence of a staff handbook or collective agreement which governs the individual's work.
- A formal induction process, or the provision of training.
- Whether the employer moves the worker around from job to job.
- If the worker receives sick pay (note: since the Working Time Regulations 1998 came into force, holiday pay is no longer a significant pointer).
- If the employer can overrule the worker, when the worker decides how or when the job is to be done.
- If the employer has exercised disciplinary powers over the worker, or if the worker has utilised a grievance procedure.
- If the contract contains restrictive covenants (either during the employment period or post termination).

Specific pointers towards self-employed status:

- The worker works from his own premises.
- The worker is responsible for his own expenses, rather than being able to reclaim them from the employer.
- The worker works for other employers/organisations.
- The worker issues invoices before receiving payment.
- The worker stands to make (or lose) money depending on how well he does his job (such a contractor should not be confused with an employee who is paid commission).
- The worker has invested his own money in being able to perform the job properly (e.g. purchased equipment, paid for his own training).
- The worker has his own business cards (rather than company business cards) or has his own advertisements (e.g. in Yellow Pages).
- The worker had some influence over his rate of pay (e.g. tendered against others for the work).

HMRC provides first-class guidance on the employee/self-employed distinction (see **www.hmrc.gov.uk/employment-status/index.htm**). Note that tribunals will not adopt a checklist approach: they will look at all the factors to form an overall picture.

2.2.4 Labels

If the parties agree between themselves whether the worker is an employee or self-employed, this will be a strong indicator but will not be conclusive. The tribunal may depart from a self-imposed label where the label is manifestly wrong, or where it has been imposed to defraud HMRC (note: in such a case, an employee will be unable to benefit from many employment rights anyway because of the doctrine of illegality – *Massey* v. *Crown Life Insurance* [1978] 2 All ER 576, CA); although if the employee was not involved in illegal performance, the contract may still be relied upon (*Hall* v. *Woolston Leisure Co.* [2001] ICR 99; *Vakante* v. *Addey and Stanhope School (No. 2)* [2005] ICR 231).

It has been held that the formation of a one-person limited company as an intermediary between employer and worker does not automatically prevent the status being that of employer/employee (*Catamaran Cruisers* v. *Williams* [1994] IRLR 386). Clearly what matters is the reality of the situation. Thus an individual who provides his services to an end-user via his own service company can be the 'employee' of that end-user even though the arrangement is set up through an independent employment agency and even though the contract(s) expressly states that he or she is 'self-employed' (*Cable & Wireless plc* v. *Muscat* [2006] IRLR 354, CA).

It should be noted, however, that other cases have suggested that if the parties choose to impose a corporate intermediary, this will prevent employment status arising (*Costain Building & Engineering* v. *Smith* [2000] ICR 215; *Hewlett Packard* v. *O'Murphy* [2002] IRLR 4, neither of which are referred to in the *Cable & Wireless plc* v. *Muscat* judgment).

2.3 SPECIFIC TYPES OF WORKERS: HOW THEY FIT IN

2.3.1 Agency workers

This covers people who work for a principal but whose contracts are with a separate employment agency. Typically, the employment agency has people seeking work on its books. The agency places these workers with clients (the principal) on short-term, or sometimes longer-term, contracts. The agency pays the worker's remuneration directly, and the principal pays the agency a sum of money which covers the worker's remuneration and a profit element for the agency.

The agency worker covers the category of worker commonly known as a 'temp', no matter how long the temp may be working for a particular organisation.

An agency worker's arrangement typically has two distinctive features:

(a) the agency has contracts with its end-user client and with the worker (giving rise to what is often referred to as a 'triangular relationship') but the worker has no contract with the end-user; and
(b) control over the work done by the worker is exercised by the end-user and not by the agency.

For some years, the courts consistently held that agency workers were not employees of the end-user (as there was no contract, and thus no contract of employment), and were not employees of the agency either (due to lack of day-to-day control by the agency). However, several cases have suggested that the worker might be an employee. In *Frank* v. *Reuters Ltd* [2003] IRLR 423 and *Dacas* v. *Brook Street Bureau (UK) Ltd* [2004] ICR 1437, the Court of Appeal held that tribunals must consider whether there is an implied contract of employment between the agency worker and the end-user (a number of factors, in particular the length of the period for which the agency worker works for the end-user, might give rise to such an implied contract). Indeed, at least in theory, the same individual could conceivably be the employee of both (see *Cairns* v. *Visteon UK Ltd* [2007] IRLR 175, EAT). Even where a written agreement provides that it contains the entire agreement between the parties and that no contract of employment exists, this will not be determinative (*RNLI* v. *Bushaway* [2005] IRLR 674).

In the last couple of years, there has been a backlash which has cast considerable doubt on *Franks* v. *Reuters* and *Dacas* v. *Brook Street*, although neither case has been overruled. In *James* v. *Greenwich Council* [2008] IRLR 302, the Court of Appeal reminded tribunals that the test for implying a contract between agency worker and end-user was whether it was necessary to do so. If the relationship (including the element of control by the end-user) could be explained by a straightforward agency agreement, there would be no necessity to imply a contract between worker and end-user. The Court of Appeal concluded their judgment with a stern warning to practitioners not to bring cases asserting that agency workers are employed by the end-user unless there was something other than the normal agency relationship in place which demonstrated it was necessary to imply a contract between worker and end-user.

In a case in 2007 it was held by the EAT that a worker could be an employee of the employment agency which supplied him to an end-user client even though it was the end-user rather than the agency who exercised control over the actual operation of his work (*Consistent Group Ltd* v. *Kalwak & ors* [2007] IRLR 560, EAT. A final decision in this case, which the Court of Appeal remitted back for reconsideration by an employment tribunal in April 2008 (reported at [2008] IRLR 505) had not been reached at the time of writing).

As noted above it is possible for an individual who provides his services to an end-user via his own service company to be the 'employee' of that end-user even though the arrangement is set up through an employment agency (*Cable & Wireless plc* v. *Muscat* [2006] IRLR 354, CA).

About the only thing that is clear is that there is nothing automatic about the position. On at least two occasions since 2005 the EAT has called for Parliament to clarify the situation for protection of agency-supplied workers. There were some who hoped that the DTI 'Consultation on Measures to Protect Vulnerable Agency Workers' (February 2007) might have led to legislative change, but the resulting Conduct of Employment Agencies and Employment Businesses (Amendment) Regulations 2007, SI 2007/3575, which came into force on 6 April 2008, did not deal with the question of the employment status of agency workers.

The Conduct of Employment Agencies and Employment Business Regulations 2003, SI 2003/3319, as amended by the 2007 regulations noted above, have no direct bearing on the employment status of agency workers; however, they do provide that the agency is obliged to tell the employee whether he is employed by it (the agency) or the client company and this must be set out in a document given to the employee before he commences his assignment (see reg.14). This statement will not be determinative and the common law tests will still have to be fulfilled. The regulations make a distinction between agencies that have a direct contractual relationship with the worker in respect of the work to be performed (an employment business) and agencies that have no such contractual relationship with the work-seeker (employment agencies). Both are required to give a work-seeker a statement of his right to cancel or withdraw from additional services such as training (reg.13, as amended by the 2007 regulations). Employment businesses must furnish the work-seeker with a statement which details whether the work-seeker is or will be employed by the employment business under a contract of service or apprenticeship, or a contract for services, and in either case the terms and conditions of employment of the work-seeker which apply, or will apply (reg.15(1)).

When engaging a worker through an agency, it is prudent for the end-user to ensure that there are terms in the contract with the agency that:

- The worker is not an employee of the end-user.
- The agency has disciplinary control over the worker.
- (If possible) the supply of workers through the agency is rotated.
- The agency should complete forms such as mortgage application forms.
- The agency pays the worker directly.

Finally, looking to the future, the draft EU Directive on 'Working conditions for temporary workers', issued in November 2002 is at last making headway. For several years this draft Directive was stalled, largely because of British opposition. However, in June 2008 agreement was reached at a meeting of EC Member States in Luxembourg which should enable the Directive to proceed. The main points agreed are:

- equal treatment as of day one for temporary agency workers as well as regular workers in terms of pay, maternity leave and leave;
- possibility to derogate from this through collective agreements and through agreements between social partners at national level (the British 'social partners', government, CBI and TUC, agreed shortly before the June 2008 meeting that a 12-week qualification period would apply in Britain);
- temporary agency workers to be informed about permanent employment opportunities in the user enterprise;
- equal access to collective facilities (canteen, childcare facilities, transport service);
- Member States must improve temporary agency workers' access to training and childcare facilities in periods between their assignments 'so to increase their employability';
- Member States must ensure penalties for non-compliance by temporary agencies and enterprises.

2.3.2 Casual workers/homeworkers

The basic position is that these individuals are generally entitled to the national minimum wage, have rights under working-time protections and under discrimination legislation and are entitled to statutory maternity pay. However, generally, they are not employees as there will generally be a lack of mutuality of obligation (see, for example, *Bridges & ors* v. *Industrial Rubber plc*, EAT on 21 September 2004, the case of the 'Gosport Nine').

For most employment law purposes the important question is likely to be whether there is an ongoing umbrella contract between the parties, or merely a series of short-term contracts with gaps between them (which would break continuity of employment).

In *Nethermere Ltd* v. *Taverna* [1984] IRLR 240, the Court of Appeal held that:

> there is no reason why well-founded expectations of continuing home work should not be hardened or reinforced into enforceable contracts by regular giving and taking of work over periods of a year or more and why outworkers should not thereby become employees under contracts of service like those doing similar work at the same rate in the factory.

If mutuality of obligation does exist, it is simply a matter of applying the standard tests to determine the worker's status.

The National Minimum Wage Act 1998, s.35 specifically covers homeworkers. It defines a homeworker as 'an individual who contracts with a person for the purposes of that person's business on the execution of work to be done in a place not under the control or management of that person'. In that context, in *James* v. *Redcats (Brands) Ltd* [2007] IRLR 296, the EAT held that:

the fact that there is a lack of any mutual obligations when no work is being performed is of little, if any, significance when determining the status of the individual when work is performed. At most it is merely one of the characteristics of the relationship which may be taken into account when considering the contract in context. It does not preclude a finding that the individual was a worker, or indeed an employee, when actually at work.

James v. *Redcats* was remitted back to a new employment tribunal to decide whether on the facts Mrs James was a worker in the light of guidance on the law provided by the EAT. In February 2008, the Cardiff employment tribunal ruled that she was indeed a worker and also a homeworker for purposes of the NMW legislation.

There is an International Labour Organisation (ILO) Convention 177 on Homework which provides that 'national policy on home work shall promote, as far as possible, equality of treatment between homeworkers and other wage earners, taking into account the special characteristics of home work and, where appropriate, conditions applicable to the same or a similar type of work carried out in an enterprise'. At the time of writing this Convention had not been ratified by the United Kingdom and ratification is not expected in the near future (in a House of Commons debate in January 2008 the government said it has no present intention to change or add to this area of employment law).

2.3.3 Workers under 'zero hour contracts'

There is no legal definition of a 'zero hours contract'. It is a day-to-day name for a contract under which the employer does not guarantee to provide work and pays only for work actually done.

A zero hours contract thus enables employers to call on staff at any time and not pay them when they are not needed. There are no specific rules covering the position of persons working under such contracts, although the Secretary of State would be able to make such rules under powers provided by the Employment Relations Act 1999, s.23 – see **section 2.4**).

As a general rule persons working under zero hours contracts are unlikely to be able to accrue continuity of employment but can do so if, in practice, they work regularly. Thus in *Colley* v. *Corkindale* [1995] ICR 964, EAT, an employee worked only once a fortnight (every other Friday) but was held to accrue continuity of employment.

A 1998 White Paper *Fairness at Work* noted the potential for abuse of zero hours contracts which can, at least in theory, be used to deprive individuals of those employment rights which require continuity of employment.

2.3.4 Ministers of religion

Traditionally ministers of religion did not normally come within the definition of 'employee'. This was on the basis that a minister is an office holder and there is no express employment contract between a minister and his church (*Diocese of Southwark* v. *Coker* [1998] ICR 140, CA).

That traditional position has now changed. In December 2005 in *Percy* v. *Church of Scotland Board of National Mission* [2006] IRLR 195, HL the House of Lords ruled that a Church of Scotland Minister's relationship with her church constituted employment for purposes of SDA 1975. That Act gives a wider meaning to 'employment' than ERA 1996, which was not then under consideration as Ms Percy had dropped an unfair dismissal claim at an earlier stage. Nevertheless two of the five Law Lords suggested that the traditional position noted above might now need to be reconsidered. This happened in October 2006. The EAT then ruled that a minister, this time a minister of the New Testament Church of God, was an employee of that church and could claim unfair dismissal, a decision which was later upheld by the Court of Appeal (*New Testament Church of God* v. *Stewart* [2008] IRLR 134).

Section 19 of SDA 1975 excludes religions where the appointment of a minister of the 'wrong' gender would offend its followers.

2.3.5 Civil servants

There is debate about whether civil servants should properly be regarded as office holders or as ordinary employees or even as both (see *Robinson* v. *City of London Territorial and Auxiliary Forces Association* [1967] 2 ITR 652 and *R* v. *Lord Chancellor's Department, ex parte Nangle* [1991] ICR 743).

However, this question is largely academic as ERA 1996 s.191 expressly provides that the majority of rights under that Act (including the right to claim unfair dismissal) apply to Crown servants. In addition, the discrimination statutes apply to civil servants. However, Crown servants are not entitled to written particulars of employment, a statutory minimum notice period or a statutory redundancy payment.

A difficult problem has arisen by virtue of recent decisions by the courts and tribunals concerning agency workers showing that in some situations a worker provided by an agency can be an employee of the end-user (see **section 2.3.1**). The Civil Service Order in Council 1995 (as amended) provides that, generally speaking, people cannot lawfully become civil servants other than by selection on merit via fair and open competition. This provision is fundamental to Civil Service recruitment. If a court or tribunal finds that an agency worker used by a government department is, or has evolved into being, an employee of that department it could thereby be making people civil servants. This would be contrary to the strict requirements of the Order in Council noted above, that appointment must be on merit via fair and open competition.

In an effort to prevent escalation of the problem the President of the Employment Tribunals issued a Practice Direction on 15 November 2007.

This provides that cases where the Order in Council noted above applies shall be stayed pending the outcome of two test cases due to be heard at the London Central Employment Tribunal. These cases will address the question of whether the Order in Council precludes a contract of employment ever being implied where the agency worker is working for the Crown.

2.3.6 Overseas workers

The right to claim under the discrimination legislation applies only to workers 'in relation to employment . . . at an establishment in Great Britain'.

The position is more complicated for claims under the ERA 1996, including unfair dismissal, and other miscellaneous employment rights. It is examined in **Chapter 11** on unfair dismissal, at **section 11.3.12**.

2.3.7 Apprentices

As seen from the definition above (**section 2.1.2**), apprentices fall within the definition of employee under the discrimination statutes and TUPE. They do not, strictly, fall within the definition of employee for the purposes of the ERA 1996 (including the right to claim unfair dismissal) or the Maternity and Parental Leave etc. Regulations 1999; however, 'contract of employment' is defined in ERA 1996, s.230(2) so as to include a (common law) apprenticeship.

The fact that an 'apprenticeship' is a modern apprenticeship in terms of the Learning and Skills Act 2000, i.e. where there is a tripartite agreement between 'apprentice', 'employer' and a government-sponsored service provider, does not preclude it being an 'apprenticeship' in the traditional sense (*Thorpe* v. *Dul* [2003] ICR 1556). The Court of Appeal held in 2006 that the question is one of fact which has to be determined by an employment tribunal (*Flett* v. *Matheson* [2006] IRLR 277, CA).

The Law Society's training solicitor contracts are 'apprenticeship' contracts which give trainees broader rights than other employees. However, it seems they do not generally provide unfair dismissal rights because they cannot be terminated by the employer and therefore there cannot be a 'dismissal' within the meaning of ERA 1996 s.95. The pupilage, under which a barrister trains, is a common law contract of apprenticeship (*Edmonds* v. *Lawson* [2000] ICR 567, CA).

2.3.8 Police

Police service is not 'employment' for the purposes of the ERA 1996. Accordingly police officers do not qualify for the statutory protections against unfair dismissal, redundancy and/or unlawful deduction from wages (for members of the statutory police forces, see **section 11.3.8**).

However, special rules extend the sex and race discrimination legislation and health and safety rules to police officers (see SDA 1975, s.17 and RRA 1976, s.76A). The extent to which the police force can be vicariously liable for acts of sex and race discrimination by one police officer against another is historically complicated, and is addressed in **section 14.9**. It is no longer in doubt, however, that the chief constable is vicariously liable for claims of race harassment which occurred after April 2001, or sex harassment which occurred after July 2003.

From 1 August 2004, police officers have had whistleblowing protection in the same way as other workers (ERA 1996, s.43KA inserted by Police Reform Act 2002, s.37). The Independent Police Complaints Commission has been added to the list of 'prescribed persons' to whom disclosures (i.e. disclosures concerning conduct of police officers) can be made (Public Interest Disclosure (Prescribed Persons) (Amendment) Order 2004, SI 2004/3265).

DDA 1995 has applied to police officers since 1 October 2004 (Disability Discrimination Act 1995 (Amendment) Regulations 2003, reg.25).

2.3.9 Company directors

The position of company director is an office not an employment. A director may be an employee as well as being a director but this is not automatic – indeed, it is common practice for companies to have non-executive directors who are not employees, have no service agreement and no employment relationship of any sort with the company.

Whether a shareholder/working director of a company is an employee depends on the facts of each case. Relevant considerations include the reasons for the contract, whether it was made when insolvency loomed, what each party actually did pursuant to the contract and importantly the degree of control exercised by the company over the individual. At the end of the day, the most important single test is likely to be whether the individual concerned is in reality answerable only to himself. If 'yes', and as a result a tribunal finds that the contract under which he works is not in reality a 'contract of service' and therefore that he is not an employee within the meaning of ERA 1996, s.230 of the company concerned, it is unlikely that the EAT will overturn the decision (*Morrison* v. *ODS Business Services Ltd & ors* (unreported, EAT, 21 June 2007)).

Whilst a controlling shareholding is significant it is not on its own determinative of the issue (see *Secretary of State (DTI)* v. *Bottrill* [1999] ICR 592, CA, *Hauxwell & anor* v. *Secretary of State of Trade and Industry & ors* (unreported, EAT, 19 June 2002) and *Nesbitt* v. *DTI* [2007] IRLR 847. It may raise doubts as to whether that individual concerned is truly an employee, is always relevant and may be decisive. However, it will not on its own justify a finding that there was no contract of employment (*Clark* v. *Clark Construction Initiatives Ltd & anor* [2008] IRLR 364, EAT).

EMPLOYMENT LAW HANDBOOK

The fact that a director has guaranteed a company's debts to a bank is not inconsistent with his being its employee (*Neufeld* v. *A&N Communication in Print Ltd* (unreported, EAT, 11 April 2008)).

2.3.10 Partners

Leaving aside Limited Liability Partnerships (LLPs) established under the Limited Liability Partnerships Act 2000, 'partnership' is defined as 'the relationship which subsists between persons carrying on a business in common with a view of profit' (see Partnership Act 1890, s.1).

There are current proposals for a Partnerships Bill which, if pursued, will mean that partnerships in England and Wales can become legal entities as they already are in Scotland. The long-established and well-known definition of 'partnership' noted above will also be changed (in wording if not meaning) when and if the Bill is passed.

Partners in a firm, other than salaried partners, are not normally employees — quite the contrary, they are the employers. Their status is different from (say) executive directors of a company, who usually will be employees. Whilst most of the employment protection legislation does not apply to partners, the sex and race (not disability) discrimination legislation does (SDA 1975, s.11 and RRA 1976, s.10).

Salaried partners (who, usually, will not be partners within the strict meaning of the Partnership Act) are normally employees, and qualify for all employment rights.

In general the Age Discrimination regulations, in effect from 1 October 2006, apply to the partners in partnerships as much as to employees. However, there is an important difference in respect of retirement. The 'exception for retirement' rule which enables an employer to require an employee to retire at age 65 does not apply to partners in a partnership (see **Chapter 16** and Employment Equality (Age) Regulations 2006, regs. 17 and 30).

2.4 THE FUTURE

The government has power, under Employment Relations Act 1999, s.23, to issue secondary legislation redefining who is to be treated as an employee or employer and what rights extend to what categories of workers. This is a surprisingly potent power to be exercised by statutory instrument — particularly one which (as in this case) does not need to be laid before Parliament for approval.

The government issued a discussion document in July 2002 on employment status in connection with statutory employment rights but no further action has been taken.

A dedicated website at **www.emplaw.co.uk/lshandbook** provides links to judgments and other source material referred to in this chapter.

CHAPTER 3
Contracts of employment

3.1 GENERAL INFORMATION

Every employee has a contract of employment. It may not be in writing, and the employer and employee may disagree about some of the terms. Nevertheless, the relationship is contractual. Where the terms are not expressed, they are those standard in the trade or as can be inferred from the parties' conduct. Where the terms are disputed, the employment tribunal has jurisdiction to make declarations as to the terms of contracts of employment (ERA 1996, s.11).

All employers are obliged to provide a written statement of particulars of employment which contains basic information for the employee such as salary, dates of employment, job title and disciplinary procedures (ERA 1996, ss.1–3). Other than the right to seek a declaration, above, there is no free-standing financial penalty for an employer who fails to provide the written statement. However, if an employee successfully brings another type of tribunal claim, an additional two or four weeks' pay (capped at the current statutory maximum, £330 from 1 February 2008) may be awarded if the employer has not provided a written statement of terms and conditions in accordance with ss.1–3 (Employment Act 2002, s.38).

Contractual claims can be brought in the county court or High Court or, since July 1994, in employment tribunals (Employment Tribunals (Extension of Jurisdiction) Order 1994, SI 1994/1623). Only employees can commence breach of contract claims in the employment tribunal, although an employer can counterclaim once a contract claim has been raised by the employee. A claim can only be brought once the employment has come to an end (art.3(c) of the 1994 Order; *Miller Bros & FP Butler Ltd* v. *Johnston* [2002] IRLR 386). Tribunals cannot award more than £25,000. Any excess over the statutory maximum of £25,000 cannot be recovered in a civil court even if the claimant, in his claim form to the tribunal, expressly reserved the right to pursue a claim for the excess over £25,000 in the civil court. This is essentially because once an employment tribunal has given judgment on a wrongful dismissal claim it ceases to exist independently of the judgment and becomes *res judicata* so the claimant no longer has a cause of action to pursue in a civil court (*Fraser* v. *HLMAD Ltd* [2006] IRLR 687, CA). As a practical matter wrongful dismissal claims in excess of £25,000 should therefore always be brought in the High Court and not in the employment tribunal. However, all is not necessarily lost if this is not done – provided a claimant has expressly reserved the right to bring a claim in the civil courts and provided there has not yet been a hearing on the merits, a contract claim in the employment tribunal can be withdrawn without *res judicata* difficulties (*Sajid* v. *Chowdhury* [2002] IRLR 113, CA).

Like all contracts, a contract of employment can be tainted with illegality. The most common example is where employer and employee attempt to evade income tax (*Colen* v. *Cebrian (UK) Ltd* [2004] ICR 568). The employee will, however, only be precluded from relying on the provisions of a contract tainted with illegality where the employee was involved in illegal performance (*Hall* v. *Woolston Hall Leisure Co.* [2001] ICR 99; *Vakante* v. *Addey and Stanhope School (No.2)* [2005] ICR 231, CA). Further, nothwithstanding arguments to the contrary by HM Revenue Commissioners, the employee must have been aware that there was some form of misrepresentation or some attempt to conceal the true facts of the relationship before the contract is rendered illegal (*Enfield Technical Services Ltd* v. *Payne* and *Grace* v. *BF Components Ltd* [2008] EWCA Civ 393 on 22 April 2008).

In exceptional circumstances, the tribunal may take the employee's basic knowledge of English into account in assessing whether there was illegal performance (*Wheeler* v. *Quality Deep Ltd* [2005] ICR 265).

Dismissal of an employee who is not permitted to work in the UK is not normally unfair dismissal (it will be 'some other substantial reason for dismissal' falling within ERA 1996, s.98(2)(d)).

Rules in effect from 29 February 2008 under the Immigration, Asylum and Nationality Act 2006 (replacing the Asylum and Immigration Act 1996) make it an offence knowingly to employ a person aged 16 or over who is subject to immigration control and who has not been granted leave to enter or remain in the United Kingdom (or whose leave to do so is invalid, has ceased or is subject to a condition preventing him from accepting the employment). Employers have a defence if they can prove that, before the employment began, a document was produced to them in terms of the Immigration (Restrictions on Employment) Order 2007, SI 2007/3290. A contract to supply the labour of illegal immigrants may be similarly tainted with illegality, preventing any monies being recovered under it (*Dowling & Rutter* v. *Abacus Frozen Foods (No. 2)* 2002 SLT 491, OH; *Rutter* v. *Abacus Frozen Foods (No. 1)* (2000) *The Times*, 26 April).

3.2 WHERE DO CONTRACT TERMS COME FROM?

3.2.1 Statute

A number of terms are implied into the contract of employment by statute. For example, an equality clause is implied into all contracts of employment to

CONTRACTS OF EMPLOYMENT

ensure men and women receive the same remuneration for like work (or work of equal value) (EqPA 1970, s.1); another term implied by statute is the right to a minimum period of paid holiday (*Barber* v. *RJB Mining (UK) Ltd* [1999] ICR 679, QBD).

An employee cannot contract out of basic statutory employment rights and any attempt to do so is void (ERA 1996, s.203). Some subsidiary rights can be contracted out of – for example, the 48-hour maximum working week.

3.2.2 Express terms

Where a contract of employment is in writing, the majority of the terms will be expressly set out. Employment contracts range from basic statements (complying merely with the obligation to set out basic particulars of employment: see **section 3.1**) through to complex and lengthy documents, such as a service contract for a company director. The longer and more detailed a contract, the greater the scope for argument on interpretation or allegations of breach.

Express terms can also be agreed verbally. Thus, when an employee accepts a job offer based on a verbal guaranteed minimum commission of £10,000 per annum, this will be an enforceable express term of the contract.

Express terms are often incorporated into a contract of employment by reference to other documents; however, a lack of clear drafting can lead to confusion and, ultimately, litigation.

In the previous edition of this book, we said it was now clear that the Unfair Contract Terms Act 1977 applies to employment contracts. However, this proposition, which was based on the decision of the High Court in *Brigden* v. *American Express Bank Ltd* [2000] IRLR 94, has subsequently been questioned, although not expressly overruled, by the Court of Appeal. In the case in question the Court of Appeal ruled that an ex-employee of a bank was not dealing as a consumer and therefore could not use the Unfair Contract Terms Act 1977, s.3 to render void a contract term under which he forfeited his right to a bonus if he was no longer an employee at the date of bonus payments (*Commerzbank AG* v. *Keen* [2007] IRLR 132, CA).

In any event, even if the Unfair Contract Terms Act 1977 does not apply, an employee who has signed a written contract of employment will not normally succeed in a claim that one of its terms was unduly onerous (*Peninsula Business Services Ltd* v. *Sweeney* [2004] IRLR 49, EAT).

Collective agreements

These are agreements between the employer and a recognised trade union. A collective agreement is not legally enforceable unless it is in writing and contains a provision stating that the parties intend it to be a legally enforceable contract (TULRCA 1992, s.179).

The basic rule was set out in *Alexander* v. *Standard Telephones and Cables Ltd (No. 2)*[1991] IRLR 286, HC as follows:

> The principles to be applied can therefore be summarised. The relevant contract is that between the individual employee and his employer; it is the contractual intention of those two parties which must be ascertained. In so far as that intention is to be found in a written document, that document must be construed on ordinary contractual principles. In so far as there is no such document or that document is not complete or conclusive, their contractual intention has to be ascertained by inference from the other available material including collective agreements. The fact that another document is not itself contractual does not prevent it from being incorporated into the contract if that intention is shown as between the employer and the individual employee. Where a document is expressly incorporated by general words it is still necessary to consider, in conjunction with the words of incorporation, whether any particular part of that document is apt to be a term of the contract; if it is inapt, the correct construction of the contract may be that it is not a term of the contract. Where it is not a case of express incorporation, but a matter of inferring the contractual intent, the character of the document and the relevant part of it and whether it is apt to form part of the individual contract is central to the decision whether or not the inference should be drawn.

Selection procedures for redundancy are not apt for implied incorporation as they are not part of the day-to-day activities between employers and the employees (*LTI Ltd* v. *Radford* (unreported, EAT, 19 July 2001)). However, 'selection processes' are different from 'severance terms'. In a case in 2008 the EAT ruled that redundancy severance terms set out in a collective agreement were contractually binding but that the redundancy selection process or procedure set out in the same collective agreement was not binding (*Martland & ors* v. *Cooperative Insurance Society Ltd* (unreported, EAT, 10 April 2008)).

In general it is probably true that in recent years there has been an increased willingness by courts and tribunals to find that the terms of collective agreements have been incorporated into individual contracts of employment. Incorporation may be achieved in two ways: first, by an express term; second, on the view that the collective agreement represents the standard terms in the industry and that both parties, if questioned by the officious bystander, would have said 'of course we intended them to be included' (*Lee* v. *GEC Plessey Telecommunications* [1993] IRLR 383, HC; *Marley* v. *Forward Trust Group* [1986] IRLR 369, CA).

The Court of Appeal has stressed the importance of establishing the need for clear evidence to establish a custom and practice of incorporation of collectively negotiated terms (*Henry* v. *London General Transport Services Ltd* [2002] IRLR 472, CA). A shop steward or union representative will usually have ostensible authority to negotiate on behalf of union members, even if the union's internal procedures require that the proposed amendments be put to the individual employees and authorised by a higher officer within the union (*Harris* v. *Richard Lawson Autologistics* [2002] IRLR 476, CA). Indeed, a collective agreement negotiated by a union for its members can apply for the benefit of all employees, even those not a member of the union concerned (*Stewart* v. *The Moray Council* [2006] IRLR 168, Central Arbitration Committee).

On a TUPE transfer, where the terms of the contract incorporated a collective agreement, it is only the terms of the collective agreement at the date of the transfer that are relevant. The TUPE regulations do not require a transferee undertaking to adopt post-transfer changes in a collective agreement made with the transferor (*Ackinclose* v. *Gateshead Council* [2005] IRLR 79, EAT).

Staff handbooks

In the absence of a contractual term expressly incorporating the provisions of a staff handbook, it is difficult to predict whether courts will regard the contents of the handbook as having contractual status. Recent cases suggest that it is becoming easier for employees to establish that it was intended that the contents of a staff handbook should have contractual force (*Keeley* v. *Fosroc International Ltd* [2006] IRLR 961, CA and *Home Office* v. *Evans & Laidlaw* [2008] IRLR 59, CA).

The question of whether a provision in a staff handbook is incorporated into an employee's contract of employment can be crucial in enabling the employee to bring a claim of constructive dismissal since to do so the employee needs to prove that the employer breached a contractual term. The employee may circumvent the difficulty by arguing that there was an implied term that the employer should not arbitrarily disregard the provisions of the staff handbook (*Petrie* v. *MacFisheries Ltd* [1940] 1 KB 258; *Dal* v. *Orr* [1980] IRLR 413; but see *Secretary of State for Employment* v. *ASLEF* [1972] 2 QB 455).

Employers' policies which are not formally set out in a staff handbook are less likely to be found to be contractual terms. The most important factor appears to be clarity: a vague statement of intent is less likely to achieve contractual status than a clearly defined and detailed policy. However, again a breach of a policy may amount to a breach of the implied term of trust and confidence (see **section 3.3.2**) (*Dryden* v. *Greater Glasgow Health Board* [1992] IRLR 469, EAT (not contractual), *Grant* v. *South-West Trains Ltd* [1998] IRLR 188, HC (not contractual); but see *Secretary of State for Scotland* v. *Taylor* [1999] IRLR 362, CS (contractual)).

3.2.3 Implied terms

The law of contract recognises implied terms in a variety of situations: because they are necessary to give business efficacy to an agreement; because they are customary in the trade; or because the term is so obvious that the courts assume the parties must have intended it (the well-known 'officious bystander' test). Employment contracts are no different. Terms will be implied into the contract of employment when necessary to ensure it makes sense, or when such a term is common practice, or because the employer and employee must have intended it (*Devonald* v. *Rosser & Sons* [1906] 2 KB 728).

The courts will not lightly imply a term into a contract. Thus if there is an omission from a carefully drawn up agreement the natural inference will be that it 'was omitted advisedly from the terms of that agreement on the ground that it was seen as too controversial or too complicated . . .' and the court will not fill the gap with what it considers reasonable (*Ali* v. *Christian Salvesen Food Services Ltd* [1997] ICR 25, CA).

Because of the importance of establishing a contractual term in order to found a claim of constructive dismissal, a significant body of case law has arisen dealing with terms that are customarily implied into contracts of employment. Examples of these are set out in **section 3.3**.

3.3 COMMON CONTRACTUAL TERMS

3.3.1 Introduction

A number of terms are central to the employment relationship and are implied into all contracts. The most frequently encountered of these are set out below. **Section 3.3.2** contains terms which are implied into all employment contracts. **Sections 3.4** and **3.5** relate to terms involving fidelity (such as the duty of confidentiality) and restrictive covenants. The law will only imply limited terms relating to fidelity; anything more should be regulated by express provision.

3.3.2 Terms implied into all employment contracts

Mutual trust and confidence

An employer may not, 'without reasonable and proper cause conduct itself in a way calculated and likely to destroy or seriously damage the relationship of trust and confidence between employer and employee' (*Malik* v. *BCCI* [1997] IRLR 462, HL). The obligation is phrased in several different ways within the body of the five opinions within the House of Lord's report, for example, 'the employer shall not without reasonable and proper cause, conduct itself in a manner calculated and likely to destroy or seriously damage the relationship of confidence and trust between employer and employee' (this is from Lord Steyn's judgment in *Malik* v. *BCCI*, above). An important point here was the use of the word 'and' in the phrase 'calculated and likely to destroy . . .'. Other formulations have used the word 'or'. This clearly is far less restrictive and has had support from the EAT which said recently that the '. . . use by Lord Steyn of the word "and" instead of "or" in his formulation of the implied term is an example of Homer nodding' (*Baldwin* v. *Brighton and Hove City Council* [2007] IRLR 232, EAT).

In practice, the existence of the implied term of mutual trust and confidence comes close to an obligation on employers to act 'reasonably'. Indeed the term has been called an obligation of 'fair dealing' (*Shiner Ltd* v. *Hilton* [2001] IRLR 727, EAT). However, it does not go so far as to impose a general obligation on an employer to act sensitively in his dealings with an employee – although the employer must, of course, be careful not to breach the common law duty to take reasonable care to avoid causing foreseeable harm to the employee (*Deadman* v. *Bristol City Council* [2007] EWCA Civ 822).

It has been held that breach of the implied term of trust and confidence will always be repudiatory and therefore will always entitle the employee to resign in response to that breach (*Morrow* v. *Safeway Stores plc* [2002] IRLR 9, EAT and *Sime* v. *Imperial College London* (unreported, EAT, 20 April 2005). However, this proposition is probably of little practical significance as of course not every action of an employer that causes an employee to feel that trust and confidence has been undermined will amount to a breach of the implied term.

It is generally accepted that an employee who is not a director has no general positive duty to disclose his own misconduct to his employer (*Bell* v. *Lever Brothers* [1932] AC 161, HL and *BCCI* v. *Ali* [1999] IRLR 226, HC), save that he must disclose fraudulent conduct of fellow employees even if that will reveal his own misconduct (*Sybron Corp.* v. *Rochem* [1983] 2 All ER 706). However, more recently the High Court has suggested that senior employees as well as company directors have a positive duty to disclose breaches of duties owed to the employers (*Tesco Stores* v. *Pook* [2004] IRLR 618, HC in which it was held that a senior manager involved in defrauding his employers was under a positive obligation to disclose bribes taken in breach of his fiduciary duty).

Examples where an employer has been in breach of trust and confidence include: verbal abuse of an employee (*Palmanor Ltd* v. *Cedron* [1978] IRLR 303, EAT; *Cantor Fitzgerald International* v. *Bird* [2002] IRLR 867, HC); arbitrary refusal to award a pay increase (*FC Gardner Ltd* v. *Beresford* [1978] IRLR 63, EAT); failing to provide support for employees (*Wigan Borough Council* v. *Davies* [1979] IRLR 127, EAT); unreasonable accusations of theft (*Robinson* v. *Crompton Parkinson Ltd* [1978] IRLR 61, EAT); undermining a supervisor in front of subordinates (*Hilton International Hotels* v. *Protopapa* [1990] IRLR 316, EAT); persistently trying to vary an employee's terms and conditions of employment (*Woods* v. *WM Car Services (Peterborough) Ltd* [1982] IRLR 413, CA); failing to investigate allegations of sexual harassment (*Bracebridge Engineering* v. *Darby* [1990] IRLR 3, EAT); and failing to make reasonable adjustments as required by the Disability Discrimination Act (*Greenhof* v. *Barnsley MBC* [2006] IRLR 98, EAT). The mutual trust and confidence term is particularly important in regulating how an employer exercises a discretion with respect to an employee; for example, when awarding a bonus (*Horkulak* v. *Cantor Fitzgerald International* [2005] ICR 402, CA; *Commerzbank AG* v. *Keen* [2007] IRLR 132, CA and *Ridgway* v. *JP Morgan Chase Bank National Association* [2007] EWHC 1325 (QB)) or providing a bridging loan for relocation expenses (*French* v. *Barclay's Bank plc* [1998] IRLR 646, CA).

In exceptional circumstances it can be a breach of the implied term of trust and confidence for an employer to insist on strict compliance with express terms of an employment contract (*GMB Union* v. *Brown* (unreported, EAT, 16 October 2007), in which the GMB's insistence on strict compliance with its standard grievance procedures amounted to breach of trust and confidence as it was unreasonable to require the employee to discuss her grievance with the manager who was himself the perceived source of her problems).

There is no general implied obligation on an employer to advise the employee of his economic well-being, such as ways to maximise pension or insurance benefits (*Crossley* v. *Faithful and Gould Holdings* [2004] ICR 1615, CA).

If an employer treats one employee less well than others in a particular case, this may amount to breach of the term of trust and confidence: the duty extends to failing to take positive steps (e.g. not offering generous redundancy terms to one employee) as well as taking those positive steps (*Transco* v. *O'Brien* [2003] IRLR 441, CA; *Turner Coulston* v. *Janko* (unreported, EAT, 3 September 2001)).

A constructive dismissal case can be brought by an employee on the basis that a course of conduct by the employer culminated in a 'last straw which broke the camel's back' and cumulatively amounted to a fundamental breach of the implied term of trust and confidence. In such a case it is not necessary for the incidents which make up the course of conduct to be themselves breaches of contract (*Barke* v. *SEETEC Business Technology Centre Ltd* (unreported, EAT, 13 January 2006)). Nevertheless the resignation must be in response to an act which contributed something to the chain of events and which was not entirely innocuous (see *Omilaju* v. *Waltham Forest LBC* [2005] ICR 481, CA and *GAB Robins (UK) Ltd* v. *Triggs* [2007] ICR 1424, EAT).

Reasonable exercise of duties under disciplinary and grievance procedures

The statutory dismissal and grievance procedures (which came into force on 1 October 2004) require all stages of the process to be conducted 'without unreasonable delay' (Employment Act 2002, Sched.2, para.12). Section 30 of the Act provides for these procedures to be incorporated into all contracts of employment but has not been brought into force. The entire compulsory statutory dispute resolution system is due to be repealed and replaced with effect from April 2009 by a Code of Practice (see **section 4.1**) so it can safely be assumed that s.30 never will come into force.

Regardless of whether the statutory procedures apply or not, the courts will imply a term that grievances must be resolved within a reasonable period. Thus an employer who failed to hear a grievance over a two-month period, despite repeated requests from two employees, was found to be in breach (*WA Goold (Pearmak) Ltd* v. *McConnell* [1995] IRLR 516, EAT). In *McClory* v. *Post Office* [1993] IRLR 159, HC an employer, who suspended three employees for six months whilst investigating charges of violence, was found to be in breach of contract. The court implied a term that an employer would only suspend on reasonable grounds and would continue the suspension only for so long as there were reasonable grounds for doing so.

Likewise, it is an implied term not to impose a disciplinary sanction which is out of all proportion to the employee's offence (*BBC* v. *Beckett* [1983] IRLR 43, EAT; *Stanley Cole (Wainfleet) Ltd* v. *Sheridan* [2003] IRLR 885, CA).

An employer's refusal to allow an employee to appeal against dismissal can by itself justify a finding of unfair dismissal save in the exceptional cases such as where the employee accepts he has been guilty of serious misconduct, where there really is no point whatsoever in even entertaining an appeal (*West Midlands Co-operative Society Ltd* v. *Tipton* [1986] ICR 192, HL).

References

Normally there is no implied term requiring an employer to provide a reference for ex-employees. However, in circumstances where the employment is of a type where it is normal practice to require a reference from a previous employer before the job is offered, and where the employee cannot be expected to obtain new employment in the absence of a reference, there is an implied term that a reference will be provided. The most common example of this is employment in the financial services sector (*Spring* v. *Guardian Assurance* [1994] IRLR 460, HL).

If an employer does provide a reference, there is an implied term that the reference should be 'true, accurate and fair in substance' (*Bartholomew* v. *London Borough of Hackney* [1999] IRLR 246, CA). It need not, however, be 'full and comprehensive' (*Cox* v. *Sun Alliance* [2001] IRLR 448, CA). To minimise the risk of litigation, an increasing number of employers now provide references merely setting out the dates of employment, job title, salary and the reason for termination of employment.

Providing a safe working environment

Employers must provide a reasonably safe system and place of work, including ensuring that the equipment and fellow employees are reasonably safe. Failure to comply, or to offer alternative employment when it is not practical to comply, may amount to a constructive dismissal (*Thanet District Council* v. *Websper* (unreported, EAT, 30 September 2002) and *Marshall Specialist Vehicles* v. *Osborne* [2003] IRLR 672, EAT).

However, there are limits to an employer's duty in this respect. An employer is not a 'nanny' and has no duty to prevent an adult employee from doing work which the employee knows carries an element of risk (*Buck & ors.* v. *Nottinghamshire Healthcare NHS Trust* [2006] EWCA Civ 1576 and *Withers* v. *Perry Chain Co Ltd* [1961] 3 All ER 676).

This subject is addressed in more detail in **Chapter 8**.

Paying wages

This is so obvious, it hardly requires stating! An employer cannot avoid paying wages by asserting that no wages were ever agreed. In the absence of express agreement, the law requires a reasonable wage to be paid.

Providing work

As yet, the courts have not recognised a general 'right to work'. The traditional view is of a 'work–wage bargain'. The employee is entitled only to his wages; as Asquith J. put it: 'provided that I pay my cook her wages regularly, she cannot complain if I take all or any of my meals out' (*Collier* v. *Sunday Referee Publishing Co Ltd* [1940] 2 KB 647).

The position is different where the employee needs to be able to exercise his skills in order either to maintain them, or to protect his reputation (*Herbert Clayton and Jack Waller Ltd* v. *Oliver* [1930] AC 209, HL; *Land Securities Trillium Ltd* v. *Thornley* [2005] IRLR 765, EAT). Suspension of a professional person even on full pay 'inevitably casts a shadow over the employee's competence' and the courts can interfere by granting an injunction in appropriate cases (*Mezey* v. *South West London and St George's Mental Health NHS Trust* [2007] IRLR 244, CA).

Further, an employer must not without reasonable or proper cause arbitrarily or capriciously deny the employee the opportunity of working (see *Langston* v. *Amalgamated Union of Engineering Workers* [1974] IRLR 15, EAT; *William Hill Organisation Ltd* v. *Tucker* [1999] ICR 291, CA; *TFS Derivatives Ltd* v. *Morgan* [2005] IRLR 246, HC and D. Brodie, 'The Right to Work' (1998) Juridical Review 311–323).

Doing the work

An employee is obliged to work. Save to the extent specifically agreed, if at all, an employee may not delegate his duty to another (*Bunce* v. *Potsworth Ltd* [2005] IRLR 557, CA).

An employee is not obliged to obey instructions to do a job which is different from that which he was employed to do (*O'Brien* v. *Associated Fire Alarms Ltd* [1969] 1 All ER 93 and *Bull* v. *Nottinghamshire and City of Nottingham Fire and Rescue Authority* [2007] ICR 1631, CA).

Of course an employee who is unable to work through ill health or who exercises the right to paid holiday, parental or maternity leave, etc. will not be in breach of this term. Statutory terms trump implied common law terms (*O'Grady* v. *Saper* [1940] 3 All ER 527).

Exercising reasonable care

Employees must take reasonable care when performing their duties. In principle, an employee who causes loss to his employer by failing to take reasonable care could be sued by the employer (*Janata Bank* v. *Ahmed* [1981] IRLR 457, CA). However, it is unlawful for an employer to make deductions for any losses caused from the employee's wages unless the requirements of Part II of the ERA 1996 have been complied with (see **section 9.6**).

Obeying instructions

An employee is under an implied obligation to carry out the employer's reasonable and lawful orders. Failure to do so will place the employee in breach of contract and is usually listed as a disciplinary offence in the employee's contract (although a first offence is unlikely to justify dismissal). An order is lawful if it falls within the employee's job description and does not break the law; for example, an instruction to a lorry driver to drive at 100 mph would be an unlawful order, and the driver could not be justifiably disciplined for refusing to follow it (*Morrish* v. *Henlys (Folkestone) Ltd* [1973] IRLR 61, EAT; *Cresswell* v. *Inland Revenue* [1984] ICR 508, HC).

Where a written contract clearly defines an employee's contractual duties there can be an implied obligation on him to carry out duties outside of the express terms if, but only if, there are exceptional circumstances justifying the requirement, the work is suitable and the employee suffers no detriment in terms of contractual benefits or status and the change in duties is only temporary (*Luke* v. *Stoke on Trent City Council* [2007] IRLR 305, EAT).

Whether an instruction is reasonable will depend on all the circumstances: the classic case involves an instruction to an employee to visit Turkey, where he had been sentenced to be executed (*Ottoman Bank* v. *Chakarian* [1930] AC 277). Unsurprisingly, this was held to be an unreasonable instruction. In other words, the employer will be subject to the implied obligation of trust and confidence when giving instructions: an employer is likely to be in breach of the obligation in so far as he demands of the employee an impossible, criminal or ludicrous act.

3.4 DUTIES OF FIDELITY

This is a complex and rapidly developing area of the common law, often involving litigation of some urgency. Although we summarise the relevant principles, for a detailed study of these duties the reader is referred to specialist practitioners' textbooks.

3.4.1 Confidential information

Employers should express unambiguously the information which they require to be kept confidential and make it clear that the obligation of confidence persists after the employment relationship has ended. Such information might include customer lists or trade secrets. If the clause is sufficiently precise, injunctive relief will be granted to prevent employees from misusing this confidential information during, or after, their employment.

The law implies a term preventing employees from misusing confidential information during their employment. The duty of confidentiality owed by an ex-employee to his former employer is considerably less onerous than that owed by a continuing employee to his employer. Ex-employees are permitted to use their full skill and knowledge for their own benefit, even if that is in competition with the ex-employer and once the employment finishes, the law will protect only the trade secrets of the ex-employer. In the absence of an express term, it will not restrict use by ex-employees of other information accumulated during their employment. What amounts to a trade secret is a question of fact and degree – the Coca-Cola formula would qualify – and so is difficult to define (*Faccenda Chicken* v. *Fowler* [1986] IRLR 69, CA; *Lansing Linde Ltd* v. *Kerr* [1991] 1 All ER 418, CA; and *SBJ Stephenson* v. *Mandy* [2000] IRLR 233, QBD).

The courts will not imply a confidentiality term which goes beyond that set out above, no matter how reasonable it might be to do so (*Brooks* v. *Olyslager OMS (UK) Ltd* [1998] IRLR 590, CA).

If employees disclose confidential information during their employment, this will often justify summary dismissal (depending on the level of confidentiality/importance of the information, and whether this is listed as a dismissible offence in the employer's disciplinary code). However, employees are afforded considerable protection if they disclose confidential information in good faith in order to reveal some misdeed by the employer (Public Interest Disclosure Act 1998). This whistleblowing protection is examined in more detail in **section 9.25**.

3.4.2 Competition during employment

An implied term prevents employees from setting up in competition with the employer, or from working for a competitor (even outside working hours, if such employment truly competes with the employer), whilst the employment subsists. Often contracts include restrictive covenants which define the geographic areas or type of work in which the employee is prohibited from competing. The law distinguishes between actual competition (which an employee cannot engage in) on the one hand and steps taken in anticipation of competition – i.e. preparing to compete – on the other. The law does not imply a term to prevent the latter (*Hivac Ltd* v. *Park Royal Scientific Instruments* [1946] All ER 350; *Marshall* v. *Industrial Systems* [1992] IRLR 294, EAT; and *Foster Bryant Surveying Ltd* v. *Bryant* [2007] IRLR 425, CA).

Directors *(Item Software (UK) Ltd* v. *Fassihi* [2005] ICR 450, HC) and senior employees (*Tesco Stores* v. *Pook* [2004] IRLR 618, HC) are fiduciaries. They have an obligation to disclose any conflict of interest (*Shepherds Investments Ltd & Anor* v. *Walters & ors* [2007] IRLR 110, ChD). As a general rule the duties and responsibilities of a director to a company end when he stops being a director (*Keisner* v. *Terrus Group Ltd* [2006] EWHC 2765, ChD). Employees, on the other hand, are not fiduciaries; they have no duty to inform the employer of work they do for a third party in breach of contract (*Nottingham University* v. *Fishel* [2000] ICR 1462, QBD).

Secret profits

Employees who abuse their position of employment to make a secret profit must account for this to their employer (*Tesco Stores* v. *Pook* [2004] IRLR 618, HC).

3.4.3 Competition after employment

On termination of employment, subject to any enforceable post-termination restrictive covenant in his contract, an employee is free to compete with his employer. However, and importantly, if the termination resulted from a breach of contract by the employer (for example, in a constructive dismissal situation) the general rule is that any restrictive covenants, even if otherwise reasonable and enforceable, will fall away with the rest of the contract and so not be enforceable (*General Billposting Co. Ltd* v. *Atkinson* [1909] AC 118, HL; but see *Rock Refrigeration* v. *Jones* [1997] ICR 938, CA and *Campbell* v. *Frisbee* [2003] ICR 141, CA). This is addressed in greater detail in **section 3.5**.

3.5 RESTRICTIVE COVENANTS

3.5.1 Introduction

Restrictive covenants, which prevent workers from engaging in their trade or profession after the termination of their employment, are anticompetitive and in restraint of trade. In the absence of contrary policy arguments, they would be void.

However, the law also recognises that contracts freely entered into (where the employee agreed to a restrictive covenant) should normally be enforced. Thus the courts have reached a compromise: restrictive covenants are void unless the ex-employer can show that they do no more than is reasonable to protect its legitimate business interests.

The courts will not imply restrictive covenants; they must be expressed (*Wallace Bogan & Co Ltd* v. *Cove* [1997] IRLR 453, CA).

3.5.2 Legitimate business interests

The onus is on the employer to demonstrate that it is seeking to protect a legitimate business interest.

Trade secrets

This is addressed above under 'Confidential information' (see **section 3.4.1**).

Customers and suppliers

To establish that the employer is seeking to protect a legitimate business interest, the restrictive covenant should normally identify (either as a class or – ideally – by name) the customers and suppliers with whom the ex-employee has had contact within the recent past. Given these might change as time elapses, it is common to agree that the employer can provide a list at regular intervals. If the ex-employee has had no contact with particular customers, then the employer has no business interest to protect in relation to them, and a clause that purports to do so will be going further than is necessary to protect the employer's interests (*Herbert Morris Ltd* v. *Saxelby* [1916] 1 AC 688, HL).

Staff

Despite a number of authorities to the contrary pre-1990, the courts are now accepting that employers have a legitimate business interest in maintaining a stable workforce. Thus it is permissible to restrain ex-employees from soliciting people they used to work with to join their new enterprise. However, as with customers and suppliers, the clause must be carefully drafted (*Alliance Paper Group* v. *Prestwich* [1996] IRLR 25, HC; *Dawnay Day & Co Ltd* v. *De Braconier D'Alphen* [1997] IRLR 442, CA).

3.5.3 No more than is reasonable to protect the employer's interests

If a restrictive covenant is held to be unreasonable, it is void and unenforceable. Minor phrases or clauses can be severed, leaving the remainder of the clause intact. However, in the absence of any ambiguity, the courts cannot 'read-down' an otherwise unreasonable covenant to render it enforceable (*TFS Derivatives* v. *Morgan* [2005] IRLR 246, HC).

Extent of covenants

Courts will permit a prohibition on a senior ex-employee from working for a direct competitor; but, in order to be upheld, such a clause will have to be subject to strict geographical and temporal limits (*Dentmaster (UK) Ltd* v. *Kent* [1997] IRLR 636, CA). As a rule of thumb, a 6 to 12-month restriction will be reasonably safe, a 12 to 24-month restriction will be dubious, and a restriction in excess of 24 months is unlikely to be upheld.

The reasonableness of any geographical restriction will depend on the nature of the trade and the competition. A court might uphold a restrictive covenant preventing a print shop manager in Yorkshire from competing within seven miles of an ex-employer's premises; but a one-mile radius clause in central London is likely to be struck down: it would effectively prohibit a print shop manager from earning a living anywhere in central London (*Scully UK Ltd* v. *Lee* [1998] IRLR 259, CA). A solicitors' post-termination 6 mile geographical competition restriction was void as too wide but a 12 month anti-client-poaching restriction was valid in *Allan Janes LLP* v. *Johal* [2006] ICR 742, ChD. A 12-month post-termination restrictive covenant in the employment contract of the managing director of a firm of insurance brokers was valid in *Thomas* v. *Farr Plc & anor* [2007] ICR 932, CA.

When drafting a restrictive covenant clause, the employer should carefully consider how the geographical and temporal restrictions will affect the individual employee, taking into account the employee's occupation/profession (*Office Angels Ltd* v. *Rainer-Thomas* [1991] IRLR 214, CA; *Spencer* v. *Marchington* [1988] IRLR 392, HC; *Hollis & Co* v. *Stocks* [2000] IRLR 712, CA). Worldwide restrictive covenants, which used to be almost always regarded as excessive, may now be permitted in suitable cases such as high-tech industries (*Poly Lina* v. *Finch* [1995] FSR 751).

Two important factors are the seniority of the employee and the effect that the restriction will have on the employee's ability to earn a living. Courts will be more willing to enforce a restrictive covenant against a senior employee than against a junior one. It is not sufficient that the clause is reasonably necessary to protect the employer's interests. The court will undertake a balancing act to weigh the prejudice to the employer in striking down the covenant, against the prejudice to the employee in enforcing it (*Empire Meat Co. Ltd* v. *Patrick* [1939] 2 All ER 85, CA).

Dismissal of an employee for refusing to accept new reasonably required restrictive covenants can count as 'some other substantial reason' for dismissal and thus be a potentially fair reason for dismissal (*Willow Oak Developments Ltd t/a Windsor Recruitment* v. *Silverwood & ors* [2006] IRLR 607, CA).

Standard form clauses

It is important that the employer provides evidence that it has weighed up the need for the clause, and the extent to which it impacts on the ex-employee. A post-termination non-competition clause failed in one case mainly because the wording was the company's standard form (*Wincanton Ltd* v. *Cranny* [2000] IRLR 716, CA).

Specific consideration

The fact that the employer makes a specific termination payment to an ex-employee (a golden handshake) in order to secure his agreement to restrictive covenants does not override the public interest test that the clause go no further than is reasonable to protect the employer's legitimate business interests (*Turner* v. *Commonwealth & British Minerals Ltd* [2000] IRLR 114, CA). However, the employee's agreement in these circumstances will be a factor in determining what is reasonable (*J.A. Mont (UK) Ltd* v. *Mills* [1993] IRLR 172, CA; *TSC Europe (UK) Ltd* v. *Massey* [1999] IRLR 22, HC at para.49).

3.5.4 TUPE transfers

Following a TUPE transfer, all contracts of employment will be transferred to the purchaser. The basic position is that valid restrictive covenants in the employees' contracts can be enforced by the new owner of the business (*New ISG Ltd* v. *Vernon & ors* [2008] IRLR 115, ChD, although in that case there were other reasons for the court finding that the benefit of the covenants did not transfer to the new owner). However, a restriction forbidding solicitation of the employer's customers will not automatically cover customers of the new owner (*Morris Angel & Son Ltd* v. *Hollande* [1993] ICR 71, CA).

3.6 VARYING CONTRACT TERMS

Employers frequently need to vary contract terms. Business reorganisation, or harmonisation of employment contracts amongst different workers, might require reconsideration of the employment contract. Any unilateral change of terms and conditions (operating to the employee's detriment) will usually entitle the employee to resign and claim constructive dismissal. The advisor's responsibility is to obtain the employee's consent or, if consent is not forthcoming, to ensure that any constructive dismissal will be fair rather than unfair.

An employee who has signed an agreement, but added the words 'under duress', cannot be taken to have agreed to the changes (*Hepworth Heating Ltd* v. *Akers* (unreported, EAT, 21 January 2003).

CONTRACTS OF EMPLOYMENT

It may sometimes be possible for an employee to agree to continue to work on new terms under protest and at the same time claim constructive unfair dismissal on the basis that he was constructively dismissed under one contract and is now working under a new one on new terms (*Hogg* v. *Dover College* [1990] ICR 39, EAT). However, an employee who wishes to work on 'under protest' while reserving the right to resign and claim constructive dismissal if the employer insists on enforcing the changes has to be very careful. If, under protest, he works on under the new terms and then subsequently refuses to do so the employer will have grounds to dismiss him and successfully resist a claim of unfair dismissal simply because the employee did not keep his side of the bargain (*Robinson* v. *Tescom Corporation* [2008] IRLR 408 which the EAT said was wholly different from the *Hogg* v. *Dover College* case because Mr Robinson's original contract of employment still existed).

3.6.1 Does the variation need the employee's consent?

Sometimes the employer will be changing policy rather than contractual terms. The latter requires consent, the former does not. In addition, some contracts of employment contain a clause entitling the employer to make changes without the employee's express consent; if so, the employees' consent need not be obtained again, subject to an implied obligation not to vary the terms arbitrarily or unreasonably (*Lee* v. *GEC Plessey Telecommunications* [1993] IRLR 383).

3.6.2 Consultation

If agreement has yet to be obtained, the employer should explain the proposed changes, the reasons behind them and what will happen if the changes do not occur. Employees should be encouraged to raise concerns and these concerns should be assessed and considered. It is prudent to consult with employee representatives at this stage because if, eventually, any employees do not agree to the changes and are dismissed, the duty of collective consultation will arise prior to the dismissal. This has become particularly important since the Information and Consultation of Employees Regulations 2004, SI 2004/3426 came into force on 6 April 2005. A failure to engage in collective consultation could result in a protective award of up to 90 days' pay per employee being made against the employer (TULRCA 1992, s.188) if changes are being made to more than 20 employees' contracts (see *GMB & Amicus* v. *Beloit Walmsley Ltd* [2003] ICR 1396, EAT).

3.6.3 Obtaining agreement

Any variation should be supported by consideration (except in Scotland, where no requirement for consideration exists). This can take the form of a pay rise or, when that is not practical, a one-off incentive (e.g. a bonus or an extra day's paid holiday). If the employee's agreement is not supported by consideration, it may be invalid (although the employer may still be able to argue that the employee's employment on the old terms was terminated and a new contract came into existence on the new terms).

Employees who agree changes, however reluctantly, will be bound by them and there will not be any employment law problem. Agreement can be inferred by continuing in employment on the altered terms without raising any objection (see, for example, *GAP Personnel Franchises Ltd* v. *Robinson* (unreported, EAT, 16 October 2007)).

3.6.4 If agreement cannot be obtained

Changes should not simply be imposed, as that would risk giving the employee the right to resign and claim unfair and/or wrongful constructive dismissal. Note, however, that if a good, sound business reason for an important change can be shown and proper consultation has been undertaken (particularly if a sizeable proportion of the workforce has agreed to the change) then the constructive dismissal is likely to be fair (*Willow Oak Developments Ltd t/a Windsor Recruitment* v. *Silverwood & ors* [2006] IRLR 607, CA and *Forshaw* v. *Archcraft Ltd* [2005] IRLR 600, EAT in both of which an employee had resigned after refusing to sign a new restrictive covenant).

An employee cannot be expected to confront the employer over an issue which will only be relevant in the future, for example, a change to pension rights or sickness benefits; thus continued working cannot be automatically taken as an acceptance of that type of variation (*Davies* v. *MJ Wyatt Decorators Ltd* [2000] IRLR 759, EAT). Nor is it sufficient merely to notify employees of the change and ask them to acknowledge receipt of the letter. Acknowledgement of receipt is not agreement.

The only safe route for the employer is to comply with the general law of contract: to give notice of termination to all employees who have refused to consent to the change, coupled with an offer of a new contract, with the variations, to start immediately on termination of the old contract. However, this can be highly damaging to staff morale and, of course, may result in unfair dismissal claims being brought (although, as set out above, the employers have a good argument that the dismissal was fair). If more than 20 employees are dismissed, collective consultation is required (see **section 3.6.2**).

3.6.5 Written statement of changes

An employer must provide an employee with a written statement of any changes to the main terms and conditions of employment within one month of the variation (ERA 1996, s.4).

3.6.6 Variations following a TUPE transfer

With effect from 6 April 2006 the 1981 TUPE regulations were replaced by the Transfer of Undertakings (Protection of Employment) Regulations 2006, SI 2006/246 (TUPE 2006). So far as this section of this book is concerned, the new regulations have made no material changes.

It is unlawful to vary any terms and conditions, except those relating to pension rights, following the acquisition of new staff pursuant to a TUPE transfer. Any significant variation adverse to employees will entitle them to claim constructive dismissal which will be automatically unfair (TUPE 2006, reg.7(1)). Changes which are to the benefit of the employee will not have this effect (*Regent Security Services* v. *Power* [2008] IRLR 66, CA); nor will minor changes which would not (in the absence of a transfer) entitle employees to claim constructive dismissal (*Rossiter* v. *Pendragon* [2002] IRLR 483, CA and *Viggosdottir* v. *Islandspostur HF* [2002] IRLR 425, EFTA Court) although the position has been changed in favour of employees by a new provision introduced as TUPE 2006, reg.4(9) (see **section 13.6**).

Employers are not usually entitled to rely on the normal TUPE defence, that the dismissals were for some 'economic, technical or organisational reason entailing changes in the workforce' since variations to terms and conditions will generally not involve changes in the workforce (*Delabole Slate Ltd* v. *Berriman* [1985] IRLR 305, CA and *Green* v. *Elan Care* (unreported, EAT, 4 March 2002); but see *Crawford* v. *Swinton Insurance Brokers Ltd* [1990] IRLR 42, EAT).

A compromise agreement settling redundancy terms and concluded after a business transfer does not vary the terms of the contract (*Solectron Scotland Ltd* v. *Roper* [2004] IRLR 4, EAT).

For a variation to be prohibited under TUPE, the change must occur because of the TUPE transfer. Thus when contracts of fixed-term transferred employees expire and are renewed on different terms which harmonise with those routinely used by the transferee, the variation is not prohibited under TUPE. This is because new terms in new contracts resulted from expiry of the previous fixed-term contracts rather than from the TUPE transfer (*Ralton* v. *Havering College* [2001] IRLR 738, EAT).

A dedicated website at **www.emplaw.co.uk/lshandbook** provides links to judgments and other source material referred to in this chapter.

CHAPTER 4

Problems during employment

4.1 GENERAL INFORMATION

Problems during employment are best dealt with as swiftly and informally as possible. Relaxed assistance by a supervisor is likely to be more effective than a formal warning for poor performance. However, difficulties inevitably arise on both sides of the employment relationship. Employers sometimes need to invoke disciplinary proceedings, and employees have grievances that they wish to have resolved. The importance of clear lines of communication cannot therefore be overstated.

The Employment Act 2002 and supporting regulations (the Employment Act 2002 (Dispute Resolution) Regulations 2004, SI 2004/752, which came into force from 1 October 2004) provided for a new pre-tribunal compulsory dispute resolution system. The core elements are:

1. Mandatory disciplinary procedures which, should the employer fail to follow them, render a dismissal automatically unfair.
2. Mandatory grievance procedures which, should the employee fail to invoke them, may prevent the lodging of a claim at the employment tribunal.
3. Boosting or reducing tribunal awards to reflect compliance – or non-compliance – with the procedures.

In practice this compulsory pre-tribunal dispute resolution system, while well intentioned, caused more problems than it solved. It is due to be scrapped and replaced by a voluntary system, probably with effect from April 2009, under what at the time of writing is the Employment Bill. In early May 2008 Acas issued a revised draft of its Code of Practice, CoP1 on Disciplinary and Grievance Procedures, which is likely to become a more important part of a new voluntary system than its predecessor. The Employment Bill (cl.3) provides that if an employer has unreasonably failed to follow 'a relevant Code of Practice', including this one, there will be a discretionary power for an employment tribunal to increase compensatory award on unfair dismissal by up to 25 per cent if it considers it just and equitable to do so

Because the statutory dispute resolution system will soon be consigned to history we have decided to omit commentary on the disciplinary and grievance procedures that it introduced from this book. Even though they are not dealt with here it is important to note that the statutory disciplinary and grievance procedures will continue to be obligatory for a while after publication of this book. For reference purposes the procedures are set out at Sched.2 to the Employment Act 2002. A draft Employment Act 2008 (Commencement No.1 and Transitional and Saving Provisions) Order 2008 has already been prepared by the BERR and proposes 6 April 2009 as the operative date for the changes (the draft order is included in a schedule to the BERR 'Dispute Resolution: secondary legislation consultation', July 2008).

Useful and comprehensive information concerning operation of the 2004 dispute resolution procedures is easily and freely available from various websites and booklets including those provided by organisations such as the BERR, Acas and Citizens Advice Bureaux. Readers who require more detailed legal information could refer to the previous edition of this book, where available, or there are various other websites and books which can help (a selection is available from this book's companion website at **www.emplaw.co.uk/lshandbook**).

4.2 THE RIGHT TO BE ACCOMPANIED

4.2.1 Introduction

It has always been a basic principle of a reasonable disciplinary procedure for an employee to have a right to be accompanied by a representative. This right was crystallised by the Employment Relations Act 1999, ss.10–15.

All workers – including agency workers and homeworkers – have a right to be accompanied by a representative during any disciplinary hearing. A disciplinary hearing is widely defined as a hearing which could result in:

- the administration of a formal warning to a worker by the employer;
- the taking of some other action in respect of a worker by the employer;
- the confirmation of a warning issued or some other action taken (Employment Relations Act 1999, s.13);
- the taking of disciplinary action or dismissal under the statutory procedure.

Thus the right to a representative extends to any appeal hearing.

Any attempt to contract out of the right to be accompanied is void (Employment Relations Act 1999, s.14).

4.2.2 What representative is a worker allowed?

With effect from 4 September 2000, a worker has had the legally enforceable right to be accompanied by a fellow worker or trade union representative of his choice at any internal disciplinary procedure or grievance procedure meeting (Employment Relations Act 1999, s.10 which also provides that the representative is entitled to 'address the hearing' and to 'confer with the worker during the hearing', but is not permitted to 'answer questions on behalf of the worker', and so can be there to provide guidance and support, but not to act as an advocate).

The Act does not entitle a worker to insist on any other type of representative, such as a lawyer, a member of the family or a friend who is not a work colleague, although the worker's contract of employment might provide for wider rights of representation. The Court of Appeal has held that it is unlikely that an argument for legal representation based upon Art.6 of the European Convention on Human Rights (right to fair trial) could succeed (*R.v. Securities & Futures Authority Ltd ex. p. Fleurose* [2002] IRLR 297, CA).

There is no duty on a fellow worker or trade union official to accept a request to accompany a worker and no pressure should be brought to bear on a person if he does not wish to act as a companion. Employers should allow companions a reasonable amount of paid time off work to fulfil this responsibility (Acas Code of Practice 'Disciplinary and Grievance Procedures in the Workplace', paras.59 and 61).

If a companion cannot attend on the proposed date for the disciplinary (or grievance) hearing, the employer must adjourn the hearing date for up to five days if this will enable the companion to be present, provided the alternative time proposed by the employee is reasonable (Employment Relations Act 1999, s.10(4) and (5)).

4.2.3 What if the employer breaches the right to be accompanied?

The employee is entitled to complain to an employment tribunal, which can award up to two weeks' pay. A week's pay is capped under the statute (currently, since February 2008, at £330), thus the maximum currently payable is £660 (Employment Relations Act 1999, s.11).

Of more significance is that dismissal of a worker for exercising rights under this section, whether the worker is the person being accompanied or the companion, is automatically unfair dismissal (Employment Relations Act 1999, s.13).

Withholding the right to be accompanied even at the informal oral warning stage can be a breach of the employee's statutory right (*London Underground Ltd* v. *Ferenc-Batchelor; Harding* v. *London Underground Ltd* [2003] IRLR 252, EAT).

4.3 DISCIPLINARY PROCEDURES

4.3.1 Introduction

An employer is obliged to include, in the written particulars of employment, a note setting out details of any disciplinary rules and procedures applying to an employee. The note must also identify the person to whom an employee can appeal any disciplinary decision (ERA 1996, s.3(1)).

A disciplinary hearing is defined as a hearing which could result in:

1. The administration of a formal warning to a worker by the employer.
2. The taking of some other action in respect of a worker by the employer.
3. The confirmation of a warning issued or some other action taken (Employment Relations Act 1999, s.13).

The EAT has emphasised the importance of particularly careful investigation where there are serious allegations of criminal misbehaviour, and suggested that the obligation on the investigator is just as much to look for evidence which exculpates the individual as evidence which implicates that individual (*A* v. *B* [2003] IRLR 405).

Depending on the circumstances, if a dismissal is unfair because the employer followed unfair procedures (for example, an unfair redundancy selection process) the likelihood that the employee might have been dismissed anyway even if proper procedures had been followed can be relevant in assessing compensatory award (see *Software 2000 Ltd* v. *Andrews, Trinder, Prowse and Lawrence* [2007] IRLR 568, EAT).

4.3.2 The meetings

A disciplinary hearing should usually be conducted by the person who will take the decision whether or not to dismiss. However, this does not mean that an entire board or committee should conduct a disciplinary hearing – it is perfectly proper for one member of the board/committee to make a recommendation to colleagues (*Budgen & Co* v. *Thomas* [1976] IRLR 174, EAT).

Although some older authorities suggest that best practice requires that the decision maker should be someone other than the person investigating the disciplinary issues, the courts now recognise that 'there is nothing strange in the employer making his own enquiries and then reaching the decision whether he should or should not dismiss the employee' (*Sartor* v. *P&O European Ferries (Felixstowe) Ltd* [1992] IRLR 271, CA).

How to deal with confidential informers

A basic principle of a fair disciplinary process is that the employee should know who is making the allegations against him, so that he has the opportunity to challenge the veracity of his accuser. Many defences turn on cross-allegations that the accuser has a grudge against the accused and has manufactured the evidence against him. Whether the employer accepts this or not, it remains a fundamental principle of natural justice that the employee should know who accuses him.

However, sometimes accusers wish to keep their identity confidential. This may be for a variety of reasons, but the most common is a fear of retribution. The EAT has laid down guidelines on how to approach such a situation. *Linfood Cash & Carry Ltd* v. *Thomson* [1989] IRLR 235, EAT should be read in full, but the salient points (summarised) are:

1. A formal written statement should be taken from the informer, dealing in detail with the opportunities the informer had to see the disciplinary offence, why the informer was present and whether the informant has suffered at the hands of the accused or has any other reason to fabricate evidence.
2. The employer should then carry out further investigations with a view to corroborating or undermining the informer's evidence.
3. A decision must then be made, depending on the employer's view of the strength of the evidence, whether or not to carry on with the disciplinary process.
4. The written statement of the informant, with identifying details removed, should be made available to the accused employee.
5. The disciplinary hearing should be adjourned, if the accused employee raises any questions, for those questions to be put to the informer.

In a case in 2006, a nursery nurse was dismissed after a child's parents complained that she had slapped their child. She claimed unfair dismissal (plus another claim not relevant here). The nursery school promised anonymity to the parents. An employment tribunal chairman ordered that the parents and the child should be identified. The EAT overruled this, pointing out that the issue at the main hearing would not be about the accusers or their allegations but would be whether it had been fair for the employer to dismiss the employee on the basis of hearsay evidence from unidentified accusers. It followed that the interests of justice did not require the promise of anonymity to the parents to be breached (*Fairmile Kindergarten* v. *Macdonald* (unreported, EAT, 20 January 2006)).

At the end of the day, the ultimate test when a tribunal is considering whether an order should be made requiring disclosure of a confidential document is not whether disclosure is relevant but whether it is necessary (*Arqiva Ltd* v. *Sagoo* (unreported, EAT, 22 March 2007)).

4.4 WRITTEN STATEMENT OF REASONS FOR DISMISSAL

The general rule is that an employee is entitled to request written reasons for the dismissal (ERA 1996, s.92). A written statement must then be provided within two weeks. The law '... requires an employer to lay his cards on the table when he dismisses an employee. Whatever may have been said orally or informally or in negotiations, the reason for dismissal has to be set out with due formality' if the employee so requests (*Health Development Agency v. Parish* (unreported, EAT, 24 October 2003)).

A request may be verbal or written. If the employer unreasonably fails to provide a written statement of the reasons for dismissal within two weeks, the employee can complain to an employment tribunal. The tribunal is entitled to make an award equal to two weeks' pay. As from February 2008, the figure for a week's pay is capped at £330 (it is adjusted in line with inflation each year), thus the maximum payable is £660. The tribunal may also make a declaration as to the reasons for the dismissal.

The general rule does not apply in two situations:

1. If the employee has less than one year's continuous employment, in which case the right to a written statement does not exist (Unfair Dismissal and Statement of Reasons for Dismissal (Variation of Qualifying Period) Order 1999, SI 1999/1436).
2. If the employee is pregnant or on maternity, parental or adoption leave, in which case the employee is entitled to a written statement without making any request.

A dedicated website at **www.emplaw.co.uk/lshandbook** provides links to judgments and other source material referred to in this chapter.

CHAPTER 5

Small employers

5.1 GENERAL INFORMATION

There is no general statutory definition of a 'small employer' in UK law. However, a straw in the wind of possible harmonisation change is adoption by the European Commission of Recommendation 2003/361/EC setting out updated definitions of micro, small and medium-sized enterprises with effect from 1 January 2005. A micro-employer is defined as one with fewer than 10 employees and less than 2m euros balance sheet total or turnover; a small employer is one with less than 50 employees and less than 10m euros balance sheet total or turnover; and a medium-sized employer is one with fewer than 250 employees and less than 43m euros balance sheet total or 50m euro turnover. This EU definition has no general relevance to British employment law. Nor is it adopted as the definition of a small or medium-sized company in the Companies Act 2006, ss.382 and 465. However, it is used in connection with tax relief on research and development expenditure by companies (Finance Act 2000, Sched.20 (Definition of Small and Medium-Sized Enterprises) Order 2004, SI 2004/3267).

Although there is no general definition of 'small employer' for British employment law purposes, various statutory provisions make special rules for employers with fewer than a specified number of employees or which fall below some other threshold. As a general rule there are provisions specifying that employees of any 'associated employer' must be included in the calculation where the number of employees is the deciding factor.

In general, employers are 'associated' if one is a company controlled by the other or if both are companies over which a third person (company or individual) has direct or indirect control (ERA 1996, s.231; TULRCA 1992, s.297). It follows that to be 'associated' at least one of the employers must be an incorporated company (*Hasley* v. *Fair Employment Agency* [1989] IRLR 106, CA). A company does not have to be a UK company to be 'associated' (*Hancill* v. *Marcon Engineering Ltd* [1990] ICR 103, EAT). 'Control' for employment law purposes is not restricted to voting control in the company or tax law sense. For employment law purposes 'control' is concerned with practical rather than theoretical matters. An employment tribunal will look at all the circumstances when deciding who has control of a company (*Tice* v. *Cartwright* [1999] ICR 769, EAT).

There is a general rule in unfair dismissal cases which requires employment tribunals to take into account the size and administrative resources of the employer's undertaking when considering whether or not a dismissal is unfair. For example, smallness can justify less formality than would be required from a larger employer when consulting employees about impending redundancies (ERA 1996, s.98(4); *De Grasse* v. *Stockwell Ltd* [1992] IRLR 269, EAT).

Business Link has a small business website and publishes useful 'fact sheets' on various employment law related subjects (**www.businesslink.gov.uk**).

An EU 'Small Business Act', discussed at the Lisbon summit in December 2007, was issued on 25 June 2008. This is akin to a Code of Practice encouraging officials at EU and national levels to always consider the needs of small business.

Acas tried a pilot mediation scheme to help companies with less than 50 employees deal with employment law related problems in 2003. There are indications that Acas is likely to develop its mediation services generally as part of its new role when the 2004 statutory dispute resolution procedure is replaced, probably in April 2009.

5.2 SPECIFIC PROVISIONS

5.2.1 Consultation with employees

There is of course no exemption for small employers from the general, overall requirement that there should be proper and meaningful consultation with employees when questions of fairness arise. However, there are exemptions for smaller employers from some of the specific statutory rules regarding consultation obligations.

Works councils

Companies with fewer than 50 employees (averaged over the previous 12 months) are exempt from the requirements of the Information and Consultation of Employees Regulations 2004, SI 2004/3426, which implement the EC National Information and Consultation Directive 2002/14/EC. The consultation obligations were phased in over three years from 6 April 2005. Since 6 April 2008 they have applied to all employers with at least 50 employees (for further details see **Chapter 9**).

Redundancy

Since 1 March 1996 employers have been under a statutory duty to consult appropriate representatives of employees about impending redundancies if at least 20 employees are being dismissed at one establishment within a 90-day period (TULRCA 1992, s.188(1) as amended by the Collective Redundancies and Transfer of Undertakings (Protection of Employment) (Amendment) Regulations 1995, SI 1995/2587). This statutory obligation therefore never applies to employers with fewer than 20 employees.

5.2.2 Disability discrimination

The previous small employers' exemption from DDA 1995 was removed on 1 October 2004 by the Disability Discrimination Act 1995 (Amendment) Regulations 2003, SI 2003/1673, implementing the EC General Framework Directive 2000/78/EC in this respect.

5.2.3 Employers' liability insurance

The Employers' Liability (Compulsory Insurance) Act 1969 requires all employers to take out insurance in respect of liability to employees for bodily injury or disease sustained during employment in Great Britain. The obligation is imposed regardless of the employer's size or number of employees.

With effect from 28 February 2005 companies which employ only their owner have been exempted from the requirement to have employers' liability compulsory insurance (Employers' Liability (Compulsory Insurance) (Amendment) Regulations 2004, SI 2004/2882).

5.2.4 Fire regulations

Employers with less than five employees are exempted from the record-keeping rules set out in the Regulatory Reform (Fire Safety) Order 2005, SI 2005/1541.

5.2.5 Health and safety

Employers with fewer than five employees are exempt from the Health and Safety at Work etc. Act 1974 rule that employers must prepare a written statement of general policy with respect to the health and safety of employees and bring it to the notice of all employees (Employers' Policy Statements (Exceptions) Regulations 1975, SI 1975/1584).

5.2.6 Industrial training levies

Employers with an annual wage bill below specified amounts (basically £76,000 in the construction industry and £275,000 in engineering) are exempt from training levies payable by larger employers in those industries (Industrial Training Levy (Construction Industry Training Board) Order 2008, SI

SMALL EMPLOYERS

2008/534 and Industrial Training Levy (Engineering Construction Industry Training Board) Order 2008, SI 2008/535).

5.2.7 Maternity leave and adoption leave

Employers with five or fewer employees were previously exempt from the full rigour of the normal rule that it is automatically unfair dismissal to refuse to allow an employee to return to work after maternity leave or adoption leave. This small employers' exemption has been removed entirely in relation to employees whose expected week of childbirth begins on or after 1 April 2007 or where the child is expected to be placed for adoption or enters Great Britain before 1 April 2007 (Maternity and Parental Leave etc. and the Paternity and Adoption Leave (Amendment) Regulations 2006, SI 2006/2014).

5.2.8 Statutory maternity pay, statutory adoption pay and statutory paternity pay

An employer who pays £45,000 or less in national insurance (NI) contributions payments in a tax year can recover 104.5 per cent of any SMP paid by deducting it from future NI liability (or by direct payment from HM Revenue & Customs on request if NI liability is insufficient to enable recovery by deduction) (Statutory Maternity Pay (Compensation of Employers) Amendment Regulations 2004, SI 2004/698). 'Contributions payments' means all Class 1 NI contributions (employer and employee) which the employer is under a liability to pay (Statutory Maternity Pay (Compensation of Employers) and Miscellaneous Amendment Regulations 1994, SI 1994/1882, regs.1(4) and 2(2)).

Similar arrangements apply to recovery by small employers of statutory adoption leave pay and statutory paternity leave pay introduced from April 2003 (Statutory Paternity Pay and Statutory Adoption Pay (Administration) Regulations 2002, SI 2002/2820, reg.3(b)).

5.2.9 PAYE and NI contributions

Employers whose average monthly liability to pay NI contributions and PAYE is less than £1,500 can pay these quarterly rather than monthly. Employers who choose to pay quarterly are required to make payments for the tax quarters ending 5 July, 5 October, 5 January and 5 April by the 19th of each of those months (Income Tax (Employments) (Amendment) Regulations 2000, SI 2000/1152 and the Social Security (Contributions) (Amendment No.5) Regulations 2000, SI 2000/1149).

A scheme by which large and medium-sized employers can be required to make PAYE payments and file end-of-year PAYE returns electronically currently applies only to large (250 or more staff) and medium-sized (50 or more staff) employers (Income Tax (Pay As You Earn) Regulations 2003, SI

EMPLOYMENT LAW HANDBOOK

2003/2682, regs.191, 199, 205 and 206). The regulations do not currently apply to employers with fewer than 50 employees, but there are proposals for the scheme to be extended to them from April 2010. There are also proposals under which it will be obligatory from April 2011 for employers with fewer than 50 employees to file online Parts 1 and 3 of Form P45 (when an employee leaves or a new employee starts) and Form P46 (when a new employee starts without a P45 from previous employment).

There is a cash incentive (up to £825 tax-free spread over five years from 2004/2005 to 2008/2009) for small employers (fewer than 50 employees) to start filing tax returns online. The HM Revenue & Customs website provides full details (see **www.hmrc.gov.uk**).

5.2.10   Race discrimination in small partnerships

Racial discrimination between partners or between partners and prospective partners is normally unlawful (though a 'partner' is, of course, normally not an employee). An exemption from this rule for small partnerships was removed on 19 July 2003. However, the exemption was not completely removed but rather was removed only if discrimination is on grounds of race or of ethnic or national origins (RRA 1976, s.10 as amended by the Race Relations Act 1976 (Amendment) Regulations 2003, reg.12). The small partnership exemption as between partners therefore possibly continues if the discrimination is on grounds of colour or nationality. This possibility was doubted by the EAT in a non-partnership case in 2006 (*North East London Strategic Health Authority* v. *Nassir-Deen* (unreported, EAT, 18 December 2006)) but was later upheld by the EAT in a different context concerned with reversal of the burden of proof under RRA 1976, s.54A (*Okonu* v. *G4S Security Services (UK) Ltd* (unreported, EAT, 11 February 2008).

Whatever the position under anti-race discrimination rules, the size of a partnership does not affect the application of other types of anti-discrimination legislation (sex, religious belief, etc.).

5.2.11   Stakeholder pensions

Employers with fewer than five employees are exempt from employer obligations under the stakeholder pensions scheme, notably the obligation to facilitate employees' access to a scheme (Stakeholder Pension Schemes Regulations 2000, SI 2000/1403, reg.22(1)).

5.2.12   Trade union recognition

Employers with fewer than 21 employees cannot be required to recognise a trade union. Assessment of the number of employees for this purpose can be either as at the day when the request for recognition is received or averaged over the 13 weeks ending with that day (TULRCA 1992, Sched.A1, para.7(1) introduced by the Employment Relations Act 1999).

5.2.13 Written particulars of employment

Until 1 October 2004, the statement of written particulars of terms of employment to which almost every employee is entitled could be slightly simplified if the relevant number of employees was less than 20. As from that date the special rules for small employers concerning disciplinary procedures, exempting them from some of the normal requirements, ended. All employers are now required to have disciplinary and grievance procedures at least to a minimum specified standard and to provide details to employees in their written statement of particulars of employment. As noted earlier, these requirements are likely to be removed in 2009 (see **section 4.1**).

A dedicated website at **www.emplaw.co.uk/lshandbook** provides links to judgments and other source material referred to in this chapter.

CHAPTER 6

Trade unions

6.1 GENERAL INFORMATION

This book is concerned with individual, not collective, employment rights. Apart from the short general outline notes in the introductory section, it therefore covers trade union matters only from the standpoint of the employment law rights of individuals. In particular this book does not cover the law relating to trade union recognition, industrial action or collective bargaining. It should be noted, however, that the law relating to industrial action is assuming increased significance, as occurrences of industrial action have been increasing in recent years after a period of calm with public sector workers in particular demonstrating dissatisfaction with pay awards in 2007 and 2008.

According to figures extracted from the Government Review of the Employment Relations Act 1999 and National Statistics/Labour Market Trends (since January 2007, Economic & Labour Market Review) the number of working days lost to industrial action in recent years were as shown in the table below.

Year	Days lost from stoppages arising from labour disputes
1997	235,000
1998	282,000
1999	242,000
2000	499,000
2001	525,000
2002	1,322,000
2003	499,100
2004	905,000
2005	157,400
2006	745,500
2007	1,041,100

As a general rule, in UK law (in contrast to law in other EU Member States), collective employment 'rights' are not legally enforceable by individuals. In the UK the theory is that employees and their employers make their own individual employment agreements with each other and employment terms which have been negotiated collectively are therefore only enforceable if and to the extent that they are incorporated into an individual's employment contract (*Hulland* v. *Sanders* [1945] KB 78, CA, *Alexander* v. *Standard Telephones and Cables Ltd (No. 2)* [1991] IRLR 286 and TULRCA 1992 ss.178 and 179). However, as noted above, more recently it has become more likely in appropriate cases that courts and tribunals will recognise that the terms of a collective agreement are incorporated into individual contracts of employment as implied terms (*Lee* v. *GEC Plessey Telecommunications* [1993] IRLR 383 and *Healy & ors* v. *Corporation of London* (unreported, EAT, 24 June 1999)).

The European Convention on Human Rights provides that everyone has rights to 'freedom of peaceful assembly and to freedom of association with others', including the right 'to form and join trade unions for the protection of his interests', and to 'freedom of expression' (European Convention on Human Rights, Arts.10 and 11; Human Rights Act 1998, s.6 and Sched.1). In Britain employees of public authorities (as defined in the Human Rights Act 1998) can enforce these, and all other, Convention rights directly against their employers. In practice the Convention has proved less useful for trade unions than many expected. For example, in *Unison* v. *UK* [2002] IRLR 497, the European Court of Human Rights rejected a trade union's request to, in effect, overturn a UK Court of Appeal decision that a proposed strike would be political rather than a 'trade dispute'. On the other hand, a direct consequence of the application of the Convention, Art.11 by the European Court in a case in 2007 will be a change to British law to increase the rights of trade unions to exclude or expel a member because he takes part in political activities which are inconsistent with the union's principles (*ASLEF* v. *UK* [2007] IRLR 361, ECtHR). ASLEF had expelled Mr Lee, a member of the British National Party who had stood as a BNP candidate in local elections. ASLEF had had to readmit Mr Lee to membership after an employment tribunal ruled that his expulsion was unlawful (under TULRCA 1992, s.174). The case eventually went to the European Court of Human Rights. The court was not persuaded that expulsion from ASLEF had impinged in any significant way on Mr Lee's exercise of freedom of expression or his lawful political activities and ruled that British law (TULRCA 1992, s.174) does not strike a proper balance between the rights of a trade union and the rights of individuals who are, or might wish to be, members of it. The Employment Bill before Parliament at the time of writing therefore includes a provision (cl.18) to correct the position and make it easier for a trade union to expel someone who is a member of a political party which stands for fundamental principles of which the union disapproves.

Most UK statute law relating to trade unions was consolidated into one Act in 1992, TULRCA 1992. This has frequently been amended (notably by the Trade Union Reform and Employment Rights Act 1993, the Employment Relations Act 1999, the Employment Act 2002, the Employment Relations Act 2004 and prospectively by the current Employment Bill).

The general background is that until 1901 it was generally assumed that legal action could only be taken against individual union officers and/or members and that trade unions as such could not be sued as they are unincorporated associations with no legal 'persona'. This assumption was shown to be wrong in *Taff Vale Railway Co.* v. *Amalgamated Society of Railway Servants* [1901] AC 426, in which the House of Lords ruled that legal action could be taken against a trade union by persons who suffered economic loss as a result of the union's activity. Not surprisingly, this decision upset trade unions and a few years later, with support from the embryo Labour Party, a new (Liberal) government passed the Trade Disputes Act 1906. Although this Act did not override *Taff Vale* it did grant trade unions and their members immunity from most civil actions arising from trade disputes.

This 1906 Act forms the basis of the modern law, which provides trade unions with a unique immunity from legal action in respect of the consequences of activities done 'in contemplation or furtherance of a trade dispute', as defined, provided various conditions (we think there are around 30 conditions in all) are fulfilled (TULRCA 1992, s.219).

The rules work by providing that certain specific acts are 'not protected' by TULRCA 1992, s.219 and therefore do not qualify the union for immunity from legal action. The acts which are 'not protected' are essentially:

- secondary industrial action (other than lawful picketing) (TULRCA 1992, s.224);
- action taken against an employer because he 'is employing, has employed or might employ' a person who is not a member of a trade union (TULRCA 1992, s.222);
- action taken in support of an employee who has been lawfully dismissed for taking part in unofficial industrial action (TULRCA 1992, s.223);
- action taken in an attempt to force a business to deal (or not to deal) with another business by reason of that other business's recognition or non-recognition of a trade union (TULRCA 1992, s.225).

Importantly, even an official strike will be action which is 'not protected' if proper procedures required by the law are not followed. The procedures include a requirement to conduct a ballot of members before taking industrial action such as a strike (TULRCA 1992, s.226). The ballot must conform to strict conditions, including that the employer is given at least seven days' advance notice of the ballot. The requirements for giving relevant notices and the precise detail of what the notices must contain are set out in TULRCA 1992, ss.226A and 234A as amended (most recently by the Employment Relations Act 2004, ss.22 and 25 which came into effect on 1 October 2005 – see the Employment Relations Act 2004 (Commencement No. 4 and

Transitional Provisions) Order 2005, SI 2005/2419). There is no requirement for the names of the employees concerned to be provided to the employer. A ballot which approves industrial action is valid to cover action started during the next four weeks, with possible extension up to eight weeks if the union and employer agree (TULRCA 1992, s.234).

Special rules governing the position of police and prison officers are worth noting. It is a criminal offence for anyone to do 'any act calculated to induce any member of a police force to withhold his services' (Police Act 1996, s.91). This effectively prevents the police from going on strike. Similar rules which formerly applied to prison officers were relaxed in 2005 when a voluntary agreement under which they agreed not to go on strike came into effect. This voluntary agreement did not work as intended and came to an end on 8 May 2008. The previous legal ban on strikes by prison officers was reintroduced on the same day (Criminal Justice and Immigration Act 2008).

An important part of the changes introduced by the Employment Relations Act 1999 was to give trade unions a new statutory right to be 'recognised' by employers for purposes of collective bargaining, notably in relation to pay, hours and holidays (Employment Relations Act 1999, Sched.1 inserting a new Sched.A1 into TULRCA 1992). These provisions came into effect on 6 June 2000. A new semi-judicial role was assigned to the old Central Arbitration Committee, rejuvenated for the purpose, to assist in resolution of recognition disputes. The essential idea was to use the statutory procedure as an encouragement to employers to recognise trade unions voluntarily, and this strategy appears to have been successful. A government review of the Employment Relations Act 1999 in July 2002 stated that 'a thousand deals for recognition have been voluntarily agreed between employers and unions since 1998' while during the whole period from June 2002 to end March 2005 the Central Arbitration Committee made just 116 awards for recognition (source: *CAC Annual Report for 2004/2005*). The CAC received 66 applications for recognition in the year ended 31 March 2007 (source: *CAC Annual Report for 2006/2007*).

6.2 INDIVIDUAL EMPLOYMENT RIGHTS

6.2.1 Right to join a trade union

Until 1993 trade unions were able to specify any qualification for membership, so in practice they effectively had carte blanche to decide who should and who should not be a member (*Boulting* v. *ACTAT* [1963] 1 All ER 716).

As from 30 November 1993 individuals have had an absolute right not to be excluded from or expelled by a union save in four particular cases (TULRCA 1992, s.174).

The four cases in which it is legitimate for a union to reject an applicant are in outline where:

(a) the individual is not employed in a specified trade, industry or profession, or does not fulfil an occupational description such as grade, level or category of appointment or who does not have specified trade, industrial or professional qualifications or work experience; and/or
(b) the individual does not work in a specified area of Great Britain; and/or
(c) the individual does not work for a particular employer or employers; and/or
(d) the individual engages in specified types of conduct.

The last case has given rise to great problems concerning the right of a union to refuse membership to politically-motivated extremists whose views are contrary to the principles of the union. Until 31 December 2004 the legislation specifically precluded a trade union from excluding or expelling an individual because of membership of a political party. As from that date this was refined to enable a union to exclude or expel an individual for political activities although it continued to be unlawful to exclude or expel him because of membership of a political party (see TULRCA 1992, s.174(4A) and (4B) introduced by Employment Relations Act 2004, s.33(3)). The intention was to give unions a degree of freedom in the criteria they set out for membership whilst protecting the fundamental rights of individuals to belong to political parties. The new rules were prompted by concern that without them concerted groups of extremists might use the rules which specify a minimum level of compensation to be paid by a union which has unlawfully excluded a person from membership (see below) to attempt to bankrupt trade unions with whose principles they disagreed. In the February 2007 case noted above (*ASLEF* v. *UK* [2007] IRLR 361, ECtHR) the expulsion of BNP activists from ASLEF had taken place before the distinction between political activities and membership of a political party had been introduced by the Employment Relations Act 2004.

In 2007 the European Court of Human Rights considered the case in relation to the law which applied both before and after the 2004 changes. The court decided that even the post-2004 version of TULRCA 1992, s.174 failed to strike the right balance between the rights of the individual and those of the union in that it did not give enough weight to the general principle that trade unions must be free to decide, in accordance with their rules, questions concerning admission to or expulsion from the union. Hence the further changes to that section being made by the current Employment Bill.

Compensation can be awarded on a 'just and equitable' basis for unlawful infringement of the right to join a trade union, subject to a top limit of 30 times the maximum week's pay which can be taken into account for the unfair dismissal basic award plus an amount equal to the maximum unfair dismissal compensatory award. The absolute maximum is therefore £72,900 (i.e. (30 × £330) + £63,000) as from 1 February 2008 (see TULRCA 1992, s.176(6) and the Employment Rights (Increase of Limits) Order 2007, SI 2007/3570). There is also a lower limit of £6,900 (from 1 February 2008) if a union persists in the exclusion or expulsion after an employment tribunal order unless the exclusion or expulsion was attributable mainly to membership of a political party (TULRCA 1992, s.176(6A) and (6B) as introduced with effect from 31 December 2004 by the Employment Relations Act 2004, s.33). A rule that applications for compensation had to be made to the EAT rather than to an employment tribunal was abolished by the Employment Relations Act 2004, s.34.

6.2.2 Right not to join a trade union

Every trade union member has the statutory right on giving reasonable notice and complying with any reasonable conditions to terminate his membership of the union (TULRCA 1992, s.69).

If a union pressurises an employer to refuse anyone employment or to dismiss anyone because that person is not a union member, an employment tribunal has power to order the union to pay or contribute to compensation (TULRCA 1992, ss.142 and 160).

Dismissal of an employee because he is not a member of a trade union, or of a particular trade union, is automatically unfair dismissal (TULRCA 1992, s.152(1)(c)). At one time there was an exception under which an employee could be fairly dismissed for refusing to join a particular union provided there was a 'union membership agreement' in force (a type of agreement under which an employer and a trade union agreed that only members of that union would be employed). This exception was repealed by the Employment Act 1988, effectively bringing an end to the era in which the 'closed shop' could flourish. Any reader interested in the closed shop is referred to the clear exposition of the system by the European Court of Human Rights in *Young, James and Webster v. United Kingdom* [1981] ECHR 4.

The European Court of Human Rights has held that Art.11 of the ECHR should be interpreted as meaning that individuals have the right not to join a trade union as well as the right to join one (*Sigurour A. Sigurjonsson v. Iceland* (1993) EHRR 462).

6.2.3 Right not to be unjustifiably disciplined by trade union

Regardless of anything in a trade union's rules, its members have the statutory right not to be 'unjustifiably disciplined' by the union for specified conduct (TULRCA 1992, s.64(1)). 'Disciplined' is defined. It means, *inter alia*, expulsion, fining, reallocation of subscriptions, deprivation of benefits, services or facilities, advice to another union not to accept a person as a member and subjection to 'some other detriment' (TULRCA 1992, s.64(2)).

There is a long statutory list of conduct which is 'unjustifiable' (TULRCA 1992, s.65(2)). This includes matters such as refusing to take part in a strike or other industrial action, joining another union and working for a non-unionised employer. However, it specifically does not include conduct which is professionally improper thus enabling a union to discipline a member who is guilty of professional impropriety (TULRCA 1992, s.65(5)).

Compensation can be awarded on a 'just and equitable' basis for unlawful infringement of the right to join a trade union, subject to a top limit of 30 times the maximum week's pay which can be taken into account for unfair dismissal basic award plus an amount equal to maximum unfair dismissal compensatory award. The absolute maximum is therefore £72,900 (i.e. (30 × £330) + £63,000) as from 1 February 2008 (TULRCA 1992, s.67 as amended by the Employment Relations Act 2004, s.34).

In 2007 there was an example of a case in which the Court of Appeal increased the element of compensation awarded for injury to feelings from £7,500 to £12,500 because a claimant who had been unjustifiably disciplined by her trade union was able to show that she had suffered to an unusual extent (*Massey* v. *Unifi* [2007] IRLR 902, CA).

The rule that an application for compensation had to be made to the EAT if the union persisted in infringing a member's right not to be unjustifiably disciplined was abolished with effect from 31 December 2004 (TULRCA 1992, s.67 as amended by the Employment Relations Act 2004, s.34). In those circumstances the application can now be made to an employment tribunal but there is a minimum level of compensation (£6,900 from 1 February 2008 – TULRCA 1992, s.67(8A)).

6.2.4 Right not to be discriminated against by a trade union

Political fund contributions

A trade union member who opts out of making political fund contributions must not 'be placed in any respect either directly or indirectly under a disability or at a disadvantage as compared with other members of the union (except in relation to the control or management of the political fund)' (TULRCA 1992, s.82(1)(c)(ii)). Contribution to the political fund must not be a condition for admission to the union (TULRCA 1992, s.82(1)(d)).

There are rules setting out the methods by which an individual union member must be allowed to exercise his right not to contribute to the union's political fund. In the final analysis a complaint can be made to the Certification Officer and if the complaint is upheld the person who made it, and also (with effect from 6 April 2005) any other union member who was a member when the complaint was made, can enforce his rights through the county court (or in Scotland, in the same way, as an order of the sheriff) (TULRCA 1992, s.82 as amended by the Employment Relations Act 2004, s.57 and Sched.1 para.6).

Sex, race and disability

A trade union (more specifically any 'organisation of workers') must not discriminate on sex, race or disability grounds in admission to membership, terms of admission to membership, access to benefits or by subjecting a member to 'any other detriment' (SDA 1975, s.12; RRA 1976, s.11; DDA 1995, ss.13–15). Similar rules apply in relation to discrimination on grounds of sexual orientation (Employment Equality (Sexual Orientation) Regulations 2003, SI 2003/1661, reg.15); on grounds of religion or belief (Employment Equality (Religion or Belief) Regulations 2003, SI 2003/1660, reg.15; and on grounds of age (Employment Equality (Age) Regulations 2006, SI 2006/1031, reg.18).

The rules in SDA 1975, s.12 have led to unions being sued by female council workers who accepted union advice to settle equal pay claims out of court on what later transpired to be less favourable terms than could have been achieved if they had sued. In the most important of these cases an employment tribunal found in favour of the women claimants that the GMB union was in breach of the Act. This decision was overruled by the EAT in 2007 on the basis that the GMB's advice had been justified as a 'proportionate means of achieving a legitimate aim' (*GMB* v. *Allen* [2007] IRLR 752, EAT). The EAT went so far as to indicate that the fact that the means used were unlawful, even dishonest, did not necessarily mean that they were 'disproportionate' – this decision is under appeal to the Court of Appeal.

EC law

A worker employed in the UK who is a national of another EC Member State must be afforded the same rights to union membership as a British national. This is one of the provisions of the Regulations concerning freedom of movement for workers (EC Council Regulation 1612/68, Art.8).

6.2.5 Right not to be subjected to detriment for a trade union related reason

A worker has the right not to 'be subjected to any detriment as an individual by any act, or any deliberate failure to act, by his employer' done to prevent him from, or penalise him for, joining or taking part in the activities of an independent trade union. The worker also has the right not to be compelled by the employer to join a trade union or a particular trade union (TULRCA 1992, s.146 as amended by the Employment Relations Act 1999, Sched.2 para.2 and by the Employment Relations Act 2004, ss.30 and 31).

Exactly what is a 'deliberate failure' is unclear – the government said during the passage of the 1999 Employment Relations Bill that the expression is intended to cover 'both conscious and unconscious failures to act' and refused to agree an amendment to change it to 'wilful failure' (House of Commons, Standing Committee E, 18 March 1999).

Until October 2004 there were certain loopholes. Firstly, the provision protected only those within the legal definition of 'employee' and did not cover other 'workers'. Secondly, there was no protection if the purpose of the employer's action or failure to act: (i) was to prevent the individual concerned from making use of services provided by his trade union (including raising a matter on his behalf); or (ii) included the purpose of seeking to 'further a change in his relationship with all or any class of his employees' unless the act was one which 'no reasonable employer would take' (TULRCA 1992, s.148(3) – the 1993 'Ullswater amendment').

With effect from 1 October 2004, the Employment Relations Act 2004 blocked the loopholes noted above and strengthened the protections provided to unions and to their members and prospective members against interference by employers in relation to union membership and activity. The single biggest part of this 'blocking and strengthening' is s.29 of the Employment Relations Act 2004 which introduces appropriate new provisions into TULRCA 1992, as ss.145A–F.

Action can count as being against a person 'as an individual' even if it is taken against him in his capacity as a union official (*Farnsworth (F.W.) Ltd* v. *McCoid* [1999] ICR 1047, CA). Exactly what amounts to a 'detriment' is not certain but in the context of sex discrimination law the Court of Appeal has held that the expression has the wide meaning of 'putting at a disadvantage' (*Ministry of Defence* v. *Jeremiah* [1980] ICR 13).

Compensation for breach of this right can be awarded without limit on a 'just and equitable' basis and an employment tribunal has power to order a trade union to pay or contribute to compensation if it pressurised the employer into subjecting the individual to the detriment in respect of which a complaint has been brought (TULRCA 1992, ss.149 and 150). In assessing compensation for injury to feelings in a case under TULRCA 1992, s.146 the EAT has held that the same sort of considerations apply as in race and sex discrimination cases and similar levels of compensation are appropriate (*London Borough of Hackney* v. *Adams* [2003] IRLR 402).

An example of the effect of the provisions noted above is the successful claim made by an employee elected to be full-time branch secretary of her trade union, who found that she would not be entitled to a salary increase from her employer until she ceased full-time union activities (*Southwark LBC* v. *Whillier* [2001] ICR 1016, CA).

6.2.6 Right not to be dismissed for a trade union related reason

Separate from, but similar to, the right of a worker not to be subjected to a detriment on account of trade union related matters, is the right of an employee not to be dismissed for a trade union related reason. Thus dismissal of an employee because the employee is not a member of an independent trade union, or of a particular trade union, is automatically unfair dismissal.

Selection for redundancy on these grounds is also automatically unfair dismissal (TULRCA 1992, ss.152(1)(c) and 153).

Dismissal is also automatically unfair if the principal reason for it was that the employee 'had taken part, or proposed to take part, in the activities of an independent trade union at an appropriate time' or since 1 October 2004 was that the employee 'had made use, or proposed to make use, of trade union services at an appropriate time' or had turned down an offer made by his employer in an attempt to influence him in matters relating to his union membership or activity. Selection for redundancy on these grounds is also automatically unfair dismissal (TULRCA 1992, ss.152(1) and 153).

Similarly, dismissal of an employee is automatically unfair dismissal if the principal reason for it is that the employee took or is taking part in 'protected industrial action' and the dismissal takes place during what is called 'the protected period'. 'Protected industrial action' is essentially industrial action induced by acts which carry immunity from action in tort because of TULRCA 1992, s.219: meaning for most practical purposes official strikes called after a proper balloting process has been carried out. Since 6 April 2005, the 'protected period' is 12 weeks (previously eight weeks) from the start of the 'protected industrial action' plus an extension equal to the length of any lock-out the employer might impose (TULRCA 1992, s.238A, as amended by the Employment Relations Act 2004).

If an employee who is an active trade union official is dismissed for misconduct there may be a fine line to draw in deciding whether the real reason for the dismissal was the employee's conduct or his trade union-related activities. In such a case an employment tribunal will look to what the employer considered to be the reason for the dismissal and will give little weight to an employee's unsupported belief as to the reason (*Port of London Authority* v. *Payne* [1994] ICR 555, CA and *South West Trains Ltd* v. *McDonnell* (unreported, EAT, 7 August 2003) where it was held that the reason for dismissal of a trade union official was his misconduct rather than his union activities or membership).

In a case in 2006 an employment tribunal found that the reason for a dismissal was, as argued by the employer, the employee's misconduct. However, the tribunal had gone on to state that because of the employee's trade union activities it would have been impossible for him to defend any allegation 'for his employers had a closed mind arising out of their attitude to those activities'. The EAT overruled the tribunal's decision as the logical conclusion of this was that he was dismissed because of his trade union activities (*Afzal* v. *Europackaging Ltd* (unreported, EAT, 25 October 2006)).

It is unlawful for an employer to refuse a person employment 'because he is, or is not, a member of a trade union'. This is a specific separate right since by definition the claim cannot be for unfair dismissal (TULRCA 1992, s.137). The argument that a refusal to employ a person was because of his past trade union activity rather than because of his trade union membership is unlikely to succeed as it will normally be impossible to draw a sensible distinction between the two (*Fitzpatrick* v. *British Railways Board* [1992] ICR 221, CA and *Harrison* v. *Kent County Council* [1995] ICR 434, EAT).

The normal minimum service qualification for unfair dismissal and statutory redundancy pay rights does not apply if a dismissal is automatically unfair under TULRCA 1992, s.152. With effect from 6 April 2005 this qualification is irrelevant (Employment Relations Act 2004, s.35).

Minimum compensation for a person dismissed because that person is a trade union member or took part in trade union activities is £4,400 (with a possible reduction for contributory fault in redundancy cases) (TULRCA 1992, s.156 and the Employment Rights (Increase of Limits) Order 2007, SI 2007/3570).

6.3 MISCELLANEOUS

6.3.1 Check-off

Provided that a 'subscription deduction arrangement' exists between an employer and a trade union, a worker can request the employer to deduct union dues, at rates current from time to time, directly from wages. The employee can withdraw the request at any time and has the right to require that the deduction is not to include any political fund contribution. It is unlawful for the employer to avoid administrative inconvenience resulting from some employees exercising this right by refusing to operate check-off arrangements for them (TULRCA 1992, ss.68 and 86(3)).

Previous rules that authorisations for check-off deductions could not last more than three years and that increases in trade union subscriptions could not be deducted by an employer without at least one month's advance notice to the worker concerned were abolished by the Deregulation (Deduction from Pay of Union Subscriptions) Order 1998, SI 1998/1529.

6.3.2 Time off work for trade union related duties or activities

See **section 7.3.11**.

6.3.3 Inspection

Union register of members

A trade union is required to keep a register of the names and addresses of members and to allow any member to check, without charge, whether there is an entry relating to him (TULRCA 1992, s.24).

Union accounts

A trade union is required to keep proper accounts and to have them available for inspection by members 'until the end of the period of six years beginning with 1 January following the end of the period to which they relate'. A member can insist on being accompanied by an accountant (who can be required to sign reasonable confidentiality terms) and the union can charge a reasonable fee (TULRCA 1992, ss.28, 29 and 30).

Provision of rules

Any person, not just a member of the union, can require a trade union to supply a copy of its rules. The union can charge a reasonable fee (TULRCA 1992, s.27).

6.3.4 Penalties

If on a complaint of unfair dismissal either the employer or the complainant claims that the employer was induced to dismiss the complainant because of pressure (such as a threat of industrial action) applied because the complainant was not a union member then an employment tribunal has power to penalise whoever applied the pressure if the complainant wins his case.

In that situation the tribunal may, if it considers it just and equitable to do so, order the person (including a trade union) who applied the pressure to contribute to or pay the whole of any compensation awarded for the unfair dismissal. Compensation in such cases involves a minimum basic award of £4,400 if the appropriate date falls on or after 1 February 2008 (TULRCA 1992, s.160; Employment Relations Act 1999, s.33; Employment Rights (Increase of Limits) Order 2007, SI 2007/3570).

6.4 PROBLEM AREAS

A TUC-sponsored Trade Union Rights and Freedoms Bill was introduced in the House of Commons in December 2006 marking the centenary of the 1906 Trades Disputes Act, which first introduced the UK system for immunities from tortious liability for unions when organising industrial action. Although this 2006 Bill failed to become law its contents throw light on recent trade union thinking.

The main proposals were:

- to make it automatically unfair dismissal 'if the reason or one of the reasons for the dismissal is that the employee has participated, is participating or proposes to participate in lawful industrial action or a lawful

strike', with an automatic right in such circumstances to reinstatement and re-engagement orders;
- to make it unlawful to use temporary workers to replace strikers;
- to restrict the circumstances in which the courts can grant an injunction to prevent industrial action;
- to impose a duty on employers to cooperate generally with union ballots and in particular 'to supply to a trade union in good time information reasonably requested by the trade union for the purposes of establishing the names, addresses, categories and workplaces of those members whom it wishes to ballot';
- to legitimise secondary action; and
- repeal of TULRCA 1992, s.226A which requires unions to give employers seven days' notice of industrial action ballots.

It is also worth noting that the changes introduced by the Employment Relations Act 2004 did *not* include:

- any sanction against unfair practices during union recognition campaigns;
- any special provision for union recognition rights in small firms (i.e. those employing less than 21 workers);
- any change to the three-year bar on union re-application for recognition and no change to the position that there is no appeal from a decision of the Central Arbitration Committee (CAC) save by judicial review.

A dedicated website at **www.emplaw.co.uk/lshandbook** provides links to judgments and other source material referred to in this chapter.

CHAPTER 7
Working time and time off work

7.1 GENERAL INFORMATION

An employee's fundamental obligation is to be ready, willing and able to work. However, this is subject to qualifications. Employees are entitled under statute to time off work and are also entitled to regular breaks within their working day. Until October 1998 this was governed mainly by contract, subject to overriding duties arising out of the common law duty to maintain a safe place and system of work, breach of which might give rise to a personal injury claim if the employee suffered physical or psychological injury (*Johnstone* v. *Bloomsbury Health Authority* [1991] ICR 269, CA and *Marshall Specialist Vehicles Ltd* v. *Osborne* [2003] IRLR 672, EAT).

The government issued a consultation paper on 18 June 2008 ('Time to train') proposing a new right for employees to request time off work for training. This is unlikely to come into operation before April 2010. The proposal is that the new right should work in a similar way to that already in operation in relation to the right that some employees have to request flexible working. Employers will not be required to pay for training when they agree to a request for time to train, though the consultation paper says the government 'expects that many will be happy to do so'. This new right will be separate from and additional to the existing rights to time off work noted below for young people needing study leave and for Union Learning Representatives.

An Employment Retention Bill designed to retain newly disabled people in work had a first reading in the House of Commons on 29 January 2008. If this Bill becomes law it will amend the Employment Rights Act 1996 to provide an entitlement to 'rehabilitation leave' for newly disabled people and people whose existing impairments change.

This chapter addresses the entitlement of employees to have their hours at work regulated. It also addresses their entitlement to time off for various purposes, the most common of which are holiday, sickness, maternity leave, trade union activities, parental leave and looking after dependants in an emergency. A number of less common entitlements are also dealt with.

7.2 THE WORKING TIME REGULATIONS

7.2.1 Introduction

The Working Time Regulations 1998, SI 1998/1833 (WTR 1998) came into force on 1 October 1998. They implement in Britain EC Directives introduced in the early 1990s, now consolidated as the EC Working Time Directive 93/104/EC.

The 1998 Regulations have been amended by: the Working Time Regulations 1999, SI 1999/3372; the Working Time (Amendment) Regulations 2001, SI 2001/3256; the Working Time (Amendment) Regulations 2002, SI 2002/3128; the Working Time (Amendment) Regulations 2003, SI 2003/1684; the Working Time Regulations 1998 (Amendment) Regulations 2004, SI 2004/2516; the Working Time Regulations 1998 (Amendment) Order 2005, SI 2005/2241; and the Working Time (Amendment) Regulations 2007, SI 2007/2079.

There are also separate 'sector specific' regulations: the Merchant Shipping (Hours of Work) Regulations 2002, SI 2002/2125; the Merchant Shipping (Working Time: Inland Waterways) Regulations 2003, SI 2003/3049; the Civil Aviation (Working Time) Regulations 2004, SI 2004/756; and the Road Transport (Working Time) Regulations 2005, SI 2005/639.

The European Commission succeeded in having the original Working Time Directive adopted under the health and safety provisions of the EC Treaty. This meant it could be adopted by qualified majority vote. The UK considered this to be deliberate sleight of hand designed to impose on it a measure which should have been adopted under the social policy provisions and therefore be subject to UK opt-out. The view was that this backdoor method for adopting the Directive resulted from a desire to reduce UK competitive advantage than from genuine health and safety considerations. Although the Directive required that it should be implemented by November 1996, the UK delayed implementation for almost two years while pursuing an ultimately unsuccessful challenge to its legality in the ECJ (*United Kingdom* v. *EU Council* [1997] IRLR 30, ECJ). In the meantime, some public sector workers sought direct enforcement of the Directive in the UK. They failed as the Court of Appeal ruled that the Directive was not sufficiently precise and unconditional to be directly enforceable (*Gibson* v. *East Riding of Yorkshire Council* [2000] IRLR 598, CA).

Subject to very minor exceptions, all workers (mobile and non-mobile) in all sectors are now covered either by the Working Time Directive or sector specific Directives and by regulations implementing them in the UK.

Working time limits set out in WTR 1998 take effect as implied contractual terms: accordingly workers can enforce their rights to paid holiday or rest breaks in the same way that they can enforce any other contractual right (*Barber* v. *RJB Mining (UK) Ltd* [1999] ICR 679, QBD).

The provisions of WTR 1998 apply to 'workers', not just 'employees'. A worker is defined as (WTR 1998, reg.2(1)):

an individual who has entered into or works under (or, where the employment has ceased, worked under) (a) a contract of employment or (b) any other contract, whether express or implied and (if it is express) whether oral or in writing, whereby the individual undertakes to do or perform personally any work or services for another party to the contract whose status is not by virtue of the contract that of a client or customer of any profession or business undertaking carried on by the individual.

In other words, the regulations apply to all employees and self-employed individuals unless they are sole traders running a business on their own account.

The EAT has found that reg.2(1)(b) created a 'hybrid' category of worker falling between the position of the individual employee and the individual who is a genuinely self-employed contractor, and stated that so long as someone who falls into this hybrid category was not carrying on a profession or business undertaking, they would be a 'worker' for the purposes of WTR 1998 (*Torith Ltd* v. *Flynn* [2003] All ER 45). The important question is not 'whether the individual is in business on his own account' but is, as the regulations state, whether the other party to the contract is a 'client or customer or client of any profession or business undertaking carried on by the individual' (*Byrne Brothers (Formwork) Ltd* v. *Baird & Ors* [2002] ICR 667, EAT and *Redrow Homes (Yorkshire) Ltd* v. *Wright* [2004] ICR 1126, CA).

7.2.2 Luxembourg agreement – June 2008

On 10 June 2008 the EU Member States reached agreement on several long-standing problems which have arisen in practice in implementation of the Working Time Directive. Subject to approval by the European Parliament, it can therefore be expected that at least some of the issues noted in this chapter will be resolved in the foreseeable future.

The main points of agreement in relation to the Working Time Directive were:

- on-call time to be split into active and inactive on-call time, with active on-call time to be counted as working time;
- inactive on-call time may not be counted as rest time and can be counted as working time if national laws or social partners agree;
- standard maximum limit remains at 48 working hours per week unless an individual worker chooses otherwise (opt-out);
- new protective limit (cap) for workers who opt out: maximum working week of 60 hours unless social partners agree otherwise;
- new cap for workers who opt-out if inactive on-call time is counted as working time: maximum working week of 65 hours;
- the cap protects all workers employed for longer than 10 weeks with one employer;
- opt-out only under certain conditions, such as: no signature during first month of employment, no victimisation for not signing or withdrawing

opt-out, and employers must keep records on working hours of opted-out workers.

7.2.3 Maximum 48-hour working week

The opening part of reg.4 of WTR 1998 provides:

> 4(1) Unless his employer has first obtained the worker's agreement in writing to perform such work, a worker's working time, including overtime ... shall not exceed an average of 48 hours for each seven days;

Calculating the number of hours

The Regulations are concerned with limiting the average number of hours in a working week. To calculate the average number of hours, one looks at the average over a rolling 17-week period (WTR 1998, reg.4(3)).

Alternatively, the employer can agree a different period with the workforce for calculating the average weekly working hours, either in a workforce agreement, a collective agreement or in the worker's contract of employment. However, this can only be done for 'objective or technical reasons' and is subject to a maximum reference period of 52 weeks (WTR 1998, reg.4(3) read with reg.23(b)).

For certain categories of workers, such as those who live a long distance away from their place of work (including offshore workers), or where there is a need for continuity of service (such as work at hospitals, docks or airports), or where there are periodic surges of activity (such as in the tourism or postal industries), or where the worker's working time is spent on board trains with intermittent activities and their hours are linked to transport timetables, the average hours are taken over a 26-, rather than 17-week reference period (WTR 1998, regs.4(5) and 21, as amended).

If the worker has been employed for less than 17 (or, if applicable, 26) weeks, the weekly working hours are averaged out from when employment started (WTR 1998, reg.4(4)).

Adjustments are made to the number of days within the reference period to take account of any absences owing to 'excluded days' *viz.* days consisting of any period of annual leave taken as part of the statutory right to four weeks' leave, any period of sick or maternity, paternity, adoption or parental leave, or any period when the 48-hour limit was disapplied by reason of the worker opting out (WTR 1998, reg.4(6) and (7)).

What time counts?

Regulation 4(1) makes it clear that overtime is included as worked time for the purpose of the 48-hour week.

The ECJ has ruled that all time spent by a doctor on call in a hospital constitutes working time for the purposes of the Working Time Directive (*Sindicato Medicos Publica* v. *Valenciana*, Case C-303/98 [2001] ICR 1116 and *Landeshaupstadt Kiel* v. *Jaeger*, ECJ Case C-151/02 [2003] IRLR 805).

These decisions caused considerable practical difficulty. The EC Commission, and the EC Employment, Social Policy, Health and Consumer Affairs Council recommended that the rules should be changed to ensure that inactive on-call time is not counted as working time (but adding that it should not count as rest time). The issue proved particularly difficult to resolve as it became linked in the normal EC horse-trading process with other issues, notably differences of view concerning the 'opt-out' and the 'reference period' over which the average 48-hour weekly limit on working time is calculated. Many attempts to get agreement failed, including as recently as December 2007 but as noted above (see **section 7.2.2**) agreement was finally reached on 10 June 2008. Appropriate amendments to the Working Time Directive can therefore be expected in the near future.

In 2006, the EAT ruled that on-call time spent by a care-worker was working time for purposes of the WTR 1998 even though she was allowed to sleep while on call. The worker in question was provided with tied accommodation at her workplace but was required to be available on site to answer calls (*Macartney* v. *Oversley House Management* [2006] ICR 510, EAT).

Apart from the obvious direct problems caused by the European Court of Justice 'on-call' working time decisions, they also lead to problems in connection with the national minimum wage and with provision of rest breaks for workers (see *Anderson* v. *Jarvis Hotels plc* (unreported, EAT, 30 May 2006) and *Miles* v. *Linkage Community Trust Ltd* [2008] IRLR 602, EAT).

Keeping records

There is an obligation to keep records (and to retain them for two years) to see whether the 48-hour maximum working week is being complied with. There is also an obligation to keep records identifying workers who have signed an 'opt-out' agreement from the 48-hour maximum working week (see below) but the wording of the Regulations suggests there is no requirement to keep records of time worked by such workers (WTR 1998, regs.9 and 4(2)).

Exclusions and special provisions

Some workers are excluded from the maximum 48-hour working week provisions of WTR 1998 and there are special provisions for others, notably as follows:

- *Unmeasured working time.* Workers whose working time is neither measured nor pre-determined, or whose hours can be determined by the workers themselves, are excluded. The Regulations give examples of managing executives, or others with autonomous decision-taking powers, family workers, or ministers of religion (WTR 1998, reg.20). Specific provision to cover situations where working time was partly determined by the worker was criticised by the European Court of Justice in 2006 (*EC Commission* v. *United Kingdom*, Case C-484/04, [2006] IRLR 888, ECJ). The UK government considered the offending provision (WTR 1998, reg.20(2)) had never been needed in the first place and removed it even before the ECJ delivered its judgment (Working Time (Amendment) Regulations 2006, SI 2006/99).

- *Domestic workers.* Those employed as domestic servants in private households are excluded (WTR 1998, reg.19).
- *Opting out* – see below (WTR 1998, reg.5).
- *Armed forces and police* are excluded 'where characteristics peculiar to' their services inevitably conflict with WTR 1998 (WTR 1998, reg.18(2)).
- *Seafarers.* Special rules apply (Merchant Shipping (Hours of Work) Regulations 2002, SI 2002/2125).
- *Offshore workers.* As from 1 October 2006, new regulations changed the definition of offshore work in the WTR 1998 (Working Time (Amendment) (No.2) Regulations 2006, SI 2006/2389). The new definition makes it clear that those employed on rigs outside UK 'territorial waters' but within the UK sector of the continental shelf (except one or part of one in which the law of Northern Ireland applies) are covered by WTR 1998. In 2008 an employment tribunal in Aberdeen held that annual leave entitlement of offshore oil rig workers under the WTR 1998 is entitlement to leave from what would otherwise be working time. As the 'two weeks off' part of their normal 'two weeks on/two weeks off' rota was not in most cases working time, it followed that most of the workers concerned were entitled to annual holiday based on an average working week of 3.5 days, not 5 days.
- *Most 'travelling personnel' on Inland Waterways.* Special rules apply (Merchant Shipping (Working Time: Inland Waterways) Regulations 2003, SI 2003/3049).
- *Aircrew on civil aircraft.* Special rules apply (Civil Aviation (Working Time) Regulations 2004, SI 2004/756).
- *Sea fishermen.* Special rules apply (Fishing Vessels (Working Time: Sea-fishermen) Regulations 2004, SI 2004/1713).
- *Mobile workers in road transport.* Special rules apply (Road Transport (Working Time) Regulations 2005, SI 2005/639).
- *Doctors in training.* Special phasing-in rules apply (WTR 1998, reg.25A inserted by the Working Time (Amendment) Regulations 2003, SI 2003/1684). From 1 August 2004 to 31 July 2007 the maximum permitted average working week for doctors in training was 58 hours; from 1 August 2007 to 31 July 2009 it is 56 hours; and from 1 August 2009 it will be the normal 48 hours.
- *Young workers.* Special rules apply (WTR 1998, reg.5A and see below at **section 7.2.6**).

Previous exclusions covering non-mobile workers in transport industries (e.g. office staff), offshore workers and non-aircrew workers in aviation were ended on 1 August 2003 by the Working Time (Amendment) Regulations 2003 noted above.

Opting out

As the law currently stands, an individual worker and his employer can validly agree to opt out of the permitted working hours limits imposed by WTR 1998 (WTR 1998, reg.5, permitted by Art.22 of the consolidated Working Time Directive 2003/88/EC). At least in theory a worker has protection against being forced to work long hours because it is unlawful to subject the worker to any detriment for refusing to sign an opt-out agreement (ERA 1996, s.45A). Further, any opt-out agreement must be cancellable on not more than three months' notice (seven days' notice if nothing else has been agreed).

An opt-out agreement must be in writing (WTR 1998, reg.4(1)). A cancellation notice must also be in writing (WTR 1998, reg.5(2)(b)).

A worker's consent to the opt-out agreement must be by the individual concerned, and cannot be 'given by trade-union representatives in the context of a collective or other agreement' (*SIMAP* v. *Conselleria de Sanidad y Consumo de la Generalidad Velenciana* [2000] IRLR 845, ECJ). There is some indirect indication from the EAT that if an employee who has signed an opt-out agreement later changes his mind and insists on enforcing his right to work no more than the 48-hour maximum, it is likely to be lawful for his employer to make an appropriate reduction in his salary (*Clamp* v. *Aerial Systems* (unreported, EAT, 6 October 2004)).

It is understood that in practice, the UK is the only country in the EU where employees and employers make extensive use of the opt-out facility. The European Parliament and some Member States, notably France, Belgium, Sweden, Spain, Greece and Finland, are on record as wanting to remove the facility. The British government has confirmed that the EU Treaty signed, subject to ratification, in Lisbon in December 2007 will not affect the ability of the UK to allow individual opt-outs from the permitted working hours limits imposed by WTR 1998 (Hansard HC col. 804, 3 July 2007).

7.2.4 Holidays

General

Until WTR 1998, workers had no statutory right to holiday. Most workers were then given a statutory right to a minimum of four weeks' paid annual leave (in other words, 20 days for a person who works five days a week and proportionately less for a person who works fewer days per week).

There is no statutory right to time off on bank holidays nor for extra pay in respect of them if they fall during normal paid annual holidays.

EMPLOYMENT LAW HANDBOOK

In 2005 the government announced that it would give workers a statutory right to bank holidays in addition to their existing entitlement under WTR 1998. In the event it did not do so, and instead introduced rules to increase the basic statutory holiday entitlement without changing the rule that there is no statutory entitlement to bank holidays. The increase is phased in but will be fully effective from 1 April 2009 when the statutory right will be to a minimum of 5.6 weeks' paid annual leave (in other words 28 days for a person who works five days a week and proportionately less for a person who works fewer days per week).

How much holiday?

Regulation 13 of WTR 1998 provides that workers are entitled to four weeks' holiday leave in any leave year. A leave year is deemed to commence on the date that employment started (and each successive anniversary) unless the worker began work prior to 1 October 1998, in which case his leave year will begin each year on 1 October. This can be varied to achieve consistency amongst the workforce (WTR 1998, reg.13).

Regulation 13A, introduced by the Working Time (Amendment) Regulations 2007, SI 2007/2079 with effect from 1 October 2007, provides for entitlement to additional annual leave as follows:

(a) in any leave year beginning on or after 1 October 2007 but before 1 April 2008, 0.8 weeks;
(b) in any leave year beginning before 1 October 2007, a proportion of 0.8 weeks equivalent to the proportion of the year beginning on 1 October 2007 which would have elapsed at the end of that leave year;
(c) in any leave year beginning on 1 April 2008, 0.8 weeks;
(d) in any leave year beginning after 1 April 2008 but before 1 April 2009, 0.8 weeks and a proportion of another 0.8 weeks equivalent to the proportion of the year beginning on 1 April 2009 which would have elapsed at the end of that leave year;
(e) in any leave year beginning on or after 1 April 2009, 1.6 weeks.

Adding the 1.6 weeks to the four weeks means that (from 1 April 2009) a worker who works five days a week will be entitled to 5.6 × 5 days' paid annual holiday *viz.* 28 days.

As there are generally eight bank and public holidays in a year, the practical overall effect of the 2007 changes for full-time workers whose employer previously allowed them to take off bank and public holidays with pay in addition to the statutory four weeks minimum is 'no change' (unless of course the employer agrees to provide more holiday than is required by the new rules). A full-time worker in that position had 28 days' paid leave before October 2007 (i.e. 20 days' statutory holiday plus by agreement eight paid bank and public holidays). Unless the employer agrees an increase, the same worker will still have 28 days' paid leave when the new rules are fully in force, but it will then be a statutory entitlement to 28 days' paid leave including the bank and public holidays.

Perhaps a little oddly there is no definition of a 'week' in the regulations but it is clearly meant to mean the same amount of time as the working week for the individual concerned.

Originally workers did not become entitled to paid holiday leave until they had been continuously employed for 13 weeks. This was changed in 2001. The right to paid holiday now accrues from the first day of employment and workers are entitled to take one-twelfth of their annual holiday entitlement for every month that they have worked (Working Time Amendment Regulations 2001, SI 2001/3256).

Calculation problems

There are two main areas of difficulty in calculating the statutory minimum number of days holiday to which a worker is entitled in a year. One concerns entitlement during the reg.13A phasing-in period until April 2009 and the other concerns workers who work irregular hours. These difficulties acquire a special significance when a worker leaves employment during a leave year as he is then entitled to pay in lieu of any untaken holiday (see below).

An overriding point to bear in mind is that 28 days is the absolute maximum statutory holiday entitlement (WTR 1998, reg.13A(3)). So even if someone works six days per week, their maximum statutory entitlement to paid holiday when the new rules are fully in force will be 28 days not 33.6 days (i.e. not 5.6 × 6).

The table below should help resolve any difficulty in calculating entitlement in respect of the phasing-in period under reg.13A. Multiply the weeks number given below by the number of days per week usually worked by the person concerned. For example, 4.8 weeks × 5 days = 24 days, 4.8 weeks × 4 days = 19.2 days.

While calculation of the statutory holiday entitlement of someone who works full days is quite straightforward using the table below, the calculation for those who work irregular hours can be complicated. The BERR website provides the following answer to the question: 'How do you calculate the holiday entitlement for someone working casually or working very irregular hours?'

> It may well be easiest to calculate the holiday entitlement that accrues as hours are worked. The holiday entitlement of 4.8 weeks is equivalent to 10.2% of hours worked. The 10.2% figure is 4.8 weeks' holiday, divided by 47.2 weeks (being 52 weeks – 4.8 weeks). The 4.8 weeks have to be excluded from the calculation as the worker would not be present during those 4.8 weeks in order to accumulate annual leave. So if someone has worked 10 hours, they would be entitled to 61 minutes paid holiday. The holiday entitlement is just over 6 minutes for each hour worked.

Leave year starts:	2007-08	2008-09	2009-10
1 November	4.8 weeks	5.26 weeks	5.6 weeks
1 December	4.8 weeks	5.33 weeks	5.6 weeks
	2008	**2009**	**2010**
1 January	4.8 weeks	5.4 weeks	5.6 weeks
	2008-09	**2009-10**	**2010**
1 February	4.8 weeks	5.47 weeks	5.6 weeks
1 March	4.8 weeks	5.53 weeks	5.6 weeks
1 April	4.8 weeks	5.6 weeks	5.6 weeks
1 May	4.87 weeks	5.6 weeks	5.6 weeks
1 June	4.93 weeks	5.6 weeks	5.6 weeks
1 July	5 weeks	5.6 weeks	5.6 weeks
1 August	5.07 weeks	5.6 weeks	5.6 weeks
1 September	5.13 weeks	5.6 weeks	5.6 weeks
1 October	5.2 weeks	5.6 weeks	5.6 weeks

A part-time worker who never works on Mondays is not entitled to pro-rata time off or pay in lieu in respect of bank holidays which fall on a Monday. In one case a worker failed in his claim that this rule contravened his rights under the Part-time Workers (Prevention of Less Favourable Treatment) Regulations 2000, SI 2000/1551 (*McMenemy* v. *Capita Business Services Ltd* [2007] IRLR 400, CS).

Other changes introduced by the Working Time (Amendment) Regulations 2007

Other changes introduced by the Working Time (Amendment) Regulations 2007, SI 2007/2079 with effect from 1 October 2007 are:

- any additional holiday over and above the minimum required by the EC Working Time Directive 2003/88/EC (20 days per year for a full-time worker) can be carried over to the following leave year, subject to agreement between employer and worker (new reg.13A(7) inserted into WTR 1998);
- although payment in lieu is not allowed in respect of the statutory minimum holiday entitlement this does not apply until 1 April 2009 and payment in lieu is permissible in respect of any contractual holiday entitlement greater than the statutory minimum (new reg.13A(6) inserted into WTR 1998);

- part days' holiday entitlement will not be rounded up to the nearest full day (WTR 1998, reg.13(6) is revoked);
- the new 2007 Regulations extend to all workers covered by WTR 1998 including agency workers; they do not extend to those covered by the Civil Aviation (Working Time) Regulations 2004, SI 2004/756 nor the Merchant Shipping (Hours of Work) Regulations 2002, SI 2002/2125; nor to agricultural workers in Scotland (new reg.13A(8) inserted into WTR 1998);
- there is provision to ensure that an employee who is contractually entitled to time off for bank and/or public holidays will usually not be entitled to the new statutory increase in holiday entitlement as well – 'usually' as this will only be so provided the conditions in new reg. 26A are fulfilled (new reg. 26A inserted into WTR 1998).

When can holiday be taken?

Subject to any agreement to the contrary, a worker must give the employer notice of intention to take holiday and the notice must be at least twice as long as the amount of holiday to be taken (WTR 1998, reg.15(1) and (4)(a)). So if the employee is taking two weeks' holiday, the regulations provide that the employee should give the employer four weeks' advance notice. The employer then has half that amount of time to object and refuse permission for the holiday to be taken at that time (WTR 1998, reg.15(4)(b)).

An employer can require workers to take holiday to which they are entitled (WTR 1998, reg.15(2)(a)). This can be especially relevant on dismissal when a worker may prefer to take pay in lieu rather than holiday (see below). If the employer is unhappy about this, the employer can require the worker to take the holiday subject to giving appropriate notice, which again must be at least twice the amount of holiday involved (WTR 1998, reg.15(4)(a)).

Holiday pay

The statutory holiday is paid holiday (WTR 1998, reg.16). Under reg. 16 holiday pay is calculated by reference to normal working hours and therefore overtime does not have to be taken into account in calculating holiday pay unless it is contractually guaranteed. This is so even if in practice the employer regularly works considerable amounts of overtime (*Bamsey & ors* v. *Albon Engineering Ltd* [2004] EWCA Civ 359; *Evans* v. *Malley Organisation Ltd t/a First Business Support* [2003] IRLR 156).

However, if an employee who works normal hours is paid at a variable rate (usually because the employee is a piece worker) the calculation of a week's pay must include any commission or similar payment which varies in amount. If a commission or bonus varies with output it must therefore be taken into account in the calculation (*May Gurney Ltd* v. *Adshead & 95 ors* (unreported, EAT, 3 July 2006)).

In the absence of any provision to the contrary, a full-time salaried worker whose contract provides for a specified number of days' holiday per year is entitled to holiday pay on the basis that five days equals one week. Thus where a worker on an annual salary was contractually entitled to 10 days' holiday his holiday pay entitlement was 14/365ths, not 10/365ths (*Taylor* v. *East Midlands Offender Employment* [2000] IRLR 760). Another way of putting this is to say that the daily rate of accrued holiday pay due to an employee should be calculated by reference to the total of 233 working days in a year rather than by reference to 365 days (*Leisure Leagues UK Ltd* v. *Maconnachie* [2002] IRLR 600, EAT and *Yarrow* v. *Edwards Chartered Accountants* (unreported, EAT, 8 June 2007)).

A worker has no right to carry forward untaken holiday to the next year and normally cannot claim pay in lieu (WTR 1998, reg.13(9)(b)). The European Court of Justice has confirmed that holidays cannot lawfully be swapped for cash even if the holiday year has expired and the holiday allowance was carried forward to the next year (*Federatie Nederlandse Vakbeweging* v. *Staat der Nederlanden*, Case C-124/05, 6 April 2006). The logic is that an interpretation of the EC Working Time Directive which would allow pay in lieu of holiday entitlement would be self-contradictory as it would be tantamount to encouraging a practice which runs counter to the Directive's basic health and safety objectives.

However, the position is different when employment is terminated. The worker is then entitled to compensation for loss of holiday pay in respect of holiday accrued but untaken at the date of termination. This will usually be the value of the outstanding pay, although that may be varied in the contract of employment, or in a workforce or collective agreement (WTR 1998, reg.14). There is no statutory cap on the amount of a week's pay for this purpose (and, specifically, ERA 1996, s.227 does not apply).

If the worker had not taken his full statutory holiday entitlement in previous years (i.e. before the final leave year) that is simply history and the worker's bad luck – the worker cannot claim back holiday pay for those years (*Apex Masonry Contractors Ltd* v. *Everitt* (unreported, EAT, 26 September 2005)). On the other hand if the worker had taken more paid holiday than the statutory pro rata annual entitlement, the employer cannot recover the excess holiday pay unless there is express provision for this via a 'relevant agreement' (WTR 1998, reg.14(4) and *Hill* v. *Chapell* [2003] IRLR 19).

The question of whether a worker who is absent on long-term sick leave is entitled to accrue paid holiday rights is a 'hot potato' which was referred by the House of Lords to the European Court of Justice in December 2006. In January 2008 an Advocate General of the ECJ gave a preliminary opinion to the effect that such a worker is entitled to holiday which has accrued during his absence, but can take it only after he has returned to work (A-G's opinion in *Stringer, Kilic, Thwaites, Ainsworth and Khan* v. *HMRC*, ECJ Case C-520/06 and in *Schultz-Hoff* v. *Deutsche Rentenversicherung Bund*, ECJ Case

C-350/06, both on 24 January 2008). The Advocate General also suggested that if the worker is dismissed then he is entitled to a compensatory payment as a replacement for leave which accrued but was not taken due to the sickness absence and that this 'allowance in lieu' should be equivalent to normal pay. Whether the ECJ itself will agree with this opinion remains to be seen.

A worker who is dismissed for dishonesty remains entitled to pay in lieu of untaken holiday (*Witley & District Men's Club* v. *McKay* [2001] IRLR 595, EAT).

'Rolled-up' holiday pay

'Rolled-up' holiday pay refers to remuneration paid on account of holiday pay as a regular sum throughout the course of a year as part of a worker's hourly, daily or weekly wage. This can be administratively convenient, especially in industries such as construction where there can be a frequent turnover of workers, on the basis that the employer will then not have to pay holiday pay when the workers are taking leave.

The introduction of WTR 1998 led to problems with this system as reg.16 provides that the statutory minimum holiday must be paid holiday. Could a worker who had already received rolled-up holiday pay claim that reg.16 also entitled him to pay while taking his statutory minimum holiday?

The European Court of Justice provided an answer in 2006. It ruled that it is unlawful for an employer to roll up statutory holiday pay. However, provided the employer has made it completely plain that additions to regular pay were on account of holiday pay and were clearly identified and recognised as such by the employee then they could be set-off against holiday pay (*Robinson-Steele* v. *R.D. Retail Services Ltd* Case C-131/04 and *Clarke* v. *Frank Staddon Ltd* Case C-257/04 and *Caulfield & ors* v. *Hanson Clay Products Ltd, formerly Marshalls Clay Products Ltd* [2006] IRLR 386).

The net practical effect is thus that rolling up statutory holiday pay is unlawful but that an employee cannot get away with claiming it twice over provided the arrangement is completely transparent and comprehensible. The burden of proof is expressly on the employer to show that the arrangement was 'transparent and comprehensible'. If he can do so it seems that he will be entitled to set off rolled-up holiday pay against amounts due to an employee who is absent on the mandatory holiday to which he is entitled under the EC Working Time Directive 2003/88/EC, Art.7, certainly in respect of periods before March 2006.

There is still some uncertainty as to the future. Clearly it is undesirable that the law should be that on the one hand a practice (i.e. rolling up holiday pay) is unlawful, but on the other hand that it does not matter that it is unlawful provided it is done openly and above board. The Court of Appeal did not give further guidance when it reconsidered the matter in the light of the ECJ ruling above – it merely remitted the case in question back to the original tribunal and made a costs order in favour of the employee (*Clarke* v. *Frank*

Staddon Ltd [2006] EWCA Civ 1470, 17 October 2006). The DTI (now BERR) stated that in its view the ECJ ruling simply means that rolled-up holiday pay arrangements must now stop although 'whilst employers are in the process of changing their pay arrangements in order to eliminate rolled-up holiday pay, payments which are transparent and comprehensible can continue to be offset against what has to be eventually paid'.

A practical solution which some employers are understood to have adopted is to set up a separate bank account into which rolled-up holiday pay is paid week by week, allocated to the worker(s) concerned but not physically paid to them until either they leave employment or take their holiday.

Time limits for claims

A complaint to a tribunal concerning failure to provide paid annual leave must be made within three months of the date on which the alleged payment should have been made (WTR 1998, reg. 30).

At one time it seemed possible that a claim could be made under the unlawful deduction from wages provisions of ERA 1996, in which case the more favourable time limit of three months from the last of a series of deductions might apply (*List Design Group Ltd* v. *Douglas* [2002] ICR 686, EAT). However, the Court of Appeal later ruled that claims to enforce entitlement to holiday pay provided by the WTR 1998 can be pursued only under those Regulations, and not as claims for unlawful deduction of wages under ERA 1996. This Court of Appeal ruling was in the case now known as *Stringer, Kilic, Thwaites, Ainsworth and Khan* v. *HMRC* in which as noted above an ECJ decision, albeit on a different point, is still awaited.

7.2.5 Rest breaks and weekends

The WTR 1998 provide minimum rest breaks for all workers. The provisions differ for adult workers and young workers. Adult workers are over 18, young workers are workers who have attained the age of 15 but not the age of 18 and are over compulsory school age (WTR 1998, reg.2(1) – see **section 7.2.6**).

There are special cases, such as in an emergency, in which the obligation to provide rest breaks is relaxed (WTR 1998, reg.21) but the provision is strictly construed (*Gallagher* v. *Alpha Catering Services Ltd (t/a Alpha Flight Services)* [2005] ICR 673, CA). The intention and effect of the regulations is that even in these special cases workers will have the right to a minimum of 90 hours of 'compensatory rest' in a week but that their rest can be taken in a different pattern from that set out in the basic regulations (WTR 1998, reg.24).

Employers must make sure that workers can take their rest. However, they are under no legal obligation to make sure that workers do so (in a nice example of how EU law operates differently from the common law system, the ECJ ruled in 2006 that it was 'incompatible with the objective' of the

Working Time Directive for the British government to draw attention to this and so the DTI, now BERR, amended its official guidance accordingly – *EC Commission* v. *United Kingdom*, Case C-484-04, 7 September 2006).

Daily rest

A worker must have a minimum of 11 consecutive hours' rest during each 24-hour period for which he works for an employer. A young worker must have at least 12 consecutive hours' rest during each 24-hour period (WTR 1998, reg.10(1) and (2)).

Weekly rest

Workers must have an 'uninterrupted rest period' of not less than 24 hours in each seven-day period during which they work for their employer. This is extended to 48 hours for young workers (WTR 1998, reg.11(1) and (3)).

For adult workers, there is an alternative (at the option of the employer) of using a two-week base period, in which case the rest period must be at least 48 uninterrupted hours or two separate uninterrupted 24-hour periods (WTR 1998, reg.11(2)).

Rest breaks

Every worker must have an uninterrupted rest break of not less than 20 minutes (or such longer period as may be agreed in a collective agreement or a workforce agreement) per six hours of working time. A young worker is entitled to not less than 30 minutes of rest break per four and a half hours of working time (WTR 1998, reg.12).

If the pattern according to which an employer organises work is such as to put the health and safety of a worker at risk, in particular because the work is monotonous or the work-rate is pre-determined, the employer must ensure that the worker is given 'adequate rest breaks' (WTR 1998, reg.8). This can be helpful, for example, to workers who run the risk of developing repetitive strain injury.

Records

There is no statutory obligation to keep a record of breaks, although it is an ancillary task to the exercise of keeping records of worked time for the purpose of the 48-hour maximum working week.

Special rules and exclusions

There are special rules for workers covered by 'sector specific' regulations as noted above (the Merchant Shipping (Working Time: Inland Waterways)

Regulations 2003; the Civil Aviation (Working Time) Regulations 2004; the Fishing Vessels (Working Time: Sea-fishermen) Regulations 2004; and the Road Transport (Working Time) Regulations 2005). The last of these extends to all crew members the daily rest requirements which already applied to commercial road transport drivers under the Community Drivers' Hours Regulations 3820/85/EEC. In February 2008 the Department for Transport announced a review of the road transport working time regulations and associated guidance, and thus amending regulations can be expected.

Workers employed in a domestic capacity in a private household are excluded from the statutory entitlement to rest breaks deriving from monotonous work putting their health and safety at risk. They remain entitled to daily rest, weekly rest and the 20 minutes rest break every six hours (WTR 1998, reg.19).

Workers whose working time is not measured, or where it is determined by themselves, are excluded from the statutory entitlement to daily rest, weekly rest and the 20 minutes rest break every six hours (WTR 1998, reg.20).

7.2.6 Young workers

Special provisions in respect of young workers (basically those aged between 15 and 18 who are above compulsory school age) are included in WTR 1998.

New rules for young workers came into force on 6 April 2003 (Working Time (Amendment) Regulations 2002, SI 2002/3128). The main effect is that the working time of a young worker must not exceed eight hours a day and 40 hours a week (WTR 1998, reg.5A introduced by SI 2002/3128, reg.6) and that no young worker may work during a 'restricted period' (defined as the period between 10 pm and 6 am, or, in a case where the worker is contracted to work after 10 pm the period between 11 pm and 7 am (WTR 1998, reg.6A introduced by SI 2002/3128, reg.8).

There are potentially important exceptions to these rules (in WTR 1998, reg.27A, inserted by SI 2002/3128, reg.17) if three conditions are fulfilled. These are:

(a) the young worker's employer requires him to undertake work which is necessary either to maintain continuity of service or production or to respond to a surge in demand for a service or product;
(b) no adult worker is available to perform the work; and
(c) performing the work would not adversely affect the young worker's education or training.

If those three conditions are all fulfilled then the 'eight hours a day and 40 hours a week' rule (WTR 1998, reg.5A) will not apply.

Children of compulsory school age are not covered by WTR 1998 (*Addison (t/a Brayton News)* v. *Ashby* [2003] ICR 667). They are, of course, protected by other legislation. In the context of holiday entitlement the result is merely that child workers must have two consecutive weeks' holiday without employment during the school holidays (Children and Young Persons Act 1933, s.18(1)(j)).

In Scotland, the Children and Young Persons (Scotland) Act 1937 (as amended e.g. by the Children (Protection at Work) (Scotland) Regulations 2000, SI 2000/149) applies. An amendment made by the Children (Protection at Work) (Scotland) Regulations 2006, SSI 2006/140 with effect from 18 April 2006 places a 12-hour limit on the number of hours that a child may be employed in any week in which the child is required to attend school.

The government published a DfES (now DCFS) consultation paper on 'Increasing the School Leaving Age' on 25 April 2007. Proposals to increase to 17 and then 18 the minimum age at which young people in England and Wales can leave education or training are included in the Education and Skills Bill introduced in the House of Commons on 28 November 2007.

7.2.7 Night work

Who is a night worker?

A 'night worker' is defined as a worker 'who, as a normal course, works at least three hours of his daily working time during night time'.

'Night time' is defined (WTR 1998, reg.2(1)) as a period:

(a) the duration of which is not less than seven hours, and
(b) which includes the period between midnight and 5 a.m., which is determined for the purposes of these Regulations by a relevant agreement, or, in default of such a determination, the period between 11 p.m. and 6 a.m.

A worker on a rotating shift who, once every three weeks, worked at least three hours at night, fell within the above definition (*R* v. *Attorney General for Northern Ireland, ex parte Burns* [1999] IRLR 315).

A doctor who is 'on-call' at night is not automatically thereby a 'night worker' for the purposes of WTR 1998 (*SIMAP* v. *Conselleria de Sanidad y consumo de la Generalidad Velenciana* [2000] IRLR 845, ECJ).

What rights do night workers have?

An employer is required 'to take all reasonable steps, in keeping with the need to protect the health and safety of workers, to ensure that' the normal hours of work of any night worker employed by him do not exceed an average of eight for each 24 hours in any reference period applicable in his case (WTR 1998, reg.6(1) and (2)).

The reference period is the same 17- (or 26-) week period that is used for the computation of the 48-hour maximum working week.

If the night work involves a significant risk to the health and safety of workers employed by the employer (note: not just to the worker involved) or involves special hazards or heavy physical or mental strain, then there is an absolute limit of eight hours' night work during any individual period of 24 hours (WTR 1998, reg. 6(7) and (8)).

An employer must ensure that each night worker has the opportunity of a confidential, free health assessment before starting night work and at regular intervals 'of whatever duration may be appropriate in his case' (WTR 1998, reg.7). DTI Guidance suggests that a questionnaire prepared by a qualified occupational health practitioner and completed by the worker may suffice.

Where practical, a night worker has the right to be transferred to suitable day work if a registered medical practitioner informs the employer that the worker is suffering from health problems connected with working at night (WTR 1998, reg.7(6)).

Keeping records

There is an obligation to keep night time work records and retain them for two years. The same applies to records concerning offers of free health assessments (WTR 1998, reg.9).

7.2.8 Workforce agreements

Employers and workers can vary some provisions of WTR 1998 by use of a workforce agreement. A workforce agreement is a non-unionised alternative to a collective agreement as a method for agreeing changes on behalf of the whole of the workforce, or to a 'particular group' of workers who share a workplace, function or organisational unit within a business (WTR 1998, Sched.1, paras.1(c), 2).

The provisions of the WTR 1998 that can be varied by a workforce agreement are aspects of the night work and rest break rules. In addition, a workforce agreement can increase the 17-week period (by reference to which average weekly working hours are calculated for the purpose of the maximum 48-hour working week) to anything up to 52 weeks. However, an employer cannot enter into a collective 'opt-out' of the maximum 48-hour working week by way of a workforce agreement (*SIMAP* v. *Conselleria de Sanidad y Consumo de la Generalidad Velenciana* [2000] IRLR 845, ECJ).

To be valid, the workforce agreement must be signed by elected representatives of the workforce. The number of representatives can be determined by the employer, but workers must be entitled to vote for as many candidates as there are representatives to be elected. Voting should take place in secret and all workers should be entitled to stand for election. The exception is where the employer employs fewer than 20 workers, when at least half the workers must sign the workforce agreement (WTR 1998, Sched.1, paras.1(d), 3).

In addition, to be valid, the workforce agreement must state that it has effect for a period not exceeding five years and it must be circulated to all workers to whom it is intended to apply, prior to it being made available for signature by the elected representatives (WTR 1998, Sched.1, para.1(b), (e)).

7.2.9 Enforcement

There are four ways of enforcing rights provided by the WTR 1998.

The first of these is by criminal sanctions. The local authority, or the Health and Safety Executive, is entitled to bring prosecutions arising from breaches of regulations imposing the 48-hour maximum working week, night work, record keeping and some of the rest break provisions (WTR 1998, regs.28 and 29 and Health and Safety (Enforcing Authority) Regulations 1998, SI 1998/494).

Second, a worker can lodge a complaint with an employment tribunal alleging that his rights have been infringed. If a complaint is well-founded, a tribunal must make a declaration to that effect and may make an award of compensation. No upper limit for compensation is specified (WTR 1998, reg.30). Compensation is not mandatory but is expressly a matter for the tribunal's discretion to be considered in the light of financial loss suffered by the worker and the 'default of the employer' (*Miles* v. *Linkage Community Trust Ltd* [2008] IRLR 602, EAT which is also authority for the proposition that the right to compensation only arises once the worker has complained and the employer has refused to rectify the problem – until the matter has been raised there can be no 'refusal', which is the trigger for compensation under WTR 1998, reg.30).

Third, the worker can bring a claim in the employment tribunal if he suffers a detriment because of asserting, or attempting to assert, a right under WTR 1998. It does not matter whether he actually has that right, provided he purports to exercise it in good faith (ERA 1996, s.45A).

Fourth, if the worker is dismissed because he asserts, or attempts to assert, his rights under WTR 1998, the dismissal will be automatically unfair (ERA 1996, s.101A).

An attempt by public sector employees to use a fifth possible method, direct enforcement of the Working Time Directive, failed as the Court of Appeal held that the definition of 'working time' in Art.2 of the Directive was not sufficiently precise to enable a court to determine the period an employee had to have worked before the employee was entitled to the specified period of annual leave (*Gibson* v. *East Riding of Yorkshire Council* [2000] ICR 890, CA).

Additionally, a worker may have rights under general law resulting from a breach by his employer of WTR 1998. The worker can also bring a claim for breach of contract, although financial loss or personal injury would have to be demonstrated (*Barber* v. *RJB Mining (UK) Ltd* [1999] ICR 679). For example, in 2007 the Court of Appeal dealt with the case of a young man driving a van on the M1 at night who lost control, was flung out when the van overturned and was paralysed. He is reported to have received £400,000 as an interim award against his employer because the accident was caused by tiredness after working non-stop for 19 hours. The Court of Appeal overturned a High Court ruling that the young man was to blame, finding he was only one-third responsible (because he was not wearing a seat belt). The case will no doubt go down in folk-lore because of the employer's approach to how employees should work, summarised as 'Eating's cheating' and 'You can sleep when you're dead' (*Eyres v. Atkinsons Kitchens and Bedrooms Ltd* [2007] EWCA Civ 365, 24 April 2007).

7.3 TIME OFF WORK

7.3.1 Introduction

All workers are entitled to time off work in prescribed circumstances. The most important are set out below. An employer's obligations as to pay and other contractual terms during an employee's time off work vary depending on the reason for the time off.

7.3.2 Time off for sickness

The right

There is no statutory right to be off work when sick: however, in the absence of suspicion of malingering, no reasonable employer would insist an employee attend work when ill. Such a requirement would probably be a breach of the term of trust and confidence and any dismissal (whether actual or constructive) would be likely to be unfair dismissal (see **Chapter 11**).

Pay

The employee is entitled to statutory sick pay (SSP), payable to most employees for 28 weeks at a rate of £75.40 per week (from April 2008) after the first three days of sick absence. After seven days of absence, the employer is entitled to demand a medical certificate signed by a doctor (Social Security and Benefits Act 1992, Pt XI; Statutory Sick Pay (Medical Evidence) Regulations 1985, SI 1985/1604). The employer must issue a form SSPI(T) by the end of the twenty-third week to let the employee know when SSP will be ending. Incapacity benefit may then be claimed by an employee who is still too ill to work.

In practice many employers offer enhanced sickness rights. Care must be taken to ensure that any contractual provisions do not amount to unjustified less favourable treatment of persons with a disability, thereby breaching DDA 1995.

Some employers offer Permanent Health Insurance (PHI) schemes as a perk. If a PHI scheme is available through employment, there is an implied term that the employer will not dismiss the worker so as to deprive him of the benefits from the PHI policy (*Aspden* v. *Webbs Poultry & Meat Group (Holdings) Ltd* [1996] IRLR 521).

As noted above the question of whether a worker who is absent on long-term sick leave is entitled to accrue holiday pay is under consideration by the ECJ. The A-G's opinion is that a worker in that situation would be entitled to pay in lieu of holiday if he is dismissed (*Stringer, Kilic, Thwaites, Ainsworth and Khan* v. *HMRC*, ECJ Case C-520/06 and in *Schultz-Hoff* v. *Deutsche Rentenversicherung Bund*, ECJ Case C-350/06, both on 24 January 2008). Whether the ECJ itself will agree with this opinion remains to be seen.

7.3.3 Time off for ante-natal care

An employee who is pregnant and 'has, on the advice of a registered medical practitioner, registered midwife or registered health visitor, made an appointment to attend at any place' for ante-natal care is entitled 'to be permitted by her employer to take paid time off during the employee's working hours in order to enable her to keep her appointment' (ERA 1996, s.55(1)). No minimum qualifying service is necessary.

The employer is entitled to request a certificate confirming pregnancy before allowing the employee to take time off, with the exception of the first appointment during her pregnancy (since, at that stage, the employee might not have had the pregnancy formally confirmed) (ERA 1996, s.55(2) and (3)).

The right to time off for ante-natal care is restricted to employees. Employees excluded from the right to paid time off under ERA 1996, s.55 are those employed in the armed forces, the police service and in share fishing.

Although this right to time off is an absolute one, the enforcement provisions weaken it. A claim can only be brought if an employer has 'unreasonably refused' to allow it and the only remedy is a declaration that the employer has acted unreasonably plus compensation reflecting the pay the worker would have received if she had been allowed the time off.

Women are entitled to be paid at their normal hourly rate whilst absent for ante-natal appointments (ERA 1996, s.56).

7.3.4 Time off for maternity leave

An excellent summary of maternity rights generally is provided on the BERR website (**www.berr.gov.uk/files/file34285.pdf** – employees' version; **www.berr.gov.uk/files/file34286.pdf** – employers' version).

The right

All female employees are entitled to up to 52 weeks' maternity leave regardless of length of employment (Work and Families Act 2006 and Regulations thereunder – see below).

Maternity leave comes in three forms:

1. *Compulsory.* It is a criminal offence for an employer to permit an employee to work during the two weeks from the day on which she gives birth (ERA 1996, s.72 and Maternity and Parental Leave etc. Regulations 1999, SI 1999/3312, reg.8). Compulsory maternity leave is part of the 26 weeks' ordinary maternity leave (see immediately below).
2. *Ordinary.* Ordinary maternity leave (OML) is twenty-six weeks' leave starting from the earliest of: (i) the date the mother selects by notice to her employer, not being before the beginning of the eleventh week before the expected week of childbirth; or (ii) the first date on which she is absent from work wholly or partly because of her pregnancy, not being before the beginning of the fourth week before the expected week of childbirth; or (iii) the day after childbirth occurs (ERA 1996, s.71 and Maternity and Parental Leave etc. Regulations 1999, SI 1999/3312, regs.4 and 6). A woman is normally entitled to all contractual benefits except pay during OML (but is entitled to statutory maternity pay (SMP) or maternity allowance – see below).
3. *Additional.* Additional maternity leave (AML) is a further 26 weeks' leave from the end of ordinary maternity leave (ERA 1996, s.73 and Maternity and Parental Leave etc. Regulations 1999, SI 1999/3312, regs.6(3) and 7(4)). The previous requirement to have completed a minimum period of continuous employment to qualify for AML has been removed in relation to employees whose expected week of childbirth began on or after 1 April 2007 (Maternity and Parental Leave etc. and the Paternity and Adoption Leave (Amendment) Regulations 2006, SI 2006/2014).

A new employee who was pregnant when she was interviewed for her new job can insist on taking a full year off work, not 26 weeks as previously, even starting shortly after the new job began – and if she does not get the job and thinks the reason had something to do with her maternity leave rights she will be able to claim unlawful sex discrimination (see **Chapter 14**). This results from a change to the rules made in 2006. Any employee whose expected week of childbirth begins on or after 1 April 2007 and who qualifies for OML (26 weeks) will automatically also qualify for AML (a further 26 weeks). The previous requirement that she must have completed 26 weeks of continuous employment with the same employer (or an associated employer) at the beginning of the fourteenth week before the expected week of childbirth was abolished by the Maternity and Parental Leave etc. and the Paternity and Adoption Leave (Amendment) Regulations 2006, SI 2006/2014, reg.6. The resulting risk for employers, and opportunity for employees, may be less than it superficially appears to be because the government, looking after its own finances, did not change the rule making SMP conditional on the mother having completed at least 26 weeks' continuous employment (Social Security Contributions and Benefits Act 1992, s.164(2)(a)).

It should be noted that a woman is entitled to her statutory minimum annual holiday in addition to any maternity leave to which she may be entitled (*Merino Gómez* v. *Continental Industrias del Caucho SA,* ECJ Case C-342/01 [2004] IRLR 407).

Pay during maternity leave

An employee on maternity leave is not entitled to contractual pay (see SDA 1975, s.6A and **Chapter 14**). However, she is normally entitled to SMP for 39 weeks – increased from 26 weeks where the expected week of confinement fell on or after 1 April 2007 (Social Security Contributions and Benefits Act 1992, ss.164–171, the Statutory Maternity Pay (General) Regulations 1986, SI 1986/1960 and the Statutory Maternity Pay, Social Security (Maternity Allowance) and Social Security (Overlapping Benefits) (Amendment) Regulations 2006, SI 2006/2379, reg.3).

If she does not qualify for SMP (e.g. because she has not completed 26 weeks' continuous employment with the employer or because her average weekly earnings were less than the NI lower earnings limit – £90 from April 2008) she may qualify instead for maternity allowance (see below).

The government hopes to extend both SMP and maternity allowance (and statutory adoption pay) from 39 weeks to 52 weeks. In October 2007 HMRC stated that it is planning implementation when babies are due on or after April 2010.

SMP is a state benefit administered and paid by employers who recover (most of) the cost by making deductions from NI contributions and PAYE due. Smaller employers recoup 100 per cent plus a 'handling charge' of 4.5 per cent (Statutory Maternity Pay (Compensation of Employers) Amendment Regulations 2002, SI 2002/225) but larger employers may only recoup 92 per cent. A small employer is defined as one whose NI contributions payments for the qualifying tax year do not exceed £45,000 (Statutory Maternity Pay (Compensation of Employers) Amendment Regulations 2004, SI 2004/698). Small employers who cannot afford SMP payments can get 'recoupment' in advance via their tax office.

SMP is payable at two rates, earnings related for the first six weeks and a standard rate for the remaining (normally 33) weeks (Social Security Contributions and Benefits Act 1992, s.166(4)). The earnings related rate is 90 per cent of average weekly earnings earned during the eight weeks immediately before the qualifying week (i.e. during the eight week 'reference period' ending 15 weeks before the expected week of childbirth). As from April 2008 the standard rate payable for the remaining 33 weeks is £117.18 a week, subject always to a maximum of 90 per cent of previous earnings (see the Social Security Benefits Up-rating Order 2008, SI 2008/632, art.10 – these regulations also apply the same rate of £117.18 per week to maternity allowance, statutory adoption pay and statutory paternity pay from April 2008).

To qualify for SMP, a woman must have been an employee in continuous employment with the same employer (or an associated employer) for at least 26 weeks up to, and including at least one day during, her qualifying week, i.e. the fifteenth week before the expected week of childbirth (Social Security Contributions and Benefits Act 1992, s.164(2)(a)). If an employee is reinstated or re-engaged after a statutory dispute resolution procedure, her continuity of employment will be treated as unbroken for SMP purposes (see the Statutory Maternity Pay (General) and the Statutory Paternity Pay and Statutory Adoption Pay (General) (Amendment) Regulations 2005, SI 2005/358).

SMP is not payable to those whose average earnings are less than £90 per week (from April 2008). In that case, provided she was employed for at least 26 of the previous 66 weeks and had earned an average of at least £30 per week, she will be entitled instead to maternity allowance (Social Security (Maternity Allowance) (Earnings) Regulations 2000, SI 2000/688, as amended). From April 2008, maternity allowance is £117.18 per week for 39 weeks.

A woman whose expected week of confinement began on or after 1 April 2007 can work up to a maximum of 10 days during maternity leave (known as Keeping in Touch days or 'KIT' days) without losing SMP (see below). Working for more than 10 days results in loss of one week's SMP for each week or part week during which work is carried out (the Maternity and Parental Leave etc. Regulations 1999, SI 1999/3312, reg.12A inserted by the Maternity and Parental Leave etc. and the Paternity and Adoption Leave (Amendment) Regulations 2006, SI 2006/2014, reg.9).

New rules in force from 6 April 2008 provide that a woman whose expected week of childbirth begins on or after 5 October 2008 must receive any contractual remuneration to which she is entitled as a result of being pregnant or being on maternity leave even though, as noted above, she is not generally entitled to contractual remuneration during maternity leave (Sex Discrimination Act 1975 (Amendment) Regulations 2008, SI 2008/656 introducing a new version of SDA 1975, s.6A which, along with the changes noted in the next paragraph, ensure full implementation of the EC Equal Treatment Directive 2002/73/EC after criticism by the High Court in *Equal Opportunities Commission v. DTI* [2007] IRLR 327, QBD).

Other contractual terms during leave

Draft Maternity and Parental Leave etc and the Paternity and Adoption Leave (Amendment) Regulations 2008 were issued on 27 June 2008. These will amend the Maternity and Parental Leave etc. Regulations 1999 (and the Paternity and Adoption Leave Regulations 2002) for the benefit of parents of children expected to be born (or placed for adoption) on or after 5 October 2008. The amendments remove the distinctions between the rights of employees on OML and those on AML (similar distinctions between the rights of employees on ordinary adoption leave and additional adoption leave are also removed).

We have noted in the preceding section that since 6 April 2008 there has also been a minor modification to the rule that a woman is not entitled to remuneration during maternity leave to benefit women whose expected week of childbirth begins on or after 5 October 2008 (Sex Discrimination Act 1975 (Amendment) Regulations 2008, SI 2008/656).

Previously (that is for women whose expected week of childbirth was before 5 October 2008) only the implied obligation of trust and confidence, any contractual notice, redundancy or discipline terms and the employee's obligation of good faith continued during AML.

As the contract of employment continues to exist during maternity leave, a woman is entitled to her full statutory holiday entitlement as well as to OML and AML.

Commencement and duration of leave

The employee can choose when her OML is to start, although it cannot begin earlier than 11 weeks before the expected date of childbirth. No later than the end of the fifteenth week before her expected week of childbirth, or as soon as is reasonably practicable, the employee must notify her employer of:

- her pregnancy;
- her expected week of childbirth (on request the employee must produce a supporting certificate from a registered medical practitioner or midwife); and
- the date on which she intends her OML to start (Maternity and Parental Leave etc. Regulations 1999, reg.4).

If an employee fails to give any or all of the required notifications or has given them late and cannot satisfy a 'reasonably practicable' test, she will lose her right to OML.

There are two exceptions to the rule noted above that an employee must notify her employer no later than the end of the fifteenth week before her expected week of childbirth of the date on which she intends her maternity leave to start. Firstly, if she has not started her maternity leave four weeks before the expected date of childbirth and then is absent from work on grounds related to her pregnancy, that absence automatically triggers the start of her maternity leave. Secondly, if the child is born early, this too will automatically trigger the start of maternity leave. In either case, the employee must notify the employer as soon as reasonably practicable that she is absent because of pregnancy-related sickness or because she has given birth (Maternity and Parental Leave etc. Regulations 1999, regs.4(3)–(4) and 6).

Right to return to work – 'KIT days'

A woman whose expected week of confinement began on or after 1 April 2007 can work up to a maximum of 10 days (known as Keeping in Touch days or 'KIT days') without bringing her maternity leave to an end. Taking advantage of this new provision will not extend the 52 weeks maximum maternity leave and she will be protected from any detriment or dismissal connected with these 'keeping in touch days' (appropriate amendments to the Maternity and Parental Leave etc. Regulations 1999, regs.19 and 20 were made by the Maternity and Parental Leave etc. and the Paternity and Adoption Leave (Amendment) Regulations 2006, SI 2006/2014, regs.10 and 11).

Right to return to work – full-time

An employee whose expected week of childbirth begins on or after 5 October 2008 is entitled to return to work after ordinary or additional maternity leave to the job in which she was employed before she started her leave, with her seniority, pension rights and similar rights intact (Maternity and Parental Leave etc. Regulations 1999, reg.18(2) and 18A(1)(a) as amended). If it is not reasonably practicable for the employer to permit her to return to that job then he must offer her another job which is 'suitable for her and appropriate for her in the circumstances' (Maternity and Parental Leave etc. Regulations 1999, reg. 18(2)). There is special provision to take care of the position if a redundancy situation has arisen (Maternity and Parental Leave etc. Regulations 1999, regs. 10 and 18(4)).

If an employee wishes to wait until the end of her OML (or AML) period to return to work, she does not need to give any notice to the employer: she just returns to work on the expiry of her leave. If she wishes to return to work sooner, she must give at least 28 days' notice to the employer (Maternity and Parental Leave etc. Regulations 1999, regs.7 and 11).

Dismissal in those circumstances (i.e. refusal to allow return to work) will normally be automatically unfair dismissal if it is for a 'prescribed reason' connected with pregnancy, maternity or taking maternity leave (or parental leave) (see ERA 1996, s.99(2)). 'Prescribed' means prescribed by regulations (i.e. the Maternity and Parental Leave etc. Regulations 1999, reg 20(3) as amended).

If 'it is not practicable by reason of redundancy for [a woman's] employer to continue to employ her under her existing contract of employment', then it will not be unlawful to refuse to allow her to return to work (Maternity and Parental Leave etc. Regulations 1999, reg.10). However, the employer is under an obligation to offer a suitable alternative vacancy, or with an associated employer, on terms that are not substantially less favourable than her old terms of employment. To this extent, during a redundancy exercise, a woman on maternity leave has rights which 'trump' those of other workers when the employer is considering to whom limited numbers of suitable alternative vacancies should be offered.

Right to return to work – part-time or job share

The Employment Act 2002, s.47 gives parents of children under six (or parents of disabled children who are under 18) the right to request flexible working. This right is subject to the employee having been continuously employed for a period of not less than 26 weeks. Subject to this qualifying period any woman returning from maternity leave may make a request for flexible working which will then need to be seriously considered by her employer, who must provide reasons for any refusal (see **section 9.10**).

Apart from this statutory right to have a request for flexible working considered seriously, a woman whose employer refuses a request to allow her to return to work part-time or on a job share basis may find that he is 'guilty' of unlawful indirect sex discrimination unless he can justify the refusal.

Thus in a case in 2007 an employer refused to allow a woman to work part-time on her return from maternity leave. She resigned in protest and brought claims of sex discrimination and constructive unfair dismissal. She won on both counts. The discrimination was not justified and amounted to a repudiation of contract which she had accepted promptly and had resigned for that reason. That was constructive dismissal. There was no explanation or defence of fairness and so the dismissal was unfair (*Shaw* v. *CCL Ltd* [2008] IRLR 284, EAT).

If the employer can objectively justify the refusal to allow a previously full-time employee to return part-time then the position is different. In considering justification, an employment tribunal must objectively balance the needs of the employer against the discriminatory effect of the refusal rather than apply the 'range of reasonable responses' test used in unfair dismissal cases (*Hardys & Hansons Plc* v. *Lax* [2005] EWCA Civ 846).

Enforcement

An employee is entitled not to be subjected to any detriment by her employer because she was pregnant or because she took maternity leave. A tribunal has power to make a declaration and award compensation (ERA 1996, ss.47C, 48 and 49).

Moreover, if a woman is dismissed for a reason related to her pregnancy (or because she sought to take maternity leave), the dismissal is automatically unfair (ERA 1996, s.99; Maternity and Parental Leave etc. Regulations 1999, reg.20). This is subject to the 'not practicable by reason of redundancy' exception noted above (Maternity and Parental Leave etc. Regulations 1999, reg.10).

Until 1 April 2007 there was also a small employer (up to five employees) exemption from the normal 'automatically unfair' dismissal rule. This exemption has been removed by the Maternity and Parental Leave etc. and the Paternity and Adoption Leave (Amendment) Regulations 2006, SI 2006/2014, reg.11(b)).

With effect from 24 November 2002, a new provision was added to the Maternity and Parental Leave etc. Regulations 1999, reg.20(3) (by the Maternity and Parental Leave (Amendment) Regulations 2002, SI 2002/2789). The new provision is sub-paragraph (ee). This applies if an employer fails to notify a woman on maternity leave of the end date of that leave as required by the Maternity and Parental Leave etc. Regulations 1999, reg.7(6) and (7)). The new provision makes it automatically unfair dismissal in such circumstances to dismiss a woman because she failed to return on the correct date.

In practice, any detriment or dismissal will also give the woman the right to claim unlawful sex discrimination.

It is quite likely that an employer will have to take on new staff to cover for any employee(s) away on maternity leave. Dismissal of such staff on return to work of a woman away on maternity leave, is *prima facie* 'fair dismissal' for 'some other substantial reason', provided they had been informed accordingly, in writing, when engaged (ERA 1996, s.106).

7.3.5 Suspension from work on maternity grounds

Under health and safety legislation, an employer is obliged to undertake risk assessments of the risk of working to new or expectant mothers. If a risk is identified which cannot be averted by altering working hours or conditions of work, the employer is obliged to suspend the employee from work but since a change in the law in 1994 it will be automatically unfair dismissal to dismiss her.

A new mother is defined as one who has given birth within the last six months, or who is breastfeeding. Further, if a pregnant night-worker has a certificate from her doctor stating that she cannot work at night for health and safety reasons, she must be suspended from work.

Obviously an employer should not be penalised for failing to employ a person when health and safety rules make it illegal for him to do so. Accordingly special rules apply if an employee is suspended on 'maternity grounds'. However, these rules only apply if the suspension is on 'maternity grounds' as defined. The effect is that they only cover suspensions required by law or which are recommended in a Code of Practice issued under s.16 of the Health and Safety at Work etc. Act 1974 if specified by the Secretary of State as a 'relevant provision' (ERA 1996 s.66(1) and see *Iske* v. *P & O European Ferries (Dover) Ltd* [1997] IRLR 401, EAT). Relevant provisions are the Suspension from Work on Maternity Grounds Order 1994, SI 1994/2930; Suspension from Work on Maternity Grounds (Merchant Shipping and Fishing Vessels) Order 1998, SI 1998/587; and the Management of Health and Safety at Work Regulations 1999, SI 1999/3242, regs.16–19.

The employer is required to record the findings of the assessment and give information about the findings but can do so by word of mouth. There is no stipulation as to what form the information must take and no requirement that the assessment must be in writing (*Stevenson* v. *J M Skinner & Co* (unreported, EAT, 6 March 2008)).

Suspension must be on full pay unless the worker unreasonably refused suitable alternative work (ERA 1996, s.68).

A failure to conduct a risk assessment also amounts to discrimination under SDA 1975 (*Hardman* v. *Mallon (t/a Orchard Lodge Nursing Home)* [2002] IRLR 516). No male comparator is needed because of the rule that a pregnant woman seeking to establish sex discrimination related to her pregnancy need not point to a male comparator simply because pregnancy is a uniquely female condition (i.e. the rule in *Webb* v. *Emo Air Cargo (UK) Ltd* [1995] ICR 1021, HL).

7.3.6 Paternity leave

Preliminary

Fathers have been entitled to take up to 13 weeks' unpaid parental leave since 1999. The Employment Act 2002, s.1 introduced a new right for fathers (and other partners) to take one or two weeks' paid paternity leave on the birth or adoption of a child. Details are in the Paternity and Adoption Leave Regulations 2002, SI 2002/2788 (PAL 2002). The right is restricted to 'employees'.

It has been suggested that the ECJ ruling in *Land Brandenburg* v. *Sass* [2005] IRLR 147, ECJ Case C-284/02 implies that current UK law may infringe the EC Equal Treatment Directive 76/207/EC, Art 2(3) by providing mothers but not fathers with 26 weeks' AML. This is on the basis that (unlike OML) the additional 26 weeks is for looking after the baby not for recuperation from the physical and mental effects of giving birth. Whether or not influenced by this ECJ ruling in May 2007 the British government started – or more accurately continued – consultation on plans to provide fathers with a right to up to 26 weeks' additional paternity leave, some of which would be with pay, if the child's mother has returned to work.

The proposal is for the new right to be available during the second six months of the child's life and to provide parents with the option of dividing a period of paid leave entitlement between them. The father and mother will have to jointly notify the father's employer not less than eight weeks before the start of the additional paternity leave. The precise start date for the new regime is not fixed but it is unlikely to apply in respect of babies due before April 2010.

The right

The name of the PAL 2002 and the way they are drafted can cause confusion in two respects. Firstly, the regulations sub-divide paternity leave (PAL 2002, regs.4–14) into 'paternity leave (birth)' and 'paternity leave (adoption)', which is quite separate from adoption leave. Secondly, the name gives the impression that a person must be a father to qualify for paternity leave. This is not so. A woman can be entitled to paternity leave (birth) if she is the partner of the birth mother and to paternity leave (adoption) if the adoptive father (or mother in same-sex relationships) takes up the separate entitlement to adoption leave.

The basic eligibility criterion for the right to paternity leave (birth) and paternity leave (adoption) is that the employee has or expects to have responsibility for the upbringing of the child (PAL 2002, regs.4 and 8). Being the biological father is insufficient – responsibility for upbringing is also needed.

To qualify an employee must (PAL 2002, regs.4 and 8):

(a) have been continuously employed for at least 26 weeks ending either with the fifteenth week before the expected week of birth, or with the week in which the child's adopter is notified of having been matched with the child;
(b) be the father of the child or be the mother's husband or civil partner or partner, or be married to or the partner of the adopter;
(c) have, or expect to have, responsibility for the upbringing of the child.

A 'partner' is a person of either sex who lives with the mother and child in an enduring family relationship but is not a relative of the mother (a relative being a parent, grandparent, sister, brother, aunt or uncle).

Pay and other contractual terms during leave

Employees on paternity leave are not automatically entitled to contractual pay. However, they are entitled to statutory paternity pay if they earn more than the NI lower earnings limit (currently £90 a week). Full details of the qualification are in the Social Security Contributions and Benefits Act 1992, ss.171ZA–171ZK and the Statutory Paternity Pay and Statutory Adoption Pay (General) Regulations 2002, SI 2002/2822). From April 2008 it is payable at the lesser of £117.18 per week or 90 per cent of the employee's normal weekly earnings (Statutory Paternity Pay and Statutory Adoption Rates (Weekly Rate) Regulations 2002, SI 2002/2818, reg.2 and Social Security Benefits Up-rating Order 2008, SI 2008/632).

When on paternity leave, an employee's terms and conditions remain unchanged save for those relating to remuneration (PAL 2002, reg.12).

To receive statutory paternity pay, the employee must have continuous employment between the fifteenth week before the expected week of confinement and the date of the child's birth. From 6 April 2005, if an employee is reinstated or re-engaged after a statutory dispute resolution procedure, the continuity of employment will be treated as unbroken for statutory paternity pay purposes (Statutory Maternity Pay (General) and the Statutory Paternity

Pay and Statutory Adoption Pay (General) (Amendment) Regulations 2005, SI 2005/358).

Commencing leave and duration of leave

An employee who is entitled to paternity leave may choose whether to take one week's leave or two consecutive weeks' leave (PAL 2002, reg.5(1)). The leave must not start before the child is born and must be finished within 56 days of the birth.

An employee must give his employer notice of his intention to take paternity leave (the employer can request the notice in writing) before the fifteenth week before the expected week of birth, or as soon as reasonably practicable. The notice must specify the expected week of the child's birth or the date on which the child is expected to be placed with the adopter, the length of the absence, and the date on which the employee has chosen to begin his leave (PAL 2002, regs.6, 10). Where paternity leave is taken on the adoption of a child the notice must also include the date on which the adopter was notified they had been matched with a child.

The employer can request, and the employee must give, a signed declaration that the employee satisfies the conditions of entitlement for paternity leave and the purpose of the absence (PAL 2002, regs.6(3) and 10(3)). Note that, unlike maternity leave, self-certification is sufficient; there is no equivalent of the woman's MatB1 form.

Right to return to work

Employees who return to work after a period of paternity leave, if the whole period of their leave did not include any additional maternity or adoption leave or parental leave of more than four weeks, are entitled to return to the same job they were employed in before the leave commenced (PAL 2002, reg.13(1)). If the employee returns from paternity leave in any other situation he is entitled to his old job unless his return to that post is not reasonably practicable. The onus is then on the employer to place the returning employee in another job which is both suitable and appropriate for the employee to do in the circumstances (PAL 2002, reg. 13(3)).

Enforcement

An employee is entitled not to be subjected to any detriment by his employer because he took or sought to take paternity leave. He may present a complaint to a tribunal within three months of suffering any such detriment. If an employee is dismissed for a reason relating to paternity leave the dismissal is automatically unfair (ERA 1996, s.47A, PAL 2002, reg.29) unless his job is redundant and the employer has complied with its obligations to look for alternative work.

In 2008 the EAT considered the applicability of PAL 2002, reg.29 in some detail. It makes a dismissal automatically unfair if it is 'connected with' the taking of paternity leave. The question was whether this means that there must be a causal connection or whether it is sufficient that dismissal was 'associated with' the taking of paternity leave. In the case in question a man was dismissed while on paternity leave but the reason for his dismissal was that he had an argument on the telephone with his employers, partly brought about because he was short of sleep as a result of helping to look after a new baby. He lost his 'automatically unfair dismissal' claim. The EAT took the view that there must be a causal connection with paternity leave for a dismissal to be automatically unfair under reg.29 and that in this case there was no such connection (*Atkins* v. *Coyle Personnel plc* [2008] IRLR 420, EAT).

7.3.7 Adoption leave

The right

The Employment Act 2002 also introduced a new statutory right for employees who are matched with a child for adoption to take time off work to build a relationship with the child when the child starts living with them. Employees are entitled to 26 weeks' 'ordinary adoption leave' and 26 weeks' 'additional adoption leave', conceptually similar to OML and AML (see above). The details are in PAL 2002.

Adoption leave is separate from the one or two weeks' paternity leave (adoption) provided for by the same regulations (see above).

Technical provisions ensure that an adopting parent is entitled to adoption leave regardless of whether or not the adoption is a domestic UK adoption or an inter-country adoption.

Qualification

Ordinary adoption leave may be taken by employees only. The employee must be the child's adopter, have been continuously employed for at least 26 weeks ending with the week in which the employee was notified of having been matched with the child and has notified the adoption agency that he agrees that the child should be placed with him and the date of placement (PAL 2002, reg.15).

An employee is only entitled to additional adoption leave if the employee took ordinary adoption leave in respect of the same child and that leave did not end prematurely. The wording of the regulations implies that the right is only available when the child is a new placement; i.e. step-parents and fosterparents who formally adopt will not be eligible.

Only one parent is entitled to adoption leave; the other parent is usually entitled to statutory paternity leave (see above).

Pay and other contractual terms during leave

There is no statutory right to contractual pay during adoption leave. However, an employee's contract of employment continues during any ordinary adoption leave and except with regard to remuneration the employee must be treated in all respects as if the employee were not absent.

Draft Maternity and Parental Leave etc. and the Paternity and Adoption Leave (Amendment) Regulations 2008 were issued on 27 June 2008. These will amend the Paternity and Adoption Leave Regulations 2002 (and the Maternity and Parental Leave etc. Regulations 1999) for the benefit of parents of children placed for adoption (or expected to be born) on or after 5 October 2008. The amendments remove the distinctions between the rights of employees on ordinary adoption leave and additional adoption leave (similar distinctions between the rights of employees on OML and those on AML are also removed).

Previously (that is for adoptions before 5 October 2008) only the implied obligation of trust and confidence, any contractual notice, redundancy or discipline terms and the employee's obligation of good faith continued during additional adoption leave (PAL 2002, reg.12).

Statutory adoption pay (SAP) is available during an ordinary adoption leave period. It is payable in the same manner and at the same rate as SMP. As with SMP, employers can recoup from the state most, or in the case of smaller employers all, of the cost of SAP by offset against tax/NI payments due, or in cash if these are insufficient.

The employee must give the employer at least 28 days' notice (which must be in writing if the employer requests) stating proposed start date, the expected date of placement, evidence of the adoption and a declaration that SAP is required rather than statutory paternity pay.

Where adoption placement is on or after 1 April 2007 the payment period for SAP is 39 weeks (Statutory Paternity Pay and Statutory Adoption Pay (General) and the Statutory Paternity Pay and Statutory Adoption Pay (Weekly Rates) (Amendment) Regulations 2006, SI 2006/2236). As for SMP and maternity allowance, the government has a goal to extend this to 52 weeks before the end of the current Parliament – but this is an aspiration rather than a commitment. Under the same regulations (SI 2006/2236) SAP continues to be payable if the employee comes back to work for up to 10 'Keeping in touch' days during adoption leave.

Commencing leave

The employee chooses the date on which ordinary adoption leave should start, either from the date on which the child is placed or a predetermined date no more than two weeks before the child is expected (PAL 2002, reg.18).

Within seven days of receiving notification of a match, or as soon as is reasonably practicable, the employee must give the employer notice of the date on which the child is expected to be placed, and the date on which the employee has chosen for ordinary adoption leave to begin. If the employer requests it, the employee must provide evidence of their entitlement to adoption leave including the name and address of the adoption agency, the name and date of birth of the child, the date on which the employee was notified of match and the date on which the agency expects to place the child (PAL 2002, reg.17).

On receiving an employee's notice the employer must, within 28 days of receipt, notify the employee of the date on which the employee's entitlement to leave ends, including any additional adoption leave the employee may be entitled to.

Problems with the adoption

The regulations provide the employee with some protection should the adoption of the child not go according to plan. Where the child is not placed with the employee when the employee has already begun adoption leave, or the child dies during the leave, or the child is returned to the agency whilst the employee is on leave, then the employee's adoption leave will end eight weeks after the week in which one of the above happened (PAL 2002, reg.22) or, if earlier, at the end of the ordinary or additional adoption leave period.

Right to return to work

Unless it is impracticable by reason of redundancy an employee is entitled to have his job back at the end of adoption leave (PAL 2002, reg.26). If the employee is redundant and there is a 'suitable alternative vacancy' the employer (or associated employer or successor) must offer alternative employment on terms which 'are not substantially less favourable to him than if he had continued . . .' in his old job (PAL 2002, reg.23).

An employee who for whatever reason (including because, for example, the child died or was returned to the adoption agency) intends to return to work before taking the full 52 weeks of adoption leave to which he would normally be entitled must give his employer eight weeks' notice. If he does not do so the employer can postpone his return for up to eight weeks, or until the date on which the additional adoption leave would normally have ended if sooner (PAL 2002, reg.25 as amended by the Maternity and Parental Leave etc. and the Paternity and Adoption Leave (Amendment) Regulations 2006, SI 2006/2014).

A previous provision enabling an employer to request the name and date of birth of a child in respect of whom adoption leave is taken (PAL 2002, reg.17 (3)(b)) has been removed (Paternity and Adoption Leave (Amendment) Regulations 2004, SI 2004/923). As from the same date all terms and conditions applying in relation to an employee returning to work from adoption leave, not just those relating to remuneration, must be as favourable as those which would have applied if the employee had not been absent (PAL 2002, reg.27(1)(b) as amended by SI 2004/923).

Enforcement

Employees are entitled not to be subjected to any detriment by the employer because they took or sought to take adoption leave, or the employer believed they were likely to take adoption leave. There has been at least one example (in February 2007) of a case in which a woman has succeeded in an employment tribunal claim that she was dismissed because she planned to adopt a child.

An employee may present a complaint to a tribunal within three months of suffering any such detriment. If an employee is dismissed for a reason relating to adoption leave the dismissal is automatically unfair (ERA 1996, s. 47A, PAL 2002, reg.29) unless the employee's job is redundant and the employer has complied with its obligations to look for alternative work.

7.3.8 Parental leave

Parental leave is a separate right for parents of young or recently adopted children to have unpaid time off. It is in addition to maternity leave: thus a mother can take statutory maternity leave and follow it immediately with a period of parental leave.

The basic rules are in ERA 1996, ss.71–80 and the Maternity and Parental Leave etc. Regulations 1999, SI 1999/3312 as amended by Maternity and Parental Leave (Amendment) Regulations 2001, SI 2001/4010 and Maternity and Parental Leave (Amendment) Regulations 2002, SI 2002/2789.

The right

Any employee who has completed one year's continuous employment and who 'has, or expects to have responsibility, for a child' has a legally enforceable right to take up to four weeks' unpaid parental leave per year while the child is under the age of five, subject to an overall maximum of 13 weeks' leave in respect of each child.

If disability living allowance is payable in respect of the child the age of five restriction is increased to the age of 18, the 13 weeks overall maximum is increased to 18 weeks and the parent can then, but only then, take parental leave in blocks of less than one week (*Rodway v. South Central Trains Ltd* [2005] IRLR 583, CA and Maternity and Parental Leave etc. Regulations 1999, SI 1999/3312, Sched.2, para.7 and reg.15 inserted into SI 1999/3312 by SI 2001/4010).

If the child is adopted, the right to parental leave can be exercised up to the fifth anniversary of the placement, provided the child is still under 18.

Qualification

To qualify for parental leave, an employee must have at least one year's continuous employment and have (or expect to have) responsibility for a child (Maternity and Parental Leave etc. Regulations 1999, reg.13). In general an employee who has changed jobs has to requalify under the one year's continuous employment rule to be entitled to take any balance of the 13 weeks' leave not previously taken.

Default provisions

An employer can agree to grant more favourable provisions than those provided by the regulations, but not less favourable ones (Maternity and Parental Leave etc. Regulations 1999, reg.16). Subject to that, the default scheme set out in Sched.2 to the regulations will automatically apply.

Employees must give at least 21 days' notice that they intend to take parental leave, informing the employer of the proposed dates for leave. An exception is where an expectant father intends to take parental leave when his child is born, in which case the notice should specify the expected week of childbirth and the duration of the leave (Maternity and Parental Leave etc. Regulations 1999, Sched.2, paras.3 and 4).

Other than in the case of an expectant father or a placement for adoption, the employer may postpone the period of leave for up to six months if the employer considers that 'the operation of his business would be unduly disrupted if the employee took leave during the period specified in his notice'. In such a case, the employer must serve a counter-notice within seven days of the employee's notice, specifying the reason for postponing the leave and giving dates when the employer agrees to permit the employee to take the leave (Maternity and Parental Leave etc. Regulations 1999, Sched.2, para.6). The employer cannot postpone leave indefinitely.

An employer can insist on evidence of the child's date of birth (or adoption), of the child's disability (if leave is being claimed beyond the child's fifth birthday) and of the employee's responsibility for that child (Maternity and Parental Leave etc. Regulations 1999, Sched.2, para.2).

Right to return to work

If parental leave is taken for a period of four weeks or less, other than immediately after taking AML, employees are entitled to return from leave to the same job they were doing before their absence (Maternity and Parental Leave etc. Regulations 1999, regs.18 and 18A).

If parental leave is taken for a period of more than four weeks (which can only occur if the employer agrees as the default provisions provide for a maximum of four weeks' leave in one year), employees are entitled to return from leave to the same job they were doing before their absence or, if that is not reasonably practicable, to another job which is both suitable and appropriate for them to do in the circumstances (Maternity and Parental Leave etc. Regulations 1999, reg.18(2)–(5)).

Enforcement

Employees are entitled not to be subjected to any detriment because they have taken, or sought to take, parental leave. On a successful complaint to a tribunal, the tribunal has the power to make a declaration and order compensation (ERA 1996, ss.47C, 48 and 49; Maternity and Parental Leave etc. Regulations 1999, reg.19).

Any dismissal of employees for taking, or seeking to take, parental leave will be automatically unfair. The only exception is where it ceases to be reasonably practicable for the employer to allow them to return to a suitable and appropriate job and either they accept or unreasonably refuse a suitable and appropriate job from an associated employer (ERA 1996, s.99; Maternity and Parental Leave etc. Regulations 1999, reg.20).

7.3.9 Time off for dependants

An employee is permitted:

> a reasonable amount of time off work during [his] working hours in order to take action which is necessary –
>
> (a) to provide assistance on an occasion when a dependant falls ill, gives birth or is injured or assaulted;
> (b) to make arrangements for the provision of care for a dependant who is ill or injured;
> (c) in consequence of the death of a dependant;
> (d) because of the unexpected disruption or termination of arrangements for the care of a dependant;
> (e) to deal with an incident which involves a child of the employee and which occurs unexpectedly in a period during which an educational establishment which the child attends is responsible for him.
>
> ERA 1996, s.57A(1)

Item (c) above does not give a right to compassionate leave as such on death of a dependant. Although it may be in consequence of the death it is not 'action which is necessary', which refers to matters such as making funeral arrangements, registering the death and if there is a Will applying for probate (see *Forster v. Cartwright Black* [2004] IRLR 781, EAT).

The right to time off under ERA 1996, s.57A does not include taking regular time off to care for a sick dependant but would extend to taking time off to make arrangements for others to care for the ill dependant (*Qua* v. *John Ford Morrison Solicitors* [2003] IRLR 184, EAT).

'Dependant' is defined as meaning an employee's spouse, child or parent. It also includes any person who lives in the same household as the employee (other than his employee, tenant, lodger or boarder). Civil partners were added to the list by the Civil Partnership Act 2004, Sched.27, para.151. Further, it includes anybody who reasonably relies on the employee for assistance on occasions when they fall ill, or for assistance with care arrangements. This would include, for example, an elderly neighbour or relative (ERA 1996, s.57A(3)–(5)).

An employee is entitled to a reasonable amount of time off work in order to assist a dependant in any of the above situations. A period as long as one month for care by a parent will 'rarely, almost never', fall within ERA 1996, s.57A (*Cortest Ltd* v. *O'Toole* (unreported, EAT, 7 November 2007)).

The time off work is unpaid. Employees must tell their employer the reason for the absence as soon as reasonably practicable (which does not necessarily have to be before the employee leaves work) and, unless they have already returned to work, give an estimate of the length of their absence (ERA 1996, s.57A(2)). Tribunals are likely to make a fairly generous (to the employee) interpretation of these requirements (see *Truelove* v. *Safeway Stores plc* [2005] ICR 589, EAT).

7.3.10 Health and safety activities

Safety representatives appointed by a recognised trade union are entitled to take such time off during working hours as is necessary to: (i) enable them to perform their statutory functions; and (ii) undergo reasonable training (Safety Representatives and Safety Committee Regulations 1977, SI 1977/500). As from 1 October 1996, non-union appointed representatives chosen by employees for health and safety duties have similar rights (Health and Safety (Consultation with Employees) Regulations 1996, SI 1996/1513).

Safety representatives are entitled to pay during such time off (Safety Representatives and Safety Committees Regulations 1977, reg.4 and Health and Safety (Consultation with Employees) Regulations 1996, SI 1996/1513, reg.7).

7.3.11 Trade union duties and activities and employee representatives

Trade union officials

Employees who are trade union officials have the statutory right to reasonable time off from their normal work for attending to specified trade union duties. This includes conducting negotiations with the employer on terms and conditions of employment. There is an Acas Code of Practice CoP 3 on Time Off for Trade Union Duties and Activities (TULRCA 1992, s.168; Employment Protection Code of Practice (Time Off) Order 1998, SI 1998/46).

The right is a right to time off with pay (TULRCA 1992, s.169)

Following a 2006 review of facilities provided to workplace representatives, the DTI issued a consultation paper on 'Workplace Representatives: a review of their facilities and facility time', January 2007. Conclusions were published in November 2007. No major changes were proposed but there was a recommendation that the Acas Code of Practice should be revised and updated.

A trade union official is entitled to compensation if he is not allowed to exercise this statutory right to time off for attending to trade union duties whether or not he has suffered loss (*Skiggs* v. *South West Trains Ltd* [2005] IRLR 459, EAT).

Dismissal for attempting to exercise the statutory rights given by TULRCA 1992, ss.168 and 169 is automatically unfair dismissal (ERA 1996 s.104(4)(c)).

Trade union members

An employee who is a member of an independent recognised trade union is entitled to reasonable unpaid time off during working hours to take part in trade union activities (TULRCA 1992, s.170).

There is no definition of what constitutes 'trade union activities' for this purpose. Attending union meetings and acting as a union representative are examples of 'activities' for which time off can be claimed but trade union activities for this purpose specifically exclude strikes or other industrial action (TULRCA 1992, s.170; Employment Protection Code of Practice (Time Off) Order 1998, SI 1998/46). Lobbying Parliament is covered provided that the purpose is relevant to the employment concerned and is for 'the presentation of arguments intended to persuade a member of Parliament to vote in a particular way on a particular issue' (*Luce* v. *Bexley London Borough Council* [1990] ICR 591, EAT).

It seems clear that a person does not have to be a union representative to be engaged in trade union activities (*Hamilton* v. *Arriva Trains Northern Ltd* (unreported, EAT, 4 August 2004)), a case under TULRCA 1992, s.146 'Right not to be subjected to detriment for a trade union related reason', but presumably the same is true for the purposes of s.170).

Preparation for and participation in unofficial industrial action is clearly not participation in trade union activity. However, preparation for official industrial action can be participation in trade union activity (*Britool* v. *Roberts* [1993] IRLR 481).

Dismissal for attempting to exercise the statutory rights given by TULRCA 1992, s.170 is automatically unfair dismissal (ERA 1996, s.104(4)(c)) as is dismissal on other grounds related to trade union membership or activities (TULRCA 1992, s.152).

Trade union learning representatives

Trade union 'learning representatives' have had a legally enforceable right to paid time off work for fulfilling their duties as such since 27 April 2003 (Employment Act 2002, s.43). A person is a learning representative of a trade union 'if he is appointed or elected as such in accordance with its rules'. There are various pre-conditions for exercising this right, chief among them being that the trade union must have given the employer written notice that the employee is a learning representative and that the employee has undergone or will within six months undergo sufficient training to enable him to perform his function (TULRCA 1992, s.168A).

The right is a right to time off with pay (TULRCA 1992, s.169)

In any question concerning the right to time off for trade union duties and activities, Acas Code of Practice CoP 3 on Time Off for Trade Union Duties and Activities should be taken into account.

Dismissal for attempting to exercise the statutory rights given by TULRCA 1992, ss.168A and 169 is automatically unfair dismissal (ERA 1996, s.104(4)(c)).

7.3.12 Suspension on medical grounds

Some statutory instruments require or recommend employers to suspend employees on health grounds in particular circumstances. Currently there are only three such instruments, the Control of Lead at Work Regulations 1998, SI 1998/543, the Ionising Radiations Regulations 1999, SI 1999/3232 and the Control of Substances Hazardous to Health Regulations 1999, SI 1999/437 (ERA 1996, s.64).

Provided the employee has worked for at least one month when the suspension commences, he is entitled to full pay for up to 26 weeks, unless he falls ill during that period (when normal sick pay provisions will apply). However, if the employee declines suitable alternative work, or refuses to comply with reasonable requirements imposed by the employer with a view to ensuring his services are available, he ceases to be entitled to normal pay. Short term (less than three months) and casual staff are excluded from the right to payment (ERA 1996, ss.64(4) and 65).

7.3.13 Time off for public duties

An employer is obliged to allow employees to take a reasonable amount of time off work for performing certain public duties. The employee does not need to have achieved any qualifying period of employment. The time off work is not paid.

The duties are tightly defined in s.50 of ERA 1996, but can be summarised as duties as a justice of the peace, as a member of a local authority, a statutory tribunal, a police authority, a board of prison visitors or a prison visiting committee, a health authority or an education authority, the environment agency or a water authority.

Justices of the peace are permitted time off from work for discharging any of their functions. Employees falling within the other categories are permitted time off only for attendance at committee meetings or undertaking duties authorised by the body (ERA 1996, s.50(1) and (3)). The DTI provided a useful booklet entitled 'Time Off for Public Duties' (Booklet PL702) which is now available from the BERR website (**www.berr.gov.uk/employment/employment-legislation/employment-guidance/page16377.html**).

There is no statute requiring an employer to allow employees time off work for jury service (but there are sanctions for failing to do so – see **section 7.3.19**).

What is a reasonable amount for time off for public duties must be determined in accordance with ERA 1996, s.50(4). This specifies three 'circumstances' which can be summarised as:

(i) how much time off will be needed to perform a particular duty compared to how much time off is needed to perform the duties of the office generally;
(ii) how much time off the employee has already had for public duties or for trade union duties/activities;
(iii) the effect on the employer's business of the employee taking time off.

It is for the tribunal to determine reasonableness by an objective consideration of these and any other factors it considers relevant (*Riley-Williams* v. *Argos* (unreported, EAT, 29 May 2003)).

7.3.14 Time off for pension fund trustees and members

An employer which operates an occupational pension fund is obliged to permit a reasonable amount of time off to employees who are trustees of that pension fund. The time off should be paid at normal pay rates. Time off is permitted for performing duties as a trustee and for training in connection with those duties (ERA 1996, ss.58 and 59).

Employees can complain to a tribunal if they are denied a reasonable amount of time off, or if they are not paid during such time off. Employees also have a right not to be subjected to any detriment for performing their duties as pension fund trustees and any dismissal for that reason is automatically unfair (ERA 1996, ss.46, 60 and 102).

There are analagous provisions entitling employees to time off work, with pay, for acting as 'consulted representatives' of employees under the Occupational and Personal Pension Schemes (Consultation by Employers and Miscellaneous Amendment) Regulations 2006, SI 2006/349 (see Sched.5 of SI 2006/349).

7.3.15 Time off for study or training

In addition to the right to time off for training in connection with many of the matters listed above, there exists a free-standing right to time off for training for 16 and 17-year-olds who have left school but have failed to achieve a satisfactory standard of achievement whilst at school/college (ERA 1996, s.63A).

In essence, 16 and 17-year-olds who have failed to reach a prescribed standard of academic achievement (for example, five GCSE passes) are entitled to paid time off work to attend courses at specified institutions. Although there are minor exceptions, in general they are entitled to be paid by the employer at their normal rate (ERA 1996, s.63B; Teaching and Higher Education Act 1998, ss.32 and 33; Right to Time Off for Study or Training Regulations 2001, SI 2001/2801). An 18-year-old who commenced a course under these provisions whilst younger is entitled to finish the course (and continue to be paid whilst doing so). Once he reaches 19, he loses the right to paid time off for study (ERA 1996, s.63A(4)).

Employees can complain to an employment tribunal if the employer fails to allow time off, or fails to pay them in respect of that time off. Moreover, employees have a right not to be subjected to any detriment for invoking these rights (ERA 1996, ss.63C and 47A).

In 2004 the government commissioned a report to consider how best to develop skills in the UK. The result (published in December 2006 as the Leitch report on 'Prosperity for all in the Global Economy: World Class Skills') includes recommendations for employees to have a statutory right to workplace training unless employers make appropriate arrangements voluntarily by 2010.

7.3.16 Information and consultation

Employees who are information and consultation representatives or who have actual or prospective duties under the Transnational Information and Consultation of Employees Regulations 1999, SI 1999/3323, the European Public Limited-Liability Company Regulations 2004, SI 2004/2326 or the Information and Consultation of Employees Regulations 2004, SI 2004/3426 are entitled to reasonable time off work with pay to attend to their duties as such.

Employment tribunals are given jurisdiction to consider any complaint to the effect that this right has been unreasonably refused or that pay has been withheld.

7.3.17 Accompanying a worker at a disciplinary or grievance hearing

As discussed in **section 4.2**, employees are entitled to be represented by a trade union official or workplace colleague during any disciplinary or grievance hearings. Such a right would be ineffective unless the accompanying employee were entitled to time off work to discharge this function. The right was introduced in the Employment Relations Act 1999. Employees can complain to an employment tribunal if the employer fails to allow them time off to accompany a colleague, or subjects them to a detriment for doing so. Moreover, any dismissal for accompanying a colleague at a disciplinary or grievance hearing will be automatically unfair (Employment Relations Act 1999, ss.10(6) and 12).

7.3.18 Time off for redundant workers to seek new work

An employee who has been given notice of dismissal due to redundancy (note: warnings about impending redundancies are insufficient) is entitled to take a reasonable amount of time off work to look for new employment or make arrangements for re-training. To qualify for this right, the employee must have been employed for two years at the date on which notice expires (this period was not reduced to one year when many of the main employment qualifying periods were reduced) (ERA 1996, s.52).

The time off work is paid, but limited to 40 per cent of a week's pay. This is a cap on the total amount paid, irrespective of the number of weeks during which the employee is searching for a new job whilst under notice, rather than a cap on the total amount to be paid per week (ERA 1996, s.53). An employee can complain to an employment tribunal if the employer refuses to allow reasonable time off work or to pay him during such time. However, the maximum compensation is again limited to 40 per cent of one week's pay for the employee (ERA 1996, s.54).

7.3.19 Areas not covered by a statutory right to time off

Jury service

Surprisingly, no statute requires an employer to allow employees time off work for jury service. However, a provision introduced with effect from 6 April 2005 makes it automatically unfair dismissal if an employee is dismissed for taking time off work for jury service (subject to exceptions and safeguards if the employer's business would be badly affected by allowing the employee to take time off). There is no qualification period of employment required and no upper age limit for claiming unfair dismissal in such a case (ERA 1996, s.98B introduced by Employment Relations Act 2004, s.40).

Even before 6 April 2005, an employer who refused to allow an employee time off for jury service could be fined for contempt of court, and it would have normally (but not automatically) been unfair dismissal if an employer refused to allow an employee back to work after jury service.

Reserve forces

There is no legal obligation on employers to allow an employee time off for territorial army training and many employers expect workers to do this during annual leave. The Reserve Force Act 1996 updates the law regarding call up of reservists generally. It includes a power of call-out for non-fighting purposes such as peacekeeping and humanitarian and disaster relief operations. There is statutory provision for payments to reservists and their employers in respect of loss suffered as a result of call-out or recall (Reserve Forces (Call-out and Recall) (Financial Assistance) Regulations 2005, SI 2005/859).

Employers of reservists who are called up are obliged to re-employ them afterwards provided they make written application within six months, complying with conditions set out in s.3 of the Reserve Forces (Safeguard of Employment) Act 1985.

An employer who dismisses an employee because he is a reservist can be committing a criminal offence under the Reserve Forces (Safeguard of Employment) Act 1985, s.17 (as amended by the Reserve Force Act 1996, s.122(3)). There is no provision to prevent employers discriminating against job applicants by refusing to employ them on grounds of membership of the reserve forces.

Toilet breaks

Although the Workplace (Health, Safety and Welfare) Regulations 1992, SI 1992/3004, require employers to provide 'suitable and sufficient sanitary conveniences' at 'readily accessible places', there is no specific law which gives employees the right to take time off work to go to the lavatory. Clearly this right is implied into any employment contract.

Specific categories of employment

1. Employees ordinarily working outside the UK generally have no statutory rights to time off work, except for attending to duties as employee-trustees of an occupational pension scheme (TULRCA 1992, s.285).
2. Merchant seamen do not have the normal statutory rights to time off work for public duties or for training and to look for work if under notice of dismissal for redundancy (ERA 1996, s.199(2)).

3. Profit-sharing fishermen do not have the normal statutory rights to time off work for public duties or for training and to look for work if under notice of dismissal for redundancy (ERA 1996, s.199(2)) or to time off for trade union duties and activities (TULRCA 1992, s.284).
4. Police officers have limited rights to time off work (ERA 1996, s.200(1) and TULRCA 1992, s.280).
5. Members of the armed forces have limited rights to time off work (ERA 1996, s.192, Sched.2, para.16 and TULRCA 1992, s.274(1)).
6. Civil servants whose terms of employment restrict their rights to take part in 'certain political activities' or 'activities which may conflict with [their] official functions' are not allowed time off for public duties connected with any such activities (ERA 1996, s.191(5)).

A dedicated website at **www.emplaw.co.uk/lshandbook** provides links to judgments and other source material referred to in this chapter.

CHAPTER 8

Health and safety at work

8.1 GENERAL INFORMATION

This chapter considers the main obligations for an employer in connection with the health and safety of his workers. The law imposes both criminal and civil sanctions upon employers who fail to take reasonable care for the health and safety of workers. For more detailed consideration of these obligations, readers should consult an appropriate textbook such as Redgrave et. al, *Redgrave's Health and Safety* (5th editon), Butterworths, 2007. This chapter sets out a summary of common law and statutory obligations, and then considers a number of specific health and safety issues such as asbestos, young workers and stress.

The Health and Safety Commission (HSC) and the Health and Safety Executive (HSE) were merged into a single national regulatory body (called the Health and Safety Executive) on 1 April 2008 (by the Legislative Reform (Health and Safety Executive) Order 2008, SI 2008/960).

Two useful sources of information, which can often point readers to the answer more swiftly than a textbook, are:

1. *The Health and Safety Executive*: they publish many free leaflets and books. They have a comprehensive (and constantly expanding) website at **www.hse.gov.uk** and can be contacted on their information line on 0845 345 0055.
2. *The Institution of Occupational Safety and Health*: this has an international membership of over 28,000 health and safety professionals and maintains a register of health and safety consultants. It is 'an independent, not-for-profit organisation which offers authoritative guidance on health and safety issues'. It can be contacted at The Grange, Highfield Drive, Wigston, Leicestershire LE18 1NN (tel: 0116 257 3100) or via its website (**www.iosh.co.uk**).

8.2 COMMON LAW DUTIES

An employer owes a duty of care to employees to: (i) select proper staff; (ii) provide adequate materials; (iii) provide safe premises; and (iv) provide a safe system of work (*Wilsons and Clyde Coal Co Ltd* v. *English* [1938] AC 57, HL). Not only are these duties in tort but they are also implied terms under the contract of employment so that if an employer is in breach of these terms (and the breach is sufficiently serious), the employee can resign and claim constructive dismissal (*Graham Oxley Tool Steels Ltd* v. *Firth* [1980] IRLR 135 and *Marshall Specialist Vehicles Ltd* v. *Osborne* [2003] IRLR 672).

A higher than normal standard of care is expected of employers with non-English speaking employees to ensure they fully understand safety instructions (*Tasci* v. *Pekalp of London Ltd* [2001] ICR 633, CA).

The Court of Appeal has held that an employer cannot require an employee to work excessively long hours so that it was reasonably foreseeable that the work might damage his health, irrespective of the fact that an express term required the employee (a junior doctor) to work such long hours (*Johnstone* v. *Bloomsbury Health Authority* [1991] IRLR 118, CA).

The duty to take care for the well-being of employees extends to mental as well as physical health (*Walker* v. *Northumberland County Council* [1995] IRLR 35).

Employers cannot simply sit back and wait for their employees to complain – they have a duty to be proactive, at least to some degree, and also to keep abreast of current awareness on matters such as best practice on prevention of occupational stress (*Barber* v. *Somerset County Council* [2004] ICR 457, HL).

However, there are limits to an employer's common law duties in this respect. An employer is not a 'nanny' and has no duty to prevent an adult employee from doing work which the employee knows carries an element of risk (*Buck & ors* v. *Nottinghamshire Healthcare NHS Trust* [2006] EWCA Civ 1576). Similarly an employer does not have a legal duty specifically to warn a qualified senior secretary that she should intersperse other work with her typing to avoid risk of repetitive strain injury (*Pickford* v. *ICI plc* [1998] IRLR 435, HL).

8.3 STATUTORY DUTIES

The statutory position is governed by the Health and Safety at Work etc. Act 1974 (HSWA 1974) and the Management of Health and Safety at Work Regulations 1999, SI 1999/3242 (MHSWR 1999). A vast number of industry-specific and other regulations exist, which are in general outside the scope of this book. Recent regulations of general interest include the Provision and Use of Work Equipment Regulations 1998, SI 1998/2306, the Control of Vibration at Work Regulations 2005, SI 2005/1093, the Control of Noise at Work Regulations 2005, SI 2005/1643, the Work at Height Regulations 2005, SI 2005/735 (amended by the Work at Height (Amendment) Regulations 2007, SI 2007/114), the Control of Asbestos Regulations 2006, SI 2006/2739 and the Construction (Design and Management) Regulations 2007, SI 2007/320.

Until 27 October 2003 there was a 'civil liability exclusion' which meant that employees could not sue their employers for injury resulting from a breach of the regulations. As from that date employees can claim damages from their employer in a civil action if they suffer injury or illness as a result of the employer breaching MHSWR 1999 or the Fire Precautions (Workplace) Regulations 1997, SI 1997/1840. This change was implemented by the Management of Health and Safety at Work and Fire Precautions (Workplace) (Amendment) Regulations 2003, SI 2003/2457.

A subsequent amendment expressly removed the (unintended and probably remote) possibility of third parties suing employees for any breach of duty arising under MHSWR 1999 (Management of Health and Safety at Work (Amendment) Regulations 2006, SI 2006/438, in force from 6 April 2006).

A Corporate Manslaughter and Corporate Homicide Act 2007 criminalising gross failures in the management of health and safety causing death came into force on 6 April 2008.

8.3.1 Health and safety policies

Every employer with five or more employees has a statutory obligation to prepare and keep up to date a 'written statement of his general policy with respect to health and safety at work of his employees ... and to bring the statement and any revision of it to the notice of all his employees' (HSWA 1974, s.2(3), Employers' Health and Safety Policy Statements (Exemptions) Regulations 1975, SI 1975/1584).

In addition, all employers (irrespective of the number of employees) must provide an approved leaflet or health and safety poster at a place reasonably accessible to all employees or provide all employees with a copy (Health and Safety Information for Employees Regulations 1989, SI 1989/682 and the Health and Safety Information for Employees (Modifications and Repeals) Regulations 1995, SI 1995/2923).

8.3.2 Risk assessments

Every employer (irrespective of the number of employees) must carry out a 'risk assessment for the purpose of identifying the measures he needs to take to comply with ... the relevant statutory provisions' (MHSWR 1999, reg.3).

The Health and Safety Executive have produced a useful booklet entitled Five Steps to Risk Assessment (revised June 2006, available at **www.hse.gov.uk/pubns/raindex.htm**). It points out that 'a risk assessment is simply a careful examination of what, in your work, could cause harm to people so that you can weigh up whether you have taken enough precautions or should do more to prevent harm'. It sets out five steps to be taken, namely:

(a) identify the hazards;
(b) decide who might be harmed and how;

(c) evaluate the risks and decide on precautions;
(d) record the findings and implement them; and
(e) review the assessment and update it if necessary.

There are special obligations regarding risk assessments for new or expectant mothers. They are considered at **section 7.3.5**.

8.3.3 Health and safety representatives/consultation with employees

Employers are obliged to consult on health and safety matters with any duly elected safety representatives of the workforce. If there are no elected safety representatives, then the employer is obliged to consult all employees: thus it is in the employer's interests to ensure representatives are elected. There is no 'small employer' exemption (Safety Representatives and Safety Committees Regulations 1977, SI 1977/500 amended by the Management of Health and Safety at Work Regulations 1992, SI 1992/2051 and the Health and Safety (Consultation with Employees) Regulations 1996, SI 1996/1513, reg.4).

The consultation must be 'in good time' and must cover health and safety matters generally, including the provision of health and safety information, planning and organising of health and safety training, and consultation regarding the health and safety implications of any new technologies in the workplace (Health and Safety (Consultation with Employees) Regulations 1996, reg.3).

The employee representatives have the right to paid time off work for training and carrying out their duties. They are protected against victimisation (i.e. being subjected to a detriment for performing their functions) and any dismissal connected with their duties will be automatically unfair. Victimisation and dismissal are also prohibited for employees (not necessarily elected employee representatives) who exercise their rights under health and safety legislation or who brought health and safety issues to the employer's attention if there is no safety representative whose attention could have been drawn to the matter. Finally, victimisation and dismissal are prohibited in respect of any employees who leave (or propose to leave) their place of work, or take appropriate steps, because they reasonably believe there to be 'serious and imminent danger' within the workplace (ERA 1996, ss.44(1) and 100). No qualifying period of continuous employment is required to bring a claim of unfair dismissal on these grounds (ERA 1996, s.108(3)(c)).

If at least two safety representatives ask the employer in writing to establish a 'safety committee', the employer must do so within three months (Safety Representatives and Safety Committees Regulations 1977, SI 1977/500, reg.9(1)).

8.3.4 Reporting obligations

Employers must report all work-related health and safety incidents specified in the Reporting of Injuries, Diseases and Dangerous Occurrences Regulations

1995, SI 1995/3163 (RIDDOR). In summary, this covers any 'major injury' or 'dangerous occurrence', as defined in the regulations. A dedicated reporting centre has been set up for this purpose at Caerphilly Business Park, Caerphilly CF83 3GG (0845 300 99 23), and reports can be logged via the website (**www.hse.gov.uk/riddor/**).

8.4 SPECIFIC EXAMPLES

8.4.1 Asbestos

Exposure to asbestos, particularly long-term exposure, causes mesothelioma and other pulmonary diseases, often fatal. It causes 3,000 deaths a year (most of these result from asbestos exposure during the 1950s and 1960s). It is a criminal offence to import or use asbestos (subject to minor exceptions, such as in the interests of national security, or for the purpose of disposal of asbestos).

In March 2003, the EC issued a new Directive 2003/18/EC to amend and tighten up Directive 1983/477/EC (on the protection of workers from the risks related to exposure to asbestos at work). An important provision (Art.8) is that employers must ensure that no worker is exposed to an airborne concentration of asbestos in excess of 0.1 fibres per cm^3 as an eight-hour time-weighted average (TWA). The new (generally tighter) rules should have been implemented in all Member States by 15 April 2006. The UK missed that date but implementing British regulations came into force from 13 November 2006 (Control of Asbestos Regulations 2006, SI 2006/2739, replacing the Control of Asbestos at Work Regulations 2002, SI 2002/2675). An HSE Approved Code of Practice and guidance to the Control of Asbestos Regulations 2006, an HSE Guide to management of asbestos in non-domestic premises 2006 and an HSE Guide for safety representatives 2006 were issued at around the same time.

A new 'duty to manage' asbestos came into effect on 21 May 2004 (Control of Asbestos at Work Regulations 2002, SI 2002/2675, reg.4).

A single asbestos fibre can cause mesothelioma and possibly death. There have been particular legal problems for employees who suffered injury as a result of exposure to asbestos fibres but who could not prove which of several employments led to the injury (*Fairchild* v. *Glenhaven Funeral Services Ltd & ors* [2002] UKHL 22). The House of Lords ruled that in such cases liability should be apportioned between the employers (and thus their insurers) by reference to the duration of the respective employments (*Barker* v. *Corus (UK) plc* [2006] ICR 809). This 2006 decision was not well received by many, the fundamental problem being that mesothelioma claims are frequently based on events which took place many years ago and some of the employers concerned may have gone into liquidation. The effect of the House of Lords decision was to let (insurers of) the liquidated employers off the hook in such cases and make it impossible for many sufferers to claim compensation, however negligent their employers might have been. The government reacted by changing the law. A section was introduced into a Bill which was conveniently going through Parliament at that time, the effect of which is to make all relevant employers jointly and severally liable, with of course the right for any one of them who is sued to claim appropriate contribution from the other or others of them (Compensation Act 2006, s.3 and the Compensation Act 2006 (Contribution for Mesothelioma Claims) Regulations 2006, SI 2006/3259). The legislation is retrospective to 3 May 2006, the date of the House of Lords decision in the *Barker* case. It provides a right for the parties to seek variation of any settlement or determination made before that date and opens the way for any employer who had been unjustly forced to pay 'too much' compensation to seek contribution from the other various employers if they are still in existence.

In Scotland the relatives of a person who has died from mesothelioma can claim damages even if the victim settled their own claim while alive (Rights of Relatives to Damages (Mesothelioma) (Scotland) Act 2007 amending the Damages (Scotland) Act 1976).

In order to win an asbestosis/mesothelioma claim the employee (or his estate) must produce evidence to show, or to support an inference, that the employer he is suing was in breach of its duty to take reasonable care to protect its workers from inhaling asbestos dust (*Brett* v. *University of Reading* [2007] EWCA Civ 88).

There is an on-going problem in relation to pleural plaques (scars formed in lung tissue as a consequence of the inhalation of asbestos). Pleural plaques are not thought to lead directly to any serious asbestos-related condition, only rarely are any symptoms noticed by the individual concerned, and medical opinion is generally to the effect that they do not carry an increased risk of asbestosis, mesothelioma or other lung cancer. The House of Lords has ruled that the mere presence of asbestos fibres in employees' lungs cannot found a cause of action in a personal injury claim – some form of physical injury has to be shown. Even an employer who negligently exposed employees to asbestos is not liable to compensate employees who have pleural plaques but whose only 'injury' is anxiety at the prospect of contracting an asbestos-related illness (*Johnston* v. *NEI International Combustion Ltd; Rothwell* v. *Chemical & Insulating Co Ltd* [2007] ICR 1745).

In February 2008 the Scottish government announced it would 'overrule' this House of Lords decision so far as Scotland is concerned by introducing an appropriate Bill before the 2008 summer recess (it is able to do this as the law of damages was 'devolved' to the Scottish Parliament by the Scotland Act 1998). Shortly afterwards Gordon Brown told the House of Commons in London that his government would 'publish a consultation document soon'.

8.4.2 Children and young workers

Child. For employment law purposes a child is defined as a person who is not over compulsory school age (Education Act 1996, s.558).

Young worker. The Working Time Regulations 1998 define a 'young worker' as someone aged between 15 and 18 who is over compulsory school age (WTR 1998, reg.2(1)).

Compulsory school age. Pupils must stay at school until the end of the summer term after they reach 16 (whether or not they are sitting any exams) unless their sixteenth birthday is during the summer holidays (for England and Wales, Education Act 1996, s.8 as amended by Education Act 1997; for Scotland, Education (Scotland) Act 1980, s.31 as amended by Standards in Scotland's Schools etc. Act 2000 and the School Education (Amendment) (Scotland) Act 2002).

There is a general statutory duty on every employer to 'ensure that young persons employed by him are protected at work from any risks to their health or safety which are a consequence of their lack of experience, or absence of awareness of existing or potential risks or the fact that young persons have not yet fully matured' (Management of Health and Safety at Work Regulations 1999, SI 1999/3242). In addition it is prohibited to employ a child in various types of activity, notably:

- a child may not be employed to work in mines and quarries, manufacturing industries, shipbuilding, electricity generation and distribution, building works and road, rail and canal transport (Employment of Women, Young Persons and Children Act 1920);
- it is an offence to cause or permit a child to ride on or drive a vehicle, machine or agricultural implement (Agriculture (Safety, Health and Welfare Provisions) Act 1956, s.7);
- a young person may not clean machinery if to do so would expose him to risk of injury (Offices, Shops and Railway Premises Act 1963, s.18);
- persons under 18 may not be employed in effecting any betting transaction or in a licensed betting office (Betting, Gaming and Lotteries Act 1963, s.21);
- persons under 18 may not be employed in a licensed bar (Licensing Act 1964, s.170), reduced to 16 if the employment is under an approved training scheme (Licensing Act 1964, s.170(1A));
- persons under minimum school leaving age may not be employed on a ship registered in the UK save as permitted by regulations made under the Merchant Shipping Act 1970 (s.51 of that Act).

The minimum age at which a child may be employed in any work, other than as an employee of his parent or guardian in occasional light agricultural or horticultural work, is 14 (increased from 13 by the Children (Protection at Work) Regulations 1998, SI 1998/276, reg.2(2)(a), amending the Children and

Young Persons Act 1933, s.18(1) – for Scotland, the Children and Young Persons (Scotland) Act 1937).

There are special rules governing performances by child actors. In essence a licence from the local education authority is required for a child to take part in professional performances except in two cases, namely performances on up to three days in any six-month period (Children and Young Persons Act 1963, s.37(3)(a)) and performances arranged by a school, the relevant local authority or a 'body of persons' approved by the Secretary of State which involve no payment to or for the child, other than expenses (Children and Young Persons Act 1963, s.37(3)(b)). There is a total ban on any child taking part in any performance in which his life or limbs are endangered and there is no power for licences to be granted for such performances (Children and Young Persons Act 1933, s.23).

In December 2007, in answer to a question in the House of Commons, the government said that child employment legislation 'is more than adequate and not in need of review' but that 'new guidance is necessary to support employers, young people and those advising them in understanding the law ... we have undertaken to publish improved best practice guidance next year' (Hansard, 17 December 2007).

We understand that, in addition, the Department for Children, Schools and Families (DCSF) is currently working on a consolidation of the current mish-mash of child employment legislation. Indeed a comprehensive consolidating and amending Act dealing with child employment was passed many years ago (the Employment of Children Act 1973) but was never brought into force and was repealed in July 2008 by the Statute Law (Repeals) Act 2008.

Working Time

CHILDREN (DEFINED AS ABOVE)

Main provisions are set out in the Children and Young Persons Act 1933, s.18 as amended (notably by the Children and Young Persons Act 1963, s.34, the Children Act 1972, s.1 and the Children (Protection at Work) Regulations 1998, SI 1998/276).

It is important to note that the Children and Young Persons Act 1933, s.18 (as amended) applies subject to by-laws and licences and that it applies in respect of performances by the child actors only if a licence is required (see above). So far as working time is concerned it provides that:

- Children may not be employed before 7.00 am or after 7.00 pm, are entitled to a minimum of one hour's rest after four consecutive hours of work and must not be employed unless they have had (or could still have) at least two weeks per year free from any employment during school holidays.
- During school term, an overall weekly limit of 12 hours' work applies. Subject to that weekly limit, maximum working hours on Sundays and

weekdays are two hours. On Saturdays this is increased to five hours for those under 15 (eight hours for those aged 15 or over). Children may not be employed before the end of school hours on any school day, save that local bye-laws can allow employment for up to one hour before the start of school hours on a school day (Children and Young Persons Act 1933, ss.18(1)(b) and 18(2)(a)(ii)).

- During school holidays an overall weekly maximum limit of 25 hours' work applies (35 hours for those aged 15 or over). Subject to that weekly limit, maximum working hours on weekdays (including Saturdays) are five hours for those under 15 and eight hours for those aged 15 or over. Maximum working time on Sundays is the same as in school terms, i.e. two hours.

YOUNG WORKERS (DEFINED AS ABOVE)

Regulation 5A of WTR 1998 (inserted by the Working Time (Amendment) Regulations 2002, SI 2002/3128) provides that:

(1) A young worker's working time shall not exceed –

  (a) eight hours a day, or
  (b) 40 hours a week.

(2) If, on any day, or, as the case may be, during any week, a young worker is employed by more than one employer, his working time shall be determined for the purpose of paragraph (1) by aggregating the number of hours worked by him for each employer.

(3) For the purposes of paragraphs (1) and (2), a week starts at midnight between Sunday and Monday.

(4) An employer shall take all reasonable steps, in keeping with the need to protect the health and safety of workers, to ensure that the limits specified in paragraph (1) are complied with in the case of each worker employed by him in relation to whom they apply.

Young workers must have an 'uninterrupted rest period' of not less than 48 hours in each seven-day period during which they work for their employer (WTR 1998, reg.11(3)).

8.4.3 New or expectant mothers

This is discussed at **section 7.3.5**.

8.4.4 Stress

A study of stress falls outside the scope of this book. However, the starting point for any advisor is to consider the landmark judgment in *Walker* v. *Northumberland County Council* [1995] ICR 702, which provides that employers have a duty not to cause psychiatric damage to employees by requiring them to undertake too much work and providing insufficient backup. Both the EAT and the Court of Appeal have emphasised that it is not enough for an employee merely to prove 'stress' to support claims. There must be a demonstrable injury to health (*Morgan* v. *Staffordshire University* [2002] IRLR 190, EAT and *Sutherland* v. *Hatton* [2002] EWCA Civ 76, CA).

The latter of those two cases shows that the ordinary principles of employer's liability apply to work-related stress claims. As a general rule an employer can assume that an employee can withstand normal job pressures and signs of stress must have been obvious to the employer if a worker is to succeed in a stress-related claim – it is only foreseeable injury which gives rise to an employer's liability for stress (*Hartman* v. *South Essex Mental Health and Community Care NHS Trust* [2005] IRLR 293, CA). The onus is normally on a worker to complain about stress and to bring it to the attention of the employer. There is no breach of duty in allowing a willing worker to continue in a stressful job if the only alternative is dismissal or demotion.

The guidelines in *Sutherland* v. *Hatton* were later approved by the House of Lords but with the important difference that the House of Lords emphasised that employers have a duty to be pro-active rather than simply adopt a reactive 'wait and see' position (*Barber* v. *Somerset County Council* [2004] ICR 457). Thus although in *Sutherland* v. *Hatton* the Court of Appeal suggested that an employer who offers a confidential counselling service is likely to have a complete defence to a stress-related claim by a worker, it was later held that mere provision of a counselling service is not enough to discharge an employer's duty to take reasonable steps to prevent an overworked employee's breakdown (*Intel Corporation (UK) Ltd* v. *Daw* [2007] IRLR 346, CA).

The essentials for determining whether an employer is liable in negligence for psychiatric injury suffered by an employee have been stated by the High Court (*Barlow* v. *Borough of Broxbourne* [2003] EWHC 50, QB quoted with approval in *Green* v. *DB Group Services (UK) Ltd* [2006] EWHC 1898, QB), to be:

- whether the claimant has established that the conduct complained of . . . took place and, if so, whether it amounted to bullying or harassment in the ordinary connotation of those terms. In addressing this question it is the cumulative effect of the conduct which has to be considered rather than the individual incidents relied on;
- did the person or persons involved in the victimisation or bullying know, or ought they reasonably to have known, that their conduct might cause the claimant harm;
- could they, by the exercise of reasonable care, have taken steps which would have avoided that harm and
- were their actions so connected with their employment as to render the defendant vicariously responsible for them.

Damages for stress-related injury can be very high. In a case in 2006 a City bank was held vicariously liable for a prolonged campaign of bullying and harassment at work suffered by a female secretary who was awarded in excess of £850,000 (*Green* v. *DB Group Services (UK) Ltd* [2006] IRLR 764, HC).

While in general stress claims are matters for the courts rather than employment tribunals, it is important to note that if an employee resigns and claims constructive unfair dismissal the normal rule is that compensation will only be available for financial loss (*Dunnachie* v. *Kingston upon Hull City Council* [2004] IRLR 727, HL). However, the position is different in discrimination cases as statute then specifically gives employment tribunals power to award compensation for injury to feelings.

Recommended sources of information include the HSE guidance 'Managing the causes of work-related stress – A step-by-step approach using the Management Standards' with CD-ROM (priced at £10.95 available from HSE Books (tel: 01787 881165; **www.hsebooks.com**)). The HSE also provides a useful website (**www.hse.gov.uk/stress**).

A dedicated website at **www.emplaw.co.uk/lshandbook** provides links to judgments and other source material referred to in this chapter.

CHAPTER 9
Miscellaneous matters

9.1 BANK AND PUBLIC HOLIDAYS

Technically, there is a difference between bank holidays and public holidays although in common parlance the two expressions are frequently used interchangeably. Bank holidays are days specified as days for closure of banks by the Banking and Financial Dealings Act 1971 (which repealed and replaced the old Bank Holidays Act 1871) or since 1974 by Royal proclamation. There are also two common law public holidays, Good Friday and Christmas day.

There is no statutory right to holiday, with or without pay, on bank or public holidays. However, many workers are entitled to paid leave on bank and public holidays either under customary arrangements (which may be implied terms of contract) or under express contract provisions (Banking and Financial Dealings Act 1971; Shops (Early Closing Days) Act 1965).

If an employer allows staff to take bank and public holidays with pay those days count towards the minimum statutory annual holiday pay entitlement under the Working Time Regulations (an increase in which is being phased in from 2007 – see **section 7.2.4**).

The eight regular public and bank holidays in England and Wales are:

- New Year's Day (by Royal proclamation, since 1974);
- Good Friday
- Easter Monday;
- first Monday in May (by Royal proclamation, since 1978);
- last Monday in May (Spring Bank Holiday);
- last Monday in August (Summer Bank Holiday);
- Christmas Day; and
- Boxing Day.

If Christmas Day, Boxing Day or New Year's Day fall on a Saturday or Sunday the holiday is postponed until the Monday (and Tuesday if necessary).

Scotland has the same except that New Year's Day is a bank holiday under the Act rather than by Royal proclamation, 2 January is an additional bank holiday, the first rather than the last Monday of August is a bank holiday and an additional bank holiday on St Andrew's Day (30th November) was added by the St Andrew's Day Bank Holiday (Scotland) Act 2007. Setting bank holidays is a specific exception from the list of 'reserved matters' under the Scotland Act 1998 (see Sched.5, Pt II, A3). Scottish ministers therefore have the responsibility for setting bank holidays in Scotland and can make adjustments if appropriate in rather the same way as adjustments can be made by Royal proclamation in England and Wales (Banking Act 1971, s.1(2)).

There are regular attempts to introduce an extra bank holiday in England and Wales, the latest being a private member's Autumn Bank Holiday Bill which had a first reading in the House of Commons on 4 March 2008.

For notes on the special position of shop assistants see **section 9.24** on Sunday trading.

9.2 BULLYING AT WORK

There is no general UK legislation specifically to protect those who may be suffering, or have suffered, from bullying at work. This does not mean they have no legal protection. It does mean, however, that to get legal protection or redress they must look to those parts of employment-related law which may be relevant or to the general law (*Wigan Borough Council* v. *Davies* [1979] ICR 411, and *Waters* v. *Commissioner of Metropolitan Police* [2000] ICR 1064, HL).

Chapter 14 deals with SDA 1975 and RRA 1976. They provide the principal employment law protection against bullying at work.

The Emergency Workers (Obstruction) Act 2006, which came into effect on 20 February 2007, makes it an offence to assault or impede persons providing specified emergency services.

More general statutory protection is afforded by the Criminal Justice and Public Order Act 1994, the Public Order Act 1986 and the Protection from Harassment Act 1997. There have been two failed private members' attempts since 1996 to get a Dignity at Work Act, which would effectively be an anti-bullying statute, passed into law. If it ever becomes law, a Dignity at Work Act would probably give employment tribunals the power which they do not currently have to award compensation in unfair dismissal cases for non-financial loss such as for injury to feelings or stress (see *Dunnachie* v. *Kingston upon Hull City Council* [2004] ICR 1052, HL).

There is an implied term in employment contracts that 'the employer shall render reasonable support to an employee to ensure that the employee can carry out the duties of his job without harassment and disruption by fellow workers'. Thus employees who suffer from bullying at work may be able to bring a breach of contract or constructive dismissal claim against their employers (Arnold J. in *Wigan Borough Council* v. *Davies* [1979] ICR 411, quoted with approval by the House of Lords in *Waters* v. *Commissioner of Metropolitan Police* [2000] ICR 1064, HL).

An employer can be liable for the consequences of any harassment committed by an employee in the course of his employment in breach of the Protection from Harassment Act 1997, s.1 (*Majrowski* v. *Guy's & St Thomas's NHS Trust* [2005] IRLR 695, HL, in which the House of Lords confirmed that s.3 of the Protection from Harassment Act 1997 has this effect). A single instance of bullying or harassment does not amount to a contravention of that Act because there must be an offending 'course of conduct' and 'a "course of conduct" must involve conduct on at least two occasions' (Protection from Harassment Act 1997, ss.1 and 7 and *Banks* v. *Ablex Ltd* [2005] IRLR 357, CA). An occurrence does have to be criminal to count (*Conn* v. *The Council of the City of Sunderland* [2007] EWCA Civ 1492).

Acas provides two booklets on Bullying and Harassment at Work, one being for employees and the other for managers and employers (available for download from the Acas publications website at **www.ecacas.co.uk**).

9.3 COMPANY DIRECTORS

The position of 'company director' is an 'office' not an employment. A director may be an employee as well as being a director but this is not automatic. Indeed, it is common practice for companies to have non-executive directors who are not employees, have no service agreement and no employment relationship of any sort with the company.

Depending on the circumstances, a person who is the controlling shareholder of a private company, and who is also a director or 'shadow director', may or may not be an employee. In practice the question tends to arise when a one-man company goes to the wall and the director/chief shareholder applies for a contribution towards unpaid salary, etc. under the rules noted below under 'insolvency guarantees' (*Secretary of State (DTI)* v. *Bottrill* [1999] ICR 592, CA and *Sellars Arenascene Ltd* v. *Connolly* [2001] ICR 760, CA).

The question of control is not on its own determinative of the issue as to whether a shareholder or director of a company is an employee. The EAT has pointed out that liability to be dismissed by a liquidator shows that even in a 'one-man company' the majority shareholder employee does not have absolute control of his destiny (*Nesbitt* v. *DTI* [2007] IRLR 847, EAT). Although the existence of a controlling shareholding may raise doubts as to whether the individual concerned is truly an employee, is always relevant and may be decisive, it will not on its own justify a finding that there was no contract of employment (*Clark* v. *Clark Construction Initiatives Ltd & anor* [2008] IRLR 364 in which the EAT also said that if a contract purports to be a contract of employment, the onus is on the party seeking to deny its effect to satisfy the court that it is not what it appears to be; this is particularly so where the individual has paid PAYE tax and NI as an employee 'as on the face of it he has earned the right to take advantage of the benefits which employees may derive from such payments').

The fact that the individual has guaranteed a company's debts to a bank is not inconsistent with his being its employee (*Neufeld* v. *A&N Communication in Print Ltd* (unreported, EAT, 11 April 2008), which is also authority for the proposition that the status of the individual has to be considered as at the time which is relevant to the case in point, not as at the date when that person first began working for the company).

If the conduct of a director of a company which has become insolvent (either while he was a director or subsequently) 'makes him unfit to be concerned in the management of' a company the court must order a minimum of two years' disqualification – the maximum disqualification period is 15 years (Company Directors Disqualification Act 1986, ss.6 and 8). The Insolvency Act 2000 introduced a fast-track system enabling the Secretary of State to accept undertakings with the same legal effect as a disqualification order made by a court. The consequences of breaching a disqualification undertaking are the same as those for breaching a disqualification order: a fine or imprisonment for up to two years.

A director owes fiduciary duties to his company. As a general rule these end when he stops being a director. However, it will be different if he resigns in order to exploit an opportunity or to use for his own benefit information which has come to him in his capacity as a director (*Keisner* v. *Terrus Group Ltd* [2006] EWHC 2765, ChD). In 2007 company directors of a company were found to be in breach of both their fiduciary duties as directors and their duty of fidelity as employees as a result of diverting a business opportunity and establishing a potentially rival business whilst still employed by that company (*Shepherds Investments Ltd & Anor* v. *Walters & ors* [2007] IRLR 110, ChD). However, each case turns on its own facts and there is no absolute rule that acts done by a director which are preparatory to competition after he leaves are necessarily a breach of the implied term of loyalty and good faith (*Foster Bryant Surveying Ltd* v. *Bryant* [2007] IRLR 425, CA, in which a company director who was effectively forced to resign and who, before his notice period had expired, agreed with the company's best client that he would continue to service it, was held not to be in breach of his fiduciary duties to the company).

9.4 CONSULTATION

There are at least eight sets of circumstances in which employers have specific legal obligations to consult with employees and/or their representatives.

MISCELLANEOUS MATTERS

9.4.1 Dismissal generally

Employers have a general duty to consult any employee before dismissing that employee and failure to do so is likely, save in exceptional circumstances, to result in the dismissal being treated as unfair dismissal if the employee complains to an employment tribunal. Since 1 October 2004 there has been a statutory obligation on an employer to operate a formal dismissal/disciplinary procedure before dismissing an employee.

When consultation is required it must not be merely a matter of form. The employee(s) concerned must have an opportunity to understand properly what it is that they are being consulted about, to consider the matter and to express their views (*Rowell v. Hubbard Group Services Ltd* [1995] IRLR 195, EAT).

9.4.2 Redundancy

Employers must consult appropriate representatives of employees if 20 or more employees at one establishment are to be dismissed as redundant within a period of 90 days (TULRCA 1992, s.188, as amended). When deciding whether the number of employees to be dismissed by reason of redundancy is 20 or more, any who have accepted voluntary redundancy in the knowledge that if they did not do so they would have to accept compulsory redundancy must be included (*Optare Group Ltd v. TGWU* [2007] IRLR 931, EAT).

The penalty for failure to consult in such a case is an order to pay each affected employee a 'protective award' of up to 90 days' pay with no maximum limit. If there is a recognised trade union the consultation must be with trade union representatives (Collective Redundancies and Transfer of Undertakings (Protection of Employment) (Amendment) Regulations 1999, SI 1999/1925).

Consultation must begin in good time and in any event 30 days before the first of the dismissals takes effect or 90 days if 100 or more employees are to be dismissed (TULRCA 1992, s.188(1A)). The European Court of Justice has held that giving a notice of dismissal by reason of redundancy constitutes 'redundancy' for purposes of the EC Collective Redundancies Directive 98/59/EC even though the notice will not expire for some time. The result is that if 20 or more employees at one establishment are to be made redundant a notice of dismissal given during the consultation period may be invalid even if it expires after the end of that period (*Junk v. Wolfgang Kuhnel*, ECJ Case C-188/03, 28 January 2005).

Where a business is closing, consultation over redundancies extends to the reasons for the closure causing them. Older authorities have held, effectively, that the duty to consult is concerned only with how a redundancy programme would be carried out, not whether there should be redundancies. The EAT held in September 2007 that this no longer applies where a business is closing: '... the obligation to consult over avoiding the proposed redundancies inevitably involves engaging with the reasons for the dismissals, and that in turn requires consultation over the reasons for the closure.' Only in the rare situation where there is to be closure but redundancies could be avoided will consultation over the closure decision itself not be needed (*UK Coal Mining Ltd* v. *NUM & British Association of Colliery Management* [2008] IRLR 4, EAT).

9.4.3 Business transfers

The seller and the purchaser of any business or undertaking must inform and generally consult with appropriate representatives of affected employees about any proposed sale or purchase of the business/undertaking or other 'relevant transfer' which may affect employees (TUPE 2006, regs.13–16). If any of the employees are members of an independent trade union which is also a recognised trade union then this means the representatives of that union.

Specified information must be given in all cases and if there are any 'measures in relation to an affected employee' being taken then there must also be proper consultation. The specified information includes the proposed date of the transfer and the reasons for it; the legal, economic and social implications of the transfer for any affected employees; and details of any measures affecting employees which are likely to be taken in connection with the proposed transfer.

The regulations provide that if an employer fails to inform and/or consult in good time a disaffected employee may present a complaint to an employment tribunal which can award compensation of up to 13 weeks' pay, subject to the statutory cap (currently set at £330 for each week).

The EAT has held that where a transfer is in prospect and no trade union is recognised and there are no employee representatives in post, there is a duty on the employer to initiate an election for representatives and then inform and consult them or, failing that, to inform and consult individuals (*Howard* v. *(1) Millrise Limited t/a Colourflow (In Liquidation) and (2) S G Printers t/a Colourflow* [2005] IRLR 84, EAT).

An employer's failure to inform employees about a proposed transfer of the business in which they are employed will not prevent them exercising their rights (under TUPE 2006, reg.4(7)) to opt out of the automatic transfer of their employment contracts to the new owner provided they exercise those rights as soon as reasonably possible – the result may be that the new owner will not be able to take the benefit of restrictive covenants in those contracts (*New ISG Ltd* v. *Vernon & Ors* [2008] IRLR 115, ChD).

9.4.4 Occupational pension scheme arrangements

Employers have a statutory duty to consult any relevant recognised trade union on specified matters concerning occupational pension schemes (Pension Schemes Act 1993, ss.11(5) and 113 and the Occupational Pensions

Schemes (Disclosure of Information) Regulations 1996, SI 1996/1655). This covers basic general information which must be made available to those eligible within two months of request (reg.4) and more detailed information about specific benefit entitlements which must be made available to the person entitled 'within 1 month after the date on which benefit becomes payable, or within 2 months after such date where that person is retiring before normal pension age' (reg.5).

Any significant changes to occupational or personal pension schemes are prohibited unless consultation about the change is carried out beforehand (Occupational and Personal Pension Schemes (Consultation by Employers and Miscellaneous Amendment) Regulations 2006, SI 2006/349).

9.4.5 Health and safety

Employers have a statutory duty to consult safety representatives appointed by a recognised trade union on health and safety matters (Safety Representatives and Safety Committees Regulations 1977, SI 1977/500, as amended). They must also consult non-union members and any employees who are not represented by safety representatives 'in good time on matters relating to health and safety and, in particular, with regard to' a list of five specified items (Health & Safety (Consultation with Employees) Regulations 1996, SI 1996/1513).

9.4.6 Collective bargaining

Employers have a statutory duty to provide any relevant recognised trade union which is an independent trade union with information for the purposes of collective bargaining (TULRCA 1992, s.181).

9.4.7 European Works Councils

Large companies with operations in more than one EU Member State are obliged to inform and consult employees in a wide variety of circumstances (Transnational Information and Consultation of Employees Regulations 1999, SI 1999/3323). The regulations, which implement the EC Works Council Directive 94/45, require companies whose central management is based in the UK and which have more than 1,000 employees in total in EU Member States (plus Iceland, Liechtenstein, and Norway) with at least 150 employees in each of two of those States to have or set up Works Councils. The maximum penalty for breach of the regulations is £75,000.

9.4.8 Information and Consultation Regulations 2004

The Information and Consultation Regulations 2004, SI 2004/3426 apply to employers with 50 or more employees. They implement the EC National

Information and Consultation Directive 2002/14. The regulations were phased in over the three years from 6 April 2005.

Since 6 April 2008 the regulations have applied to undertakings with 50 or more employees. They give employees the right to request their employer to inform them of, and consult with them about, a wide range of business matters affecting employment and to require the employer to set up a regular system for information and consultation within the (fairly flexible) framework set out in the regulations. The EAT has power to impose a maximum penalty of £75,000 on employers who do not comply with the regulations. The CAC has monitoring and enforcement powers.

The regulations are generally fairly easy to avoid if an employer is concerned about their effect. This is because there is no 'associated employer' provision for calculating the number of employees. As the BERR Guidance (January 1996 edition at para.6) points out 'The fact that an undertaking may be part of a group of companies is not relevant for working out whether that undertaking has enough employees to be covered by the legislation. It is the number of employees employed by an individual company that is relevant, not those employed by a subsidiary of the company, a parent company, or a fellow-subsidiary of a common parent company.'

The Information and Consultation of Employees (Amendment) Regulations 2006, SI 2006/514 remove the obligation to inform and consult under the 2004 regulations if an employer is under a duty to inform and consult with employees in respect of pension matters (see above).

9.5 DATA PROTECTION

The general effect of the Data Protection Act 1998 is to give individuals, including employees, rights of 'subject access', namely the right to have access to information held about them, called 'personal data', and to have that information corrected or deleted where appropriate. An employer (known as a 'data controller' for this purpose) may charge a fee of up to £10 for providing the information (Data Protection (Subject Access) (Fees and Miscellaneous Provisions) Regulations 2000, SI 2000/191). The right is enforceable by complaint to the Information Commissioner (previously known as the Data Protection Commissioner) who has power to prosecute or to serve an enforcement notice on a defaulting 'data user.'

The Data Protection Act 1998 repeals and replaces the Data Protection Act 1984. Whereas the 1984 Act only applied to computerised records, the new law applies to personal data recorded manually or in print with effect from 24 October 2001 (save for a minor exception, relating to some manual data in existence at 24 October 1998, which came into effect on 24 October 2007).

Between 2002 and 2004 the Information Commissioner published a four-part 'Data Protection Code of Practice' for employers, followed by a consolidated version published in June 2005. The Code covers:

- recruitment and selection;
- employment records;
- monitoring of employees; and
- information about workers' health.

The right of data subjects to access personal data (Data Protection Act 1998, s.7) is provided so that they can check that there has not been an unlawful invasion of their privacy, and the courts frown on any attempt to use the right for 'fishing expedition' purposes, i.e. trawling for information which may be of assistance in an unrelated court case. With that in mind a fairly restricted, narrow meaning has been given to 'personal data'. The Court of Appeal has ruled that it '. . . is information that affects [a person's] privacy, whether in his personal or family life, business or professional capacity'. The Court of Appeal suggested two considerations should be taken into account: first, whether the information is biographical in a significant sense, that is 'going beyond the recording of [the individual's] involvement in a matter or an event which has no personal connotations' and, second, whether the information has the individual as its focus (*Durant* v. *Financial Services Authority* [2003] EWCA Civ 1746).

Following the *Durant* judgment and publication in June 2007 by the EU Data Protection Working Party of an 'opinion on the concept of personal data', the UK Information Commissioner's Office published new guidance on the meaning of personal data in August 2007 (available from **www.ico.gov.uk**). This includes a flowchart designed to take users through the factors to consider when determining whether they are processing 'personal data'.

In November 2007 the High Court ruled that a refusal to disclose personal information in response to a subject-access request by a data subject on the ground that 'supply of . . . a copy . . . would involve disproportionate effort' (Data Protection Act 1998, s.8(2)(a)) is lawful if the search for the data would be disproportionate (*Ezsias* v. *The Welsh Ministers* [2007] All ER (D) 65).

On a related topic, the Privacy and Electronic Communications (EC Directive) Regulations 2003, SI 2003/2426 generally forbid invasive use of electronic communications without the informed consent of the 'target' computer user.

9.6 DEDUCTIONS FROM WAGES

The Employment Tribunal Service Annual Report for the year to 31 March 2007 shows that 34,857 unlawful deduction from wages claims were filed in that year, making them the third 'most popular' type of claim, behind unfair dismissal (44,491) and equal pay (44,013).

Employers are statutorily forbidden from making deductions from wages save in specific cases (ERA 1996, ss.13–27). The rules do not, of course, remove an employer's right to recover money properly due from an employee (e.g. to recover an overpayment of expenses). They merely mean that, save in a few special cases, employers are not allowed to recover the money by taking the law into their own hands and deducting it from future wages without consent.

If an employer reduces wages without agreement of the employees this is an unlawful deduction from wages contrary to the statute as well as being a breach of contract. Employees will be taken to have waived their right to complain if they continue to work at the lower wage for a reasonable length of time without making it plain that they are doing so 'under protest' (see, for example, *Henry & ors* v. *London General Transport Services Ltd* [2002] ICR 910, CA in which bus conductors worked on at reduced pay for two years before making an unsuccessful claim). However, a worker's breach of contract is not a good defence to a claim for unlawful deduction of wages (*Asif* v. *Key People Ltd* (unreported, EAT, 7 March 2008)).

'Wages' includes fees, commissions, bonuses, holiday pay, statutory sick pay and statutory maternity pay. However, an employment tribunal has no jurisdiction to rule on whether a person is entitled to statutory sick pay or similar statutory payments – that is a job for HM Revenue & Customs – and an employee cannot get around that by trying to use the 'unlawful deductions from wages' rules (*Taylor Gordon & Co Ltd* v. *Timmons* [2004] IRLR 180, EAT). Pay in lieu of notice counts as 'wages' if payable under a contractual provision but not if genuinely paid as compensation for failing to give notice (*Delaney* v. *Staples* [1992] ICR 483, HL).

In practice the provisions can be more valuable to employees in dispute with their employer than one might at first sight suppose. For example, an employer is not entitled to deduct overpaid holiday from an employee's final salary payment, in the absence of a 'relevant agreement' under WTR 1998 authorising such a deduction (*Hill* v. *Howard Chapell* [2003] IRLR 19, EAT). Similarly the amount of pay which an employer is entitled to deduct from an employee's wages because the employee has been on strike is the amount for which the employee would be entitled to sue if the deduction were unlawful and therefore the employer is not able to take holidays into account in calculating the deduction (*Cooper & ors* v. *The Isle of Wight College* [2008] IRLR 124, QBD).

Where a person, usually a woman, may have a claim under EqPA 1970 it may sometimes be more appropriate for her claim to be framed as one for unlawful deduction from wages instead. The relative differences, with a 10-point comparative list of relative advantages and disadvantages, were considered in detail by the Court of Appeal in *Alabaster* v. *Barclays Bank plc and the Secretary of State for Social Security* [2005] EWCA Civ 508.

A claim by a former employee that he was dismissed for complaining about unauthorised deductions from wages will amount to an assertion of a statutory right within the meaning of the ERA 1996, s.104(4)(c) with the result that if the claim is proved, the dismissal will be automatically unfair (*Pearce and Pearce* v. *Dyer* (unreported, EAT, 20 October 2004)).

Exceptions to the general rule forbidding deductions from wages are:

1. Deductions required or authorised by law (such as PAYE or under an attachment of earnings order) or by the worker's contract (ERA 1996, s.13(1)(a)).
2. Deductions authorised by the employee in advance of the event in respect of which they are made (ERA 1996, s.13(1)(b)).
3. Deductions to reimburse the employer for overpayment of wages or expenses (ERA 1996, s.14(1)).
4. Deductions made 'on account of the worker's having taken part' in a strike or other industrial action (ERA 1996, s.14(5)).

If an employer overpays an employee in error and the employee, genuinely not realising that there has been a mistake, innocently uses the overpayment to pay ordinary expenses and 'changes his position' as a result, the employer will not be entitled to recover the overpayment (*Lipkin Gorman (a firm)* v. *Karpnale Ltd* [1992] 4 All ER 512).

Errors in computation of wages which result in an underpayment do not count as 'deductions' and so a tribunal will have no jurisdiction if a deficiency in wages results. The deficiency must, of course, be made good but the statutory remedies for unlawful deductions will not apply (*Morgan* v. *Glamorgan County Council* [1995] IRLR 68).

To be covered by the unlawful deduction from wages rules the amount of the deduction must be quantified. If and to the extent that the amount claimed to have been deducted is uncertain, the claim has to be for breach of contract rather than for unlawful deduction from wages (*Tradition Securities & Futures SA* v. *Mouradian* (unreported, EAT, 14 December 2007)). This would mean that in an extreme case where the deduction was more than £25,000 an employee should claim in the civil courts rather than in an employment tribunal.

9.7 DIPLOMATIC IMMUNITY

Foreign states are immune from the jurisdiction of the UK courts, including employment tribunals, except insofar as the State Immunity Act 1978, the Diplomatic Privileges Act 1964 or the Consular Relations Act 1968 provide to the contrary (State Immunity Act 1978, ss.1, 4 and 16). Some important international organisations nominated by Orders in Council, for example, the United Nations, NATO and WHO, enjoy a similar immunity under the International Organisations Act 1968.

This immunity of foreign states is removed in employment cases if the employment contract was made in the UK or the work is to be wholly or partly performed in the UK for 'an office, agency or establishment maintained . . . for commercial purposes'. Even in that case the immunity is not removed if the employee was 'habitually resident' in the foreign state at the time the contract was made.

A foreign state can waive its immunity in any particular case (State Immunity Act 1978, s.2). However, solicitors acting for a foreign state can waive their client's immunity '. . . only if they have been authorised by the State, which includes authority exercised or conferred by the head of the State's diplomatic mission' (*Aziz* v. *Republic of Yemen* [2005] ICR 1391, CA).

9.8 EMPLOYMENT AGENCIES

Workers supplied by an agency may either simply be introduced by the agency to an employer or alternatively they may be employees of the agency temporarily seconded or supplied to a 'client employer'. For the purposes of the Employment Agencies Act 1973, the former type of agency is called an 'employment agency' whereas the latter is called an 'employment business'.

The EAT and the Court of Appeal have given considerable attention recently to the question of the employment law status of workers supplied to end-users by employment agencies and employment businesses. Depending on the facts, the worker may be an employee of the agency, of the end-user, of neither (perhaps self-employed) – or even of both, although this is unlikely (see *Cairns* v. *Visteon UK Ltd* [2007] IRLR 175, EAT). The question is obviously of considerable practical importance, especially if, for example, a temp wishes to claim unfair dismissal. There are, of course, guiding principles but the employment law status of a particular individual can be very difficult to determine in any particular circumstances.

Case law shows that the key factor in determining who is the employer of an agency-supplied worker is not so much what may be in writing as identification of who in practice has day-to-day control over the activities of the worker. Frequently this will be the end-user employer rather than the agency (see *Bunce* v. *Postworth Ltd t/a Skyblue* [2005] IRLR 557, CA and *Dacas* v. *Brook Street Bureau (UK) Ltd & Anr* [2004] IRLR 358, CA). These cases have been followed by a host of others up to and including *James* v. *Greenwich Council* [2008] IRLR 302. Some cases have gone one way, some another. In the *James* case the Court of Appeal confirmed that the mutuality of obligation requirement for establishing whether there is a contract of employment remains important and that passage of time is not by itself sufficient to mean that a contract of employment can or should be implied between an agency-supplied worker and the end-user.

In 2006, 2007 and 2008 both the EAT and the Court of Appeal have called for Parliament to clarify the position. In the *James* case noted above the EAT said that the common law can only tinker with the problem on the margins and a '. . . careful analysis of both the problems and the solutions, with legislative protection where necessary, is urgently required' and the Court of Appeal said that the matter is one of 'controversial social and economic policy for debate in and decision by Parliament informed by discussions between the interested parties'. Given the legislative proposals noted below, the fluidity of the case law and that a broad selection of relevant cases is noted on the website accompanying this book (**www.emplaw.co.uk/lshandbook**) we have taken the view that no useful purpose would be served by further examination here of questions concerning the employment status of agency workers.

The Conduct of Employment Agencies and Employment Businesses (Amendment) Regulations 2007, SI 2007/3575 which came into force on 6 April 2008, did not deal with this issue. A private member's Temporary and Agency Workers (Equal Treatment) Bill, introduced in the House of Commons in December 2007, proposed that 'both the employment business, or employment agency, and the end user: (a) shall be deemed to be the employer of the agency worker; and (b) shall have joint and several liability for any award of compensation that might be ordered in respect of such a complaint'. This Bill was withdrawn in May 2008 immediately after the government announced that it had come to an agreement with the TUC and the CBI on amending the law in relation to the rights of agency workers generally.

At the time of writing little is known of the detail of what will be in the legislation which will follow this agreement. It is clear that agency workers will be given the statutory right to 'equal treatment' after 12 weeks in a job ('equal treatment' being defined to mean 'at least the basic working and employment conditions that would apply to the workers concerned if they had been recruited directly by [the end-user] to occupy the same job. It will not cover occupational social security schemes' (BERR Press Release, 20 May 2008). The government also announced that after many years of unsuccessful negotiation it will now engage with its European partners to seek agreement on the terms of the proposed Agency Workers Directive which was drafted in 2002 with a view to necessary UK implementing legislation to be introduced in the next parliamentary session.

Apart from the question of the employment status of agency workers, there are some clear general rules.

It is a criminal offence for an agency to charge a fee to a work-seeker for finding him work, subject to exceptions in the Conduct of Employment Agencies and Employment Businesses Regulations 2003, SI 2003/3319, as amended from 6 April 2008 by the Conduct of Employment Agencies and Employment Businesses (Amendment) Regulations 2007, SI 2007/3575. The exceptions allow agencies to charge fees to certain categories of worker such as a writer, model or professional sportsperson, provided that the employer is not also charged a fee. The rules are enforced by the BERR's Employment Agency Standards Inspectorate (tel: 0845 955 5105).

EMPLOYMENT LAW HANDBOOK

An employment tribunal can ban persons from running an employment agency for up to 10 years for misconduct or any other sufficient reason (Employment Agencies Act 1973, s.3A).

The Conduct of Employment Agencies and Employment Businesses Regulations 2003, SI 2003/3319 flesh out the detail of the 1973 Act and revoke previous detailed rules. Minor improvements in protection for agency workers are made by the Conduct of Employment Agencies and Employment Businesses (Amendment) Regulations 2007, SI 2007/3575 which came into force on 6 April 2008. Significant provisions of the 2003 regulations include the following:

- Prohibition against bureaux requiring a work-seeker to use additional services (reg.5) or imposing contract terms which have the effect of binding a work-seeker to them (reg.6). An amendment made by SI 2007/3575 (above) provides that a bureau must ensure that a work-seeker who takes up additional services can give notice to cancel or withdraw from those services without incurring any detriment or penalty.
- Temp-to-perm fees. Fees payable to an agency by an employer who offers full-time work to a temp supplied by an agency are not banned, as originally proposed. Instead if terms are not agreed at the start of a posting, the regulations impose a minimum (eight) and a maximum (up to 14) number of weeks before workers are free to take up a permanent post without the employer having to pay a fee to the agency (reg.10).
- The position as to who is (or is meant to be) the employer must be agreed and set out in a single document before the hiring starts (regs.13–17).
- Agencies are obliged to have full information from the proposed hirer and work-seeker before introducing one to the other, and to make specified information available to each of them. This includes special rules on verification of qualifications of agency-supplied workers (regs.18–22).
- There are rules for protection of au pairs, with special protection for those under 18, including prohibition of loans on unfair terms (reg.24).

There is a potential problem in the interaction of reg.20 (requiring an agency to inform a client if information comes to light suggesting that a work-seeker is not suitable for an assignment) with reg.28 (confidentiality). The official view is that 'The express provision of Regulation 20 on disclosing information where it becomes clear that the worker is unsuitable will prevail over Regulation 28, in the same way as the disclosure provisions in the Act prevail' (Hansard, HL, 18 December 2003, col.1335). Whether this view is correct may have to be decided by the courts in due course.

9.9 EMPLOYERS' LIABILITY INSURANCE

Employers are required by statute to take out insurance in respect of liability to employees for bodily injury or disease sustained during employment in the UK. The minimum cover required was raised from £2 million to £5 million on

1 January 1999 (Employers' Liability (Compulsory Insurance) Act 1969 and the Employers' Liability (Compulsory Insurance) Regulations 1998, SI 1998/2573).

A copy of the insurance certificate must be displayed at each place of business where relevant employees work and the employer is required to retain each certificate or a copy 'for a period of 40 years beginning on the date on which the insurance to which it relates commences or is renewed'. The 40 year rule is not enforced as there is no penalty for breach. It is currently under review.

The Employers' Liability (Compulsory Insurance) Act 1969 does not guarantee an employee compensation for injury or disease sustained during employment as an employee must prove the employer's liability. However, it does ensure that if there is a liability the employer will have funds to meet it.

A minor change exempts very small companies that employ only their owner from the requirement to have employers' liability insurance, with effect from 28 February 2005 (Employers' Liability (Compulsory Insurance) (Amendment) Regulations 2004, SI 2004/2882).

9.10 FLEXIBLE WORKING

Since 6 April 2003 parents and others responsible for looking after children aged under six (under 18 if the child is disabled) have had the right for requests for flexible working arrangements to be taken seriously by their employers. The request must be to enable the employee to care for the child and is subject to the employee having been employed in the job for at least 26 weeks (Flexible Working (Eligibility, Complaints and Remedies) Regulations 2002, SI 2002/3236, reg.3(1)(a)). There is no set time for making an application but as from 6 April 2007 it must be made before the day on which the child concerned reaches the age of six or, if disabled, 18 (Flexible Working (Eligibility, Complaints and Remedies) (Amendment) Regulations 2006, SI 2006/3314, reg.5).

Since 6 April 2007 the right has been extended to cover requests for flexible working by employees with responsibility for caring for: (i) spouses/ partners; (ii) adult relatives as defined; and (iii) adults living at the same address as the employee (Flexible Working (Eligibility, Complaints and Remedies) (Amendment) Regulations 2006, SI 2006/3314).

A private member's Flexible Working Bill was introduced in the House of Commons in March 2007 proposing that the right to request flexible working should be extended to all parents with children under the age of 18. The Bill failed to become law but in May 2008 the government issued a draft legislative programme which includes proposals for a similar measure.

The request must be to enable the applicant to look after a person 'in respect of whom he satisfies such conditions as to relationship as the Secretary of State may specify by regulations'. An employee caught abusing the right would be likely to be subject to the employer's disciplinary procedures and might be faced with dismissal.

EMPLOYMENT LAW HANDBOOK

The request must relate to hours and/or time of work, to the place of work 'as between his home and a place of business of his employer' or such other type of change as may be specified in regulations (ERA 1996, s.80F(1)(a)). There are various grounds on which an employer can lawfully refuse such a request (ERA 1996, s.80G(1)(b)). Otherwise an employee will have a right to compensation and/or an order that the employer reconsider the refusal. An employment tribunal is entitled to examine the factual correctness of the grounds which the employer asserts are the reasons for refusal but does not have power to consider whether the employer acted fairly or reasonably in rejecting the request (*Commotion Ltd* v. *Rutty* [2006] IRLR 171, EAT).

Unless the employer agrees the application (and notifies the employee accordingly, in writing), he must 'within 28 days after the date on which the application is made' hold a meeting to discuss the application (Flexible Working (Procedural Requirements) Regulations 2002, SI 2002/3207, reg.3). The employer then has 14 days to notify the employee, in writing, of the decision. If the decision is a refusal, it must specify the grounds for refusal. The employee then has 14 days to appeal. The appeal must be in writing and must be heard by the employer within 14 days of receiving it (time limits can be varied by agreement between employer and employee, which must be recorded in writing by the employer (SI 2002/3207, reg.12)).

If the reason or principal reason for dismissal of an employee is that the employee made (or proposed to make) an application for flexible working arrangements as above, the dismissal will be automatically unfair (ERA 1996, s.104C). Although the normal qualification period of employment required before an employee can claim unfair dismissal does not apply (Employment Relations Act 2004, s.41) the basic requirement noted above that an employee must have been continuously employed for at least 26 weeks before having the right to request flexible working does apply.

There is nothing in the 'flexible work' provisions noted above to alter existing sex discrimination law under which in recent years it has frequently been possible for employees, especially women returning to work after maternity leave, to negotiate flexible working arrangements with their employers.

The main relevant law is in ERA 1996, ss.47E, 80(F) –(I) and 104C and the regulations noted above.

Both Acas, with a helpline on 08457 474747, and the BERR have excellent information on flexible working available on their websites. The BERR site provides forms for employers and employees to use in connection with applications for flexible work.

9.11 FREEDOM OF MOVEMENT

Freedom of movement of workers is one of the four basic freedoms of the EU. The overall effect is that 'a worker who is a national of a Member State may not, in the territory of another Member State, be treated differently from national workers by reason of his nationality in respect of any conditions of employment and work, in particular as regards remuneration, dismissal and, should he become unemployed, reinstatement or re-employment' (*Ninni-Orasche* v. *Bundesminister für Wissenschaft, Verkehr und Kunst*, ECJ Case C-413/01, 6 November 2003).

EC Directive 2004/38/EEC 'on the right of citizens of the Union and their family members to move and reside freely within the territory of the Member States' had to be implemented in Member States by 30 April 2006. It replaces and consolidates the various previous rules. In the UK the Directive is implemented by the Immigration (European Economic Area) Regulations 2006, SI 2006/1003 and the Immigration (Notices) (Amendment) Regulations 2006, SI 2006/2168. A whole raft of previous regulations is revoked. The other main changes are: (i) inclusion of civil partners as family members; (ii) introduction of a three-month initial right of residence is no longer conditional on the EU national being a worker or self-employed; and (iii) introduction of a permanent right of residence which generally applies after five years' residence.

Bulgaria and Romania joined the EU on 1 January 2007. The British government did not want to repeat the mistake it made in May 2004 when it did not take advantage of 'phase in derogations' which would have allowed it to postpone full freedom of access to citizens of the 10 countries which then joined the EU – there was a considerable underestimate of the numbers involved and quite serious problems followed. This time around, the European Union (Accessions) Act 2006 and the Accession (Immigration and Worker Authorisation) Regulations 2006, SI 2006/3317 (as amended) provide for a phasing-in period until December 2011 for full applicability of EU freedom of movement rules to people coming from Bulgaria and Romania to work in the UK.

There are detailed UK rules concerning recognition of professional qualifications in Member States (the European Communities (Recognition of Professional Qualifications) Regulations 2007, SI 2007/2781 and the European Qualifications (Health and Social Care Professions) Regulations 2007, SI 2007/3101). They cover a wide range of professions including accountants, barristers, solicitors, chiropractors, actuaries, civil engineers, physiotherapists and surveyors (auditors are still covered by the European Communities (Recognition of Professional Qualifications) (First General System) Regulations 2005, SI 2005/18, which was otherwise revoked by SI 2007/2781).

The European Court of Justice has ruled that a Member State is entitled to restrict a person who has a professional qualification in another Member State to carrying out only activities which his qualification allows him to do in the Member State in which it was obtained (*Colegio de Ingenieros de Caminos, Canales y Puertos* v. *Administracion del Estado*, ECJ Case C-330/03, 19 January 2006).

9.12 GUARANTEE PAYMENTS

Employees have a statutory right to a minimum level of 'fall back' pay from their employers in respect of any normal working day for which the employer provides no work. This is called a 'guarantee payment' (ERA 1996, ss.28–35). As from 1 February 2008 the normal maximum level of guarantee payment works out at £102 in any three-month period so, in practice, this is not a very valuable right. Jobseeker's allowance is far more important, and in any event many employees are entitled under their employment contracts to full wages/salary regardless of whether or not they are provided with work.

9.13 INSOLVENCY GUARANTEES

EC Directive 80/987/EEC requires Member States to set up and finance 'guarantee institutions' (Art.3) to ensure a degree of State-guaranteed financial protection for employees if their employer becomes insolvent.

This Directive has been amended so that as from 8 October 2005 Member States must ensure that they use a definition of 'insolvency' which includes insolvency proceedings other than liquidation and that part-time employees, fixed-term workers and temporary workers are not excluded from the rights legislated for by the Directive (Amending Directive 2002/74/EC).

Pursuant to these EC provisions if on insolvency of the employer an employee whose employment is terminated applies in writing to the Secretary of State then, subject to conditions and limits, the employee is entitled to recover from the National Insurance Fund certain amounts which the employer has failed to pay (ERA 1996, ss.182–190). These are:

- up to eight weeks' arrears of pay, subject to an overall maximum since 1 February 2008 of £2,640;
- unpaid pay for the minimum statutory notice period;
- up to six weeks' unpaid holiday pay in respect of the last 12 months;
- basic award (for unfair dismissal);
- repayment of premiums paid by an apprentice or articled clerk; and
- statutory redundancy pay, maternity pay, sick pay, paternity pay and adoption pay.

Arrears of pay for this purpose includes any protective award which a tribunal may order an employer to pay if proper consultation does not take place when 20 or more employees are being made redundant at one establishment. The EAT seemed to suggest in *Evans, Motture & Hutchins* v. *Permacell Finesse Ltd (in administration)* (unreported, EAT, 23 October 2007) that there is no statutory cap on the amount of a week's pay which can be taken into account when calculating the Secretary of State's liability in such a case. This is simply wrong (ERA 1996, ss.184(1)(a) and 186).

The starting point for enquiries is to telephone the Redundancy Payments Office helpline (tel: 0845 145 0004).

Separately, the Pensions Act 2004 established a Pension Protection Fund (PPF) with a view to protecting members of private sector defined benefit schemes whose employers become insolvent with insufficient funds in their pension scheme.

Following conflicting decisions in the High Court it was held by the Court of Appeal in August 2005 that when a company is in administration the fees and costs of the administrator, including those of an administrator who has ceased to act as such, take priority over amounts due to employees in respect of protective award and/or genuine pay in lieu of notice (*In re Ferrotech Ltd (and Other Cases)* [2006] ICR 205, CA).

9.14 ITEMISED PAY STATEMENTS

Employees have the right to a written itemised pay statement at or before the time at which any payment of wages or salary is made. This must contain details of gross and net wages or salary and any deductions (ERA 1996, s.8). They are entitled to a s.8 pay statement whether or not it is requested (*Coales v. John Wood & Co* [1986] ICR 71, EAT).

Writing includes typing, printing, lithography, photography and 'other modes of representing or reproducing words in a visible form' (Interpretation Act 1978, Sched.1). Presumably therefore an e-mail pay statement satisfies the requirements.

9.15 JOB ADVERTISEMENTS (ANTI-DISCRIMINATION RULES)

It is unlawful to publish or cause to be published an advertisement inviting applications for (amongst other things) employment, promotion or transfer of employment which indicates or might reasonably be understood to indicate that an application will or may be determined to any extent by reference to the applicant's gender, sexual orientation, colour, race, nationality or ethnic origins or to the applicant not being disabled or not having any particular disability (SDA 1975, s.38; RRA 1976, s.29; DDA 1995, s.16B; Equality Act (Sexual Orientation) Regulations 2007, SI 2007/1263).

In each case there is an exception if the discrimination would be lawful (so, for example, it might be lawful to advertise for a white male hunchbacked actor to play the role of Quasimodo in a production of the Hunchback of Notre Dame).

There is no specific mention of job advertisements in the religious discrimination regulations (Employment Equality (Religion or Belief) Regulations 2003, SI 2003/1660 or in the Employment Equality (Age) Regulations 2006,

SI 2006/1031. However, both sets of regulations make it clear that the discrimination they outlaw includes discrimination in connection with offers of employment.

The disability discrimination rules regarding job advertisements also ensure that a job advertisement will be unlawful if it suggests reluctance to make reasonable adjustments to accommodate an applicant's disability. In contrast to the sex and race discrimination rules, the disability discrimination rules permit positive discrimination (but note that the White Paper 'Framework for a Fairer Future – The Equality Bill' published on 26 June 2008 includes proposals to legitimise some positive discrimination in sex and race anti-discrimination legislation).

Third-party publishers (e.g. newspapers) have been liable for knowingly publishing discriminatory advertisements since 5 December 2005 when the Disability Discrimination Act 2005, s.10 came into effect. Publishers are not liable if they reasonably rely on a statement from the advertiser that the advertisement is permissible under DDA 1995. An advertiser who knowingly or recklessly makes such a statement which is false or misleading in a material respect commits an offence and can be liable to a fine of up to £5,000.

The law does not give individual job applicants the right to take legal action in respect of discriminatory advertisements. Such action may only be taken by the Commission for Equality and Human Rights (Equality Act 2006, Sched.3, paras.8, 23, 42 making appropriate amendments to SDA 1975, RRA 1976 and DDA 1995). In 2008 an ECJ Advocate General gave his opinion that the Belgian equivalent of the CEHR could bring a race discrimination claim against a company which publicly stated it would not employ Moroccans even though there was no evidence that it had ever refused to employ one (*Centrum voor Gelijkheid van Kansen en voor Racismebestrijding* v. *Firma Feryn NV*, ECJ case C54/07, 12 March 2008).

The discrimination Acts do not impose a legal duty on an employer to advertise a post (*Coker & Osamor* v. *Lord Chancellor* [2002] ICR 321, CA).

The employment law anti-discrimination rules are considered generally at **Chapters 14** to **17**.

9.16 LAY OFF AND SHORT TIME

In most 'normal' salaried jobs an employee has no legally enforceable right to work. The employer's only obligation is to pay the agreed salary.

When suspension or lay off is in point the important question is thus usually not whether an employer has the right temporarily to suspend or lay off an employee, but whether the employee is entitled to receive pay during the suspension period. The answer to this will normally depend on the terms of the employee's contract and any conditions which may apply (e.g. a collective agreement). For this purpose it is important to remember that implied terms in employment contracts are just as relevant as express terms.

If an employer purports to suspend or lay off an employee without pay when the employer has no right to do so, the suspension may amount to a fundamental breach of contract. In that case the employee will be entitled, if she wishes, to treat the contract as repudiated by the employer and treat herself as constructively dismissed.

An employee who is laid off without pay may be entitled to a statutory guarantee payment from the employer (see above). Further, if the employee has completed two years' continuous employment and is laid off for at least four consecutive weeks (or six non-consecutive weeks in a 13-week period) she will be entitled to claim statutory redundancy pay. This right also applies if the employee was put on short time for similar periods (a week of short time is one in respect of which she has received less than half a normal week's pay).

An improperly handled suspension can give an employee legitimate grounds for resigning and claiming unfair constructive dismissal on the basis that the employer was in breach of the implied term of trust and confidence (*Camden & Islington Mental Health and Social Care Trust* v. *Atkinson* (unreported, EAT, 20 August 2007) and see notes under 'Implied terms in employment contracts/duties of employer' at **section 3.2.3**).

If an employee is suspended pending an enquiry (e.g. dismissed for misconduct but suspended while an appeal is being considered), the employee's legal rights will be affected by the eventual outcome of the enquiry/appeal. If the dismissal is then confirmed it will take effect from the day of the original dismissal which will in law be the effective date of termination ('edt') of the employment (*J. Sainsbury Ltd* v. *Savage* [1981] ICR 1, CA). If on the other hand the enquiry/appeal results in the employee being reinstated the dismissal will be deemed to have been of no effect with the result that he will be entitled to full back-pay for the period of the suspension (and as he has not been dismissed he will not be able to mount an unfair dismissal claim) (*Ladbrokes Betting & Gaming Ltd* v. *Ally* (unreported, EAT, 11 May 2006)).

9.17 MINIMUM WAGE

In March 2008 the government announced increases in the National Minimum Wage (NMW) to take effect from 1 October 2008 as follows (figures in italics apply before that date):

- £5.73 (*£5.52*) per hour for adults aged 22 and over
- £4.77 (*£4.60*) per hour for 18 to 21 year olds; and
- £3.53 (*£3.40*) per hour for 16 and 17 year olds.

The maximum amount which can be taken into account when determining whether the minimum wage has been paid where the employer provides a worker with accommodation, commonly called the 'accommodation offset', is £4.46 per day or £31.22 per week with effect from 1 October 2008 (previously £4.30 per day or £30.10 per week).

There are special rules for farm (and related) workers set out in annual Agricultural Wages Board Wages Orders.

A person qualifies for the NMW if he ordinarily works in the UK under his contract and has ceased to be of compulsory school age. Workers, as defined, qualify for the NMW even if they are not employees. In determining whether, for the purposes of the minimum wage legislation, a person is a worker rather than self-employed, the test to be applied is to ask whether the 'dominant purpose' of the contractual relationship is the provision of personal services. If so, the person is likely to be a worker and therefore covered by the minimum wage legislation. The fact that there is no mutuality of obligation when the work is not being performed is of little significance in determining the status of the relationship when the person is actually at work. It is simply one of the factors to take into account in deciding whether a person is a worker, an employee or is 'self-employed' (*James* v. *Redcats (Brands) Ltd* [2007] IRLR 296). The general question of worker and employee status is considered in **Chapter 2**.

- *Agency workers* are covered (National Minimum Wage Act 1998, s.34).
- *Apprentices*. The basic position is that apprentices aged below 19 do not qualify for the NMW and older ones do not qualify during the first 12 months of their employment if they are under 26 (see National Minimum Wage Regulations 1999, reg.12(2) and *HM Revenue & Customs* v. *Rinaldi-Tranter* (unreported, EAT, 13 September 2007). Nevertheless, in 2005 an apprentice succeeded in showing that as a matter of contract he was entitled to be paid at the rate of the NMW, although as an apprentice he was excluded from the statutory right (*Garrett Electrical Ltd* v. *Cotton* (unreported, EAT, 15 November 2005)). A new class of persons in respect of whom special NMW rules can be made, namely persons who have attained the age of 26 and are 'undertaking a course of further education requiring attendance for a period of work experience' has been added by the National Minimum Wage Act 1998 (Amendment) Regulations 2007, SI 2007/2042. The Solicitors Regulation Authority sets minimum rates of pay for solicitors under training contracts. As of 1 August 2008 these are £18,420 for trainee solicitors in central London and £16,500 elsewhere.
- *Carers and workers 'on-call'*. In a decision welcomed by care sector employers, the Court of Appeal held in February 2003 that a carer who worked a seven-hour day for three duty days and then had three days off but had to be in residence and available 24 hours per day during her three duty days should be treated as engaged in 'unmeasured work' (National Minimum Wage Regulations 1999, reg.6) rather than 'time work' (National Minimum Wage Regulations 1999, reg.3). The result was that the carer's daily pay, at the rate of £31.40 per day, had to be divided by seven for NMW purposes (meaning that it was lawful as being just over the then applicable NMW). The carer had argued that her daily pay should be divided by 24 (which would have produced an hourly rate well below the NMW). The case was

brought under the 'unlawful deductions from wages' provisions of ERA 1996, s.23 but is relevant in the context of the NMW (*Walton* v. *Independent Living Organisation Ltd* [2003] ICR 688, CA).

A subsequent EAT judgment went the other way. In January 2006 the EAT ruled that on-call time spent by a care-worker worker was 'salaried hours work' within the meaning of National Minimum Wage Regulations 1999, reg.4 even though she was allowed to sleep while on call. The worker in question was provided with tied accommodation at her workplace but was required to be available on site to answer calls (*Macartney* v. *Oversley House Management* [2006] IRLR 514, EAT).

Overruling an employment tribunal, the EAT has held that a person can be regarded as working even though he is asleep. This will be so if he is sleeping at his employer's premises and the reason he is sleeping there is that his employer requires him to be in those premises for the employer's purposes (*Anderson* v. *Jarvis Hotels plc* (unreported, EAT, 30 May 2006)). Although the NMW rules are not the same as those applied by the Working Time Regulations useful comparisons can be drawn when considering the position of workers 'on call' (see **Chapter 7**). Care must always be taken to ensure that the two are kept intellectually separate.

- *Homeworkers* are covered by the National Minimum Wage Act 1998 even if they do not come within the normal definition of 'worker' because they are not obliged to perform their work personally (National Minimum Wage Act 1998 s.35 and *Bridges & ors* v. *Industrial Rubber plc* (unreported, EAT, 21 September 2004), the case of 'the Gosport Nine'). In the important *James* v. *Redcats (Brands) Ltd* case noted above the final decision (February 2008) of the employment tribunal to which the EAT remitted the case was that Mrs James was not only a 'worker' but also was a 'home worker' for NMW purposes. See also 'Piece workers' below.
- *House sitters*. In at least one case an employment tribunal has held that a house sitter was entitled to be paid at NMW rates for all the time when present in the house except when sleeping or free to leave the premises. The 'Resident family workers and resident home helps' exemption noted below did not apply.
- *Piece workers*. There are obviously special difficulties in ensuring that a piece worker is paid a minimum wage.

The old requirement for employers to make an estimate of the hours needed to complete a task and the related 'four/fifths rule' were abolished from 1 October 2004. Since then anyone doing what is technically called 'output work' must be paid either the NMW for all hours worked or alternatively be paid under a system called 'rated output work' (National Minimum Wage Regulations 1999 (Amendment) Regulations 2004, SI 2004/1161). Under this system the employer must pay each worker for the number of hours that a person working at the 'mean hourly output rate' takes to produce the number of pieces made. There are complicated rules for calculation of the mean hourly rate. As from 6 April 2005, the minimum was increased by a multiplier of 120 per cent.

Employers must give piece workers a comprehensive written notice making it clear that they are entitled to be paid a fair piece rate, providing the telephone number of the NMW helpline and setting out various other details prescribed by the regulations.

- *Resident family workers, au pairs and resident home helps* are excluded. Resident family members (but not others) working for a family business are also excluded (National Minimum Wage Regulations 1999, reg.2(3) and (4)).
- *Self-employed workers*. It goes without saying that the self-employed do not have rights under the NMW rules.
- *Trainees on government training schemes* are excluded from entitlement to the NMW while under age 19 or during the first 12 months if they are 19 or over (National Minimum Wage Regulations 1999 (Amendment) Regulations 2001, SI 2001/1108 and see 'Apprentices' above).

Enforcement of NMW legislation is effected by HM Revenue & Customs on behalf of the BERR. They claim to have helped over 78,000 workers recover around £27 million in unpaid wages since 1999 (BERR Press Release, 6 December 2007 'Government signals crackdown on rogue employers who avoid minimum wage'). There were no prosecutions under the National Minimum Wage Act until August 2007 when a woman was convicted for obstruction, contrary to the National Minimum Wage Act 1998, s.31(5). In October 2007 Torbay Council pleaded guilty to the offence of neglecting to furnish information contrary to the National Minimum Wage Act 1998, s.31(5)(b).

Currently employers face a penalty only if they continue to pay below the NMW after having been caught. The enforcement rules are to be toughened under proposals in the 2008 Employment Bill. In particular there will be a new 'notice of underpayment' which will include an obligatory financial penalty of 50 per cent of the amount of NMW outstanding, subject to a minimum penalty of £100 and a maximum of £5,000. Employment tribunals will have jurisdiction to hear appeals against these notices.

The complex record-keeping requirements in the original draft of the National Minimum Wage Regulations were removed and replaced by the much simpler provisions which are now in reg.38. Records must be kept for at least three years and must be in a form which enables the information kept about a worker in respect of a pay reference period to be produced in a single document. A worker has the right to require his employer to produce records and to inspect and copy those records (National Minimum Wage Act 1998, s.10). This applies notwithstanding that at the time of the request the worker had ceased to work for the employer (*Madani* v. *Spirit SSR Ltd* (unreported, EAT, 18 November 2003)).

Tips paid directly by a customer to staff do not count as wages for minimum wage purposes (National Minimum Wage Regulations 1999, reg.31(1)(e)). However, if the tips are collected and distributed centrally through the employer's payroll system, as is normal if a restaurant adds a service charge to a bill and shares the total service charges received amongst staff such as in the 'tronc' system, the amount paid to an employee is treated as part of his wages (*Nerva & Ors* v. *Paradiso E Inferno Wine Bar* [2002] IRLR 815, ECtHR).

There is an NMW helpline on 0845 6000 678 (Monday to Friday 9 am to 5 pm).

9.18 NOTICE PERIODS

Any employees who have completed one month or more continuous employment with the same employer (or an associated employer) are entitled to a statutory minimum period of notice. They will, of course, be entitled to longer notice than the statutory minimum if the contract so provides (either expressly or by implied term) (ERA 1996, s.86). If employed for less than one month, a common law requirement of reasonable notice applies.

The statutory minimum notice entitlement ranges from one to 12 weeks as follows:

- one week if period of continuous employment is between one month and two years;
- one week for each year of continuous employment between two and 12 years;
- 12 weeks if period of continuous employment is 12 years or more.

An employee who is being dismissed by reason of redundancy is entitled to the same notice period as that to which the employee would be entitled if being dismissed for any other reason.

Quite apart from the minimum statutory notice periods required by ERA 1996, common law requires that subject to any express agreement an employment contract may only be lawfully terminated (by either party) if reasonable notice is given. What is reasonable will depend on all the facts and circumstances including the employee's status and, if relevant, the notice arrangements agreed for other employees in similar positions with the same employer. One month's notice was too little and three months was reasonable in a case in 2000 in which a senior employee was dismissed only three months after starting work (*Fahrenheit 451 (Communications) Ltd* v. *Clark* [2000] All ER 849, EAT).

In general, the length of notice which might be found reasonable at common law if none has been agreed might be approximately as follows, subject in every case to the statutory minimum and depending on (amongst other matters) length of service:

- Weekly paid staff: a week's notice.
- Monthly paid staff: a month's notice.

- Middle management: three months' notice.
- Senior management: three to six months' notice.
- Directors: six to 12 months' notice.

At least in Scotland, there is no general implied term giving an employer a right to dismiss an employee on zero or shorter notice by providing 'pay in lieu of notice' (*Morrish* v. *NTL Group Ltd* [2007] CSIH 56, 3 July 2007).

There is an argument that if an employee is wrongfully dismissed without notice and as a result does not complete the qualifying period required for claiming unfair dismissal, but would have completed that period if he had been given and served out proper notice, damages for the wrongful dismissal should be increased to take account of the loss of chance of making a successful unfair dismissal claim. This argument found favour with the EAT in 1999 (*Raspin* v. *United New Shops Ltd* [1999] IRLR 9), but was criticised by the Court of Appeal in 2004 (*Virgin Net Ltd* v. *Harper* [2004] EWCA (Civ) 271). It was finally killed off by the EAT in 2005 (*Wise Group* v. *Mitchell* [2005] ICR 896).

9.19 OVERSEAS EMPLOYMENT

Former statutory rules, which spelled out that most employees who ordinarily work outside the UK were not entitled to unfair dismissal and some other rights, were abolished on 25 October 1999 (ERA 1996, s.196 was repealed by the Employment Relations Act 1999, s.32(3) and Sched.9).

Since then the position has been governed generally by the common law. Subject to some statutory provisions in discrimination cases, the government is on record as taking the view that special rules are not needed as '... the principles of our own domestic law are enough to ensure that our legislation does not apply in inappropriate circumstances' (Hansard, HL, 8 July 1999, cols.1089/1090). No doubt in straightforward cases that is true, but in the many less straightforward ones which are common in the age of easy travel in which we live this was an invitation to argument and litigation. Not surprisingly a whole series of cases has followed in rapid succession to test what exactly this meant in practice.

The House of Lords clarified the position in January 2006, making it clear that for an employment tribunal to have jurisdiction in an unfair dismissal case it is not essential that the employment in question should have been in Great Britain. Rather, it is sufficient that the employment relationship is closely connected with Great Britain (*Lawson* v. *Serco* [2006] IRLR 289, HL). Although it will only be in unusual circumstances that an employee who works and is based abroad comes within the scope of the unfair dismissal provisions, the House of Lords gave two examples of situations in which the employment relationship might be sufficiently closely connected with Great Britain to enable an employment tribunal to entertain an unfair dismissal claim: (i) where an employee is posted abroad to work for a business conducted in Britain; and/or (ii) where he is working in a political or social British enclave abroad.

The EAT later ruled that the principles in *Lawson* v. *Serco* (above) apply in disability discrimination cases as well as in unfair dismissal cases (*Williams* v. *University of Nottingham* [2007] IRLR 660, EAT). They also apply in cases under the Fixed-Term Employees (Prevention of Less Favourable Treatment) Regulations 2002, SI 2002/2034 (*Collins & Ashbourne* v. *Department for Constitutional Affairs* (unreported, EAT, 12 October 2007)).

However, the *Lawson* v. *Serco* principles do not apply to breach of contract claims nor to claims under WTR 1998 (see *Bleuse* v. *MBT Transport Ltd & anor* [2008] IRLR 264, EAT). In contract claim cases this is simply because *Lawson* v. *Serco* applies to statutory claims only. In claims under the Working Time Regulations, which of course are statutory claims, the logic is that the rule in *Lawson* v. *Serco* has to be modified because the statutory right is British implementation of a directly enforceable right given by EU law. If this were not so the principle of effectiveness would not be satisfied and there would be no effective UK remedy for a breach of the EU right.

There are specific statutory provisions in the anti-discrimination legislation which generally applies in the employment field if employment is 'at an establishment in Great Britain' (EqPA 1970, s.1; SDA 1975, s.6; RRA 1976, s.4; DDA 1995, s.4(6); Employment Equality (Sexual Orientation) Regulations 2003, SI 2003/1661, reg.6; Employment Equality (Religion or Belief) Regulations 2003, SI 2003/1660, reg.6; Employment Equality (Age) Regulations 2006, SI 2006/1031, reg.10).

At least for SDA 1975 (and EqPA 1970) purposes 'employment is to be regarded as being at an establishment in Great Britain unless the employee does his work wholly outside Great Britain' (SDA 1975, s.10(1) as amended by the Equal Opportunities (Employment Legislation) (Territorial Limits) Regulations 1999, SI 1999/3163, reg.2(2), dropping the word 'mainly' from the previous 'wholly or mainly').

If an employment is wholly outside Great Britain, it is not covered by SDA 1975 or EqPA 1970 (*Haughton* v. *Olau Line (UK) Ltd* [1985] ICR 711, EAT). In determining this question regard must be had not only to where the employee was working at the time of the alleged discrimination but throughout the whole period of employment (*Saggar* v. *Ministry of Defence* [2005] ICR 1073, CA). The practical effect is that the test as to whether a tribunal has jurisdiction in discrimination cases is similar to that which applied in unfair dismissal cases under ERA 1996, s.196 until its repeal as noted above.

The October 1999 change noted above has not altered rules (in ERA 1996, s.215) which ensure that employees will not break a period of continuous employment by temporarily going to work overseas (even though they are not always entitled to include time spent abroad towards counting the length of that continuous employment).

9.20 PATENTS AND INVENTIONS

Ownership of inventions made by employees in the course of their duties belongs to the employer if either 'an invention might reasonably be expected to result from the carrying out [by the employee] of his duties' or if at the time of making the invention the employee had 'a special obligation to further the interests of the employer's undertaking'.

An employee is not automatically entitled to any royalty or other reward derived from an invention he has made if the invention was made in the course of his work (*Sterling Engineering Co Ltd* v. *Patchett* [1955] 1 All ER 369).

However, if the employer refuses to make an acceptable voluntary arrangement the employee can apply to the court or to the Comptroller of Patents at the Patent Office for a compensation order (Patents Act 1977 s.40 as amended by Patents Act 2004, s.10). Procedure is set out in the Patents Rules 2007, SI 2007/3291.

The conditions for an employee/inventor to be entitled to claim a payment from his employer are:

- he must have made an invention belonging to the employer for which a patent has been granted;
- the patent must be one which is of outstanding benefit to the employer 'having regard among other things to the size and nature of the employer's undertaking'. To count as an 'outstanding benefit' it must be something out of the ordinary when looked at in the context of the activities of the employer concerned and more than just 'substantial' or 'good' (*In Memco-Med Ltd's Patent* [1992] RPC 403). In addition it must be an actual, not merely a potential, benefit (*British Steel plc's Patent* [1992] RPC 117);
- that 'by reason of those facts it is just that the employee should' have compensation from the employer;
- the employee must have made an application 'within the prescribed period' to the court or the Comptroller (the period beginning with the date of grant of the patent and ending one year after the patent ceased to have effect – Patents Rules 2007, SI 2007/3291, r.91).

The amendment made to the Patent Act 1977, s.40 by the Patent Act 2004 ensures that a patented invention can qualify an employee for compensation regardless of whether it is the invention or the patent which is of outstanding benefit to the employer, blocking a previous loophole.

Disputes as to ownership of an invention can be brought as 'entitlement proceedings' before the Comptroller (i.e. the Comptroller General of Patents, Designs and Trade Marks).

9.21 RIGHT NOT TO WORK

It is specifically provided that no court shall make any order which compels 'an employee to do any work or attend at any place for the doing of any work' (TULRCA 1992, s.236).

This is a statutory assertion of what was long considered to be the common law position. However, in the 1960s and 1970s there were suggestions that the position was not quite so simple (*C.H. Giles & Co Ltd* v. *Morris* [1972] 1 All ER 960). Trade unions became concerned that the courts might order specific performance of employment contracts on a regular basis and that failure to obey could be contempt of court. This would have made it difficult for them to organise lawful strikes or other withdrawals of labour. Accordingly, at union behest, what is now TULRCA 1992, s.236 was enacted.

Of course if an employee exercises his right not to work he will normally be in breach of contract and risk disciplinary proceedings and even dismissal.

The circumstances in which an employee has a legal right to time off work, sometimes with pay, are considered at **section 7.3**.

9.22 RIGHT TO WORK

There is no UK law which gives a person a 'right to work' although there are laws, outside the scope of this book, which make it illegal to prevent a person from going to work if that person wishes to do so. Deliberate confusion of the two 'rights' may be common as a debating ploy but has no substance in law.

As a general rule, courts will not grant an injunction requiring an employer to employ someone where an award of compensation or damages would be an adequate remedy. Compensation or damages will normally be adequate compensation to an employee for breach of contract by the employer and are the normal awards made by courts and tribunals in employment cases (*American Cyanamid Co* v. *Ethicon Ltd* [1975] AC 396 and *Powell* v. *London Borough of Brent* [1988] ICR 176, CA).

The three classic examples of types of employment in which the employee can claim that the employer is obliged to provide him with work, failing which he may be able to claim constructive dismissal, are:

(a) pieceworkers (*Devonald* v. *Rosser & Sons* [1906] 2 KB 728);
(b) actors who need publicity to keep their earning power and reputation (*Herbert Clayton and Jack Waller Ltd* v. *Oliver* [1930] AC 209); and
(c) workers who are paid 'by commission' (*Bauman* v. *Hulton Press Ltd* [1952] 2 All ER 1121).

It is clear that an employee who has a particular skill or training and who needs work to 'keep in practice' is entitled to be provided with that type of work and can resign and claim constructive dismissal if it is available but passed to other employees or is outsourced (*Breach* v. *Epsylon Industries Ltd* [1976] ICR 316, EAT, a case involving an engineer and *Land Securities Trillium Ltd* v. *Thornley* [2005] IRLR 765, EAT, a case involving an employed architect but the same principle would presumably apply in, for example, the case of a computer programmer or an aircraft pilot).

However, little in the law is completely black and white and more recent cases suggest a refinement. Even though an employer has no obligation to provide work for an employee, the employer may have a duty not to withhold work if work of the type for which the employee was employed is available and the employee wishes to do it (*William Hill Organisation Ltd* v. *Tucker* [1999] ICR 291, CA, and *Woodfine* v. *British Telecom plc* (unreported, EAT, 10 December 2003)).

The High Court has recently ruled that, in principle, a doctor is entitled to an injunction requiring his hospital employer to continue employing him while disciplinary procedures are completed (*Gryf-Lowczowski* v. *Hinchingbooke Healthcare NHS Trust* [2006] IRLR 100 (QBD) and *Kircher* v. *Hillingdon Primary Care Trust* [2006] EWHC 21 (QBD)). The Court of Appeal has confirmed that it is proper for the courts to grant such an injunction provided there is no risk to patients, pointing out that suspension of a professional person even on full pay inevitably casts a shadow over the employee's competence (*Mezey* v. *South West London and St George's Mental Health NHS Trust* [2007] IRLR 244, CA).

The Court of Appeal has also stated that the right to earn a living is not a 'possession' capable of protection under the European Convention on Human Rights. It confirmed this in 2006 when it was one of the points raised by the Countryside Alliance in its unsuccessful attempt to have the Hunting Act 2004 declared unlawful (*R* v. *The CountrySide Alliance & ors*) v. *Attorney-General & ors* [2006] EWCA Civ 817).

9.23 SMOKING AT WORK

New statutory rules have applied since 1 July 2007. Nearly all enclosed and substantially enclosed public places and workplaces in England, including enclosed parts of vehicles, have been smoke free since 6 am on 1 July 2007. As it is hard to imagine an enclosed space which is not 'substantially enclosed' the distinction can in practice be disregarded.

Premises are 'smoke-free' if they are enclosed or substantially enclosed and the circumstances set out in Health Act 2006, s.2 apply. This provides that they must be smoke free when open to the public or all the time:

... if they are used as a place of work –

(a) by more than one person (even if the persons who work there do so at different times, or only intermittently), or

(b) where members of the public might attend for the purpose of seeking or receiving goods or services from the person or persons working there (even if members of the public are not always present).

Under the rules it is an offence to:

- smoke in any such place (the ban covers being in possession of anything lit which contains tobacco, or 'being in possession of any other lit substance in a form in which it could be smoked' not just smoking tobacco as was intended at one stage (Health Act 2006, s.1(2)(b));
- allow smoking in any such place; or
- fail to display a 'no-smoking sign' of a type and size and in a position specified in the regulations in any smoke-free premises or vehicle – in practice this is the most generally relevant of the three offences as it is committed automatically unless positive action is taken to display appropriate notices in the form and manner required and because it can involve a heavier fine or penalty than smoking where smoking is forbidden.

Indoor smoking rooms at work are no longer allowed. If people wish to smoke at work, they will have to go outside. Employers can of course build a shelter outside but if they do so they must take care to ensure that it does not become a 'substantially enclosed' area. There is nothing in the regulations requiring smokers to be any specific distance away from an enclosed place but if smokers were to gather under an office window there could be health and safety issues quite separate from the smoke-free regulations.

Special provision is made for fixed penalties to apply in most cases of infringement, with special discounts for speedy payment. Thus in most cases, and provided they pay the appropriate fixed penalty within the specified period (basically 29 days), offenders will not be formally prosecuted and will not get a criminal record.

The rules for smoke-free vehicles are complicated (especially as, amazingly, England, Wales and Scotland each have slightly different rules about signs in vehicles) but essentially the position throughout Great Britain is that it is now an offence for an employee with a company vehicle to smoke while carrying a work colleague or if the vehicle is used by more than one employee (even if only occasionally and even if all the users are smokers). The position is slightly different if the vehicle is a convertible.

The various smoke-free regulations are made under provisions of the Health Act 2006. This provides for various possible defences, including one to the effect that it was not reasonable to comply with the rules.

The smoke-free regulations in England are as follows:

- Smoke-free (Premises and Enforcement) Regulations 2006, SI 2006/3368;
- Smoke-free (Vehicle Operators and Penalty Notices) Regulations 2007, SI 2007/760;

- Smoke-free (Penalties and Discounted Amounts) Regulations 2007, SI 2007/764;
- Smoke-free (Exemptions and Vehicles) Regulations 2007, SI 2007/765;
- Smoke-free (Signs) Regulations 2007, SI 2007/923.

Similar 'smoke-free' rules have applied in Wales from 2 April 2007 (Smoke-free Premises etc. (Wales) Regulations 2007, SI 2007/787 W.68) and in Northern Ireland from 30 April 2007 (Smoking (Northern Ireland) Order 2006, SI 2006/2957 NI 20 and the Smoking (2006 Order) (Commencement) Order (Northern Ireland) 2007, SR 2007/118). Scotland has had its own no-smoking (in public and workplaces) rules since 26 March 2006 (Smoking, Health and Social Care (Scotland) Act 2005).

9.24 SUNDAY TRADING

The Sunday Trading Act 1994 allows large shops to open for six hours between 10 am and 6 pm on Sundays for serving retail customers (a large shop as defined is basically a shop whose internal floor area exceeds 280 sq. metres/3,000 sq. ft.). Special provisions allow certain large shops such as motorway service stations to stay open all day on Sundays and a Sunday Trading (Horticulture) Bill was introduced in the House of Lords in March 2008 to allow garden centres and similar establishments to stay open for longer hours.

There are no restrictions on smaller shops opening on Sundays.

The Christmas Day (Trading) Act 2004 combined with the Sunday Trading Act 1994 make it illegal for a large shop in England or Wales to open on Christmas Day.

Shop workers and betting workers have special employment law rights in relation to Sunday working (ERA 1996, ss.36–43, 45, 101 and 232, as extended to Scotland by the Sunday Working (Scotland) Act 2003, include protections for employers against arbitrary refusals to work).

These special rights of qualifying shop workers and betting workers are rights not to be:

(a) dismissed, or selected for redundancy because of refusal to work on Sundays, or on any particular Sunday (contravention is automatically unfair dismissal);

(b) 'subjected to any detriment' for refusing to work on Sundays, or on any particular Sunday.

No qualifying period of employment is required.

These special rights of a shop worker depend on the shop worker being either a protected shop worker or an opted-out shop worker.

In essence, an 'opted-out shop worker' is a shop worker (as defined) who has given her employer written notice (signed and dated – called an opting-out notice) that she objects to Sunday working and who since doing so has worked continuously as a shop worker without giving an opting-in notice (ERA 1996, s.40 and s.41).

An opting-in notice is effectively the mirror image of an opting-out notice, stating that the shop worker wishes to work on Sunday or does not object to doing so (ERA 1996, s.36(6)).

It is worth noting that although in employment law generally the term 'worker' is wider than the term 'employee', the definitions of shop worker (in ERA 1996, s.232) and betting worker (in ERA 1996, s.233) are different. Only employees come within these special definitions. It follows that an employee who works in a shop can be a shop worker and thus have the right to opt out of Sunday working but that a self-employed worker who works in a shop will not be a shop worker as defined and will therefore not have that right.

Employers must give an explanatory statement in the prescribed form to any shop worker who may be required to work on a Sunday as well as on other days (ERA 1996, s.42). This does not apply to any employee who is employed to work only on Sundays (ERA 1996, s.40(3)(b) applied by ERA 1996, s.42(1)).

Shop workers are entitled to an 'early closing day' once a week (Shops (Early Closing Days) Act 1965, s.3).

9.25 WHISTLEBLOWING

Whistleblowing is defined in Chambers Dictionary as 'giving information (usually to the authorities) about illegal and underhand practices'.

ERA 1996, ss.43A–43L (inserted by the Public Interest Disclosure Act 1998) give legal protection to any worker against dismissal or other detriment as a result of his making a 'protected disclosure'. Essentially, this refers to disclosing information relating to crimes, breaches of a legal obligation, miscarriages of justice, dangers to health and safety or the environment and to the concealing of evidence relating to any of these. The rules were introduced in response to disasters and scandals such as the Bristol Royal Infirmary heart operations, North Wales child abuse, Matrix Churchill, Maxwell, Clapham Rail and Zebrugge affairs after each of which official enquiries revealed that workers had been aware of dangers but were too scared to sound the alarm.

The EAT has ruled that the expression 'legal obligation' in this context can refer to obligations arising out of a contract of employment as well as statutory obligations (*Parkins* v. *Sodexho Ltd* [2002] IRLR 109, EAT, a ruling with potentially wide significance as it suggests a way for some dismissed employees who have not completed the one year qualifying period of employment needed for unfair dismissal to bring a claim). It is enough that the worker honestly believed that the matter in respect of breach of which he was blowing the whistle was a genuine legal obligation even if in fact it was not (*Babula*

v. *Waltham Forest College* [2007] ICR 1026, CA). Previous case law suggesting the contrary (*Kraus* v. *Penna plc & anor* [2004] IRLR 260, EAT) is wrong.

To qualify for whistleblowing protection, the worker must act in good faith and have reasonable grounds for believing that the information disclosed indicates the existence of one of the above problems. However, a disclosure is not made in good faith if 'the dominant or predominant purpose of making it was for some ulterior motive' (*Street* v. *Derbyshire Unemployed Workers Centre* [2005] ICR 97, CA).

A person employed by his own company which supplies his services to an employment agency, which in turn provides his services to an end-user, still counts as a 'worker' for whistleblowing law purposes and can bring a claim against the end-user (*Croke* v. *Hydro Aluminium Worcester Ltd* [2007] ICR 1303, EAT).

There is a statutory list of 'prescribed persons' to whom protected disclosures can be made (Public Interest Disclosure (Prescribed Persons) Order 1999, SI 1999/1549 as amended). To be protected the disclosure must be made to a person who is reasonably believed to have 'ongoing legal responsibility for dealing with it at the time the disclosure is made' (*Premier Mortgage Connections Ltd* v. *Miller* (unreported, EAT, 14 September 2007)).

Members of the Armed Forces and persons who normally work outside the UK are excluded from 'whistleblowing' protection. Police officers were previously excluded as well but have been protected from 1 April 2004 (Police Reform Act 2002, s.37) and the Independent Police Complaints Commission has been added to the list of 'prescribed persons' to whom disclosures can be made (Public Interest Disclosure (Prescribed Persons) (Amendment) Order 2004, SI 2004/3265).

The Financial Services Authority (FSA) has shown particular concern to encourage 'whistleblowing' where appropriate in the financial services industry and its Code on Corporate Governance, which applies to listed companies, includes a whistleblowing protection clause.

There is no cap on the amount an employment tribunal can award in a whistleblowing case. Compensation will be calculated in the same way as under the anti-discrimination legislation (*Virgo Fidelis Senior School* v. *Boyle* [2004] IRLR 268, EAT). Very large amounts have been awarded – in July 2005 the Leeds Tribunal awarded £477,000 to a prison officer named Carol Lingard who had reported bullying and intimidation of inmates and in one of the very first whistleblowing cases an accountant, Tony Fernandes, was awarded almost £300,000 for blowing the whistle against his managing director at Netcom Consultants in Reading.

9.26 WRITTEN STATEMENT OF PARTICULARS OF EMPLOYMENT

An employer must give each employee a written statement of employment particulars within two months of employment commencing (ERA 1996, s.1, implementing the EC Written Particulars Directive 91/553/EEC). If the employee is dismissed before the two months is up he is not entitled to a written statement of employment particulars (*RKS Services* v. *Palen* (unreported, EAT, 2 November 2006)).

The two-month period is reduced if the employee is going to work abroad for more than one month. In that case the written statement must be given to the employee before he leaves to start his overseas job if he will depart before expiry of the two months. ERA 1996, s.1 sets out a lengthy list of items as required by Directive 91/553/EEC which must be included in the statement, including the names of the parties and the date on which the employee's period of continuous employment began, taking into account any employment with a previous employer which counts towards that period (meaning, essentially, employment by an associated employer).

There is no legal requirement for a contract of employment itself to be in writing. It is, of course, normal and highly desirable for there to be a written contract. In practice, if there is no formal written employment contract a written statement of particulars of employment will usually be good evidence of contractual terms. This will certainly be so if the particulars so provide (*Parker* v. *Northumbrian Water* (unreported, EAT, 12 May 2008)).

Although the legal requirement is to provide employees with a 'written statement of particulars of employment' rather than a written contract, the law provides that if there is a written contract there is no need for a separate written statement provided that the contract contains all the required details (ERA 1996, s.7A inserted by the Employment Act 2002, s.37). A 'contract of employment or letter of engagement' given by an employer to an employee before the employment starts will normally count as being given within the time limits (ERA 1996, s.7B inserted by the Employment Act 2002, s.37).

At one time, failure to provide an employee with a written statement of particulars of his employment was a criminal offence, but this has not been the case for many years. An employee can, however, apply to an employment tribunal to ensure compliance (ERA 1996, s.11). As from 1 October 2004 the tribunal normally has to award either two or four times a week's pay (as defined) if an employer has failed to provide written particulars of employment to an employee. However, this is not a free-standing right and only applies if the failure is established in the course of other proceedings before the tribunal (Employment Act 2002, s.38). The maximum on a week's pay for this purpose is the same as for a basic award on unfair dismissal, currently £330.

Employers must also give employees a written statement of any changes to their terms of employment (ERA 1996, s.4). An employee who is dismissed having completed at least one year's continuous employment can require the employer to give him a written statement 'giving particulars of the reasons for the employee's dismissal'. The employer has 14 days to comply. If the employee is dismissed while pregnant or on maternity leave or adoption leave, the normal rule is that the one year's continuous employment qualification is not required and the employer must provide the written statement of reasons even if no request is made (ERA 1996, s.92).

A dedicated website at **www.emplaw.co.uk/lshandbook** provides links to judgments and other source material referred to in this chapter.

CHAPTER 10
Termination of employment

10.1 GENERAL INFORMATION

Contracts of employment can be terminated in a number of ways. The classic examples of termination involve dismissal or resignation. However, termination can also occur by the death or insolvency of one of the parties, or by frustration of the contract. Constructive dismissal is a hybrid between dismissal and resignation. Termination can also occur by mutual agreement (a common form of which is the expiry of a fixed-term contract).

Particular problems are seen where an employee resigns in the heat of the moment and then asks for her job back. Other problems are seen when words of dismissal/resignation are ambiguous, for example, when an employer tells the employee to 'get out of here'. Is that a dismissal, or is it an instruction to take the rest of the day off? Problems also exist with pressured resignations and ultimatums to resign (e.g. 'resign or be sacked').

For the purpose of unfair dismissal or a redundancy payment, an employee must establish that she was dismissed within the definition of a dismissal in the ERA 1996, ss.95 and 136.

As previously noted the Employment Act 2002 (Dispute Resolution) Regulations 2004, which govern obligatory procedural aspects, have not been a success and are being revoked in their entirety. They are to be replaced with less prescriptive measures. In particular the Acas Code of Practice on Disciplinary and Grievance procedures is to be reviewed and given teeth. The normal position is that employment tribunals do little more than take note of official Codes of Practice but new rules will provide that if an employer has failed to follow various Codes of Practice including in particular this Acas Code there will be specific power to increase the unfair dismissal compensatory award by up to 25 per cent if it is considered just and equitable to do so (the 2008 Employment Bill, cl.3 provides for a new TULRCA 1992, s.207A to implement this proposal).

10.2 UNAMBIGUOUS DISMISSALS AND RESIGNATIONS

We deal here with straightforward dismissals and resignations, where the employer says 'you are dismissed' or the employee utters words to the effect of 'I resign'. Such terminations can either be with notice or in the case of summary dismissal or wrongful dismissal, without notice. Notice periods, and the consequences of failing to give proper notice, are addressed in **section 9.18**.

The contract can be terminated on notice by either side (ERA 1996, s.86). The length of the notice period will be set out in the contract (subject to the minimum notice periods imposed by statute: see **section 9.18**) or, if not set out, implied as being of a 'reasonable' length (*Hill* v. *C A Parsons* [1972] Ch 305). Usually, the contract will terminate on the date that the notice period expires. Occasionally, for example, when the dismissal/resignation is without notice and it is made clear that it is meant to take effect immediately, then it will take place on the date the termination is communicated to the other side. This date is important, because many employment claims have to be brought within three or six months of the effective date of termination of employment (ERA 1996, s.97).

A straightforward dismissal, as envisaged here, will count as a dismissal for the purpose of unfair dismissal and redundancy rights. A straightforward resignation will not.

10.3 AMBIGUOUS AND HEAT OF THE MOMENT DISMISSALS

Sometimes an employer will utter words in the heat of the moment which were not intended to amount to a dismissal, but the employee takes them as a dismissal and leaves. Is that a dismissal, enabling the employee to claim unfair dismissal? Or was there no dismissal, and the employee should be regarded as having resigned (hence no claim for unfair dismissal, unless constructive dismissal can be established)?

In an oldish case, the foreman in a fish filleting factory said to a worker 'If you don't like the job, fuck off'. The worker thought he had been dismissed, the foreman said not. The employment tribunal held that there was no dismissal because that was common language in the fish market and the employee should have known that the dismissal process was a much more formal one (*Futty* v. *D&D Brekkes Ltd* [1974] IRLR 130). However, in another case in 2008 in which a manager had told an employee during an argument that 'You're fucking sacked' a tribunal held that although the manager spoke in the heat of the moment and had no intention of dismissing the employee nevertheless the employee had been dismissed (*Atkins* v. *Coyle Personnel plc* [2008] IRLR 420, EAT).

The authorities are not all consistent but it seems that where the employer uses words which are genuinely ambiguous, a tribunal will decide what an objective and reasonable listener (who knows all the facts and circumstances) would have thought the employer meant. The test is a purely objective one: the tribunals will not look at what the employer secretly intended, nor at what the employee unreasonably understood. This approach does not lend itself to certainty when advising litigants, but it must be correct (*Sothern* v. *Franks Charlesly* [1981] IRLR 278; *J & J Stern* v. *Simpson* [1983] IRLR 52 and *Atkins* v. *Coyle Personnel plc* [2008] IRLR 420, EAT).

10.4 AMBIGUOUS AND HEAT OF THE MOMENT RESIGNATIONS

A problem sometimes occurs where the employee, in a moment of anger, shouts 'I resign' (usually adopting less salubrious terminology). Ordinarily, an unambiguous resignation should be taken at face value and the employee taken to have resigned and not dismissed (meaning an employee would be unable to claim unfair dismissal unless able to establish constructive dismissal). If an employee resigns, the law adopts a rather paternalistic approach and the employee will generally be given a second chance, i.e. the resignation is not immediately binding (*Southern* v. *Frank Charlesly & Co* [1981] IRLR 278 and *Burton* v. *Glycosynth Ltd* (unreported, EAT, 11 February 2005)).

The courts have held that if an employee utters words of resignation in circumstances where the employer knew, or ought to have known, that the employee might not have meant them, then the employer is obliged to give the employee a reasonable opportunity to clarify the resignation. If the employee makes it clear within that reasonable period that he did not intend to resign, then the employer must have him back. If the employer refuses to have him back, that refusal amounts to a dismissal (and, probably, an unfair dismissal) (*Sovereign House Security Services Ltd* v. *Savage* [1989] IRLR 115).

So, what is a reasonable period? It is only likely to be relatively short, a day or two. The employer is obliged to hold the employee's job open for a day or two to see if the employee comes back and makes it clear that she did not really intend to resign. An employer is not obliged to investigate whether the resignation is genuinely intended (*Kwik-Fit (GB) Ltd* v. *Lineham* [1992] IRLR 156).

10.5 PRESSURED RESIGNATIONS AND ULTIMATUMS TO RESIGN

Often employers pressure their employees to resign, or offer them the Hobson's choice of 'resign or be sacked'. They then triumphantly wave the letter of resignation as a defence to an unfair dismissal claim. But matters are rarely so straightforward.

In such circumstances, courts will hold there to have been a dismissal, since it was the employer, not the employee, who caused the employment relationship to terminate (*East Sussex County Council* v. *Walker* (1972) 7 ITR 280; *Beevor* v. *Humberside Fire Brigade* (unreported, EAT, 19 November 2003)). However, the existence of pressure on the employee to resign does not mean that there will always be a dismissal at law. Sometimes an employee's resignation will be genuine: because the employee would prefer to resign rather than continue in employment. An example is where an employee is facing serious disciplinary proceedings that are likely to result in dismissal. An employer's invitation to resign, rather than go through the disciplinary process, would not necessarily convert the employee's subsequent resignation into a dismissal (*Staffordshire County Council* v. *Donovan* [1981] IRLR 108).

10.6 CONSTRUCTIVE DISMISSAL

10.6.1 Introductory

Constructive dismissal is the name commonly given to a form of dismissal. It is not a separate cause of action. An employee is constructively dismissed if he:

> terminates the contract under which he is employed (with or without notice) in circumstances in which he is entitled to terminate it without notice by reason of the employer's conduct.
>
> ERA 1996, ss.95(1)(c) and 136(1)(c)

In other words, an employee is constructively dismissed when he resigns because the employer's conduct amounts to a repudiatory breach of the employment contract. Most constructive dismissal claims arise from allegations of a breach of the implied term of mutual trust and confidence, followed (a long way behind) by resignations due to the employer's failure to pay wages.

The guiding principle is to look for the cause of the resignation, which means looking for the *causa causans* rather than a *causa sine qua non* – old fashioned legal terminology but perhaps easier to understand than the modern 'but for' test equivalent. For a constructive dismissal claim to succeed the employee must show that there was a causal link between the employer's wrongful action and the employee's resignation (*Bunning* v. *GT Bunning & Sons Ltd* [2005] EWCA Civ 983).

The 2004 statutory dismissal procedures (soon to be abolished) do not apply to cases of constructive dismissal. However, until they are removed an employee must normally lodge a grievance with his (ex-) employer and wait 28 days before being permitted to present a constructive dismissal claim to an employment tribunal (Employment Act 2002, s.32).

A constructive dismissal may be fair or unfair. This is an important point because it is often assumed that employees are entitled to compensation just because they have been constructively dismissed. Not so. Firstly, a resignation which is in response to conduct by the employer which falls short of being a breach of a fundamental term would simply be a resignation (but note the 'last straw' doctrine: resignation in response to a series of minor misdeeds by an employer can sometimes entitle an employee to resign and claim constructive dismissal – see **section 10.6.2**). Secondly, although relatively uncommon, a tribunal can sometimes find that the employer's breach of contract was itself a response to misconduct by the employee with the result that the constructive dismissal was reasonable – thus fair – in all the circumstances of the case (*Savoia* v. *Chiltern Herb Farms Ltd* [1982] IRLR 166).

Because unfair dismissal, unlike wrongful dismissal, does not necessarily involve any breach of contract it follows that all constructive unfair dismissals are also constructive wrongful dismissal. At one stage the EAT suggested that there could be constructive unfair dismissal even if there was no breach of contract, and therefore no wrongful dismissal, but the Court of Appeal pointed out that this was wrong (*Rossiter* v. *Pendragon plc* [2002] ICR 1063, CA).

To claim constructive dismissal, the employee must establish that:

- the employer was in breach of a term of the contract of employment; and
- the breach was a repudiatory one, entitling the employee to resign; and
- the employee resigned because of that breach of contract.

The burden of proof is on the employee to establish each of the above. If he fails at any stage, he will not establish a constructive dismissal and will be held to have resigned.

An employment tribunal's decision as to the reason for an employee's resignation is a decision on a question of fact and therefore, assuming that the tribunal could reasonably have come to its decision, there can be no appeal (*O'Shea* v. *Coventry City Council* (unreported, EAT, 15 February 2005)).

In *Cape Industrial Services Ltd* v. *Ambler* [2002] EWCA Civ 1264, the Court of Appeal suggested the following questions to bear in mind when considering whether there has been an unfair constructive dismissal:

1. What were the relevant term(s) of the contract said to be breached?
2. Are the breaches, or any of them, made out?
3. If so, are the breaches (or breach) fundamental?
4. If so, did the employee resign in response to such breach or breaches? If so, then he was constructively dismissed.
5. In that event, has the employer shown a potentially fair reason for the constructive dismissal?
6. If so, did the employer act reasonably or unreasonably in treating that reason as a sufficient one for dismissal?

Finally in this introductory section, it is worth noting that if an employer sends a 'without prejudice' letter to an employee in an attempt to settle a dispute that letter will not be admissible in evidence and therefore cannot be used by the employee in an attempt to persuade a tribunal that her subsequent resignation was in fact constructive dismissal (*Brodie* v. *Ward t/a First Steps Nursery* (unreported, EAT, 7 February 2008)).

10.6.2 Employer's breach of contract

It is very tempting for tribunals to find that somebody has been constructively dismissed because the employer has acted unreasonably. However, this is not the test. An employee must demonstrate that the employer has breached a term of the contract of employment, such as the implied duty of trust and confidence (*Western Excavating Ltd* v. *Sharp* [1977] IRLR 25, CA).

It should be noted that it cannot be constructive dismissal if an employee resigns because of conduct of someone who was neither employer nor fellow employee (*Yorke & Anor (t/a Yorkes of Dundee)* v. *Moonlight* (unreported, EAT, 19 January 2007) in which the employer's father, who was not a fellow employee, had verbally abused an employee who resigned in consequence). Further, breach of an employee's statutory rights is not a breach of contract so if he resigns in consequence he will not normally be able to claim constructive dismissal (*Doherty* v. *British Midland Airways* [2006] IRLR 90).

Wages

The most obvious breach of contract is the failure to pay wages, or a unilateral decision by the employer to reduce wages. It is likely that an employer's refusal to pay the NMW would also be a breach of contract, either of an incorporated term or of an implied term that the employer will pay the minimum wage (*Industrial Rubber Products* v. *Gillon* [1977] IRLR 389). Failure to make a payment under a discretionary severance scheme will not amount to an unauthorised deduction from wages (*Campbell* v. *Union Carbide Ltd* [2002] Emp LR 1267, EAT/0341/01).

Trust and confidence

This is the most common implied term that is used in constructive dismissal claims. It is addressed in detail at **section 3.3.2**. A breach of the term of trust and confidence will always be repudiatory (*Morrow* v. *Safeway Stores plc* [2002] IRLR 9).

Duties

An employer is entitled to issue lawful and reasonable orders. The employer may also be entitled to vary a worker's job description if there is a contractual right to do so. However, a significant unilateral variation of an employee's job duties will amount to a breach of contract (*Coleman* v. *S & W Baldwin* [1977] IRLR 342).

Working hours

Insistence that the employee works overtime when there is no contractual obligation to do so, or a unilateral variation of an employee's working hours, will be a breach of contract (*Derby City Council* v. *Marshall* [1979] IRLR 261).

Job location

There will be a breach of contract if employees are required to change place of work, beyond a reasonable commuting distance from their home, unless there is an express mobility clause in the contract of employment (*Courtaulds Northern Spinning Ltd* v. *Sibson & TGWU* [1988] IRLR 305).

Unlawful sex (or other) discrimination

The EAT has specifically confirmed that an employee who resigns because of unlawful discrimination can in appropriate circumstances have a claim for constructive dismissal (*Shaw* v. *CCL Ltd* (unreported, EAT, 22 May 2007)).

Suspension without pay

Suspension without pay during a disciplinary process will always be a breach of contract, unless there is an express right to suspend without pay in the contract (*Warburton* v. *Taff Vale Rly Co* (1902) 18 TLR 420).

Swearing at or criticising employee

Unjustified or excessive swearing at an employee may be a breach of the implied term of mutual trust and confidence (*Palmanor Ltd* v. *Cedron* [1978] ICR 1008; *Horkaluk* v. *Cantor Fitzgerald* [2004] ICR 697, QBD). Likewise, humiliating criticism of an employee in front of other staff may be a breach of trust and confidence. The likelihood of a breach is increased if the swearing or criticism is directed at a manager in the presence of their subordinates (*Hilton International Hotels* v. *Protopapa* [1990] IRLR 316; *Ogilvie* v. *Neyrfor-Weir Ltd* (unreported, EAT, 15 May 2003)).

Refusing a pay rise

The arbitrary refusal to award a pay rise to a particular employee could be a breach of trust and confidence (*F C Gardner Ltd* v. *Beresford* [1978] IRLR 63). This may present problems for employers when trying to vary contractual terms and conditions. If they offer a pay rise only to those who accept amended terms, any subsequent finding of constructive dismissal is likely to be unfair, not fair (*Imperial Group Pension Trust Ltd* v. *Imperial Tobacco Ltd* [1991] IRLR 66, Ch D). Likewise, offering increased pension benefits to members of one trade union but not another might be a breach of trust and confidence (*BG plc* v. *O'Brien* [2001] IRLR 496, EAT). Failing to implement a nationally agreed pay rise may also be a breach of trust and confidence (*Glendale Managed Services Ltd* v. *Graham* [2003] EWCA Civ 773).

In a case in 2005 the Court of Appeal held that a 'promise' of a pay increase made at a Christmas party was not intended to create a legally binding obligation so there was no breach of contract, let alone a repudiatory breach, when the employer later changed his mind (*Judge* v. *Crown Leisure Ltd* [2005] IRLR 823, CA).

Inadequate support

In appropriate circumstances, not giving adequate support to a member of staff might amount to a breach of trust and confidence (*Seligman* v. *McHugh* [1979] IRLR 130).

Dealing with grievances and disciplinary matters promptly

If the employer fails to deal with grievances and disciplinary matters promptly – particularly if the employee is suspended without pay – this may be a breach of contract (see **section 3.3.2**). Issuing an unjustified final written warning may also amount to a repudiatory breach, entitling a constructive dismissal claim (*Stanley Cole (Wainfleet) Ltd* v. *Sheridan* [2003] IRLR 52).

Failing to provide a suitable working environment

If an employer fails to provide a suitable working environment it may breach an implied term of the contract of employment. This could include an excessively stuffy environment (*Waltons & Morse* v. *Dorrington* [1997] IRLR 488, which pre-dates anti-smoking legislation) or even in some circumstances failing to offer alternative employment to an employee to alleviate stress (*Thanet DC* v. *Websper* (unreported, EAT, 30 October 2002)). Either of these might entitle an employee to resign and claim constructive dismissal.

Changing terms and conditions following a TUPE transfer

The 2006 TUPE regulations include at reg.4(5) a provision which was not in the 1981 version which they replace. Under the 2006 provision a variation to terms of employment will be permissible if 'the sole or principal reason for the variation is (a) a reason connected with the transfer that is an economic, technical or organisational reason entailing changes in the workforce; or (b) a reason unconnected with the transfer'.

In practice it is hard to see that this will make much difference and ordinarily a change to terms and conditions following a TUPE transfer will be a repudiatory breach of contract. If the employee resigns as a result, it will therefore generally lead to a finding of an automatic unfair dismissal (see **section 3.6.6**).

An important rider to the general rule is that where the old employer could legitimately have made changes to working practices without breach of contract the employee will not be entitled to resign and use the TUPE regulations to claim unfair constructive dismissal simply because it is the new employer who made those changes (*Rossiter* v. *Pendragon* [2002] IRLR 483, CA).

10.6.3 Repudiatory breach

Not every breach of contract will entitle an employee to resign and claim constructive dismissal. The breach must be a serious, or a repudiatory, one. An isolated incident of paying wages one day late will not suffice, although constant late paying of wages might be serious enough to amount to a repudiatory breach (*Hutchings* v. *Coinseed Ltd* [1998] IRLR 190). Likewise, a short delay in paying sick pay, where there was a genuine dispute over whether the employee was malingering and the employer was seeking medical evidence, is not a repudiatory breach of contract (*Rugamer* v. *Sony Music Entertainment UK Ltd* [2001] IRLR 644, EAT).

It has been held that a comparatively minor unilateral reduction of wages (from £60 to £58.50 per week) was not an unfair repudiatory breach by the employer. Such a reduction might sometimes amount to a constructive dismissal but, on the facts of the particular case, was held to be 'marginal' (*Gillies* v. *Richard Daniels & Co Ltd* [1979] IRLR 457).

A breach of the term of mutual trust and confidence will always amount to a repudiatory breach of contract (*Morrow* v. *Safeway Stores plc* [2002] IRLR 9).

A repudiatory breach by the employer will usually release the employee from all obligations under the contract, including confidentiality and restrictive covenant clauses (see **section 3.4** for more detail).

Cumulative acts – the last straw doctrine

The cumulative effect of a number of incidents, leading to a 'last straw', can amount to repudiatory breach of the implied term of trust and confidence even if the individual incidents are not breaches of contract (*White* v. *Reflecting Roadstuds Ltd* [1991] IRLR 331; *Lewis* v. *Motorworld Garages Ltd* [1985] IRLR 465). There is no requirement that the last straw itself has to be a breach of contract (*Barke* v. *SEETEC Business Technology Centre Ltd* (unreported, EAT, 13 January 2006)) but it must be more than utterly trivial and must contribute something to the breach (*GAB Robins (UK) Ltd* v. *Triggs* [2008] ICR 529, CA).

GAB Robins (UK) Ltd v. *Triggs* is also authority for the important proposition that whilst an employer's repudiatory conduct is an essential condition of a constructive dismissal claim, it is the employee's acceptance of the repudiation that effects the dismissal. It follows that damage (e.g. stress) caused by antecedent breaches of the implied term of trust and confidence is not damage suffered 'in consequence' of the dismissal (see ERA 1996, s.123) but rather is damage in respect of which the employee, prior to dismissal, has already accrued as a cause of action to sue for damages. Compensation for such damage cannot therefore be awarded as part of a compensatory award if the constructive dismissal was unfair.

There is no particular timescale within which the various incidents culminating in a 'last straw' must take place. The Court of Appeal has held that an employment tribunal was wrong when it decided that a gap of 18 months between the acts complained of was too long for the 'last straw' doctrine to apply (*Logan* v. *Commissioners of Customs & Excise* [2003] EWCA Civ 1068). However, the 'last straw' approach cannot be used to link together matters which took place before an employee affirmed his contract and matters which took place afterwards – the slate is effectively wiped clean by an affirmation of contract by the employee (*Gibson (t/a Blandford House Surgery)* v. *Hughes* (unreported, EAT, 13 September 2006)).

10.6.4 Employee must resign in response to the breach

It is not enough for the employee to resign soon after the employer's breach of contract. In order to fall within the definition of constructive dismissal, the resignation must be because of the repudiatory breach (*Norwest Holst Group Administration Ltd* v. *Harrison* [1984] IRLR 419 and *Bunning* v. *GT Bunning & Sons Ltd* [2005] EWCA Civ 983).

There is no statutory requirement for the employee to tell the employer of the reason for resignation at the time of leaving, although a failure to do so might throw into doubt the reasons for leaving if they are challenged later (*Weathersfield Ltd* v. *Sargent* [1999] IRLR 94, CA).

There is also no need for the breach to be the sole cause of the employee's resignation. Once a repudiatory breach is established, if the employee leaves then, even if he may have done so for a whole host of reasons, he can claim that he has been constructively dismissed if the repudiatory breach is one of the factors relied upon (*Abbey Cars (West Horndon) Ltd* v. *Ford* (unreported, EAT, 23 May 2008)). An employee who leaves partly because of the employer's breach, and partly because of a better job offer, will still be able to claim constructive dismissal (*Jones* v. *F Sirl & Son (Furnishers) Ltd* [1997] IRLR 493).

Waiving the breach

The employee does not have to resign immediately on becoming aware of the breach. Employees are permitted a reasonable time to consider their position.

However, if they wait too long, they are regarded as having waived the breach and therefore would be unable to resign and claim constructive dismissal.

How long can the employee wait? There is no fixed rule. Delay by the employee in resigning is of itself neutral. It may indicate that the employee is not resigning in response to the employer's breach of contract but it does not by itself constitute affirmation of contract (*Allen* v. *Robles* [1969] 1 WLR 1193 and *Bass* v. *Travis Perkins Trading Company Ltd* (unreported, EAT, 15 December 2005)).

Factors to be taken into account include the employee's length of service, whether the employee has protested at the breach, how serious the breach is and whether the employee has been taking steps to mitigate his loss (by using a grievance procedure, or by looking for another job). The employee is entitled to a reasonable time to decide whether to leave or not (*Air Canada* v. *Lee* [1978] IRLR 392; *G W Stephens & Son* v. *Fish* [1989] ICR 324), but three weeks has been held to be too long (*Cow* v. *Surrey and Berkshire Newspapers Ltd* (unreported, EAT, 7 March 2003)).

10.7 TERMINATION BY MUTUAL AGREEMENT

Theoretically, the employer and employee can agree to terminate the employment contract. However, as this avoids a dismissal (and hence a claim for unfair dismissal), courts strain to avoid finding that a consensual dismissal has taken place. In practice, unless the initiative for the termination has come from the employee, courts and tribunals are likely to find that it was a classic dismissal by the employer, because the employer was the effective cause of the termination.

The legal rationale for this approach is as follows. Employees cannot contract out of their employment rights unless they comply with one of the two recognised methods of compromising claims, i.e. a settlement via Acas or a formal compromise agreement (ERA 1996, s.203). Therefore an agreement to terminate employment cannot be effective to sign away the right to claim unfair dismissal (unless the agreement complies with the requirements for a compromise agreement, which it inevitably will not) (*Igbo* v. *Johnson Matthey Chemicals* [1986] IRLR 215, CA).

However, occasionally a tribunal will find that there was a genuine, mutually agreed termination, for example, an occasion when university lecturers applied for their employment to be terminated early in order to receive the benefit of an enhanced early retirement scheme. The Court of Appeal held that their dismissal under the scheme was a genuine mutual termination, not a dismissal at the behest of the employer (*Birch & Humber* v. *University of Liverpool* [1985] IRLR 165, CA).

10.7.1 Fixed-term contracts

If a contract is for a fixed period of time, it will terminate when that period of time expires and is deemed a dismissal. Under the Fixed-Term Employees (Prevention of Less Favourable Treatment) Regulations 2002, SI 2002/2034, those on task-related contracts share the same protection as those working on fixed-term contracts. The expiry of such a contract is deemed to be a dismissal for the purpose of unfair dismissal and redundancy legislation (ERA 1996, ss.95(1)(b) and 136(1)(b)). A tribunal then needs to consider whether the dismissal is fair or unfair. This prevents employers from trying to avoid unfair dismissal legislation by awarding a series of short fixed-term contracts. Under the regulations a fixed-term contract is normally automatically converted by law into a contract of indefinite duration once the employee has completed four years' continuous employment under it (or renewals of it) (Fixed-Term Employees (Prevention of Less Favourable Treatment) Regulations 2002, reg.8).

10.8 FRUSTRATION

Frustration is a well-known concept in contract law, which has been applied somewhat haphazardly to employment law.

Frustration of contract occurs when there is an event which makes continued performance of the employment contract impossible, or something completely different from what the parties agreed, i.e. working in an employer/employee relationship. For there to be frustration of a contract there must be some outside event or extraneous change of situation, not foreseen or provided for by the parties to the contract. This includes long-term sickness or imprisonment of the employee and death of the employee or employer (*Egg Stores* v. *Leibovici* [1976] IRLR 376; *F C Shepherd* v. *Jerrom* [1986] IRLR 358, CA; *G F Sharp* v. *McMillan* [1998] IRLR 632; *Ward* v. *Cambridgeshire County Council* (unreported, EAT, 26 July 2001); *Aspden* v. *Webbs Poultry & Meat Group (Holdings) Ltd* [1996] IRLR 521).

Where employees are unable to perform their contractual obligations, the contract may be frustrated. This terminates the employment relationship automatically and the termination is not a dismissal for the purpose of unfair dismissal legislation. However, a slightly different definition of dismissal in redundancy legislation ensures that frustration amounts to dismissal for the purpose of entitling the employee to statutory redundancy pay (ERA 1996, s.139).

It will be appreciated that the doctrine of frustration can, theoretically, be invoked to avoid a claim of unfair dismissal in any long-term sickness situation, no matter how arbitrary the employer's decision to dismiss. It is now settled that it will not apply where the contract of employment contains a long-term disability scheme (often known as permanent health insurance), since the existence of a scheme means that long-term absence through sickness was envisaged at the time of contracting (*Villella* v. *MFI Furniture Centres* [1999] IRLR 468). Thus as a general rule it has become harder to establish frustration in sickness cases in recent years particularly because most contracts allow for a period of sick leave and therefore it is difficult to say that long-term sickness was not foreseen (*Four Seasons Healthcare Ltd* v. *Maughan* [2005] IRLR 324).

In an oldish (1972) case the old National Industrial Relations Court explained that:

> In the context of incapacity due to sickness, the question of whether or not the relationship has come to an end by frustration sounds more difficult than it is. The tribunal must ask itself: 'Was the employee's incapacity, looked at before the purported dismissal, of such a nature, or did it appear likely to continue for such a period, that further performance of his obligations in the future would either be impossible or would be a thing radically different from that undertaken by him and agreed to be accepted by the employer under the agreed terms of his employment?'
>
> *Marshall* v. *Harland & Wolff Ltd* [1972] ICR 101, NIRC

This was quoted with approval by the EAT in *Jones* v. *Friction Dynamics Ltd* (unreported, EAT, 28 March 2007), when the EAT overruled an employment tribunal's conclusion that a sick employee's contract had been terminated by frustration. The employee had recovered and even though he did not come back to work the employer did not dismiss him until two years later when it went into administration. The EAT ruled that by then it was too late for the employer to claim that the contract had been frustrated and so the employee could proceed with an unfair dismissal claim.

The employer must not be at fault in causing the employee's inability to work. If an employee is off sick long-term through stress, caused by the employer's breach of health and safety duties, the employer will not be able to rely on the doctrine of frustration (*Paal Wilson & Co A/S* v. *Parfenreederei Hannah Blumenthal (The Hannah Blumenthal)* [1983] 1 AC 854, HL). However, in that situation dismissal of the employee may be *prima facie* fair dismissal on grounds of lack of capability – this will depend on whether dismissal was or was not within the range of reasonable responses for the employer in all the circumstances which of course include questions of responsibility for the incapability (*McAdie* v. *Royal Bank of Scotland plc* [2007] EWCA Civ 806 and see **section 11.4.4**).

The duration of a potentially 'frustrating event' is not of itself enough to determine whether it frustrates a contract – other relevant factors including in particular the length of the employee's service must be taken into account (*Gryf-Lowczowski* v. *Hinchingbooke Healthcare NHS Trust* [2006] IRLR 100, QBD).

10.9 DEATH AND INSOLVENCY

10.9.1 Death of employee

An employee is obliged to provide personal service. Death will frustrate the contract of employment. A particular exception to this is where the employee is already under notice of dismissal. In that case, death does not frustrate the contract, but the dismissal is treated as having occurred on the date of death. This is so that the employee's estate is not prevented from bringing a claim of unfair dismissal simply because the employee died whilst already under notice (ERA 1996, s.133(1)).

An employee's estate is able to bring claims for breach of contract, unfair dismissal or discrimination after the employee's death. Likewise, claims issued before death can be pursued by the employee's estate after death (Law Reform (Miscellaneous Provisions) Act 1934, s.1; ERA 1996, s.206; *Lewisham & Guy's Mental Health NHS Trust v. Andrews* [2000] ICR 707, CA).

10.9.2 Death of employer

The death of an employer (where the employer is an individual, as contrasted with a limited company) will frustrate the contract of employment. At common law this would mean that no monies were payable. However, statute provides that in these circumstances a termination is deemed to be a dismissal due to redundancy. A redundancy award will then be payable, unless the employer's personal representatives make an offer of suitable alternative employment within eight weeks of death. Notice pay will not be payable (ERA 1996, ss.136(5)(b), 138 and 174).

Partnerships

The death of a partner presents a theoretical problem. Technically, the partnership changes its identity and the old employer no longer exists. The contract should be frustrated and the right to a redundancy payment triggered. In practice, a tribunal would readily find an implied term (on the officious bystander test) that the parties intended the employment relationship to continue when periodic changes in the partnership take place. The position is different when a partnership dissolves, although it is not entirely clear whether this amounts to a frustrating event or an ordinary dismissal (*Briggs v. Oates* [1990] IRLR 473). Where a solicitors' firm is dissolved due to intervention by the Law Society, the employee's status will depend on whether continued employment remains lawful and whether the intervenor is trying to sell the practice as a going concern (*Rose v. Dodd* [2005] EWCA Civ 957).

10.9.3 Insolvency/dissolution of company

Winding up

A compulsory winding-up order will terminate any employment contracts. An employee will usually have a claim for redundancy (and notice pay), which will be met by the BERR if the company lacks sufficient funds (see below) (*Re Oriental Bank Corpn* (1886) 32 Ch D 366). A voluntary winding-up order (passed by members) will not automatically terminate employment contracts (*Midland Counties Bank* v. *Attwood* [1905] 1 Ch 357).

Appointment of administrator/receiver

Administrators and administrative receivers appointed by debenture holders act as agents of the company concerned (Insolvency Act 1986, ss.14(5) and 44(1)(a) respectively). In both cases, they are personally liable in respect of employment contracts 'adopted by them'. They have 14 days from their appointment to make other arrangements (Insolvency Act 1986, ss.19(5) and 44(2)). Their appointment does not automatically terminate employment contracts of the company with its employees (*Griffiths* v. *Secretary of State for Social Services* [1974] QB 468).

A court-appointed receiver, on the other hand, is an officer of the court and is not the agent of the company. His appointment terminates any employment contracts (*Reid* v. *The Explosives Co Ltd* (1887) 19 QBD 264) and therefore may give rise to unfair and/or wrongful dismissal claims.

An administrator or receiver becomes personally liable for employment contracts 'adopted' by him, i.e. where he has acted in a way which indicates the employment contract is ongoing. Employees will then be deemed to have entered into new contracts of employment. There is a statutory immunity from this deemed adoption during the first 14 days following appointment (*Powdrill* v. *Watson* [1995] ICR 1100, HL (the 'Paramount Airways' case) partly overturned by the Insolvency Act 1986, ss.19 and 44(2)).

'Wages or salary' are payable prior to the administrator's own fees and expenses (Insolvency Act 1986, Sched.B1, para.99, inserted by the Enterprise Act 2002, s.248 and Sched.16) so administrators are rightly cautious about adopting employment contracts. Neither statutory redundancy pay nor unfair dismissal compensation count as 'wages or salary' for this purpose (see *Re Allders Department Stores (in adminstration)* [2005] ICR 867, ChD). Similarly, damages for wrongful dismissal do not count as 'wages or salary' for this purpose (*In re Leeds United Association Football Club Ltd* [2007] ICR 1688, HC) and nor do amounts payable to employees in respect of protective award or genuine pay in lieu of notice (*Ferrotech (in re) & other cases* [2006] ICR 205, CA – this was an urgent appeal following conflicting High Court judgments in 2005 which led to some panic within the insolvency community).

The National Insurance Fund

Subject to various limits, the fund (administered by the BERR) will pay certain sums to employees which an employer is unable to pay by reason of its insolvency/dissolution, etc. In outline, the important limits are:

- up to eight weeks' wages;
- any unpaid pay for the minimum statutory notice period;
- up to six weeks' unpaid holiday pay in respect of the last 12 months;
- basic award for unfair dismissal (*DTI* v. *Walden* [2000] IRLR 168).

For this purpose a week's pay is limited to £330 per week for terminations on or after 1 February 2008 (Employment Rights (Increase of Limits) Order 2007, SI 2007/3570).

In a case in 2007 the EAT said of the State guarantee of protective award that 'it is not subject, apparently, to the statutory cap . . . in a week's pay provided for by ERA 1996, s.227' (*Evans, Motture and Hutchins* v. *Permacell Finesse Ltd (In administration)* (unreported, EAT, 23 October 2007). While technically correct, this can best be described as misleading – the cap does apply in such a case but it is imposed by a different section, ERA 1996, s.186, which was not mentioned.

The cap provided for by ERA 1996, s.186 is normally adjusted annually to ensure it is the same as the cap in a week's pay provided by ERA 1996, s.227 It must be applied before deductions for tax and national insurance (*Titchener* v. *DTI* [2002] IRLR 195, EAT).

A website at **www.emplaw.co.uk/lshandbook** provides links to judgments and other source material referred to in this chapter.

CHAPTER 11
Unfair dismissal

11.1 GENERAL INFORMATION

There were 44,491 unfair dismissal claims to employment tribunals in the most recent period for which statistics are available (Employment Tribunal and EAT Statistics (GB) 1 April 2006 to 31 March 2007). This is more than for any other jurisdiction (although there was an enormous jump in the number of equal pay claims filed during the same period, running a close second at 44,013 claims).

There are a number of conditions that need to be satisfied before somebody can bring a claim for unfair dismissal. Most importantly, the claimant must be an employee (as defined by ERA 1996, s.230) and must have been continuously employed for at least a year, although this requirement is subject to exceptions.

As noted at **Chapter 4** the compulsory dismissal procedures introduced in October 2004 which apply to both employers and employees are soon to be abolished (by the 2008 Employment Bill, before Parliament at the date of writing). We are therefore not covering them in this edition but it must be remembered that they will still apply for at least a few months after publication of this book, probably until April 2009. The consequences for both employers and employees who fail to abide by these procedures can be severe, so they must not be overlooked for so long as they continue to be required.

11.2 QUALIFICATIONS

11.2.1 Is the claimant an employee?

Whereas the tendency for recent employment legislation has been to provide various protections and benefits for most workers, unfair dismissal law remains firmly wedded to the concept of 'employee'. The definition of 'employee' in ERA 1996 is not particularly helpful (it refers to 'an individual who has entered into or works under (or, where the employment has ceased, worked under) a contract of employment'). So what is a 'contract of employment'? The Act defines it as 'a contract of service or apprenticeship, whether express or implied, and (if it is express) whether oral or in writing' (s.230). This is considered in more detail in **section 2.2**.

11.2.2 Qualifying period of employment

The general rule is that an employee must have been continuously employed for a period of not less than one year before obtaining the right to claim unfair dismissal (ERA 1996, s.108; Unfair Dismissal and Statement of Reasons for Dismissal (Variation of Qualifying Period) Order 1999, SI 1999/1436). There are exceptions so that in some cases (generally cases in which a dismissal is automatically unfair) there is no qualifying period and in a few special cases it is just one month.

Continuous employment

An employee (normally) has to complete one year's continuous employment in order to qualify to bring an unfair dismissal claim. In determining whether employment is continuous, each individual week must, theoretically, be examined although in practice a more global view is usually taken (ERA 1996, s.210).

In order to qualify as a week of continuous employment, the week in question must have been governed – either during part or all of it – by a contract of employment. However, if the employee is incapable of work due to sickness or injury, or is absent from work due to a temporary cessation of work (or in circumstances where, by arrangement or custom, he is regarded as continuing in employment), the week still counts as a 'filler' week of continuous employment even if there is no governing contract of employment. No more than 26 filler weeks can count before continuity of employment is broken (ERA 1996, s.212), even if the employer has guaranteed re-employment at the end of a career break (*Curr v. Marks & Spencer* [2003] IRLR 74).

Employment with the same employer, or an associated employer, during any period is presumed to be continuous unless the contrary is shown (ERA 1996, s.210(5)).

The employee must have worked for the same employer during the period of continuous employment, or the clock resets to zero. The employee is deemed to have been working for the same employer where there has been a transfer of undertakings, a move between associated employers, a change of partners in a partnership or where the employee is kept on by personal representatives after the death of an employer (ERA 1996, s.218).

If an employee was on strike during any week, or part of a week, then the entire week is excluded for the purpose of calculating the number of weeks of continuous employment. This does not, however, reset the clock to zero. Likewise, any period during which an employee is locked out by the employer does not count when calculating the number of weeks of continuous employment (ERA 1996, s.216).

Extension of period

If an employee is dismissed without notice after 51 weeks of employment (but before a full year's employment has been achieved), the statutory minimum period of notice of one week, as set out in ERA 1996, s.86, is added to the actual time worked. This takes the employee past the one-year threshold and enables a claim for unfair dismissal to be brought (ERA 1996, s.97(4)).

The above only extends the period of employment by the statutory minimum period of one week, not the contractual notice period. Thus an employee who has worked for 11 months, and who is summarily dismissed in breach of a three-month notice clause, cannot extend the period of employment by three months to claim unfair dismissal. Furthermore, if a dismissed employee has not completed sufficient continuous employment to qualify for unfair dismissal but would have done so if he had been given the contractual notice to which he was entitled, he is not entitled to damages for loss of the chance to claim unfair dismissal (*Wise Group* v. *Mitchell* [2005] ICR 896, EAT; *Virgin Net* v. *Harper* [2003] IRLR 831).

Exceptions to the one-year qualification requirement

There are a number of exceptions to the one-year qualifying period. For the most part, they are for dismissals that are automatically unfair, namely:

1. Reasons set out in TULRCA 1992, s.154(1), that is dismissal on grounds related to trade union membership, non-membership or activities.
2. Dismissal for any of the reasons set out in ERA 1996, s.108(3). These are essentially:

    (a) dismissal related to pregnancy, childbirth or maternity;
    (b) dismissal relating to compulsory, ordinary or additional maternity leave;
    (c) dismissal relating to ordinary or additional adoption leave;
    (d) dismissal relating to paternity or parental leave;
    (e) dismissal for certain health and safety reasons;
    (f) dismissal in connection with a health and safety representative's role;
    (g) dismissal of a protected shop worker, opted-out shop worker or a betting shop worker who refuses to work on Sundays;
    (h) dismissal for refusing to comply with a requirement imposed in contravention of WTR 1998 or to forgo a right conferred under the regulations;
    (i) dismissal of an employee who is a trustee of his employer's pension scheme for performing his duty as such;
    (j) dismissal of employee representatives, or candidates for election, for performing their functions as such;
    (k) dismissal relating to an employee's role as a member of, or candidate for election to, a 'special negotiating body' or European Works Council;

EMPLOYMENT LAW HANDBOOK

(l) dismissal relating to part-time status;
(m) dismissal for exercising rights as a fixed-term worker;
(n) dismissal for 'assertion of a statutory right';
(o) dismissal for making a 'protected disclosure';
(p) dismissal for enforcing the right to be paid the minimum wage;
(q) dismissal for enforcing the right to tax credits;
(r) selection for redundancy for any of the reasons set out as (a) to (p) above;
(s) dismissals as a result of carrying out jury service (see ERA 1996, s.98B);
(t) dismissal on grounds related to the right to request flexible working.

The normal qualifying period is reduced to one month if the dismissal is by reason of a requirement specified under ERA 1996, s.64(2), such as a requirement under a prescribed statutory instrument dealing with dangerous chemicals or radioactive substances. Although the qualifying period threshold is reduced to just one month, it is likely that any dismissal for this reason will be fair (ERA 1996, s.108(2)).

Note that the normal one-year qualifying period is required under the TUPE regulations. Although a 'TUPE related' dismissal is automatically unfair (TUPE 2006, reg.7(1)), the effect of TUPE 2006, reg.7(6) is that the employee must have completed the normal qualifying period of employment.

11.3 EXCEPTIONS

11.3.1 Employee aged 65 or over

Until 1 October 2006, save in a few special cases, there was an absolute bar against a person claiming unfair dismissal if they were aged 65+ when dismissed (ERA 1996, s.109). From 1 October 2006 the position has been different (Employment Equality (Age) Regulations 2006, SI 2006/1031 implementing the anti-age discrimination parts of the EC Equal Treatment Framework Directive 2000/78 in Britain). ERA 1996, s.109 has been repealed and the 65-year age limit for unfair dismissal claims has been abolished – but it lives on in modified form as it has been replaced by other rules which ensure that enforced retirement of an employee at age 65 or over is generally not unfair dismissal.

This comes about because the Age Regulations 2006, reg.30(2) provides an exception to the general rule that age discrimination in the employment field is unlawful. It provides that it is not unlawful to dismiss an employee at or over the age of 65 where the reason for the dismissal is retirement, albeit this is subject to certain conditions.

The conditions include that the employee must be given six months' written notice which must inform him that he has the legal right to require the employer to consider a request to defer his retirement. If the conditions are not fulfilled then even though retirement takes place on or after the employee's 65th birthday the employer will be liable to a penalty and in some cases the enforced retirement will be unfair dismissal.

The practical effect is that the following steps are involved in a retirement on or after 1 October 2006:

- six to 12 months before intended retirement date the employer must give the employee written notice of that date and of the right to request to continue to work after that date;
- three to six months before intended retirement date the employee can make a written request to continue to work after that date, specifying whether or not this is for a particular period or until a particular date;
- if the employee makes a written request as above, a meeting must be held with her to discuss it unless it is simply granted without question;
- if the request is granted the employer must remember to put the revised contract terms in writing (see **section 16.1**).

There is a legal argument to the effect that the Equal Treatment Framework Directive 2000/78/EC does not allow employers to make retirement compulsory at any age and that therefore the UK regulations are contrary to EU law in so far as they allow enforced retirement at age 65. If that argument is correct the 2006 Age Regulations will have to be amended. The question has been referred to the ECJ following an application by the Heyday organisation (part of Age Concern). The ECJ's Attorney-General is expected to publish his opinion in September 2008. It will then be considered by the full court and the result is likely to be known around the end of the year or in the first part of 2009. It seems unlikely that the Heyday challenge will be successful as the ECJ has already ruled that a similar provision in Spanish law was justified as being a proportionate means to achieve a legitimate aim and was therefore compatible with EC rules (*Palacios de la Villa* v. *Cortefiel Servicios SA* [2007] IRLR 989, ECJ Case C-411/05) – but that was Spain. It is at least possible that the ECJ will rule that what is justified in Spain is not justifiable in the UK.

Pending a ruling from the ECJ in the Heyday case, the President of the Employment Tribunals issued a direction on 8 November 2007 directing that all unfair dismissal claims by persons aged 65 and over should be stayed – in other words, claims can be lodged so that they are not barred as 'out of time' but they will not be heard until after the ECJ has given its ruling.

Note that a partner in a partnership is not an employee. As the provisions of the Age Regulations 2006, reg.30 noted above apply only to employees it follows that, subject to the defence of justification, it is unlawful to require a partner to retire at any age (see Age Regulations 2006, reg.17 and *Seldon* v. *Clarkson Wright & Jakes* (unreported, Ashford employment tribunal, 4 December 2007)). The same applies to an 'office holder' (see the Age Regulations 2006, reg.12 and *Hampton* v. *Lord Chancellor and MoJ* [2008] IRLR 258).

11.3.2 Members of the Armed Forces

Members of the Armed Forces cannot, at present, claim unfair dismissal. Section 192 of ERA 1996 permits certain claims to be brought by members of the Armed Forces, including unfair dismissal: however, this section has not yet been brought into force (s.192 and Sched.2, para.16).

If and when it is brought into force, members of the Armed Forces will not be able to claim unfair dismissal until 'the person aggrieved has made a complaint to an officer under the service procedures for the redress of complaints applicable to him' and there will be a time limit of one month. Once implemented, the unfair dismissal provisions will be broadly similar to those for civilians, save that certain automatically unfair dismissal provisions (such as the right to claim automatic unfair dismissal if the dismissal occurs from the individual's refusal to expose himself to danger) will not apply (ERA 1996, s.192(4)).

11.3.3 Civil servants if national security is involved

Prior to 16 July 2001, there was a general power for a minister to issue a certificate exempting categories of civil servants from the right to claim unfair dismissal (ERA 1996, s.193). From 16 July 2001, this has been replaced with a provision that unfair dismissal rights do not apply to staff within the Security Service, the Secret Intelligence Service or GCHQ (Employment Relations Act 1999 (Commencement No. 8) Order 2001, SI 2001/1187).

However, there remains a general power for ministers to issue exemption certificates in any unfair dismissal case where issues of national security are involved (Employment Tribunals Act 1996, s.10).

A Registrar of births, deaths and marriages is not an employee of the local authority for which he works but rather is an office holder under the Registration Services Act 1953, s.6(4) and therefore cannot claim unfair dismissal (*Lincolnshire CC* v. *Hopper* [2002] ICR 1301, EAT).

11.3.4 Diplomatic immunity and international organisations

This is complicated and is governed by a number of different Acts. In a nutshell, foreign states are able to claim diplomatic immunity from a claim of unfair dismissal if:

- the employee is working for 'an office, agency or establishment maintained ... for commercial purposes' and was 'habitually resident in [the foreign] State' at the time the contract was made; or
- the employee is not employed for commercial purposes (e.g. is employed in a diplomatic mission) and, at the time proceedings were brought, was a national of the foreign state; or
- the employee is not employed for commercial purposes (e.g. is employed in a diplomatic mission) and, at the time he became employed, he was neither

a UK national nor habitually resident there (State Immunity Act 1978 (particularly s.4); Diplomatic Privileges Act 1964; Consular Relations Act 1968).

Notwithstanding the normal rules regarding a solicitor's ostensible authority, solicitors acting without authority cannot waive immunity on behalf of a foreign state client. They can waive their client's immunity '. . . only if they have been authorised by the State, which includes authority exercised or conferred by the head of the State's diplomatic mission . . .' (*Yemen* v. *Aziz* [2005] ICR 1391, CA).

Certain international organisations are also exempt from legal suit. Orders in Council can be made under the International Organisations Act 1968 to grant immunity to certain categories of international organisation. In practice, many of these organisations will waive immunity: however, it is there to be claimed should they so desire.

Organisations in respect of which Orders in Council have been made include:

- United Nations;
- North Atlantic Treaty Organisation (NATO);
- World Health Organisation;
- World Trade Organisation;
- International Monetary Fund (IMF);
- International Labour Organisation (ILO);
- European Bank for Reconstruction and Development.

11.3.5 Dismissal procedures agreement in force

The Secretary of State can make an Order exempting certain industries from unfair dismissal legislation, provided a suitable alternative remedy has been set up by agreement between the industry and independent trade unions (ERA 1996, s.110). There are no dismissal procedure agreements currently in force.

11.3.6 Expiry of a fixed-term contract

The coming to an end of a fixed-term contract counts as dismissal for unfair dismissal and redundancy purposes (ERA 1996, ss.95 and 136). Until 25 October 1999 an agreement to opt out of this special protection was legally valid if in writing and the fixed term was for a minimum of one year. That 'unfair dismissal opt out option' was terminated by the Employment Relations Act 1999, s.18.

Whether a particular dismissal is unfair must then be decided according to the normal rules.

If it is shown that there was a genuine purpose for the contract being set up as a fixed-term contract, that fact was known to the employee and that the specific purpose has ceased to be applicable, then the employer may be able to win an argument that the deemed dismissal on expiry was 'some other substantial reason' and the employee may then not be able to win a claim that it was unfair dismissal (*Terry* v. *East Sussex County Council* [1976] ICR 536, EAT and *North Yorkshire County Council* v. *Fay* [1985] IRLR 247, CA).

Prior to allowing the fixed term to elapse, employers should consult with employees about whether there is any alternative employment available for them.

Note that under the Fixed-term Employees (Prevention of Less Favourable Treatment) Regulations 2002, SI 2002/2034, a fixed-term contract is normally automatically converted by law into a contract of indefinite duration once the employee has completed four years' continuous employment under it or under renewals of it (SI 2002/2034, reg.8).

11.3.7 Illegal contracts and tax evasion

A basic principle of contract law is that a party to an illegal contract should not be able to sue on that contract. Thus a contract to employ somebody to commit a crime is unenforceable – as an extreme example, a contract killer cannot claim unfair dismissal. Accordingly, the courts have held that where a contract of employment is tainted with illegality, then the basic position is that employment rights flowing from that contract, including the right to claim unfair dismissal, cannot be enforced (*Newland* v. *Simons & Willer (Hairdressers) Ltd* [1981] IRLR 359).

If a particular employment is illegal by statute, involves criminality or is unenforceable as being contrary to public policy, that is an end of the matter. Knowledge or lack of knowledge of these matters will not make any difference to whether the employee can bring any claim – the answer is just plain 'no'. For example, if an employee who comes from outside the EC works in Britain without a work permit, then the contract of employment is illegal from the outset and the employee will be unable to claim unfair dismissal (*Bamgbose* v. *The Royal Star and Garter Home* (unreported, EAT, 26 November 1996)).

However, if the illegality lies in the way an employment contract is performed the employee's knowledge and the degree of his participation in the illegality can be very relevant to deciding whether or not the contract is illegal and thus whether a claim derived from the employment is unenforceable (*Bakersfield Entertainment Limited* v. *Church and Stuart* (unreported, EAT, 4 November 2005)).

For some years it seemed that the position differed depending on whether the claim was a discrimination claim or one of the other types of employment law claim such as unfair dismissal. It seemed that in discrimination cases a claim by an employee could be defeated on grounds of illegality only if the employee both knew that there had been a deliberate attempt to set up arrangements in a way which was illegal and actively participated in their illegal performance (*Hall* v. *Woolston Hall Leisure Ltd* [2001] ICR 99 – subject to an exception that if the illegality was so closely connected with the alleged discrimination that allowing the claim to proceed would be tantamount to condoning it, then the employee will not be allowed to proceed, see *Vakante* v. *Addey and Stanhope School* [2004] EWCA 1065). However, in non-discrimination cases it seemed that mere knowledge of the facts giving rise to the illegality was enough to prevent an employee bringing a claim even if he was unaware that there was anything wrong in what was being done (*Salvesen* v. *Simons* [1994] ICR 409, EAT).

Now, following a decision of the EAT in an unfair dismissal case in 2007, upheld by the Court of Appeal in April 2008, it seems that the true position is that the 'doctrine of illegality' operates in unfair dismissal cases in much the same way as in discrimination cases (*Enfield Technical Services Ltd* v. *Payne and Grace* v. *BF Components Ltd* [2007] IRLR 840, upheld by the Court of Appeal [2008] IRLR 500). In that case Elias P. said 'there must be some form of misrepresentation, some attempt to conceal the true facts of the relationship, before the contract is rendered illegal . . .'.

In practice, in the authors' view, the combined result of these judgments is likely to mean that in both unfair dismissal and discrimination cases for an employer to be able to use 'illegality of contract' as a defence to a claim by an employee he would have to be able to demonstrate at least that the employee knew something 'shady' was going on even if the employee did not know it was actually illegal. Clearly, however, each case has to be considered on its own facts and merits.

Illegality of contract issues most frequently arise where tax evasion is occurring. A tribunal will draw a distinction between illegal tax evasion and lawful tax avoidance. Thus an arrangement by an employee to evade PAYE and NICs will taint his contract with illegality with the result that he will not be able to bring an unfair dismissal claim even if the arrangement was made in good faith (*Daymond* v. *Enterprise South Devon* (unreported, EAT, 6 June 2007)). Even minor or short-term tax evasion, such as claiming that income is taxable under Schedule D rather than Schedule E (with its deferred payment) will prevent a claim of unfair dismissal (*Salvesen* v. *Simons* [1994] ICR 409, EAT and *Hunt* v. *Power Resources Ltd* (unreported, EAT, 10 February 2005)). Likewise, an employee who colludes with the employer by pretending to be self-employed so as to qualify for legal aid and obtain the benefit of deferring income tax and paying lower Class 4 NI contributions was held to have disqualified himself from the right to bring a claim for unfair dismissal (*Beauvale Furnishings Ltd* v. *Chapman* [2001] Emp LR 501 and *Soteriou* v. *Ultrachem* [2004] IRLR 870, QBD).

However, the employee will remain able to claim unfair dismissal if:

- greater public policy arguments exist, for example, to provide protection for employees against being dismissed when they blow the whistle on their employer's unlawful practices (*Hewcastle Catering Ltd* v. *Ahmed & Elkamah* [1992] ICR 626, CA); or
- the unlawfulness of the employee's position is minor and pales into insignificance beside that of the employer; a court may decide that it would be proper to allow the employee to have enforceable rights (*Saunders* v. *Edwards* [1987] 1 WLR 1116); or
- the illegality is minor and one-off, for example, the non-deduction of PAYE from a one-off payment which did not form part of the employee's regular remuneration. The court held that the conduct was unlawful, but not so bad as to result in the whole contract being treated as illegal/unenforceable (*Annandale Engineering* v. *Samson* [1994] IRLR 59, EAT).

The burden of proof is on the employer to establish illegality, not on the employee to prove he can bring a claim (*Colen* v. *Cebrian (UK) Ltd* [2004] ICR 568, CA).

11.3.8 Police and prison officers

The position here is more complex than it need be. Traditionally police officers are not employees within the meaning of ERA 1996: their service is governed by statute not contract. Accordingly, they cannot claim, for example, unfair dismissal or for unlawful deductions from wages under ERA 1996. However, special rules extend the sex, race and disability discrimination legislation, and whistleblowing and health and safety rules to police officers.

Under the Prisons Act 1952, prison officers have the powers and privileges of a constable so if it were not for special provision in the Criminal Justice and Public Order Act 1994 they would be subject to the same employment law rules as are applicable to police officers. The 1994 Act ensures that prison officers are treated differently from the police and that they are not excluded from employment protection rights.

If internal police disciplinary rules are not followed, the police officers may have remedies under the law of judicial review (*R* v. *Sec'y of State for Home Dep't ex p Benwell* [1984] ICR 723, QBD and *Commissioner of the Metropolitan Police* v. *Lowrey-Nesbit* [1999] ICR 401, EAT). Further, the Police Act 1996 provides for disciplinary rules and appeals to a police appeals tribunal (Police Act 1996, ss.50 and 85).

By contrast, employees of the four statutory police forces not maintained by Home Office grant (the British Transport Police, the Ministry of Defence Police, the Royal Parks Constabulary and the UK Energy Authority Police) are employees. However, they are specifically excluded from claiming unfair dismissal, with the exception that they are entitled to claim if the reason for their dismissal is an automatically unfair health and safety reason within ERA 1996, s.100 (ERA 1996, s.200; S*pence* v. *British Railways Board* [2001] ICR 232, EAT; *Sweeney* v. *Chief Constable of the Ministry of Defence* (unreported, EAT, 28 May 2001)).

11.3.9 Profit-sharing fishermen

No employment law textbook would be complete without a reference to profit-sharing fishermen. Employment 'as a master or as a member of the crew of a fishing vessel where the employee is remunerated only by a share in the profits or gross earnings of the vessel' is excluded from unfair dismissal rights (ERA 1996, s.199(2)). This has been interpreted strictly: a fisherman whose remuneration is a share of the profits of the employer's fleet (as contrasted with the profits of the vessel) is entitled to the benefit of unfair dismissal legislation (*Goodeve* v. *Gilsons* [1985] ICR 401, CA).

11.3.10 Striking workers

As a general rule, employees taking part in unofficial industrial action cannot claim unfair dismissal unless the reason for dismissal is pregnancy, maternity or other automatically unfair reason (TULRCA 1992, s.237(1)).

An employee taking part in official industrial action can only complain of unfair dismissal if there has been selective dismissal of employees taking part in the action, or there have been selective offers of re-engagement to employees taking part in the action. If the employer dismisses all employees taking part in the action, they cannot claim unfair dismissal (TULRCA 1992, s.238).

However, an employer cannot dismiss employees engaged in official industrial action during an initial protected period. The protected period is usually 12 weeks from the date when the industrial action started. This period is extended if the employer is stonewalling and not taking reasonable steps to resolve the dispute. Dismissal of employees during the protected period is automatically unfair (TULRCA 1992, s.238A).

11.3.11 Temporary replacements for women on maternity leave

Strictly, this is not an exclusion from the right to claim but a defence to a claim of unfair dismissal. However, it is convenient to deal with it at this stage.

If an employee is employed upon a temporary basis to cover for a woman on maternity leave, and is dismissed when the woman returns, then the reason for the dismissal is deemed to be 'some other substantial reason' within s.98(1) of ERA 1996. However, to fall within this rule, the temporary worker must have been informed in writing, at the time the job is offered, that the employment will be terminated when the original worker resumes work (ERA 1996, s.106).

A point to watch out for is that if temporary replacements are engaged on fixed-term contracts, they are likely to be entitled to the same wages as the new mother they are standing in for. This follows from the terms of the Fixed-Term Employees (Prevention of Less Favourable Treatment) Regulations 2002, SI 2002/2034 (see **section 11.4**). We are aware of at least one case in which a tribunal has made an award on this basis.

11.3.12 Workers ordinarily outside Great Britain

Prior to 25 October 1999, s.196 of ERA 1996 contained complex provisions disentitling persons who worked outside the UK from claiming unfair dismissal. This was repealed by the Employment Relations Act 1999.

The position is now governed by general law. In debate on the matter in the House of Lords, a government spokesman (Lord Highbury) said 'After careful consideration, we have concluded that the complexities are unnecessary. International law and the principles of our own domestic law are enough to ensure that our legislation does not apply in inappropriate circumstances' (Hansard, 8 July 1999, cols.1089/1090). Since then lawyers, tribunals and the courts have found great difficulty in establishing what are 'inappropriate circumstances'.

The House of Lords clarified the position in January 2006. The all-important question is whether an employment tribunal has jurisdiction. The House of Lords made it clear that for a tribunal to have jurisdiction it is not essential that the employment in question should have been in Great Britain. It is sufficient that the employment relationship is closely connected with Great Britain (*Lawson v. Serco* [2006] IRLR 289, HL).

Although it will only be in unusual circumstances that an employee who works and is based abroad comes within the scope of the unfair dismissal provisions, the House of Lords gave two examples of situations in which the employment relationship might be sufficiently closely connected with Great Britain to enable an employment tribunal to entertain an unfair dismissal claim as: (i) where an employee is posted abroad to work for a business conducted in Britain; and/or (ii) where he is working in a political or social British enclave abroad.

Later in the joined cases of *Burke v. The British Council; ADT Fire & Security plc v. Speyer; Cameron v. Navy, Army and Air Force Institutes* (unreported, EAT, 14 December 2006), the EAT gave further more particularised guidance in the light of the House of Lords' judgment in *Lawson v. Serco*. The EAT said there are 'five gateways' to jurisdiction:

a) The standard case; the employee is working in Great Britain at the time when he is dismissed with the focus on that time rather than on the time the contract was made.
b) The peripatetic employee; the employee's base i.e. the place where he is ordinarily working, as judged not so much by the terms of the contract but by the conduct of the parties, is in Great Britain.

c) The expatriate (1); the employee who works and is based abroad and who is the overseas representative, posted abroad by an employer for the purposes of a business carried on in Britain e.g. foreign correspondent of the Financial Times . . .
d) The expatriate (2); the employee who works in a British enclave abroad; jurisdiction will be established provided the employee was recruited in Britain;
e) The expatriate (3); the employee who has equally strong connections as the above two with Britain and British employment law.

11.4 CAPABILITY OR QUALIFICATIONS

11.4.1 Introduction

Under ERA 1996, one of the potentially fair reasons for dismissal is that the reason 'relates to the capability or qualifications of the employee for performing work of the kind which he was employed by the employer to do' (ERA 1996, s.98(2)(a)).

When relying on this reason, the employer needs to demonstrate that the employee's capability or qualifications were the reason, or principal reason, for the dismissal. The tribunal then has to be satisfied that the dismissal was fair in all the circumstances. Guidance can be found in the Acas Code of Practice on Disciplinary and Grievance Procedures (CoP 1). A new version of this Code is currently under preparation, and a draft was prepared for consultation in May 2008. Whilst the Code does not apply directly to capability dismissals, the courts have said that it provides the starting point for establishing procedural fairness in capability as well as conduct dismissals (*Lewis Shops Group* v. *Wiggins* [1973] IRLR 205).

When dismissing for reasons relating to capability, an employer must bear in mind the effect of DDA 1995. If the employee qualifies as disabled within the meaning of the Act and it is possible for the employer to make reasonable adjustments to enable the employee to perform the job, then the employer will probably be in breach of DDA 1995 if he fails to make such adjustments. In addition, the employer will probably be found to have acted unfairly in all the circumstances, thus also rendering the dismissal unfair under ERA 1996. However, the tests for disability discrimination and unfair dismissal are separate and breach of one Act does not automatically entail breach of the other (*Kent County Council* v. *Mingo* [2000] IRLR 90, EAT).

A peculiar aspect of the law relating to capability/qualification dismissals is that the authorities almost all date back to the early and mid-1970s. This is probably because the principles of law are straightforward: investigate, warn, wait, dismiss. Cases tend to turn on the facts rather than points of law.

It is important to remember that the intended repeal of the compulsory dispute resolution procedures introduced in 2004 is unlikely to be effective until April 2009 (see **Chapter 4**). Until they have been repealed they must be carefully observed in every case.

11.4.2 Qualifications

'Qualification' is defined by ERA 1996 in the following terms: ' "qualification", in relation to an employee, means any degree, diploma or other academic, technical or professional qualification relevant to the position which he held' (s.98(3)).

There are very few cases dealing with lack of qualifications as a reason for dismissal. Often, if an employee has misled an employer about qualifications on an application form, the matter will become clear – and the employee will be dismissed – before accruing the one year's continuous employment needed to bring a claim of unfair dismissal. When the employee has accrued the necessary qualifying period of employment, many employers will treat the case as one relating to conduct (i.e. lying on the application form) and deal with it under that route.

Qualification has been interpreted as relating to aptitude or ability. A mere licence, permit or other authorisation does not fall within the definition of qualification unless it is substantially concerned with the aptitude or ability of the person to do the job. Thus the dismissal of a seafarer who was not registered was not a reason relating to his qualifications (*Blue Star Ship Management Ltd v. Williams* [1979] IRLR 16). However, the holding of a driving licence can be a qualification within the statutory definition (*Tayside Regional Council v. McIntosh* [1982] IRLR 272) as can the holding of a pilot's licence (*Sayers v. Loganair Ltd* (unreported, EAT, 17 May 2005)).

11.4.3 Capability: incompetence

'Capability' is defined in the ERA 1996 in the following terms: ' "capability", in relation to an employee, means his capability assessed by reference to skill, aptitude, health or any other physical or mental quality' (ERA 1996, s.98(3)).

In practice, as well as in the statutory definition, a distinction is drawn between cases involving incapability due to the employee's incompetence and cases involving incapability due to the employee's inability to work through ill health. This section deals with the former, the latter is dealt with in **section 11.4.4**.

Issues of 'capability' and issues of 'conduct' (see **section 11.5**) should not be confused. Persistently poor job performance can amount to misconduct entitling the employer to dismiss an employee but it does not normally come within the 'capability and qualifications' head considered above (*London Borough of Hackney v. Benn* [1997] IRLR 157, CA). Incompetence and laziness are not the same thing. Laziness will usually be conduct rather than capability (*Sutton & Gates (Luton) v. Boxall* [1979] ICR 67, EAT).

For an employer to dismiss for reasons of incompetence, the employer must have evidence that the employee was, in fact, incapable of doing the work. Often incompetence will be evident long before the employee has accrued the year's continuity of employment needed to bring a claim for unfair dismissal. However, in certain cases (such as a promotion, or moving to a different job with an associated employer), the employee may have already accrued a year's continuity of employment before the inability to discharge job functions becomes evident.

It is not for a tribunal to decide whether it thinks the employee is capable of doing the job. Provided the employer has formed a genuine and reasonably held belief that the employee is not meeting the required standards, the tribunal must not substitute its views for those of the employer. Thus where an airline pilot was involved in a faulty landing causing damage to the aircraft (and, as bad luck would have it, a senior executive from the airline was on the flight), the pilot's dismissal was held to be fair. As Lord Denning said:

> Whenever a man is dismissed for incapacity or incompetence it is sufficient that the employer honestly believes on reasonable grounds that the man is incapable and incompetent. It is not necessary for the employer to prove that he is in fact incapable or incompetent.
>
> *Taylor* v. *Alidair Ltd* [1978] IRLR 82, CA

In practice, to demonstrate that its belief was genuinely held on reasonable grounds, an employer will have to provide evidence of the employee's inability to perform adequately. Sometimes an assertion of the employee's incompetence by a sensible manager will suffice and the courts have held that tribunals are entitled to accept such evidence at face value and not insist on corroboration. However, a tribunal would normally expect to see at least one warning letter to the employee setting out the ways in which the employer asserts that he is failing to meet standards (*Cook* v. *Thomas Linnell & Sons Ltd* [1977] IRLR 132).

Evidence which may assist an employer in establishing that it held a reasonable belief in the employee's incompetence includes staff appraisals (*Cook* v. *Thomas Linnell & Sons Ltd* [1977] IRLR 132), complaints by customers (*Dunning & Sons (Shop Fitters)* v. *Jacomb* [1973] IRLR 206) or staff members (*Hopper* v. *Feedex Ltd* [1974] IRLR 99), or a general fall-off in trade (*Cook*).

It is important that employees are judged only in respect of matters which are part and parcel of the job they were employed to do. Thus the dismissal of an assistant accountant for lacking management ability was held to be unfair, because he had been employed to assist with accounts, not to be a manager (*Woods* v. *Olympic Aluminium Co Ltd* [1975] IRLR 356).

Warnings

The employer is under an obligation to warn the employee of the respects in which he is failing to do his job adequately, warning him of the possibility or likelihood of dismissal on this ground and giving him an opportunity to improve his performance (*James* v. *Waltham Holy Cross UDC* [1973] IRLR 202).

It is uncommon for a dismissal to be found fair if the employer has not warned the employee that performance is unsatisfactory. The authorities make it clear that a reasonable employer is expected to give the employee at least one opportunity to improve. An isolated careless act will rarely justify dismissal. This is of valuable social benefit as well, because studies demonstrate that the cost of recruiting and training a new employee will usually exceed the cost of retaining and retraining an existing one (*Scottish Co-Operative Wholesale Society Ltd* v. *Lloyd* [1973] IRLR 93; *Jones* v. *GEC Elliott Automation Ltd* [1972] IRLR 111; *Jones* v. *London Co-operative Society* [1975] IRLR 110).

It can be reasonable for an employer to dismiss without giving a warning in rare circumstances. There exists old authority suggesting that if the employee will not change his ways, and a warning would be futile, it is not necessary to warn him (*Retarded Children's Aid Society* v. *Day* [1978] IRLR 128, CA; *Grant* v. *Ampex (Great Britain) Ltd* [1980] IRLR 461). The authors consider that it would be dangerous to rely on these authorities nowadays, because – particularly in the light of cases such as *Polkey* v. *AE Dayton Services Ltd* [1988] AC 344, HL – a tribunal is likely to say that an employer cannot know that a warning would be futile until it has tried to warn. As Sir Hugh Griffiths said in a well-known passage in *Winterhalter Gastranom Ltd* v. *Webb* [1973] ICR 245, 'many [employees] do not know that they are capable of jumping the five-barred gate until the bull is close behind them'.

The probable futility of a warning would go to compensation rather than fairness. If the consequences of the employee's act of incompetence were particularly serious, the employer may be justified in dismissing without warning because it cannot risk any repetition of the incompetent or careless job performance. Thus, in the *Taylor* case referred to above, the airline was entitled to dismiss Mr Taylor without warning because the potential consequences of another faulty landing were so serious (*Taylor* v. *Alidair Ltd* [1978] IRLR 82, CA). In *Taylor*, the EAT gave other examples where no warning would necessarily be expected, such as the scientist operating a nuclear reactor, the driver of the London to Manchester express or the driver of an articulated lorry full of sulphuric acid. It can be seen that this exception only applies to employment involving the greatest danger to the public and, indeed, the Court of Appeal has refused to apply this principle to a teacher who was dismissed without warning (*Inner London Education Authority* v. *Lloyd* [1981] IRLR 394, CA).

Opportunity to improve

A warning is pointless without giving the employee an opportunity to improve. If no period is offered then, subject to establishing one of the reasons for not giving any warning (above), the dismissal will probably be unfair.

How long a period ought to be given? This is a question of fact and a tribunal will decide whether it considers the period provided to be reasonably sufficient to allow the employee to achieve (or demonstrate) a satisfactory level of improvement. Factors taken into account are the nature of the job, the employee's length of satisfactory service and the turnaround time for demonstrating improvement. Thus tribunals have held that three months is reasonable for a sales director with two years' employment (*Winterhalter Gastronom Ltd* v. *Webb* [1973] IRLR 120), five weeks is insufficient for a manager of six years' experience (*Evans* v. *George Galloway & Co* [1974] IRLR 167) and three years is a reasonable period for a salesman with almost 20 years' satisfactory service (*Sibun* v. *Modern Telephones Ltd* [1976] IRLR 81). In *Stolt Offshore Ltd* v. *Fraser* (unreported, EAT 0041/02, 26 February 2003) a dismissal based on a final written warning issued two years earlier to an employee engaged on a series of fixed-term contracts was found to be justified.

Alternative employment

An employer should be able to show that it has considered alternative employment; even if the end result is that it does not think that there is anything suitable for the incompetent employee. The extent of the obligation to seek alternative employment will depend on factors such as the size of the company and whether the employee had a history of being able to do another job competently (*Henderson* v. *Masson Scott Thrissel Engineering Ltd* [1974] IRLR 98).

11.4.4 Capability: ill-health

An employee will be incapable of performing his job properly if he is absent through ill-health: either through an on-going series of short-term absences, or a single lengthy episode of absence. Ill-health dismissals are the most frequently encountered examples of capability dismissals.

In very limited situations, there is a statutory obligation to suspend employees rather than dismiss them. This is considered in **sections 7.3.5** and **7.3.12**. Note that a lengthy absence may, in rare circumstances, frustrate the contract of employment. Frustration is not an argument that often wins favour with tribunals: see *Four Seasons Healthcare Ltd* v. *Maughan* [2005] IRLR 324, EAT and *Jones* v. *Friction Dynamics Ltd* (unreported, EAT, 28 March 2007). This is dealt with in **section 10.8**.

Note that the provisions of DDA 1995 must be considered when considering dismissal on grounds of long-term illness: in particular, the duty to make reasonable adjustments (see **Chapter 15**).

The crucial point to bear in mind in ill-health dismissals is that tribunals are not particularly concerned with what has happened in the past. They are far more interested in whether the employer has taken reasonable steps to investigate what is likely to happen in the future. Even if an employee has been absent for many, many months, if his return is imminent an employer will act unfairly in dismissing him.

Particular difficulty can arise if the reason for the employee's illness was work-related (for example, inhalation of noxious fumes or – as now commonly seen – stress). At one time the EAT suggested that 'an employer's treatment of an employee which causes ill-health which in turn causes incapability which the employer treats as a reason for dismissal can never make the dismissal unfair' (*London Fire & Civil Defence Authority* v. *Betty* [1994] IRLR 384). However, it subsequently said that such a black and white statement of the position is wrong (*Edwards* v. *Governors of Hanson School* [2001] IRLR 733, EAT).

The correct position is that an employer's treatment of an employee which causes ill-health which in turn causes incapability which the employer treats as a reason for dismissal does not of itself make a dismissal unfair. The proper approach is to apply ERA 1996, s.98 in the normal way and decide whether dismissal was or was not within the range of reasonable responses for the employer in the circumstances – which of course include the nature and extent of the responsibility of the employer for the incapability. As the EAT has pointed out, if it were otherwise it would mean that in practice employers could be obliged to retain indefinitely employees who were incapable of any useful work (*Royal Bank of Scotland plc* v. *McAdie* (unreported, EAT, 29 November 2006), the logic and the decision in this case being subsequently confirmed by the Court of Appeal in *McAdie* v. *Royal Bank of Scotland plc* [2007] IRLR 895, CA).

A dismissal may be justified if the risk of future illness places the health and safety of other employees in jeopardy. Thus a sole wireless operator at risk of a heart attack on a ship could be fairly dismissed, due to the risk to his fellow sailors if he suffered acute coronary disease (*Converfoam (Darwen) Ltd* v. *Bell* [1981] IRLR 193, EAT).

Timing

The EAT has stated that: 'The basic question which has to be determined in every case is whether, in all the circumstances, the employer can be expected to wait any longer and, if so, how much longer?' The relevant circumstances included 'the nature of the illness, the likely length of the continuing absence, the need of the employers to have done the work which the employee was engaged to do' (*Spencer* v. *Paragon Wallpapers Ltd* [1976] IRLR 373, EAT quoted with approval by the Court of Appeal in *O'Donoghue* v. *Elmbridge Housing Trust* [2004] EWCA Civ 939, CA, 16 June 2004).

Making enquiries

In order to form a view on the likelihood of the employee's return to work (or the probability of continuing short-term absences), the employer must make reasonable enquiries. Failure to do so will almost always result in the dismissal being unfair.

This involves two distinct stages. First, the employer should consult fully with the employee so as to establish the reason for the absence(s) and the employee's view of when he is likely to return to work (*East Lindsey District Council* v. *Daubney* [1977] IRLR 181). Note that the obligation to remain in contact is that of the employer: the employer cannot avoid this obligation by saying 'the employee never contacted me' (*Mitchell* v. *Arkwood Plastics (Engineering) Ltd* [1993] ICR 471).

The employee should be made aware that the employer is contemplating dismissal if the employee does not return to work. This is not so much a disciplinary warning as giving the employee full notice of the potential outcome if her health does not improve.

Second, the employer will normally be expected to undertake some level of consultation with a doctor. A good example is a case in 2007 in which a bus driver suffered a suspected stroke. His PSV licence was rescinded and his employers dismissed him without waiting for medical reports to confirm whether he was permanently incapacitated. The EAT agreed with an employment tribunal that this was unreasonable and that the dismissal was unfair (*First West Yorkshire t/a First Leeds* v. *Haigh* [2008] IRLR 182, EAT). However, an employee cannot be compelled to undergo medical examination or submit to disclosure of medical records (unless the employee has agreed to do so in the contract of employment) and if the employee refuses to consent, the employer will not be criticised provided it has attempted to obtain medical advice.

In practice, tribunals are sometimes willing to overlook a failure to gain medical advice in cases of repeated short-term absences, when there have been warnings for those absences. The reason is not clear: it seems to be partly because the absences are treated as conduct (rather than capability) issues, and partly because medical opinion will rarely be helpful when the causes of absence are temporary and transient (*International Sports Co Ltd* v. *Thompson* [1980] IRLR 340).

Depending on the nature of the illness, the employer must decide whether to seek the opinion of a specialist or simply to rely on a GP's report. There is danger in relying on a GP's report for anything other than small companies: a tribunal may consider that it was unreasonable to limit investigation to a medical expert who does not specialise in the relevant medical field. Further, in practice, GPs' reports rarely contain clear prognoses and an employer will be criticised if it dismissed based upon an unclear prognosis (*Crampton* v. *Dacorum Motors Ltd* [1975] IRLR 168).

The employer must ensure that the instructions sent to the medical expert are clear. If it transpires that the medical expert was not provided with all relevant information (even if the omission was inadvertent), any dismissal will probably be unfair (*Ford Motor Car Co Ltd* v. *Nawaz* [1987] IRLR 163).

If the medical opinion demonstrates that the employee is unlikely to return to work in the near future, and the employer is satisfied that its business interests require dismissal of the employee, it will normally be fair to dismiss.

Alternative employment

An employer should always consider alternative employment in cases of ill-health dismissals. Is there a job which the employee could undertake from home? Is there light work available that the employee could do? A failure to consider alternatives will often render a dismissal unfair (although the compensatory award will be nil if there were, in fact, no suitable alternative positions available) (*Merseyside & North Wales Electricity Board* v. *Taylor* [1975] IRLR 60).

11.5 CONDUCT

11.5.1 General

It is important to remember that intended repeal of the compulsory dispute resolution procedures introduced in 2004 is unlikely to be effective until April 2009 (see **Chapter 4**). Until they have been repealed they must be carefully observed in every case.

Misconduct by an employee is a ground frequently relied on by employers to justify dismissal. If the principal reason for a dismissal is serious misconduct which the employer reasonably believes has been committed by the employee, then the dismissal can be regarded as potentially fair (ERA 1996, s.98(2)(b)).

Whether the dismissal is, in fact, fair or unfair will then turn on whether the employment tribunal considers that the employer acted reasonably in the circumstances (which include the size and administrative resources of the employer's undertaking) in treating it 'as a sufficient reason for dismissing the employee'. There is no onus of proof on employer or employee here and the matter has to be determined by the tribunal 'in accordance with equity and the substantial merits of the case'. Each case has to be looked at on its own particular facts and, although some general principles can be drawn from case law, past cases should generally be treated only as examples and not as establishing that a particular type of misconduct does or does not justify dismissal (ERA 1996, s.98(4)).

A well-established three-limb test known as the 'Burchell guidelines' shows that in coming to its decision on whether a dismissal for misconduct was fair or unfair an employment tribunal must consider: (i) whether the employer genuinely believed that the employee had been guilty of the misconduct when it dismissed him; (ii) if so, were there reasonable grounds for the belief; and (iii) did the employer carry out as much investigation into the matter as was reasonable in all the circumstances before dismissing the employee? (*British Home Stores* v. *Burchell* [1980] ICR 303, EAT).

Case law further establishes that even if the matter is finely balanced an employment tribunal must not substitute its own view for that of the employer. The correct test is not whether a reasonable employer would have dismissed the employee as opposed to imposing a lesser penalty, but whether dismissal fell within the range of reasonable responses of a reasonable employer in all the circumstances. The dismissal will be unfair only if the employer's decision to dismiss was outside this band of reasonable responses (*Midland Bank plc* v. *Madden* [2002] 2 All ER 741 and *Post Office* v. *Foley* [2000] ICR 1283, CA) (see also **section 11.10**). It is also established that the test of whether a decision to dismiss falls within the band of reasonable responses to the employee's conduct which a reasonable employer could adopt is a test which applies to each of the three limbs of the Burchell guidelines noted above (see *Iceland Frozen Foods Ltd* v. *Jones* [1983] ICR 17, EAT). Thus the test applies not only in determining whether it was procedurally or substantively fair or unfair for an employer to dismiss an employee but also in determining whether investigations carried out by the employer were reasonable in all the circumstances (*Sainsbury (J.) Ltd* v. *Hitt* [2002] EWCA Civ 1588, [2003] ICR 111, CA).

Readers looking for a clear and relatively simple example of the way the Burchell guidelines are applied in practice might care to look at the EAT judgment in *Tesco Stores Ltd* v. *Pryke*, 10 May 2006 – this case includes a very clear summary by the EAT of the principles which must be taken into account in deciding whether a dismissal is fair or unfair in conduct cases. Tesco dismissed an employee of 15 years, during the last seven of which he had worked as a lorry driver, accident free. In June 2004 his lorry overturned at a roundabout. He said the lorry had been badly loaded. Speed could not be confirmed as his tachograph was missing. After proper procedures he was dismissed. An employment tribunal found that he been unfairly dismissed on the basis that Tesco's failure to interview two trainee loaders meant that Tesco's investigation had not been reasonable. The EAT remitted the case back to a different tribunal for rehearing on the basis that the tribunal had substituted its own view of what was a reasonable investigation for the 'range of reasonable responses' test which it should have applied.

Even if an employment tribunal decides that an employer's decision to dismiss an employee for misconduct was within the range of reasonable responses open to the employer, the dismissed employee may still be able to claim that his dismissal was unfair if he can show that the employer did not really believe that dismissal was appropriate on the particular facts of the case

(*Hicks* v. *Allied Glass Containers Ltd* (unreported, EAT, 25 March 2003) and to justify dismissal the employer must have reasonable grounds for that belief (see e.g. *Porter* v. *Oakbank School* [2004] 5C 603, IH (Ex Div)).

The basic rule is that it is for the employer to show the reason (or, if more than one, the principal reason) for a dismissal (ERA 1996, s.98). A particular danger for employers when dismissing an employee for misconduct is that the employee may claim that misconduct was not the real reason for the dismissal. A good example is *East Lancashire Coachbuilders* v. *Hilton* (unreported, EAT, 24 August 2006) in which a director was dismissed ostensibly on the grounds of misconduct which had clearly taken place but a tribunal found the real reason for his dismissal was quite different, had nothing to do with misconduct and was unfair.

In *Queen Elizabeth Hospital NHS Trust* v. *Ogunlana* (unreported, EAT, 6 October 2006), the EAT neatly summarised the overall position as follows:

> It is for the employer to show a genuine belief in the misconduct alleged, and that that belief was the reason for dismissal;
>
> Having established that potentially fair reason for dismissal, it is for the Tribunal to determine, the burden of proof being neutral, whether the employer carried out a reasonable investigation and had reasonable grounds for that belief. In answering those questions the Tribunal must apply the range of reasonable responses approach. It must not substitute its view as to whether a reasonable investigation was carried out or whether there were reasonable grounds for that belief, for that of the Respondent employer;
>
> A similar approach must be taken to questions of procedural unfairness;
>
> Finally the question is whether dismissal fell within the range of reasonable responses open to the employer.

If an employee has unequivocally admitted the misconduct in question, the employer will generally be able to take that at face value and not have to investigate the matter further (*Millbrook Proving Ground Ltd* v. *Jefferson* (unreported, EAT, 11 March 2008). If the misconduct is not admitted the amount of investigation which an employer should make before deciding to dismiss can be a problem. In 2007 the EAT (overruling an employment tribunal) held that if an employer with responsibility for vulnerable children or adults becomes aware of facts which lead it to lose full confidence in an employee and (after due process) dismisses him, the fact that the employer does not investigate further will not of itself make the dismissal unfair. The EAT emphasised that it was not setting a general rule and that each case must be determined on its own facts (*B* v. *A* (unreported, EAT (Scotland), 3 April 2007)).

If one of a group of employees is guilty of the misconduct but the employer, having made reasonable enquiries, genuinely cannot ascertain which individual(s) was/were responsible it can be fair to dismiss the whole group (*Monie* v. *Coral Racing Ltd* [1980] IRLR 464, CA), or the whole group other than any who the employer genuinely and justifiably believes were not responsible (*Frames Snooker Centre* v. *Boyce* [1992] IRLR 472, EAT).

Similarly if several employees are guilty of the same misconduct and some are sacked but not others then it does not follow that those who were sacked must have been unfairly dismissed. Disparity in treatment is no more than one factor to be taken into account along with other factors. Thus the employer can properly take into account different circumstances such as length of service and/or previous conduct in deciding to dismiss some and not dismiss others. Good examples are *UK Coal Mining Ltd* v. *Raby* (unreported, EAT, 30 January 2003) in which two employees were caught fighting at work and one was dismissed whilst the other was not – the disparity in treatment was justifiable as the one not dismissed was acting in self defence and had an unblemished record which the other did not; and *Enterprise Liverpool plc* v. *Bauress & anor* (unreported, EAT, 30 January 2006) in which three joiners employed by Enterprise Liverpool were caught 'doing a foreigner', that is working for other employers and using their real employer's tools when doing so – two were relatively new employees and were sacked, the other was not. The EAT found that the dismissals were fair.

By the same token the fact that a person ('A') who has been dismissed because of some particular form of misconduct can show that on a previous occasion another employee ('B') had not been dismissed even though B had been guilty of the same type of misconduct is simply one matter to take into account in deciding whether the dismissal was fair or unfair. It certainly does not follow that the dismissal of A is therefore unfair – in every case what matters is the statutory test under ERA 1996, s.98(4) (*Hadjioannou* v. *Coral Casinos Ltd* [1981] IRLR 352 and *Levenes Solicitors* v. *Dalley* (unreported, EAT, 23 November 2006)).

The law differentiates between gross misconduct and misconduct generally. Gross misconduct is an old common law expression which refers to conduct so serious that it justifies instant dismissal without notice. Misconduct can justify dismissal even though it is not gross misconduct in that sense. However, a dismissal for misconduct which was not gross misconduct will normally be an unfair dismissal if the employer failed to discuss the matter properly with the employee, failed to apply any relevant disciplinary procedures or failed to give the employee a chance to correct matters.

Dismissal will usually be a fair sanction in cases of gross misconduct. Offences of violence or dishonesty are taken very seriously and will almost always amount to gross misconduct. Thus, for example, in 2003 the Privy Council dismissed an appeal by a doctor against the General Medical Council's decision to strike him off after conviction for dishonestly claiming £6,300 locum fees, even though he had repaid the money and had an otherwise exemplary record (*Patel* v. *General Medical Council* [2003] IRLR 316, PC).

It is normally incumbent on an employment tribunal to positively consider whether dismissal of an employee came within the band of reasonable responses for an employer in the position of the employer and if the tribunal comes to a decision without such consideration then an appeal by the losing party is likely to succeed to the extent that the EAT would be likely to remit the matter back for a rehearing (*Retirement Care Group Ltd* v. *Greener* (unreported, EAT, 22 May 2002)).

If a tribunal decides in a particular case that the misconduct for which an employee was dismissed was not a sufficient reason for dismissing him the dismissal will have been 'unfair'. Nevertheless if the misconduct contributed to the dismissal it must be taken into account in assessing the compensatory award component of compensation and may be taken into account in assessing the basic award component (ERA 1996, s.123(6); *Optikinetics Ltd* v. *Whooley* [1999] ICR 984, EAT).

11.5.2 Examples

1. An employee refused to work on a day which, under his contract, was a holiday. The work was commercially urgent: this could be conduct justifying dismissal (*Brandon and Goold* v. *Murphy Bros* [1983] IRLR 54).
2. An employee refused to falsify invoices: this was not conduct justifying dismissal (*Morrish* v. *Henlys (Folkestone) Ltd* [1973] IRLR 61).
3. A long-serving member of staff in a shop was caught shoplifting in another shop: this could be conduct justifying dismissal (*Moore* v. *C&A Modes* [1981] IRLR 71).
4. Lateness for work without good reason can be conduct justifying dismissal if it continues over a period of time and is not corrected in spite of warnings (*Hallett & Want* v. *MAT Transport Ltd* [1976] IRLR 5).
5. Being spotted at a function while allegedly absent on sick leave can be conduct justifying dismissal (*Hutchinson* v. *Enfield Rolling Mills Ltd* [1981] IRLR 318, EAT).
6. Unauthorised use of employer's computer equipment can be conduct justifying dismissal (*Denco Ltd* v. *Joinson* [1991] ICR 172, EAT).
7. Unauthorised use of employer's telephone system can be conduct justifying dismissal (*East Berkshire Health Authority* v. *Matadeen* [1992] ICR 724, EAT).
8. A resident social worker slapped an inmate at a young person's residential home: this could be conduct justifying dismissal (*Boys & Girls Welfare* v. *McDonald* [1997] ICR 693, EAT).
9. One-off use of obscene language is unlikely to amount to conduct justifying dismissal (*Wilson* v. *Racher* [1974] ICR 428, CA).
10. A foreman working for a cleaning company applied personally to one of the customers to carry out a cleaning contract for that customer: this was conduct justifying dismissal (*Adamson* v. *B & L Cleaning Services Ltd* [1995] IRLR 193, EAT).
11. An employee normally worked overtime but was not obliged to do so by the terms of his contract. He decided he would in future work overtime

only on days which suited him, which placed his local authority employer in a difficult position. The EAT held that in the circumstances this amounted to conduct justifying his dismissal (*Horrigan* v. *Lewisham Council* [1978] ICR 15, EAT).

12. A bank employee's contract provided that he could be required to work at any of the bank's branches in the UK. He refused to move at short notice from Leeds to Birmingham, resigned and claimed constructive unfair dismissal. The EAT held he had been constructively dismissed and his conduct did not justify that dismissal (*United Bank* v. *Akhtar* [1989] IRLR 507, EAT).
13. A clause in a consultant's contract under which he could be dismissed if he was guilty of conduct tending to bring the 'employer' into disrepute entitled the 'employer' to dismiss him even though the misconduct had taken place before the date of the contract (*Bland* v. *Sparkes* (1999) *The Times*, 17 December).
14. Fighting at work with a fellow employee is likely to be regarded as conduct justifying dismissal even though the employee concerned had previously had a long unblemished record (*Beedell* v. *West Ferry Printers* [2000] IRLR 650, EAT).
15. Private use of telephone at work. Whilst unauthorised private use of a telephone might in some circumstances justify dismissal, this will depend on all the facts and would very seldom if ever justify dismissal without warning. The same thinking would no doubt apply to unauthorised use of the Internet by an employee (*John Lewis plc* v. *Coyne* [2001] IRLR 139, EAT).
16. An employee used a company vehicle for private purposes without permission. The EAT overruled the tribunal's finding of unfair dismissal largely because of the employee's previously unblemished long service but was itself overruled by the Court of Appeal (*Strouthos* v. *London Underground Ltd* [2004] IRLR 636, CA).
17. An employer did not have reasonable grounds for its belief that fraud had been committed and failed to carry out sufficient investigation (*Panama* v. *London Borough of Hackney* [2003] IRLR 278, CA).
18. An employer's use of covert surveillance to get evidence that an employee was falsifying time-sheets was held to be proportionate and not an unlawful infringement of the employee's right to privacy under the Human Rights Act 1998 (*McGowan* v. *Scottish Water* [2005] IRLR 167, EAT).
19. Downloading pornography from the Internet. An example is *London Borough of Hillingdon* v. *Thomas* (2002) *The Times*, October 4, in which the EAT held that an employer's decision to dismiss an HR manager with many years' unblemished service for downloading porn from the Internet in breach of the very rules he was meant to enforce was within the band of reasonable responses open to an employer and was therefore not unfair dismissal.

20. Pretending to be unfit to return to work when video footage showed that he was not so unfit (*Corus UK Ltd* v. *A M Mainwaring* (unreported, EAT, 22 June 2007), which also establishes that there is no absolute requirement for the employer to get a doctor's report in such circumstances).

11.6 RETIREMENT

Since 1 October 2006 enforced retirement of an employee is not unfair dismissal provided that certain conditions are fulfilled (ERA 1996, ss.98(2)(ba) and 98(3A)). The rules relating to age discrimination generally are in the Employment Equality (Age) Regulations 2006, SI 2006/1031 which are considered in more detail at **section 16.1**.

In essence the conditions which must generally be fulfilled for enforced retirement not to be unfair dismissal are that the employee is aged 65 or more (ERA 1996, s.98ZA) and (ERA 1996, s.98ZG) that the employer:

(i) has given the employee notice of the right to request deferred retirement and the date on which he intends the employee to retire;
(ii) has considered any request by the employee not to be retired;
(iii) has considered any appeal against a decision to refuse such a request.

11.7 REDUNDANCY

Redundancy is a potentially fair reason for dismissal. In order to qualify, the employer will need to have undergone a reasonable period of consultation and selection. This is addressed in detail in **Chapter 12**.

11.8 CONTRAVENTION OF A STATUTORY DUTY

Another potentially fair reason for dismissal under ERA 1996 is: 'that the employee could not continue to work in the position which he held without contravention (either on his part or on that of his employer) of a duty or restriction imposed by or under an enactment' (ERA 1996, s.98(2)(d)). This is most commonly seen in cases where a commercial driver, or an on-the-road salesperson, loses his driving licence. However, the mere fact that it becomes a breach of statute to continue employing the worker in that position does not automatically mean any dismissal will be fair: it merely means it is potentially fair. A tribunal will still consider the overriding test of fairness in ERA 1996, s.98(4), the principal factors being whether the employer considered the possibility of alternative employment and whether modifications to the job description would have removed the element of breach of duty (*Appleyard* v. *Smith (Hull) Ltd* [1972] IRLR 19; *Fearn* v. *Tayford Motor Co Ltd* [1975]

IRLR 336; *Sutcliffe & Eaton* v. *Pinney* [1977] IRLR 349, EAT; *Sandhu* v. *Department of Education and Science* [1978] IRLR 208, EAT).

Note that it is necessary for there to be a breach of statute: an honestly and reasonably held belief by the employer will not suffice (although it may suffice to establish dismissal for 'some other substantial reason' – see **section 11.9**) (*Bouchaala* v. *Trusthouse Forte Hotels Ltd* [1980] IRLR 382, EAT and *Klusova* v. *London Borough of Hounslow* [2008] ICR 396, CA). This is in contrast to the position in whistleblowing cases where an employee can claim protection under the whistleblowing legislation if he honestly believed that the matter in respect of breach of which he was blowing the whistle was a genuine legal obligation even if in fact it was not (see *Babula* v. *Waltham Forest College* [2007] ICR 1026, CA and **section 9.25**).

Dismissals on this ground are not matters arising out of capability or conduct so the 2004 statutory disciplinary procedures (see **Chapter 4**) have never applied.

11.9 DISMISSAL FOR SOME OTHER SUBSTANTIAL REASON

11.9.1 General

If an employer can show that the reason for dismissal of an employee was a 'substantial reason of a kind such as to justify the dismissal of an employee holding the position which that employee held' (ERA 1996, s.98(1)(b)), then the dismissal is regarded as potentially fair even if it is not one of the specific potentially fair reasons set out in ERA 1996, s.98(2), i.e. reasons related to capability, qualifications, conduct, retirement or redundancy or which would lead to contravention of a statutory duty or restriction.

Whether the dismissal is, in fact, fair or unfair will then turn on whether the employment tribunal considers that the employer acted reasonably in the circumstances (which include the size and administrative resources of the employer's undertaking) in treating it 'as a sufficient reason for dismissing the employee' (ERA 1996, s.98(4)). There is no onus of proof on employer or employee here and the matter has to be determined by the tribunal in accordance with equity and the substantial merits of the case.

The 'some other substantial reason' provision is a wide mop-up provision designed to ensure that employers are not unduly restricted by having to consider detailed legalistic rules in deciding whether or not it is appropriate to dismiss an employee. Some general principles can be drawn from case law but past cases should generally be treated only as examples and each new case must be looked at on its own particular facts and merits.

Tribunals are required to take into account rights under the European Convention on Human Rights (ECHR) in deciding what is fair. This may have a particular effect on cases in which an employer claims that a dismissal was fair under the 'some other substantial reason' provisions (Human Rights Act 1998, ss.3 and 6).

For example, the European Court of Human Rights held in 1999 that dismissal of a person because he is homosexual infringes Art.8(1) of the ECHR (*Lustig-Prean & Beckett* v. *UK and Smith & Grady* v. *UK* [1999] IRLR 734). Under the Human Rights Act 1998 this would now have to be taken into account by an employment tribunal. Cases such as one in 1980 in which it was held to be fair for an employer to have dismissed a homosexual handyman at a children's camp simply because he was homosexual might therefore now be decided differently unless the employer could also show that it was reasonable for him to believe that the employee posed an actual threat to the children (*Saunders* v. *Scottish National Camps Association Ltd* [1980] IRLR 174). It should also be noted that discrimination on grounds of sexual orientation in an employment or vocational context became unlawful in Britain on 1 December 2003 (under the Employment Equality (Sexual Orientation) Regulations 2003, SI 2003/1661).

It should be noted here that the Human Rights Act 1998 does not give private individuals or companies rights against other private individuals or companies. Rather it enables private citizens to enforce Convention rights against public authorities through the domestic courts, requires that all legislation must be interpreted as far as possible in a way which is compatible with the ECHR and gives the UK courts power in very exceptional cases to make a declaration of incompatibility, stating that a particular piece of UK legislation is incompatible with the ECHR (Human Rights Act 1998, ss.4 and 6; *R.* v. *A.* [2001] UKHL 25).

11.9.2 Examples

1. *Company reorganisations:* if an employer carries out a general reorganisation of its business to improve efficiency and in doing so dismisses an employee then the dismissal may be potentially fair under the 'some other substantial reason' heading (*Catamaran Cruisers Ltd* v. *Williams & anor* [1994] IRLR 386). It is enough for the employer to establish a 'reasonable belief' which is more than 'whimsical, unworthy or trivial' that the reorganisation has advantages (*Scott & Co* v. *Richardson* (unreported, EAT, 26 April 2005)).
2. *Business transfers:* if a dismissal takes place in connection with transfer of ownership of a business it will be automatically unfair unless it can be shown to have been for an 'economic, technical or organisational reason entailing changes in the workforce'. In that case it will be treated as a dismissal for 'some other substantial reason' and thus be potentially a fair dismissal (TUPE 2006, reg.7(3)(b)).
3. *Disclosure of information:* an employee whose spouse worked for a competitor of the employer was held to have been fairly dismissed because of

the risk of disclosure of confidential business information (*Skyrail Oceanic t/a Goodmos Tours* v. *Coleman* [1981] ICR 864, CA). However, the risk must be demonstrably real if dismissal is to be within the range of reasonable responses open to the employer (*Chandlers (Farm Equipment) Ltd* v. *Rainthorpe* (unreported, EAT, 8 February 2005) in which the 'SOSR defence' therefore failed).

4. *Employee changing mind about proposed resignation:* an employee stated that he was intending to emigrate and would be resigning so the employer recruited and trained a successor. The employee then decided not to emigrate but was dismissed. The industrial tribunal, the EAT and the Court of Appeal all found his claim that the dismissal was unfair failed on the basis that his expressed intention to resign was 'some other substantial reason' justifying his dismissal (*Ely* v. *YKK Fasteners Ltd* [1994] ICR 164, CA).
5. *Business disruption:* an employee was held to have been fairly dismissed when the reason was that antagonism between him and another worker in a small business was causing disruption to the business (*Triangle Cars* v. *Hook* (unreported, EAT 1340/98, 1 July 1999)).
6. *Temporary worker covering for a woman on maternity leave, etc.:* provided the temporary worker was informed in writing of the position before being taken on, dismissal when the permanent employee returns from maternity leave (or after a pregnancy or maternity-related absence) will be treated as a dismissal for 'some other substantial reason' and thus be potentially fair. This also applies if a permanent employee has been suspended on medical grounds not connected with pregnancy or maternity (ERA 1996, s.106).
7. *Customer objecting to employee:* provided the employer has been careful to take all the circumstances into account, including the length of time the employee has been working, the likelihood of the employee being able to find alternative employment and the general quality of the employee's work, dismissal of an employee whose continued employment could result in loss of a valued customer or client can be 'some other substantial reason' justifying the dismissal (*Dobie* v. *Burns International Security Services (UK) Ltd* [1984] ICR 812, CA). The employer in such a situation is not required to justify the decision taken by the third party (see e.g. *Scott Packing & Warehouse Co Ltd* v. *Paterson* [1978] IRLR 166 and/or *Grootcon (UK) Ltd* v. *Keld* [1984] IRLR 302, quoted with approval by Burton P. in *B* v. *BAA plc* [2005] IRLR 927, EAT).
8. *Company takeover:* the Court of Appeal ruled that dismissal of a company chief executive by new owners of the employing company was fair after a takeover battle in which the chief executive had strongly fought against the new owners and had even mounted a competing bid (*Cobley* v. *Forward Technology Industries plc* [2003] ICR 1050, CA).
9. *Shift changes for business needs:* the dismissal of an individual who refuses to work on a Sunday for religious reasons, when the business

needs necessitate that she occasionally work on a Sunday, is fair provided the employer balances the prejudice to it of not having her working on a Sunday, against the prejudice to her of imposing the rule (*Copsey* v. *WWB Devon Clays* [2005] IRLR 811).

10. *New restrictive covenants:* The Court of Appeal in 2006 agreed with the EAT that an employee's refusal to sign a new contract of employment containing restrictive covenants could be 'some other substantial reason' for unfair dismissal law purposes provided the requirement for the covenants was genuine and not 'whimsical or capricious' or a put-up job designed to get rid of the employee (*Willow Oak Developments Ltd t/a Windsor Recruitment* v. *Silverwood & ors* [2006] ICR 1552 overruling *Forshaw* v. *Archcraft Ltd* [2005] IRLR 600).

11. *Unsuitability for work with children or vulnerable adults:* an employee who was responsible for care of children was dismissed after receipt by the employer of an enhanced disclosure letter containing adverse information about the employee. The EAT said that an employment tribunal 'should have had no difficulty in holding that that was "some other substantial reason" for the purposes of ERA 1996, s.98(1)(b)' (see *B* v. *A* (unreported, EAT (Scotland), 3 April 2007)).

12. *Dismissal because of pressure from a customer or important third party on the employer:* whether third party pressure justifies dismissal in any particular case will, as always, depend on the particular circumstances. This will include especially whether the employee was warned on accepting the job that he might be dismissed if customers/clients of the employer so requested (*Dobie* v. *Burns International Security Services (UK) Ltd* [1984] ICR 812, CA, in which the Court of Appeal held that a security guard had been unfairly dismissed when the reason for his dismissal was the insistence of the local authority which controlled Liverpool Airport that his employer should not allow that particular individual to do the job). The EAT has said that in this type of situation failure by the employer to consider whether the dismissal would cause an injustice to the employee would be an indication of the fact that the employer had not acted reasonably in all the circumstances (*Greenwood* v. *Whiteghyll Plastics Ltd* (unreported, EAT, 6 August 2007)).

11.10 REASONABLENESS OF DISCIPLINARY SANCTIONS

As part of considering the overall fairness of a dismissal, the tribunal will consider whether dismissal was an appropriate sanction. In cases not involving misconduct, for example, dismissal due to incapability or contravention of a statutory duty, an employer will not act reasonably unless it considers whether there is any alternative employment available for the employee, both within the employer's organisation and within any associated employers.

However, in conduct dismissal the tribunal will always be concerned with reviewing the fairness of the level of sanction imposed. In other words, was dismissal excessive? Would a warning (or some other sanction) have sufficed?

In deciding this question, a tribunal should not substitute its own view for that of the employer. On any given set of facts, one employer might think dismissal is warranted whereas another might not. This does not mean that the stricter employer is acting unreasonably. An employer will only be found to have acted unreasonably if the tribunal thinks that no reasonable employer would have dismissed in those circumstances.

Thus the courts have developed the range of reasonable responses test. If the decision to dismiss falls within the band of reasonable responses to the employee's conduct which a reasonable employer could adopt, the dismissal would be fair (*Iceland Frozen Foods* v. *Jones* [1982] IRLR 439, EAT; *Nkengfack* v. *London Borough of Southwark* [2002] EWCA Civ 711; *Sainsbury's Supermarkets Ltd* v. *Hitt* [2003] IRLR 23; *Stolt Offshore* v. *Fraser* (unreported, EAT 0041/02, 26 February 2003)). Although the courts discourage use of the word 'perverse', it is essentially a perversity test: if the decision to dismiss was perverse, the dismissal will be unfair (*Foley* v. *The Post Office* [2000] IRLR 827, CA).

It is only in exceptional circumstances that it could be said to be within the band of reasonable responses for an employer to avoid giving an employee notice of a charge against him and giving him an opportunity to know what evidence there was against him (*Pudney* v. *Network Rail Ltd* (unreported, EAT, 22 March 2006)).

A disciplinary sanction short of dismissal can entitle the employee to resign and claim unfair and/or wrongful constructive dismissal if the sanction is out of all proportion to the employee's offence (*Stanley Cole (Wainfleet) Ltd* v. *Sheridan* [2003] IRLR 52).

In a case in 2006, a full-time lecturer at Thames Valley University was dismissed because she had another part-time job elsewhere. Thames Valley said the reason for her dismissal was misconduct but she claimed it was really on grounds of competence – and she was able to do both jobs so she claimed the dismissal was wrongful and unfair. She lost before an employment tribunal and again on appeal at the EAT, where Elias P. said 'Dismissal was an appropriate sanction and one which a reasonable employer could impose' (*Guernina* v. *Thames Valley University* (unreported, EAT, 21 December 2006)).

Dismissal will usually be a fair sanction in cases of gross misconduct, unless unusual circumstances exist (for example, particular mitigating circumstances or a history of the employer having a policy of overlooking such offences: *Post Office* v. *Fennell* [1981] IRLR 221, CA). Offences of violence or dishonesty will almost always amount to gross misconduct. The dismissal of an employee for testing positive in a drug test, even though she had smoked cannabis at the weekend before coming on duty and was no longer under its influence, may be found fair (*O'Flynn* v. *Airlinks the Airport Coach Co Ltd* [2002] Emp LR 1217).

If an act of misconduct does not amount to gross misconduct, it will be rare for a tribunal to ratify a decision to dismiss as fair unless:

- there exist unambiguous disciplinary rules making it clear that breach of that rule will result in dismissal, even for a first offence (*Meyer Dunmore International Ltd* v. *Rogers* [1978] IRLR 167, EAT; *W Brooks & Son* v. *Skinner* [1984] IRLR 379, EAT; *Asda Stores Ltd* v. *Malyn* (unreported, EAT, 6 March 2001)); or
- there is a history of warnings for that employee, either in respect of a similar or, indeed, wholly different, disciplinary matter (*Retarded Children's Aid Society* v. *Day* [1978] IRLR 128, CA; *Auguste Noel* v. *Curtis* [1990] IRLR 326, EAT). Note that warnings should lapse after a given period of time (the Acas Code of Practice says that a final written warning should normally be disregarded for disciplinary purposes after a specified period, for example, 12 months). Until quite recently it was thought that once a warning had expired it had to be totally disregarded. However the Court of Appeal has said in 2008 that this is going too far – the existence of an expired warning is a circumstance which an employer can take into account in deciding whether to dismiss an employee but this should not be taken as 'encouraging reliance on expired warnings as a matter of course' (*Airbus UK Ltd* v. *Webb* [2008] ICR 561, CA).

11.11 AUTOMATICALLY UNFAIR DISMISSALS

11.11.1 General

A dismissal is automatically unfair dismissal if the reason for it is what used to be called an inadmissible reason. That expression was generally dropped in the consolidation of employment law in the ERA 1996 but is still used (in TULRCA 1992, s.154) in connection with dismissals which are automatically unfair by reason of trade union membership or activity (ERA 1996, ss.99–104 and TULRCA 1992, ss.152 and 153).

A dismissal can also be automatically unfair whether it is a dismissal in the ordinary sense or a dismissal in the form of a redundancy. In other words, if the employees concerned are selected for redundancy for an automatically unfair reason, the redundancy is automatically unfair (ERA 1996, s.105 and TULRCA 1992, s.153).

As a preliminary it should be noted that the statutory dismissal procedures introduced in 2004 are very relevant to consideration of automatically unfair dismissal. Although these procedures are being abolished, probably with effect from April 2009, and are therefore not considered in detail in this book (see **Chapter 4**), any dismissal which does not comply with them while they are still in force will normally be automatically unfair.

The normal rule in ERA 1996, s.98 that in unfair dismissal cases the onus of proof is on the employer to show the reason for dismissing an employee applies in cases in which the employee alleges that dismissal was automatically unfair in the same way as it does in other unfair dismissal cases (*Povey* v. *Dorset County Council* (unreported, EAT, 10 October 2002)). Notwithstanding this, there is at least one example of a case in which the EAT accepted that where a claimant relied on an automatically unfair reason for dismissal it was for him to establish that the reason on which he relied was the reason, or if there was more than one reason, the principal reason for the dismissal (*Griffiths & ors* v. *Perco Engineering Services* (unreported, EAT, 14 March 2006)).

The House of Lords has held that there is no rule to the effect that a dismissal made as the result of a mistaken view of the law is automatically unfair dismissal (*Halfpenny* v. *IGE Medical Systems Ltd* [2001] IRLR 96, HL).

An important practical consequence of a dismissal being categorised as automatically unfair is that, in most cases, such claims can be brought by new employees who have not completed the minimum period of employment, currently one year, required for bringing a normal unfair dismissal claim. There are a few exceptions (see **section 11.2.2**).

More specifically, the consequences of a dismissal being automatically unfair are:

- the normal criteria for determining whether a dismissal is fair do not apply;
- in almost all cases the employee does not have to have completed any qualifying period of continuous employment (see **section 11.2.2**);
- in certain cases there is a minimum basic award of £4,400 (ERA 1996, s.120, TULRCA 1992, s.156 and Employment Rights (Increase of Limits) Order 2007, SI 2007/3570).

Many of the situations noted in **section 11.11.2** in which dismissal is automatically unfair provide for exceptions in particular circumstances. This does not mean that a dismissal in those circumstances is fair. It merely means that the dismissal is not automatically unfair and leaves the question of whether it is fair or unfair for a tribunal to decide according to ordinary principles of unfair dismissal law.

It is worth noting that the regulations noted in **section 11.11.2** which make it automatically unfair dismissal to dismiss a person for a family-related reason use feminine or masculine references. It is irrelevant which is used, as words importing the feminine gender automatically include the masculine and vice versa unless specific provision is made to the contrary (Interpretation Act 1978, s.6).

'Special award' which used to be ordered in certain automatically unfair dismissal cases has been abolished if the dismissal took place on or after 25 October 1999 (Employment Relations Act 1999, s.33).

11.11.2 Reasons

Adoption leave

The same automatically unfair dismissal rules apply in relation to refusal to allow an employee to return to work after adoption leave as apply for refusing to allow an employee to return to work after maternity leave (Paternity and Adoption Leave Regulations 2002, SI 2002/2788, reg.29) and see the notes below in this section at 'Maternity leave and pregnancy'.

Assertion of statutory rights

If an employee is dismissed for making an allegation that the employer has infringed one or more of the employee's relevant statutory rights then this is automatically unfair dismissal (ERA 1996, s.104).

This is so whether or not the employee has taken proceedings to enforce the right. It is immaterial whether the employee has the right or whether it has been infringed provided the claim is made in good faith (ERA 1996, s.104(3) and *Mennell* v. *Newell & Wright* [1997] IRLR 519, CA).

Relevant statutory rights are set out in ERA 1996, s.104(4) by reference to other sections. Reference should be made to the Act for the precise detail but examples include:

- rights to a minimum notice period;
- statutory rights to time off work;
- the right to itemised pay statements or payslips;
- the right to a written statement of particulars of employment;
- the right not to have unlawful deductions from wages, etc.;
- the rights under WTR 1998 to annual paid holiday and not to be required to work excessive hours;
- the right to time off work for trade union activities or duties or as a trade union learning rep;
- the right not to have unauthorised deductions from wages in respect of union contributions or union political funds;
- the right to be consulted under the terms of TUPE 2006.

The EAT has set out three steps which must be considered to support an automatically unfair dismissal claim on the basis of assertion of a statutory right. First, has the employee alleged that the employer had infringed a right of his which is a relevant statutory right? Second, decide whether or not he has that right and whether it has been infringed? Third, decide whether the claim to the right and the claim to the fact that it has been infringed has been made in good faith (*Danlardy* v. *Southwark Race Equalities Council* (unreported, EAT, 19 May 2006)).

It is irrelevant that the employee did not realise until after he had been dismissed that he had been asserting a statutory right. It is enough that the employee refused to accede to a requirement that would have breached regulations giving him statutory rights and that the dismissal is because of that refusal see *McLean* v. *Rainbow Homeloans Ltd* [2007] IRLR 14, EAT (Scot), in which an employment tribunal rejected an unfair dismissal claim on the basis that the employee had not completed the required one year qualifying period of continuous service. The EAT overruled the tribunal as the employee claimed he was dismissed for refusing to work more than the 48 hours per week referred to in WTR 1998 – this was assertion of a statutory right covered by ERA 1996, s.104(4) and no qualification period was required (ERA 1996, s.108(3)(dd)).

Business transfers

Dismissal of an employee for a reason connected with a sale or other transfer of a business is automatically unfair dismissal, whether it takes place on, before or after the sale or transfer unless the dismissal is for an economic, technical or organisational (ETO) reason involving changes in the workforce (TUPE 2006, reg.7).

If a dismissal would have taken place even if there had been no transfer it is unlikely that that dismissal will be categorised as having been for a reason connected with the transfer (*Matthews (t/a Anton Motors)* v. *Smith & ors* [2002] EWCA Civ 1722).

It makes no difference whether the dismissal was on, before or after the transfer or whether it was by the transferor or the transferee or whether it was actual dismissal or constructive dismissal (*Morris* v. *John Grose Group Ltd* [1998] IRLR 499, EAT and *CAB Automotive Ltd* v. *Blake, Singh & ors* (unreported, EAT, 12 February 2008)). If the dismissal was for a reason connected with the transfer, it will be automatically unfair unless it can be justified on the ETO grounds entailing changes in the workforce noted above.

It should be noted that the normal qualification period of continuous employment, currently one year, applies if an employee claims automatically unfair dismissal under TUPE 2006, reg.7. This is provided for by TUPE, reg.7(6) which makes it clear that the automatically unfair dismissal provisions in those regulations benefit only employees who are eligible to claim unfair dismissal in the 'ordinary way'.

Companion at certain meetings with the employer

A worker (as defined by Employment Relations Act 1999, s.13) has the right to be accompanied by a fellow worker or trade union representative of his choice at internal disciplinary procedure and grievance procedure hearings (Employment Relations Act 1999, s.10).

Similarly, an employee who exercises his right to make a request to his employer not to retire on the intended date of retirement is entitled to have a fellow worker accompany him at any meeting arranged to consider his request or at any subsequent appeal meeting (Employment Equality (Age) Regulations 2006, SI 2006/1031, reg.47).

Dismissal of an employee for exercising this right or of the companion for accompanying that employee is automatically unfair dismissal (Employment Relations Act 1999, s.12 and Employment Equality (Age) Regulations 2006, SI 2006/1031, Sched.6, para.13(5)).

Employee representatives

Duly elected employee representatives have certain rights to be consulted in the event of proposed multiple redundancies on sale or transfer of the employing business. Dismissal of an employee who has been so elected for performing or proposing to perform any functions as an employee representative is automatically unfair dismissal. It is also automatically unfair to dismiss an employee for being a candidate for election as an employee representative or for voting in an election of employee representatives (ERA 1996, s.103; Collective Redundancies and Transfer of Undertakings (Protection of Employment) (Amendment) Regulations 1995 and 1999, (SI 1995/2587, reg.14 and SI 1999/1925, reg.13)).

European Public Limited-Liability Company Regulations

As from 8 October 2004 companies operating in more than one EU Member State have been able to establish a 'single European company' or 'SE' to operate in all Member States (EC Regulation 2157/2001). In Great Britain the related regulations include a complete section entitled 'Employee Involvement' which give employees certain rights in relation to the setting up and running of 'SEs'. Dismissal for exercising or attempting to exercise these rights is automatically unfair dismissal (European Public Limited-Liability Company Regulations 2004, SI 2004/2326, reg.42). See also 'Information and Consultation of Employees Regulations' and 'Works councils' below in this section.

Failure to follow statutory disciplinary procedures

Until the statutory dismissal procedures introduced in 2004 are finally abolished (probably in April 2009 – see **Chapter 4**), a dismissal is automatically unfair if any of these procedures applies, has not been completed, and that non-completion is wholly or mainly attributable to the failure of the employer to comply with the requirements. Note that an employee will still require one year's continuity of employment to claim; this is not an exception to the one-year rule.

UNFAIR DISMISSAL

Fixed-term work regulations

Dismissal is automatically unfair if it is in connection with an attempt to exercise any right under the Fixed-Term Employees (Prevention of Less Favourable Treatment) Regulations 2002, SI 2002/2034.

Flexible working

If the reason or principal reason for dismissal of an employee is that the employee made (or proposed to make) an application for flexible working arrangements (under ERA 1996, s.80F), or for related reasons, the dismissal will be automatically unfair dismissal (ERA 1996, s.104C).

No qualification period of employment is required, other than the one imposed by the rules which require an employee to have been in continuous employment for a period of not less than 26 weeks with the employer in order to have the right to be considered for flexible working in the first place (Employment Relations Act 2004, s.41).

Health and safety

A dismissal is automatically unfair dismissal if it is for one of six specified health and safety-related reasons (EC Directive 89/391/EEC and ERA 1996, s.100):

1. The employee was carrying out or proposed to carry out activities in connection with prevention of health and safety risks at work, having been designated to do so by the employer.
2. The employee, being one of the duly appointed safety representatives on the workforce, performed or proposed to perform his duties as such.
3. The employee was exercising rights under the Health and Safety (Consultation with Employees) Regulations 1996, SI 1996/1513.
4. The employee brought directly to 'his employer's attention, by reasonable means, circumstances connected with his work which he reasonably believed were harmful or potentially harmful to health or safety' if there was no safety representative or safety committee whose attention could be drawn to the matter. This refers to the raising of the health and safety issue rather than to the safety of the employee (*ABC News Intercontinental Inc* v. *Gizbert* (unreported, EAT, 21 August 2006) in which a journalist had brought to ABC's attention the dangers of travelling to a war zone but that was not the principal reason for his dismissal, which was his refusal to go to a war zone). 'Reasonable means' for this purpose is unlikely to include an instant unofficial strike (*Balfour Kilpatrick Ltd* v. *Acheson & ors* [2003] IRLR 683, EAT).
5. The employee left or proposed to leave his place of work because he reasonably believed there was serious and imminent danger which he could not reasonably be expected to avert.

6. The employee took or proposed to take appropriate steps to protect himself or others from danger which he reasonably believed to be serious and imminent, unless those steps were so negligent that dismissal would be justified because of them.

Industrial action

Dismissal of an employee for taking part in 'protected industrial action', which normally means an official strike, is automatically unfair dismissal (TULRCA 1992, s.238A(2) and (3)) if:

- it takes place within the period of 12 weeks beginning with the day on which the employee started to take protected industrial action; or
- it takes place after the end of that period and the employee had stopped taking protected industrial action before the end of that period; or
- it takes place after the end of that period and the employee had not stopped taking protected industrial action before the end of that period, and the employer had not taken such procedural steps as would have been reasonable for the purposes of resolving the dispute to which the protected industrial action relates.

There is no statutory definition, as such, of 'official industrial action' or 'official strike'. However, there is a kind of definition – although more of a description than a definition – of 'unofficial strike' and 'unofficial industrial action'. Any strike or other industrial action which is not authorised or endorsed by a trade union will generally be 'unofficial' (TULRCA 1992, s.237(2)).

Information and Consultation of Employees Regulations

It is automatically unfair dismissal for an employer to dismiss an employee for seeking to exercise rights to which he is entitled under the Information and Consultation of Employees Regulations 2004, SI 2004/3426 (see reg.30). Since April 2008 these regulations have applied where an employer has 50 or more employees. For notes on the rights provided by the regulations, see **section 9.4.8**. See also 'European Public Limited-Liability Company Regulations' above in this section and 'Works councils' below.

Jury service

Dismissals as a result of carrying out jury service are automatically unfair, subject to exceptions and safeguards if the employer's business would be badly affected by allowing the employee to take time off (ERA 1996, s.98B). No qualification period of employment is required for claiming unfair dismissal in such a case (ERA 1996, s.108(3)(aa)).

Maternity leave and pregnancy (and adoption, paternity or parental leave – see above and below).

It is automatically unfair dismissal if a woman is dismissed for a reason connected with pregnancy, childbirth or maternity (or is selected for redundancy for that reason). Subject to the exemption noted below this includes refusing to allow her to return to work at the end of maternity leave (ERA 1996, s.99 and Maternity and Parental Leave etc. Regulations 1999, SI 1999/3312, reg.20(3), as amended by the Maternity and Parental Leave etc. and the Paternity and Adoption Leave (Amendment) Regulations 2006, SI 2006/2014). The nature of the right itself depends on whether the leave was compulsory, ordinary or additional maternity leave (see **section 7.3.4**).

There is an exemption from the normal automatically unfair dismissal provisions for not allowing a person to return to work after maternity leave (or parental or paternity leave) if the employer can demonstrate: (i) that it is not reasonably practicable for a reason other than redundancy for him to offer the individual a job which is both suitable for her and appropriate for her to do in the circumstances; (ii) that an associated employer has done so; and (iii) that she unreasonably refused that offer, or accepted it (Maternity & Parental Leave etc. Regulations 1999, reg.20(7); Paternity and Adoption Leave Regulations 2002, reg.29(5)).

If the exemption applies it is not automatically unfair to refuse to allow the employee to return to work. Whether it is unfair or not in any particular case will instead depend on the judgment of an employment tribunal.

The previous small employer's exemption (five or less employees) from the obligation to allow a woman to return to work after maternity leave (or parental leave – it never existed in relation to paternity leave) has been removed with effect from 1 April 2007 (by the Maternity and Parental Leave etc. and the Paternity and Adoption Leave (Amendment) Regulations 2006, SI 2006/2014).

In addition to being automatically unfair under ERA 1996, a dismissal for a reason connected with pregnancy, childbirth or maternity is also likely to be unlawful sex discrimination contrary to SDA 1975 (see **Chapter 14**).

National minimum wage

Dismissal is automatically unfair if it is in connection with an attempt to exercise any right under the National Minimum Wage Act 1998 or to bring a defaulting employer to book or because the worker might qualify for the NMW (ERA 1996, s.104A; National Minimum Wage Act 1998, s.25).

Parental leave

The same automatically unfair dismissal rules apply in relation to refusal to allow an employee to return to work after parental leave as apply for refusing to allow an employee to return to work after maternity leave (Maternity and Parental Leave etc. Regulations 1999, SI 1999/3312, reg.20(3)(e)(ii)) – see above in this section at 'Maternity leave and pregnancy'.

Part-time work regulations

Dismissal is automatically unfair if it is in connection with an attempt to exercise any right under the Part-Time Workers (Prevention of Less Favourable Treatment) Regulations 2000, SI 2000/1551.

Paternity leave

The same automatically unfair dismissal rules apply in relation to refusal to allow an employee to return to work after paternity leave as apply for refusing to allow an employee to return to work after maternity leave (Paternity and Adoption Leave Regulations 2002, SI 2002/2788, reg.29 – see the notes above at 'Maternity leave, pregnancy and parental leave').

Linguistics, some might say casuistry, and skilled advocacy can be important in establishing or denying rights under the regulations. In an EAT case in 2008 an employee on paternity leave, tired after looking after his partner and their new baby, was woken from his sleep to take a telephone call from his employer. A heated argument followed and ultimately the employee was dismissed as a result of that argument. The employee claimed his dismissal was automatically unfair under reg.29 on the basis that, as required by that regulation, it was 'connected with' the fact that he took paternity leave. He lost at the employment tribunal and again on appeal. The EAT rejected his contention that it was sufficient that his dismissal was 'associated with' his taking paternity leave (*Atkins* v. *Coyle Personnel plc* [2008] IRLR 420, EAT).

Pension scheme trustees

The dismissal of an employee who has been appointed trustee of a relevant occupational pension scheme is automatically unfair dismissal if the reason (or principal reason) for the dismissal was that he performed (or proposed to perform) any functions as such trustee (ERA 1996, s.102(1)).

The same applies in respect of an employee who is dismissed for activity connected with being a 'consulted representative' under the Occupational and Personal Pension Schemes (Consultation by Employers and Miscellaneous Amendment) Regulations 2006, SI 2006/349, or for exercising rights under those regulations (see SI 2006/349, Sched.5).

Redundancy selection (improper)

If one employee rather than another is selected for redundancy for a reason which unfair dismissal law treats as automatically unfair dismissal, then subject to one condition the resulting dismissal is automatically unfair dismissal, even though technically the reason for it was redundancy (which is *prima facie* a fair reason for dismissing an employee) (ERA 1996, s.105). The condition is that 'the circumstances constituting the redundancy applied equally to one or more other employees in the same undertaking who held positions similar to that held by the employee and who have not been dismissed by the employer' (ERA 1996, s.105(1)(b)).

Spent convictions

Dismissal because of failure to disclose a spent conviction is automatically unfair dismissal, subject to a few exceptions intended to protect the public (Rehabilitation of Offenders Act 1974, s.4(3) and *Property Guards Ltd* v. *Taylor and Kershaw* [1982] IRLR 175, EAT). Rejection of a job applicant for that reason is also unlawful.

The exceptions cover jobs involved with looking after the young, the old, the sick and the handicapped, the administration of justice, banking and insurance and national security (Rehabilitation of Offenders Act 1974 (Exceptions)(Amendment) Order 1975, SI 1975/1023 as frequently amended, most recently by the Rehabilitation of Offenders Act 1974 (Exceptions) (Amendment) (England and Wales) Order 2007, SI 2007/2149).

The normal requirement that an employee must have completed at least a year's continuous employment to qualify for unfair dismissal is generally disapplied in respect of dismissals which are automatically unfair. However, there is no mention of 'spent convictions' in the disapplying section (ERA 1996, s.108) so in the authors' view it follows that the normal requirement must be satisfied.

Sunday work

Dismissal of shop workers or betting workers because of refusal to work on Sundays or on a particular Sunday is automatically unfair dismissal unless they agreed to do so (in which case they can normally revoke that agreement on giving three months' notice) (ERA 1996, s.101).

Tax credits

Dismissal of an employee is automatically unfair dismissal if the principal reason relates to a claim for tax credit. There are also specific provisions in the Tax Credits Act 1999 making it unlawful for an employer to subject an employee to any detriment for that reason. The Act provides that an employee cannot claim under both heads (i.e. unfair dismissal and detriment) but it may nevertheless be possible to do exactly that as 'employee' is defined differently for purposes of the Act and ERA 1996 (ERA 1996, s.104B; Tax Credits Act 1999, ss.6 and 18 and Sched.3)).

Time off for dependants

Subject to the same exception as noted above in connection with additional maternity leave and parental leave, it is also automatically unfair dismissal if employees are dismissed for a reason connected with them exercising their rights under ERA 1996, s.57A to take time off work for looking after dependants (ERA 1996, ss.57A and 99(3)(d); Maternity and Parental Leave etc. Regulations 1999, SI 1999/3312, reg.20(3)(e)(iii)).

Time off for union learning representatives

Dismissal is automatically unfair if it is in connection with attempts by trade union learning representatives to exercise rights under TULRCA 1992, s.168A to time off for training and other similar purposes (ERA 1996, s.104(4)(c)).

For general notes on the right to time off for trade union learning representatives see **section 7.3.11**.

Trade union activities

Dismissal is automatically unfair dismissal if the principal reason for it (or for the selection for redundancy) was that the employee 'had taken part, or proposed to take part, in the activities of an independent trade union at an appropriate time' (TULRCA 1992, ss.152–154). The normal length of service requirement for exercising unfair dismissal rights does not apply. The provisions making a dismissal automatically unfair where it was because the employee was asserting a statutory right may also be relevant (ERA 1996, s.104(4)(c) and see 'Assertion of statutory rights' above in this section)

For general notes on the right to time off for trade union-related duties and activities see **section 7.3.11**.

Trade union membership

If employees are dismissed for the negative reason that they are not a member of any trade union or of a particular trade union or because they refused, or proposed to refuse, to become or remain a member, this will automatically be unfair dismissal. It is also automatic unfair dismissal if they were dismissed for the positive reason that they were a member of (or proposed to join) a union, or because they had taken part (or proposed to take part) in union activities 'at an appropriate time', but in these cases the union must be an independent trade union for employees to have automatic unfair dismissal rights. The normal minimum service rule for unfair dismissal does not apply in such cases (TULRCA 1992, ss.152–154).

The provisions making a dismissal automatically unfair where it was because the employee was asserting a statutory right may also be relevant

(ERA 1996, s.104(4)(c) and see 'Assertion of statutory rights' above in this section).

Refusal to employ a person because he is or is not a member of a trade union obviously is not dismissal at all. There is therefore separate provision to make this unlawful (TULRCA 1992, s.137).

Whistleblowing

Since 2 July 1999, it has been automatically unfair dismissal to dismiss a worker for making a qualifying disclosure in good faith to someone to whom the worker is entitled to make it (Public Interest Disclosure Act 1998, s.5 inserted a new ERA 1996, s.103A accordingly).

Working time regulations

Dismissal is automatically unfair if it is in connection with an attempt to exercise any right under WTR 1998 (ERA 1996, ss.101A and 104(4) and WTR 1998, reg.32).

Works councils

Dismissal is automatically unfair if it is in connection with activities as a member of (or candidate for membership of) a European Works Council (Transnational Information and Consultation of Employees Regulations 1999, SI 1999/3323, reg.28). The same applies in relation to dismissals in connection with activities as a member of (or candidate for membership of) a 'European Cooperative Society' (European Cooperative Society (Involvement of Employees) Regulations 2006, SI 2006/2059, reg 31). See also 'Information and Consultation of Employees Regulations' and 'European Public Limited-Liability Company Regulations' above in this section.

A dedicated website at **www.emplaw.co.uk/lshandbook** provides links to judgments and other source material referred to in this chapter.

CHAPTER 12

Redundancy

12.1 GENERAL INFORMATION

To a non-lawyer, the word 'redundancy' is associated with a dismissal where there is no allegation of misconduct. Sometimes the phrase 'made redundant' can even be used as a euphemism for being dismissed. This is wrong. Redundancy is no more than one of many possible reasons for dismissal.

Just to complicate matters, in law there are two different definitions of redundancy. The first, and better known, definition applies to an employee's entitlement to a redundancy payment and to establishing redundancy as a potentially fair reason for dismissal. The second, much wider, definition applies when considering whether it is necessary to consult a trade union (or employee representatives) when redundancies are contemplated by an employer.

Official figures show that the number of redundancies in 2007 was far greater (at least 470,000) than the 145,000 recorded for 2006 (see *Economic & Labour Market Review*, Vol.2, issue 5, May 2008).

Useful official information from the BERR (formerly DTI) is available online (see **www.berr.gov.uk/employment/redundancy/index.html**).

12.2 WHEN IS AN EMPLOYEE REDUNDANT?

Redundancy is defined in ERA 1996, s.139 as follows:

> an employee who is dismissed shall be taken to be dismissed by reason of redundancy if the dismissal is attributable wholly or mainly to –
>
> (a) the fact that his employer has ceased, or intends to cease –
>
>   (i) to carry on the business for the purposes of which the employee was employed by him, or
>
>   (ii) to carry on that business in the place where the employee was so employed, or
>
> (b) the fact that the requirements of that business –
>
>   (i) for employees to carry out work of a particular kind, or

(ii) for employees to carry out work of a particular kind in the place where the employee was employed by the employer,

have ceased or diminished or are expected to cease or diminish.

If a 'redundancy' does not fall within this definition, it will not count as a redundancy for ERA 1996 purposes (*Lesney Products & Co Ltd* v. *Nolan* [1977] IRLR 77).

'Business' includes the business of an associated employer. 'Cease' and 'diminish' can each be either permanent or temporary for the above definition (ERA 1996, s.139(1)).

The EAT spelled out the practical position clearly in a case in 2005, saying:

> It is now well-established that a three-stage process is involved in determining whether an employee is redundant under ERA 1996, s.139(1)(b). First, ask if the employee was dismissed. Second, ask if the requirements of the employer's business for employees to carry out work of a particular kind had ceased or diminished or were expected to cease or diminish. Third, ask whether the dismissal of the employee was caused wholly or mainly by that state of affairs.
>
> *Hachette Filipacchi UK Ltd* v. *Johnson* (unreported, EAT, 14 December 2005)

Note that a business reorganisation which does not entail a reduction in the number of employees (just a redistribution of responsibilities) may not fall within the s.139 definition. Subject to a fair procedure having been followed, however, a dismissal arising from a reorganisation will probably count as 'some other substantial reason for dismissal' within ERA 1996, s.98(1), and the employees will not be entitled to any statutory redundancy payment. The failure to appreciate this distinction can involve employers making significant and unnecessary redundancy payments and, indeed, has led to claims of professional negligence against advisors for erroneous advice (*Port of Sheerness Ltd* v. *Brachers* [1997] IRLR 214).

Likewise, dismissals for refusing to accept new contract terms will not normally be redundancies because there will still be a need for the same number of employees to carry out work of a particular kind (*Aylward* v. *Glamorgan Holiday Hotels* (unreported, EAT, 5 February 2003)).

Similarly the General Manager of a group of hotels was not dismissed by reason of redundancy when he was replaced, on a business reorganisation, by a combination of senior Area General Manager and a junior Resident Manager as, subject to slight changes, the hotel group's requirements for his work to be done had not ceased or diminished (and *Corus & Regal Hotels plc* v. *Wilkinson* (unreported, EAT, 28 June 2004)).

It is possible, although not common, that in law a change from full-time employment to part-time employment can count as a dismissal by reason of redundancy followed by re-engagement on new terms. The question depends on whether on the facts of any particular case the statutory definition of redundancy is satisfied. There is a fine (arguably artificial) line between a situation where the employee's new job is the same as his original full-time job save that certain terms and conditions of employment have been altered in which case there is no redundancy (*Johnson* v. *Nottinghamshire Combined Police Authority* [1974] ICR 170, CA) on the one hand and on the other hand a situation where the requirement for a full-time employee to carry out work of a particular kind has gone and instead is to be replaced by a requirement for a part-time employee in which case there may be redundancy as there was in *Halliday* v. *Archdiocese of Southwark* (unreported, EAT, 5 March 2001).

Historically, lawyers and courts spent a vast amount of time considering an issue known as the 'contract' versus 'function' test for redundancy, in order to decide precisely what work an employee carried out for the purposes of s.139(1)(b). The contract test requires an analysis of what the employee's contract said, and this is contrasted with the function test, i.e. what the employee did in practice on a day-to-day basis. This distinction is no longer drawn (*Murray* v. *Foyle Meats Ltd* [1999] ICR 827, HL).

12.3 WHO ARGUES REDUNDANCY?

Redundancy legislation was introduced in 1965. Unfair dismissal legislation was introduced in 1971. For the intervening six years, many cases were brought by employees trying to establish that they were entitled to a redundancy payment. A combination of the erosion of the value of a statutory redundancy payment (the maximum possible payment as at 1 July 2008 being £9,900), coupled with the change in culture which has led to employers rarely seeking to avoid paying statutory redundancy payments, has resulted in disputed claims for statutory redundancy pay being comparatively unusual (around 7,000 a year or about 3.5 per cent of all tribunal claims in each of the years 2004 to 2007).

The argument that a dismissal was by reason of redundancy is now more commonly used by employers than by employees as redundancy is one of the potentially fair reasons for a dismissal (ERA 1996, s.98(2)(c)).

A significant incentive for an employee to issue a claim for unfair dismissal (rather than for a redundancy payment) is the considerably higher possible maximum unfair dismissal award (£63,000 plus up to £9,900 basic award with effect from 1 February 2008). Moreover, employees need to have been employed for two years before they become entitled to a redundancy payment (ERA 1996, s.155). They only need one year's employment to claim unfair dismissal, or even none in some cases (ERA 1996, s.108).

When employees bring a claim for a redundancy payment, they are presumed to have been dismissed because of redundancy unless the employer proves otherwise (ERA 1996, s.163(2)). By contrast, no such presumption exists when an employee claims unfair dismissal and the employer seeks to establish redundancy as a defence (ERA 1996, s.98).

12.4 QUALIFYING FOR A STATUTORY REDUNDANCY PAYMENT

In order to qualify for a statutory redundancy payment, the worker must:

1. Be an employee, rather than self-employed (ERA 1996, s.156). This distinction is discussed in **Chapter 2**.
2. Have accrued two years' continuity of employment (ERA 1996, s.155).

Until 1 October 2006, service before a person's 18th birthday did not count for statutory redundancy pay. Both this lower age limit and the age 65 upper age limit were removed by the Employment Equality (Age) Regulations 2006, SI 2006/1031, Sched.8.

Redundancy rights are available to fixed-term employees working under a contract signed after 1 October 2002, even if the contract contains a written agreement to waive a redundancy payment. However, those on a fixed-term contract of at least two years' duration signed before 1 October 2002 do not have this protection (Fixed-Term Employees (Prevention of Less Favourable Treatment) Regulations 2002, SI 2002/2034).

Many companies offer enhanced redundancy payments under the contract of employment. Depending on construction these may be applicable to all employees, or the employees may need to qualify for a statutory redundancy payment before becoming entitled to a contractual enhancement. Enhanced terms offered in the past can mean that they become implied contractual terms to which other employees are in future entitled (*Albion Automotive* v. *Walker & ors* [2002] EWCA Civ 946).

A further, distinct situation which gives rise to a right to redundancy pay can arise under the rules relating to 'lay off ' or 'short time'. Employees whose pay is linked to hours worked or output achieved may be able to claim redundancy pay even though there has been no dismissal if they are laid off or put on short time (ERA 1996, s.135(1)(b) combined with ERA 1996, ss.147 and 148). These provisions have their roots in the days before unfair dismissal was 'invented' and were originally designed to prevent unscrupulous employers avoiding liability for redundancy pay by laying off an employee rather than dismissing him.

12.5 CHALLENGING THE FAIRNESS OF REDUNDANCIES

The fact that an employee was dismissed by reason of redundancy does not, of course, mean that the dismissal was not unfair dismissal. Redundancy is no more than a potentially fair reason for dismissal (ERA 1996, s.98(2)(c)).

An important point for advisors to bear in mind is that an employee is normally only entitled to challenge the fairness of the decision to select him or her for redundancy. The law regards the primary decision (i.e. the decision to make redundancies in the first place) as a business decision on which tribunals should not sit in judgment. This is justified, rightly or wrongly, on the basis that it is not for employment tribunals to investigate the merits of industrial disputes (*Moon* v. *Homeworthy Furniture (Northern) Ltd* [1976] IRLR 298 and *James W Cook & Co (Wivenhoe) Ltd* v. *Tipper* [1990] IRLR 386, CA). For discussion of consultation see *UK Coal Mining Ltd v. NUM and anov* [2008] IRLR 4, EAT and **section 12.8.4.**

There are three basic methods of attacking the fairness of a redundancy dismissal:

1. Proving that the reason for selection was automatically unfair: usually a reason connected with pregnancy, trade union activities or the assertion of various statutory rights.
2. Where the reason for selection is not automatically unfair, proving that the dismissal was nevertheless unfair because of the method of selection: often the subject of an argument that the employer failed to utilise an objective method of selecting redundant candidates, or that the employer had a hidden agenda and used the redundancy situation as a device to engineer the dismissal of particular employees.
3. Even if the method of selection is objective, proving that the redundancy process itself was unfair. This will most commonly be seen where inadequate consultation is carried out or where alternative work exists but is not offered.

12.6 AUTOMATICALLY UNFAIR REASONS FOR REDUNDANCY

Where the reason (or principal reason) for selecting employees for redundancy falls within a prescribed category, the dismissals will be automatically unfair (ERA 1996, s.105). Questions of whether the employer has acted reasonably in other ways, for example, by investigating alternative employment, simply do not arise. These unfair reasons are covered in **section 11.11**.

12.7 UNREASONABLE METHOD OF SELECTION

Even if a redundancy situation exists, a dismissal will be unfair if it fails to meet the overriding test of fairness set out in the legislation:

> the determination of the question whether the dismissal is fair or unfair (having regard to the reason shown by the employer) –
>
> (a) depends on whether in the circumstances (including the size and administrative resources of the employer's undertaking) the employer acted reasonably or unreasonably in treating it as a sufficient reason for dismissing the employee, and
>
> (b) shall be determined in accordance with equity and the substantial merits of the case. (ERA 1996, s.98(4))

A tribunal may not substitute its own views of what constitutes reasonableness either in respect of redundancy selection criteria or implementation of those criteria for the views of the employer, but must ask itself the wider question of whether the selection was one that a reasonable employer acting reasonably could have made (*Drake International t/a Drake Ports Distribution Services* v. *O'Hare* (unreported, EAT, 2 September 2003) and *Look Ahead Housing & Care Ltd* v. *Odili and Mendes* (unreported, EAT, 28 January 2008)).

In a classic decision which has withstood the test of time, the EAT set out the core factors that will usually exist before an employer can be regarded as having acted fairly (*Williams* v. *Compair Maxam Ltd* [1982] IRLR 83, EAT). These are:

1. The employer will seek to give as much warning as possible of impending redundancies so as to enable the union and affected employees to take early steps to inform themselves of the relevant facts, consider possible alternative solutions and, if necessary, find alternative employment in the undertaking or elsewhere.
2. The employer will consult the union as to the best means by which the desired result can be achieved fairly and with as little hardship to the employees as possible. In particular, the employer will seek to agree with the union the criteria to be applied in selecting the employees to be made redundant. When a selection has been made, the employer will consider with the union whether the selection has been made in accordance with those criteria.
3. Whether or not criteria have been agreed with the union, the employer will seek to establish criteria for selection which so far as possible do not depend solely upon the opinion of the person making the selection but can be objectively checked against such things as attendance record, efficiency at the job, experience or length of service.
4. The employer will seek to ensure that the selection is made fairly in accordance with these criteria and will consider any representations the union may make as to such selection.
5. The employer will seek to consider whether instead of dismissing an employee it could offer alternative employment.

Three points must be noted:

1. Although the case involved an employer where a union was recognised, the same basic principles apply where the employer does not recognise a union.
2. If the employer omits a stage, it will not automatically render the dismissal unfair; however, it is likely to do so.
3. The above test is not a substitute for the overriding test in the statute; it must be regarded as an indication of ordinary principles of fairness rather than a statement of legal hurdles which must be overcome (*Rolls-Royce Motors Ltd* v. *Dewhurst* [1985] IRLR 184, EAT).

The requirements set out in *Williams* v. *Compair Maxam* have been restated, more succinctly, by the House of Lords as follows:

> in the case of redundancy, the employer will normally not act reasonably unless he warns and consults any employees affected or their representatives, adopts a fair decision on which to select for redundancy and takes such steps as may be reasonable to minimise a redundancy by redeployment within his own organisation. (*Polkey* v. *AE Dayton Services Ltd* [1988] AC 344, HL, per Lord Bridge)

Finally, guidance can be found in the Acas advisory booklet 'Redundancy Handling'. This is a useful source of guidance for both employers and employees and highlights the key points when selecting for redundancy as:

1. Agree the selection criteria with employee representatives.
2. Be objective, fair and consistent.
3. Establish an appeals procedure.

12.8 CONSULTATION

12.8.1 Introduction

Consultation is an all-embracing and ongoing obligation. If an employer fails to consult with employees during the redundancy process, a tribunal is highly likely to find that it has failed to act reasonably, thus any dismissals for redundancy will be unfair.

There is a statutory obligation to consult with trade unions or elected employee representatives if an employer proposes to make 20 or more people redundant from one establishment within a period of 90 days (TULRCA 1992, s.188). For consultation purposes, redundancy is given a much wider meaning than in ERA 1996. It is defined as 'a reason not related to the individual concerned or for a number of reasons all of which are not so related' (TULRCA 1992, s.195(1)). This comes close to the traditional layman's understanding of redundancy as dismissal where the individual is not personally at fault.

Note that the associated employer provisions do not apply here, so when determining how many employees are being made redundant, one looks at the employees of individual corporate employers, rather than the corporate group as a whole (*Green & Son (Castings) Ltd* v. *ASTMS* [1984] ICR 352).

The EAT has held that when deciding whether the number of employees to be dismissed by reason of redundancy is 20 or more, any who have accepted voluntary redundancy in the knowledge that if they did not do so they would have to accept compulsory redundancy are to be included (*Optare Group Ltd* v. *TGWU* [2007] IRLR 931, EAT).

The word 'establishment', does not merely refer to a physical location. A purposive construction is adopted. Thus a bakery and 28 shops have been held to count as one establishment for the purpose of redundancy consultation requirements (*Clarks of Hove Ltd* v. *Bakers Union* [1978] ICR 1076, CA and *Rockfon AS* v. *Nielson* [1996] ICR 673, ECJ).

This statutory obligation is absolute. The EAT has summarised the obligation to consult as follows.

1. Where no consultation about redundancy has taken place with either the trade union or the employee the dismissal will normally be unfair, unless the tribunal finds that a reasonable employer would have concluded that consultation would be an utterly futile exercise in the particular circumstances of the case.
2. Consultation with the trade union over selection criteria does not of itself release the employer from consulting with the employee individually regarding his being identified for redundancy.
3. It will be a question of fact and degree for the tribunal to consider whether consultation with the individual and/or the union was so inadequate as to render the dismissal unfair. A lack of consultation in any particular respect will not automatically lead to that result. The overall picture must be viewed by the tribunal up to the date of termination to ascertain whether the employer has or has not acted reasonably in dismissing the employee on the grounds of redundancy (*Mugford* v. *Midland Bank* [1997] IRLR 208, EAT and *Hachette Filipacchi UK Ltd* v. *Johnson* (unreported, EAT, 14 December 2005)).

Employers must also take into account the Information and Consultation of Employees Regulations 2004, SI 2004/3426, which implemented the National Information and Consultation Directive 2002/14/EC. These require affected employers to have in place arrangements giving employees the opportunity to be informed and consulted on management decisions affecting their future, such as decisions relating to changes in work organisation or contractual relations, including redundancies. As from 1 April 2008 these regulations apply to any employer with 50 or more employees.

12.8.2 With whom should employers consult?

Since 1 November 1999, an employer must consult with any trade union that it recognises. Prior to 1 November 1999, the employer could choose whether to consult with the recognised union or with elected employee representatives (Collective Redundancies and Transfer of Undertakings (Protection of Employment) (Amendment) Regulations 1999, SI 1999/1925).

If there is no trade union, the employees must be given the opportunity to elect employee representatives. The procedure for this is set out in TULRCA 1992, s.188A. If the employees fail to elect representatives, the employer must give all the affected employees the information they would have had to give to the representatives.

The minimum statutory requirements are set out above. However, having chosen criteria for redundancy selection, an employer who fails to discuss an individual's scores with that individual, and give her the opportunity to make representations prior to being dismissed, is likely to be held to have acted unreasonably (*Walls Meat Co* v. *Selby* [1989] ICR 601, CA). Indeed, sometimes tribunals have found even more fundamental consultation to be necessary with employees: in *Rolls-Royce Motor Cars Ltd* v. *Price* [1993] IRLR 203, the union refused to discuss a change in redundancy procedures with the employer. The tribunal found the employer acted unreasonably in failing to consult the employee, despite having attempted to consult with the union.

This obligation is taken so seriously by tribunals that it can lead to apparently harsh results for employers. Thus in *Ferguson* v. *Prestwick Circuits* [1992] IRLR 266 it was held that the employer should have consulted the employee, even though previous experience suggested that the employee would prefer it not to do so.

The EAT held in *Grant* v. *BSS Group plc* (unreported, EAT, 13 March 2003) where an employer was making one person redundant out of a pool of two, failure to consult with both rendered the dismissal unfair. However, in *Mugford* v. *Midland Bank* [1997] ICR 399, EAT Judge Peter Clark stated (at para.36) that the consultation requirement obliges an employer to consult with those 'identified for redundancy ... before a final decision to dismiss is reached'. He did not suggest there is an obligation to consult with all employees in the pool whether or not they are provisionally selected for redundancy. It therefore seems that there is a straightforward conflict between *Grant* and *Mugford*, resulting in tribunals being free to choose which authority to follow. Consequently, tribunals will be at liberty to disregard *Grant* and pursue the traditional approach that the detailed consultation need take place only with those provisionally selected for redundancy, rather than all those in the pool.

12.8.3 How long should consultation take?

Despite what UK employers might consider to be onerous consultation obligations, Parliament has acknowledged that:

> The suggestion that it is easier and cheaper to dispose of employees in the UK than elsewhere seems to us to have been shown to be factually correct ... in many European countries, there is a long drawn out process of notification and consultation which may well involve more cost to the employer who is continuing to pay wages ...
>
> Third Report of the House of Commons Select Committee on Trade and Industry, February 2001

As noted above there is a statutory obligation to consult with trade unions or elected employee representatives if an employer proposes to make 20 or more people redundant from one establishment within a period of 90 days

(TULRCA 1992, s.188). Where the statutory rules apply (i.e. if 20 or more people are being dismissed at one establishment by reason of redundancy), TULRCA 1992, s.188(1A) requires that the employer must begin consultation in good time and in any event 30 days before the first of the dismissals takes effect, increased to 90 days if the number of redundancies is 100 or more.

In January 2005 the European Court of Justice held that where collective consultation is required prior to redundancies being made, the consultation must be completed before notice of dismissal is given to any of the employees concerned (*Junk* v. *Wolfgang Kuhnel* [2005] IRLR 310, ECJ). The effect of this is that an employer proposing to dismiss 20 or more employees by reason of redundancy must complete the 30 or 90 days consultation required by the EC Collective Redundancies Directive 98/59/EC before he gives any of them notice of dismissal. Later in 2005 the EAT had no problem in giving TULRCA 1992, s.188 this meaning (*Leicestershire County Council* v. *Unison* [2005] IRLR 920, EAT). Previously it had generally been thought that s.188 would be complied with if an employer gave notice to employees during the 30 (or 90) day consultation period provided the notice did not expire until after the consultation period had ended.

An employer has a separate obligation, under TULRCA 1992, s.193, to give advance notice to the BERR (formerly DTI) if he proposes to make 20 or more employees redundant within a 90-day period. Following the ruling by the European Court in the *Junk* case these rules were changed to state specifically that the notice to be given to the Secretary of State must be given at least 30 days before notice is given to employees to terminate their contracts of employment, increased to 90 days if 100 or more are being dismissed (Collective Redundancies (Amendment) Regulations 2006, SI 2006/2387, effective from 1 October 2006). This notice should be given on Form HR1 (available at **www.insolvency.gov.uk/pdfs/rpforms/hr1.pdf**). Failure to notify the BERR is a criminal offence, albeit rarely prosecuted (TULRCA 1992, s.194). However, it will not affect the fairness or unfairness of any dismissals.

The phrase 'in good time' replaced the previous 'at the earliest opportunity' in 1995. The new test of 'in good time' is slightly less stringent than the old test of 'at the earliest opportunity' (*MSF* v. *Refuge Assurance plc* [2002] IRLR 324 and *Amicus* v. *Nissan Motor Manufacturing (UK) Ltd* (unreported, EAT, 26 July 2005)). Failure to consult sufficiently early may lead to an enhanced compensatory award (*Elkouil* v. *Coney Island Ltd* [2002] IRLR 174, EAT), in addition to a protective award under the statutory collective consultation requirements (TULRCA 1992, s.188).

There is no specific expiry time for consultation although s.188 is not indefinitely 'elastic'. In one case an employer was held to have complied with s.188 when consultation started in January 2003 but the redundancy dismissals did not take place until almost two years later. This was because, throughout the intervening period, there was an ongoing meaningful and effective consultation about the employees and that consultation dealt with the same employees and the same prospective redundancies (*Vauxhall Motors Ltd* v. *Transport and General Workers Union* [2006] IRLR 674, EAT).

The adequacy of consultation required if the statutory provisions do not apply (for example, because less than 20 people are to be made redundant) is of course a matter of fact and degree, for the tribunal to determine. The EAT has stated that 'in our judgment it falls short of an adequate and reasonable standard of consultation for an employee to be told on Monday that he is selected for redundancy dismissal intended to take place on Friday' (*Chronos Richardson Ltd* v. *Watson* (unreported, EAT, 27 March 2001)).

12.8.4 What should the consultations consist of?

The consultation must include specific items. These are ways of:

- avoiding the dismissals;
- reducing the number of employees to be dismissed; and
- mitigating the consequences of the dismissals.

It is also common (albeit not obligatory under statute) to consult with unions and representatives over the selection criteria. Many unions avoid discussion about selection criteria for internal political reasons: they do not want to be seen supporting criteria that might favour some members over others. Provided an employer has tried to consult over selection criteria, it will have acted reasonably (TULRCA 1992, s.188(4) and (6)).

Consultation must be 'with a view to reaching agreement', so employers must give unions/employees adequate information and time to respond. Any response must be conscientiously considered by the employer. This does not mean that the employer is obliged to accede to the union's/employees' demands: provided it acts in good faith, gives proper consideration to their arguments and does not unreasonably reject suggestions, the employer will have complied with its duty to consult (TULRCA 1992, s.18(6); *R.* v. *British Coal Corp, ex parte Price (No. 3)* [1994] IRLR 72; *Rowell* v. *Hubbard Group Services Ltd* [1995] IRLR 195).

In *Lambe* v. *186K Ltd* [2004] EWCA Civ 1045, Wall LJ confirmed the criteria for fair consultation set out by the EAT in *King* v. *Eaton* [1996] IRLR 199, CS, namely that fair consultation means:

(a) consultation when the proposals are still at a formative stage;
(b) adequate information on which to respond;
(c) adequate time in which to respond;
(d) conscientious consideration by [the employer] of the response to consultation.

The larger the employer (and the greater the number of proposed redundancies), the more formal the consultation process should be. Smallness does not justify a failure to consult, but it will justify less formality (*De Grasse* v. *Stockwell Ltd* [1992] IRLR 269, EAT).

Where a business is closing, consultation over redundancies must extend to the reasons for the closure causing them. On the basis of older authorities, notably *R* v. *British Coal etc ex p Vardy & ors* [1993] ICR 720, QBD, it had seemed that the duty to consult is concerned only with how a redundancy programme would be carried out and never with whether there should be redundancies. The EAT held in 2007 that where a business is closing this is no longer good law. In that situation '. . . the obligation to consult over avoiding the proposed redundancies inevitably involves engaging with the reasons for the dismissals, and that in turn requires consultation over the reasons for the closure'. Therefore where redundancies are going to follow from closure of a business it will only be in the rare situation where redundancies could be avoided that consultation over the closure decision itself will not be needed (*UK Coal Mining Ltd* v. *NUM & British Association of Colliery Management* [2008] IRLR 4, EAT). The extent to which, if at all, this case has any application in a 'non-closure' context is uncertain.

12.9   ESTABLISHING THE POOL OF REDUNDANCY CANDIDATES

Before selection of employees can occur, the employer will need to establish the pool from which the selection will take place. Sometimes this will be obvious: if an entire workforce or building is closing down, the pool might be that workforce or those who work in the building. Alternatively, in a small company, if two secretaries are to be made redundant, the pool may comprise all of the secretaries. Failure to consider employees doing similar work from more than one division of an enterprise can be considered unreasonable (*Kvaerner Oil and Gas Ltd* v. *Parker & ors* (unreported, EAT 0444/02, 28 January 2003)). Similarly, where a group of six workers skilled in operating a specific machine but also skilled in other activities of their department were selected for redundancy when the machine was decommissioned, it was held that the pool of employees from which redundancies were to be made should have included the other employees of the department, rendering the dismissals unfair (*Hendy Banks City Print Ltd* v. *Fairbrother & Ors* (unreported, EAT/0691/04, 21 December 2004)).

Provided the employer can provide a sensible explanation for the pool it chooses, the employee cannot criticise the choice of pool before the tribunal. Again, this is a fundamental business decision and is not one with which tribunals will interfere unless the decision is perverse (e.g. employees with red hair), discriminatory (e.g. part-time workers) or taken in bad faith (*Earl of Bradford* v. *Jowett (No. 2)* [1978] IRLR 16).

12.10 THE SELECTION PROCESS

The first stage in the selection process is to establish the selection criteria. If consulting with a union or employee representatives, this may form a significant part of the consultation process.

Until 3 January 1995, the selection of an employee for redundancy in contravention of a customary arrangement or agreed procedure would render the dismissal automatically unfair. Such selection is no longer automatically unfair (Deregulation and Contracting Out Act 1994, s.36) but under the test of reasonableness an employer would often be hard-pressed to justify departure from customary or agreed procedures.

The crucial point about the criteria is that they should be capable of some element of objective assessment. 'Length of service' is capable of objective assessment. 'Strategic implementation planning ability' would mean wholly different things to different people, therefore any assessments could be inconsistent and unfair.

An employment tribunal must not substitute its own views of what constitutes reasonableness either in respect of redundancy selection criteria or implementation of those criteria, for the views of the employer. What matters is whether the selection was one that a reasonable employer acting reasonably could have made (see most recently *Look Ahead Housing & Care Ltd* v. *(1) Odili (2) Mendes* (unreported, EAT, 28 January 2008)).

Tribunals are not always consistent when deciding whether criteria can be objectively assessed. The authors' experience suggests that a finding that criteria cannot be objectively justified is often linked with poor performance by the employer in the witness box. Equally, some very nebulous criteria have been held to be capable of objective justification, such as, 'quality of work, efficiency in carrying it out and the attitude of the persons evaluated to their work' (*Graham* v. *ABF Ltd* [1986] IRLR 90).

12.10.1 Last in, first out

'LIFO' was the standard redundancy criterion during the 1970s. It was a simple method of selection – employees would be selected for redundancy in the order they joined the company, the most recent joiners being dismissed first. Because of the difficulties this sometimes caused when employers found themselves employing a predominantly middle-aged/elderly workforce, an occasional alternative was first in, first out (FIFO).

Selection for redundancy on the basis of age has been unlawful since 1 October 2006 (Employment Equality (Age) Regulations 2006, SI 2006/1031). The Acas guide to the regulations, 'Putting the Employment Equality (Age) Regulations 2006 into practice', points out that therefore 'practices such as last in first out (LIFO), and using length of service in any selection criteria are likely to be age discriminatory'. This will be especially likely if 'the last' in are generally the youngest. However, if the age discrimination can be justified as 'a proportionate means of achieving a legitimate aim' it will not be unlawful.

There is also a risk that a LIFO approach might be regarded as indirect sex or race discrimination if the business is traditionally male or white-dominated and women and non-white employees have only been recruited in recent years. In that case, LIFO might have a disproportionate impact on women and non-white employees. To avoid a finding of discrimination an employer would have to show that the choice of LIFO as the selection criterion was objectively justified.

12.10.2 The matrix method

Nowadays, a common method of redundancy selection is to draw up a list of criteria and assign scores to each employee under each criterion. The scores are added up and the employees with the lowest cumulative score will be selected for redundancy.

Common criteria include:

- length of service;
- disciplinary record;
- qualifications;
- leadership skills;
- productivity;
- cost to the business.

Some of these, notably leadership skills and productivity run the risk that they may not be capable of objective assessment and if they are used, the scores should be supported by independent evidence.

Attendance and time-keeping records should be used with caution as redundancy criteria. If they are used, any periods off work relating to maternity or parental leave should be ignored, as should any periods off work occurring when workers exercise their right to time off to care for dependants in an emergency.

Special consideration must be given to those who suffer from a disability within the meaning of DDA 1995 (see **Chapter 15**). Whether a disabled employee is at a substantial disadvantage in a process of redundancy selection is a question of fact. That involves considering the extent to which the disabled employee's chances of scoring as well as an employee who is not disabled is adversely affected by the disability and making any reasonable adjustments which may be required to ensure that the disabled person is not at a disadvantage because of his disability (*NTL Group Ltd* v. *Difolco* (unreported, EAT, 27 January 2006)).

Selection of a part-timer for redundancy in preference to a full-time employee would be a breach of the Part-Time Workers (Prevention of Less Favourable Treatment) Regulations 2000, SI 2000/1551 unless it could be justified on objective grounds (*Hendrickson Europe Ltd* v. *Pipe* (unreported, EAT, 15 April 2003)).

12.10.3 Consultation and disclosure of selection criteria to employees

It is good practice to consult with individual employees on their scores, so as to enable them to comment on whether they feel they have been unfairly marked down in any categories. This raises a controversial question: is it necessary to show the employees the scores of others? To disclose other employees' scores breaches principles of confidentiality and can result in an enormous amount of management time justifying minor discrepancies in scores between employees. To withhold details of other scorings renders the entire process of limited value, because it is difficult to comment on what are, effectively, comparative markings.

The authorities are not consistent, making it difficult to provide clear advice. One approach is seen in *Eaton* v. *King* [1995] IRLR 75, EAT, upheld in *British Aerospace plc* v. *Green* [1995] IRLR 433, CA in which it was held that there was no obligation to disclose scores to employees.

The opposite approach is seen in *John Brown Engineering Ltd* v. *Brown* [1997] IRLR 90, EAT. In that case, employees were not even given their own assessments when invited to comment on their selection for redundancy. The tribunal described the process as a 'sham' and the EAT upheld that decision. It commented that 'it may be invidious to publish the whole identified "league tables", but in choosing not to do so the employer must run the risk that he is not acting fairly in respect of individual employees'.

A sensible compromise in a small company might be to make all scores available to employees whilst anonymising all the identities. In a larger company, a representative sample of (anonymised) scores should be made available. The employees' own scores should always be given to them for comment.

12.10.4 Are there exceptions to the need to consult?

If an employer can persuade the tribunal that consultation would have been 'utterly useless or futile', then the employer might have acted reasonably in not consulting and the dismissals will be fair. It is not necessary for a deliberate decision that consultation would be futile to be taken at the time, the question is whether a reasonable employer would have dismissed without consultation in the circumstances.

One case in which a failure to consult was upheld as reasonable was where the employer's business was vulnerable to industrial espionage and it had been agreed with the unions that staff who were made redundant would leave the employer's premises immediately (*Duncan* v. *Marconi Command & Control Systems Ltd* (unreported, EAT, 1988)). Similarly, an employer was able to justify departure from best practice on consultation where the business was small and failing and consultation was pointless (*Warner* v. *Adnet Ltd* [1998] ICR 1056, CA). These are exceptional cases, however, and in practice it is all but impossible to persuade a tribunal that consultation would have been 'utterly useless or futile' (*Polkey; Duffy* v. *Yeomans & Partners Ltd* [1994] IRLR 642, CA).

12.11 SUITABLE ALTERNATIVE EMPLOYMENT

12.11.1 Introduction

Legal wisdom dictates that an employer will always strain to avoid dismissing employees. When the spectre of redundancy raises its head, any reasonable employer would always look for, and offer, suitable alternative employment to affected employees. Further, a reasonable employer would seek out suitable alternative employment within the companies of any associated employers. Therefore, any employer who fails to offer suitable alternative employment when available is acting unreasonably, thereby rendering the dismissal unfair.

Note that employees lose the right to claim a redundancy payment if they accept an offer of alternative employment (subject to a four-week trial period, see below) or unreasonably refuse an offer of suitable alternative employment from the employer or an associated employer (ERA 1996, ss.138 and 141).

In all but the smallest companies, the employer should be able to demonstrate that it has considered alternative employment (if appropriate, with associated employers) and discussed it with the employee. The employer should also raise alternative employment at the consultation stage: it may be that the employee is aware of suitable alternative work that the employer is unaware of.

12.11.2 What is suitable alternative employment?

This is an objective test (*Jones* v. *MEM Marketing Retail Services* (unreported, EAT, 19 October 2007)). It is for the employer to prove that the offered employment is suitable.

Whether it is suitable is a question of fact and degree for employment tribunals to consider. Employees disentitle themselves from receiving statutory redundancy pay if they unreasonably refuse an offer of suitable alternative employment. When deciding whether refusal is unreasonable, a tribunal may take into account matters specific to the employee, and a small reduction in pay or status may be more relevant here. Examples of relevant issues to both questions are: loss of status (*Taylor* v. *Kent County Council* [1969] 2 QB 560 and *Cambridge & District Co-operative Society Ltd* v. *Ruse* [1993] IRLR 156, EAT); travel (*Bass Leisure Ltd* v. *Thomas* [1994] IRLR 104 and *Douce* v. *F Bond & Sons Ltd* [1966] 1 ITR 365); working arrangements (*Morrison &*

Poole v. *Cramic Engineering Co Ltd* [1966] 1 ITR 404 and *O'Connor* v. *Montrose Canned Foods Ltd* [1966] 1 ITR 171); and family circumstances (*Bainbridge* v. *Westinghouse Brake & Signal Co Ltd* [1966] 1 ITR 55).

In order to ensure that an offer of suitable alternative employment is handled reasonably (failing which the redundancy dismissal will be unfair dismissal) an employer must give priority to potentially redundant employees and appoint them to vacancies for which they are suited even though there may be better external candidates (*Corus Hotels Plc* v. *Williams* (unreported, EAT, 28 June 2006)). This obligation does not, of course, extend to meaning that an employer must make an appointment to a post for which someone is not suitable.

Each case has to be considered on its own merits and precedent is not of great help but it is likely that a redundancy dismissal will amount to unfair dismissal if the employer fails to provide the employee concerned with full information (including salary levels if known) about alternative jobs available within the same group. In such a case the employee's failure to express interest or to request further information can be a factor to be taken into account to reduce any compensatory award on grounds of contributory fault (*Fisher* v. *Hoopoe Finance Ltd* (unreported, EAT, 13 April 2005)).

The offer of alternative employment need not be in writing (although, for evidential purposes, it is prudent for an employer to put it in writing). It should contain sufficient information for the employee to make a decision on whether or not to accept and should be made before the original employment ends. In order to qualify so as to disentitle the employee to a redundancy payment, the new job must start immediately or within four weeks of the old job finishing.

The EAT has held that the further up the seniority ladder an employee is, the more proactive an employer can expect the employee to be when it comes to coming forward with suggestions for alternative employment – particularly if the senior employee wishes to be considered for a less senior or well-paid post. In *Whittle* v. *Parity Training* (unreported, EAT, 1 July 2003) the EAT approved the proposition that 'the duty on an employer is only to take reasonable steps, not to take every conceivable step possible, to find the employee alternative employment' and that it follows that if 'an employee at senior management level who is being made redundant is prepared to accept a subordinate position, he ought, in fairness, to make this clear at an early stage so as to give his employer an opportunity to see if that is a feasible solution'.

12.11.3 Employees on maternity or adoption leave

Special rules apply to parents on maternity or adoption leave. If a woman on maternity leave is to be made redundant, she 'is entitled to be offered' suitable alternative employment (Maternity and Parental Leave etc. Regulations 1999). It seems that this will be so even if he or she is not the best candidate (*Archibald* v. *Fife Council* [2004] ICR 954, HL – an important disability discrimination case but the same general principle may well apply). In other words, a woman on maternity leave comes first in the queue and 'trumps' all other employees when the employer decides to whom a limited number of suitable alternative posts should be offered. The same wording has been used in the Paternity and Adoption Leave Regulations 2002 in the section covering redundancy during adoption leave. Failure to offer suitable alternative employment will render the dismissal automatically unfair.

It used to be that in the case of small employers (five or fewer employees, inclusive of employees of an associated employer) it was not automatically unfair dismissal if the employer could show it was not reasonably practicable to permit her to return. However, this is no longer the case (Maternity and Parental Leave etc. Regulations 1999, reg.20(6) was revoked by the Maternity and Parental Leave etc. and the Paternity and Adoption Leave (Amendment) Regulations 2006, SI 2006/2014 in respect of employees whose expected week of childbirth began after 1 April 2007).

12.11.4 Trial period

Any person offered suitable alternative employment is entitled to a statutory trial period of four calendar (as opposed to working) weeks, thus time continues to run even when the workplace is closed for a seasonal holiday. If either party terminates the employment during the trial period, then the dismissal is deemed to be for reason of redundancy. However, if the employee unreasonably resigns, and if the alternative employment was suitable, he ceases to be entitled to a redundancy payment (*Benton v. Sanderson Kayser Ltd* [1989] IRLR 19, CA).

It is unreasonable, and may render any (constructive) dismissal unfair, to insist that the employee accepts or rejects the new job offer without allowing a four-week trial period (*Elliott v. Richard Stump Ltd* [1987] IRLR 215).

The statutory four-week trial period may be extended for longer than four weeks if, and only if:

- it is for the purpose of retraining the employee for the new job;
- it is in writing, setting out the date on which the period of retraining ends;
- it was agreed before the employee started work in the new job; and
- it specifies the terms and conditions of employment which will apply to the employee at the end of the trial period (ERA 1996, s.138(6)).

If there is to be an extended (i.e. beyond four weeks) trial period the specified conditions must be strictly observed for the employee to remain entitled to statutory redundancy pay if he decides not to continue (*O'Hara v. Reality (White Arrow Express) Ltd* (unreported, EAT, 18 November 2003)).

There is no room for a 'common-law reasonable' period to run alongside the statutory four weeks (*Optical Express v. Williams* [2008] ICR 1, EAT).

12.12 BUMPING

There is a question as to whether 'transferred redundancies' (known as 'bumping') fall within the statutory definition of redundancy. Bumping is where an employee is dismissed to make way for another employee whose position no longer exists.

There are two views as to whether a 'bumped' employee has or has not been dismissed by reason of redundancy. Back in 1981 the EAT said:

> ... experienced as we are in this general area of industrial relations law, our immediate reaction was that a dismissal on the grounds of redundancy must ... relate the cessation or diminution of work to the dismissal of the particular man. We were soon shown to be wrong when we were referred to *W. Gimber & Sons Ltd.* v. *Spurrett* (1967) 2 ITR 308 ... Lord Parker ... giving the leading judgment, quoted and approved the words used by the industrial tribunal:
> 'If there is a reduction in the requirements for employees in one section of an employer's business and an employee who becomes surplus or redundant is transferred to another section of that business, an employee who is displaced by the transfer of the first employee and is dismissed by reason of that displacement is dismissed by reason of redundancy.'
> *Elliott Turbomachinery Ltd* v. *Bates* [1981] ICR 218

Nowadays this seems to be the generally accepted position. However, in *Church* v. *West Lancashire NHS Trust* [1998] IRLR 4, the EAT held that a bumped employee does not fall within the definition of redundancy, because there was no diminution in the requirement for work of the particular kind he was employed to do. Although the EAT gave permission to appeal to the Court of Appeal, the case was not pursued further.

In a later House of Lords case the generally accepted position seemed to be restored (*Murray & anor* v. *Foyle Meats Ltd* [1999] ICR 827, HL). However, as *Murray* was not directly concerned with 'bumped redundancies' (it was concerned with closely related issues about proper selection of employees for redundancy dismissal) and as the House of Lords made no reference to *Church* in their judgment there is perhaps still scope for arguing that the EAT was right in its controversial ruling in *Church* that a 'bumped redundancy' dismissal is not 'by reason of redundancy'.

The EAT has held that there is no obligation on an employer to consider bumping, and that a redundancy dismissal cannot be attacked as being unfair simply because bumping was not considered (*Dixon* v. *Automobile Association* (unreported, EAT, 20 April 2004)). However, in order to minimise the risk of a redundancy dismissal being found by a tribunal to be unfair dismissal a prudent employer should at the very least consider whether it would be appropriate to dismiss some other employee, even from a more junior position, and offer his job to the potentially redundant employee (see *Lionel Levanthal Ltd* v. *North* (unreported, EAT, 27 October 2004) and *Alvis Vickers Ltd* v. *Lloyd* (unreported, EAT, 5 August 2005)).

12.13 TIME OFF WORK

An employee who is under notice of redundancy and who has accrued two years' continuity of employment is entitled to time off work in order to look for a new job or arrange training for future employment. There is no limit to the amount of time off work that can be taken, save that it must be reasonable (ERA 1996, s.52).

However, the time off is not well remunerated. Employees are entitled to be paid on a *pro rata* hourly basis for each hour taken off, save that there is an absolute maximum of 40 per cent of one week's pay (the statutory cap on a week's pay which applies for some purposes does not apply for this purpose). This maximum applies to the entire notice period. Thus an employee earning £52,000 per annum who is under one month's notice of redundancy, and who takes a total of two weeks off, will only be entitled to a maximum of £400 (i.e. 40 per cent of one week's pay). In such circumstances, one should investigate whether the contract provides greater rights to payment than does statute (ERA 1996, s.53).

A few categories of employees are not entitled to time off under ERA 1996, s.52. In outline these are some fishermen and merchant seamen, police officers and members of the armed forces.

12.14 APPEALS

Until the statutory dismissal procedures are revoked (probably April 2009 – see **Chapter 4**), failure to offer an appeal will normally be automatically unfair. However, if the employer can establish that the appeal would be unlikely to have made a difference, any compensatory award will be small and can even be reduced to zero (*Alvis Vickers Ltd* v. *Lloyd* (unreported, EAT, 5 August 2005) and see **Chapter 19**). Whilst an effective appeal procedure can cure a procedural defect from an earlier stage (*Lloyd* v. *Taylor Woodrow Construction* [1999] IRLR 782) a defective process can contribute to a finding of unfair dismissal (*Alstom Traction Ltd* v. *Birkenhead* (unreported, EAT, 17 June 2002)).

There is no obligation, as a matter of general fairness, to provide an appeal against a redundancy decision. Therefore if the statutory dismissal procedures do not apply (most commonly, until they are revoked, because more than 20 redundancies are taking place), then the failure to offer an appeal against selection for redundancy is unlikely to render a dismissal unfair (*Robinson* v. *Ulster Carpet Mills* [1991] IRLR 348, which is still good law – see *Alvis Vickers Ltd* v. *Lloyd* (unreported, EAT, 5 August 2005)). Nevertheless it is undoubtedly good practice to offer an appeal (Acas advisory booklet 'Redundancy Handling').

A dedicated website at **www.emplaw.co.uk/lshandbook** provides links to judgments and other source material referred to in this chapter.

CHAPTER 13

Transfer of undertakings

13.1 INTRODUCTION

Under the common law an employment contract is a personal contract between employee and employer. One result is that under common law when a person sells or otherwise transfers a business that he owns to a new owner, the employees remain his employees. Unless the new owner re-employs them, at best they will have to accept different jobs with the original employer (if he has any available) and at worst will find themselves dismissed as redundant (*Nokes* v. *Doncaster Amalgamated Collieries Ltd* [1940] 3 All ER 549).

An incorporated company is, in law, a person and so the common law position described above applies in the same way regardless of whether the business or undertaking being sold or otherwise transferred is owned by an incorporated company or by an individual. It will thus be seen that under the common law there is an enormous difference for employees between an incorporated company transferring ownership of its business to a new owner and the company's shareholders transferring their shares to a new owner. In both cases the employees' contracts remain with the company and in both cases the new owner takes over the running of the business. But in the first case the company has disposed of the business in which they worked so they may well be redundant, whereas in the second case they go on working as before.

Regulations first introduced in the UK in 1981 (the Transfer of Undertakings (Protection of Employment) Regulations 1981, SI 1981/1794 (TUPE 1981)) to implement the EC Acquired Rights Directive 77/187/EEC reversed the common law position for protection of employees. With effect from 6 April 2006, TUPE 1981 have been revoked and replaced by the Transfer of Undertakings (Protection of Employment) Regulations 2006, SI 2006/246 (TUPE 2006) (see TUPE 2006, regs.20 and 21).

The main effects of the TUPE rules are:

1. The contract of employment of any employee covered by the rules is automatically 'novated' to the new owner of the business (TUPE 1981, reg.5 replaced by TUPE 2006, reg.4).

2. With a few exceptions, all the former employer's liabilities to such an employee arising from the employment pass to the new employer (TUPE 1981, reg.5 replaced by TUPE 2006, reg.4).
3. An employee who is dismissed for a reason connected with the transfer will automatically be treated as unfairly dismissed unless the employer can show that the reason for the dismissal was 'an economic, technical or organisational reason entailing changes in the workforce' in which case the question of whether or not the dismissal was unfair has to be assessed in accordance with normal unfair dismissal rules (TUPE 1981, reg.8 replaced by TUPE 2006, reg.7).
4. For the above to apply not only when a business or undertaking is transferred but also when there is a change in provision of services (case law and TUPE 2006, reg.3(1)(b)).

The TUPE regulations apply only in respect of employees. The same definition of 'employee' is used in TUPE 2006, reg.2 as was previously used in TUPE 1981, reg.2. This is a little wider than the definition in ERA 1996, s.230 but does not include 'anyone who provides services under a contract for services' and thus does not include self-employed people who are working for someone else.

The TUPE regulations apply even if the party to which a business is transferred is outside the EU/UK notwithstanding the potential difficulty of workers enforcing their rights against a non-EU/non-UK transferee (*Holis Metal Industries Ltd* v. *GMB & Newell Ltd* [2008] IRLR 187, EAT).

There is no exception in the TUPE regulations for inter-group transfers. The European Court of Justice has held that the Acquired Rights Directive applies where a business is transferred between two companies in the same group even if they have the same ownership, management and premises and are engaged in the same works (*Allen & ors* v. *Amalgamated Construction Co Ltd* [2000] ICR 436, ECJ).

Replacement of the 1981 regulations by TUPE 2006 followed lengthy consultation by the DTI (now BERR) which began in September 2001. The exercise proved more complicated than had originally been expected and in one sense was not urgent as its main purpose was to clarify and tidy up the law rather than make radical changes to it. It was not until March 2005 that the draft new regulations were issued and it took another year before they were finalised. Meanwhile the original EC Acquired Rights Directive and a 1998 amending directive, Directive 98/50/EC, had themselves been revoked and replaced by a new Acquired Rights Directive 2001/23/EC.

As previously, the TUPE 2006 rules do not apply when an incorporated company is taken over. As noted above in that situation the employer continues to be the same limited company as previously (TUPE 1981, reg.3(1), TUPE 2006, reg.3(1)(a) and *Brookes* v. *Borough Care Services* [1998] ICR 1198, EAT). In December 2007 a Private Equity (Transfer of Undertakings and Protection of Employment) Bill was introduced in Parliament to extend

EMPLOYMENT LAW HANDBOOK

the TUPE rules to cover employees of incorporated companies which are taken over. Eventually the Bill was withdrawn – those in favour of it presumably came to understand, as was explained by other MPs, that the TUPE regulations have nothing whatsoever to do with the mischief which the well-intentioned proposer of the Bill sought to correct.

Three supplementary points need to be made to complete this introduction:

- the TUPE regulations do not apply to employee rights under company pension schemes (TUPE 2006, reg.10). However, similar rules are applied by the Transfer of Employment (Pension Protection) Regulations 2005, SI 2005/649 (see **section 13.12**).
- special TUPE-plus codes of practice apply in the public sector whether or not the TUPE regulations themselves apply (the most important currently being the Code of Practice on Workforce Matters in Public Sector Service Contracts, March 2005; and the Cabinet Office Statement of Practice 'Staff Transfers in the Public Sector', November 2007 – see **section 13.14**).
- immigration rules operating from 29 February 2008 will be relevant if there are any immigrant workers amongst those whose employment is transferred to the new owner of a business as a result of a TUPE transfer. A new 'points-based' immigration system started on 29 February 2008 and the Home Office guidance states in relation to TUPE transfers that 'if the new owner is not a licensed sponsor, it must apply for a licence within 28 calendar days of taking over the business. If it does not, we are likely to curtail the leave of the sponsored migrants, as they will not be working for or studying with a licensed sponsor' (para.156 of the 'Home Office (BIA) Licensing Guidance: Sponsorship under the Points Based System', February 2008).

13.2 DIFFERENCES BETWEEN TUPE 1981 AND TUPE 2006

As noted above the main purpose of introducing new TUPE regulations was to clarify and tidy up the law rather than make radical changes to it. Nevertheless there are differences and for those familiar with TUPE 1981 it may be convenient to summarise the main changes, as follows:

- Case law under TUPE 1981 ensured that the regulations operated to protect employees involved in outsourcing of services. A main purpose of TUPE 2006 is to codify that position. This is done by extending the definition of a 'relevant transfer' by adding new wording to cover a 'service provision change', specifically extending TUPE protection to employees involved in outsourcing or insourcing and in a change of service contractors (TUPE 2006, reg.3(1)(b)).
- New provisions require a transferor employer to provide to a transferee employer information about employees whose employment will be automatically transferred under TUPE (TUPE 2006, regs.11 and 12).

- Bringing into the TUPE regulations themselves the rules about informing and consulting employees and/or their representatives about a TUPE transfer (these rules were previously contained in separate regulations) (TUPE 2006, regs.13 - 16).
- A partial removal of TUPE protection for employees to help insolvent businesses survive (TUPE 2006, regs.8 and 9).
- Watering down the possibility of a transferee employer claiming that a change imposed on employees taken over as a result of a TUPE transfer was merely a change in working conditions and not a change in terms of contract (TUPE 2006, reg.4(9)).

As the BERR Guide to the 2006 TUPE regulations says 'The rights and obligations in the 1981 regulations remain in place, though the 2006 regulations contain revised wording at some points to make their meaning clearer, as well as reflecting developments in case law since 1981.'

13.3 CONTINUITY OF EMPLOYMENT

If the trade or business in which employees are employed is transferred to a new owner and the employees were employed in it at the time of the transfer their employment before the transfer 'counts as a period of employment with the transferee, and . . . the transfer does not break the continuity of the period of employment' (ERA 1996, s.218).

Contrary to previous thinking, the phrase 'at the time of the transfer' in ERA 1996, s.218(2) must be strictly construed so that it refers to a particular point in time, being the time when responsibility as employer for carrying on a particular undertaking moves from the transferor to the transferee. The House of Lords has held that this interpretation is required to ensure conformity with the EC Acquired Rights Directive 77/187/EEC, Art 3(1) as interpreted by the European Court of Justice (*Celtec Ltd* v. *Astley & ors* [2006] ICR 992, HL 29). Previously it had been thought that a transfer for relevant purposes might be a process spread over a period of time (*Clark Tokeley Ltd (t/a Spell Brook Ltd)* v. *Oakes* [1999] ICR 276, CA).

The fact that the TUPE regulations ensure that on transfer of a business an employee is treated as having been continuously employed by the new owner since the date of commencement of the original employment does not entitle the employee to the benefit of better terms provided to its own previous employees. In the words of HHJ McMullen in the EAT 'one cannot use TUPE to advance upon a position which was not there on the date of the transfer . . . Nor can TUPE be brought in respect of a criticism of post-transfer variations, unless it is to safeguard a pre-transfer right' (*Computershare Investor Services plc* v. *Jackson* [2008] IRLR 70, CA).

13.4 INFORMATION AND CONSULTATION (EMPLOYEES)

TUPE 2006, reg.13 requires an employer to inform appropriate representatives of any 'affected employees' (defined to include all those affected, whether employed by the transferor or the transferee and whether or not they are amongst those whose employment is to be transferred) of:

- the fact that the transfer is to take place, the date or proposed date of the transfer and the reasons for it;
- the legal, economic and social implications of the transfer for any affected employees;
- the measures which he envisages he will, in connection with the transfer, take in relation to any affected employees or, if he envisages that no measures will be so taken, that fact; and
- if the employer is the transferor, the measures, in connection with the transfer, which he envisages the transferee will take in relation to any affected employees who will by virtue of the TUPE regulations become employees of the transferee after the transfer or, if he envisages that no measures will be so taken, that fact.

In addition an employer must consult appropriate representatives of any 'affected employees' if it is envisaged that he will be 'taking measures' in relation to affected employees (TUPE 2006, reg.13(6)). There is no definition of 'measures' but the word is likely to be construed widely to include 'any action, step or arrangement' (*IPCS* v. *Secretary of State for Defence* [1987] IRLR 373). Whether the resulting distinction between the duty to inform and the duty to consult has any practical relevance is beyond the scope of this book.

The obligation to 'inform' is to do so 'long enough before a relevant transfer to enable the employer of any affected employees to consult the appropriate representatives of any affected employees' (TUPE 2006, reg.13(2)). The obligation to 'consult' is to do so with a view to seeking agreement of the appropriate representatives to the 'intended measures' (TUPE 2006, reg.13(6)). Either way this would seem to mean that leaving it to the last minute would be a breach of the regulations.

The information and consultation rules in TUPE 2006 derive from the Collective Redundancies and Transfer of Undertakings (Protection of Employment) (Amendment) Regulations 1995 and 1999, SI 1995/2587 and SI 1999/1925. This pedigree makes it relevant to add three points for avoidance of possible confusion:

- SI 1995/2587 and SI 1999/1925 continue in force, without change to their names, but no longer have any effect in relation to transfers of undertakings. In that respect they operated by making amendments to TUPE 1981 which has been revoked.

- SI 1995/2587 and SI 1999/1925 apply in redundancy cases only if at least 20 employees are being dismissed. The TUPE information and consultation rules apply regardless of the number of affected employees.
- In cases where SI 1995/2587 and SI 1999/1925 apply they always require consultation whereas the TUPE regulations require consultation only if it is envisaged that the employer will be 'taking measures'.

There is a definition of 'appropriate representatives' in TUPE 2006, reg.13(3) and there are rules for electing them if there is no recognised independent trade union in TUPE 2006, reg.14. The obligation to inform is taken very seriously, to such an extent that if a TUPE transfer is in prospect and no trade union is recognised and there are no employee representatives in post, the employer must initiate an election of representatives and then inform them (and consult if appropriate) or, failing that, must inform (and consult if appropriate) affected employees individually (TUPE 2006, reg.13(11) and *Howard* v. *Millrise Limited t/a Colourflow (In Liquidation) & Anor* [2005] IRLR 84, EAT).

If an employer fails to inform and/or consult as required by TUPE 2006, reg.13 (or to arrange an election of 'appropriate representatives' in situations where that is required) an employment tribunal can award compensation. The detail of who can apply to a tribunal in particular circumstances is set out in TUPE 2006, reg.15 which also provides a three-month time limit for applying to a tribunal. Compensation means 'such sum not exceeding thirteen weeks' pay for the employee in question as the tribunal considers just and equitable having regard to the seriousness of the failure of the employer to comply with his duty' (TUPE 2006, reg.16(3)). The EAT has ruled that 'compensation' for failure to consult as required by the TUPE regulations is not 'compensation' at all (i.e. is not compensation for loss) but is a punitive award and meant as a deterrent. Therefore unless there are mitigating factors the award should be the maximum thirteen weeks' pay (*Sweetin* v. *Coral Racing* [2006] IRLR 252). Assuming this is good law it presumably also applies to compensation for failure to inform.

A change from TUPE 1981 is that under TUPE 2006, reg.16(4) a 'week's pay' for this purpose is made subject to the statutory cap set out in ERA 1996, s.227 (currently £330, making a maximum of £4,290 per employee).

In the past there were differences of opinion as to whether liability to pay compensation for failure to inform and/or consult employees before a TUPE transfer was one of the (very few) types of liability which remains with the transferor when ownership of an undertaking is transferred or whether it is a liability which is transferred to the new owner (under what is now TUPE 2006, reg.4). The arguments for both points of view were extensively rehearsed by the EAT in *Alamo Group* v. *Tucker* [2003] ICR 829. TUPE 2006 disposes of this knotty question once and for all, at least so far as employees are concerned, simply by making the outgoing and incoming employers jointly and severally liable (TUPE 2006, reg.15(9)).

Finally it should be noted that if in any case there are special circumstances which render it not reasonably practicable for an employer to perform any of the duties noted above it will be sufficient for him to 'take all such steps towards performing that duty as are reasonably practicable in the circumstances' (TUPE 2006, reg.13(9)).

13.5 INFORMATION AND CONSULTATION (BETWEEN EMPLOYERS)

An intending transferor must provide the intending transferee with what TUPE 2006 refers to as 'employee liability information' about any person employed by him who is assigned to the organised grouping of resources or employees that is the subject of that transfer (TUPE 2006, reg.11(1)). This includes information about employees who have been dismissed for a reason connected with the transfer that is not 'an economic, technical or organisational reason entailing changes in the workforce' (TUPE 2006, reg.11(4) and see **section 13.7**).

This information must be provided at least 14 days before a relevant transfer unless special circumstances make this not reasonably practicable. It can then be done as soon as reasonably practicable thereafter (TUPE 2006, reg.11(6)). There is of course provision to make sure that changes in employee liability information must also be provided (TUPE 2006, reg.11(5)).

'Employee liability information' in relation to each employee means

(a) identity;
(b) age (if the employer does not know the age of an employee he will presumably have to rely on the 'Exception for statutory authority' provision in reg.27(1) of the Age Discrimination regulations – see **section 16.1** – to justify taking any steps necessary to find out);
(c) the particulars of employment that an employer is obliged to give to an employee under ERA 1996, s.1 (see **section 9.2.6**);
(d) information of any disciplinary or grievance procedure relevant to the employee concerned within the previous two years 'in circumstances where the Employment Act 2002 (Dispute Resolution) Regulations 2004 apply' (as noted at **Chapter 4** these regulations are due to be revoked, probably on 6 April 2009, so an appropriate change will no doubt be made to this item);
(e) information of any court or tribunal case, claim or action: (i) brought by an employee against the transferor, within the previous two years; (ii) that the transferor has reasonable grounds to believe that an employee may bring against the transferee, arising out of the employee's employment with the transferor; and
(f) information of any collective agreement which will have effect after the transfer, in its application in relation to the employee, pursuant to TUPE 2006, reg.5.

The penalty for failure to comply with the duty to provide employee liability information can be heavy (TUPE 2006, reg.12(4)–(6)). The regulations provide for it to be such amount as an employment tribunal considers just and equitable in all the circumstances having regard to 'any loss sustained by the transferee which is attributable to the matters complained of' and any relevant contractual terms – but give a strong steer that it should not generally be less than £500 per employee. A tribunal must take into account that the transferee is under the normal obligation to mitigate his loss (TUPE 2006, reg.12(6)).

13.6 CHANGES TO TERMS OF EMPLOYMENT ON TRANSFER OF OWNERSHIP

A variation in terms of employment can occur at any time but is especially likely when a business is sold or otherwise transferred to new owners. Under TUPE 2006, reg.4(4) the variation will be 'void if the sole or principal reason for the variation is (a) the transfer itself; or (b) a reason connected with the transfer that is not an economic, technical or organisational reason entailing changes in the workforce' (as to which see below). Whether the employee has or has not agreed the change makes no difference to the change being void.

In 2007 the Court of Appeal, agreeing with the EAT, put an important gloss on this to the effect that the variation will not be void if it is for the benefit, rather than to the detriment, of the employee (*Regent Security Services* v. *Power* [2008] ICR 442). In practice this probably means that if shortly after a 'TUPE transfer' an employee's contract is varied, even with his agreement, the employee will for some time afterwards be able to have a change of mind and pick and choose which variations to accept – and refuse to abide by others.

If a change other than one which is insignificant is made to the detriment of employees in their terms and conditions of employment they will be entitled to resign and claim unfair constructive dismissal (TUPE 2006, reg.4(11)).

The overall result is that it can be extremely difficult for an employer to harmonise the terms and conditions of employment of new employees it has just taken on as the result of a TUPE transfer with those of existing employees.

Clearly any link between a change in terms of employment and the transfer will eventually disappear. However, there is no set period (two years was not long enough to sever the link in *London Metropolitan University* v. *Dr Sackur & Ors* (unreported, EAT, 17 August 2006)). There is no guidance on this point in the regulations nor in the official guide to TUPE 2006 issued by BERR in March 2007 (which unhelpfully but accurately states that the matter has to be assessed in the light of all the circumstances of the individual case and will vary from case to case). The absence of a specified time does make it clear that time is not the only, or indeed the main, consideration. Therefore if the employer is carrying out a general reorganisation anyway involving a change in the terms of employment of existing staff as well as of new employees taken on as the result of a TUPE transfer it might well be possible for him to demonstrate that the change was not for a reason connected with the transfer.

Under TUPE 1981 an employer could validly make changes to working conditions (as opposed to terms of contract) of staff taken on as the result of a TUPE transfer if the changes could lawfully have been made by the previous employer without breach of contract (*Rossiter* v. *Pendragon plc* [2002] ICR 1063, CA, overruling an EAT decision to the contrary). However, even this minor semi-exception to the general rule must now be regarded with suspicion. A new provision in TUPE 2006 provides that 'if a relevant transfer involves or would involve a substantial change in working conditions to the material detriment of a person whose contract of employment is or would be transferred . . .' under the regulations then the employee may treat himself as having been dismissed (TUPE 2006, reg.4(9)).

This would seem to be in line with ECJ rulings which have held that an employee can enter into a valid agreement with his new employer to alter employment terms provided that the alteration is one which could have been lawfully made 'in situations other than those involving the transfer of an undertaking' and 'provided that the transfer of the undertaking itself may never constitute the reason for that amendment' (see *Viggosdottir* v. *Islandspostur HF*, EFTA Court Case E-3/01 [2002] IRLR 425 and *Collino & Anor* v. *Telecom Italia SpA* Case C-343/98 [2000] IRLR 788, ECJ).

If adverse changes made to an employee's terms of employment because of the transfer of the employing business are part of a package it is not open to the new employer to argue that the adverse changes are binding on the basis that the package as a whole was beneficial to the employee (*Torgeir Langeland* v. *Norske Fabricom A/S*, Case E-3/95 [1997] 2 CMLR 966; *Foreningen* v. *Daddy's Dance Hall AS* [1988] ECR 739, ECJ; *Wilson & Sanders* v. *St Helens BC* [1998] ICR 1141, HL; and *Credit Suisse First Boston (Europe) Ltd* v. *Lister* [1999] ICR 794, CA).

The only 'defences' likely to be open to an employer facing a claim by an employee based on a contention that changes in terms of employment are invalidated by the TUPE rules are: (i) that the transfer of the employing business was not the reason for the changes being made; and/or (ii) that the reason or principal reason for the changes was an 'economic, technical or organisational reason entailing changes in the workforce' and that it would have been fair to dismiss the employee if he had not agreed to the changes (the ETO defence – see **section 13.7**).

13.7 DISMISSAL CONNECTED WITH A TUPE TRANSFER

If an employee is dismissed and the principal reason for the dismissal is a TUPE transfer or a reason connected with a TUPE transfer then he will automatically be treated as unfairly dismissed unless the employer can show that the reason for the dismissal was 'an economic, technical or organisational [ETO] reason entailing changes in the workforce' (TUPE 2006, reg.7). This applies whether the dismissal is before or after the transfer and whether it is actual dismissal or constructive dismissal, for example, a resignation in response to the new employer's attempt to impose a change in terms of employment.

The effect of an employer calling in aid this ETO defence is not to make an otherwise unfair dismissal fair. Rather it is to remove the normally automatic unfairness of a TUPE-related dismissal. Whether or not the dismissal or constructive dismissal is in fact unfair in such circumstances will be decided by applying normal rules and principles. Technically, if the ETO defence to a finding of automatically unfair dismissal has been made out, then in considering whether the dismissal is fair or unfair the normal rules in ERA 1996, s.98 will apply with the dismissal being regarded as being for 'some other substantial reason' or, in appropriate cases, as being by reason of redundancy (TUPE 2006, reg.7(3)).

The Court of Appeal has held that if there was more than one reason for a dismissal and one of them was an ETO reason it is up to the employment tribunal to decide as a question of fact whether that was the principal reason within the meaning of the TUPE regulations (*Whitehouse* v. *Blatchford & Sons Ltd* [2000] ICR 542, CA).

13.8 WHAT UNDERTAKINGS AND TRANSFERS ARE COVERED?

The TUPE regulations apply to 'a transfer of an undertaking, business or part of an undertaking or business situated immediately before the transfer in the UK to another person where there is a transfer of an economic entity which retains its identity' (TUPE 2006, reg.3(1)(a)). Although the wording is slightly different, the above is essentially the same as was previously provided by TUPE 1981.

A significant new provision is added as TUPE 2006, reg.3(1)(b). This covers 'a service provision change' where the services are provided by an 'organised grouping of employees . . . which has as its principal purpose the carrying out of the activities concerned on behalf of the client' (TUPE 2006, reg.3(3)(a)).

13.8.1 Transfer of an undertaking or business

There are two separate questions to be asked. The first is 'was there an identifiable economic entity which counts as an undertaking for the purpose of the regulations?' The second question is 'was there a relevant transfer of any such entity?' These two questions should normally be considered separately and in turn (*Whitewater Leisure Management Ltd* v. *Barnes & ors* [2000] IRLR 456, EAT).

Rulings by the European Court and the UK Court of Appeal and EAT clarify the position to the extent that they make it clear that the most important consideration for deciding the first question noted above is whether there is a recognisable, stable and continuing economic entity. The correct approach is 'multifactorial', that is all relevant factors must be considered (*Cheesman* v. *Brewer Contracts* [2001] IRLR 144, EAT and *P & O Trans European Ltd* v. *Initial Transport Services Ltd* [2003] IRLR 128, EAT).

It is not essential that there should be a discrete and identifiable stable economic entity before the transfer – it is sufficient if a part of a larger stable economic entity becomes identified for the first time as a separate economic entity on the occasion of the transfer separating it from the rest (*TGWU* v. *Swissport (UK) Ltd (in administration) & Aer Lingus Ltd* [2007] ICR 1593, EAT).

The transfer does not have to be a sale and the undertaking transferred can be involved in any form of activity. At one time the UK TUPE regulations were worded so that undertakings which were 'not in the nature of a commercial venture' were excluded. However, the ECJ held that this exclusion was unlawful and the regulations were therefore changed accordingly (Trade Union Reform and Employment Rights Act 1993, s.33).

Tribunals and the courts will seek to ascertain whether there was a continuing economic entity before and after a transfer to help them decide whether the TUPE regulations apply in any particular situation. In particular the regulations apply regardless of whether any tangible assets are transferred. By the same token it does not follow that the regulations apply just because tangible assets have been transferred (*Landsorganisationen i Danmark* v. *Ny Molle Kro* [1989] ICR 330, ECJ).

For a while, following a European Court case in early 1997, it was thought that an employer might be able to avoid the EC/UK TUPE regulations altogether if it was able to arrange that no employees at all would be transferred with the business in which they had previously been employed (*Süzen* v. *Zehnacker Gebaudereiningung Gmbh Krankenhausservice* [1997] ICR 662, ECJ). This possible 'escape route' for employers was soon closed. The argument that if no staff and no assets are taken over it must automatically follow that no undertaking has been transferred has been held to be wrong (*Abler & Ors* v. *Sodexho Catering Gesellschaft mbH* [2004] IRLR 168, ECJ). If it were otherwise, it would sometimes be possible for purchasers of businesses to avoid the TUPE regulations by deliberately refusing to take on any of the staff employed by the previous owner (for example, by buying assets and goodwill only) thus thwarting the very object of the regulations (*ECM (Vehicle Delivery Services) Ltd* v. *Cox & Ors* [1999] IRLR 559, CA). The Court of Appeal has held that if no employees are taken on by the new owner it is legitimate for a tribunal to consider the reason why, with a strong hint that if the reason was to avoid the TUPE regulations then that itself is an indication that the regulations apply, at least if the relevant activity is a labour-intensive one (*ADI (UK) Ltd* v. *Willer & Ors* [2001] IRLR 542, CA). In *ADI* Dyson LJ said (at para.52):

> ... if the circumstances of an alleged transfer of undertaking are such that an actual transfer of labour would be a relevant factor to be taken into account in deciding whether there has been a transfer of undertaking, then the Tribunal will not only be entitled but will be obliged to consider the reason why the labour was not transferred if that has been raised as an issue.

This statement of the law was specifically approved in *Astle & Ors* v. *Cheshire County Council & Anor* [2004] IRLR 12.

In 2007 the European Court of Justice held that a group of 40 temporary workers employed by an Austrian employment agency (or what in Britain would technically be called an employment business) amounted to a 'stable economic entity'. The workers were all supplied to one particular client. The agency which provided them hit financial difficulties and the owners set up a new business, PPS, and transferred the employment of the workers in question to the new business. Their work remained the same as before. These employees were owed unpaid salaries from the original agency. They claimed against their new employer, PPS, for the amounts due. The ECJ held that a stable economic entity had been transferred even though it comprised only temporary workers and no other assets. The workers therefore had rights under the EC Acquired Rights Directive 2001/23/EC and thus could make their claims against PPS (*Jouini & ors* v. *Princess Personal Service GmbH* [2007] IRLR 1005, ECJ).

The question of whether there is a 'stable economic entity' is essentially one of fact for an employment tribunal to determine. Unless the tribunal's decision is so clearly wrong that it can be categorised as 'perverse' it will therefore not be overturned on appeal (see, for example, *Thomas* v. *On Reflection Ltd & ors* (unreported, EAT, 1 February 2006), in which the parlous financial state of the putative transferor was one factor a tribunal had taken into account in deciding that there was no 'stable' undertaking).

13.8.2 Service provision changes

Although the introduction of a specific regulation (TUPE 2006, reg.3(1)(b)) governing service provision clarifies, and makes some changes to, the previous position it would be wrong to think that it makes any radical change. Thus, for example, TUPE 1981 was held to apply to the outsourcing to an independent contractor of activities such as cleaning or security previously carried on in-house, commonly known as 'first generation contracting-out', and the subsequent transfer of such a contract to a new contractor, commonly known as 'second generation contracting out' (*Argyll Training Ltd* v. *Sinclair (1) and Argyll & The Islands Enterprise Ltd (2)* [2000] IRLR 630, EAT).

EMPLOYMENT LAW HANDBOOK

The new regulations in TUPE 2006, reg.3(1)(b) cover specifically:

1. First generation contracting out or outsourcing ('activities cease to be carried out by a person ('a client') on his own behalf and are carried out instead by another person on the client's behalf ('a contractor')).
2. Second generation contracting out ('activities cease to be carried out by a contractor on a client's behalf (whether or not those activities had previously been carried out by the client on his own behalf) and are carried out instead by another person ('a subsequent contractor') on the client's behalf).
3. Contracting in or insourcing ('activities cease to be carried out by a contractor or a subsequent contractor on a client's behalf (whether or not those activities had previously been carried out by the client on his own behalf) and are carried out instead by the client on his own behalf).

Examples given in the BERR Guidance are labour-intensive services such as office cleaning, workplace catering, security guarding, refuse collection and machinery maintenance. However, lawyers, accountants and others can be included. Thus at least in theory if a major client of law firm A is dissatisfied with the service it is receiving and decides to instruct a new law firm B, then if the unsatisfactory service was provided by a dedicated group of lawyers who worked pretty well exclusively on that client's business, the employment contracts of those lawyers will be automatically transferred under TUPE 2006 to law firm B. This might please law firm A, and perhaps the lawyers concerned, but is unlikely to be what either the client or law firm B had in mind. At one stage, to avoid this result, there was a suggestion that there should be a 'professional services exception' to the new rules, but this was dropped.

The first case involving the new 'service provision change' regulation of which the authors are aware involved a similar scenario. Boots Healthcare transferred its advertising account from agency A to agency B. Agency A was reported to be arguing that staff who had serviced the Boots account were an 'organised grouping of employees' and that when it lost the Boots account the employment contracts of those staff had automatically transferred to agency B. Given that the basic purpose of TUPE is to provide protection to employees it is somewhat bizarre that the first reported use of the new regulations should be by an employer seeking to save employment costs.

We understand that the advertising industry has developed a 'voluntary protocol' in an attempt to enable advertising agencies to club together to avoid unintended consequences resulting from the application of TUPE 2006 with a view to providing mutual 'protection' in the event of a TUPE staff transfer.

In a separate case an employment tribunal, applying *Schmidt* v. *Spar und Leikhasse of Bordesholm etc* [1995] ICR 237, ECJ, decided that a single person, H, could count as 'an organised grouping of employees' for the purposes of TUPE 2006, reg.3(1)(b). A client of the PR agency for which she worked transferred its account to another PR agency and the tribunal held that H's employment, and liability in respect of certain claims she wished to bring in respect of her past employment, automatically passed to the new agency under TUPE 2006 (*Hunt* v. *Storm Communications Ltd & ors* (unreported, Reading Employment Tribunal, 1 June 2007)).

13.9 WHAT RIGHTS AND OBLIGATIONS ARE TRANSFERRED?

When TUPE 2006 applies all the transferor's rights, powers, duties and liabilities under or in connection with any contract of employment of any person employed by the transferor and assigned to the organised grouping of resources or employees that is subject to the transfer are automatically transferred to the purchaser/transferee. Employment contracts are thus treated as if they had been originally made with the new employer (TUPE 2006, reg.4(1) and (2)).

Thus for practical purposes if the TUPE regulations apply the new employer simply steps into the shoes of the old and takes on all continuing obligations to the staff involved. Thus a new owner of a business would automatically find that he had liability for settling personal injury claims arising from an accident which happened while the business was owned by a previous owner. In this case the new owner would also take the benefit of any claim under the previous employer's employers' liability insurance policy in respect of such claims (*Bernadone* v. *Pall Mall Services Group Ltd* [2001] ICR 197, CA and *Martin* v. *Lancashire County Council* [2001] ICR 197, CA). Similarly, a new owner would take on liability to an employee in respect of an alleged wrongful act such as an act of race or sex discrimination committed by the previous owner (*DJM International Ltd* v. *Nicholas* [1996] IRLR 76, EAT).

This broad statement is subject to three important exceptions:

1. The employee can object to his employment being automatically transferred to the new owner/employer (TUPE 2006, reg.4(7) and see **section 13.11**).
2. Criminal liabilities are not transferred to the new owner/employer (TUPE 2006, reg.4(6)).
3. Pension obligations are not transferred to the new owner/employer under EC/UK TUPE (but see **section 13.12** for notes on the Transfer of Employment (Pension Protection) Regulations 2005, SI 2005/649).

Another important exception was suggested in a German case in 2006. It suggests that employees' rights to favourable terms for purchase of products produced by their employer or with which the employer's business is closely concerned are not rights which necessarily transfer if ownership of the business is transferred. A German court ruled that the right of employees in a division of Daimler-Benz to buy Mercedes cars on special terms could not be exercised against the new owner of that division after what in the UK would be a 'TUPE transfer' (*Endres* v. *T-Systems International GmbH*, Federal Labour Court Germany).

13.10 WHO CAN BENEFIT?

Employees benefit from the TUPE rules provided they were employed in the transferred undertaking 'immediately before the transfer' (TUPE 2006, reg.4(3)).

Even an employee who is dismissed before the transfer of the employing business will be treated as employed 'immediately before the transfer' if he was dismissed for a reason connected with the transfer so that his dismissal is automatically unfair (TUPE 2006, reg.7 and *Litster* v. *Forth Dry Dock and Engineering Co Ltd* [1989] ICR 341, HL).

The wide purposive interpretation of the words 'employed immediately before the transfer' adopted in *Litster* is in point only if the principal reason for the dismissal was the transfer or a reason connected with it (in which case the automatically unfair dismissal provisions of the TUPE regulations apply). If the dismissal was for some other reason the words 'employed immediately before the transfer' will be interpreted literally.

The effect of TUPE 2006, reg.4(3) is that employees dismissed before a business transfer for a reason connected with the transfer which is an economic, technical or organisational reason entailing changes in the workforce do not have the normal protections provided by that regulation. In deciding what was the reason for the dismissal, only the thought process of the person making the dismissals, and why the decision to dismiss was reached, should be taken into account. Thus where the administrator of a company dismisses employees for sound ETO reasons (within the meaning of TUPE 2006, reg.7(1)) which were not related to the transfer of the business, the fact that behind the scenes the owners of the business deliberately kept secret their plan that the administrator would dismiss employees did not scupper that plan. They were to arrange a transfer of the employing business to other companies they owned without liability to the dismissed employees dismissed by the administrator (*Dynamex Friction Ltd & Ferotec Realty* v. *Amicus & Ors* [2008] IRLR 515).

By the same token, employees dismissed before a sale of the business they work for do not have their right to claim unfair dismissal automatically transferred to the purchaser if they were dismissed because the business was overstaffed, inefficient and insolvent and could only be made viable and continue as a going concern if the workforce was reduced. Again, this would normally amount to an ETO reason within the meaning of TUPE 2006, reg.7(1) and the employees would have to pursue their claims against the original employer – which might be fruitless if that employer is insolvent, leaving them to fall back on the State 'insolvency guarantee' scheme noted in **section 9.13** (*Thompson* v. *SCS Consulting Ltd & ors* [2001] IRLR 801, EAT).

13.11 OPTING OUT

While the basic rule is that any agreement between an employer and an employee to the effect that the TUPE regulations shall not apply to that employee is void this does not mean that an employee is obliged to go to work for a new employer if ownership of the employing business is transferred. What is now TUPE 2006, reg.4(7) was introduced in 1993 after an ECJ case (*Katsikas v. Konstantinidis* [1993] IRLR 179, ECJ). It ensures that the employee has the right to resign if she objects to the transfer. However, if she does so, she will not have been dismissed and will forfeit any rights to statutory compensation.

The harshness of this rule has been mitigated by case law. If an employee resigns because of genuine fears that the new owner of the employing business will impose employment terms substantially worse than those provided by the current owner she will be able to resign and bring a complaint of constructive wrongful dismissal against the current owner (*University of Oxford v. Humphreys & Anor* [2000] ICR 405, CA). However, if a well-meaning employee agrees to go to work for the new employer for a while then even if all parties were aware before the date of the relevant transfer that this was to be for a short period only, the EAT has held that her contract will automatically transfer under TUPE. The benefit of the principle established in *University of Oxford v. Humphreys* will not be available to her (*Capita Health Solutions v. BBC and McLean* [2008] IRLR 595, EAT).

The owner of a business who is considering disposing of it (by a relevant transfer) must inform employees about the proposals before he does so (see **section 13.2**). Failure to do this might mean that the employees concerned could not exercise their opt-out rights because they did not know what was happening but in that situation they will be allowed to 'opt-out' after the transfer provided they do so with minimum delay (*New ISG Ltd v. Vernon & Ors* [2008] IRLR 115, ChD).

13.12 PENSIONS

Pension rights have always been outside the scope of the TUPE regulations and continue to be so (TUPE 2006, reg.10).

Although this is strictly correct there are two extremely important qualifications. One is *Beckmann v. Dynamco Whicheloe MacFarlane Ltd* [2003] ICR 50, ECJ and the other is the Transfer of Employment (Pension Protection) Regulations 2005, SI 2005/649, which came into effect on 6 April 2005.

Beckmann established that the pensions exclusion must be narrowly construed. The question was whether benefits payable under General Whitley Council conditions of service on redundancy of an employee after age 50, including the right to an early retirement pension, should have transferred with the employee when she was transferred from the NHS to the private sector. The ECJ held that such rights are not old-age, invalidity or survivors' benefits within the meaning of Art.3(3) of Council Directive 77/187/EEC. Therefore such rights do pass under (and are not treated as pension rights excluded from) the TUPE regulations. This contradicted previous British thinking on the subject (see *Frankling* v. *BPS Public Sector Ltd* [1999] ICR 347, EAT). It follows that the liability to provide such benefits is automatically transferred to the new employer in cases where the TUPE regulations apply.

The second and even more fundamental qualification to the statement that pension rights have always been outside the scope of the TUPE regulations is provided by the Pensions Act 2004, ss.257–259, and the Transfer of Employment (Pension Protection) Regulations 2005, SI 2005/649. The basic effect is that if in a TUPE situation the previous employer provided a pension scheme then the new employer will have to provide some form of pension arrangement for employees who were members of (or eligible for membership of) the old employer's scheme. It will not have to be the same as the arrangement provided by the previous employer but will have to be of a certain minimum standard. As a general rule employer contributions must equal employee contributions subject to an upper limit of 6 per cent of basic pay (see reg.3 of the Transfer of Employment (Pension Protection) Regulations 2005).

Similar arrangements have been operating since 2003 under a Code of Practice applying to the transfer of staff from the public sector to a private sector employer when services are outsourced (see **section 13.14**).

Importantly, the arrangements include an opt-out provision. The employee and the new owner are free to agree whatever pension terms (or none) they want at any time after the time when the employee becomes employed by the new owner (Pensions Act 2004, s.258(6)).

13.13 INSOLVENT COMPANIES

Special provision is contained within TUPE 2006 designed to enable assets of a failing business to be transferred to a purchaser without the purchaser taking on employees' contracts or other liability to employees (TUPE 2006, reg.8).

The most important provision is that the automatic transfer of contracts of employment and employee liabilities and the automatic unfair dismissal provisions normally effected by TUPE 2006, regs.4 and 7 'do not apply to any relevant transfer where the transferor is the subject of bankruptcy proceedings or any analogous insolvency proceedings which have been instituted with a view to the liquidation of the assets of the transferor and are under the supervision of an insolvency practitioner' (TUPE 2006, reg.8(7)).

Other (more lengthy) provisions apply where insolvency proceedings have been opened in relation to the transferor not with a view to the liquidation of the assets of the transferor and which are under the supervision of an insolvency practitioner (called 'relevant insolvency proceedings' – TUPE 2006, reg.8(6)). In that case, employees' contracts do automatically transfer to the new employer but some liabilities which would normally pass under TUPE do not. Essentially, these are debts payable by the government from the National Insurance Fund when an employer becomes insolvent, including arrears of pay, pay in lieu of notice and statutory redundancy pay. In addition, subject to conditions, 'permitted variations' in contract terms of transferred employees are allowed (TUPE 2006, reg.9). Essentially a 'permitted variation' is one which is 'designed to safeguard employment opportunities by ensuring the survival of the undertaking, business or part of the undertaking or business that is the subject of the relevant transfer' ((TUPE 2006, reg.9(7)).

For these provisions to apply the transfer in question must have taken place after the date on which insolvency proceedings commence. In *Secretary of State for Trade and Industry* v. *Slater & ors* [2007] IRLR 928, EAT, a TUPE transfer took place before an insolvency practitioner had been appointed, before the shareholders' winding-up resolution and before the meeting of creditors. The EAT said that, applying normal rules, the company was therefore not technically insolvent at the time of the transfer. Therefore reg.8 did not apply, the liablity for back pay and holiday pay fell on the employer and there was no liability on the Secretary of State.

13.14 PUBLIC SECTOR

TUPE 2006 applies to public and private undertakings engaged in economic activities whether or not they are operating for gain. Three public sector documents take this a stage further. They are:

- A Cabinet Office Statement of Practice 'Staff Transfers in the Public Sector', first issued in January 2000, updated in November 2007 to take account of TUPE 2006.
- A Code of Practice on workforce matters in public sector service contracts – March 2005 version.
- An Alternative Dispute Resolution Procedure re Code of Practice on Handling Workforce Issues, March 2004.

The Cabinet Office Statement of Practice noted above concerns transfers of staff between one public sector employer and another while the March 2005 Code of Practice concerns the transfer of staff from a public sector employer to a private sector employer when services are outsourced. In effect, where these Codes apply they 'gold plate' TUPE. They are commonly known as the 'TUPE-plus' provisions.

When a public body outsources an activity to a private sector employer (for example, a local authority contracting out provision of school lunches) the private sector employer will be required by the TUPE regulations to continue to provide the same terms and conditions of employment for the staff transferred to his employment under the TUPE regulations. However, TUPE would not prevent the employer from taking on new staff on less favourable terms. With a view to ending the possibility of a 'two-tier workforce' in such situations, the government issued a Code of Practice in February 2003, effective in respect of all local authority outsourcing contracts advertised on or after 13 March 2003. The Code provides that the local authority, as part of its arrangements with the private sector employer, must require that employer to 'demonstrate its support for [the principles of the Code] and its willingness to work with the local authority fully to implement them'. The Local Government Act 2003, ss.101 and 102 gave legal backing to this requirement. The same rules were extended to cover the public sector generally as from 18 March 2005 when the 'Code of Practice on workforce matters in public sector service contracts – March 2005 version' came into effect (available online at **www.ogc.gov.uk/documents/Code_of_Practice_on_workforce_matters.pdf**).

Three points relating to the Code of Practice are worth particular note:

1. The Code requires that the new staff must be offered 'fair and reasonable terms and conditions which are, overall, no less favourable than those of transferred employees' but does not require that new staff have clause-by-clause identical terms to the inherited staff.
2. The Code applies not only when staff are transferred from a local authority to a private sector employer but also when staff so transferred are moved on to a new provider under a retender of the contract to which TUPE applies (i.e. the Code applies to what is sometimes called a 'second generation TUPE transfer').
3. Pension benefits must be available to the new staff. Unless they are able to join the local government scheme (which will depend on whether the new employer has admitted body status) they must be offered membership of a 'good quality employer pension scheme' which, if it is a defined contribution or stakeholder scheme, provides for the employer to match employee contributions up to 6 per cent.

There is no statutory sanction if, contrary to the Code of Practice, the private employer takes on new staff on less favourable terms than those of staff inherited from the local authority. Of course, if there is a relevant clause in the outsourcing contract there may be some legal comeback for breach of contract either directly by the local authority or by the transferred staff under the Contracts (Rights of Third Parties) Act 1999.

In an effort to provide some sort of mechanism for resolving disputes which might arise, the Office of the Deputy Prime Minister announced dispute resolution proposals in June 2003. These form the basis of the Alternative Dispute Resolution (ADR) procedure which is now found at Annex A to the Code of Practice (Code of Practice on Workforce Matters: Alternative Dispute Resolution Procedure). The Code provides for a three-stage ADR procedure (e.g. mediation and ADR) supervised by an independent person appointed from an approved list supplied by Acas.

The original version of the ADR procedure was agreed by the LGA, the Employers' Organisation for Local Government, the TUC and the CBI and was finally agreed in March 2004 as a document entitled 'Alternative Dispute Resolution Procedure re Code of Practice on Handling Workforce Issues'. All the parties agree that the ADR procedure should be a last resort and to make their best efforts to resolve problems by agreement. In practice the real teeth in the arrangement are commercial rather than legal – a contractor who, in contravention of the Code, takes on new staff on terms which are less beneficial than the terms applicable to staff he has taken on from the local authority will take the risk of being effectively blackballed from making tenders for future contracts.

A dedicated website at **www.emplaw.co.uk/lshandbook** provides links to judgments and other source material referred to in this chapter.

CHAPTER 14

Sex and race discrimination

14.1 GENERAL INFORMATION

Discrimination cases remain high in number. The latest figures show that there were 28,153 complaints of sex discrimination and 3,780 of race discrimination lodged in the year to 31 March 2007.

Sex and race discrimination are governed primarily by the Sex Discrimination Act 1975 (SDA 1975) and the Race Relations Act 1976 (RRA 1976), although a number of supplementary Acts and statutory instruments have modified these over time.

Despite slight diversion in language and interpretation, the two Acts are broadly similar in principle (this is in contrast to the DDA 1995 (**Chapter 15**), which has very different principles and statutory language). It is therefore convenient to deal with sex and race discrimination together, highlighting any differences between the two Acts where appropriate.

Historically, sex discrimination law has also been more heavily influenced by European Community legislation, in particular the EC Equal Treatment Directive and Art.141 (previously known as Art.119) of the Treaty of Rome. As a result, interpretation of similar wording within the two Acts can differ because SDA 1975 must be interpreted in accordance with EC principles. Recently the European Community has been more active with regard to race discrimination law and new anti-discrimination rules laid down by the EC Race Directive (Directive 2000/43/EC) have been incorporated into RRA 1976 by the Race Relations Act 1976 (Amendment) Regulations 2003, SI 2003/1626.

In October 2005, the Employment Equality (Sex Discrimination) Regulations 2005, SI 2005/2467 came into force. These regulations implement the amended Equal Treatment Directive (2002/73/EC) and brought sex discrimination law closer in line with the amended RRA 1976. The High Court ruled in March 2007 that the 2005 regulations failed properly to implement the EC Directive 76/207/EC in three technical but important ways: (i) re harassment – association with sex, not causation by it, should define harassment; (ii) re pregnancy/maternity – any suggestion that any comparator is needed is wrong; and (iii) in general there must be no differences between contractual benefits during compulsory, ordinary and additional maternity leave. Further regulations were made to correct the position in these three respects (Sex Discrimination Act 1975 (Amendment) Regulations 2008, SI 2008/656 and Maternity and Parental Leave etc. and the Paternity and Adoption Leave (Amendment) Regulations 2008, SI 2008/1966).

The Equal Opportunities Commission and the Commission for Racial Equality, along with the Disability Rights Commission, were subsumed into a new single Equality Commission with effect from 1 October 2007. This was established under the Equality Act 2006 as the 'Commission for Equality and Human Rights' (CEHR). Shortly before it started operations it informally changed its name to the 'Equality and Human Rights Commission' (EHRC).

It should be remembered that the equal pay legislation is a specific aspect of sex discrimination legislation. This book follows the normal convention of dealing with equal pay and terms of employment separately from sex discrimination (**Chapter 17**). Since the previous edition of this book there has been a mushrooming of equal pay claims mainly by relatively low-paid female staff employed by local authorities – there were 44,013 such claims lodged in the year ended 31 March 2007 compared with 8,229 in 2004/2005.

Discrimination law recognises the two different concepts of direct and indirect discrimination. Direct discrimination is treating somebody less favourably because of their sex or race. Indirect discrimination involves imposing a condition or requirement that a considerably smaller proportion of persons of a certain colour or nationality will be able to comply with; for example, a condition that job applicants have blond hair (which may discriminate against those of African or Indian nationalities), or applying a provision, criterion or practice which puts persons of one sex or of a defined race, ethnicity or national origin at a particular disadvantage when compared with other persons (RRA 1976, s.1(1A) and SDA 1795, s.1(2), as amended by the Employment Equality (Sex Discrimination) Regulations 2005, SI 2005/2467 (EE(SD)R 2005)

In a sex and race discrimination context, the most important difference between the two is that direct discrimination can never be justified whereas indirect discrimination is not unlawful if it can be justified as a proportionate means of achieving a legitimate aim (Sex Discrimination Act 1975, s.1(1)(b)(iii) as introduced by EE(SD)R 2005, reg.3 with effect from 1 October 2005 – different wording achieved a generally similar result before 1 October 2005).

A person is liable for unlawful discrimination if he discriminates against others (directly or indirectly):

- in the arrangements he makes for the purpose of determining who should be offered employment;
- in the terms on which he offers that employment;
- by refusing or deliberately omitting to offer them that employment;
- in the way the employer affords access to opportunities for promotion, transfer or training, or to any other benefit, facilities or services, or by refusing or deliberately omitting to afford access to them;

EMPLOYMENT LAW HANDBOOK

- by subjecting them to a detriment;
- by dismissing them; or
- by subjecting them to harassment (SDA 1975, s.6; RRA 1976, s.4).

Note that a slightly different list of prohibited actions applies for contract workers.

Protection against discrimination does not cease when the employment relationship has come to an end if an act of discrimination by an employer arises out of and is closely connected to the employment relationship (SDA 1975, s.20A, s.35C; RRA 1976, s.27A(2) and *Relaxion Group plc* v. *Rhys-Harper* [2003] IRLR 484, HL).

Under RRA 1976 it is also unlawful to discriminate against an employee on grounds of race 'in the terms of the employment which he affords him', although this adds little to the provisions listed above which appear in both Acts (RRA 1976, s.4(2)(a)).

14.1.1 Victimisation

Victimisation has a special meaning in anti-discrimination law. In the context of this chapter it is unlawful activity which takes place if an employee is treated less favourably than others because the employee has:

- brought proceedings (whether against the employer or a third party) under EqPA 1970, SDA 1975 or RRA 1976;
- given evidence or information in connection with such a claim; or
- alleged that the employer (or a third party) has done an act which would amount to a breach of EqPA 1970, SDA 1975 or RRA 1976.

The rules and principles applying are the same as for normal acts of discrimination (SDA 1975, s.4; RRA 1976, s.2).

The protection does not apply if the activity which the employee is complaining about is in reaction to an allegation which was 'false and not made in good faith' (RRA 1976, s.2(2)). For example, an employee who brought discrimination proceedings in order to harass his employer would not be bringing the proceedings in good faith. Therefore his doing so would not be a protected act and his dismissal for that reason would not be unlawful victimisation (*HM Prison Service* v. *Ibimidun* (unreported, EAT, 2 April 2008)).

An employer is not guilty of victimisation if taking action designed to protect its position in pending litigation. Thus refusal by an employer to provide a reference to an ex-employee who is claiming race discrimination will not amount to victimisation if it is genuinely done to protect its position in the litigation, rather than maliciously (*Chief Constable of West Yorkshire Police* v. *Khan* [2001] IRLR 830, HL). However; an employer will be able to justify what might otherwise be seen as victimisation only in respect of acts genuinely done to preserve their position in pending discrimination proceedings

(*Chief Constable of Norfolk & anor* v. *Arthurton* (unreported, EAT, 6 December 2006)). An employer's refusal to allow an employee time off work to consult advisors about pending sex (or race) discrimination proceedings against the employer could well be unlawful victimisation if the employee can show that his employer generally allows employees who are involved in legal proceedings time off to consult advisors (*TNT Express Worldwide (UK) Ltd* v. *Brown* [2001] ICR 182, CA).

The House of Lords ruled in 2007 that it is not unlawful victimisation for an employer to write a letter to staff who are bringing an equal pay claim warning them of job losses and other consequences if their claims succeeded (*St Helens MBC* v. *Mrs J. Derbyshire* [2007] IRLR 540, HL). The Court of Appeal had ruled that this was not unlawful provided that the employer's action is an 'honest and reasonable' response to protect its interests and provided that the letter is not sent until after the claim has been formally started. The House of Lords held that this was the wrong test and that under the statute what matters is the likely effect of the letter on recipients rather than the honesty or reasonableness of the employer in sending it.

It should be noted that the 'reversal of the burden of proof' rules which normally apply in discrimination cases do not apply to victimisation claims under RRA 1976 (see **section 14.3.4**).

14.2 QUALIFICATIONS FOR BRINGING A CLAIM

14.2.1 Employee or agency worker

To bring a claim of sex or race discrimination, claimants need to demonstrate that they are or were an employee or are applying for a job as an employee. Employee is defined more widely than is the case for unfair dismissal. It refers to somebody who works 'under a contract of service or of apprenticeship or a contract personally to execute any work or labour'. This covers self-employed workers who are employed personally to carry out a job, as well as conventional employees (SDA 1975, s.82(1); RRA 1976, s.78(1); *Mirror Group Newspapers Ltd* v. *Gunning* [1986] IRLR 27).

No qualifying period of employment is required to bring a claim. Indeed, many claims of discrimination are brought by job applicants who, obviously, will not have accrued any continuity of employment.

Unlike claims of unfair dismissal, an illegal contract of employment will not normally prevent an employee from claiming sex discrimination (*Hall* v. *Woolston Hall Leisure Ltd* [2001] ICR 99, CA). Although there is no recent authority in point for race discrimination, there is no reason to draw a distinction between sex and race discrimination in this regard.

By the same token illegal conduct of an employee will not prevent him from claiming race discrimination unless his claim is so inextricably linked to his own illegal conduct that a tribunal should not permit him to recover because it would appear to condone the conduct (*Governing Body of Addey and Stanhope School* v. *Vakante* [2003] ICR 290, EAT where an asylum seeker took up employment in breach of his conditional leave to remain in the UK).

In addition, SDA 1975 and RRA 1976 apply to contract workers, i.e. persons who work for a principal under a contract made with a third party. This benefits agency workers, i.e. those whose services are supplied as temporary workers through an agency (SDA 1975, s.9; RRA 1976, s.7). The Acts also apply to partners in a partnership (SDA 1975, s.11; RRA 1976, s.10 – although note RRA 1976, s.10 applies only if there are six or more partners) and to barristers and, in Scotland, to advocates (SDA 1975, ss.35A and 35B; RRA 1976, ss.26A and 26B). Specific provision to cover office holders was added into SDA 1975 with effect from 1 October 2005 (by EE(SD)R 2005). For convenience, however, the word 'employee' will be used throughout this chapter.

14.2.2 Who is protected?

Claims can only be brought if an employee (or job applicant) has been discriminated against on one of a number of prescribed grounds relating to sex or race. Applicants have to establish, if claiming direct discrimination, that they were treated less favourably because one or more of the prescribed grounds apply. If claiming indirect discrimination, they have to establish that the condition or requirement imposed by the employer is one that a considerably smaller proportion of people who are of that category (i.e. female, black, etc.) can comply with. The grounds are listed below.

Sex

If a woman is treated less favourably than a man on grounds of her gender, that will amount to discrimination (SDA 1975, s.1(1)(a)). Likewise, if a man is treated less favourably than a woman on grounds of his gender, that will also amount to discrimination. There is an exception where an employer provides special benefits to women in connection with pregnancy or childbirth: failure to offer these benefits to men is not treated as sex discrimination (SDA 1975, s.2).

Gender reassignment

It is discriminatory to treat a person less favourably on the grounds that they have undergone or are undergoing treatment for gender reassignment. This specifically includes denying somebody a period of absence to undergo treatment if they would have been permitted a period of absence if ill or injured (SDA 1975, s.2A, inserted by the Sex Discrimination (Gender Reassignment) Regulations 1999, SI 1999/1102).

The Court of Appeal has held that there was no unlawful sex discrimination when an employer required a male employee who, after 10 years or so, took to dressing as a female, to use the male lavatory. The employee resigned because the employer refused to let them use the female toilets. The important point was that the employee concerned was still a 'pre-operative' transsexual. In addition to claiming sex discrimination unfair constructive dismissal was also claimed. The employee failed in that claim as well (*Croft* v. *Royal Mail Group plc* [2003] EWCA Civ 1045).

Both the European Court of Justice and the European Court of Human Rights have ruled that it is unlawful to refuse a retirement pension until age 65 for a post-operative male-to-female transsexual who would have been entitled to a retirement pension at the age of 60 if she had been born female (*Richards* v. *Secretary of State for Work and Pensions*, ECJ Case C-423/04, 27 April 2006 and *Grant* v. *The United Kingdom*, ECtHR Case 32570/03, 23 May 2006). These rulings are of little practical effect as in Britain a male-to-female transsexual person who has been issued with a gender recognition certificate and who has attained the age at which a woman of the same age is entitled to a pension is treated as attaining pensionable age when the certificate is issued (Gender Recognition Act 2004, Sched.5).

Homosexuality

Until 1 December 2003, it was not unlawful to discriminate on grounds of homosexuality (although it may have been unlawful for public body employers to discriminate on grounds of homosexuality, because they must act in accordance with Art.8 of the ECHR – *MacDonald* v. *Advocate General for Scotland and Pearce* v. *Governing Body of Mayfield Secondary School* [2003] IRLR 512).

On 1 December 2003 discrimination on the grounds of sexual orientation became unlawful. The Employment Equality (Sexual Orientation) Regulations 2003, SI 2003/1661 then came into effect. These regulations are discussed in more detail in **section 16.3**.

Marriage and civil partnership

It is unlawful sex discrimination to treat a married person or a civil partner (whether male or female) less favourably than a single person (SDA 1975, s.3 as substituted by the Civil Partnership Act 2004, s.251). Under this provision it has been held that it was unlawful for a police force to refuse to employ two police officers in the same division because they were married to each other (*Graham* v. *Chief Constable of the Bedfordshire Constabulary* [2002] IRLR 239, EAT).

Colour

This is self evident: if a person is treated less favourably because of that person's colour, it will amount to race discrimination (RRA 1976, s.3(1) which applies to discrimination on grounds of 'colour, race, nationality or ethnic or national origins').

Race

This is likewise self evident: if a person is treated less favourably because of their race, it will amount to race discrimination. Note that 'race' does not mean religion (for notes on the Employment Equality (Religion or Belief) Regulations 2003, see **section 16.2**).

Discrimination on the grounds of race includes either an employer or a tribunal making assumptions with regard to cultural differences without proper evidence, however benign the intention (*Bradford Hospitals NHS Trust* v. *Al-Shabib* [2003] IRLR 4, EAT).

An employer will not be liable for race discrimination if he dismisses an employee because the employee's racist views are likely to cause violence in the workplace (*Serco Ltd* v. *Redfearn* [2006] ICR 1367, CA).

Nationality or national origins

This covers a person's geographic origin or their legal nationality (RRA 1976, s.3(1)).

The component parts of the UK are regarded as separate nations for this purpose. Thus a Scottish company that refuses to hire an English worker will be guilty of discrimination (*BBC Scotland* v. *Souster* [2001] IRLR 150). The authors are aware of at least two cases at which employment tribunals have confirmed this in respect of Welsh people (*Griffiths* v. *Reading University Students Union* (unreported, ET case 16476/96, 24 October 1996) and *Williams* v. *Cowell and anor* [2000] ICR 85, CA).

Ethnic origins

The concept of an ethnic group is not always easy to identify (RRA 1976, s.3(1)). In *Mandla* v. *Dowell Lee* [1983] IRLR 209 the House of Lords identified seven relevant characteristics one or more of which 'will commonly be found and will help to distinguish the group from the surrounding community'. These are:

(a) a long shared history, of which the group is conscious as distinguishing it from other groups, and the memory of which it keeps alive;
(b) a cultural tradition of its own, including family and social customs and manners, often but not necessarily associated with religious observance;

(c) either a common geographical origin, or descent from a small number of common ancestors;
(d) a common language, not necessarily peculiar to the group;
(e) a common literature peculiar to the group;
(f) a common religion different from that of neighbouring groups or from the general community surrounding it;
(g) being a minority or being an oppressed or a dominant group within a larger community.

In *Mandla* Sikhs were held to be an ethnic group and thus entitled to the protection of RRA 1976. The same is true of Jews (*Seide* v. *Gillette Industries Ltd* [1980] IRLR 427, EAT). Muslims do not constitute an ethnic group, being a group of people united in religious beliefs – but direct discrimination against Muslims might amount to indirect discrimination against Arabs (*Walker* v. *Hussain* [1996] IRLR 11). Gypsies have been held to be an ethnic group (*Commission for Racial Equality* v. *Dutton* [1989] IRLR 8, CA), but Rastafarians are not (*Crown Suppliers (PSA) Ltd* v. *Dawkins* [1993] ICR 517, CA) because their shared history only goes back to the 1930s and they are otherwise indistinguishable from other Afro-Caribbeans.

In 2007 a question arose as to whether calling a group of people 'bloody foreigners' and telling them to 'go back to your own country' demonstrated hostility by reference to race, colour, nationality or ethnic or national origins. This was for the purposes of the Crime and Disorder Act 1998 not RRA 1976. The fact that the House of Lords decided that persons who are not of British origin constitute a racial group and that therefore a reference to 'foreigners' was a reference to a racial group for the purposes of that Act may, however, be relevant in the context of RRA 1976 (*R* v. *Rogers* [2007] UKHL 8).

Religion or belief

Discrimination on grounds of religion or belief became unlawful when the Employment Equality (Religion or Belief) Regulations 2003 came into effect on 2 December 2003. The detail of these regulations is dealt with in **section 16.2**.

The provisions of RRA 1976 already allowed some protection against discrimination on the grounds of religion where discrimination against a particular religion might amount to indirect discrimination on grounds of race. Thus an employer who refused Muslim employees time off work for a religious festival was found to have indirectly discriminated on grounds of race (*JH Walker Ltd* v. *Hussain* [1996] IRLR 11). Public authorities are obliged to respect freedom of religion under the Human Rights Act 1998, but this has relatively little practical effect.

It should be borne in mind that the defence of justification is available for indirect discrimination, unlike for direct discrimination.

14.3 DIRECT DISCRIMINATION

14.3.1 Introduction

Direct discrimination occurs when a person 'treats another less favourably than he treats or would treat' another person (i.e. a man, or a person from a different racial group) (SDA 1975, s.1(1)(a); RRA 1976, s.1(1)(a)).

The concept of direct discrimination is based around a comparator. This is a real or hypothetical fellow employee (or job applicant) who is in the same position as the applicant, but who is of a different gender, race, nationality, etc.

Note that segregation on racial grounds is discrimination (RRA 1976, s.1(2)). The practice followed in the United States during the 1950s and 1960s of separate but equal rights/facilities for black people is not permitted. However, if a particular racial group chooses to segregate itself, this will not amount to discrimination. Thus, in *FTATU* v. *Modgill* [1980] IRLR 142, EAT, the 16 Asians who staffed a company's paint shop (which was dirty work) had not been segregated from the company's other workers because they were a self-perpetuating group, with friends or relatives of existing workers applying for a job when they knew that somebody was considering leaving.

14.3.2 Selecting the comparator

It is not sufficient for applicants to establish that they have been treated badly. An employer does not discriminate against women by treating women badly, if it treats men equally badly. Rather, when claiming direct discrimination, applicants must establish that they have been treated less favourably than somebody of the other gender or a different racial group.

Save in one situation a comparator is essential. However, it is not essential that an actual comparator be identified. The House of Lords has found that, in the absence of an actual comparator whose relevant circumstances are the same or not materially different from the applicant, it would defeat the purpose of SDA 1975 if the question of discrimination could not be addressed simply because the complainant cannot point to anyone else who was in the same position, and so a hypothetical comparator should be constructed (*Shamoon* v. *Chief Constable of Royal Ulster Constabulary* [2003] IRLR 285, HL). With regard to race discrimination claims, the Court of Appeal has expressly approved the use of a hypothetical comparator finding that if a tribunal did not direct itself to the need for a hypothetical comparator that failure would cause the tribunal to err in principle (*Balamoody* v. *UK Central Council for Nursing, Midwifery and Health Visiting* [2002] IRLR 288, CA).

In *Law Society* v. *Kamlesh Bahl* [2003] IRLR 640 the EAT held that it is not necessarily an error of law if the tribunal fails to identify a hypothetical comparator. However, in another case the EAT found that failure to construct a comparator had led to a wrong conclusion that there was unlawful sex discrimination when a male manager went into the female toilets at work and shouted at a woman cleaner there who he suspected of skiving (*Kettle Produce Ltd* v. *Ward* (unreported, EAT, 8 November 2006)).

A clear example of the need to establish a comparator is provided by a case in 2007 in which a solicitor had dismissed his female personal assistant. The solicitor had been having an affair with her and then found that she was also having an affair with another man. Her dismissal was clearly unfair dismissal and this was not disputed. However, an employment tribunal also found that the dismissal was unlawful sex discrimination on the basis that 'but for' the fact that the assistant was female she would not have been dismissed. The EAT said this 'but for' test was the wrong test to apply. Rather, the tribunal should have constructed a male comparator. It would then have been obvious that, in equivalent circumstances, the solicitor would have dismissed a gay male personal assistant and that the reason for the dismissal was jealousy (and no doubt concern over infidelity), not sex discrimination. Application of the proper test, using a hypothetical male comparator, demonstrated that sex discrimination law was simply not engaged (*B* v. *A* (unreported, EAT, 9 January 2007)).

The comparator must be selected so that the relevant circumstances in one case are the same as, or not materially different from, the other. Thus it would be incorrect to select the male managing director as the comparator if asserting that the pay rise given to a female clerical worker is discriminatory: the correct comparator would be a male clerical worker (SDA 1975, s.5(3); RRA 1976, s.3(4); *Showboat Entertainment Centre Ltd* v. *Owens* [1984] IRLR 7 (race); *Chief Constable of West Yorkshire* v. *Vento* [2001] IRLR 124, EAT (sex)).

The one situation in which a comparator is not required is where the discrimination is against a woman on grounds related to her pregnancy or maternity. There can be no question of comparing her situation with that of a man as pregnancy and maternity are uniquely female conditions (*Webb* v. *Emo Air Cargo (UK) Ltd* [1994] ICR 770, ECJ). With effect from 6 April 2008, amendments were made to SDA 1975 s.3A to make this clear (Sex Discrimination Act 1975 (Amendment) Regulations 2008, SI 2008/656).

14.3.3 Less favourable treatment

The applicants must prove that they were treated less favourably than their comparator. Dismissal will always amount to less favourable treatment. Often proving less favourable treatment will be straightforward, for example, if a female shop assistant is given a 3 per cent pay rise and a male assistant an 8 per cent pay rise. It may be that this is for perfectly proper reasons, such as the male assistant being more productive, but the reason is immaterial at this stage (it becomes relevant when determining whether the less favourable treatment was on grounds of sex, race, etc.).

Subject to one exception, in addition to less favourable treatment, applicants must also show that they have suffered dismissal, less favourable terms and conditions, or some other detriment. It cannot automatically be assumed that a target of racial abuse has been subjected to a detriment: the EAT has recognised that in some work environments racial abuse is 'given and taken in good part by members of different ethnic groups' (*Thomas & Anor* v. *Robinson* [2003] IRLR 7, EAT). The exception is that if the complaint is of sex or race discrimination by way of harassment there is no requirement for the claimants to show that they have been subjected to any detriment (SDA 1975, s.6(2A); RRA 1976, s.4(2A)).

It is important to note that different treatment is not necessarily less favourable treatment (except with racial segregation: see **section 14.3.1**). Thus if a woman is asked questions in an interview that would not have been asked if she were a man, that will only amount to direct discrimination if less favourable treatment results (*Chief Constable of Greater Manchester Police* v. *Hope* [1999] ICR 338, EAT).

Dress codes

A person is not treated less favourably than a person of the other gender if they are both required to wear uniforms but the men are required to wear one uniform and the women a different one (*Schmidt* v. *Austicks Bookshop* [1978] ICR 85, EAT). However, if an employer's dress code requires all staff, both male and female, to dress in a professional and business-like way, it will be for an employment tribunal to decide whether a further specific requirement that men should wear a collar and tie is unlawful sex discrimination. Whether the further requirement is unlawful or not would turn on whether an equivalent level of smartness to that required of the female members of staff could only be achieved, in the case of men, by requiring them to wear a collar and tie (*Thompson* v. *DWP (Job Centre Plus)* [2004] IRLR 348). This question would be one for an employment tribunal to decide in the light of current attitudes and mores (*Smith* v. *Safeway plc* [1996] ICR 868, CA).

Pregnant women

Discrimination is expressly forbidden on grounds of pregnancy or because a woman is exercising (or seeking to exercise or has exercised or sought to exercise) a statutory right to maternity leave (SDA 1975, s.3A). This section was inserted into SDA 1975 by the EE(SD)R 2005. It did not create any new rights or duties, merely spelling out the position already developed by caselaw in order to implement the EC Equal Treatment Directive (Directive 76/207/EC, as amended). As noted above, the High Court ruled in March 2007 that s.3A should be recast to make it quite clear that no comparator is needed and appropriate changes were made with effect from 6 April 2008 (by the Sex Discrimination Act 1975 (Amendment) Regulations 2008, SI 2008/656).

EE(SD)R 2005 also inserted a new s.6A into SDA 1975. This ensured that a woman would not be entitled to normal contractual benefits while absent on maternity leave, the detail varying depending on whether the leave was ordinary or additional maternity leave. The March 2007 High Court ruling noted above found that this section also failed properly to implement Directive 76/207/EC (as amended) and suggested it should be recast to make it clear that there must be no differences between contractual entitlements during compulsory, ordinary and additional maternity leave.

Accordingly a new version of s.6A has been substituted which applies where a woman's expected week of childbirth begins on or after 5 October 2008 (Sex Discrimination Act 1975 (Amendment) Regulations 2008, reg.5). Under this new version a woman's contractual entitlements while on maternity leave are the same regardless of whether the leave is compulsory, ordinary or additional maternity leave. The basic result is that while absent on any form of maternity leave a woman is not entitled to contractual pay but is entitled to contractual non-cash benefits.

Inevitably there are exceptions, set out in SDA 1975, s.6A:

(i) she is entitled to any 'remuneration to which she is entitled as a result of being pregnant or being on maternity leave'; this is called 'maternity-related remuneration';
(ii) 'maternity-related remuneration' includes remuneration which 'falls to be calculated by reference to increases in remuneration that the woman would have received had she not been on maternity leave'; this is called 'increase-related remuneration';
(iii) she is entitled to any bonus in respect of times when she is on compulsory maternity leave.

During maternity leave a woman is entitled to the benefits of non-cash contract terms such as use of a company car (unless provided solely for business) or mobile phone (unless provided solely for business), gym membership, participation in share schemes, disciplinary or grievance procedures, membership of pension schemes, contractual notice period, and, importantly, any obligation of trust and confidence. She is also entitled to compensation in the event of redundancy.

A woman on maternity leave is of course entitled to SMP (a state benefit paid by the employer and wholly or mainly recouped from the government – see **section 7.3.4**) or generally to maternity allowance if she does not qualify for SMP.

The case law that follows was, of course, established before the new provisions came into force, but it is instructive nonetheless in gauging which actions are considered discriminatory.

For a while it was thought that dismissal of a woman prevented from working by illness would not be unlawful sex discrimination if a man would be dismissed in similar circumstances even if the woman's illness was attributable to her pregnancy (*Handels-og* v. *Dansk Ag (Hertz case)* [1992] ICR 332, ECJ). However, the ECJ subsequently ruled that dismissal of a woman in this situation is unlawful direct sex discrimination (*Brown* v. *Rentokil Ltd* [1998] IRLR 445, ECJ Case C-394/96).

A female teacher of RE and morals at a Roman Catholic (RC) School became pregnant by an RC priest. She was held to have been unfairly dismissed even though the reason for her constructive (she resigned) dismissal was NOT that she had become pregnant but was that the governors felt she would no longer have the respect of her pupils in teaching morals and RE and therefore could no longer perform her duties properly. The immediate reason for the dismissal was therefore not sex discrimination. Further, as the governors pointed out, they would have treated a male RE teacher in just the same way if he made an RC nun pregnant so there was no 'discrimination' involved at all. Nevertheless the EAT (following *Webb* v. *Emo Air Cargo (UK) Ltd* [1994] ICR 770, ECJ, ECJ Case C-32/93) held that the dismissal was automatically unfair. The woman had been (constructively) dismissed for a reason 'connected with her pregnancy' and this was therefore automatically an unfair dismissal (*O'Neill* v. *Governors of St Thomas More RC School* [1997] ICR 33, EAT).

It is discriminatory to refuse to engage a pregnant woman, or dismiss her once her pregnancy is discovered, when she is engaged on a short fixed-term contract and she would be unable to fulfil the majority of it due to maternity leave (*Tele Danmark A/S* v. *Handels* [2001] IRLR 853, ECJ). It is discriminatory to apply a provision which removes individuals from a list of 'bank' staff when they have not worked for 12 months where the operator of the 'bank' knew the abstention from work was pregnancy-related (*Johnson* v. *Queen Elizabeth Hospital NHS Trust* (unreported, EAT, 11 September 2003)).

A reduction in a woman's bonus because she is absent during part of the year with pregnancy-related sickness and on maternity leave will amount to unlawful sex discrimination (*GUS Home Shopping Ltd* v. *Green & McLaughlin* [2001] IRLR 75, EAT), as will a failure to carry out a proper risk assessment for a pregnant employee, as required by the Management of Health and Safety Regulations 1999 (*Hardman* v. *Mallon (t/a Orchard Lodge Nursing Home)* [2002] IRLR 516, EAT). However, it seems that a failure to consult with an employee who is absent on maternity leave will not necessarily amount to sex discrimination: the employee must also show that she suffered a detriment (*Ojinnaka* v. *Sheffield College* (unreported, EAT, 18 May 2001)).

It was established by the European Court of Justice in February 2008 that the Pregnant Workers' Directive 92/85/EC does NOT protect a woman in circumstances where, albeit in-vitro fertilised ova were actually in existence, they had not yet been transferred into her uterus *Mayr* v. *Backerei und Konditorei Gerhard Flöckner OHG* [2008] IRLR 387). However, the Equal Treatment

Directive (76/207/EC) would protect a woman at such an advanced stage of IVF treatment if it can be established that the reason for her dismissal is the fact she has undergone such treatment because this stage of the treatment affects only women and so dismissal for it would amount to direct sex discrimination under the principle established in *Webb* v. *Emo Air Cargo (UK) Ltd* (above).

14.3.4 The burden of proof – establishing that less favourable treatment was on grounds of gender or race

Once applicants have established less favourable treatment has occurred, they must establish that it has occurred on grounds of gender, race, etc. This will frequently be obvious in harassment cases. In other cases, it will rarely be obvious from the actions or words of the employer. An employer might discriminate, when deciding to offer a job or promote an employee, on grounds of gender or race. However, one will rarely see a letter from the employer rejecting an applicant on the grounds that 'we do not wish to appoint a black female to this post'.

For both sex discrimination and race discrimination concerning race or ethnic or national origin once the applicant has established a *prima facie* case of discrimination on the balance of probabilities the burden of proof shifts on to the respondent who must establish a credible, non-discriminatory reason for the less favourable treatment (SDA 1975, s.63A as inserted by the Sex Discrimination (Burden of Proof) Regulations 2001, SI 2001/2660; RRA 1976, s.54A as inserted by the Race Relations Act 1976 (Amendment) Regulations 2003, SI 2003/1626). If it can do so, then no finding of discrimination will be made. Thus, in the above hypothesis, if the employer established that the reasons for the differing pay rises were due to different levels of productivity, this will amount to a credible, non-discriminatory reason and the applicant's claim will fail.

The 'reversal of the burden of proof' provisions in RRA 1976, s.54A apply to discrimination on grounds of race, ethnic and national origin. As there is no mention there of discrimination on grounds of colour or nationality, it follows that in the unlikely event of a discrimination claim being based only on colour or nationality then the reversal of the burden of proof rules would not apply (*Okonu* v. *G4S Security Services* [2008] ICR 598, EAT). The government is on record as saying it recognises that this is an anomaly and it is likely to make an appropriate change to the law when an opportunity arises (Hansard, HL, col.1536, 21 May 2008).

If a claim is for unfair dismissal under ERA 1996, then ERA 1996, s.98 applies in the normal way (see **Chapter 11**). The special 'reversal of the burden of proof' rules noted here are then neither relevant nor necessary (*Kuzel* v. *Roche Products Ltd* [2008] IRLR 530, CA).

The EAT, in *Barton* v. *Investec Henderson Crosthwaite Securities Ltd* [2003] IRLR 332, set out 13 points as guidelines to be followed when dealing with reversal of the burden of proof. These guidelines were amended slightly in *Igen Ltd* v. *Wong* [2005] ICR 931, CA. It is wrong to use them as a basis for sophisticated arguments which 'significantly and artificially complicate the fundamentally simple question of asking why the employer acted as he did'. This does not meet with judicial approval (*Laing* v. *Manchester City Council* [2006] IRLR 748, EAT) and the Court of Appeal has expressed surprise that there should still be difficulties with the burden of proof in sex and race discrimination cases given the 'clear and sound detailed guidance' in *Igen* v. *Wong* (see *Madarassy* v. *Nomura International Plc* [2007] ICR 867, CA).

In practice a 'two stage' approach is frequently adopted by tribunals (*EB* v. *BA* [2006] IRLR 471, CA). First, they look for some evidence that the claimant was treated less favourably than others; second, if that is shown, the burden of proof then passes to the employer to demonstrate that the reason for the less favourable treatment was other than an unlawfully discriminatory reason. However, there is no absolute rule that this two-stage approach must be followed. Thus especially in cases where use of a hypothetical rather than an actual comparator is appropriate it can be sufficient for a tribunal to focus simply on the reason why a claimant was treated in a particular way rather than specifically using the two-stage approach (*Brown* v. *London Borough of Croydon* [2007] ICR 909, CA).

It would be wrong to interpret SDA 1975, s.63A or RDA 1976, s.54A to mean that the burden of proof shifts just because it is possible that a tribunal might be able to make a finding of unlawful discrimination. For the burden of proof to shift so that an employer is assumed 'guilty' of discrimination unless he proves to the contrary, the employee must first show facts from which 'a reasonable tribunal could properly conclude' that there has been unlawful discrimination (*Appiah & anor* v. *Bishop Douglass Roman Catholic High School* [2007] IRLR 264, CA and *Atabo* v. *Kings College London & Ors* [2007] EWCA Civ 324, 19 April 2007).

All surrounding circumstances are relevant. Employment tribunals must consider all allegations relating to the way the employer treated the applicant (or other employees), irrespective of whether they form part of the direct claim, as material to go into the 'melting pot' when deciding whether to draw an inference (*Anya* v. *University of Oxford* [2001] ICR 847, CA). This can lead to extraordinarily lengthy tribunal hearings and since *Anya* was decided, the courts have been busy trying to limit its application (whilst denying that they are doing so – see *Wheeler* v. *Durham County Council* [2001] EWCA Civ 844 and *Prospect Care Services* v. *Curtis* (unreported, EAT, 6 November 2001)). Where complaints are crystallised into a series of specific incidents, it is still proper for the tribunal to look at all the material before them as a whole. This material can then inform their conclusions as to whether unlawful discrimination occurred (*Rihal* v. *London Borough of Ealing* [2004] IRLR 642).

Inferences of discrimination can be drawn from an employer's failure to answer a statutory questionnaire (**section 14.6**), or from a failure to follow any relevant Codes of Practice.

The Court of Appeal has held that once an employee has shown a *prima facie* case of discrimination by reason of sex-change, the burden of proof shifts to the employer to disprove it (*EB* v. *BA* [2006] IRLR 471, CA and see **section 14.2.2**).

By way of exception, the reversal of the burden of proof rules do not apply to victimisation claims under RRA 1976 (*Serco Ltd t/a Education Bardford & ors* v. *Quarshie* (unreported, EAT, 17 January 2006)). This follows from the specific wording used in the 'reversal of the burden of proof' rule in RRA 1976, s.54A, which is not exactly the same as that used in the similar provisions in other discrimination legislation. As the Court of Appeal later put it, this means 'that (counter-intuitively) the reverse burden of proof provision does not apply to a case of victimisation in the context of racial discrimination although it may well apply to victimisation cases in other discriminatory contexts' (*Oyarce* v. *Cheshire County Council* [2008] EWCA Civ 434, 2 May 2008).

Justification in direct discrimination cases

The defence of justification is not available in direct discrimination cases. However in practice the 'genuine occupational qualification' exemption achieves a similar result (see **section 14.7.2**).

14.4 INDIRECT DISCRIMINATION

14.4.1 Introduction

Indirect discrimination embraces the concept of the employer imposing a requirement or condition (note: the precise wording differs for sex and some types of race discrimination) which a particular gender or racial group finds it difficult to comply with. More precisely, indirect discrimination occurs where an apparently neutral provision, criterion or practice would put persons of one sex [race] at a particular disadvantage compared with persons of the other sex [or different race], unless that provision, criterion or practice is objectively justified by a legitimate aim, and the means of achieving that aim are appropriate and necessary. This wording, taken from the EC Equal Treatment Directive 76/207/EEC has been adapted to suit SDA 1975 and RRA 1976 (by respectively the EE(SD)R 2005 and the Race Relations Act 1976 (Amendment) Regulations 2003, SI 2003/1626).

Thus a requirement that an employee be over six feet tall is likely to discriminate indirectly against both women and smaller races/nationalities (such as Indians or orientals). This is because a considerably smaller proportion of women than men are over six feet tall and because a considerably smaller proportion of Indian/oriental persons than (say) Caucasian/African will be over six feet tall and thus women and Indian/oriental persons would be at a disadvantage. The employer will only be able to avoid liability by demonstrating that the provision, criterion or practice is a proportionate means of achieving a legitimate aim (SDA 1975, s.1(2)(b)(iii); RRA 1976, s.1(1A)(c)).

Examples of cases that have been held to amount to indirect discrimination include an advertisement for people with a degree in engineering (which in 1977 women were less likely to possess – *Price* v. *Civil Service Commission* [1977] IRLR 291, EAT). A requirement that workers work long or uncertain hours is indirectly discriminatory against women (*London Underground Ltd* v. *Edwards (No. 2)* [1998] IRLR 364, CA), or a requirement to work a particular shift system (*Chief Constable of Avon and Somerset* v. *Chew* [2002] Emp LR 370 – 2.26 per cent difference between genders). A refusal to consider flexi-time arrangements may be discriminatory against women (*Robinson* v. *Oddbins* (unreported, EAT, 19 June 1996)), as may be a refusal to allow job sharing (*British Telecommunications plc* v. *Roberts* [1996] IRLR 601, EAT). A company rule under which only women can be taken on for particular part-time work will be indirect sex discrimination against women if part-time workers are excluded from benefits for which full-time staff are eligible (*Nikoloudi* v. *Organismos Tilepikinonion Ellados*, ECJ Case C-196/02, 10 March 2005).

It is particularly important to be clear about the distinction between direct and indirect discrimination when bringing a tribunal claim. The Court of Appeal has said that 'it is well established on authority and in practice that the material facts for the separate causes of action need to be separately pleaded, proved and ruled on. Section 1 of the [RRA 1976] cannot be construed as collapsing two causes of action into a single cause of action . . .' (*Secretary of State for Defence* v. *Elias* [2006] IRLR 934, CA). Nonetheless the distinction is not always clear or easy to draw (*HM Prison Service* v. *Potter* (unreported, EAT, 14 November 2006)).

The main practical importance of the distinction between direct and indirect sex discrimination has long been and still is that, as can be seen from the definition at the start of this section, justification is a defence in indirect sex and race discrimination cases but not in cases of direct sex or race discrimination.

14.4.2 Nature of the provision

Traditionally both Acts required the imposition of a requirement or condition. However, SDA 1975 and RRA 1976 have both been amended to comply with EC legislation (by respectively the EE(SD)R 2005 and the Race Relations Act 1976 (Amendment) Regulations 2003). The position now is that to prove a claim of indirect sex discrimination or discrimination on grounds of race or ethnic or national origins, the existence of a provision, criterion or practice has to be established, rather than a requirement or condition. Confusingly, the old wording ('requirement or condition') still applies to claims under RRA 1976 based on colour or nationality.

To establish a requirement or condition, applicants had to prove that compliance was a necessary factor to enable them to obtain the job or promotion, etc. (still required if the claim is based on colour or nationality rather than race or ethnic or national origins). Thus if assessment criteria included such factors as age, practical experience in England and ability to speak English, but none of these were decisive, a claim for race discrimination would fail because they did not amount to a requirement or condition (*Perera v. Civil Service Commission* [1983] IRLR 166, CA).

So far as we are aware there is, as yet, no considered authority on the meaning of the new wording, 'provision, criterion or practice' used in SDA 1975 and RRA 1976. It is, however, apparent that it is wider than the old wording because it will include an informal practice within the employer's organisation as well as more formal conditions and requirements. Thus a policy of a police force that partners should not have roles which involved one of them being supervisor and the other being subordinate was accepted as being a 'provision, criterion or practice' in *Faulkner v. Hampshire Constabulary* (unreported, EAT, 2 March 2007).

An example given in the statutory Code of Practice on Racial Equality in Employment is of a woman of Nigerian origin who is informed of a vacancy for a managing director. She phones and is told that the company's normal practice is to use head-hunters for recruitment to senior management posts. If she 'can show that this practice makes it more difficult for people of Nigerian origin than others to get senior management jobs in this company, and that this puts her at a disadvantage, the practice could amount to unlawful indirect discrimination'.

14.4.3 A 'considerably smaller proportion' of one group can comply

As with direct discrimination, the concept of comparison is important; however, here it is comparison of one group (e.g. black people) against another group (e.g. white people).

Whilst statistical evidence is not always necessary (because the tribunal can make findings of fact arising from general descriptions or simply from their own experience), it will assist in many cases. The Court of Appeal has made it clear that a flexible approach should be taken when deciding whether a disparate effect had been established; statistical evidence may disclose a percentage figure which of itself is inherently unlikely to establish a disparate effect but when read as part of a combination of factors may demonstrate the required disparate effect (*Chief Constable of Avon and Somerset v. Chew* [2001] All ER 101).

There is no technical definition of 'considerably smaller', and the appellate courts (including the European Court of Justice) have repeatedly shied away from attempting to define it. It is therefore a matter left for the judgment of the employment tribunal.

One does not look at the number in each group who can comply with the condition, nor does one look at the ratio between the groups. Instead, one looks at the proportions (number of black people who can comply against total number of black people, versus the number of white people who can comply against the total number of white people). It is wrong to say 27 white persons can comply but only four black persons, thus the condition is discriminatory. What must be done is to examine the proportions, e.g. 72 per cent of white people can comply whereas only 22 per cent of black people can comply, thus a considerably smaller proportion of black people can comply with the condition (*Perera* v. *Civil Service Commission* [1983] IRLR 166, CA, but see *Harvest Town Circle* v. *Rutherford* [2001] IRLR 599 and *Secretary of State for Trade and Industry* v. *Rutherford* [2003] IRLR 858).

It is normally a matter for the tribunal to determine what the total pool is, i.e. when deciding the total number of white people who can comply, does one look at the entire country, the county, the industry, the employer's entire undertaking or just the people undertaking the particular job? Provided the tribunal's decision as to the pool is not perverse, the appellate courts will not interfere (*Kidd* v. *DRG (UK) Ltd* [1985] IRLR 190; *Greater Manchester Police Authority* v. *Lea* [1990] IRLR 372, EAT).

Part-time workers

Historically, part-time workers were forced to rely on establishing claims of indirect sex discrimination if they were treated less favourably because they were part time. This was based on an argument (usually successful) that a considerably smaller proportion of women than men were able to work full time, because many more women had responsibilities for children which prevented full-time work. However, this argument sometimes failed if the statistical evidence was not available and, in any event, did not avail men. To remedy this anomaly, the Part-Time Workers (Prevention of Less Favourable Treatment) Regulations 2000, SI 2000/1551, were introduced. These are dealt with in **section 14.10**.

14.4.4 Persons at a 'particular disadvantage'

In order to bring a claim of sex discrimination or race discrimination on the grounds of race or ethnic or national origins an employee will have to show that the provision, criterion or practice in question 'puts or would put persons of the same race or ethnic or national origins as that other at a particular disadvantage when compared with other persons' (RRA 1976, s.1(1A)(a)) or 'puts or would put women [or men] at a particular disadvantage when compared with men [or women]' (SDA 1975, s.1(2)(b)(i)).

There is no requirement to demonstrate a proportion differential between groups. This enables tribunals to adopt a flexible, non-statistical approach in order to determine whether a provision, criterion or practice puts persons of one race or sex at a particular disadvantage when compared with others.

14.4.5 It is to the employee's detriment

In claims for race discrimination on grounds of colour or nationality a person cannot complain of a discriminatory practice unless it affects him personally. This stage does not now apply to cases of sex discrimination or to cases of race discrimination on grounds of race or ethnic or national origin. In *Mandla (Sewa Singh) & anor* v. *Dowell Lee & ors* [1983] ICR 385, HL which concerned a requirement that school pupils remove their turbans, it was held that this was indirectly discriminatory against Sikhs. However, the Sikhs who had been prepared to discard their turbans had no claim because the requirement or condition had not prevented them from becoming pupils and therefore had not been to their detriment.

14.4.6 Justification

The most important practical difference between direct and indirect discrimination is the existence of the justification defence. Except in age discrimination cases (as to which see **section 16.1**) an employer can never justify direct discrimination although in practice the 'genuine occupational qualification' exemption achieves a similar result (see **section 14.7.2**). The position is different in indirect discrimination cases. The employer is entitled to raise a defence of justification to defeat a claim of indirect discrimination.

The burden of proof is on the employer to establish justification (Sex Discrimination (Indirect Discrimination and Burden of Proof) Regulations 2001, SI 2001/2660, amending SDA 1975, s.1(2)(b)(ii); RRA 1976, s.1(b)(ii)).

In claims of racial discrimination on the grounds of race or ethnic or national origins and in claims of sex discrimination, the provisions, criteria or practices which have been applied and which are alleged to be unlawful will be justified if they are 'a proportionate means of achieving a legitimate aim' (SDA 1975, s.1(2)(b)(iii); RRA 1976, s.1(1A)(c)).

Technically the position is different in claims of racial discrimination on the grounds of colour or nationality. In those cases the justification must be on objective grounds, such as economic grounds or administrative efficiency. In those cases justification requires 'an objective balance between the discriminatory effect of the condition and the reasonable needs of the party who applies the condition' (*Webb* v. *Emo Air Cargo (UK) Ltd* [1995] IRLR 645, HL). In practice the difference may have little or no effect but it is worth noting that the EAT has ruled unequivocally that the wording of RRA 1976, s.1(1A) means that that section applies only 'to discrimination on the grounds of race, ethnic or national origin and not to colour or nationalities' (*Okonu* v. *G4S Security Services (UK) Ltd* [2008] ICR 598, EAT).

A recent example of a race discrimination case in which it was successfully argued that a provision, criteria or practice was a proportionate means of achieving a legitimate aim is *Azmi* v. *Kirklees Metropolitan Borough Council* [2007] ICR 1154, EAT. The EAT ruled that a decision to suspend a Muslim teaching assistant for refusing an instruction not to wear her veil when in class with pupils assisting a male teacher was indirectly discriminatory but was lawful as a proportionate means in support of a legitimate aim.

Controversially, the EAT has even gone so far as suggest that the fact that means used are unlawful, even dishonest, will not necessarily prevent them being a proportionate means of achieving a legitimate aim (*GMB* v. *Allen* [2007] IRLR 752, EAT, in which women sued their union for advising them to accept equal pay settlements which they later found were for considerably lower amounts than those to which they were legally entitled; the union successfully defended the claim on the basis that the advice it had given was in the best interests of union members as a whole – although it is understood that the women have appealed to the Court of Appeal).

Justification defences have also succeeded where the employer proved that a job needed a full-time member of staff (*Greater Glasgow Health Board* v. *Carey* [1987] IRLR 484, EAT); where the employer has different retirement ages for different jobs (*Bullock* v. *Alice Ottley School* [1993] ICR 138, CA); where the employer bases redundancy payments on length of service (*Barry* v. *Midland Bank plc* [1999] IRLR 581, HL); where the employer refused to employ orthodox Sikhs on the basis that their beards would be unhygienic in a chocolate factory (*Panesar* v. *Nestlé Co Ltd* [1980] ICR 144, CA) or where they needed to wear protective headgear rather than turbans (*Singh* v. *British Rail Engineering Ltd* [1986] ICR 22, EAT); and where jobs filled mainly by women and men respectively had different pay structures because of different collective bargaining processes (*Enderby* v. *Frenchay Health Authority* [1993] IRLR 591, ECJ). The ECJ has held that indirect sex discrimination against part-timers can be justifiable if the employer can show that part-timers generally take longer than full-time staff to acquire relevant job-related skills (*Gerster* v. *Freistaat Bayern* [1998] ICR 327, ECJ – whilst this is an accurate statement of the law, tribunals are likely to require statistical evidence before making factual findings to that effect in any individual case).

Cases in which the justification defence has failed include where the convenience of a school uniform was not sufficient justification for a 'no turbans' rule (*Mandla* v. *Dowell Lee* [1983] IRLR 209, HL); requiring a non-English telex operator to be proficient with obscure jargon and UK geography without any training within six months (*Bayoomi* v. *British Railways Board* [1981] IRLR 431); reduction of the qualifying period for unfair dismissal from two years to one year would add to business costs (*R.* v. *Secretary of State, ex parte Seymour-Smith* [1995] IRLR 464, CA (overturned on different grounds in the House of Lords)).

14.5 HARASSMENT

14.5.1 Sexual harassment

Until 1 October 2005 sexual harassment at work was not specifically dealt with as such by legislation. However, this changed on 1 October 2005. On that date a new s.4A was introduced into the SDA 1975 by the EE(SD)R 2005. This was to implement the EC Equal Treatment Directive 2002/73/EC.

The High Court found in March 2007 that the wording of SDA 1975, s.4A did not reflect as accurately as it should have done the requirements of the EC Directive. Amendments were therefore introduced with effect from 6 April 2008 (by the Sex Discrimination Act 1975 (Amendment) Regulations 2008, SI 2008/656). The new amended version of SDA 1975, s.4A provides that a person subjects a woman to harassment if *'he engages in unwanted conduct that is related to her sex or that of another person'* which has unwanted effects such as violating her dignity. The words in italics were introduced on 6 April 2008 replacing the previous wording which was 'on the ground of her sex, he engages in unwanted conduct'.

Also with effect from 6 April 2008 there is specific provision to make an employer liable for sex harassment of employees by third parties such as customers, subject to two important let-outs. These are that the employee has been subject to third-party harassment at least twice before and that the employer had failed to take reasonably practicable steps to prevent such harassment.

In Scotland, there are proposals for a new statutory offence of 'communicating indecently'. If the Sexual Offences (Scotland) Bill introduced on 17 June 2008 becomes law it will criminalise those who send malicious and unwanted sexually offensive e-mails and texts, as well as other verbal and written messages.

14.5.2 Racial harassment

Section 3A(1) of RRA 1976 (introduced by the Race Relations Act 1976 (Amendment) Regulations 2003, SI 2003/1626) states that harassment occurs where:

> on grounds of race or ethnic or national origins, [a person] engages in unwanted conduct which has the purpose or effect of (a) violating [another] person's dignity, or (b) creating an intimidating, hostile, degrading, humiliating or offensive environment for him.

This section therefore does not apply where discrimination is on grounds of colour or of nationality (other than national origins). Omission of the words 'colour' and 'nationality' is unlikely to be generally significant if only because colour and nationality are normally inextricably linked with race. Nevertheless the EAT has ruled unequivocally that it follows from the wording, which the Race Relations Act 1976 (Amendment) Regulations 2003 applies in various circumstances, that 'the new definitions of indirect discrimination and harassment ... will apply only to discrimination on the grounds of race, ethnic or national origin and not to colour or nationalities' (*Okonu* v. *G4S Security Services (UK) Ltd* [2008] ICR 598, EAT).

Conduct will only be regarded as racial harassment if, having regard to all the circumstances, including in particular the perception of the complainant, it should reasonably be considered as having the effect described in s.3A(1) (RRA 1976, s.3A(2)).

Thus while overt sexual or racial remarks will always suffice as less favourable treatment (subject to *de minimis* principles), as will unwanted touching (*Chief Constable of Lincolnshire Police* v. *Stubbs* [1999] IRLR 81, EAT), if the recipient of the harassment is hypersensitive and an ordinary person would not perceive the treatment as amounting to harassment, then it will not amount to less favourable treatment (*Driskel* v. *Peninsula Business Services Ltd* [2000] IRLR 151).

Harassment will only fall within SDA 1975 or RRA 1976 where claimants can show they were harassed as a result of their gender or race and so must establish a comparison between the way the alleged discriminator treated the complainant and a person of different gender or race. The doctrine of discrimination *per se* – the idea that if the form of the harassment is sexual or gender specific, such as verbal abuse in purely sexual terms, that on its face constitutes less favourable treatment on the ground of sex – has been specifically rejected by the House of Lords (*MacDonald* v. *Advocate General for Scotland and Pearce* v. *Governing Body of Mayfield Secondary School* [2003] IRLR 512).

14.6 QUESTIONNAIRES

Section 74 of SDA 1975 and s.65 of RRA 1976 lay down a questionnaire procedure whereby those aggrieved can question an employer if they believe that they have been discriminated against.

Both the Sex Discrimination (Questions and Replies) Order 1975, SI 1975/2048, and the Race Relations (Questions and Replies) Order 1977, SI 1977/842, set out forms for both the questions of the aggrieved and the reply by the respondent. It is not obligatory to use these forms, and the exchange of questions and answers may be by letter. Whatever form the exchange takes all documentation relating to it is admissible as evidence in proceedings.

A respondent cannot be compelled to provide answers to any questions asked in this form but the tribunal can draw adverse inferences from a failure to respond within a reasonable period or any evasive or equivocal responses.

Further, in *Dattani v. Chief Constable of West Mercia Police* [2005] IRLR 327 the EAT held in a race discrimination case that tribunals have a duty to consider drawing an inference of unlawful discrimination from 'evasive or equivocal' replies given by an employer to an employee's written questions, regardless of whether or not those replies are in the usual statutory format. However, this is a matter for the tribunal to judge – failure to answer a questionnaire, or indeed to provide other information or documents, does not automatically raise an inference of unlawful discrimination (*D'Silva v. NATFHE (University & College Union) & ors* [2008] IRLR 412, EAT).

Section 65 of RRA 1976 was amended by the Race Relations Act 1976 (Amendment) Regulations 2003 to provide that 'where the question [asked by the aggrieved person] relates to discrimination on the grounds of race or ethnic or national origins, or to harassment' the respondent must, in order to avoid the possibility of adverse inferences being drawn, respond within a period of eight weeks beginning with the day on which the question was served on him. Further, EE(SD)R 2005, reg.32 amended s.74 of SDA 1975 to provide that questions relating to sex discrimination in the employment field must also be answered within the period of eight weeks if the respondent is to avoid the possibility of an adverse inference being drawn.

14.7 DEFENCES AND EXEMPTIONS

14.7.1 Justification

This is a defence to a claim of indirect, but not direct discrimination, and is dealt with in **section 14.4.6**.

14.7.2 Genuine occupational qualification and genuine occupational requirement

Section 7 of SDA 1975 and s.5 of RRA 1976 each provide for certain exceptions from the normal rules if genuine occupational qualifications are appropriate (for example, waiters/waitresses, actors/actresses, photographic, etc. models and employees whose jobs involve providing personal services).

The exceptions are not blanket exceptions. They operate as exceptions only to the rules which outlaw racial discrimination in connection with the offering of employment and access to certain benefits and opportunities, notably concerned with training and promotion. They are not relevant to other forms of discrimination, for example, in the terms on which employment is offered or in relation to a decision to dismiss an employee. In a racial discrimination context, these are covered by a separate section, RRA 1976, s.4A, which provides a separate exception where race or ethnic or national origins is a genuine and determining occupational requirement, subject to it being proportionate. There is no equivalent to RRA 1976, s.4A in SDA 1975.

Where gender and race are 'genuine occupational qualifications' for the job, it is not unlawful to discriminate in failing to offer the job, or in failing to promote or train for that job. Advertisements can therefore lawfully state that applications will only be considered from persons of a particular gender or race.

The genuine occupational qualification defence does not apply to the filling of a job vacancy if the employer already employs a person of the relevant gender or racial group who could reasonably be expected to carry out those duties without undue inconvenience (SDA 1975, s.7(4); RRA 1976, s.5(4)).

The most common examples of genuine occupational qualification are hiring waiters of a particular race for restaurants (e.g. Indian or Chinese), or for authenticity when acting (thus it is not discriminatory to insist on a man to play the role of Hamlet) (SDA 1975, s.7; RRA 1976, s.5).

There are various categories of 'genuine occupational qualification' listed in the SDA 1975 and RRA 1976 two of which appear in both Acts. Unless the category is listed in the relevant Act, an employer cannot argue that sex or race is a genuine occupational qualification for that position (*Grieg* v. *Community Industry* [1979] ICR 356, EAT). These are dealt with below.

Both sex and race

- *Actors*. 'Participation in a dramatic performance or other entertainment' where authenticity requires the person to be a man or a woman or a member of a particular racial group (SDA 1975, s.7(2)(a); RRA 1976, s.5(2)(a)). This exemption extends to freelance actors because of the wide definition of employee within the Acts (see **section 14.2.1**).
- *Models*. 'Participation as an artist's or photographic model' is listed as a genuine occupational qualification in RRA 1976, s.5(2)(b). Whilst not expressly identified in SDA 1975, the sex discrimination legislation does include a category where 'the essential nature of the job calls for a man [or woman] for essential reasons of physiology', which can include being a model (SDA 1975, s.7(2)(a)).
- *Personal services*. Both sex and race can be genuine occupational qualifications for a job involving provision of personal services promoting the welfare of persons of a gender or racial group, where those services 'can most effectively be provided by a person of that' gender or racial group. In fact, the sex legislation goes slightly further than the race legislation by covering provision of 'welfare, education or similar personal services' rather than just welfare. This appears to cover jobs involving counselling where the client would prefer to be counselled on a woman-to-woman, or black-to-black basis (SDA 1975, s.7(2)(e); RRA 1976, s.5(2)(d)).

Race only

An additional job where race can amount to a genuine occupational qualification is listed in RRA 1976. This is where the job involves 'working in a place where food or drink ... is ... provided' in a setting where authenticity requires the person to be of a particular racial group. This covers Chinese waiters in Chinese restaurants, or an Irish publican in an Irish bar (RRA 1976, s.5(2)(c)).

Sex only

Section 7 of SDA 1975 lists other categories of job for which sex can be a genuine occupational qualification.

- *Physiology (but not strength)*. There is a genuine occupational qualification 'where the essential nature of the job calls for a man [or woman] for reasons of physiology (excluding physical strength or stamina)'. This covers models, as above, but would also cover other categories such as strippers. Note that it does not assist an employer who simply wants a physically strong employee: women may be able to fulfil their requirements and they are obliged to consider women as well as men for any job requiring strength or stamina (SDA 1975, s.7(2)(a)).
- *Decency and privacy*. It is a genuine occupational qualification if a job needs to be done by one gender to preserve decency or privacy (SDA 1975, s.7(2)(b)). The courts have held that this does not extend to a shop assistant in a man's tailor (*Wylie* v. *Dee & Co (Menswear) Ltd* [1978] IRLR 103). Note that there are special rules relating to gender reassignment. In this connection a person whose gender has become the acquired gender under the Gender Recognition Act 2004 is treated as being of the acquired sex (see SDA 1975, ss.7A(4) and 7B(3) inserted by the Gender Recognition Act 2004 following cases such as *Goodwin* v. *The United Kingdom,* ECtHR, 3 July 2002).
- *Private homes*. It is a genuine occupational qualification if a job is in a private home and objection might reasonably be taken to one sex having the job because of 'the degree of physical or social contact' with a person living there or because of the knowledge that the employee will obtain of 'the intimate details of such a person's life'. This is a heavily watered-down version of the pre-1986 exemption for any private households containing fewer than five employees (SDA 1975, s.7(2)(ba)).
- *Certain 'sleeping in' jobs*. It can be a genuine occupational qualification if a job can only be practically done by someone living in premises provided by the employer. This will be so if: (a) there are no separate male/female sleeping accommodation and sanitary facilities; and (b) the employer cannot reasonably be expected to adapt the premises or provide separate premises. This is intended to cover structures that cannot really be

extended such as lighthouses and oil rigs, although the employer will need to prove that it was not practical to provide separate male/female accommodation (SDA 1975, s.7(2)(c)).
- *Caring jobs.* Subject to a reasonableness test, it can be a genuine occupational qualification if a job involves providing special care or supervision for one gender, where all the inhabitants are of one gender. This is intended to cover places of work such as prisons or single-sex hospital wards (SDA 1975, s.7(2)(d)).
- *The 'Saudi exemption'.* It is a genuine occupational qualification if a job involves work in a country whose laws/customs are such that the job could only be done effectively by members of one sex (SDA 1975, s.7(2)(g)).
- *Married couples.* This genuine occupational qualification defence applies if a job is 'one of two to be held by a married couple' or by civil partners (SDA 1975, s.7(2)(h)).

14.7.3 Particular types of employment

Compliance with other statutory requirements

There is a general exemption for conduct which would otherwise be discriminatory, if it is necessary in order to comply with legislation. This can be any legislation under RRA 1976, but must specifically be legislation 'for the protection of women' to attract the exemption under SDA 1975 (SDA 1975, s.51; RRA 1976, s.41).

Election candidates

The Sex Discrimination (Election Candidates) Act 2002 inserted a new s.42A into SDA 1975, permitting political parties to select candidates on grounds of gender, i.e. allowing women-only shortlists.

A private member's Race Relations (Election Candidates) Bill had its first reading in the House of Commons on 6 February 2008. If this becomes law it will allow for the creation of shortlists on the grounds of ethnicity in the selection of parliamentary candidates. Under current law this would normally amount to unlawful positive race discrimination (see **section 14.8**).

Ministers of religion

Religions are entitled to insist on a minister being of a particular gender (or not having undergone gender reassignment) if necessary to avoid offending religious doctrine (SDA 1975, s.19(1)).

Police

Both sex and race discrimination are prohibited in the police force, except that regulations discriminating between male and female constables are permitted in so far as they concern height, uniform or equipment (SDA 1975, s.17(3)).

Prison officers

Again, both sex and race discrimination are prohibited for prison officers, except that any requirement as to height is excluded from the provisions of SDA 1975. No such exclusion appears in RRA 1976 and so the prison service would need to establish that any indirect discrimination against physically smaller racial groups was justified (SDA 1975, s.18).

Private households

Section 4(3) of RRA 1976 was amended in 2003 so that the 'domestic employment' exemption no longer applies if the discrimination is 'on grounds of race or ethnic or national origins' (see Race Relations Act 1976 (Amendment) Regulations 2003, SI 2003/1626, reg.6(2)(b)). However, discrimination on grounds of colour or nationality (as opposed to national origins, if the distinction can be drawn) is still lawful in a private household employment context (so presumably an advertisement for a nanny stating that only those of Filipino nationality need apply would be lawful).

Discrimination by victimisation is unlawful under RRA 1976, s.2, and it makes no difference whether or not it is connected with employment in a private household (RRA 1976, s.4(3)).

A 'private household' exemption used to be contained in SDA 1975, but this was removed (by the Sex Discrimination Act 1986) after criticism from the ECJ in *EC Commission v. United Kingdom of GB & NI* [1982] ICR 578, ECJ Case 61/81.

Sikhs on a building site

Health and safety legislation requires all persons to wear a helmet on a building site. This was indirect race discrimination against Sikhs but was clearly justifiable. As a result special rules were made to exempt Sikhs from the obligation to wear a helmet on a building site (at their own risk). Thus employers cannot plead the need to comply with health and safety legislation to avoid employing Sikhs (Employment Act 1989, s.12).

Sports

It is not unlawful to hold single-sex sport events where women are at a disadvantage because of physical strength, stamina or physique (SDA 1975, s.44).

14.8 POSITIVE DISCRIMINATION

Positive discrimination in favour of one race or gender is, by definition, discrimination against another race or the other gender. Subject to the exceptions below, it is unlawful under UK law.

The main exception is where, for a particular type of work in the UK as a whole or within the employer's undertaking, women (or men) or a particular racial group are non-existent or significantly under-represented (or were non-existent/under-represented at any time within the last 12 months). In such a case, it is lawful to provide women-only or race-specific training to help them fit into that work. It is also lawful to encourage only women (or members of a racial group) to take advantage of opportunities for doing that work (SDA 1975, ss.47 and 48; RRA 1975, ss.37 and 38). Note this extends to training and encouragement only. If the employer holds a job open just for women (or members of a racial group) this will amount to unlawful discrimination.

There is also particular provision for providing special training for people who have been absent from regular full-time employment so as to discharge 'domestic or family responsibilities' (SDA 1975, s.47(3)).

The Sex Discrimination (Election Candidates) Act 2002 makes it lawful to have women-only shortlists at political elections, a practice which an industrial tribunal had ruled in 1996 to be unlawful sex discrimination under the then current law (*Jepson* v. *Labour Party* [1996] IRLR 116).

It has been held that positive discrimination is not permitted under the Equal Treatment Directive unless justification can be established (*EFTA Surveillance Authority* v. *Kingdom of Norway* [2003] IRLR 318).

It is understood that the Equality and Human Rights Commission and the Association of Chief Police Officers in England and Wales consider there is a distinction to be drawn between 'positive action' (considered lawful) and 'positive discrimination' (clearly unlawful). It seems that the former means encouragement of minority group applicants to come forward – and that even this is not enough to enable the police to achieve Home Office targets for 2009 for employment of women and persons from ethnic minority groups.

The White Paper 'Framework for a Fairer Future – The Equality Bill' published on 26 June 2008 includes proposals to legitimise some positive discrimination in sex and race anti-discrimination legislation.

14.9 VICARIOUS RESPONSIBILITY

14.9.1 General

For the majority of obligations imposed by SDA 1975 and RRA 1976, the primary liability is that of the person who commits the acts of discrimination, e.g. the racist interviewer or the sexual harasser. They are deemed primarily liable under the legislation and can be named as respondent in their own capacity for aiding and abetting the tort of discrimination in employment (SDA 1975, s.42(2); RRA 1976, s.33(2)). However, the employer is vicariously responsible for anything done by a person in the course of his employment (whether or not it was done with the employer's knowledge or approval) (SDA 1975, s.42(1); RRA 1976, s.32(1)).

The phrase 'in the course of employment' has a wide meaning. Not only does it include acts done whilst at work (*Jones* v. *Tower Boot Co Ltd* [1997] IRLR 168, CA), but it includes acts done by an employee who is entrusted by an employer with a duty owed by that employer to a third party. The traditional argument that an employer is vicariously responsible for the acts of an employee who was using an unauthorised method to do a job he was authorised to do but is not vicariously liable if the employee was simply doing something which was unauthorised is now regarded as semantic and should not generally allow an employer to escape liability for an employee's acts of sex abuse against children in the care of the employer. Thus a school was held liable for sexual abuse perpetrated on young boys by one of the housemasters, since the school owed a duty to the boys to look out for their well being and it had entrusted that duty to the housemaster (*Lister* v. *Hesley Hall* [2001] IRLR 472, HL).

The phrase 'in the course of employment' can extend to acts done outside of work, but having some connection to work. Thus the employer can be vicariously liable for sexual harassment occurring in the pub after work, or racist comments made at the company Christmas party (*Chief Constable of Lincolnshire Police* v. *Stubbs* [1999] IRLR 81, EAT).

In the well-known 'Bernard Manning' case, the employer was liable for not stopping a comedian who mocked two female black waitresses on grounds of their sex and race during his act (*Burton & Rhule* v. *De Vere Hotels* [1997] ICR 1, EAT). This was later disapproved by the House of Lords (*obiter dicta* in *Pearce* v. *Governing Body of Mayfield Secondary School* [2003] IRLR 512) but a similar position was later established by statute (RRA 1976, s.3A makes racial harassment an unlawful act 'in its own right', i.e. distinct from direct or indirect discrimination and see *Gravell* v. *London Borough of Bexley* (unreported, EAT, 2 March 2007)).

New rules in force from 6 April 2008 make it clear that an employer can be liable for sexual harassment of staff by third parties, for example, customers, provided it has happened at least twice before (Sex Discrimination Act 1975 (Amendment) Regulations 2008, SI 2008/656).

With effect from 2 April 2001 (as a direct consequence of the Stephen Lawrence enquiry) rules were introduced to ensure that Chief Constables have vicarious liability for acts of racial discrimination committed by police officers, including against other officers. A similar change was made to sex discrimination law with effect from 19 July 2003. The bizarre anomaly whereby a police force could not be held liable for such acts by one member upon another, which was confirmed by the Court of Appeal in *Chief Constable of*

Bedfordshire Police v. *Liversidge* [2002] EWCA Civ 894, has been removed and a Chief Constable can thus now be liable to members of his police force for acts of harassment or discrimination by another member of that force (SDA 1975, s.7(1A); RRA 1976, s.19B).

14.9.2 Vicarious liability – defence

It is a defence for the employer to establish that it 'took such steps as were reasonably practicable to prevent the employee from doing that act' or acts of that description (SDA 1975, s.41(3); RRA 1976, s.32(3)). An employee can be made personally liable for acts of unlawful discrimination committed by him in the course of his employment against a fellow employee, even though the employer is held not to be legally liable for his conduct because it took reasonably practical steps to prevent its employee from doing the act in question (*Yeboah* v. *Crofton* [2002] IRLR 634).

Tribunals do not like allowing employers to escape liability for the acts of their employees on this ground and, in practice, to succeed an employer would normally have to demonstrate properly established and monitored equal opportunities policies, with regular equal opportunities training for all staff and effective grievance/ disciplinary procedures in connection with any complaints of harassment or discrimination (SDA 1975, s.42(3); RRA 1976, s.32(3)).

The Court of Appeal has ruled (in a whistleblowing case) that an employer may be liable for the acts of an employee done in the course of his employment whether or not what the employee has done would be actionable against him (*Cumbria County Council* v. *Carlisle-Morgan* [2007] IRLR 314, EAT in which an employer was liable for detriment suffered by an employee at the hands of a fellow employee as a result of making protected disclosures).

14.10 PART-TIME WORKERS

Historically, part-time workers were forced to rely on establishing claims of indirect sex discrimination if they were treated less favourably because they were part time. The argument sometimes failed if the statistical evidence was not available and, in any event, did not avail men. To remedy this anomaly, the Part-Time Workers (Prevention of Less Favourable Treatment) Regulations 2000, SI 2000/1551 (PTWR 2000) were introduced (see **section 16.5**).

A dedicated website at **www.emplaw.co.uk/lshandbook** provides links to judgments and other source material referred to in this chapter.

CHAPTER 15

Disability discrimination

15.1 GENERAL INFORMATION

The employment related provisions of the Disability Discrimination Act 1995 (DDA 1995) make it unlawful for an employer to treat a disabled person less favourably in relation to employment at an establishment in Great Britain than others unless the employer can show that the treatment in question is justified. The rules protect job applicants and self-employed people who contract personally to provide services as well as those who come within the normal definition of employee.

The EC General Framework Directive 2000/78/EC lays down a 'general framework for combating discrimination on the grounds of religion or belief, disability, age or sexual orientation as regards employment and occupation ...' with a view to putting into effect in the Member States the principle of equal treatment. Implementation of the disability discrimination parts of this Directive in Britain were effected by the Disability Discrimination Act 1995 (Amendment) Regulations 2003, SI 2003/1673 which made substantial changes to the 1995 Act. The Disability Discrimination Act 1995 (Pensions) Regulations 2003, SI 2003/2770 deal with disability discrimination issues in relation to occupational pension schemes, essentially to make such discrimination unlawful. Further amendments were made by the Disability Discrimination Act 2005, the employment parts of which came into force on 5 December 2005 and make changes to the rules about discriminatory job advertisements and widen the definition of disability to benefit those with Aids, cancer or multiple sclerosis and those suffering from mental illness.

Two Codes of Practice came into effect on 1 October 2004, the Code of Practice on Employment and Occupation and the Code of Practice for Trade Organisations and Qualifications Bodies. A further Code of Practice on the duty of public authorities to promote disability came into effect on 5 December 2006.

An Employment Retention Bill designed to retain newly disabled people in work had a first reading in the House of Commons on 29 January 2008. If this Bill becomes law it will amend ERA 1996 to provide for 'employment retention assessments' for newly disabled people and people whose existing impairments change and for entitlement to 'rehabilitation leave'.

Employment tribunal statistics show that the number of disability discrimination claims, of which there were 924 in the first year of operation of DDA 1995, have now levelled out at around a fairly consistent 5,000 a year (4,942 DDA claims were registered in the year to 31 March 2005, 4,585 in 2005/06 and 5,533 in 2006/07). The median award in 2006/07 was £8,232 and the mean average award was £15,059. Compensation for future loss of earnings and for injury to feelings are particularly important components of disability discrimination awards.

The Act also requires employers to make reasonable adjustments to working conditions to help overcome the practical effects of disability, again unless there is justification for not doing so, and makes it unlawful to victimise employees because they have sought to enforce or help someone else to enforce rights under the Act (DDA 1995, ss.4A and 55).

Concentration on the 1995 legislation should not obscure the fact that before 1995 both common law and statute gave certain protections to disabled persons in the employment field. Those protections continue. For example, disability must be taken into account in considering the fairness of a dismissal for purposes of unfair dismissal law. Also the Chronically Sick and Disabled Persons Act 1970 requires employers to make provision for the needs of disabled persons using premises provided by them (*Seymour* v. *British Airways Board* [1983] IRLR 55).

The Disability Rights Commission was subsumed, along with the Equal Opportunities Commission and the Commission for Racial Equality into a new Equality Commission with effect from 1 October 2007. This was established under the Equality Act 2006 as the 'Commission for Equality and Human Rights' (CEHR) but shortly before it started operations it informally changed its name to the 'Equality and Human Rights Commission' (EHRC).

The original small employers' exemption from the DDA 1995 was gradually whittled down and was completely withdrawn from 1 October 2004 (Disability Discrimination Act 1995 (Amendment) Regulations 2003, repealing DDA 1995, s.7).

Any agreement is void so far as it purports to exclude or limit the operation of the DDA employment provisions (DDA 1995, Sched.3A, Part 1, para.1(3)).

It should go without saying that to make a claim under the DDA 1995 a person must be a disabled person within the meaning of DDA 1995, s.1 (as to which see **section 15.2**). Thus a man who was not disabled but who was rejected for a job on the erroneous basis that he was suffering from a disability could not bring a claim under the Act (*Hart* v. *Bolton Hospitals NHS Trust* (unreported, EAT, 9 March 2005)). Further, for an employer to be 'guilty' of disability discrimination he must be aware of the fact that the employee concerned is suffering from a disability (*Mayor and Burgesses of the London Borough of Lewisham* v. *Malcolm* [2008] UKHL 43 on 25 June 2008 finally puts this beyond doubt, even though it has been questioned in other cases such as *London Borough of Hammersmith & Fulham* v. *Farnsworth* [2000] IRLR 691).

The question of whether or not a person is a disabled person within the meaning of the Act is one of fact not of law. An appeal from an employment tribunal's ruling on that question will therefore be allowed only if the tribunal's decision was so 'perverse' that no reasonable tribunal could have come to it or was so defective that justice requires the matter to be remitted back for rehearing (*Janda* v. *Foyle and Co Ltd* (unreported, Court of Appeal, 16 November 1999)). For avoidance of any possible doubt it should be noted that 'sickness' is not the same as 'disability' and the European Court of Justice has held that therefore a person who has been dismissed by his employer solely on account of sickness does not fall within the general framework laid down by Directive 2000/78/EC for combating discrimination on grounds of disability (*Chacón Navas* v. *Eurest Colectividades SA* [2007] ICR 1, ECJ Case C-13/05).

15.2 WHAT IS A 'DISABILITY'?

A 'disabled person' for DDA 1995 purposes is someone with 'a physical or mental impairment which has a substantial and long-term adverse effect on his ability to carry out normal day to day activities' (DDA 1995, s.1). As a general rule persons who have had a disability are included (DDA 1995, s.2).

There is a formal guidance document produced under the Act on 'matters to be taken into account in determining questions relating to the definition of Disability'. A new version of the Guidance came into effect from 1 May 2006 (Disability Discrimination (Guidance on the Definition of Disability) Appointed Day Order 2006, SI 2006/1005). This takes into account the 2005 amendments which widen the definition of disability to benefit those with Aids, cancer or multiple sclerosis and those suffering from mental illness.

Like the Disability Discrimination Act Employment Code of Practice, the Guidance does not have the force of law but courts and tribunals are obliged to take it into account (DDA 1995, s.3(3) and see *Virdi* v. *Commissioner of Police of the Metropolis and Central Police Training & Development* [2007] IRLR 24, EAT). Tribunals must follow it and not substitute their own views for what is appropriate. Thus, in one case, an employment tribunal expressly disregarded part of the Guidance which states that 'playing a particular game' or 'taking part in a particular hobby' is not a normal day-to-day activity. The EAT overruled the tribunal on the basis that it had committed an error of law by disregarding the Guidance (*Coca-Cola Enterprises Ltd* v. *Shergill* (unreported, EAT, 2 September 2002)).

A consultation on possible changes to the definition of disability in anti-discrimination law took place in 2006. Any resulting changes are likely to be recommended for inclusion in the proposed 'Single Equalities Act' expected by 2010.

It is normal practice for an employment tribunal to hold a preliminary hearing, often with the chairman sitting on his own, to consider whether a person making a claim under DDA 1995 is 'disabled' within the meaning of the Act.

Non-medically instigated addictions (more accurately 'addiction to alcohol, nicotine or any other substance') and certain personality disorders (a tendency to arson, theft or physical or sexual abuse of other persons, exhibitionism and voyeurism) plus allergic rhinitis (hay fever), tattoos and ear and body piercing are excluded from the definition of 'disability' (Disability Discrimination (Meaning of Disability) Regulations 1996, SI 1996/1455). However, if they are a consequence of a disability within the meaning of DDA 1995, s.1 these matters are not excluded (*Murray* v. *Newham CAB* [2003] ICR 643, EAT). Rather than pursue *Murray* to its logical conclusion, the EAT later ruled that a person suffering from depression and who indulged in indecently exposing himself as a result, was convicted of indecent exposure offences and was then dismissed from his job, had been dismissed because of exhibitionism (an excluded condition) not because of a disability (i.e. depression) (*Edmund Nuttall Limited* v. *Butterfield* [2005] IRLR 751, EAT).

Looking through the telescope the other way (i.e. at the cause of depression rather than its results) the EAT has also ruled that depression can be a disability within the meaning of the DDA 1995 even though its cause was an excluded condition – in this case cocaine addiction (*Hutchison 3G UK Ltd* v. *Mason* (unreported, EAT, 16 July 2003)).

There are four criteria (expanded on in the formal guidance document noted above) to be considered in deciding whether a particular condition counts as disability for the purposes of DDA 1995. The four criteria, set out in s.1, are that the condition must be:

(a) an 'impairment'; which has a
(b) 'substantial effect'; which is
(c) 'long-term'; and which adversely affects ability to carry out
(d) 'normal day-to-day activities'.

15.2.1 Impairment

This may be physical or mental. How it was caused does not matter, even if it was caused by an excluded condition such as alcoholism. As noted above the previous requirement for an impairment which consists of a 'mental illness' to be clinically well-recognised has been removed by the Disability Discrimination Act 2005, s.18(2).

The following are examples of possibly borderline impairments which have been recognised as impairments for DDA 1995 purposes:

- *Asthma*. Although a House of Lords amendment extending protection to people with asthma failed to get into the Act, there has been at least one case in which a tribunal accepted that asthma was an 'impairment' (*Cox* v. *The Post Office* (unreported, IT/1301162/97)).
- *Autism* i.e. Autistic Spectrum Disorder and/or Asperger's Syndrome (*Hewett* v. *Motorola Ltd* [2004] IRLR 545, EAT). ASD and Asperger's

Syndrome are sub-categories of 'Pervasive Developmental Disorder' classified as F84 within the WHO International Classification of Mental and Behavioural Disorders in ICD-10.

- *Blindness.* A person who is certified as blind or partially sighted by a consultant ophthalmologist, or registered as blind or partially sighted in a register maintained by or on behalf of a local authority is deemed to be disabled (Disability Discrimination (Blind and Partially Sighted Persons) Regulations 2003, SI 2003/712). However, sight problems which can be corrected by spectacles or contact lenses are specifically excluded (DDA 1995, Sched.1, para.6(3)).
- *Depression and stress.* 'Stress' is not a 'clinically well-recognised illness' and therefore under pre-December 2005 law could not on its own count as an impairment for purposes of the DDA 1995 (*Morgan* v. *Staffordshire University* [2002] IRLR 190, EAT and *Beales* v. *Secretary of State for Work and Pensions* (unreported, EAT, 18 September 2006)). However, the need for 'mental illness' to be clinically well-recognised to qualify as a disability for DDA purposes was removed (with effect from 5 December 2005) by the Disability Discrimination Act 2005, s.18(2). One result is likely to be that, provided they can show that the other statutory conditions are fulfilled, employees will sometimes succeed in claims that 'stress' is a disability for DDA purposes. The authors are aware of a 2008 case in which a woman diagnosed with clinical depression after the birth of twins won a stress-related DDA claim at an employment tribunal.
- *Diabetes* (e.g. *Home Office* v. *Collins* [2005] EWCA Civ 598, CA and *British Telecommunications plc* v. *Pousson* (unreported, EAT, 5 August 2005)).
- *Dyslexia* (e.g. *Holmes* v. *Bolton Metropolitan Borough Council* (unreported, IT, December 1988)).
- *Dwarfism* (Achondroplasia Dwarfism) (*English* v. *Kwik-Save* (unreported, IT, December 2003)).
- *Epilepsy.* The authors are aware of a case in which a tribunal has accepted that epilepsy is an 'impairment'.
- *General learning difficulties* (*Dunham* v. *Ashford Windows* [2005] IRLR 608, EAT).
- *ME (Myalgic Encephalomyelitis) and CFS (chronic fatigue syndrome) and schizophrenia* (*O'Neill* v. *Symm and Co Ltd* [1998] ICR 481, EAT).
- *Obesity.* It is possible that being overweight could amount to a disability if there is a medical background. The authors are aware of a case in which the Royal Mail lost an unfair dismissal case after it had failed to make reasonable adjustments to cater for a long-service postman whose weight had almost doubled to 25 stone.
- *Obstructive sleep apnoea.* The authors are aware of a case in which a tribunal has accepted that this breathing disorder which can lead to daytime

fatigue was accepted by a tribunal as being an 'impairment' for DDA purposes.
- *Panic disorder* (*Jenkins* v. *Hugh James Solicitors* (unreported, EAT, 3 March 2005)).
- *Rheumatoid arthritis* (*Quinn* v. *Schwarzkopf Ltd* [2002] IRLR 602, Ct Sess).

The authors are aware of a case in which a tribunal ruled that baldness is not an 'impairment'.

The Act is concerned with impairment of a person's ability to carry out activities, not with whether he is able to carry them out. What matters is therefore what he cannot do rather than what he can still do. The fact that he is able to carry out normal day-to-day activities does not mean that his ability to do so is unimpaired (*Goodwin* v. *Patent Office* [1999] ICR 302, EAT; *Ekpe* v. *Commissioner of Police of the Metropolis* [2001] ICR 1084, EAT).

When considering whether an employee is disabled, a tribunal should not compare the performance of the employee with the average person in the population. The comparison should be between what the person can actually do and what that person would be able to do without the impairment (*Paterson* v. *Metropolitan Police Commissioner* [2007] ICR 1522, EAT).

A person who claims that if medical treatment were to cease he would suffer from a disability within the meaning of DDA 1995 can claim protection even though he is not actually suffering from such a disability (DDA 1995, Sched.1 para.6(1)). Thus, for example, a diabetic, if he fulfils the other conditions, could be disabled for DDA purposes even though his diabetes is in fact under control by use of insulin. However, he must produce evidence, not merely speculation, as to the effect of cessation of the medical treatment (*Woodrup* v. *London Borough of Southwark* [2003] IRLR 111, CA).

15.2.2 Substantial

The Minister for Social Security and Disabled People said in Parliament during the passage of DDA 1995 that 'substantial' in this context means 'more than minor' (Hansard, 2 February 1995). The 2006 official Guidance says 'A substantial effect is one that is greater than the effect which would be produced by the sort of physical or mental conditions experienced by many people which have only "minor" or "trivial" effects' (replacing wording in the previous 1996 Guidance, which referred to 'substantial' as meaning 'more than minor or trivial').

The 2006 Guidance also suggests that 'The time taken by a person with an impairment to carry out a normal day-to-day activity should be considered when assessing whether the effect of that impairment is substantial. It should be compared with the time it might take a person who did not have the impairment to complete an activity.'

The EAT has held that an impairment which makes it difficult for a person to carry out normal day-to-day tasks such as cooking, DIY, heavy shopping, grooming the dog or carrying suitcases counts as one which has a 'substantial' adverse effect (*Vicary* v. *British Telecom plc* [1999] IRLR 680, EAT).

Although the question of whether a particular impairment is 'substantial' within the meaning of DDA 1995 is normally one of fact rather than law it is nevertheless a matter to be decided by an employment tribunal not by a doctor (*Cave* v. *Goodwin* [2001] EWCA Civ 391, CA; *Abadeh* v. *British Telecom plc* [2001] ICR 156, EAT). It is worth noting at this point that it would be wrong for an employment tribunal to substitute its own assessment of medical evidence for that of the employer in a disability related unfair dismissal case (*Heathrow Express Operating Company Ltd* v. *Jenkins* (unreported, EAT, 9 February 2007)). Also it is not the task of an expert medical witness to address what the legal consequences are in any particular situation. His opinion on whether a person is suffering from a disability within the meaning of DDA 1995 will not be regarded as helpful (*Carden* v. *Pickerings Europe Ltd* [2005] IRLR 720, EAT).

A progressive condition which does not yet have a substantial adverse effect but which is likely to do so in the future can entitle an individual to claim protection (DDA 1995, Sched.1, para.8, which gives the following specific examples of progressive conditions: 'cancer, multiple sclerosis or muscular dystrophy or HIV infection').

The Disability Discrimination Act 2005 amends the 1995 Act so that '. . . a person who has cancer, HIV infection or multiple sclerosis is to be deemed to have a disability, and hence to be a disabled person' save for cancers of a description which can be provided by regulations (DDA 1995, Sched.1, para.6A). The effect of the amendment is that persons with HIV, cancer or multiple sclerosis are now treated as disabled for DDA 1995 purposes as from the point of diagnosis even if they are outside the normal definition in DDA 1995, s.1 (for example, because the person affected is perfectly able to carry on normal day-to-day activities).

To take advantage of these 'progressive condition' provisions of DDA 1995, Sched.1, para.8 an employee must show not only that he is suffering from the condition in question but also that it is more likely than not that at some stage in the future it will lead to an impairment which will have a substantial adverse effect on his ability to carry out normal day-to-day activities (*Mowat-Brown* v. *University of Surrey* [2002] IRLR 235, EAT).

The Court of Appeal has held that the phrase 'as a result of that condition' in DDA 1995, Sched.1, para.8 'should not be so narrowly construed as to exclude an impairment which results from a standard and common form of operative procedure'. Thus an employee who suffered from incontinence as a result of surgical treatment for prostate cancer was disabled within the meaning of DDA 1995 although the impairment resulted from the surgery and was not a direct result of the cancer (*Kirton* v. *Tetrosyl Ltd* [2003] IRLR 352, CA).

The adoption of 'coping strategies' (e.g. wearing spectacles) may alter the effects of a disability so that they are no longer substantial with the result that the disability ceases to be within the meaning of disability for purposes of the DDA 1995 (*Virdi* v. *Commissioner of Police of the Metropolis and Central Police Training & Development* [2007] IRLR 24, EAT).

The fact that an individual is receiving disability payments does not mean that his disability is 'substantial' within the meaning of DDA 1995 (*Gallier* v. *Lothian Buses plc* (unreported, EAT (Scot), 26 August 2003)).

15.2.3 Long term

This means 12 months (whether accrued or likely to accrue) or the life expectancy of the person concerned if that is less than 12 months. For the purpose of deciding whether a person has had a disability in the past, a long-term effect is one which lasted at least 12 months (DDA 1995, Sched.1, para.2 and Sched. 2, para.5).

In considering whether an impairment had lasted for at least 12 months the EAT has accepted that it is permissible for a tribunal to take into account the whole of the period until the commencement of the employment tribunal proceedings (*Heatherwood & Wrexham Park Hospitals Trust* v. *Beer* (unreported, EAT, 14 June 2006)).

If an impairment ceases to have a substantial adverse effect on a person's ability to carry out normal day-to-day activities it will be treated as continuing to have that effect if that effect is 'likely' to recur (DDA 1995, Sched.1, para.2(2)). It is not the 'impairment' or the 'disability' which must be likely to recur for an employee to be able to take advantage of this provision – rather it is that the 'substantial adverse effect' of the illness on day-to-day activities must be likely to recur (*Swift* v. *Chief Constable of Wiltshire Constabulary* [2004] IRLR 540, EAT). The EAT has held that the word 'likely' means 'more probable than not that it would happen' so if there is a 50/50 chance that the impairment will recur, it is not 'likely' to recur within the meaning of DDA 1995, Sched.1, para.2(2) and the person concerned will therefore not be classed as disabled (*Latchman* v. *Reed Business Information Ltd* [2002] ICR 1453, EAT).

The question of whether at a particular date a disability suffered by a person was 'long term' must be decided by reference to the nature of the disability as at that date and subsequent developments must not be taken into account (*Elliott* v. *Pertemps Recruitment Partnership Ltd* (unreported, EAT, 5 March 2003)). By the same token in determining whether a condition is 'long term' by reason of the likelihood of recurrence (see DDA 1995, Sched.1, para.2(2)) it is not permissible to take into account matters which took place after the date of the alleged discrimination. So if an impairment did in fact recur after the date of the alleged discrimination, that recurrence must be disregarded. If at the time of an act of discrimination on grounds of disability it was unlikely that the impairment would recur, the person concerned cannot be 'disabled'. He will thus not be able to bring a DDA claim in respect of that act of discrimination even though if precisely the same discriminatory act had taken place a few weeks later he would have been able to claim (*Richmond Adult Community College* v. *McDougall* [2008] IRLR 227, CA and *Croal* v. *Network Rail Infrastructure Ltd* (unreported, EAT, 28 February 2008)).

For purposes of deciding whether dismissal of an unsuitable employee or rejection of a job applicant is dismissal or rejection 'for a reason which relates to the disabled person's disability' it is irrelevant whether the employer knows that the unsuitability was caused by a disability and by the same token knowledge of the disability is irrelevant in considering whether the dismissal or rejection was justified and therefore lawful (*London Borough of Hammersmith and Fulham* v. *Farnsworth* [2000] IRLR 691, EAT). It follows that a tribunal can use the benefit of hindsight to decide whether it was likely at the date of termination that the adverse effect of the impairment would last for at least 12 months from the date of injury and so be 'long term' (*Barker* v. *Westbridge International* (unreported, EAT, 8 June 2000)).

15.2.4 Normal day-to-day activities

The Guidance states that 'the term "normal day-to-day activities" is not intended to include activities which are normal only for a particular person, or a small group of people. In deciding whether an activity is a normal day-to-day activity, account should be taken of how far it is normal for a large number of people, and carried out by people on a daily or frequent and fairly regular basis. In this context, "normal" should be given its ordinary, everyday meaning' (para.D5 of the Guidance). This does not mean that the percentage of the population which undertakes a particular activity is the deciding factor in whether an activity is a normal day-to-day activity. Thus putting in hair rollers is a normal day-to-day activity for DDA purposes even though 'most' (i.e. more than half the population) people do not do so (*Ekpe* v. *Metropolitan Police Commissioner* [2001] ICR 1084, EAT).

'Normal day-to-day activities' includes activities relevant to participation in professional life and therefore includes carrying out an assessment or examination of a police officer for promotion (*Paterson* v. *Metropolitan Police Commissioner* [2007] ICR 1522, EAT).

The fact that a condition may occur only at work is not a reason for excluding it from consideration when deciding whether it has a substantial adverse effect on an employee's ability to carry out normal day-to-day activities (*Cruickshank* v. *VAW Motorcast Ltd* [2002] ICR 729, EAT).

15.3 WHAT IS DISCRIMINATION UNDER DDA 1995?

A new definition of 'discrimination' has applied with effect from 1 October 2004 (DDA 1995, s.3A, inserted by Disability Discrimination Act 1995 (Amendment) Regulations 2003, reg.4(2)).

The basic part of the new definition simply restates the previous definition: 'a person discriminates against a disabled person if (a) for a reason which relates to the disabled person's disability, he treats him less favourably than he treats or would treat others to whom that reason does not or would not apply, and (b) he cannot show that the treatment in question is justified'.

The definition above is in effect a definition of 'indirect discrimination' although that expression does not appear in the Act (it appears in the EC General Framework Directive 2000/78/EC, Art.2 but we think SDA 1975 is the only British Act in which the expression is used). Importantly the new definition includes a specific definition of 'direct discrimination' (DDA 1995, s.3A(5)). This makes it clear that the appropriate comparator in a direct discrimination case is a non-disabled person whose abilities are the same as (or not materially different from) the abilities of the disabled person, not a non-disabled person with a different level of ability.

The new definition also makes it clear that failure to comply with the duty to make reasonable adjustments is discrimination (DDA 1995, s.3A(2)) and that there can be no justification of direct discrimination (DDA 1995, s.3A(4)).

Cases of 'direct disability discrimination' are rare but do occasionally happen. The authors are aware of a case in 2006 in which a veterinary nurse who was blinded after having suffered a stroke was dismissed by her employer almost immediately afterwards (*Tudor* v. *Spen Corner Veterinary Centre & anor* (unreported, Manchester ET, 11 May 2006)).

Although 'discrimination' implicitly involves making a comparison between two people, if there is no directly comparable comparator a tribunal must 'construct a picture of how a hypothetical . . . comparator would have been treated in comparable surrounding circumstances' (*Chief Constable of West Yorkshire Police* v. *Vento* [2001] IRLR 124, EAT).

The Court of Appeal has said that the approach to disability related indirect discrimination is 'quite different from that which applies to other forms of indirect discrimination. However, it still requires the Tribunal to find the subjective reason why the employer acted as he did; that must be a disability related reason. It is not enough that the disability was causally relevant if the actual reason was not disability related' (*O'Hanlon* v. *HM Revenue & Customs* [2007] ICR 1359, CA). It follows, for example, that an employer who dismisses a person who has been off work for a long period because of a disability cannot escape liability under DDA 1995 merely by showing that he would have dismissed a non-disabled employee who was absent for the same period (see *Cosgrove* v. *Caesar & Howie* [2001] IRLR 653, EAT).

If an employee (or other complainant) establishes facts from which it may be presumed that discrimination has taken place, the burden of proof is on the employer to prove that there has been no discrimination (DDA 1995, s.17A(1C)).

In keeping with new rules being introduced in the anti-discrimination legislation generally, if disability discrimination is closely connected with an employment relationship it will be unlawful even if the employment had ended at the time when the act of discrimination was 'committed' (DDA 1995, s.16A, inserted by Disability Discrimination Act 1995 (Amendment) Regulations 2003, reg.15).

There was no definition of harassment in the original version of DDA 1995. A specific definition of 'harassment' is now included in s.3B (inserted by the Disability Discrimination Act 1995 (Amendment) Regulations 2003, reg.4(2)).

15.4　WHO IS PROTECTED?

The employment-related provisions of DDA 1995 apply for the benefit of job applicants, employees, apprentices, self-employed persons working for others, pension scheme members, office holders, partners in a firm, barristers and advocates and also apply for the benefit of members and prospective members of trade organisations and similar (DDA 1995, ss.4A–14D and s.68), in all cases whether past or present (DDA 1995, s.16A).

Discriminatory acts done by an employer after termination of an employee's contract of employment are within the scope of anti-discrimination legislation generally, including DDA 1995, provided they are 'incidental' to the employment – for example, a job reference (*Kirker* v. *British Sugar Plc* [2003] ICR 867, HL).

If an individual is supplied by an employment agency under a contract with an 'end-user' (referred to as a 'principal') to work for the principal at an establishment in Great Britain, the principal is responsible to the individual for any disability discrimination in relation to the contract work. This is so even if the agency is technically the employer and even if the individual supplied by the agency has his own one-man consultancy company which is technically his employer (DDA 1995, s.4B).

The employment provisions of DDA 1995 apply to Crown and civil servants as to other employees in Great Britain (DDA 1995, s.64). Police officers, prison officers, fire fighters, members of the Ministry of Defence Police, the British Transport Police, the Royal Parks Constabulary or the United Kingdom Atomic Energy Authority Constabulary were all excluded from DDA protection before 1 October 2004 but are now protected. The same applies to partners in a partnership and applicants for partnership who since that date have the same DDA rights against the firm as employees or applicants for employment (Disability Discrimination Act 1995 (Amendment)

Regulations 2003). Barristers previously had no rights under the employment sections of DDA 1995, simply because they are not in employment within the meaning of DDA 1995, s.68 (interpretation). That, too, is changed with effect from 1 October 2004 (new DDA 1995, ss.7A–7D). However, members of the armed forces continue to be excluded (DDA 1995, ss.64(7)).

An employee who 'does his work wholly outside Great Britain' is not protected. Until late 1999 this exemption also removed the protection of DDA 1995 from those who worked 'mainly' outside Great Britain (DDA 1995, s.68(2) and (3)). However, since 16 December 1999, a worker who does at least part of his work within Great Britain, including in particular a worker posted from overseas, is protected by the DDA 1995 even though his work is done mainly elsewhere (Equal Opportunities (Employment Legislation) (Territorial Limits) Regulations 1999, SI 1999/3163). In 2007 the EAT confirmed that the rules concerning overseas employment set out by the House of Lords in *Lawson* v. *Serco* [2006] ICR 250, HL apply in disability discrimination cases as well as in unfair dismissal cases (*Williams* v. *University of Nottingham* [2007] IRLR 660, EAT and see **section 9.19**).

An employee working on board a ship, aircraft or hovercraft is not protected except in 'prescribed cases'.

A person, such as a carer, who is discriminated against because of a third party's disability cannot bring a claim, at least not under DDA 1995 itself. In a 2006 case an employee who was not disabled was primary carer for her disabled son. Her employers would not agree to her requests for flexible working arrangements to help her look after him. She resigned and claimed disability discrimination. Although given the wording of DDA 1995, s.3A(5) it is clear that she cannot win that claim as she is not herself disabled, the tribunal referred questions to the European Court of Justice for a ruling on whether UK law properly implements the Equal Treatment Framework Directive 2000/78/EC in this respect (*Attridge Law & anor* v. *Coleman* [2007] IRLR 88, EAT).

15.5 WHAT ARE THEY PROTECTED AGAINST?

For a disabled job applicant the protection is against the employer treating him worse than others:

(a) in the arrangements made for determining to whom employment should be offered; or

(b) in the terms on which employment is offered; or

(c) by refusing to offer, or deliberately not offering, employment (DDA 1995, s.4(1)).

For a disabled employee the protection is against the employer treating him worse than others:

(a) in the terms of employment afforded him; or

DISABILITY DISCRIMINATION

(b) in the opportunities afforded him for promotion, transfer, training or receiving any other benefit; or

(c) by refusing to afford him, or deliberately not affording him, any such opportunity; or

(d) by dismissing him, or subjecting him to any other detriment (DDA 1995, s.4(2)).

If there is no connection between a disabled employee's disability and his dismissal then that dismissal may be fair on the grounds, for example, of lack of capability to do the work. However, it is incumbent on an employment tribunal in such a case to set out in detail its reasons for finding that there was no causal link between the disability and the dismissal (*Edwards* v. *Mid Suffolk District Council* [2001] IRLR 190, EAT).

An employee who succeeds in claims of both unlawful disability discrimination and unfair dismissal is entitled to compensation for both. The fact that the employee has been unfairly dismissed does not mean that the employer is no longer liable for the earlier wrong of disability discrimination (*Beart* v. *H.M. Prison Service (No.2)* [2005] IRLR 568, CA).

15.6 REASONABLE ADJUSTMENTS

A most important section of DDA 1995 (as amended by the Disability Discrimination Act 1995 (Amendment) Regulations 2003, SI 2003/1673 with effect from 1 October 2004) is s.4A replacing the previous s.6. This provides that:

Where –

(a) a provision, criterion or practice applied by or on behalf of an employer, or

(b) any physical feature of premises occupied by the employer,

places the disabled person concerned at a substantial disadvantage in comparison with persons who are not disabled, it is the duty of the employer to take such steps as it is reasonable, in all the circumstances of the case, for him to have to take in order to prevent the provision, criterion or practice, or feature, having that effect.

The duty is to take such steps as it is reasonable, in all the circumstances of the case, to take. A practical effect is that tribunals are likely to impose greater obligations on large employers than on smaller employers. Failure to comply is discrimination under the Act (DDA 1995, s.3A(2)).

Confirming that the 2004 change noted above made no fundamental difference to the way DDA 1995 is applied, the EAT stated in *DWP* v. *Macklin* (unreported, EAT, 28 February 2008) that:

Before finding that an employer has discriminated against a disabled Claimant in failing to comply with the duty to make reasonable adjustments an Employment Tribunal must identify:

(a) the arrangement (now provision, criterion or practice under DDA 1995, s.4A as amended) applied by or on behalf of the employer

(b) the physical feature of premises occupied by the employer (if applicable; not this case)
(c) the identity of non-disabled comparators (if appropriate)
(d) the nature and extent of the substantial disadvantage suffered by the Claimant.

> Only then will it be possible to determine the question as to what adjustments it would be reasonable for the employer to make, bearing in mind the extent to which such adjustments would prevent the arrangements made by the employer placing the disabled Claimant at a substantial disadvantage when compared with the non-disabled comparator.

The provision enabling an employer to justify a failure to comply with a duty to make a reasonable adjustment was removed with effect from 1 October 2004. However, in the real world this is unlikely to make much practical difference as the duty is still a duty to make reasonable adjustments. In the authors' view there is little practical difference between saying on the one hand that a particular adjustment is unreasonable (a legitimate escape route for employers) and on the other hand that the employer is justified in not making it (which no longer provides the employer with an escape route).

The duty on the employer is to ensure that individual disabled employees do not suffer a substantial disadvantage in comparison with others. Thus when an employment tribunal is considering the issue of reasonable adjustments 'there is no requirement . . . to consider whether the disabled as a group are disadvantaged by the [provision, criterion or practice] in issue' (*Chief Constable of Lincolnshire Police* v. *Weaver* (unreported, EAT, 12 March 2008)).

What matters is whether the employer took reasonable steps, a test which can be satisfied even by an employer who is entirely ignorant of the existence of the statutory obligation (*British Gas Services Ltd* v. *McCaull* [2001] IRLR 60, EAT and *Stages* v. *Jackson & Canter* (unreported, EAT, 31 March 2008)).

If the employer does not know, and could not reasonably be expected to know, that the disabled person has a disability then the duty to make 'reasonable adjustments' does not apply (DDA 1995, s.4A(3)).

The EAT has held that there is no obligation on the employer to seek medical opinion and prognosis before dismissing the employee instead of making adjustments (*O'Neill* v. *Symm and Co Ltd* [1998] ICR 481, EAT and *London Borough of Camden* v. *Price-Job* (unreported, EAT, 4 July 2007)). However, it has also held that the duty to make reasonable adjustments includes a duty properly to assess an employee's medical condition and what would be required to eliminate any disadvantage the employee may suffer because of it, or adjustments that could be made to alleviate it (*Southampton City College* v. *Randall* [2006] IRLR 18, EAT). It may not be easy for an employer to persuade a tribunal that it was unaware of an employee's disability (see, for example, *Kent County Council* v. *Mingo* [2000] IRLR 90, EAT).

The EAT has held that as a matter of law an employer's failure to make reasonable adjustments in a disability discrimination case should not be regarded as a continuing act. Therefore acts or omissions which took place more than three months before the presentation of a claim will not normally be actionable as failures to make reasonable adjustments (*Humphries* v. *Chevler Packaging Ltd* (unreported, EAT, 15 June 2006)).

'Dismissal' for DDA purposes includes constructive dismissal. Failure to make reasonable adjustments can therefore give the employee concerned the right to resign and claim constructive dismissal. In that situation the three-month time limit for bringing the claim will run from the date of the resignation rather than from the date of the employer's conduct which had led to it (*Nottinghamshire County Council* v. *Meikle* [2005] ICR 1, CA).

The duty to make reasonable adjustments is a positive duty for the benefit of employees who by reason of disability have become incapable of doing the job for which they are employed if they could do another job within the same organisation. It can therefore even mean that a disabled existing employee must be allowed to 'trump' other applicants for a job even if the employee is not the best candidate (*Archibald* v. *Fife Council* [2004] ICR 954, HL). This is in contrast to the position in sex and race discrimination cases in which positive discrimination can actually be unlawful (but note that the White Paper 'Framework for a Fairer Future – The Equality Bill' published on 26 June 2008 includes proposals to legitimise some positive discrimination in sex and race anti-discrimination legislation). However, the duty does not go so far as to mean that the employer must make a vacancy by dismissing another employee (*Dixon* v. *Automobile Association* (unreported, EAT, 20 April 2004)).

Section 18B of DDA 1995 (which is headed 'Reasonable adjustments: supplementary') provides a non-exclusive list of matters to be taken into account in deciding whether it is reasonable for an employer to take particular steps to comply with his duty to make reasonable adjustments. They include the size of the undertaking, the amount of disruption which would be caused and the cost. The same section also provides a list of examples of steps which an employer may need to take to comply with the duty, including transfer to fill a vacancy, altering working hours, providing an interpreter, acquiring or modifying equipment, making adjustments to premises and allocating some duties to another employee.

The statutory duty to make reasonable adjustments does not mean that an employer is under a duty to pay more to a person who is on long-term sick leave because of a disability than is payable to a person who is on long-term sick leave for some other reason (*O'Hanlon* v. *HM Revenue & Customs* [2007] ICR 1359).

For several years there have been provisions preventing landlords stopping alterations being made to premises to enable employer-tenants to comply with their duties under DDA 1995. These provisions are now in DDA 1995, s.18A and the Disability Discrimination (Employment Field) (Leasehold Premises) Regulations 2004, SI 2004/153. An employer 'does not have to make an adjustment if it requires statutory consent which has not been given', for example, listed building consent, planning permission or fire regulations approval (DDA 1995, s.59).

Finally, on the question of reasonable adjustments, it is worth noting that there is as yet no complete certainty as to whether a failure to consult might of itself amount to a failure to make a reasonable adjustment. The majority of cases in which the issue has arisen suggest that failure to consult is not on its own a failure to make a reasonable adjustment (in particular *Tarbuck* v. *Sainsbury's Supermarkets Ltd* [2006] IRLR 664, EAT). However, there has been suggestion to the contrary (*Mid-Staffs General Hospital NHS Trust* v. *Cambridge* [2003] IRLR 566, EAT). It is to be hoped that the Court of Appeal will provide complete certainty in due course.

15.7 DEFENCE OF JUSTIFICATION

The general position is that discrimination on grounds of disability can never be justified if the disabled person is capable of doing the job in question. In more detail, it cannot be justified if it is direct discrimination within the meaning of DDA 1995, s.3A(5) which provides that 'A person directly discriminates against a disabled person if, on the ground of the disabled person's disability, he treats the disabled person less favourably than he treats or would treat a person not having that particular disability whose relevant circumstances, including his abilities, are the same as, or not materially different from, those of the disabled person.'

Apart from direct discrimination (as defined above) a person discriminates against someone if, for a reason which relates to his disability, he treats him less favourably than he treats or would treat others and 'he cannot show that the treatment in question is justified' (DDA 1995, s.3A(1)). Justification is therefore a defence in such cases.

The expression 'indirect discrimination' is not used anywhere in the disability discrimination legislation (SDA 1975 seems to be the only employment law related Act in which the expression itself does appear). It is, however, used, in the EC General Framework Directive 2000/78/EC, Art.2. Indirect discrimination is defined in the Directive as '... an apparently neutral provision, criterion or practice would put persons having a ... particular disability ... at a particular disadvantage compared with other persons'. It is thus similar if not identical to what the Code of Practice calls 'disability related discrimination' (para. 4.29 states that 'disability related discrimination' occurs 'when the reason relates to the disability but is not the disability itself').

Treatment can only be justified, and thus not be unlawful discrimination, if the reason for it is both material to the circumstances and is substantial (DDA 1995, s.3A(3)). It is for the employer to decide what is material and what is substantial and the tribunal's job is to consider whether the employer's decision fell within the range of reasonable responses to the known facts – an employment tribunal may not substitute its own view for that of the employer by making its own appraisal of the medical evidence or making its own risk assessment (*Jones* v. *The Post Office* [2001] ICR 805, CA; *Williams* v. *J Walter Thompson Group Ltd* [2005] IRLR 376, CA; and *Heathrow Express Operating Company Ltd* v. *Jenkins* (unreported, EAT, 9 February 2007)). In practice this means that the threshold of justification required to enable an employer to justify discrimination on grounds of disability is a 'surprisingly low one' (Sedley LJ in *Collins* v. *Royal National Theatre Board Ltd* [2004] IRLR 395, CA).

Thus dismissal of an HIV positive support worker for people with learning disabilities was justified in *High Quality Lifestyles Ltd* v. *Watts* [2006] IRLR 850, EAT. The EAT upheld the employer's contention that the dismissal was because of the risk of passing the condition on to others rather than because of his disability.

An example of justification given by the DRC Employment Code of Practice, October 2004 (para. 6.3) is that of a man who has severe back pain and is unable to bend being rejected for a job as a carpet fitter as he cannot carry out the essential requirement of the job, which is to fit carpets. This would be lawful as the reason he is rejected is a substantial one and is clearly material to the circumstances (the two conditions required for justification by DDA 1995, s.3A(3) above).

It should be noted that organisations which can confer a professional or trade qualification can refuse to grant the qualification to a person who does not meet a required standard if this is a 'proportionate means of achieving a legitimate aim' and the standard is applied equally to persons who do not have the disability in question (DDA 1995, s.14A).

15.8 COMPARATORS

This section attempts to highlight a topical problem, rather than to explain the law.

Clearly for there to be discrimination someone must be being treated worse than someone else. In direct discrimination cases (rare anyway but especially rare in relation to disability discrimination) there is no particular problem in identifying a comparator. It is simply someone else who is not suffering from the disability.

In indirect discrimination cases, however, it is not so easy to decide who is an appropriate comparator. Clearly it must be someone who is not suffering from the disability, but more is then required. The difficulty stems from the ambiguous language used in what is now DDA 1995, s.3A.

The problem is to decide what Parliament meant when it provided in that section that a person discriminates against a disabled person 'if for a reason which relates to the disabled person's disability, he treats him less favourably than he treats or would treat others to whom that reason does not or would not apply'.

The nub of the problem is to determine the correct meaning to give to the expression 'that reason'. It could refer either to:

(i) a reason which relates to the disabled person's disability; or
(ii) the facts constituting the reason for the treatment.

Lord Justice Mummery said in *Clark* v. *Novacold* [1999] ICR 951, CA that 'linguistically' the wording is ambiguous. He said 'The expression "that reason" is, as a matter of ordinary language, capable of bearing either of the suggested meanings. The ambiguity must be resolved by recourse to the context of the ambiguous language and to the aim of the legislation.'

Which of the two meanings is correct is fundamentally important. To take an example: two employees are absent on sick leave for seven months. One of them is 'merely' sick but not disabled for DDA 1995 purposes (e.g. perhaps because he had severe measles but is now almost recovered and will be able to come back to work well before 12 months is up); the other is suffering from a condition which is a disability for DDA purposes (e.g. he suffers from severe rheumatoid arthritis). The employer has a stated policy, applicable to all employees, of dismissing any who are absent on sick leave for six months or more. So both are dismissed.

Leaving aside any question of unfair dismissal (where compensation is restricted by statute), does either of them have a claim under DDA 1995 (where compensation is not subject to any statutory restriction)?

Obviously the man who had measles has no claim under DDA 1995 – he simply was not disabled. But what about the second man? The reason for his dismissal was his absence from work. Clearly that is not a 'disability' so clearly there is no direct disability discrimination. But the reason for his absence was his rheumatoid arthritis, so it can be argued that his case is one of indirect disability discrimination. Whether this is so and whether or not he has a claim under the Act depends on whether (i) or (ii) above is correct.

In *Clark* v. *Novacold*, in an employment context, the Court of Appeal held (in favour of the employee) that (i) above was not what Parliament had intended. It ruled that (ii) above is the correct interpretation. In the example above, it would follow that the man dismissed because of long-term absence caused by his rheumatoid arthritis would have a claim under DDA 1995.

However, in *Mayor and Burgesses of the London Borough of Lewisham* v. *Malcolm* [2008] UKHL 43 the House of Lords found it 'hard to accept that *Novacold* was rightly decided' and opted (by a majority) for (ii) as the correct interpretation.

Unhelpfully, *Malcolm* was a housing case rather than an employment case. Exactly where this leaves disability discrimination law in an employment context will require further clarification from the courts and possibly Parliament. Although the House of Lords in *Malcolm* came to a clear conclusion in that case it did so only by a majority, 'with some hesitation' and 'not without misgivings' – and the case did not involve an employer and employee.

Clues to the correct answer may be found in several places:

- The Court of Appeal in *Clark* v. *Novacold* and the House of Lords in *Malcolm* both agreed that the common-sense interpretation of 'that reason' was a 'reason which relates to the disabled person's disability'.
- The other interpretation of 'that reason' as the 'facts constituting the reason for the treatment' is quite difficult to grasp – even in *Clark* v. *Novacold* itself the Court of Appeal had to use convoluted wording to explain that interpretation. Lord Justice Mummery said that in the DDA 1995 phrase 'for a reason which relates to the disabled person's disability' the words 'which relates to the disabled person's disability' must be regarded 'as having been added not to identify or amplify the reason, but to specify a link between the reason for the treatment and his disability which enables the disabled person (as opposed to an able-bodied person) to complain of his treatment. That link is irrelevant to the question whether the treatment of the disabled person is for a reason which does not or would not apply to others'.
- Lord Justice Mummery himself, in another more recent case (*S* v. *Floyd and The Equality and Human Rights Commission* [2008] EWCA Civ 201, also a landlord and tenant case) applied logic which is consistent with that of the House of Lords in *Malcolm*. Lord Scott came to the view (at para.37 in *Malcolm*) that that logic 'is not, in my opinion, consistent with *Clark* v. *Novacold*'.
- In using the ambiguous wording ('if for a reason which relates to the disabled person's disability') it seems clear, as Lord Bingham put it in *Malcolm* 'that the draftsman . . . deliberately eschewed the conventional language of causation in favour of the broader and less precise expression "relates to". In this context I take the expression to denote some connection, not necessarily close, between the reason and the disability'.

The old way of expressing what is nowadays often called the 'but for' test can be helpful in clarifying thought on this type of problem – even though it is latin and therefore politically incorrect, the distinction between a *causa causans* and a *causa sine qua non* is easy to understand and is, perhaps, the key to grappling with an understanding of the problem, even if not to finding a solution to it.

Enough has been said here to demonstrate that the issue is not clear cut. However, one thing does seem clear: if the ambiguous words which have caused such difficulty are meant to have the meaning which Mummery LJ said in *Clark* v. *Novacold* that he thought Parliament intended them to have, then the best thing would be for Parliament to amend DDA 1995 as quickly as possible to make that completely clear.

15.9 TIME LIMITS

The basic time limit for presenting a complaint under the DDA 1995 is three months from when the act complained of was done (DDA 1995, Sched.3, para 3(1)).

An employment tribunal can grant an extension if it considers it 'just and equitable' to do so (DDA 1995, Sched.3, para.3(1) and (2)). As in sex and race discrimination cases where similar wording is used this gives more latitude to allow an extension of time than is possible in unfair dismissal cases, where the power to extend time for making a claim depends on the tribunal being satisfied that it was not 'reasonably practicable' for the claim to have been lodged within the time allowed. However, the exercise of the discretion is the exception rather than the rule and in particular there is no presumption that a tribunal should extend time for making a claim out of time on just and equitable grounds because the claimant has mental health problems (*Department for Constitutional Affairs* v. *Jones* [2008] IRLR 128).

Subject to three riders, the basic rule is that time starts to run 'when the act complained of was done'. The three riders are: (a) where an unlawful act is attributable to a term in a contract, that act is to be treated as extending throughout the duration of the contract; (b) any act extending over a period must be treated as done at the end of that period; and (c) a deliberate omission must be treated as done when the person in question decided upon it (DDA 1995, Sched.3, para.3(3)).

In deciding whether a claim that discrimination was an act extending over a period the whole substance of the complaint should be considered rather than whether the continuing act amounted to a 'policy, practice or regime' (*Pugh* v. *The National Assembly for Wales* (unreported, EAT, 26 September 2006)). An employer's failure to make reasonable adjustments in a disability discrimination case will not normally be regarded as a continuing act (*Humphries* v. *Chevler Packaging Ltd* (unreported, EAT, 24 July 2007)).

There are also time limits outside which a DDA questionnaire ceases to be admissible in evidence. To be admissible, a questionnaire must, unless an extension of time is allowed, have been served within three months of the time when the act complained of was done or, if it is served after proceedings have been started, within 28 days (until 1 October 2004, 21 days) of the complaint being presented (Disability Discrimination (Questions And Replies) Order 2004, SI 2004/1168, art.4).

15.10 VICARIOUS LIABILITY

Employers are liable for wrongs done by their employees 'in the course of employment'. In discrimination cases statute provides that it is no defence for employers to show that they were not aware of what was going on or that they had not authorised it. Their only defence is the one provided by the statute, namely that they had taken 'such steps as were reasonably practicable to prevent' the employee doing the discriminatory act(s) in question (DDA 1995, s.58).

Under the common law something is done 'in the course of employment' only if it relates to what the employee was employed to do. However, for purposes of the anti-discrimination statutes the phrase has the wider, more natural, meaning of 'done while at work' (*Jones* v. *Tower Boot Co Ltd* [1997] ICR 254, CA).

Although an employer may be liable to an employee who has suffered from discriminatory acts done by a fellow employee, this does not mean that the defaulting fellow employee is exonerated. An employee can be jointly liable with his employer (DDA 1995, s.57).

15.11 VICTIMISATION

Specific provisions to protect a person against being treated unfavourably because he has done anything to assert his rights under DDA 1995 or to help another to do so are included in the Act (DDA 1995, s.55). These anti-victimisation provisions do not apply 'to treatment of a person because of an allegation made by him if the allegation was false and not made in good faith' (DDA 1995, s.55(4)).

It is specifically provided that discrimination occurs even if there was only a belief or suspicion that one of the above things has been or is intended to be done (DDA 1995, s.55(2)(b)).

15.12 REMEDIES

If a complaint under DDA 1995 is upheld an employment tribunal must: (a) make a declaration as to the rights of the complainant; and/or (b) order compensation; and/or (c) recommend reasonable action 'for the purpose of obviating or reducing the adverse effect on the complainant of any matter to which the complaint relates' (s.17A). There is no statutory limit to compensation which a tribunal can award in disability discrimination cases.

As in sex and race discrimination cases, if compensation is awarded it must be calculated by applying 'the principles applicable to the calculation of damages in claims of tort' or in Scotland reparation for breach of statutory duty (DDA 1995, s.17A(3)). Therefore compensation can, in appropriate cases, include an amount in respect of damages for personal injury. A person making a discrimination claim before an employment tribunal who fails to include a claim for damages for personal injury where one could have been made is unlikely to be able to have a 'second bite at the cherry' and will not normally be allowed to bring a separate personal injury claim in the county court or High Court (*Sheriff* v. *Klyne Tugs (Lowestoft) Ltd* [1999] ICR 1170, CA).

Loss of future earnings is taken into account and may result in very substantial amounts being awarded. The principles applied by the courts in assessing damages in personal injury cases will generally be used by employment tribunals (*British Sugar plc* v. *Kirker* [1998] IRLR 624, EAT and *ICTS (UK) Ltd* v. *Tchoula* [2000] IRLR 642, EAT).

It is specifically provided that compensation for disability discrimination can include an amount for non-financial loss such as injury to feelings as well as compensation for any financial or other loss actually suffered (DDA 1995, s.17A(4)). In practice, compensation for injury to feelings is frequently the most important part of any financial claim under DDA 1995. This is reflected in figures from the Annual Statistics of the Employment Tribunals and Employment Appeal Tribunals for the 12 months to 31 March 2007. These show that the average award in unfair dismissal cases (in which there can be no compensation for non-financial loss) was £7,974 whereas in discrimination cases it was considerably higher – in race discrimination cases the average was £14,049 and in sex and disability discrimination cases it was £10,052 and £15,059 respectively).

Compensation can also include aggravated damages in a particularly bad case, but it may not include exemplary damages (*Alexander* v. *Home Office* [1988] ICR 685, CA; *Deane* v. *London Borough of Ealing & Anor* [1993] ICR 329, EAT).

An employment tribunal can order interest to be paid on cash awards made under the DDA 1995. If it does not order interest it must state the reasons (Employment Tribunals (Interest on Awards in Discrimination Cases) Regulations 1996, SI 1996/2803).

15.13 ADVERTISEMENTS

Until 1 October 2004 the law governing job advertising in a disability discrimination context worked by providing that an employment tribunal had to assume, unless the contrary was shown, that refusal to employ an applicant who had answered a potentially discriminatory job advertisement was unlawful.

However, DDA 1995, s.11 was repealed by the Disability Discrimination Act 1995 (Amendment) Regulations 2003, SI 2003/1673 and as from 1 October 2004 it is unlawful to publish or cause to be published an advertisement inviting applications for (amongst other things) 'employment, promotion or transfer of employment' if the advertisement indicates 'or might reasonably be understood to indicate' that an application will or may be determined to any extent by reference to the applicant not being disabled or not having any particular disability (DDA 1995, s.16B).

There is an exception if the discrimination would be lawful (e.g. because it was justified, as to which see **section 15.7** – for example, an advertisement for a telephonist would presumably be lawful if it required job applicants to have reasonably good hearing and an advertisement for a bicycle courier could lawfully say that the successful applicant must be able to ride a bicycle).

Publishers are not liable if they reasonably rely on a statement from the advertiser that the advertisement would not be unlawful (DDA 1995, s.16B(2A)). If the advertiser knowingly or recklessly makes such a statement which in a material respect is false or misleading the advertiser commits an offence (and would be liable on summary conviction to a fine not exceeding level 5 on the standard scale – currently £5,000).

The Act does not give individual job applicants the right to take legal action in respect of discriminatory advertisements. Such action may only be taken by the Equality and Human Rights Commission (DDA 1995, s.16B(5)).

A dedicated website at **www.emplaw.co.uk/lshandbook** provides links to judgments and other source material referred to in this chapter.

CHAPTER 16

Other categories of discrimination

By way of introduction, it should be noted that a June 2008 White Paper 'Framework for a Fairer Future – The Equality Bill' proposes a new Equality Bill which will 'declutter what has become a thicket of legislation and guidance. It will be written in plain English, so that those who benefit from the law, and those who need to comply with it, can see the wood for the trees'.

This is clearly an enormous task. The White Paper says that there are currently nine major pieces of discrimination legislation, around 100 statutory instruments setting out connected rules and regulations and more than 2,500 pages of guidance and statutory Codes of Practice – which on every count must be an underestimate. While in no sense comprehensive, this chapter, along with **Chapters 14** and **15**, on sex, race and disability discrimination, seeks to explain the main provisions of this mass of material with reference to sources wherever possible.

16.1 AGE DISCRIMINATION

16.1.1 Introduction

Directive 2000/78/EC required all EU Member States to outlaw age discrimination in employment by 2 December 2006. In Britain, regulations making direct and indirect discrimination on the basis of age unlawful in the employment field, including vocational training, unless objectively justified, came into effect on 1 October 2006 (the Employment Equality (Age) Regulations 2006, SI 2006/1031 (Age Regulations)).

It is worth noting that the ECJ ruled in 2005 that age discrimination could already be illegal notwithstanding that implementation of Directive 2000/78 was not compulsory until 2 December 2006 (*Mangold* v. *Helm*, ECJ Case C-144/04, 22 November 2005).

In British anti-discrimination law the Age Regulations are unique in that they provide for a defence of justification where there is what would otherwise be unlawful direct age discrimination (see **section 16.1.2**). In other discrimination legislation, the defence of justification is available only in indirect discrimination cases.

Previous law may still be relevant in some circumstances. Regardless of the Age Regulations, age discrimination against a person in the employment field can be a breach of contract (*Taylor* v. *Secretary of State for Scotland* [2000] ICR 595, HL) and selection of a person for dismissal on grounds of age can be unfair dismissal (*Price* v. *Civil Service Commissioner* [1978] ICR 27, EAT). The Sex Discrimination Act 1986 made it unlawful for an employer to have different retirement ages for men and women, a change introduced in light of the ECJ ruling in *Marshall* v. *Southampton and SW Hampshire HA (No.1)* [1986] ICR 335, ECJ and in any event if a job has one retiring age for males and another for females there will be at least a *prima facie* case of indirect sex discrimination which will be unlawful unless objectively justified (SDA 1975, s.1(1)(b) and *Bullock* v. *Alice Ottley School* [1993] ICR 138, CA).

The Working Time Regulations 1998, SI 1998/1833 make special provisions for young workers (basically those aged between 15 and 18 who are above compulsory school age). For details see **section 7.2.6**.

The National Minimum Wage Regulations 1999, SI 1999/584 make special provisions for young workers (basically those aged below 22). For details see **section 9.17**.

Different State Pension ages for men and women are temporarily allowed under EC/EU rules (Art.7 of Directive 79/7/EEC 'on the progressive implementation of the principle of equal treatment for men and women in matters of social security'). An attempt to challenge the legality of even temporary differences on the basis that they are contrary to the ECHR, Art.14 failed in *Pearson* v. *United Kingdom*, ECtHR, 22 August 2006.

16.1.2 Employment Equality (Age) Regulations 2006, SI 2006/1031

Introduction

The Age Regulations came into effect on 1 October 2006, except for the pensions related parts which came into effect on 1 December 2006. The main provisions ensure that:

- direct and indirect age discrimination is illegal in employment whether on grounds of youth or of old age and including terms of recruitment, job advertising, promotion and training;
- there is no discrimination within the meaning of the regulations if what was done was 'a proportionate means of achieving a legitimate aim';
- in deciding whether there has been discrimination a comparison must be made between two persons so that 'the relevant circumstances in the one case are the same, or not materially different, in the other';
- all retirement ages under 65 are illegal unless objectively justified;
- employers must give written notice to employees at least six months in advance of their intended retirement date;

- employers must give proper consideration to an employee's request to continue working beyond retirement; and
- the previous upper age limits for unfair dismissal rights and statutory redundancy payments have been removed (but the age-banded method of calculating statutory redundancy pay and unfair dismissal basic award remains).

Basic provisions

The precise definitions of direct and indirect age discrimination are in reg.3 of the Age Regulations. They reflect long-established discrimination law distinctions.

- *Direct discrimination* relates to a decision reached on the basis of a person's actual or perceived age (reg.3(1)(a)). The Equal Treatment Directive 2000/78/EC provides (Art.2(2)(a)) that 'direct discrimination shall be taken to occur where one person is treated less favourably than another is, has been or would be treated in a comparable situation' on grounds of age.
- *Indirect discrimination*. The Equal Treatment Directive provides (Art.2(2)(b)) that 'indirect discrimination shall be taken to occur where an apparently neutral provision, criterion or practice would put persons having a particular religion or belief, a particular disability, a particular age, or a particular sexual orientation at a particular disadvantage compared with other persons unless that provision, criterion or practice is objectively justified by a legitimate aim and the means of achieving that aim are appropriate and necessary ...'. The expression 'indirect discrimination' is not used in the Age Regulations. However, it is the normal shorthand used for describing what occurs where a provision, criterion or practice which is applied generally puts persons of a particular age or age group at a disadvantage (reg.3(1)(b)). The consultation paper which preceded the regulations gave the following example:

    Requiring applicants to pass a health or fitness test for recruitment or promotion would not constitute direct age discrimination. But it might be indirect age discrimination if people of certain ages were less likely to pass this test than other age groups (in which case the employer would have to objectively justify using the test ... using a health test will be justifiable if the test is set at a level necessary to indicate whether someone was capable of doing the job).

- *Harassment* involves unwanted conduct which has the purpose or effect either of violating a protected person's dignity or of creating an intimidating, hostile, degrading, humiliating or offensive environment for that person (reg.6). This is an example of British 'gold-plating' of a Directive as the Directive's requirement is not 'either/or' but is of the more restrictive 'both/and' variety (Art.2(3) of Directive 2000/78/EC).

- *Instructions to discriminate.* It is a form of discrimination to treat a person less favourably than another because he failed to carry out an instruction to discriminate or because he has complained about receiving such an instruction (reg.5).
- *Victimisation.* Where a person receives less favourable treatment than others by reason of the fact that he has brought (or given evidence in) proceedings, made an allegation or otherwise done anything under or by virtue of the regulations is also outlawed (reg.4).
- *Time limits.* There is a three-month time limit for bringing a complaint to an employment tribunal (regs.36 and 42).
- *Burden of proof.* There is provision for 'reversal of the burden of proof' in employment tribunal cases similar to that which applies in sex and race discrimination cases (reg.37 and see **section 14.3.4**).
- *Questionnaires.* There is a set form of questionnaire which an aggrieved person can use to ask questions of someone who he believes has discriminated against him (Age Regulations, Sched.3). To be admissible in employment tribunal proceedings, a questionnaire must be served within three months of the alleged discrimination unless proceedings have been instituted, in which case it must have been served within 21 days of the complaint being presented to the tribunal or such later time as the tribunal may direct (reg.41(4)).
- *Statutory dismissal procedures.* The compulsory dismissal procedures introduced from 1 October 2004 by the Employment Act 2002 (Dispute Resolution) Regulations 2004 do not apply if the reason or principal reason for the dismissal is retirement of an employee (Sched.8, para.64) – in any event they are likely to cease completely by April 2009 (see **Chapter 4**).
- *Occupational pension schemes.* There are extensive rules relating to age discrimination in the context of occupational pension schemes (reg.11 and Sched.2). The Employment Equality (Age) (Amendment) Regulations 2006, SI 2006/2408 and the Employment Equality (Age) (Amendment No.2) Regulations 2006, SI 2006/293 set out further details and brought the relevant rules into effect on 1 December 2006. They are not considered further here.

Who is protected?

The 2006 regulations apply when work is done at an establishment in Great Britain (which includes territorial waters 'adjacent to Great Britain' – reg.(2)) by employees and job applicants (reg.7), contract workers (reg.9), office holders including police and those seconded to the Serious Organised Crime Agency (regs.12–14), barristers and advocates (regs.15 and 16) and partners in firms (reg.17). Contract workers are defined as individuals supplied by their employer to a principal under a contract between their employer and the principal (reg.9). Ex-employees are covered where the discrimination or harassment arises out of or is closely connected with a 'relevant' relationship (reg.24). Civil servants and staff of the Houses of Parliament are covered (regs.44-46).

All these categories of person are protected not only against age discrimination by employers but also by principals (reg.9), by trustees and managers of occupational pension schemes (reg.11), by trade organisations (reg.18), by qualifications bodies (reg.19), providers of vocational training (reg.20), employment agencies (reg.21), by institutions of further and higher education (reg.23) and by anyone who knowingly aids another person to do an act which is made unlawful by the regulations (reg.26). 'Training' is given a wide meaning (Employment Equality (Sexual Orientation) (Religion or Belief) (Amendment) Regulations 2007, SI 2007/2269).

Although there is no decision on the precise nature of the geographical extent of the Age Regulations, it seems likely that the principles set out by the House of Lords in the unfair dismissal case of *Lawson* v. *Serco* [2006] ICR 250 will apply (see **section 11.3.12**). At any rate those same principles have been held to apply in disability discrimination cases and in cases under the Fixed-Term Employees (Prevention of Less Favourable Treatment) Regulations 2002, SI 2002/2034 (see respectively *Williams* v. *University of Nottingham* [2007] IRLR 660 and *Collins & Ashbourne* v. *Department for Constitutional Affairs* (unreported, EAT, 12 October 2007)).

Justification

What might otherwise be unlawful age discrimination under the regulations, whether direct or indirect, will not count as discrimination at all for the purposes of the Age Regulations if it is objectively and reasonably justified as a proportionate, appropriate and necessary means of achieving a legitimate aim (Directive 2000/78/EC, Art.6 combined with Age Regulations, reg.3).

The Age Regulations are unique in British discrimination law in that they provide a defence of justification where there is what would otherwise be direct age discrimination as well as in indirect discrimination cases. Other anti-discrimination rules only provide for justification to be a defence if the alleged discrimination is indirect discrimination. The Age Regulations also provide the normal exemptions, notably the 'genuine occupational requirement' exemption, which in practice provide something similar to a defence of justification in direct discrimination cases generally, not just in age discrimination cases.

The justification provisions do not cover unlawful victimisation, instructions to discriminate or harassment on grounds of age.

Examples of justification given by the EC Directive (in Art.6) are:

(a) the setting of special conditions on access to employment and vocational training, employment and occupation, including dismissal and remuneration conditions, for young people, older workers and persons with

caring responsibilities in order to promote their vocational integration or ensure their protection;
(b) the fixing of minimum conditions of age, professional experience or seniority in service for access to employment or to certain advantages linked to employment;
(c) the fixing of a maximum age for recruitment which is based on the training requirements of the post in question or the need for a reasonable period of employment before retirement.

As at 1 July 2008, the authors are not aware of any judgments at EAT or higher level which consider justification in the context of the Age Regulations. However, there have been at least three employment tribunal cases, all involving lawyers, in which the defence of justification has been considered in detail. The only general message which can be drawn from these is that, as one would expect, each case will turn on its own facts and merits combined with the skill and presentation abilities of the advocates involved:

1. An ex-partner in a City of London law firm alleged that restructuring of the firm's pension fund arrangements was discriminatory within the meaning of the Age Regulations. The employment tribunal ruled that in all the circumstances the arrangements were justified as a proportionate means of achieving a legitimate aim and dismissed his claim (*Bloxham* v. *Freshfields Bruckhaus Deringer* (unreported, London Central ET, 9 October 2007)). One consequence would seem to be that 'lockstep arrangements' under which the length of a partner's service is a factor taken into account in assessing the partner's share of a firm's profits are potentially capable of being justified even if they are age discriminatory.
2. The senior partner in a 20 partner law firm was required by the partnership deed to retire at 65. He complained to an employment tribunal. The tribunal found that the requirement was justified as a proportionate means of achieving a legitimate aim, essentially efficient long-term management of the firm (*Seldon* v. *Clarkson Wright & Jakes* (unreported, Ashford (Kent) ET, 4 December 2007)). It is understood that Mr Seldon is appealing to the EAT.
3. A part-time Recorder was required by Ministry of Justice standard terms to retire at age 65. The Ministry could not rely on the legally enforceable 'default' retirement age of 65 as this applies only to 'employees' and not to 'office holders'. The tribunal rejected the Ministry's argument that its policy of retiring judges at 65 was justified as a 'proportionate means of achieving a legitimate aim', failing to persuade the tribunal that enforced retirement of judges is necessary in order to ensure a 'reasonable flow' of new appointments (*Hampton* v. *Lord Chancellor and MoJ* [2008] IRLR 258). The Ministry of Justice subsequently raised the retirement age for Recorders, Deputy High Court Judges, Deputy District Judges, and Deputy Masters and Registrars from 65 to 70.

Retirement

Enforced retirement of an employee at an age below 65 is forbidden by the Age Regulations. The same applies to enforced retirement at any age of protected non-employees, for example, a partner in a professional partnership (Age Regulations, reg.3(1)). Subject to the important exception noted immediately below for a 'default retirement age' for employees, enforced retirement is therefore always unlawful unless it is justified as 'a proportionate means of achieving a legitimate aim'.

Enforced retirement of an employee at age 65 or more is allowed and is not unfair dismissal provided that certain conditions are fulfilled (Age Regulations, reg.30(2) and ERA 1996, s.98(2)(ba)). This 'default retirement age' applies to employees only not, for example, to partners or office holders. The government said when introducing the Age Regulations in 2006 that the decision to have a national default retirement age of 65 would be reviewed after five years.

There is a legal argument to the effect that the Equal Treatment Framework Directive 2000/78/EC does not allow there to be a maximum age after which retirement can be made compulsory and that therefore the Age Regulations, reg.30(2) is contrary to EU law and must be amended. This question was referred to the European Court of Justice in July 2007 (*R on application of Trustees of the National Council on Aging (Age Concern England)* v. *Dep't for BERR*, 24 July 2007, listed as Case C-388/07 ('the Heyday case')). An opinion by the ECJ Attorney-General is due to be published on 23 September 2008 and a final decision is expected by the end of the year or early 2009. British cases in which the question arises have all been stayed pending a decision in the Heyday case (by Direction of the President of the Employment Tribunals on 8 November 2007, supported by a Court of Appeal ruling in one of those cases, *Johns v. Solent SD Ltd* [2008] EWCA Civ 790, 13 June 2008).

The main conditions which must be fulfilled for enforced retirement not to be unfair dismissal are that the employee is aged 65 or more (ERA 1996, s.98ZA) and (by ERA 1996, s.98ZG and Age Regulations, Sched.6) that the employer:

- has given the employee written notice of the right to request deferred retirement and of the date on which he intends the employee to retire not more than one year and not less than six months before that date;
- has considered any request by the employee not to be retired – unless the request is granted or it is impractical to do so the employer must hold a meeting with the employee, who has a right to be accompanied, to consider the request within a reasonable period after receiving it;
- has considered any appeal against a decision to refuse such a request.

It follows that selection for redundancy on the basis of age is generally unlawful. Depending on the circumstances of the particular case, the practice of selection for redundancy by applying a LIFO (last in, first out) policy may be unlawful if in the particular employment concerned it could be said that in 'the last' in are generally the youngest.

The penalty for failure to comply with this notice requirement varies:

- if no notice is given at all, enforcement of the retirement is automatically unfair dismissal (ERA 1996, s.98ZG);
- if notice is given but only within the final two weeks before enforced retirement then again it will be automatically unfair dismissal (ERA 1996, s.98ZG);
- if notice is given but less than six months and more than two weeks before enforced retirement the employee will be entitled to 'compensation' of up to eight times' a week's pay (capped – Age Regulations, Sched.6, para.11(3) and (5)).

If the employer and employee agree a different retiring date after a notice has been given, and the new date is not more than six months after the one specified in the notice, then no further notice is required (Age Regulations, Sched.6, para.2(3)).

As noted above an employee who wants to continue working beyond retirement age must make a written request to his employer. This must be made at least three but not more than six months before the intended retirement date and include specified details (Age Regulations, Sched.6, para 5). If a valid request is made there will be an unfair dismissal if the employer fails to comply with the various, essentially procedural, requirements set out in Age Regulations, Sched.6, paras.6–9 before requiring the employee concerned to retire (ERA 1996, s.98ZG).

These requirements include the obligation noted above to hold a meeting to discuss the request. The employee has the right to have a companion at the meeting and to appeal the decision at a further meeting. In some respects the requirements were slightly watered down in the final version of the regulations – they do not specifically provide, as did the draft, that the employer must exercise 'good faith' nor do they set out a specific time limit by which the employer must notify the employee of its decision. On the other hand a new requirement was added that notification of the decision to the employee must be 'in writing and dated'.

The compulsory dismissal procedures introduced from 1 October 2004 by the Employment Act 2002 (Dispute Resolution) Regulations 2004 do not apply if the reason or principal reason for dismissal is retirement of an employee (Age Regulations, Sched.8, para.64). In any event they are due to be removed in their entirety in the near future (see **Chapter 4**).

General exemptions

- *Enforced retirement* of an employee aged 65 or more, subject to conditions (reg.30 – see above).

- *Genuine occupational requirement*. If possessing a characteristic related to age is a genuine and determining occupational requirement then, subject to conditions, the basic age discrimination rules will not apply in an employment context. The conditions are that it is proportionate to apply the requirement in the particular case and either the person to whom that requirement is applied does not meet it or the employer is not satisfied, and in all the circumstances it is reasonable for him not to be satisfied, that that person meets it (reg.8).
- *Long service benefits* provided that if the 'disadvantaged comparator' has more than five years' service provision of the benefit fulfils a business need (for example, by encouraging the loyalty or motivation or rewarding the experience of some or all of the workers involved) (reg.32(2)).
- *Variations in enhanced redundancy pay* can be lawful (reg.33).
- *Acts under statutory authority* (reg.27), for example, under the licensing laws or for national security purposes (reg.28).
- *Pay related to the national minimum wage* (reg.31).
- *Positive discrimination if* this 'prevents or compensates for disadvantages linked to age suffered by persons of that age or age group doing that work or likely to take up that work' (reg.29).
- *Cessation of life assurance cover* at normal retirement age or 65 for workers who retire or have retired early on grounds of ill-health (reg.34).

Recruitment and job advertisements, etc.

The DTI consultation document pointed out (at para.4.3.7) that there are '... age aspects of recruitment, selection and promotion besides upper age limits that are not explicitly mentioned in the Age Regulations'.

Examples given include:

- Requiring a birth date or age on job application forms. Although not age-discriminatory in itself, this could lead to problems.
- Requiring a certain length of experience. This would require objective justification.
- Requiring a certain qualification. This might require objective justification.

The consultation document was particularly interesting in its comment on graduate recruitment schemes. It said:

> an employer wishing to recruit graduates may not be able to justify setting a requirement of a certain maximum age. Students could be of any age, and it will be difficult to show why older students should be excluded from applying. However, in our view it will be easier for employers to justify indirect discrimination in the form of recruitment drives at universities ('milk rounds'), provided employers do not exclude applications from other sources.

We understand that in March 2007 an employment tribunal in Bristol struck out a claim by a member of the public that a job advertisement by the retailer

'Gap' contravened the Age Regulations on the basis that only a job applicant could bring a claim. A member of the public could not bring a claim as he had not suffered less favourable treatment as required by reg.3.

In October 2007 in Northern Ireland an industrial tribunal found that a 58-year-old job applicant had been discriminated against on grounds of age (under the Employment Equality (Age) Regulations (Northern Ireland) SR 2006/261 which are similar to the British regulations). An important factor was that the job advertisement had mentioned 'youthful enthusiasm' as a desirable attribute. There was also evidence that age-related questions regarding such matters as his drive and motivation at the age of 58 were raised at his interview. We understand that the man concerned, a Mr McCoy, later accepted £70,000 in settlement of his claim.

Vicarious liability of employers and principals

Where the action of an employee constitutes age discrimination (or harassment or victimisation) the employer will be responsible for the action of the employee. The employee in question will be liable as well. Employers may have a defence if they took reasonable steps to prevent discrimination by their employees (reg.25).

Unfair dismissal law and redundancy

Compulsory retirement is dismissal. It has been added to the list of reasons which make a dismissal *prima facie* fair (ERA 1996, s.98(2)(ba), introduced by Age Regulations, Sched.8, paras.21 and 22 with effect from 1 October 2006).

A rather convoluted process ensures that the dismissal will not only be *prima facie* fair but must be found to be fair if it is lawful under the Age Regulations. In most cases this means that if the employee was aged 65 or more at retirement and the procedures as to notice, etc. set out in the Age Regulations have been followed then the retirement will not be unfair dismissal (ERA 1996, s.98ZG).

If the compulsory retirement is unlawful under the Age Regulations the general rule is that retirement 'shall not be taken to be the reason (or a reason) for the dismissal' (ERA 1996, ss.98ZA and 98ZC). Thus s.98(2)(ba) will not apply and so the dismissal will not be *prima facie* fair.

Within this framework the rules make provision for cases in which the employee has a normal retirement age greater or less than 65, ensuring that provided the required procedures have been followed and the employee is over 65 the dismissal will be fair (ERA 1996, ss.98ZC–98ZD and 98ZE).

If an employee has a normal retirement age below 65, the question of whether the retirement dismissal is or is not automatically unfair depends on whether that normal retirement age is justified as a proportionate means of achieving a legitimate aim (see ERA 1996, s.98ZE).

EMPLOYMENT LAW HANDBOOK

The 'taper reduction' provision by which basic award on unfair dismissal and statutory redundancy pay were previously reduced by 1/12th for each complete month that the employee was past his 64th birthday at the effective date of termination have been abolished by the Age Regulations. All age limits (upper and lower) for entitlement to claim unfair dismissal and statutory redundancy pay have also been abolished (Age Regulations, Sched.8, paras.21–33).

However, the provisions by which basic award on unfair dismissal and statutory redundancy pay vary according to age have been retained (ERA 1996, ss.119 and 162 provide for $^{1}/_{2}$ a week's pay for each year worked before 22nd birthday; 1 weeks' pay for each year worked between 22nd and 41st birthday; and 1$^{1}/_{2}$ weeks' pay for each year worked after 41st birthday, subject to a statutory cap on a week's pay, which is £330 from 1 February 2008 – ERA 1996, s.227).

16.2 DISCRIMINATION ON GROUNDS OF RELIGION OR BELIEF

16.2.1 Introduction

Religious discrimination as such was not unlawful in the employment field in Britain (different rules apply in Northern Ireland) until 2 December 2003. On that date the Employment Equality (Religion or Belief) Regulations 2003, SI 2003/1660 (EE(RB)R 2003) came into effect. The regulations implement the parts of Equal Treatment Framework Directive 2000/78/EC which require all Member States to introduce legislation outlawing discrimination based on religion or belief (as well as based on disability, age or sexual orientation) in the employment field.

The regulations prohibit direct discrimination, indirect discrimination, victimisation and harassment in the employment field (including vocational training) by reason of 'any religion, religious belief, or similar philosophical belief'. They do not apply where the act(s) complained of took place before 2 December 2003 (*Bari* v. *Hashi & anor* (unreported, EAT, 27 February 2004)). The regulations do not extend to Northern Ireland (reg.1(2)).

There is nothing in the regulations specifically requiring employers to provide time off or facilities at the workplace for religious worship or observance. However, in particular circumstances employers will have to be careful in case their policy with regard to refusing time off for religious observance might amount to unjustified indirect discrimination.

The 2005 Annual Report of the Employment Tribunal service stated that there were 307 discrimination claims on grounds of religion or belief in the first full year of operation of EE(RB)R 2003, i.e. the 12 months to 31 March 2005. In the year to 31 March 2006 the number rose to 486 and in the year to 31 March 2007 it rose again to 648.

Apart from EE(RB)R 2003, discrimination on religious grounds can amount to unlawful indirect race discrimination contrary to RRA 1976. Also

ERA 1996, ss.45 and 101 give specific rights to shop and betting workers who do not wish to work on Sundays.

Religion-oriented race discrimination claims can sometimes succeed. For example, an employer who refused Muslim employees time off work for the religious festival of Eid was held liable to pay compensation for indirect race discrimination in *Walker (J.H) Ltd* v. *Hussain & ors* [1996] IRLR 11, EAT. However, since the coming into force of EE(RB)R 2003 the regulations will normally provide the preferred route for mounting a religious discrimination claim.

Religious discrimination may also involve infringement of the Human Rights Act 1998 (the ECHR, Art.9 guarantees freedom of religion). Each case depends on its own particular facts and case law suggests that employees will find it difficult to win religious discrimination cases on grounds of infringement of human rights. In *Copsey* v. *WWB Devon Clays Ltd* [2005] ICR 1789, CA a Christian employee failed in an unfair dismissal claim brought on the basis that his human rights were infringed by his being required to work on Sunday. Similarly in a non-employment law but relevant context a Muslim schoolgirl ultimately lost her claim that her school was in breach of Art.9(2) of the Convention by refusing to allow her to wear a jilbab rather than the shalwar kameeze permitted by the school's dress code (*R on application of Begum* v. *Headteacher & Governors of Denbigh High School* [2006] UKHL 15). Lord Hoffmann in the House of Lords, overruling the Court of Appeal, pointed out that 'Article Nine does not require that one should be allowed to manifest one's religion at any time and place of one's own choosing. Common civility also has a place in the religious life'.

Although not specifically related to employment law it should be noted that the Racial and Religious Hatred Act 2006 came into force on 1 October 2007. It makes 'provision about offences involving stirring up hatred against persons on racial or religious grounds'.

The regulations do not cover religious discrimination by trustees and managers of occupational pension schemes. A further set of regulations plug this gap: the Employment Equality (Religion or Belief) (Amendment) Regulations 2003, SI 2003/2828.

16.2.2 Employment Equality (Religion or Belief) Regulations 2003, SI 2003/1660

The regulations were amended with effect from 30 April 2007 (by Equality Act 2006, s.77). Under the original wording religion or belief meant 'any religion, religious belief, or similar philosophical belief' (reg.2(1)). This wording has been replaced and reg.2(1) now provides that:

(a) 'religion' means any religion,
(b) 'belief' means any religious or philosophical belief,
(c) a reference to religion includes a reference to lack of religion, and
(d) a reference to belief includes a reference to lack of belief.

As will be apparent, a main difference between the old and new wordings is omission of the word 'similar' in relation to philosophical belief. The change in wording does not have retrospective effect (*McClintock* v. *DCA* [2008] IRLR 29, EAT).

It is of course up to the courts to decide what is a 'philosophical belief'. In *Campbell and Cosans* v. *UK* (1982) 4 EHRR 293 the European Court of Human Rights considered that it is a belief that attains a certain level of cogency, seriousness, cohesion and importance that is worthy of respect in a democratic society and not incompatible with human dignity. In the House of Lords debate leading to omission of the word 'similar' the government spokesperson said that the 'term "philosophical belief" will take its meaning from the context in which it appears; that is, as part of the legislation relating to discrimination on the grounds of religion or belief'. She suggested that an example of a belief that might meet this description is humanism, and examples of something that might not would be support of a political party or 'belief in the supreme nature of the Jedi Knights' (Hansard HL, col.1105, 13 July 2005).

It is unclear whether 'fringe' religious or philosophical beliefs (vegans and rastafarians are examples) are covered, although in at least one case it has been accepted that Rastafarianism is a philosophical belief (*Harris* v. *NKL Automotive and Matrix Consultancy UK Ltd* (unreported, EAT, 3 October 2007)).

Direct and indirect discrimination (reg.3)

The meaning of 'direct discrimination' was changed with effect from 30 April 2007 (by Equality Act 2006, s.77). Under the original wording of reg.3 direct discrimination took place where 'on grounds of religion or belief, A treats B less favourably than he treats or would treat other persons'. Under the new wording it takes place where 'on the grounds of religion or belief of B or of any other person except A (whether or not it is also A's religion or belief) A treats B less favourably than he treats or would treat other persons'. The defence of justification is not available in direct discrimination cases – it is always unlawful unless one of the exemptions applies.

Indirect discrimination is where a generally applied provision, criterion or practice puts persons of a particular religion or belief at a disadvantage and cannot be shown to be a proportionate means of achieving a legitimate aim. It is a defence to a claim of indirect discrimination that the provision, criterion or practice applied is justified as a proportionate means of achieving a legitimate aim. If that is established there is no discrimination for the purposes of the regulations (reg.3(1)(b)).

Victimisation and harassment

Victimisation and harassment are specifically covered (regs.4 and 5). Victimisation is where a person receives less favourable treatment than others by reason of the fact that he has brought (or given evidence in) proceedings, made an allegation or otherwise done anything under or by reference to the regulations. Harassment is where a person is subjected to unwanted conduct on grounds of religion or belief with the purpose or effect of violating his dignity, or creating an intimidating, hostile, degrading, humiliating or offensive environment for him.

The regulations prohibit discrimination (including victimisation and harassment) in the fields of employment and vocational training. They provide protection for: employees (reg.6); contract workers (reg.8); office holders (reg.10); police officers (reg.11); barristers, advocates and their clerks and pupils (regs.12 and 13); partners (reg.14); civil servants (reg.36); and parliamentary staff (reg.38). They prohibit discrimination by: trades unions and employer organisations (reg.15); bodies conferring professional and trade qualifications (reg.16); training providers (reg.17); employment agencies (reg.18); and further and higher education institutions (reg.20). Specified higher education institutions are exempted so far as necessary '... to give preference in its admissions to persons of a particular religion or belief in order to preserve that institution's religious ethos' (see amendment to reg.20 made with effect from 1 April 2004 by the Employment Equality (Religion or Belief) (Amendment) Regulations 2004, SI 2004/437). 'Training' is given a wide meaning (Employment Equality (Sexual Orientation) (Religion or Belief) (Amendment) Regulations 2007, SI 2007/2269).

Discrimination, victimisation or harassment which occurs after the relevant relationship has ended is unlawful if it arises out of, and is closely connected to, the relationship (reg.21).

Vicarious liability

There are also normal 'vicarious liability' provisions making an employer responsible for anything done by a person in the course of his employment (reg.22) and for ensuring that if a person knowingly aids another person to do an unlawful act they are both treated as doing that act (reg.23).

Exceptions

There are various exceptions set out in EE(RB)R 2003:

- The most generally important exception is where being of a particular religion or belief is a genuine and determining occupational requirement for a post and it is proportionate to apply the requirement in the particular case. A small but significant gloss is that the requirement need not be a 'determining' requirement where an employer has an ethos based on religion or belief and 'having regard to that ethos and to the nature of the employment or the context in which it is carried out being of a particular religion or belief is a genuine occupational requirement for the job'. This

is referred to in the official explanatory notes as the 'religious organisations GOR' (reg.7). It is noteworthy that there is no specific 'domestic employment' exemption.
- Acts done for safeguarding national security, if the doing of the act was justified by that purpose (reg.24).
- Acts of positive discrimination in connection with training for, or taking advantage of opportunities for, particular work 'where it reasonably appears to the person doing the act that it prevents or compensates for disadvantages linked to religion or belief suffered by persons of that religion or belief doing that work or likely to take up that work' (reg.25).
- For the protection of Sikhs in connection with requirements as to the wearing of safety helmets (reg.26).

Remedies

Remedies for individuals include compensation by taking proceedings in employment tribunals (in most cases) or in the county or sheriff courts if the complaint is against a further and higher education institution (regs.27–32). Vicarious liability complaints can be brought in either place. There is no statutory limit to the total compensation which can be awarded. There is a 'for avoidance of doubt' provision confirming that compensation can be awarded for injury to feelings – although this appears in the section dealing with proceedings in the county and sheriff courts, it applies to employment tribunals as well (reg.30(1)(b)). The burden of proof is transferred to the employer to disprove an allegation once a complainant has established a *prima facie* case (regs.29 and 32).

Complaints must be made within three months from when the act complained of was done, extended to six months where the complaint is by a member of the armed forces or is to a county court or sheriff court, with power in either case to extend time if the tribunal or court considers that would be just and equitable (reg.34). A questionnaire procedure for employees is provided to help them get information from employers (reg.33 and Scheds.2 and 3).

Discriminatory terms in contracts and collective agreements are made void and/or unenforceable (reg.35 and Sched.4).

Examples

- Dismissal of a bus cleaner was held to be a breach of EE(RB)R 2003 by an employment tribunal in Leeds. He had taken holiday and unpaid leave to perform hajj, having had no response from his employer to his request (Case of TGWU member Mohammed Sajwal Khan, 14 January 2005).
- A Christian employee was required under a new shift rota system to work on Sunday at times which meant she could not get to church. She had expressly told her employer at her interview that she could not work on

OTHER CATEGORIES OF DISCRIMINATION

Sundays. She resigned and won both a claim that she had been discriminated against on the grounds of religion or belief and also a claim that her resignation amounted to constructive dismissal on the basis that the discrimination was a fundamental breach of her employer's implied contractual duty of trust and confidence (*Williams-Drabble* v. *Pathway Care Solutions Ltd & anor*, ET Case number 2601718/04).

- The first religious discrimination case to reach the EAT was heard in summer 2006. A Mr Mohmed, a Sikh employed by West Coast Trains Ltd, refused to tidy his beard. Another Sikh employee did keep his beard tidy. Mr Mohmed was dismissed, the employer said because of his lack of enthusiasm and he said because of his beard and appearance. An employment tribunal rejected his claim of direct discrimination on the grounds of his religion or belief by way of dismissal. The EAT dismissed his appeal on the basis that the beard issue related to tidiness only, not religion. The employer had demonstrated that it had no objection to beards or to Sikhs with beards and no *prima facie* case of unlawful religious discrimination had been made out by Mr Mohmed. Therefore there was no shifting of the burden of proof to require an explanation from the employer for the dismissal as provided for by EE(RB)R 2003, reg.29 (*Mohmed* v. *West Coast Trains Ltd* (unreported, EAT, 30 August 2006)).
- The EAT upheld an employment tribunal's decision that an atheist teacher had been subjected to unlawful discrimination after he failed to get an interview for a post at a Roman Catholic school (*Glasgow City Council* v. *McNab* [2007] IRLR 476, EAT).
- The EAT held that it was legitimate for a school to require a Muslim teaching assistant to remove her veil while in class as this was a proportionate means of achieving the proper aim of educating children (*Azmi* v. *Kirklees Metropolitan Borough Council* [2007] ICR 1154)
- The High Court ruled that a schoolgirl should not be allowed to wear a 'purity ring' which contravened her school's prohibition on wearing jewellery on the basis that it was a 'religious artefact' (*Playfoot (a minor), R (on the application of)* v. *Millais School* [2007] EWHC 1698 (Admin), 16 July 2007)).
- An employment tribunal found that Prospects, a Christian charity which previously employed a number of non-Christian staff and volunteers, had acted illegally when in 2004 it began recruiting only practising Christians for almost all posts, and told existing non-Christian staff that they were no longer eligible for promotion (*Sheridan* v. *Prospects* (unreported, Abergele ET, May 2008)).

16.2.3 Potential conflicts with other legislation

There is scope for potential conflict between the Employment Equality (Sexual Orientation) Regulations 2003 (EE(SO)R 2003)(see below) and the

EE(RB)R 2003. For example, what happens if a Bible fundamentalist is sacked for objecting to working alongside a homosexual person? A similar problem arose in the USA in *Peterson* v. *Hewlett-Packard*, USA Court of Appeals, 9th Circuit, January 2004 (the US court held that Hewlett-Packard was justified in dismissing a worker for refusing to remove a poster with various Biblical passages condemning homosexuality he had put up in response to the company's 'Diversity is Our Strength' posters welcoming African-American, Hispanic, Caucasian, elderly, and gay employees). The rationale and decision will no doubt be interesting to consider if and when the same sort of problem comes to be considered by an employment tribunal in the UK.

There is a full and detailed consideration of the factors to be taken into account when balancing the legitimate rights of supporters of freedom of religious belief and practice on the one hand and opponents of sexual orientation discrimination on the other in the judgment in a 2007 case in Northern Ireland (*Application for Judicial Review by the Christian Institute* [2008] IRLR 36, NIQB).

In an attempt to resolve the potential conflict, EE(SO)R 2003 provide a specific exemption where employment is for purposes of an organised religion provided appropriate conditions, including a requirement of reasonableness, are met (see **section 16.3**). An employment tribunal found in 2007 that this did not entitle a Church of England bishop to refuse to appoint a homosexual job applicant to the post of Diocesan Youth Officer (*Reaney* v. *Hereford Diocesan Board of Finance* (unreported, ET case 1602844/2006, Cardiff ET, 17 July 2007).

There are separate regulations enabling independent schools with a religious character to give employment preference to teachers whose religious beliefs accord with the religious tenets on which the school is based and to take their religious beliefs into account in dismissal situations (Independent Schools (Employment of Teachers in Schools with a Religious Character) Regulations 2003, SI 2003/2037). Other provisions provide for application to the BERR for designation of an independent school as having a religious character (Religious Character of Schools (Designation Procedure) (Independent Schools) (England) Regulations 2003, SI 2003/2314). The effect is to put independent religious schools in the same position as voluntary aided schools designated as having a religious character under the School Standards and Framework Act 1998, s.69 and the Religious Character of Schools (Designation Procedure) Regulations 1998, SI 1998/2535.

16.3 DISCRIMINATION ON GROUNDS OF SEXUAL ORIENTATION

As a preliminary it is worth making the point that the provisions outlawing discrimination on grounds of sexual orientation (EE(SO)R 2003) are entirely separate from the provisions which outlaw discrimination against transsexuals (introduced into SDA 1975 as s.2A by the Sex Discrimination (Gender Reassignment) Regulations 1999, SI 1999/1102 – see notes at **section 14.2.2**).

Discrimination on grounds of sexual orientation was not unlawful in the employment field in Britain until 1 December 2003 (save to the extent that a person who had been discriminated against on grounds of sexual orientation might in appropriate circumstances be able to claim for a breach of human rights under the ECHR). On that date EE(SO)R 2003 came into effect. The regulations implement the parts of EC Equal Treatment Framework Directive 2000/78/EC which require all Member States to introduce legislation outlawing discrimination based on sexual orientation (as well as based on disability, age or religion or belief) in the employment field. They specifically prohibit victimisation and harassment as well as other forms of such discrimination in employment and vocational training (EE(SO)R 2003, regs.6–21).

The interpretation provision (EE(SO)R 2003, reg.2) ensures that the phrase 'sexual orientation' covers preference for the opposite sex as well as homosexual preference. It is therefore as unlawful to discriminate against a straight person because that person is heterosexual as to discriminate against a gay man or a lesbian because that person is homosexual.

The regulations negate the position finally established in June 2003 that SDA 1975 does not cover discrimination on grounds of sexual orientation (*Pearce* v. *Governing Body of Mayfield School; MacDonald* v. *Advocate General for Scotland* [2003] ICR 937, HL).

The regulations make it important that employers ensure that any scheme which provides benefits for unmarried partners of employees does so regardless of whether they are same-sex or heterosexual partners. Also any equal opportunities policies should be reviewed to ensure compliance, especially perhaps in relation to promotion.

The 2005 Annual Report of the Employment Tribunal Service stated that there were 349 discrimination claims on grounds of sexual orientation in the first full year of operation of the 2003 regulations, i.e. the 12 months to 31 March 2005. In the year to 31 March 2006 the number rose to 395 and in the year to 31 March 2007 it rose again to 470.

The Equality Act (Sexual Orientation) Regulations 2007, SI 2007/1263 which came into force on 30 April 2007, 'protect people from being discriminated against because of their sexual orientation in the provision of goods and services'. While not directly related to employment law these regulations include provision (reg. 30) to ensure that 'Anything done by a person in the course of his employment shall be treated for the purposes of these Regulations as done by the employer as well as by the person.'

The main 2003 regulations do not cover sexual orientation discrimination by trustees and managers of occupational pension schemes. A further set of regulations plugs this gap: Employment Equality (Sexual Orientation) (Amendment) Regulations 2003, SI 2003/2827.

Direct and indirect discrimination

Direct discrimination occurs where a person is treated less favourably than another on grounds of sexual orientation. The defence of justification is not available in direct discrimination cases – it is always unlawful unless one of the exemptions applies (EE(SO)R 2003, reg.3(1)(a) and see below).

Indirect discrimination occurs where a provision, criterion or practice puts persons of a particular sexual orientation at a disadvantage and cannot be shown to be a proportionate means of achieving a legitimate aim. It is a defence to a claim of indirect discrimination that the provision, criterion or practice applied is justified as a proportionate means of achieving a legitimate aim. If that is established there is no discrimination for the purposes of the regulations (EE(SO)R 2003, reg.3(1)(b)).

Who is protected?

The 2003 regulations protect: employees (reg.6); contract workers (reg.8); office holders (including constables) (regs.10 and 11); barristers and advocates (regs.12 and 13); partnerships (reg.14); and civil servants and members of the armed forces (reg.36). As well as prohibiting discrimination by employers, they also prohibit discrimination by: trade organisations (reg.15); bodies conferring professional and trade qualifications (reg.16); training providers (reg.17); employment agencies (reg.18); and further and higher education institutions (reg.20). Training is widely defined (Employment Equality (Sexual Orientation) (Religion or Belief) (Amendment) Regulations 2007, SI 2007/2269).

Questionnaires

The 2003 regulations provide for a questionnaire for employees who believe they may have been discriminated against or subjected to harassment contrary to the regulations to serve on their employers and a suggested template for a response (EE(SO)R 2003, reg.22 and Scheds.2 and 3).

Collective agreements and trade unions

The 2003 regulations provide that a term of a contract or collective agreement or any rule made by a trade organisation will normally be either unenforceable or void if it purports to exclude or limit any provision of the regulations (EE(SO)R 2003, Sched.4).

As from 1 December 2003 the rules forbidding a trade union (more specifically any 'organisation of workers') discriminating against intending or actual members on sex, race or disability grounds are extended to outlaw discrimination on grounds of sexual orientation (EE(SO)R 2003, reg.15).

Exemptions

GENUINE OCCUPATIONAL REQUIREMENT

The regulations provide a 'genuine occupational requirement' exception. This applies where a particular sexual orientation is a genuine and determining occupational requirement (EE(SO)R 2003, reg.7).

The genuine occupational requirement exception includes a provision similar to SDA 1975, s.19 specifically for the benefit of religious organisations which have a doctrinal objection to homosexuality (reg.7(3)). This applies if the employment is for purposes of organised religion; the employer applies a requirement related to sexual orientation because of the nature of the employment and the context in which it is carried out, so as to avoid conflicting with the strongly held religious convictions of a significant number of the religion's followers; and the employer is not satisfied, and in all the circumstances it is reasonable for him not to be satisfied, that that person meets it.

There was a case in 2007 in which it was clear that but for his sexual orientation a currently non-sexually active homosexual man aged 40 would have been offered a job as a Diocesan Youth Officer. He took the bishop to an employment tribunal which accepted the bishop's argument that the requirement that the post should not be filled by a homosexual person was imposed because of the nature of the employment and the context in which it would be carried out so as to avoid conflicting with the strongly held religious convictions of a significant number of the Anglican church's followers. However, although it recognised that it should not substitute its own view for that of the bishop, the tribunal decided that in rejecting the man's application the bishop had not been reasonable in coming to the conclusion that the applicant had failed to meet this 'requirement related to sexual orientation'. The bishop was therefore not able to take the benefit of the genuine occupational requirement exemption. The diocese did not appeal and it is reported that compensation in excess of £45,000 was later awarded against it (*Reaney* v. *Hereford Diocesan Board of Finance* (unreported, case 1602844/2006, Cardiff ET, 17 July 2007)).

NATIONAL SECURITY

The regulations contain specific provision ensuring that they do not render unlawful an act done for the purpose of safeguarding security if the doing of the act was justified for that purpose (EE(SO)R 2003, reg.24).

MARITAL STATUS

There is also a general exception which provides that: 'Nothing in [the main part of the regulations] shall render unlawful anything which prevents or restricts access to a benefit by reference to marital status' (reg.25).

The legality of this exemption has been questioned, especially as it is common for retirement and occupational pension schemes, including those run by public sector employers, to provide surviving spouse pensions. These are obviously benefits 'by reference to marital status' and are therefore not available to the partners of homosexual employees.

In 2004, six trade unions failed in the High Court in their attempt to get a declaration that this marital status exception therefore means that the 2003 regulations do not properly implement the Equal Treatment Framework Directive 2000/78/EC (*R (on application of Amicus, NATFHE, UNISON, NASUWT, Public & Commercial Services Union, NURMTW and NUT)* v. *Secretary of State for Trade and Industry* [2004] IRLR 430). However, in a case in 2008 the European Court of Justice ruled that making a distinction for pension benefit purposes between marriage and a registered homosexual civil partnership is prohibited by the Directive 'if the partnership has substantially identical effect to marriage, which is a matter for decision for the national court concerned' (*Maruko* v. *Versorgungsanstalt der deutschen Bühnen* [2008] IRLR 450, ECJ Case C-267/06). In the UK, the Civil Partnership Act 2004 came fully into force on 6 April 2006 and provides for same-sex couples who are aged 16 or over and neither of whom is married to obtain legal recognition of their relationship by registering as 'civil partners' of each other.

POSITIVE ACTION

There is specific exemption for affording persons of a particular sexual orientation access to training facilities or for encouraging them to take advantage of opportunities for doing particular work (reg.26).

Examples

- So far as we are aware the first example of successful use of EE(SO)R 2003 was by a Mr Robert Whitfield who won £35,000 at the Stratford East Employment Tribunal in January 2005.
- In March 2005 a homosexual researcher employed by a Labour MP (Candy Atherton, MP for Falmouth & Camborne) failed in his tribunal claim that requesting him to make enquiries about a potential political opponent was unlawful under EE(SO)R 2003 because the potential opponent was thought to be gay.
- In February 2007 a man named Jonah Ditton, called a 'wee poof', was awarded £118,309 by an employment tribunal in Glasgow for sexual orientation discrimination following his dismissal after only eight days in his job.
- In February 2008 the EAT ruled that teasing of a heterosexual man by work colleagues because 'they perceived him as having stereotypical characteristics which they associated with a gay person' was not on grounds of

his sexual orientation and was therefore not contrary to the 2003 regulations (*English* v. *Thomas Sanderson Blinds Ltd* [2008] IRLR 342). He was given leave to appeal to the Court of Appeal.

A final comment

The technically correct word 'homosexual' does not appear in the 2003 regulations. Instead the more cumbersome phrase 'orientation towards people of the same sex' is used. Whether this is in case some might wrongly think that 'homo' comes from the latin word for 'man' rather than from the greek for 'same' and so believe that homosexuals must be male, or whether it is merely political correctness, is not clear. We do not profess to have the answer.

16.4 FIXED-TERM EMPLOYEES

The Fixed-Term Employees (Prevention of Less Favourable Treatment) Regulations 2002, SI 2002/2034 (FTER 2002) made several changes for the benefit of those on fixed contracts with effect from 1 October 2002. The basic idea is that it is unlawful to treat a fixed-term employee less favourably than a comparable permanent employee engaged in similar work, subject to a defence of objective justification. An employer can objectively justify individual terms which are less favourable if a fixed-term employee's contract taken as a whole is as favourable to that fixed-term employee as contracts of permanent employees are to them. Regulation 3 sets out the basic right and reg.2 defines a 'comparable employee'.

The right includes a right for a fixed-term employee not to be subjected to any other detriment by any act, or deliberate failure to act, of his employer (FTER 2002, reg.3(1)(b)). In 2004 the Court of Appeal rejected an argument that non-renewal of a fixed-term contract was itself a detriment (*Department for Work and Pensions* v. *Webley* [2005] IRLR 288, CA).

Other changes made by FTER 2002 include, first, that fixed-term contracts are automatically converted to contracts of indefinite length after four years (the four years cannot start before 10 July 2002) (FTER 2002, reg.8); second, the completion of a limited-term or task contract now counts as dismissal for unfair dismissal purposes (FTER 2002, reg.1(2) and Sched.2, para.3); third, fixed-term employees who consider they are being treated unfairly can require their employer to provide a written statement setting out the reasons for the treatment complained of (FTER 2002, reg.5).Only fixed-term employees can benefit from the regulations – a worker as generally widely defined is not covered. The TUC is on record as taking the view that the exclusion of workers who are not technically employees means that the regulations do not properly implement Directive 1999/70/EC on Fixed Term Contracts. It should also be noted that FTER 2002, regs.18, 19 and 20 provide for exclusions for apprentices, agency workers and those on training schemes provided under arrangements made by the government or funded in whole or part under the European Social Fund.

An important change from the original draft regulations is that FTER 2002 cover pensions. It is thus unlawful for occupational pension schemes to exclude from membership temporary employees who are on fixed-term contracts if comparable permanent employees are eligible for membership.

The regulations apply to fixed-term employees only. Thus an employer can effectively circumvent some parts (i.e. the non-discrimination parts) of FTER 2002 by the simple expedient of employing those who might previously have been employed on fixed-term contracts under normal permanent contracts instead. Subject to ensuring that there is no infringement of sex, race and disability discrimination, there is no statutory requirement that the terms of the contracts offered to one group of employees must be the same as those offered to others, so an employer might still legitimately offer different employment terms to different groups of employees who are not fixed-term employees covered by the regulations. However, disaffected employees might in some cases be able to claim parity by relying on the implied contractual term of trust and confidence rather than on the regulations, so this must be seen as uncharted territory.

Examples of cases in which employers have been found to have treated fixed-term staff less favourably than comparable permanent staff contrary to FTER 2002 are:

- a case in which a bank excluded fixed-term staff from a bonus scheme; fixed-term employees were able to use FTER 2002 to claim a bonus which their employer had decided in principle before the regulations came into force should be paid only to 'permanent' staff but the detailed application of which was not finalised until after FTER 2002 had come into force (*Coutts and Co plc & anor* v. *Cure & Fraser* [2005] ICR 1098);
- a tribunal case in 2006 in which a woman named Arlene Roy engaged by First Engineering on a short fixed-term contract to cover for another woman absent on maternity leave but at a lower salary won £7,336 on the basis that she had been discriminated against contrary to FTER 2002.

16.5 PART-TIME WORKERS

Historically, part-time workers were forced to rely on establishing claims of indirect sex discrimination if they were treated less favourably because they were part time. The argument sometimes failed if the statistical evidence was not available and, in any event, did not avail men. To remedy this anomaly, the Part-Time Workers (Prevention of Less Favourable Treatment) Regulations 2000, SI 2000/1551 (PTWR 2000) were introduced. The regulations apply for the benefit of 'workers' rather than just 'employees' (see **section 2.1.2**).

Under PTWR 2000, reg.5 a worker can claim parity with another if:

- he is a part-time worker;
- the comparator is a comparable full-time worker – this involves fulfilling three conditions (PTWR 2000, reg.2(4)): (i) that the full-time worker is employed by the same employer under the same type of contract; (ii) that both workers are engaged in the same or broadly similar work, having regard, where relevant, to qualification, skills and experience; and (iii) that both workers are based at the same establishment (unless there is no full-time worker based at the same establishment as the part-time worker, but there is one based at another establishment);
- the less favourable treatment is on the grounds that the claimant is a part-time worker;
- the treatment is not justified on objective grounds.

The regulations do not define full-time and part-time worker in any useful way. Instead, a full-time worker is described as somebody who 'having regard to the custom and practice of the employer ... is regarded as a full-time worker'. A part-time worker is defined as somebody who 'having regard to the custom and practice of the employer in relation to workers employed by the worker's employer under the same type of contract, is not identifiable as a full-time worker' (PTWR 2000, reg.2(1) and (2)).

For that purpose, in order to ascertain whether someone else is employed under the same type of contract, the regulations (PTWR 2000, reg.2(3) as amended by the Part-time Workers (Prevention of Less Favourable Treatment) Regulations 2000 (Amendment) Regulations 2002, SI 2002/2035) go on to provide that the following shall be regarded as being employed under different types of contract:

(a) employees employed under a contract that is not a contract of apprenticeship;
(b) employees employed under a contract of apprenticeship;
(c) workers who are not employees;
(d) any other description of worker that it is reasonable for the employer to treat differently from other workers on the ground that workers of that description have a different type of contract

There is an interesting debate, as yet not fully resolved, about whether a hypothetical comparator can be used in a part-time worker discrimination case, or whether an actual comparator is required (*Royal Mail Group* v. *Lynch* (unreported, EAT, 2 September 2002) and *Wippel* v. *Peek & Cloppenburg GmbH & ors* [2005] IRLR 211). The answer may be that there are two separate questions and that a hypothetical comparator can not be used when deciding the first question, whether there was less favourable treatment, but can be used when considering the second question, whether that treatment was on the ground that the claimant was a part-time worker (*McMenemy* v. *Capita*

Business Services Ltd (EAT, 8 March 2006) – later reported at [2007] IRLR 400, CS).

The regulations 'do not apply to any individual in his capacity as the holder of a judicial office if he is remunerated on a daily fee-paid basis' (PTWR 2000, reg.17). Accordingly a part-time chairman of a social security appeals tribunal was not entitled on his retirement to pension rights to which full-time chairmen were entitled (*Christie* v. *DCA & anor* [2007] ICR 1553, EAT).

16.5.1 Rights

Part-time workers have a right not to be treated less favourably than comparable full-time workers as regards the terms of their employment or being subjected to any detriment, unless the employer can prove that the less favourable treatment is justified. They are thus entitled, for example, to:

- the same hourly rate of pay;
- the same access to company pension schemes;
- the same entitlements to annual leave and maternity/parental leave on a pro rata basis;
- the same entitlement to contractual sick pay; and
- no less favourable treatment in access to training.

Part-time workers also have a right not to be dismissed or subjected to a detriment because they have either tried to enforce their rights under PTWR 2000, alleged that their employer has breached a right, or refused to forgo a right. Any dismissal for these reasons will be automatically unfair, unless the claim/allegation by the employee was false and made in bad faith (PTWR 2000, reg.7). Finally, if part-time workers consider that an employer has infringed their rights under PTWR 2000, they are entitled to receive a written statement of reasons for the less favourable treatment (PTWR 2000, reg.5).

In March 2006, in one of the first important cases under PTWR 2000, the House of Lords overruled decisions of the Court of Appeal, the EAT and an employment tribunal all of which had held that retained (i.e. part-time) firefighters cannot use the regulations to get parity of employment terms with full-time regular firefighters.

Essentially, the regulations required the part-timers to jump two hurdles: (i) to demonstrate that their contracts were the same as those of full timers; and (ii) to demonstrate that the work they were doing was the same or broadly similar. The employment tribunal and the EAT ruled that neither of these two hurdles had been jumped; the Court of Appeal thought the first but not the second had been jumped. The House of Lords confirmed the Court of Appeal's conclusion that the first hurdle had been jumped and that the types of contract are the same, given the very broad categories set out in the regulations. However, the Court of Appeal's approach to whether the second hurdle had been overcome was held to be too restrictive. The House of Lords indicated that if the differences between the work done by full-time and part-time firefighters is simply a function of the extra hours worked by full timers, and that an overall assessment shows that the differences do not materially detract from the similarities, the work done should be regarded as the 'same or broadly similar'. It would then follow that the second hurdle would have been jumped as well. Whether this was so would require further consideration of the facts so the House of Lords remitted the case back for further consideration by an employment tribunal for a final ruling (*Matthews & ors* v. *Kent and Medway Towns Fire Authority & ors* [2006] ICR 365, HL). In the event in March 2008 the South London employment tribunal ruled in favour of the retained firefighters, with the result that they became entitled to equal access to pension and sick pay, on a pro-rata basis, with their full-time colleagues.

A dedicated website at **www.emplaw.co.uk/lshandbook** provides links to judgments and other source material referred to in this chapter.

CHAPTER 17
Equal pay and terms of employment

17.1 BACKGROUND

The Equal Pay Act 1970 (EqPA 1970) gives women (or men) the right to the same pay and other terms and conditions of employment as men (or women) for doing the same work or work of equal value. For practical purposes this Act was the first modern employment-related anti-discrimination law enacted in Britain. It is the immediate forerunner of a now comprehensive body of anti-discrimination law applying to treatment of people at work which makes sex, sexual orientation, race, disability, religious and age discrimination generally unlawful.

In spite of its title, EqPA 1970 covers all sex discriminatory terms and conditions of employment. It must be contrasted with SDA 1975 which outlaws discriminatory practices in connection with recruitment, promotion and dismissal.

It should be stressed that nevertheless EqPA 1970 is part of the anti-sex discrimination legislation. Both it and SDA 1975 came into force on the same day (29 December 1975) and are only relevant if individuals show that they have had or are having less favourable employment terms than someone of the opposite sex. It should also be noted that EqPA 1970 is not concerned with whether pay is 'fair' but only with whether discrimination between the sexes is the reason why two or more individuals have unequal terms and conditions of employment.

The Act works by implying an equality clause into every contract of employment of a person employed 'at an establishment in Great Britain' if (as is usual) one is not expressly set out. Section 1(2)(a)–(c) sets out what is meant by an equality clause. In essence it is a clause which provides that men and women must have the same terms of employment if for the same or an associated employer they are doing:

(a) like work – i.e. the same job;
(b) work rated as equivalent; or
(c) work of equal value.

'Work rated as equivalent' claims and 'work of equal value' claims are two sides of the same coin. This was stressed by the EAT in 2006 when Elias P pointed out that 'There is no justification for distinguishing between work rated as equivalent and equal value claims since they have to be read together as the implementation of the Article 141 duty to provide equal pay for work of equal value. This in our judgment is plainly so, since an equal value claim is not open to a claimant whose work has been rated as equivalent. It is not, therefore, possible to treat EqPA 1970, s.1(2)(c) as the implementation of that provision and EqPA 1970, s.1(2)(b) as providing merely an additional and purely domestic remedy' (quoted with approval by the Court of Appeal in *Redcar & Cleveland Borough Council* v. *Bainbridge & ors* [2007] IRLR 984, CA).

The Act cannot establish an unqualified claim to be the first modern British anti-discrimination law as the Sex Disqualification (Removal) Act 1919 was passed almost 90 years ago and is still on the statute book. The 1919 Act makes it unlawful for 'an organisation of workers, an organisation of employers or any other organisation whose members carry on a particular profession or trade for the purposes of which the organisation exists' to discriminate on sex grounds against any person seeking to join or continue membership of that organisation or trying to obtain or keep a professional or trade qualification needed for practising that profession or engaging in that trade.

Although EqPA 1970 was enacted some two years before Britain joined the EEC it was an important precursor to joining. It did not come into force until after Britain's membership was finalised in 1972 but was inspired by the equal pay provisions of the 1957 EEC Treaty of Rome (Art. 119 as amended, and now renumbered 141).

The House of Lords held in 1982 that this equal pay Article is directly enforceable in the UK (*Garland* v. *British Rail Engineering* [1982] ICR 420, HL). The Article continues to be so important that the main part of its wording (as amended) is set out below:

> Each Member State shall ensure that the principle of equal pay for male and female workers for equal work or work of equal value is applied.
>
> For the purpose of this article, 'pay' means the ordinary basic or minimum wage or salary and any other consideration, whether in cash or in kind, which the worker receives directly or indirectly, in respect of his employment, from his employer.
>
> Equal pay without discrimination based on sex means:
>
> (a) that pay for the same work at piece rates shall be calculated on the basis of the same unit of measurement;
> (b) that pay for work at time rates shall be the same for the same job.

The distinction between the rights set out in EqPA 1970 and those set out in SDA 1975 mirrors a similar distinction in European law. The Treaty of Rome and the Equal Pay Directive 75/117/EC are concerned only with equality of 'pay'. There is another Directive which covers sex discrimination 'as regards access to employment, vocational training and promotion and working conditions'. This is the Equal Treatment Directive (76/207/EEC, itself later amended by Directive 2002/73/EC), which was adopted in 1976, using a power reserved in the Treaty of Rome to plug loopholes, as by that time it was felt that the wording of the Equal Pay Directive and of Art.119 (as it then was) was insufficiently broad.

Although in European law there is considerable overlap between the equal pay and the equal treatment rules, in Britain there is no overlap between rights and duties arising under EqPA 1970 on the one hand and SDA 1975 on the other. Indeed, not only is there no substantive overlap but also in some cases there are separate procedural requirements for bringing claims under each of them (SDA 1975, s.8 and *Glasgow City Council* v. *Marshall* [2000] ICR 196, HL).

In 1982 the ECJ ruled that British law did not properly implement EEC law in so far as 'work of equal value' claims were concerned (*EC Commission* v. *UK* [1982] ICR 578, ECJ). This was on the basis that the procedural requirements made it impracticable for an individual to pursue a complaint.

To correct the position the government introduced new 'work of equal value' provisions in 1983 and made changes to what were then called the industrial tribunals' 'complementary rules of procedure'. It was during introduction of these provisions at a renowned late evening House of Commons session that the Under-Secretary of State at the Department of Employment, the late Alan Clark MP, clearly uninterested in the detail of what he was introducing, was as ready to admit boredom with his subject as the opposition was to accuse him of being drunk.

These improvements were insufficient to remove delay and complexity. The main criticism was the requirement for an independent expert to prepare a report whenever an equal value case was brought under EqPA 1970. The UK government took heed of the criticisms and in 1996 amended the Act to give employment tribunals discretion to decide whether to appoint an independent expert or to determine an equal value case without outside assistance (save where 'there are no reasonable grounds for determining that the work is of equal value', in which case the tribunal has no discretion and must 'proceed to determine the question itself' (EqPA 1970, s.2A(1) as amended by Sex Discrimination and Equal Pay (Miscellaneous Amendments) Regulations 1996).

A new Code of Practice on Equal Pay, issued by the then Equal Opportunities Commission (now merged into the Equality and Human Rights Commission) came into force on 1 December 2003 replacing a 1997 Code of the same name. The 2003 Code includes a summary of guidance on how to carry out an equal pay review.

17.2 RECENT IMPORTANCE OF THE EQUAL PAY ACT

Equal pay claims in the public sector were just beginning to have considerable significance as we wrote the last edition of this book in 2005. Since then they have mushroomed and have put the finances of many local authorities under enormous strain. There were only 23 successful 'work of equal value' claims in the 10 years 1984 to 1994, but in 2006/07 there were very nearly as many equal pay claims as there were unfair dismissal claims. The number of claims going to employment tribunals has more than doubled each year for the last four years (there were 3,000 equal pay claims in 2003/04; 8,000 in 2004/05; 17,000 in 2005/06; and 44,000 in 2006/07). Expressed as percentages of the total number of claims to employment tribunals the figures are even starker – 5.2 per cent in 2004/05; 8.5 per cent in 2005/06 and 18.4 per cent in 2006/07.

In 2007 the government announced that 46 local authorities in England would be given permission to break normal rules and spend £500m of capital to settle equal pay claims but even this is clearly insufficient.

The underlying reason for this explosion in equal pay claims was that until 2003 successful claimants were subject to a two year back-dating limit. This was changed with effect from July 2003 (by the Equal Pay Act 1970 (Amendment) Regulations 2003, SI 2003/1656 inserting new EqPA 1970, s.2ZB for England and Wales and EqPA 1970, s.2ZC for Scotland). Since then a person making an equal pay claim has been able to claim up to six years' arrears (12 years if the employer deliberately concealed a relevant fact without knowledge of which the individual could not reasonably have been expected to institute the proceedings or if the claimant was under a disability at the time of the contravention to which the proceedings relate – 'disability' here referring to a legal disability and having nothing to do with physical or mental disability).

The changes had to be made because the European Court of Justice ruled in 1998 and 1999 that the two year back-dating restriction was inconsistent with Art.141 of the EC Treaty of Rome and the Equal Pay Directive 75/117/EC (*Levez* v. *T.H. Jennings (Harlow Pools) Ltd*, ECJ Case C-326/96 and *Magorrian and Cunningham* v. *Eastern HSS Board*, ECJ Case C-246/96). The ECJ ruled that equal pay claims could be backdated as far as 8 April 1976, the date of its ruling in *Defrenne* v. *SABENA* [1976] ICR 547. However, the EAT held (in *Levez* v. *T.H. Jennings (Harlow Pools) Ltd* [2000] ICR 58) that there should be a six-year long stop in the UK, this period being 'derived from equivalence with the six-year limitation period applicable to ordinary domestic claims' under the Limitation Act 1980. This is now reflected in EqPA 1970, s.2ZB. The introduction of this section in 2003 meant that the value of many potential equal pay claims increased by 300 per cent in one fell swoop.

Two other subsidiary factors have contributed to the huge increase in the number of claims.

Firstly, under the terms of a 'Single Status Agreement' concluded in 1997, local authorities agreed with trade unions that over the following 10 years formal job evaluations would establish which council jobs should be regarded as at the same level as each other and should therefore receive the same rate of pay. By their very nature job evaluation schemes, which in effect attempt to compare chalk with cheese, are as much an art as a science and so it is not surprising that they can lead to unexpected results. For example, cooks might be graded as equivalent to joiners. In practice there has been a pay differential of around £3 to £4 per hour between the two. Cooks are mainly female and joiners are mainly male so it is easy to see how cooks can benefit from the equal pay legislation. As equal pay awards can now be back-dated for up to six years, the aggregate amounts involved are enormous. The position can be made even worse for local authorities as in negotiating equal pay settlements with unions they are likely to agree phasing in of pay protection, thus opening the door for women who might have already agreed settlement of their original claims to make further claims.

Secondly, cut backs in legal aid in the 1990s led to lawyers developing, and being allowed to develop, other ways of helping the less affluent member of society. Conditional fee agreements, commonly known as 'no win, no fee', became popular. After the 2003 introduction of s.2ZB clever lawyers, especially in the canny north east of England, quickly realised that, combined with the lifting of advertising restrictions previously imposed on them, this provided an opportunity to help female local authority staff claim their newly increased rights to equal back pay and at the same time substantially increase their own fee income. Indeed it can thus be argued that while in theory legal aid cut backs should have led to a saving in public expense, in practice they have directly contributed to uncontrolled and massive increases in local authority costs.

One of the final recommendations of the outgoing Equal Opportunities Commission before it was merged into the Equality and Human Rights Commission in October 2007 was for a moratorium on all new equal pay claims. The EOC suggested that employers should be allowed three years to address any outstanding discriminatory pay issues because 'the flood of pay claims brought recently against local authorities is pushing the tribunal system to breaking point'. While if implemented this might provide a breathing space for tribunals, it will not address the underlying economic and cash problem for employers.

17.3 EQUAL PAY ACT BASICS

The Act operates in an unusual way. It does not take the straightforward route of providing that men and women must have 'equal pay for equal work' as Art.141 of the Treaty of Rome does. Instead, whether or not known to employers and employees, it inserts a statutory 'equality clause' into all employment contracts (for employment in Great Britain) unless there is already an express equality clause in a particular contract. Breach of this statutorily implied clause is a breach of contract (EqPA 1970, s.1(1) as substituted by SDA 1975, s.8(1)).

In essence this implied 'equality clause' is a clause which has the effect that men and women must have the same terms of employment (whether concerned with pay or not) if they are doing work of equal value, like work or work rated as equivalent. It does this by automatically modifying any clause in an individual's contract which makes for less favourable terms of employment than the terms of employment of a comparator of the opposite sex who is doing work of equal value, like work or work rated as equivalent. The modification is to be whatever is required to make sure that neither contract is less favourable than the other in so far as terms and conditions of employment are concerned (EqPA 1970, s.1(2)(a)–(c), as substituted by SDA 1975, s.8(1)).

'Employment' has a wide meaning for purposes of EqPA 1970. A person is 'employed', and therefore protected by the Act, not only if that person is an employee in the normal sense (i.e. 'employed under a contract of service or of apprenticeship') but also if he is a self-employed independent contractor working under 'a contract personally to execute any work or labour' (EqPA 1970, s.1(6)(a)).

Any term in any agreement which purports to exclude or limit any provision of EqPA 1970 is unenforceable by any person who would benefit from it (save that this does not apply if the agreement is one made with the assistance of an Acas conciliation officer to settle an EqPA 1970 complaint) (SDA 1975, s.79(3) and (4)).

17.4 COMPARATORS

It follows from the above that the entitlement of a successful applicant to an award under the equal pay legislation is an entitlement to be put in the same position as the chosen comparator. There is no right to claim additional benefit, for example, on the basis that the chosen comparator was at a junior level and his earnings would have been higher if he had had the same level of seniority as the claimant (*Enderby* v. *Frenchay Health Authority & Anor (No. 2)* [2000] ICR 612, CA).

It used to be thought that the comparator had to be someone working for the same employer but it is now accepted that this is not always essential provided that the relationship between two different employers is sufficiently close (*Allonby* v. *Accrington & Rossendale College & ors* [2001] ICR 1189, CA and *South Ayrshire Council* v. *Morton* [2002] ICR 956, CS). However, for the relationship to be sufficiently close differences in pay of the workers concerned must 'be attributed to a single source' (*Lawrence & ors* v. *Regent Office Care Ltd & ors* [2003] ICR 1092, ECJ) and the male and female workers being compared must be in 'comparable situations' (*Österreichischer Gewerkschaftsbund, Gewerkschaft der Privatangestellten* v. *Wirtschaftskammer Österreich*, ECJ Case C-220/02, 8 June 2004).

EMPLOYMENT LAW HANDBOOK

Civil servants can only use comparators from their own department. Although they are all employed by the Crown their pay cannot be attributed to a single source as the reality is that different departments are responsible for setting different levels of pay (*Department for Environment, Food and Rural Affairs* v. *Robertson & ors* [2005] ICR 750).

If comparison is being made between groups of employees, a work of equal value claim made by one group on the basis that the disparity in pay between them and a group of higher paid fellow employees who are predominantly of one sex is unlawful can succeed even if the disadvantaged group is not predominantly of the other sex (*Home Office* v. *Bailey* [2005] EWCA Civ 327, CA, 22 March 2005).

The ECJ has ruled that for purposes of the Equal Pay Directive 75/117/EC 'comparisons are confined to parallels which may be drawn on the basis of concrete appraisals of the work actually performed by employees of different sex within the same establishment or service' (*McCarthy Ltd* v. *Wendy Smith*, ECJ Case C-127/79, 27 March 1980). It therefore follows that hypothetical comparators cannot be used in Equal Pay Act cases. To do so would 'not enable the concrete appraisal which . . . is the bedrock of art 141' and would 'not provide the secure factual premise which enables the proper and precise extent of the . . . discrimination to be determined' (Elias P in *Walton Centre for Neurology and Neurosurgery NHS Trust* v. *Bewdley* [2008] IRLR 588, EAT).

For this reason it follows that no comparison can be made with a successor as opposed to a predecessor – by definition a successor must be hypothetical in relation to the period in respect of which the claim is being made (*Walton Centre for Neurology and Neurosurgery NHS Trust* v. *Bewdley* (unreported, EAT, 23 May 2008)). Previous authority to the contrary (*Diocese of Hallam Trustee* v. *Connaughton* [1996] ICR 860, EAT) is wrong.

There is an exception to the general rule that a hypothetical comparator cannot be used in equal pay cases. In pregnancy-related cases it is obviously impossible to find a direct male comparator as pregnancy is a uniquely female condition. For this reason any provisions in EqPA 1970, s.1 which impose a requirement for a male comparator must be disapplied in pregnancy-related cases (*Alabaster* v. *Woolwich plc & anor* [2005] ICR 1246, CA). A similar rule already existed in cases brought under SDA 1975 (*Webb* v. *Emo Air Cargo (UK) Ltd* [1995] ICR 1021, HL, in which the House of Lords, following the lead of the European Court, laid down that no male comparator (not even a hypothetical one) is needed in pregnancy-related cases).

17.5 EXTENDED MEANING OF 'PAY'

As noted above, the EC equal pay provisions give a wide meaning to the word 'pay'. As a result EqPA 1970 is worded so that it does not cover only 'pay' as such. Right at the outset the Act spells out that it is dealing with the terms of employment contracts 'whether concerned with pay or not'. For the practical purpose of determining exactly what forms of discrimination are outlawed by the Act in the employment field, 'pay' can therefore be regarded as synonymous with 'terms and conditions of employment' (EqPA 1970, s.1(2)).

Ex-gratia perks are pay within Art.141 of the Treaty of Rome. Even if they are post-retirement perks such as a travel concession they cannot be refused to women if they are given to men (or vice versa) simply on sex/gender grounds (*Garland* v. *British Rail Engineering* [1982] ICR 420, HL).

Both statutory and contractual severance payments, including redundancy pay, count as pay within Art.141 of the Treaty of Rome and therefore must be available on the same terms to men and women (*R.* v. *Secretary of State for Employment, ex parte EOC and Day* [1994] ICR 317, HL).

Unfair dismissal compensation is pay within Art.141 of the Treaty of Rome (*R.* v. *Secretary of State for Employment, ex parte Seymour-Smith* [1999] ICR 447, ECJ).

Statutory maternity pay (SMP) is pay within Art.141 of the Treaty of Rome (*Gillespie & Ors* v. *Northern Health and SS Board* [1996] ICR 498, ECJ).

The original version of EqPA 1970 (and of SDA 1975) exempted terms and conditions which related to death and retirement. However, this was found to be contrary to Art.119 (now renumbered 141) of the Treaty of Rome and in 1986 the UK therefore made appropriate changes to bring UK law into line with European requirements (*Garland* v. *British Rail Engineering* [1982] ICR 420, HL and Sex Discrimination Act 1986). As a result it has been illegal since 7 November 1987 for an employer to have different retirement ages for men and women doing the same job, independently of the Age Regulations introduced almost 20 years later in 2006 (*Marshall* v. *Southampton and South West Hampshire HA (No.1)* [1986] ICR 335, ECJ).

The EC originally envisaged gradual introduction over a period of six to seven years of the right of men and women to equal pension ages under occupational pension schemes. This relatively relaxed timetable was upset by a ruling of the European Court on 17 May 1990 that pensions had been 'pay' all along within the meaning of the Treaty of Rome, Art.119 and were therefore already covered by equalisation rules (*Barber* v. *Guardian Royal Exchange Assurance Group* [1990] ICR 616, ECJ). The immediate panic reaction in the UK was that most occupational pension schemes would have to give men full pensions at 60 instead of 65. The CBI estimated the cost to British industry of funding the resulting unexpected pension liabilities at around £40 billion and that massive unemployment could result.

The ECJ backpedalled when it understood the enormity of what it had done. In 1995 it mitigated the effect of the 1990 *Barber* decision noted above by holding that the ruling applies only to benefits accruing after 17 May 1990, the date of the judgment (*Ten Oever* v. *Stichting Bedrijfspensioenfonds voor het Glazenwassers en Schoonmaakbedrijf* [1995] ICR 74, ECJ Case C-109/91). In effect this gave the ECJ's seal of approval to what is called 'the Barber Protocol 2' in the 1992 Maastricht Treaty of 1992. The Barber Protocol 2 provided that, except in cases which had already been started, 'benefits under occupational social security schemes shall not be considered as remuneration if and in so far as they are attributable to periods of employment prior to 17 May 1990'.

The overall position so far as age of entitlement to benefits under occupational pension schemes is concerned is that all new schemes must adopt equal pension ages for males and females. All existing occupational pension schemes must ensure that benefits accruing after 17 May 1990 are available equally to men and women (Pensions Act 1995, ss.62 and 63; Occupational Pension Schemes (Equal Treatment) Regulations 1995, SI 1995/3183 as amended by the Occupational Pension Schemes (Equal Treatment) (Amendment) Regulations 2005, SI 2005/1923 with effect from 10 August 2005).

Where a court or employment tribunal finds that there has been a breach of an equality clause which relates to the terms on which persons become members of the scheme (including any terms concerning the age or length of service needed for becoming a member of the scheme), the court or tribunal may declare that a woman has a right to be admitted to the scheme with effect from such date as it may specify provided that, in any case, that date is not earlier than 8 April 1976 (EqPA 1970, s.2(6A) and (6D) inserted by the Occupational Pension Schemes (Equal Treatment) (Amendment) Regulations 2005, SI 2005/1923 with effect from 10 August 2005).

Local government employees' pension rights are equalised as from 17 May 1990 under separate regulations (Local Government Superannuation (Equality and Maternity Absence) Regulations 1995, SI 1995/901).

Access to occupational pension schemes for women must not be on different terms than for men simply on sex/gender grounds (*Bilka-Kaufhaus GmbH v. Weber von Hartz* [1987] ICR 110, ECJ).

In the context of a work of equal value claim by female workers, a somewhat controversial approach to the calculation of an hourly rate for comparison was applied in 2005 by the Court of Appeal. The Court of Appeal agreed with the EAT that allowances and benefits paid to male comparators should be aggregated with their basic hourly wage and divided by the total number of hours worked in order to arrive at an hourly rate for the purposes of comparison with earnings of part-time female workers (*Redcar & Cleveland Borough Council & anor v. Degnan & ors* [2005] IRLR 615, CA).

Finally in relation to pensions, state retirement pensions are temporarily excluded from EC equality obligations. Thus the UK can still lawfully require men to wait until age 65 for their state retirement pensions even though women have the right to receive them at age 60. The UK is equalising male/female state pension ages at 65, phasing in the change between 2010 and 2020 (EC Directive 79/7/EEC, Art.7 and Pensions Act 1995, s.126 and Sched.4, Part I).

17.6 DEFENCES

Employers who fail to ensure that male and female employees get equal pay for equal work, and are sued under EqPA 1970 as a result, have a good defence if the inequality is 'genuinely due to a material factor which is not the difference in sex'.

If there are different pay levels for male and female employees and the reasons for the difference are gender related, employers are automatically assumed to be infringing the EqPA 1970 implied term unless they can justify the inequality. However, the Act is concerned with sex discrimination not with fairness generally so no justification is needed if the reasons for the pay difference are not gender related (*Glasgow City Council* v. *Marshall* [2000] ICR 196, HL). This case (along with *Strathclyde Regional Council* v. *Wallace & ors* [1998] ICR 205, HL and *Parliamentary Commission for Administration* v. *Fernandez* [2004] ICR 123, EAT) suggests that there is no need for the reasons for the pay difference to be justified if they are not gender related. That has been doubted in various cases but the EAT specifically confirmed in July 2007 that under current law this is correct (*Middlesbrough Borough Council* v. *Surtees & ors (No. 1)* [2007] IRLR 869, EAT). Thus if an employer can prove a non-sex based reason for differences in pay between men and women (i.e. a reason which is not even tainted by sex-based factors) then that is a complete answer to any claim, direct or indirect, for equal pay pursuant to EqPA 1970.

Thus to establish the 'genuine material difference factor' defence it is enough for the employer to show that differences in pay are genuinely due to factors which are (a) material and (b) do not include a difference in sex. The employer does not have to show that the difference is objectively justifiable.

It follows that items such as London weighting, qualifications and productivity can be taken into account. Matters of this type make up what the Court of Appeal has called 'the personal equation' (*Fletcher* v. *Clay Cross (Quarry Services) Ltd* [1979] ICR 1, CA). This is clearly the case if the differences are totally non-sex related. However, it is not so clear when long service and greater experience are the material difference if most of those with longer service and greater experience are males and the others female. The position was partially clarified by the European Court of Justice in 2006. The ECJ ruled that a pay system under which employees with long service and more experience get higher pay than those with short service and less experience does not, save in 'inappropriate cases', infringe EU Equal Pay rules even though most of the shorter service employees are female and most of the longer service employees are male (*Health & Safety Executive* v. *Cadman* [2006] ICR 1623, ECJ). The 'inappropriate cases' exception means, of course, that the position is not black and white. The criterion seems to be whether or not in a particular case there can be 'serious doubt' that rewarding employees by reference to long service is in the commercial best interest of the employer. It has been suggested by an employment tribunal that 'the serious doubts exception seems to us only to be likely to apply in the case of a relatively unskilled worker, and not at all at a professional/managerial level' and that it must relate to the specific job not to the length of service pay scales (*Wilson* v. *Health & Safety Executive*, currently under appeal to the EAT).

Historical reasons on their own are not enough to be a 'genuine material factor other than a difference in sex' (*South Tyneside Metropolitan Borough Council* v. *Anderson & ors* [2007] IRLR 715, CA).

An automatic transfer of employment under the TUPE regulations from a previous service provider or the previous owner of a business to a replacement service provider or the new owner of the business which results in differences in pay between the transferred employees and other staff can be a 'genuine material factor' which provides a valid defence to an employee's claim under EqPA 1970 (*Nelson* v. *Carillion Services Ltd* [2003] IRLR 428,CA).

Further, a genuine mistake, such as mistakenly putting an employee on the wrong salary grade, is unlikely to be sex discriminatory at all and can be a 'genuine material factor' (*Yorkshire Blood Transfusion Service* v. *Plaskitt* [1994] ICR 74, EAT).

If there is more than one reason for male and female employees having different pay for equal work then, in so far as they include a reason which constitutes a 'genuine material factor' the effect must be calculated proportionately. Thus, in one case, male shift workers got extra pay both because they worked on rotating shifts and because they worked anti-social hours. Women who also worked anti-social hours claimed equal pay. Both the EAT and the Court of Appeal held that the employer could successfully use the 'genuine material factor' defence on the basis that the difference in pay was due to the fact that the men worked on rotating shifts even if the unsocial hours element was recognised as having some causative effect (*Calder & Ciakowsky* v. *Rowntree Mackintosh Confectionery Ltd* [1993] ICR 811, CA).

Further 'defences' are available in three specific situations:

1. Where special terms of employment are provided for women in order to comply with laws regulating the employment of women (such laws, other than gender-specific health and safety regulations, were generally repealed as from January 1990 by the Employment Act 1989).
2. Where special terms of employment provide special treatment for women in connection with pregnancy or childbirth.
3. Where there are special terms related to membership of or rights under an occupational pension scheme and which are permitted under the Pensions Act 1995 (EqPA 1970, s.6 as amended and Equal Treatment Directive 76/207/EEC, Art.2(3); *British Airways (European Operations at Gatwick) Ltd* v. *Moore and Botterill* [2000] ICR 678, EAT).

17.7 WHAT IS 'LIKE WORK'?

Men and women working for the same employer (including an associated employer) are entitled to the same pay and other terms and conditions if employed on 'like work'.

A woman is to be regarded as employed on like work with a man if their work is:

> of the same or a broadly similar nature, and the differences (if any) between the things she does and the things they do are not of practical importance in relation to terms and conditions of employment; and accordingly in comparing her work with theirs regard shall be had to the frequency or otherwise with which any such differences occur in practice as well as to the nature and extent of the differences.
>
> EqPA 1970, s.1(4)

The fact that a promoted woman undertakes more duties than her male predecessor in the same job cannot result in a conclusion that their work is not 'like work' within the meaning of EqPA 1970 and so justify her being paid less than him (*Sita UK Ltd* v. *Hope* (unreported, EAT, 8 March 2005)).

Differences in levels of responsibility can be differences of 'practical importance' justifying different levels of pay (*Eaton Ltd* v. *Nuttall* [1977] ICR 272, EAT).

The European Court of Justice has held that it can be lawful to remunerate employees on different pay scales even if most of the higher paid are men and most of the lower paid are women and they are all doing the same work if the reason for the difference is a difference in qualifications not the difference in sex (*Angestelltenbetriebsrat der Wiener Gebietskrankenkasse* v. *Wiener Gebietskrankenkasse* [2000] ICR 1134, ECJ Case C-309/97).

17.8 PROCEDURE AND TIME LIMITS

17.8.1 Time limit on bringing claim

Claims under EqPA 1970 are normally time barred if brought more than six months after the end of the employment in question. However, as from 19 July 2003, there are three circumstances in which time does not start to run until something else has happened. The three cases are essentially:

(i) where the claimant did not discover the qualifying fact (or could not with reasonable diligence have discovered it) during the period when a 'stable employment relationship' subsisted (EqPA 1970, s.2ZA(4)); or

(ii) where the employer deliberately concealed a relevant fact (called a 'qualifying fact') without knowledge of which the individual could not reasonably have been expected to institute the proceedings (EqPA 1970, s.2ZA(5)); or

(iii) where the claimant was under a disability at any time during the six months which would otherwise apply. 'Disability' for this purpose refers to a legal disability (i.e. being under age or mentally incapable) and has nothing to do with the definition used in DDA 1995 (EqPA 1970, ss.11(2A) and 2ZA(6)).

In those three cases the six months does not start to run until the claimant has become aware of the qualifying fact or the disability has ended as the case may be (EqPA 1970, s.2ZA inserted by Equal Pay Act 1970 (Amendment) Regulations 2003, SI 2003/1656, reg.4).

Thus in a 'stable employment case' the six months runs from '... the day on which the stable employment relationship ended' (EqPA 1970, s.2ZA(4)). The EAT has ruled that where there has been a series of short fixed-term contracts (typically a school teacher employed on a series of short contracts reflecting the terms in the academic year) the six months' limitation period runs from the end of the last contract forming part of that stable employment relationship not from the end of the stable employment relationship itself if that is different (*Jeffery & ors* v. *Sec'y of State for Education & anor* [2006] ICR 1062, EAT).

17.8.2 Compensation

As noted above (**section 17.2**) until July 2003 compensation in EqPA 1970 cases was restricted to back pay for the two years before the claim was made, and was then increased to six years back pay.

The 8 April 1976 long-stop noted at **section 17.2** specifically applies in cases where the complaint relates to exclusion from membership of an occupational pension scheme (Occupational Pension Schemes (Equal Treatment) Regulations 1995, SI 1995/3183, regs.5 and 10 as substituted by the Occupational Pension Schemes (Equal Treatment) (Amendment) Regulations 2005, SI 2005/1923, regs.5(2) and 6).

17.8.3 Employment tribunal rules of procedure

Technically, the ordinary civil courts have jurisdiction in equal pay cases because EqPA 1970 operates by implying an 'equality clause' into every employment contract which does not have one (EqPA 1970 s.1(1)). However, employment tribunals also have jurisdiction and it is normal to bring equal pay claims in an employment tribunal (EqPA 1970, s.2(1)) Indeed, in practice the civil courts will normally transfer any such claim to an employment tribunal (EqPA 1970, s.2(3)).

Some changes are made to the normal employment tribunal rules of procedure in 'work of equal value' cases brought under EqPA 1970, s.1(2)(c). A separate set of rules, formerly called the 'complementary rules of procedure' but now called 'the Employment Tribunals (Equal Value) Rules of

Procedure', applies in such cases. The rules are currently in the Employment Tribunals (Constitution and Rules of Procedure) Regulations 2004, SI 2004/1861, Sched.6 (added by the Employment Tribunals (Constitution and Rules of Procedure) (Amendment) Regulations 2004, SI 2004/2351). Unlike their predecessors, these rules of procedure apply in Scotland as well as in England and Wales. These rules do not apply to other claims under EqPA 1970 (e.g. claims claiming unequal pay for 'like work' or for 'work rated as equivalent').

Until 1996 the most important difference between the normal rules of procedure and what were then called the complementary rules was that the complementary rules imposed an absolute requirement on employment tribunals to commission an expert to prepare a job evaluation report before entertaining a work of equal value claim. This requirement was a cause of great delays and difficulty in the 1980s and 1990s. There were only 23 successful 'work of equal value' claims in the 10 years starting January 1984 and they could take years. For example, two 'work of equal value' cases started in industrial tribunals in 1986 were still not completed by the end of 1995 – the final decision in *British Coal Corp* v. *Smith* [1996] ICR 515, HL took 10 years and in *Enderby* v. *Frenchay Health Authority & Anor (No.2)* [2001] ICR 612, CA the final decision did not come until February 2000, some 14 years after the case started.

As a result of the criticisms the offending parts of EqPA 1970, s.2A(1) and the rules of procedure were changed with effect from 31 July 1996. Employment tribunals now have discretion as to whether or not to commission a job evaluation report in 'work of equal value' cases save where 'there are no reasonable grounds for determining that the work is of equal value', in which case the tribunal has no discretion and must 'proceed to determine the question itself' (Sex Discrimination and Equal Pay (Miscellaneous Amendments) Regulations 1996 amending EqPA 1970, s.2A(1) and the Employment Tribunals (Constitution and Rules of Procedure) Regulations 2004, SI 2004/1861, Sched.6, r.4(3)(b), as amended). There is no specific provision as to costs in such a case but the rule includes a general power for tribunals to 'consider whether any further orders are appropriate' (r.4(3)(g)). The EAT has ruled that if an employment tribunal has appointed an independent expert it is open to a party to appoint its own expert who can challenge the methodology of the tribunal-appointed expert but must not challenge facts which have already been found (*Middlesbrough Borough Council* v. *Surtees & ors (No. 2)* [2008] ICR 349, EAT).

The 2004 rules of procedure noted above give tribunals new case management powers in relation to work of equal value claims and generally attempt to simplify procedures and speed up progress of claims. They came into force on 1 October 2004 at the same time as the Equal Pay Act 1970 (Amendment) Regulations 2004, SI 2004/2352 which amend EqPA 1970, s.2A to allow the employment tribunal to choose to determine the question of equal value itself or to appoint an independent expert to prepare a report on that question. If there has already been a job evaluation study which has given different values to the work of the claimant and the comparator, the employment tribunal must strike out the claim unless it has reasonable grounds for suspecting that the study was flawed (SI 2004/2352, reg.2).

Even though this new version of the rules gives a wide discretion, an employment tribunal must nevertheless be careful not to be too cavalier in refusing to allow applicants an adjournment so as to have time to get a proper job evaluation report prepared if they believe it would assist their case (*Wood & ors* v. *William Ball Ltd* [2000] ICR 277, EAT and *Levy* v. *Dudley Bower Facilities Management Ltd* (unreported, EAT, 22 May 2002)).

17.8.4 Interest on awards

Employment tribunals have power to order interest to be paid on any awards they make under EqPA 1970. If interest is awarded it will begin to accrue from the day after the tribunal's decision is sent to the parties and the normal 42-day wait period does not apply. No interest will be payable if the full amount of the award is paid to the complainant within 14 days after the decision is sent out (Employment Tribunals (Interest on Awards in Discrimination Cases) Regulations 1996, SI 1996/2803 and Employment Tribunals (Interest) Order 1990, SI 1990/479, art.2(1)).

17.8.5 EqPA 1970 questionnaires

A new system of questionnaires to help potential claimants discover whether their employer may be providing better terms and conditions to a fellow employee who is of the opposite sex was instituted from 6 April 2003 under Employment Act 2002, s.42 (inserting a new s.7B into EqPA 1970, with details fleshed out by the Equal Pay (Questions and Replies) Order 2003, SI 2003/722).

EqPA 1970 questionnaires follow the pattern of formal questionnaires under SDA 1975, RRA 1976 and DDA 1995. The wording is in a schedule to the Equal Pay (Questions and Replies) Order 2003, SI 2003/722. It is also incorporated into an official explanatory booklet available on the government's Equalities Office website at **www.equalities.gov.uk**. The booklet also includes guidance notes and a form for the employer's reply.

In order to be admissible in evidence in tribunal proceedings, an employee must have served the equal pay questionnaire on the employer either before lodging a complaint with the tribunal or within 21 days after making such a complaint, although a tribunal has discretion to extend time (Equal Pay (Questions and Replies) Order 2003, art.3).

Employers have eight weeks to reply (Equal Pay (Questions and Replies) Order 2003, art.4). The questionnaire and replies will be admissible as evidence. Although an employer will not have a statutory obligation to reply failure to do so deliberately and without reasonable excuse or in a way which is evasive or equivocal will entitle a court or tribunal to '. . . draw any inference which it considers it just and equitable to draw, including an inference that the respondent has contravened a term modified or included by virtue of the complainant's equality clause or corresponding term of service' (EqPA 1970, s.7B(4), inserted by Employment Act 2002, s.42).

In some cases employers may not feel able to disclose specific information because it is confidential and disclosure could result in a breach of the Data Protection Act 1998. In such a case an employment tribunal can order disclosure of relevant information. An appropriate exception in the Data Protection Act 1998, Sched.2, para.3 ensures that an employer will not be in breach of that Act in complying with the tribunal's order. The government said in 2006 that it was proposing to change the form of the questionnaire 'to make clear that the Data Protection Act does not prevent the provision of pay information' (see item 36 in 'Implementing the Women and Work Commission Recommendations', September 2006).

17.9 WRONGFUL DEDUCTION FROM WAGES CLAIMS

In view of the complexity of claims under EqPA 1970 it can in some cases be more suitable to bring a case on the quite different basis that the employer has made an unlawful deduction from the employee's wages without the employee's consent, contrary to ERA 1996, s.13 (see **section 9.6**).

An extremely helpful summary of the main practical differences between bringing a claim under ERA 1996, s.13 on the one hand or EqPA 1970, s.1 on the other was set out at para.30 of the judgment of Brooke LJ in the Court of Appeal in *Alabaster v. Barclays Bank plc and Secretary of State for Social Security* [2005] ICR 1246, CA as follows:

(i) *Time limits*

    (a) ERA: three months, subject to a power to extend time where it is not reasonably practicable to present a claim within time;

    (b) EqPA: six months from the date of termination of employment, except in cases of 'concealment' and 'disability'.

(ii) *Composition of the tribunal*

    (a) ERA: Chairman sitting alone, subject to a discretion contained in s 4(5) of the Employment Tribunals Act 1996;

    (b) EqPA: Full tribunal.

(iii) *Interest to date of judgment*

    (a) ERA: No interest payable from the date of the unauthorised deduction until judgment;

(b) EqPA: interest payable from half way between the date of contravention and the date of judgment at a current rate of 6 per cent.

(iv) *Interest from date of judgment*

(a) ERA: Interest payable at judgment rate from 42 days after the relevant decision;
(b) EqPA: Interest payable at judgment rate from the relevant decision (unless full award is paid within 14 days after that date).

(v) *Free legal advice and legal services*

(a) ERA: Legal Services Commission funding not available. No assistance from the Equal Opportunities Commission ('EOC') [now part of Equality and Human Rights Commission (EHRC)];
(b) EqPA: Advice and assistance available from the EOC [EHRC].

(vi) *Provision for service of a statutory questionnaire*

(a) ERA: No provision;
(b) EqPA: Provision under s.78 of the EqPA and the Equal Pay (Questions and Replies) Order 2003, which prescribes that an adverse inference may be drawn from any failure to respond, or an evasive response.

(vii) *Victimisation during continuing employment*

(a) ERA: No protection;
(b) EqPA: Protection against discrimination (including victimisation) under SDA s.4.

(viii) *Victimisation as a reason for dismissal*

(a) ERA: Dismissal of an 'employee' for alleging that his/her statutory rights have been infringed, including a breach of ERA s.13, constitutes unfair dismissal;
(b) EqPA: Dismissal of both an 'employee' and a 'worker' by reason of victimisation constitutes unlawful discrimination.

(ix) *Victimisation post-dismissal*

(a) ERA: No protection;
(b) EqPA: Post-employment victimisation of both 'employees' and 'workers' constitutes unlawful discrimination.

(x) *Burden of proof*

(a) ERA: The burden is on the claimant to establish an unlawful deduction;
(b) EqPA. The burden of showing there has been no sex discrimination passes to the respondent once a *prima facie* case is established.

17.10 AND FINALLY . . .

A bizarre, and ongoing, twist to the equal pay saga which has developed since the last edition of this book was published in 2006 concerns trade unions. Some women who settled equal pay claims on union advice found that the settlements they had agreed were less favourable than they might have been if they had taken their claims to tribunals. Unions would commonly adopt a 'reasonable rather than maximum settlement policy' because pressing for maximum compensation for equal pay claimants would inevitably have an adverse impact on other members, both men and women – local authorities do not have unlimited funds so there would probably be redundancies as well as difficulty in negotiating future pay rises generally.

Some women decided to sue their unions for failing to act in their best interests. Knowing that there was a risk they would lose and that employment tribunals do not normally award costs, they decided the prudent course would be to bring their claims to a tribunal rather than in the courts. As most of the beneficiaries of the 'reasonable settlement' policy adopted by trade unions were men and most if not all the losers were women they could bring their claims against their union as 'normal' sex discrimination claims in the employment tribunal rather than, for example, as negligence claims in the court thus eliminating most of the cost risk.

In the lead case the women won their sex discrimination claims at an employment tribunal. However, they won only on the basis of 'indirect sex discrimination', the tribunal deciding that there had been no direct sex discrimination. The GMB appealed and the EAT ruled in its favour (*GMB* v. *Allen & Ors* [2007] IRLR 752, EAT). On appeal, the EAT held that the GMB had indeed been 'guilty' of indirect sex discrimination but it had used 'proportionate' means to achieve a 'legitimate aim' and so could successfully plead justification.

Interestingly, but entirely logically, the EAT ruled that it made no difference that the unions concerned might have been acting unlawfully in what they had done. Elias P said: '. . . the fact that the objective [i.e. making sensible settlements taking into account the interests of all members] might be achieved by using unlawful, even dishonest, practices does not necessarily mean that the means are disproportionate once it is accepted that the aim itself is legitimate . . . Once it is accepted that the objective or aim was legitimate, then in our judgment it is difficult to see how it can be alleged that the means were inappropriate'.

The Court of Appeal heard an appeal in *GMB* v. *Allen* in May 2008. Judgment was reserved. It might thus be said that this book has something in common with a detective story – save that in this case not even the authors know 'who dunnit'.

A dedicated website at **www.emplaw.co.uk/lshandbook.co.uk** provides links to judgments and other source material referred to in this chapter.

CHAPTER 18
Wrongful dismissal

18.1 GENERAL INFORMATION

'Wrongful dismissal' is a common law concept, another name for breach of contract in the employment field if the breach of contract takes the form of dismissal. Note that of course breach of an employment contract does not necessarily result in dismissal (recent examples include *Spackman* v. *London Metropolitan University* [2007] IRLR 744, Shoreditch County Court and *Wetherill & ors* v. *Birmingham City Council* [2007] IRLR 781, CA). A constructive dismissal (that is resignation by an employee in circumstances such that he is entitled to terminate his contract by reason of the employer's conduct) is by definition always wrongful dismissal. It may also be unfair dismissal and/or dismissal by reason of redundancy (see ERA 1996, s.95(1)(c) for unfair dismissal and ERA 1996, s.136(1)(c) for redundancy cases).

Unfair dismissal, on the other hand, does not exist in the common law. It is entirely a 'creature of statute' which can (and frequently does) occur even though there is no breach of contract. Many more unfair dismissal cases than wrongful dismissal cases are brought but wrongful dismissal if relevant is likely to be extremely important. As a general rule a wrongful dismissal is likely also to be unfair dismissal but this is not inevitably the case (for an example of a dismissal which was held to be 'wrongful dismissal' but not 'unfair dismissal' is *Samuel* v. *London Borough of Lewisham* (unreported, EAT, 29 November 2001)).

Typically, wrongful dismissal is most relevant in cases where employees are entitled to a long notice period or to a particularly valuable remuneration package and/or if they are subject to contractual obligations which may continue after their employment has ended (e.g. restrictive covenants). It follows that wrongful dismissal is most likely to be particularly relevant if the employee concerned was or is in a senior position. However, as indicated below, there is currently a developing trend for wrongful dismissal claims to be made by employees in less senior positions.

Technically, an employee who sues a former employer for wrongful dismissal is suing for wrongful repudiation of the employment contract by the employer. This is because as a matter of general law a party to a contract who commits a serious breach of a fundamental term is said to 'repudiate' the contract. The result is that the other party is entitled at their option to treat the contract as at an end (*Re Rubel Bronze & Metal Co Ltd and Vos Arbitration* [1918] 1 KB 315).

When the contract is an employment contract it follows that an employee who has not been dismissed can treat his contract as having been terminated by the employer if the employer acts or omits to act in a way which amounts to a serious breach of a fundamental term (whether express or implied). The employee will have been 'constructively dismissed' and will be entitled to resign and bring a wrongful dismissal claim against the employer (*Mersey Steel & Iron Co* v. *Naylor Benzon & Co* (1884) 9 App Cas 434 and *Graham Oxley Tool Steels Ltd* v. *Firth* [1980] IRLR 135, EAT). The breach must be a serious breach of contract going to the root of the employment relationship for it to have this effect – thus, for example, in one case it was held that an employer's refusal to implement a pay increase 'promised' to an employee in casual conversation at a Christmas party was not intended to create a binding obligation and did not entitle the employee to resign and claim constructive wrongful dismissal (*Judge* v. *Crown Leisure Ltd* [2005] IRLR 823, CA).

The cumulative effect of a number of incidents can amount to a fundamental breach of the implied contractual term of trust and confidence. There is no rule of law saying what circumstances suffice and what do not – it is a question of fact for the employment tribunal (*Woods* v. *W M Car Services (Peterborough) Ltd* [1982] ICR 693, CA) – and it is not necessary for any of the individual incidents, or indeed the last straw incident itself, to be a breach of contract (*Barke* v. *SEETEC Business Technology Centre Ltd* (unreported, EAT, 13 January 2006) and *GAB Robins (UK) Ltd* v. *Triggs* (unreported, EAT, 13 June 2007)). However, an entirely innocuous act on the part of the employer cannot be a 'final straw', even if the employee genuinely, but mistakenly, interprets it as hurtful and destructive of his trust and confidence in his employer – the test of whether the employee's trust and confidence has been undermined is objective (*Omilaju* v. *Waltham Forest London Borough Council* [2005] ICR 481, CA).

The 'last straw' approach cannot be used to link together matters which took place before an employee affirmed his contract and matters which took place afterwards – the slate is effectively wiped clean by an affirmation of contract by the employee (*Gibson (t/a Blandford House Surgery)* v. *Hughes* (unreported, EAT, 13 September 2006)).

The employee may instead of resigning elect to carry on, in which case he is in effect forgiving the employer for the breach and waiving his right to resign and claim constructive dismissal. How long a period must elapse before an employee who continues to work should be regarded as having waived a breach will depend on the facts – in *Bunning* v. *G.T. Bunning & Sons Ltd* [2005] EWCA Civ 983, CA, a woman who was offered and accepted different work from her employer partly because of her justified complaints about doing her previous work (she was pregnant) was held to have waived her right to claim constructive dismissal when she eventually resigned. In that case she had done the new job for two weeks without complaint. On the other hand in *Waltons & Morse* v. *Dorrington* [1997] IRLR 488 an employee who worked on for some four or five weeks before resigning in response to her employer's 'smoking at work' policy was successful in claiming that she had been constructively dismissed.

It is clear that an employee cannot have her cake and eat it. In other words she cannot affirm her contract and then change her mind later if another job opportunity comes up (*Young* v. *John D Wood & Co* (unreported, EAT, 29 September 1999)).

In *Cape Industrial Services* v. *Ambler* [2002] EWCA Civ 1264, the EAT spelt out the considerations to be taken into account in deciding whether a resignation amounts to constructive dismissal and, if so, whether that dismissal is unfair dismissal as follows:

(1) What are the relevant term(s) of the contract said to have been breached?
(2) Are the breaches alleged, or any of them, made out?
(3) If so, are those breaches or is that breach fundamental?
(4) If so, did the employee resign in response to such breach or breaches? If so, then the employee was constructively dismissed.
(5) In that event, has the employer shown a potentially fair reason for the constructive dismissal? If not, the dismissal is unfair.

Employers should not be put in a position where they are prevented from introducing improved business methods simply because of employees' refusal to accept change (*Woods* v. *W M Car Services (Peterborough) Ltd* [1982] ICR 693, CA and *Cresswell* v. *Board of Inland Revenue* [1984] ICR 508, Ch D).

It will not be constructive dismissal if an employee resigns because of conduct of someone who was neither her employer nor a fellow employee nor authorised by the employer (*Yorke & Anor (t/a Yorkes of Dundee)* v. *Moonlight* (unreported, EAT, 19 January 2007) in which the employers' father, who was not a fellow employee, had verbally abused an employee who resigned in consequence).

It is not necessary for the employee to show that the repudiatory breach by his employer was the sole cause of his resignation (*Jones* v. *Sirl and Son (Furnishers) Limited* [1997] IRLR 493). The test is not whether the breach was the sole cause, or even the effective cause of the resignation. An employee may have more than one reason for resigning and it is sufficient to entitle him to resign and claim constructive wrongful dismissal so long as the resignation is in part in response to the repudiatory breach (*Jamie* v. *Management Solution Partners Ltd* (unreported, EAT, 31 January 2006)).

Giving an employee notice of dismissal in accordance with the terms of his contract is, by definition, not a breach of contract. It follows that if the employee resigns for no good reason during the notice period he will not be able to claim wrongful constructive dismissal (*Kerry Foods Ltd* v. *Lynch* [2005] IRLR 680, EAT).

An important consequence of a wrongful dismissal, especially if it is a constructive dismissal, is that because the contract has come to an end because of the employer's own fault the employer may no longer be able to rely on any restrictive covenants in that contract (*General Billposting Co Ltd* v. *Atkinson* [1909] AC 118, HL). The practice of sending an employee home on extended 'gardening leave' can have this effect. It will be especially likely if the employee's position is such that he can claim the employer was under a duty to provide him with work and that sending him home on garden leave was a fundamental breach of contract entitling him to resign. This can sometimes catch an employer by surprise.

The law on this issue is still evolving and the rule in *General Billposting* is no longer to be regarded as of universal application. The Court of Appeal has questioned its continued relevance on the basis that it is no longer needed to give business efficacy to a contract and no longer accords with legal principles (*Rock Refrigeration Ltd* v. *Jones* [1997] ICR 938, CA).

The High Court has made it clear that an employee is not generally entitled to treat his employer's reaction to the employee's own breach as being repudiation of the employment contract by the employer. It is wrong to regard the implied term of trust and confidence as a one-way ticket for the benefit of one party regardless of the actions of the other – rather 'a balance has to be struck between an employer's interests in managing his business as he sees fit and the employee's interest in not being unfairly and improperly exploited' (*RDF Media Group Plc* v. *Clements* [2008] IRLR 207, QBD).

The remedy for 'wrongful dismissal' was traditionally to sue the employer in the county court or High Court for damages for breach of contract. Until relatively recently employment tribunals, which are entirely creatures of statute and therefore have jurisdiction only in respect of matters specifically assigned to them by statute, did not have power to consider breach of contract claims (similarly the courts had, and still have, no jurisdiction to hear claims such as unfair dismissal claims in respect of which statute gives tribunals exclusive jurisdiction) (ERA 1996, s.205(1)).

As Lord Browne-Wilkinson said in 1992, for a wronged employee 'to be forced to bring two sets of proceedings for small sums of money in relation to one dismissal is wasteful of time and money. It brings the law into disrepute and is not calculated to ensure that employees recover their full legal entitlement when wrongfully dismissed' (*Delaney* v. *Staples* [1992] ICR 483, HL).

Since July 1994 the jurisdiction of employment tribunals has been extended to deal with wrongful dismissal cases. However, there is a top limit of £25,000 on the amount of damages they can award in any particular case (Employment Tribunals Extension of Jurisdiction (England and Wales) Order 1994 and Employment Tribunals Extension of Jurisdiction (Scotland) Order 1994). There is, of course, no statutory limit on the amount that a court can award.

This cap on the amount an employment tribunal can award in a wrongful dismissal case sits oddly with the much higher top limit of compensatory award which tribunals can make in unfair dismissal cases (£63,000 since 1 February 2008), and the total absence of any cap on awards which tribunals can make in discrimination cases (Employment Relations Act 1999, s.34(4)).

This limit on the jurisdiction of employment tribunals still produces various anomalies. For example, an employment tribunal's jurisdiction to entertain contract claims does NOT extend to claims by continuing employees. Continuing employees still have to bring contract claims in the ordinary courts (*Coors Brewers* v. *Adcock* [2007] ICR 983, CA).

More obviously there is a problem if the employee is claiming more than £25,000. If an ex-employee includes a wrongful dismissal claim in his application to an employment tribunal he may be able to apply to withdraw that claim so that he can pursue it in the High Court where the £25,000 limit noted above does not apply (*Sajid* v. *Chowdhury* [2002] IRLR 113, CA). However, the High Court will only entertain a claim in these circumstances if it was formally withdrawn with the tribunal's approval rather than merely not pursued (*Sivanandan* v. *London Borough of Enfield* [2005] EWCA Civ 10, 20 January 2005).

The Court of Appeal made it clear in 2006 that if matters get to the stage where an employment tribunal has given judgment, the cause of action is then merged in that judgment. The claim ceases to exist independently of the judgment and the claimant no longer has a cause of action for any excess above £25,000. The case is then *res judicata* (the long-established rule which prevents claimants having more than one bite at the cherry in respect of one claim – *Henderson* v. *Henderson* (1843) 3 Hare 100 and *Sheriff* v. *Klyne Tugs (Lowestoft) Ltd* [1999] ICR 1170, CA). Even if the loss is considerably greater than the £25,000 maximum which the tribunal awarded the High Court will strike out any claim for the excess (*Fraser* v. *HLMAD Ltd* [2006] IRLR 687, CA). For that reason Mummery LJ pointed out in that case that:

> ... claimants and their legal advisers would be well advised to confine claims in employment tribunal proceedings to unfair dismissal, unless they are sure that the claimant is willing to limit the total damages claimed for wrongful dismissal to £25,000 or less. If the claimant wishes to recover over £25,000, the wrongful dismissal claim should only be made in High Court proceedings.

In some cases dismissed employees have brought court proceedings for breach of the implied contractual term of trust and confidence, seeking damages of hundreds of thousands of pounds, as well as unfair dismissal claims in the tribunals. It was held by the House of Lords in July 2004 that this 'two pronged' approach is permissible provided that the facts are such that it can be shown that the breach of the implied term was quite separate from the dismissal (*Eastwood & anor* v. *Magnox Electric plc; McCabe* v. *Cornwall County Council* [2004] ICR 1064, HL).

So anomalies still arise. In *Airbus UK Ltd* v. *Wilson* (unreported, EAT, 25 April 2006) an employee deliberately refrained from claiming compensatory award on unfair dismissal so that he could pursue a claim for loss of earnings in the courts.

The trend noted above for employees with unfair dismissal claims to include breach of contract (i.e. wrongful dismissal) claims when issuing proceedings if the circumstances will support a dual claim is confirmed by the annual reports of Acas and of the Employment Tribunals Service. There are generally around 25,000 such cases each year.

Because unfair dismissal unlike wrongful dismissal does not necessarily involve any breach of contract it follows that there cannot be a constructive unfair dismissal which is not also constructive wrongful dismissal. At one stage the EAT suggested that there is an exception to this general rule if the dismissal was one to which the TUPE regulations apply but this was overruled by the Court of Appeal (*Rossiter* v. *Pendragon plc* [2002] EWCA Civ 745; [2002] ICR 1063, CA). The Court of Appeal's logic was essentially that the TUPE regulations are designed to do no more than protect existing rights of employees and do not create new rights. It therefore follows that after a TUPE transfer new employers are entitled to make changes to working conditions which could lawfully have been made without breach of contract by the original employer and it is wrong to think that the position is different just because the changes were made as the result of a TUPE transfer.

Finally, it should be noted that the employment tribunal's breach of contract jurisdiction 'precisely shadows the jurisdiction of the ordinary civil courts to hear such claims' and 'is in a different category' from its normal jurisdiction. As a result where a foreign element is involved a tribunal has the same power as a court to consider the application of the *forum non conveniens* doctrine. An employment tribunal is thus able to stay a case on the basis that the proper forum for hearing it is overseas – Hong Kong in the case in point (*Dickie and Others* v. *Cathay Pacific Airways Ltd* [2004] ICR 1733, EAT).

18.2 REMEDIES

A contract of employment is traditionally regarded as (and as most employers are small employers frequently genuinely is) a personal contract between an employee and his employer. As it would be pointless to require an employer to employ a particular individual if relations between them had broken down without hope of repair the courts have traditionally not been prepared to grant injunctions requiring an employer to employ someone or restraining an employer from wrongfully dismissing an employee. The traditional view is that, on a balance of convenience, it will normally be possible for an employee to be adequately compensated by damages for a breach of contract by the employer. Applying normal rules, an injunction will therefore not normally be granted (*American Cyanamid Co* v. *Ethicon Ltd* [1975] AC 396). An award of damages is thus the principal remedy in wrongful dismissal cases.

Whilst the position set out in the preceding paragraph reflects the traditional position, the courts have occasionally been persuaded to grant an injunction to prevent an employer from wrongfully dismissing an employee (*Jones* v. *Gwent County Council* [1992] IRLR 521 and *Powell* v. *London Borough of Brent* [1988] ICR 176, CA). The Court of Appeal has recognised that suspension of a professional person even on full pay is not a neutral act and that 'it inevitably casts a shadow over the employee's competence'. The courts will therefore grant an interim injunction in appropriate cases to prevent suspension of an employee pending a proper investigation (*Kircher* v. *Hillingdon Primary Care Trust* [2006] EWHC 21 (QB) and *Mezey* v. *South West London and St George's Mental Health NHS Trust* [2007] IRLR 244, CA).

Compensation for wrongful dismissal is a payment of, or in lieu of, damages for breach of contract. It is thus different from an award for 'unfair dismissal' which is a statutory entitlement (normally basic award calculated by formula plus compensatory award). The factors to be taken into account in assessing compensatory awards in unfair dismissal claims are similar, but not identical, to those used for assessing damages for wrongful dismissal and to that extent there are therefore overlaps between the two (*Gunton* v. *Richmond-upon-Thames BC* [1980] ICR 755, CA and *Boyo* v. *Lambeth LBC* [1994] ICR 727, CA).

For a while, at the beginning of the 21st century, it seemed that there might be an important difference between compensation for unfair dismissal and damages for wrongful dismissal. It is old established law that damages for wrongful dismissal cannot include compensation for injury to feelings (*Addis* v. *Gramophone Co Ltd* [1909] AC 488) but the House of Lords suggested in 2001 that it might now be appropriate to include compensation for injury to feelings resulting from the manner of dismissal in unfair dismissal cases (*Johnson* v. *Unisys Ltd* [2001] IRLR 279, HL). Because this suggestion had come from the House of Lords it needed another House of Lords' decision to show that it was wrong (*Dunnachie* v. *Kingston upon Hull City Council* [2004] ICR 1052, HL). It is now quite clear that neither employment tribunals in unfair dismissal cases nor the courts or tribunals in wrongful dismissal cases will award compensation for any form of non-economic 'loss', including injury to feelings.

Nevertheless damages in wrongful dismissal cases may be awarded for psychiatric illness. This is so if the illness is recognised by medical opinion as an illness, was caused by the wrongful dismissal and the claim is worded to include a claim for general damages rather than just for financial loss (*Gogay* v. *Hertfordshire County Council* [2000] IRLR 703, CA).

The same basic principles apply in assessing damages for breach of employment contracts as apply for breach of any other contract. 'The rule of common law is that where a party sustains loss by reason of a breach of contract he is, so far as money can do it, to be placed in the same situation with respect to damages as if the contract had been performed.' Thus claimants will only be compensated for loss actually suffered and must normally take reasonable steps to mitigate their loss (*Robinson* v. *Harman* (1848) 1 Exch 850 and *Radford* v. *de Froberville* [1977] 1 WLR 1262).

Although the normal rule is that 'set offs' must be made to ensure that claimants are only compensated for loss actually suffered, it is important to note two exceptions, the 'benevolent exception' and the 'insurance exception'. If as a result of being dismissed employees receive a gift from a benefactor or are able to claim on an insurance policy they will not be required to bring the gift or the insurance proceeds into account in assessing damages due to them if the dismissal was wrongful dismissal.

The rationale behind the 'benevolent exception' is that 'it would be revolting to the ordinary man's sense of justice, and therefore contrary to public policy, that the sufferer should have his damages reduced so that he would gain nothing from the benevolence of his friends or relations or of the public at large' (*Parry* v. *Cleaver* [1970] 1 AC 1, a personal injury claim in tort, but the same considerations apply in an employment context – see *Hopkins* v. *Norcross plc* [1994] ICR 11, CA).

The 'insurance exception' dates back to *Bradburn* v. *Great Western Rail Co* (1874) LR 10 Ex 1 in which a claimant received a sum of money from an insurance he had taken out which compensated him for lost income resulting from an accident caused by the negligence of the defendant. It was held that he was entitled to full damages as well as the payment from the insurer.

Occupational pension entitlements are treated in the same way as insurance proceeds for this purpose and therefore are not set off against wrongful dismissal damages (see *Parry* v. *Cleaver* [1970] AC 1, HL and *Hopkins* v. *Norcros plc* [1994] ICR 11, CA). However, it seems that this rule applies to contractual payments only. Thus the EAT has held that it would be 'just and equitable' for a senior employee who had been made redundant to bring into account a lump sum of over £150,000 paid to him under a discretionary scheme set up 'to provide a superannuation gratuity to participants' (*Hodes* v. *Marks & Spencer* (unreported, EAT, 1 November 2001)).

The exceptions apply only where it is just and equitable that they should do so. In practice this seems to mean in the case of the benevolence exception that a gift was made by third parties and in the case of the insurance exception that the insurance was taken out by someone other than the person who caused the injury. The position was examined in great detail by the Court of Appeal in a case in 2004 in which the employer's negligence led to an accident which forced the employee to take early retirement. The question was whether in calculating damages payable by the employer it was proper that the employee should bring into account sums he received from the employer's group insurance policy or whether those sums fell within the 'insurance exception' to the normal rules. The Court of Appeal held that the employee had to bring the insurance monies into account (*Gaca* v. *Pirelli General plc* [2004] EWCA Civ 373).

The courts have power to award additional damages based on 'an account of profits' but will only do so in exceptional circumstances, as when the British government successfully sought a court order diverting to it royalties payable by the British publisher of a book by the spy George Blake, a former civil servant resident in Moscow, on the basis that the book was written in breach of the terms of his contract and to ensure that 'he should not enjoy any further financial fruits from his treachery' (*Attorney General* v. *Blake* [2001] IRLR 36, HL).

The first £30,000 paid as compensation for wrongful or unfair dismissal is normally exempt from tax and NI contributions (Income and Corporation Taxes Act 1988, s.188). This covers profit made from share options exercised on the termination of employment under the terms of a termination agreement (*Porter* v. *HMRC* [2005] UKSPC SPC00501, 7 September 2005 in which Mr Porter made a profit under a scheme, this profit was taxable under s.148 of the Income and Corporation Taxes Act 1988 (now Income Tax (Earnings and Pensions) Act 2003, s.403) and was not an 'emolument of his employment' as the Revenue had argued. This meant that the first £30,000 was tax-exempt). However, even the first £30,000 will be taxable if the employee was contractually entitled to it or if it counts as a payment from an unfunded non-approved pension scheme. For this purpose an employee is treated as being contractually entitled to a lump sum if it was paid to him under a clause in his employment contract which gave the employer the right to terminate employment summarily on making a payment in lieu of notice (*EMI Group Electronics Ltd* v. *Coldicott (HMIT)* [1999] IRLR 630, CA; *Richardson (HM Inspector of Taxes)* v. *Delaney* [2001] IRLR 663).

Because the purpose of damages for breach of contract is to put the injured party into the same financial position as he would have been in if the contract had been performed properly, it follows that if and to the extent that damages for wrongful dismissal are exempt from tax (see above) they must be paid 'net' (i.e. the employer can deduct an amount equal to estimated tax and employee NI contributions). If it were otherwise claimants would collect a windfall profit and be better off as a result of being wrongly dismissed than if they had continued working (*British Transport Commission* v. *Gourley* [1955] 3 All ER 796, HL).

The starting point in assessing damages for wrongful dismissal will be the amount of salary which the employee would have earned if he had been paid in full for his contractual notice period. However, there is no rule of law that damages are limited to loss of pay and benefits resulting from an employee not being given proper notice. Thus a wrongfully dismissed innocent employee who can establish that he has suffered financial loss by reason of 'stigma by association' with a former crooked employer (for example, if he is unable to get a new job because of the stigma) can claim damages from the former employer (*Malik & Anor* v. *BCCI (in liquidation)* [1997] ICR 606, HL).

Items valued in assessing damages for wrongful dismissal include: loss of wages (up to end of contractual notice period and for loss of future earnings);

membership of pension scheme; membership of permanent health insurance scheme; life insurance benefits; medical expenses insurance (e.g. BUPA); company car and ancillary benefits (road tax, servicing, etc.); any other 'fringe benefits' or perks; and accrued holiday pay.

Damages for breach of contract are assessed by reference to loss of contractual entitlements. Therefore no account can be taken of 'reasonable expectations' (unlike in cases of tort, such as negligence) and so there will be no compensation for loss of possible but non-enforceable future salary increases (*Lavarack* v. *Woods of Colchester Ltd* [1966] 3 All ER 683).

The extent to which loss of bonuses and commissions should be taken into account can be a source of difficulty, but the basic principle of compensating for loss of contractual entitlement will be followed. There is no specific requirement for an employer to act 'reasonably' when exercising a discretion as to how much bonus to award but employers must not exercise that discretion in bad faith, arbitrarily, capriciously or irrationally or in a way which will destroy the implied term of trust and confidence between them and the employee. For this reason it is prudent for employers to ensure that the criteria for awarding bonuses are as transparent and easy to ascertain as possible. Setting out the criteria clearly can considerably reduce, and at best eliminate, the risk of a court ordering very substantial damages if the employer is accused of wrongful dismissal by a dismissed employee especially if his continuing ex-colleagues were awarded large bonuses (*Clark* v. *Nomura International plc* [2000] IRLR 766, QBD).

There is an argument that an employee who is dismissed without being given the notice to which he is contractually entitled shortly before completing a year's employment should be able to include as part of a claim for damages for wrongful dismissal a claim for compensation for loss of the opportunity to claim unfair dismissal. This argument found favour with the EAT in *Raspin* v. *United New Shops Ltd* [1999] IRLR 9, EAT but was rejected by the Court of Appeal in *Virgin Net Ltd* v. *Harper* [2005] ICR 921, CA. The Court of Appeal ruled that the contractual notice to which the employee might be entitled is irrelevant in deciding whether the employee is entitled to compensation for loss of the chance to claim unfair dismissal. The only circumstances in which an employee who has been dismissed before completing the minimum unfair dismissal qualification period (currently one year's continuous employment) can claim compensation for loss of the right to claim unfair dismissal would be either: (i) that less than the statutory minimum notice had been given but the employee would have completed the minimum qualification period of employment if it had been given; and/or (ii) the dismissal took place in one of those special cases provided by statute for which no qualifying period of employment is required to qualify for unfair dismissal rights.

The EAT ruled unequivocally in February 2005 that if an employee is wrongfully dismissed, in breach of contract, before he has acquired a statutory right not to be unfairly dismissed he is not entitled to recover common law damages from his employer for the loss of the chance of bringing an unfair dismissal claim even if under his contract of employment he could only have been lawfully dismissed after completing the one year's continuous service required to qualify for unfair dismissal rights (*Wise Group* v. *Mitchell* [2005] ICR 896, EAT). The EAT said in that case: 'Although the Court of Appeal did not say so in terms in their judgments, it appears to us that their decision in *Harper* cannot be reconciled with *Raspin.*'

There is a principle of public policy which prevents a person from recovering loss which derives from an unlawful act. Thus if a claim by an employee relies on deception (for example, failure to disclose to his employer that he suffers from a particular medical condition) damages awarded to the employee for an act of negligence by the employer will be reduced appropriately (*Hewison* v. *Meridian Shipping Services PTE Ltd* [2003] ICR 766, CA).

Companies are specifically prohibited from making payments to directors as 'compensation for loss of office' without shareholder consent (Companies Act 2006, s.217). This does not prevent payments genuinely paid in lieu of damages for breach of contract (Companies Act 2006, s.220).

In practice, a senior director who is dismissed may be in a strong position to negotiate substantial compensation for breach of contract. Paradoxically the director's negotiating position can be particularly strong if he was dismissed as a consequence of a serious failure which might lead to the company being liable to pay compensation to customers or other third parties. This is because a decision by the company to contest the claim might, depending on the circumstances, be capable of being seen as an admission of responsibility. Further a director is likely to be aware of any unpleasant 'skeletons in the cupboard' and the employing company might be concerned that contesting an ex-director's demands for compensation might lead to him revealing them in open court. This might make it impossible for the company to defend itself later against far more expensive possible claims by third parties. In such circumstances a company might take the view that it would be cheaper to pay off the director handsomely than to contest his demands.

18.3 TIME LIMITS

Different time limits apply for bringing wrongful dismissal cases in the courts on the one hand or in an employment tribunal on the other.

If a wrongful dismissal claim is brought in the courts the normal Limitation Act 1980 time limits apply. These provide that 'an action founded on simple contract shall not be brought after the expiration of six years from the date on which the cause of action accrued' (although there can be extensions in special cases, e.g. if fraud is involved) (Limitation Act 1980, ss.5 and 32).

If a wrongful dismissal claim is brought in an employment tribunal the relevant time limits are set out in the Employment Tribunals Extension of

Jurisdiction (England and Wales) Order 1994, SI 1994/1623, art.7. In essence this allows the employee three months from dismissal to present his claim and gives the employer six weeks to make a counter claim, beginning with the day on which it received a copy of the employee's originating application from the tribunal office (but see below for more detail).

Employment tribunals have power to extend these three-month and six-week periods if satisfied that it was not reasonably practicable to have complied with them (Employment Tribunals Extension of Jurisdiction (England and Wales) Order 1994, SI 1994/1623, arts.7 and 8).

One of the consequences of the fact that the jurisdiction of employment tribunals is governed entirely by statute is that wrongful dismissal claims, like other claims, can be made to a tribunal only as expressly provided. In some situations this can lead to bizarre results. The Order extending the jurisdiction of employment tribunals to breach of contract cases requires any such claim to be made within three months of:

> the effective date of termination of the contract giving rise to the claim or . . .
> where there is no effective date of termination within the period of three months beginning with the last day on which the employee worked in the employment which has terminated.
> Employment Tribunals Extension of Jurisdiction (England and Wales) Order 1994, SI 1994/1623, art.7

The 'effective date of termination' is defined to mean 'the date on which the notice expires' if notice has been given. Therefore individuals who are wrongfully dismissed may have to serve out a long notice period before they can make a claim to a tribunal even though they could bring the same claim in the county court or High Court much sooner, immediately after the breach of contract took place (ERA 1996, s.97(1)).

On the other hand, if an employer takes on a new employee but changes its mind before the new employee actually starts work the employee can bring a wrongful dismissal claim at once to a tribunal. As there will have been no 'effective date of termination' as defined the tribunal will not be constrained by the use of that term and instead will be able to give a wide 'purposive' interpretation to the more general expression 'the last day on which the employee worked' (*Capek* v. *Lincolnshire County Council* [2000] ICR 878, CA and *Sarker* v. *South Tees Acute Hospitals NHS Trust* [1997] ICR 673, EAT).

18.4 MITIGATION OF LOSS

When assessing a damages award in a wrongful dismissal case the courts and tribunals apply the normal common law rules requiring a person who is seeking damages to 'mitigate his loss'. Wrongfully dismissed employees must, in other words, do what is reasonable in the circumstances to try to find other work and the remuneration from other work will go to reduce the damages for loss of future earnings to which they may be entitled from their former employer (*British Westinghouse Electric and Manufacturing Co Ltd* v. *Underground Electric Railways Co of London Ltd* [1912] AC 673).

The Court of Appeal has given specific guidance on the matters which must be taken into account in deciding whether employees have done what they should in an effort to mitigate loss (*Wilding* v. *British Telecommuncations plc* [2002] EWCA Civ 349, [2002] ICR 1079). The guidance can be summarised as follows:

- the onus is on the employer to show that the worker unreasonably refused an offer of re-employment;
- the test of unreasonableness is an objective one based on the totality of the evidence;
- in applying that test, the attitude of the employer, the circumstances in which the offer was made and refused and the way in which the employee had been treated must be taken into account; and
- the court or tribunal must not be too stringent in its expectations of the injured party.

There is a long established rule in unfair dismissal cases that a person who has been dismissed without notice should not be required to mitigate his loss by offsetting any wages he earns during what would have been the notice period against compensation (*Norton Tool Co Ltd* v. *Tewson* [1972] ICR 501, NIRC). However, this is a special and exceptional rule which applies in unfair dismissal cases only. It does NOT apply in wrongful dismissal cases. In wrongful dismissal cases the normal common law rule applies to the effect that a claimant is under a duty to mitigate his loss and so must bring into account by way of offset against damages to which he is entitled for not being given proper notice any monies he has earned during what should have been the period of notice (see, for example, *Zepbrook Ltd* v. *Magnus* (unreported, EAT, 18 October 2006)). The Court of Appeal has suggested that the time may have come to bring the unfair dismissal position in this respect into line with the common law, wrongful dismissal, position (see *Langley & anor* v. *Burlo* [2007] ICR 390, CA).

Employees have no obligation to mitigate their loss in a way which would reduce their entitlement to 'pay in lieu of notice' under the contract. If the contract contains such a provision (a 'PILON' clause) the employee's entitlement will be contractual and the employee will therefore normally be entitled to the full amount provided for by the PILON clause if dismissed without notice, regardless of whether or not he has looked for or found other work (*Abrahams* v. *Performing Rights Society Ltd* [1995] ICR 1028, CA).

In practice, tax considerations mean that a typical employment contract is unlikely to contain an enforceable PILON clause. It is more likely that a clause dealing with notice will give the employer an option to provide pay in lieu of notice. If the contract is drafted in that way, any PILON paid on summary dismissal will not be a contractual entitlement and thus (up to £30,000) will normally be free of tax (Income and Corporation Taxes Act 1988, s.188(4)).

But the employee may have to pay a price for this tax exemption. If the employee is dismissed without notice and has no contractual right to PILON, he will not be able to sue for it as a debt if the employer fails to pay it. Instead he will have to sue for breach of contract (*viz.* for damages for dismissal without notice) and will thus be under a duty to mitigate his loss if possible.

The odd consequence is that an unscrupulous employer may be able to save money by acting in breach of contract rather than by acting properly. It can be cheaper for an employer to refuse to pay PILON if the employer is not contractually bound to do so than to pay it, even though PILON was clearly envisaged when the contract was negotiated albeit, probably for tax reasons, was worded as an option rather than as a binding obligation. By a 2:1 majority, the Court of Appeal has endorsed this view of the law – although with some misgivings including a comment to the effect that '... the [employer] may have won its appeal but they win no plaudits for their behaviour. The treatment of [the employee] was a travesty of good industrial relations. This employer will not find me at all sympathetic if it applies for its costs of the appeal' (*Cerberus Software Ltd* v. *Rowley* [2001] ICR 376, CA).

Another consequence of the application of common law rules is that if a clause in an employment contract which sets out the amount of damages to be paid in the event of breach is not capable of being regarded as a genuine pre-estimate of loss or damage it will be regarded as an unlawful and therefore unenforceable penalty. In that case, normally because the amount is unreasonably large, the employer will be able to argue that damages for wrongful dismissal should be calculated in the normal way as 'unliquidated damages', the ex-employee will be under a duty to mitigate his loss and damages will be reduced to take account of any failure by the employee to do so (*Smith* v. *Giraud UK Ltd* [2000] IRLR 763, EAT).

If a dismissed employee who is under an obligation to mitigate his loss has failed to do so (e.g. by failing to seek other work) a tribunal must form a view as to when he should have found work and how much he could reasonably expect to have earned and must not simply apply a percentage reduction. Knowledge of local conditions can thus be very important (*Peara* v. *Enderlin* [1979] ICR 804, EAT). The courts will normally allow employees about three to six months to look for a job of similar status and remuneration to the one from which they have been wrongfully or unfairly dismissed. After that, they will normally be expected to start lowering their sights (*Addison* v. *Babcock FATA Ltd* [1987] ICR 805, CA). Failure to apply for a suitable alternative position offered by the employer is conduct which is likely to result in a tribunal reducing the compensatory award it otherwise would have made (see, for example, *Fulton* v. *RMC Russell plc* (unreported, EAT, 17 December 2003) in which compensatory award was reduced by 50 per cent for this reason).

If remuneration from a new job is greater than that from the old job from which the employee was dismissed, the excess is not to be taken into account to reduce compensatory award for unfair dismissal from the old job and it seems likely that the same principle would apply to wrongful dismissal damages (*Whelan (Cheers Off Licence)* v. *Richardson* [1998] ICR 318, EAT).

If the employee gets a new job shortly after dismissal at the same or better rate of pay, but is dismissed after a few months from that new job and does not get another for some time, the question may arise as to whether compensation for loss of earnings should be limited to loss suffered until the second job started or whether it should also include compensation for the period after the second job ended. The EAT has ruled that it should include compensation for the period after the second job ended (*Cowen* v. *Rentokil Initial Facility Services (UK) Ltd t/a Initial Transport Services* (unreported, EAT, 6 March 2008); *Dawes Cycles Ltd* v. *Sedgley* (unreported, EAT, 12 March 1998); and *Dench* v. *Flynn & Partners* [1998] IRLR 653, CA). While this proposition is worth noting it should be added that in wrongful dismissal cases it is normally irrelevant as loss of earnings would be awarded only in respect of the period of notice which the employer could have given to end the contract lawfully.

Finally, in regard to loss of pension rights the (Scottish) EAT has specifically commented that:

> ... without laying down any general rule, we have very serious doubts that it is a relevant consideration with regard to loss of pension rights, that the failure on the part of the dismissed employee to obtain other pensionable employment should be regarded as a failure to mitigate. There are so many extraneous factors applying to the question of pension schemes as to make this an imponderable.
> *Wincanton Trans European Ltd* v. *Whiteford* (unreported, EAT, 28 August 2003)

A dedicated website at **www.emplaw.co.uk/lshandbook** provides links to judgments and other source material referred to in this chapter.

CHAPTER 19
Remedies and compensation

19.1 INTRODUCTION

This chapter concentrates on remedies for three common types of claim brought in employment tribunals: unfair dismissal, discrimination and redundancy.

19.2 UNFAIR DISMISSAL

19.2.1 Introduction

Tribunals have three remedies available for unfair dismissal: reinstatement, re-engagement and compensation. When ordering reinstatement or re-engagement, the tribunal will also order the employer to pay the employee a sum of money reflecting the income lost during the period of unemployment. Exceptionally, there is a fourth remedy, interim relief, which can be ordered in a few specified cases (see **section 19.2.6**).

The tribunal is under a statutory duty to explain to employees about reinstatement and re-engagement and to ask them whether they wish the tribunal to make an appropriate order (ERA 1996, s.112(2)). However, a failure by the tribunal to comply with this obligation does not automatically mean the decision will be set aside (*Cowley* v. *Manson Timber Ltd* [1995] IRLR 153, CA). The tribunal cannot order reinstatement or re-engagement if the employee does not wish it and in any event is not obliged to do so (ERA 1996, s.112(3)). If it does not make such an order it must instead make an order for compensation (ERA 1996, s.112(4)).

19.2.2 Reinstatement and re-engagement

An order for reinstatement is, as the name suggests, an order that the employee be reinstated in the same job as he occupied before dismissal. On re-engagement, the employee may be employed in similar work subject to different terms. Importantly, an order for re-engagement must specify the identity of the employer (ERA 1996, s.115(2)(a)).

In practice, these orders are not often made. Few employees request them (other than as a negotiating tactic) and even fewer tribunals accede to the request. A tribunal's decision on the practicability of reinstatement or re-engagement will almost never be overturned on appeal (*Clancy* v. *Cannock Chase Technical College* [2001] IRLR 331, EAT).

When will reinstatement and re-engagement be ordered?

In exercising its discretion, the tribunal must take into account the employee's preferred remedy, whether it is practicable for the employer to comply with an order for reinstatement or re-engagement and whether it is just to make such an order if the employee contributed to her dismissal (ERA 1996, s.116).

Factors which will influence a tribunal in deciding whether to grant reinstatement or re-engagement include: the likelihood of industrial strife if the order is made and complied with (*Bateman* v. *British Leyland (UK) Ltd* [1974] ICR 403, NIRC); the disruption to personal relationships in a small company (*Enessy Co SA* v. *Minoprio* [1978] IRLR 489); distrust between the parties (*Nothman* v. *London Borough of Barnet (No.2)* [1980] IRLR 65); an inability to trust the employee when coming into contact with the public (*Inner London Education Authority* v. *Gravett* [1988] IRLR 497); or a genuine absence of vacancies (*Cold Drawn Tubes Ltd* v. *Middleton* [1992] ICR 318, EAT).

In deciding whether to order reinstatement or re-engagement, the tribunal must disregard the fact that the employer has replaced the employee save in two cases (ERA 1996, s.116(5) and (6)). These are:

- where the employer can demonstrate that the only way of arranging for the dismissed employee's work to be done was by taking on a permanent (as opposed to a temporary) replacement, or
- where the employer engaged the replacement after the lapse of a reasonable time without hearing that the dismissed employee sought reinstatement or re-engagement, and it was reasonable at that stage to engage a permanent replacement.

If a replacement employee has to be dismissed to make way for a reinstated or re-employed worker, that dismissal will usually be fair as being 'for some other substantial reason', subject to the employer considering suitable alternative employment for the bumped replacement worker.

Terms of order

When ordering reinstatement or re-engagement, the tribunal must also order the employer to pay compensation reflecting the employee's lost earnings. This includes the value of all benefits. The tribunal must give credit for any sums received such as payments in lieu of notice or salary received from another employment (ERA 1996, ss.114(2)(a) and 115(2)(d)).

An order for reinstatement may be made following a finding of unfair dismissal on the ground that there was a failure to comply with the statutory disciplinary procedure (ERA 1996, s.98A(1)), that failure being wholly or mainly attributable to the employer's failure to comply. Where the tribunal makes an order for reinstatement or re-engagement in this situation, it must also make an award of four weeks' wages to the employee, unless it appears to the tribunal that this would be unjust to the employer (ERA 1996, s.112(5) and (6)).

The tribunal must also state the date by which the order must be complied with and any rights and privileges (including seniority and pension rights) which must be restored to the employee (ERA 1996, ss.114(2) and 115(2)).

In addition, when ordering re-engagement, the tribunal must specify the terms of re-engagement, to include the identity of the employer and the remuneration for the employee (ERA 1996, s.115(2)).

What if the employer does not comply?

Where the employee is re-engaged or reinstated, but the employer does not comply with all the terms of the order, the employer will be ordered to pay the employee such compensation as the tribunal thinks fit (ERA 1996, s.117(2)). Where the employee is not re-engaged or reinstated at all, the employee will be regarded as having been unfairly dismissed (ERA 1996, s.117(3)). The tribunal must then make a compensatory award plus an additional award of between 26 and 52 weeks' pay. A week's pay is capped for these purposes (ERA 1996, s.117(3)(b) and s.227(1)(b)). The cap is currently, as from 1 February 2008, £330 per week. The most important factor in determining where in the 26–52 week range an order should be made is the employer's motive for not complying: a deliberate flouting of the order will warrant a higher additional award than a genuine belief that it was not practicable to comply (*Mabirizi* v. *National Hospital for Nervous Diseases* [1990] IRLR 133). However, if there has already been an award of four weeks' wages when the order for reinstatement or re-engagement was made, this must be deducted from any 'additional award' (see ERA 1996, s.117(3)(b)) for non-compliance: ERA 1996, s.117(2A)).

The normal duty on an employee to mitigate his loss applies so that if the employer fails to provide reinstatement as ordered but offers appropriate alternative employment instead which the employee unreasonably rejects, he will not be able to insist on reinstatement. Whether the alternative employment offered is appropriate and whether the employee acted unreasonably in not accepting it are matters of fact for an employment tribunal. It follows that as a general rule no appeal can be entertained against the employment tribunal's decision (*Sarieddine* v. *Abou Zaki Holding Company* [2008] EWCA Civ 453, CA, 17 April 2008).

The compensatory award is subject to a statutory maximum of £63,000 (as from 1 February 2008). This figure also applies to the part of the compensatory award that reflects arrears of pay and other benefits (made under ERA

1996, ss.114 and 115) in so far as any award made under those sections is less than the statutory cap. If an award under ss.114 or 115 alone would exceed the statutory cap, then that sum is recoverable so as to allow 'full reflection' of the employee's losses in terms of ERA 1996, s.124(4); however, no further compensatory award can then be made since the statutory cap has been exceeded (*Parry* v. *National Westminster Bank plc* [2005] ICR 396, CA). It may be doubted whether this approach is consistent with the purpose of ERA 1996, s.114(2), which 'was inserted to prevent employers from benefiting from the statutory limit simply by not reinstating an employee when ordered by a tribunal' (*Awotona* v. *South Tyneside Healthcare NHS Trust* [2005] ICR 958, CA at para.21 per Keen LJ).

However, there is a defence to the additional award if the employer can establish that it was not practicable to comply with the order. An employer will normally have difficulty in showing this, because to order the reinstatement or re-engagement, the tribunal must have decided that it was practicable for the employer to comply (ERA 1996, s.117(4)). In effect the 'practicability' defence allows employers a second bite at the cherry, perhaps to introduce new evidence or to argue that their circumstances have changed since the order was originally made (*Mabirizi* v. *National Hospital for Nervous Diseases* [1990] IRLR 133).

Where an order for interim reinstatement under TULRCA 1992, s.164 is made against an undertaking, which is then TUPE transferred, the order does not transmit to the transferee (*Darling* v. *ME Ilic Haulage* [2004] ICR 1176, EAT). However, it is likely that if an order for reinstatement were made under ss.113–116 of ERA 1996, this is a liability which would transfer; as would liabilities arising out of any failure to comply with such an order.

Effect on continuity of employment

If a tribunal orders reinstatement or re-engagement, or if the parties agree reinstatement or re-engagement through Acas or as a term of a compromise agreement, then continuity of employment is deemed to be preserved (Employment Protection (Continuity of Employment) Regulations 1996, SI 1996/3147). However, if the parties simply agree to reinstate or re-engage without commencing proceedings, going through Acas or entering into a formal compromise agreement, then normal rules on continuity of employment apply (see **Chapter 11**), i.e. continuity will be broken unless the employee can demonstrate a 'temporary cessation of work', or that continuity should continue 'by arrangement or custom' (*Collison* v. *BBC* [1998] IRLR 238, EAT; *Ingram* v. *Foxon* [1985] IRLR 5).

An employee who is dismissed, reinstated and then dismissed again may be able to claim that the procedure involved amounts to an 'arrangement' within the meaning of ERA 1996, s.212(3)(c). If so, he will be able to claim continuity of employment throughout even if the continuity of employment regulations do not apply (*London Probation Board* v. *Kirkpatrick* [2005] ICR 965, EAT).

An employee who is reinstated or re-engaged after a statutory dispute resolution procedure will not suffer a break in continuity of employment for purposes of statutory maternity pay (SMP), statutory paternity pay (SPP) or statutory adoption pay (Statutory Maternity Pay (General) and the Statutory Paternity Pay and Statutory Adoption Pay (General) (Amendment) Regulations 2005, SI 2005/358).

19.2.3 Compensation: basic award

Compensation for unfair dismissal is split into two parts, both of which the unfairly dismissed employee is entitled to. The (usually) smaller part, basic award, is very similar to statutory redundancy pay and is calculated according to a strict mathematical formula. The (usually) larger part, compensatory award, is harder to predict as it is intended to compensate the employee for their financial losses and often involves speculation as to future losses.

Normal calculation

The basic award is calculated by multiplying the number of years' continuous employment by a week's pay, adjusted according to the employee's age (ERA 1996, ss.220–229). A week's pay is calculated according to a strict formula set out in the legislation. In summary, this is the gross standard weekly wage, or average wage if it fluctuates from week to week, ignoring overtime (ERA 1996, s.119).

The week's pay is capped, for these purposes, at £330 (for dismissals after 1 February 2008). Thus if an employee earns £350 per week, £20 of that is disregarded when calculating the basic award. The maximum is index linked and is adjusted each year (normally with effect from 1 February each year).

For each complete year of continuous employment, working backwards from dismissal, that the employee was aged over 41, he receives one-and-a-half weeks' pay. For each complete year of continuous employment that he was aged between 22 and 41, he receives one week's pay. For each complete year of continuous employment that he was aged below 21, he receives half a week's pay. A maximum of 20 years' work, the most recent 20 years, can be taken into account for the basic award calculation (ERA 1996, s.119). The maximum possible basic award is therefore £9,900 (i.e. 20 x 1.5 x £330). The rate must not be calculated on a figure lower than the national minimum wage (NMW) (*Paggetti v. Cobb* [2002] IRLR 861).

Special cases

Basic award can be reduced if the employee's conduct contributed to his dismissal (ERA 1996, s.122(2)). It can also be reduced if the employee has unreasonably refused an offer of reinstatement (this does not apply to an offer of re-engagement). In appropriate cases, this can reduce the basic award to zero (ERA 1996, s.122(1) and (2)). Where an employee has been awarded any amount under designated dismissal procedures, the tribunal can reduce the basic award 'to such extent as it considers just and equitable' (ERA 1996, s.122(3A)).

If the employee received a redundancy payment at the time of the dismissal, this must be set off against the basic award. In most cases, they will be precisely the same amount of money (ERA 1996, s.122(4)).

If the employee was dismissed for redundancy, and unreasonably refused an offer of suitable alternative employment, the basic award is limited to two weeks' pay (ERA 1996, s.121).

If a basic award in respect of a dismissal which was unfair for a failure to follow the statutory grievance procedures (ERA 1996, s.98A(1)), is less than four weeks' wages (before any reductions are made under s.122) the tribunal will increase the award to four weeks' wages (ERA 1996, s.120(1A)). The tribunal has discretion not to do so, however, if it considers that such an increase would result in injustice to the employer. As previously noted the statutory procedures are due to be replaced, probably by April 2009.

In certain circumstances, the law provides for a minimum basic award, set at £4,400 from 1 February 2008. This occurs if the employee is dismissed for any of the following reasons: being a safety representative; being a trustee of an occupational pension fund; being an employee representative (for consultation purposes); or because of trade union activities or membership. The £4,400 minimum can only be reduced if the employee unreasonably refused reinstatement, contributed to the dismissal or to take account of redundancy pay already received (ERA 1996, s.120).

19.2.4 Compensation: compensatory award

The compensatory award is usually the larger part of the unfair dismissal compensation. It is:

> such sum as the tribunal considers just and equitable in all the circumstances having regard to the loss sustained by the complainant in consequence of the dismissal in so far as that loss is attributable to action taken by the employer
>
> ERA 1996, s.123(1)

There is normally a maximum of £63,000 (as from 1 February 2008) that a tribunal can order to be paid by way of compensatory award. This maximum is index linked and (should) increase each February (ERA 1996, s.124(1) and (1A)). However, the £63,000 maximum does not apply in cases where the reason for the dismissal was related to whistleblowing or health and safety.

There is a vast amount of jurisprudence on calculation of the compensatory award; however, in the overwhelming majority of cases, it consists of a relatively straightforward mathematical calculation (albeit involving speculation as to the employee's future income).

Normally, the greatest difficulties arise when determining the order of deductions. To take a simple example, say an employee suffered a £75,000 loss but the award was subject to a 50 per cent reduction for contributory fault (see ERA 1996, s.123(6)). If the reduction is applied before the statutory maximum, the employee will receive £37,500. However, if the statutory maximum is applied before the reduction, the employee receives only £31,500 (i.e. 50 per cent of £63,000), a difference of £6,000. The correct order in which deductions should be made is set out in *Digital Equipment Co Ltd* v. *Clements (No.2)* [1998] ICR 258, CA; [1997] IRLR 140, EAT. These steps are described in detail in **section 19.2.5**. In addition, we have included a new 'Step 7', dealing with compensatory awards in excess of £30,000. This was not considered in *Digital Equipment Co Ltd* v. *Clements* because at that time the limit on compensatory awards was £11,000 and the issue did not arise. We have also extended 'Step 4' to take into account the impact of the statutory dismissal procedures which came into effect in 2004, six years after the *Digital Equipment* case.

The statutory disciplinary and grievance procedures introduced in October 2004 by the Employment Act 2002 brought important changes to the compensation payable to those found to be unfairly dismissed but are not considered in detail here as they are due to be replaced, probably in April 2009 (see **Chapter 4**). However, if an employer fails to comply with them while they are still in existence the tribunal must increase the award it makes by 10 per cent and has power to increase it by up to 50 per cent. Conversely, if an employee fails to comply, compensation is subject to the same percentage reductions. It should be noted that in exercising its discretion as to the amount of 'uplift' a tribunal must have regard only to the employer's failure to follow the statutory procedures. Although the rules do not themselves restrict the way in which the discretion should be exercised the EAT has held that other considerations such as the size of the employer or the way in which the employee has been treated are generally irrelevant (*Aptuit (Edinburgh) Ltd* v. *Kennedy* (unreported, EAT, 4 July 2007)).

The proposal is for these statutory procedures to be replaced by less prescriptive rules. Clause 3 of the current Employment Bill provides for tribunals to be able to adjust awards up or down by 25 per cent where parties have unreasonably failed to comply with a relevant code of practice, likely to be a revised version of the Acas Code of Practice on Disciplinary and Grievance Procedures (a draft of which was issued in May 2008 for consultation – see **section 11.4.1**).

No award for injury to feelings on unfair dismissal

Compensation for unfair dismissal covers only pecuniary losses. There can be no award for injury to feelings arising out of the dismissal (*Dunnachie* v. *Kingston upon Hull Council* [2004] ICR 1052). Matters can therefore be complicated where there is a dual claim: part based on dismissal and part based on breach of a statutory right which allows an award for injury to feelings. For example, where a worker has been subjected to a detriment for making a protected disclosure, an award for injury to feelings is permitted (ERA 1996, s.49(2)). What then is the position if an employee has been subject to a detriment but then dismissed? On dismissal, the employee loses the rights accorded to him for making a disclosure (ERA 1996, s.47B(2)), but where the principal reason for the dismissal is the disclosure, the employee is regarded as having been unfairly dismissed (ERA 1996, s.103A). In *Melia* v. *Magna Kansei Ltd* [2005] ICR 874, the employee had been subjected to a detriment for making a protected disclosure. By June 2001, the employer's conduct amounted to a repudiatory breach of contract. The claimant resigned in November 2001 and claimed constructive dismissal. He argued that an award for injury to feelings should be made up to November 2001 when he terminated his contract. The EAT disagreed. If an employee is dismissed for making a protected disclosure, the right not to be subjected to a detriment is lost (ERA 1996, s.47B(2)). The cut-off date for any award for injury to feelings is, therefore, the moment at which the employer's conduct became repudiatory, not the date where the repudiation was accepted.

No damages for loss of chance to claim unfair dismissal

One year's continuity of employment is required to claim unfair dismissal. Where an employee is wrongfully dismissed before he has acquired the necessary one year of service, no damages can be awarded at common law in respect of the loss of the chance to claim unfair dismissal (*Wise Group* v. *Mitchell* [2005] ICR 896, EAT).

19.2.5 Calculating the compensatory award

Step 1: Calculate what the employee would have earned if he remained employed

The first step is to establish precisely what the employee would have earned had he not been unfairly dismissed. This entails establishing the employee's net (not gross) salary and factoring in the value of any benefits or pay rises he would have received. It is expressly provided that compensatory award payable to an unfairly dismissed employee shall include compensation for 'loss of any benefit which he might reasonably be expected to have had but for the dismissal' (ERA 1996, s.123(2)(b)). This refers to loss of benefits to which the employee was not contractually entitled as well as those to which he was entitled under his contract (*Gould* v. *Governors of Haileybury and Imperial Service College* (unreported, EAT, 19 July 2003)). This is calculated to the date of the tribunal hearing. Matters are complicated if the employer is entitled to an insurance payment to which the employee did not contribute (see **section 19.3.2**).

If a dismissal is procedurally unfair (most frequently seen in redundancy or conduct cases), the tribunal will consider whether the employee would have been dismissed anyway if a proper procedure had been followed and adjust compensation accordingly. For example, if going through the proper procedure would have taken four weeks, thus deferring the date of dismissal by four weeks, the tribunal will only award loss of earnings sustained in that four-week period (*Polkey* v. *AE Dayton Services* [1987] IRLR 504, HL; *Steel Stockholders (Birmingham) Ltd* v. *Kirkwood* [1993] IRLR 515). If, in any event, an employee would have been dismissed in the future because of closure of the business, compensatory award will not be calculated by reference to a date after the closure (*James W Cook & Co (Wivenhoe) Ltd* v. *Tipper* [1990] IRLR 386, CA). In asking the hypothetical question, 'what would have happened anyway?', the tribunal must also consider whether any subsequent decision to dismiss would have been fair or unfair (*Panama* v. *London Borough of Hackney* [2003] IRLR 278, CA).

The tribunal should then consider whether there are any ongoing losses, for example, if the employee remains unemployed or is now earning a lower salary. In practice tribunals will rarely look further than 12 months beyond the hearing date (unless the employee is within, say, two or three years of retirement age, in which case the tribunal will sometimes award compensation up until the anticipated retirement date). This will be added to the past loss of earnings figure. On occasion, a younger or middle-aged employee will be able to demonstrate that there will be a long-term future loss of earnings; perhaps because he was being paid significantly above the going market rate before being unfairly dismissed, or because he has developed an illness which means he cannot work.

Tribunals may, in such circumstances, award a long-term loss of earnings, which will usually result in compensation exceeding the statutory maximum (see Step 8). An appropriate discount should be given for accelerated receipt of monies – the presumption is a 2.5 per cent discount rate (*Bentwood Bros (Manchester) Ltd* v. *Shepherd* [2003] IRLR 364, CA).

When calculating the current value of future losses tribunals have been cautioned against using the government's 'Actuarial Tables for use in Personal Injury and Fatal Accident cases' (the Ogden Tables). In 2003, the EAT pointed out that these tables are designed for use in personal injury cases and warned against the danger of using them in other employment related cases, save for calculating pension loss, unless it has been established that the claimant is unlikely to get another job before he reaches his retirement age or that any job he gets is likely to be at a lower rate of remuneration (*Dunnachie* v. *Kingston upon Hull City Council (No. 3)* [2003] IRLR 843). The same caveats about use of the Ogden Tables also apply in discrimination cases (see *Birmingham City Council* v. *Jaddoo* (unreported, EAT, 28 October 2004).

That being said, a new, 6th edition of the Ogden Tables, came out in 2007, well after the *Dunnachie* decision. The 6th edition uses a different approach from previous editions and may be more acceptable in employment cases – the essential difference is that previous editions assumed that a person would generally have a job for life whereas the 6th edition makes use of research estimating working life expectancy.

The tribunal will add any ancillary losses, for example, costs in seeking new employment and loss of pension rights. The Court of Appeal has held that it was neither perverse nor an error of law for a tribunal to find an employee entitled to 10 years' loss of pension (*Bentwood Bros (Manchester) Ltd* v. *Shepherd* [2003] IRLR 364).

Finally, the tribunal will award a sum for loss of statutory rights, to reflect the fact that the employee's continuity of employment will have reset to zero with a new job and there will be a period during which the employee is without the protection of some of the employment laws (such as the first year of employment when unfair dismissal cannot be claimed). This loss is customarily assessed at £250 or £300.

Step 2: Deduct monies received (with exceptions)

Next, the tribunal will deduct any (net) monies actually earned by the employee. The employee is under an express duty to mitigate his loss (ERA 1996, s.123(4)). If the tribunal considers that he has taken inadequate steps to find new employment between the dismissal and the hearing, it will only award compensation up until the point at which it thinks he ought to have found a new job had he been searching properly (*Gardiner-Hill* v. *Roland Berger Technics Ltd* [1982] IRLR 498). Alternatively, it might award ongoing losses on the basis that the employee ought to have been in receipt of some salary, even if not at the level of the previous job, if he had been acting reasonably in his search for work (*Addison* v. *Babcock FATA Ltd* [1987] ICR 805, CA). Sometimes, an employee will be entitled to take a long-term view and will not breach the duty to mitigate if he engages in retraining, or enrolls in higher education; providing always that he would take any suitable job that would provide him with the same standard of living as his old one, if one arose (*Orthet Ltd* v. *Vince-Cain* [2005] ICR 374). It may be reasonable for an employee to mitigate his loss by starting up his own business. If so, the appropriate course for the tribunal is to: (1) calculate what sum represents loss of remuneration; (2) add any costs incurred by the claimant in starting up the business; and (3) subtract from the aggregate of (1) and (2) any earnings from the new business (*AON Training Ltd* v. *Dore* [2005] EWCA Civ 411).

If remuneration from a new job is greater than that from the old job from which the employee was dismissed, the excess is not to be taken into account to reduce compensatory award for unfair dismissal from the old job (*Whelan (Cheers Off Licence)* v. *Richardson* [1998] ICR 318, EAT).

If the employee gets a new job shortly after dismissal but is dismissed after a few months from that new job and does not get another for some time, compensation for loss of earnings will include compensation for a reasonable period after the second job ended (*Cowen* v. *Rentokil Initial Facility Services (UK) Ltd t/a Initial Transport Services* (unreported, EAT, 6 March 2008); *Dawes Cycles Ltd* v. *Sedgley* (unreported, EAT, 12 March 1998); and *Dench* v. *Flynn & Partners* [1998] IRLR 653, CA).

An unreasonable refusal to accept an offer of re-engagement can be deemed to be a failure to mitigate loss (*Wilding* v. *British Telecommunications plc* [2002] ICR 1079).

The EAT (sitting in Scotland) has pointed out that the onus is on a party alleging that another has failed to mitigate his loss to prove it; further:

> if the issue of mitigation is not raised by a party it is not incumbent upon the judge to consider it and, indeed, if he did so of his own volition without reference to parties, he would be required under the Practice Rules of the Court of Session to put the case out again for a further hearing to allow parties to address the matter.
>
> *Kyndal Spirits* v. *Burns* (unreported, EAT, 27 June 2002)

The tribunal will also deduct any sums received from the ex-employer as compensation for dismissal (i.e. any ex gratia payments). However, any contractual redundancy payments which exceed the basic award will not be deducted at this stage – they are deducted at a later stage (see Step 5 below and *Digital Equipment Co Ltd* v. *Clements (No.2)* [1998] ICR 258, CA; reversing [1997] IRLR 140, EAT).

No deduction is made in respect of insurance payouts or early pension benefits received as a result of the dismissal (*Parry* v. *Cleaver* [1970] AC 1, HL; *Hopkins* v. *Norcros plc* [1994] ICR 11, CA).

Further no deduction is made in respect of income support, jobseeker's allowance or housing benefit received whilst the employee was unemployed. This is because it will be recouped by the DWP from the compensatory award after the tribunal hearing (Employment Protection (Recoupment of Jobseeker's Allowance and Income Support) Regulations 1996). It seems that incapacity benefit should be deducted from compensatory award on the basis that it should fully compensate the claimant but should not provide a bonus (*Morgans* v. *Alpha Plus Security Ltd* [2005] ICR 525). However, there are conflicting authorities on this point (cf. *Rubenstein* v. *McGloughlin* [1997] ICR 318 and *Puglia* v. *C James & Sons* [1996] ICR 301).

There is also conflicting authority on whether deductions should be made from any PILON if the employee finds new employment within the period for which he was entitled to PILON. The EAT in *Voith Turbo Ltd* v. *Stowe* [2005] ICR 543 has suggested that there should be no deduction for monies earned during the notice period. In so doing, the tribunal refused to follow a decision that any monies earned are deductible (*Hardy* v. *Polk (Leeds) Ltd* [2004] IRLR 420). This decision does not fit easily with *Morgans* v. *Alpha Plus Security Ltd* [2005] ICR 525.

The uncertainty has been recognised as unsatisfactory. Dealing with this and related points the Court of Appeal (Mummery LJ) said:

I do not think that *Dunnachie* [*Dunnachie* v. *Kingston upon Hull City Council* [2004] ICR 1052, HL] is express or implied authority for the proposition that the ET, in calculating compensation under ERA 1996, s.123 for unfair dismissal, must ... require the employee to give credit for wages that were, or could have been, earned by the employee during the notice period ... I appreciate that uncertainty about an everyday legal point like this is not satisfactory for tribunals, practitioners, employers or employees. The sooner that the House of Lords can settle the law one way or the other the better, dealing also, if possible, with a related controversy on the duty to mitigate under ERA 1996, s.123(4), another point which has not arisen for decision in this case: (see, for example, the decisions of the EAT in *Hardy* v. *Polk (Leeds) Ltd* [2005] ICR 557 and *Morgans* v. *Alpha Plus Security Ltd* [2005] ICR 525; cf *Voith Turbo Ltd* v. *Stowe EAT* [2005] ICR 453)

Langley & anor v. *Burlo* [2007] ICR 390, CA, paras.87–89

Step 3: Procedural fairness

Before October 2004, a tribunal could consider that even had a fair procedure been followed, the employee may still have been dismissed. When that occurred the tribunal was entitled to apply a percentage reduction to the award to reflect the chance that dismissal would have occurred in any event. This was known as a '*Polkey* reduction' (*Polkey* v. *AE Dayton Services* [1988] ICR 142, HL; *Wolesley Centres Ltd* v. *Simmons* [1994] ICR 503, EAT).

As part of the statutory dispute resolution procedures introduced in October 2004, a new ERA 1996, s.98A was introduced. The overall effect was that a dismissal would be automatically unfair if an employer had not completed the new statutory procedures but that the employer's failure to comply with other (e.g. contractual) procedures in respect of the dismissal would not be taken into account if the employment tribunal was satisfied that following them would have had no effect on the employer's decision to dismiss. This is therefore currently the position.

However, as noted above the 2004 statutory dispute resolution rules will be revoked once the current Employment Bill has become law. As part of this process ERA 1996, s.98A is to be repealed (Employment Bill, cl.2). When this comes into force, probably in April 2009, the position will probably revert to that established by the House of Lords in *Polkey*.

Step 4: Adjustment for non-compliance with statutory disciplinary procedures

Following the coming into force of the Employment Act 2002 on 1 October 2004, a failure to comply with the statutory disciplinary procedure will result in potentially substantial adjustments to the award.

If the employer has failed to comply with the minimum procedures imposed by statute, the award will be increased by a presumed 10 per cent. However, a tribunal has the discretion to increase the award by up to 50 per cent, or to make no increase if exceptional circumstances apply. Likewise, if the employee has failed to comply with the minimum procedures imposed by statute, the award will be reduced by a presumed 10 per cent. However, a tribunal has the discretion to reduce the award by up to 50 per cent, or to make no reduction if exceptional circumstances apply (Employment Act 2002, s.31). Any adjustment made under this provision must be made before reductions for contributory fault or redundancy are made (ERA 1996, s.124A).

As noted above, the statutory disciplinary procedure introduced in October 2004 is to be replaced (probably from April 2009) by less prescriptive arrangements. In essence a tribunal will take into account the extent to which an employer has followed guidelines to be set out in a revised Acas Code of Practice and if it finds that those guidelines have not been followed it will have a discretion to increase compensation by up to 25 per cent (appropriate provision is in cl.3 of the Employment Bill currently before Parliament).

Step 5: Contributory fault reduction

When the dismissal was 'caused or contributed to by any action of the complainant', the tribunal must 'reduce the amount of the compensatory award by such proportion as it considers just and equitable having regard to that finding' (ERA 1996, s.123(6)).

The tribunal can reduce the award by such percentage as it considers appropriate to reflect the employee's fault, even on occasion by 100 per cent (*Perkin* v. *St Georges Healthcare NHS Trust* [2005] IRLR 934, CA). It is rare for the EAT to change the percentage reduction applied by a tribunal for contributory fault (*Charles Robertson* v. *White* [1995] ICR 349, EAT; *Havering Primary Care Trust* v. *Bidwell* (unreported, EAT, 22 April 2008)).

Misconduct by an employee does not itself have to be serious enough to justify dismissal to be relevant as contributory fault warranting a reduction in unfair dismissal compensation (*Trafford Housing* v. *(1) Hughes (2) Burke* (unreported, EAT, 8 August 2007). However, there must be an element of moral culpability or 'blameworthiness' (*Gibson* v. *British Transport Docks Board* [1982] IRLR 228). It would not be correct to reduce compensatory award when an employee was unfairly dismissed for refusing to obey the employer's instructions to falsify records (*Morrish* v. *Henlys (Folkestone) Ltd* [1973] IRLR 61).

It is legitimate for an employment tribunal to take into account the conduct before it of an employee to support its conclusions about his earlier behaviour but its decision must not be based on that (*Bell* v. *The Governing Body of Grampian Primary School* (unreported, EAT, 24 August 2007)).

Drunkenness at work, even if the employee is an alcoholic, can be contributory conduct for the purposes of deductions from compensation for unfair dismissal (*Sinclair* v. *Wandsworth Council* (unreported, EAT, 4 October 2007)).

In deciding whether a dismissal is unfair a tribunal cannot have regard to matters of which the employer was unaware at the time of the dismissal but the position is different when it comes to assessing compensation. When assessing compensation a tribunal can take into account evidence of misconduct which came to light after the dismissal and reduce the compensation which would otherwise have been awarded, even to zero (*W Devis & Sons* v. *Atkins* [1977] IRLR 314, HL). This can be so even if the misconduct takes place after dismissal if it is relevant and therefore results in it being 'just and equitable', the overriding condition set out in ERA 1996, s.123(6), for a reduction to be made (*Soros & Soros* v. *Davison & Davison* [1994] ICR 590, EAT).

A reduction for contributory fault on the basis that the employee has been engaged in lawful industrial action is not permitted (ERA 1996, s.123(5)), although if the employee's conduct has gone beyond ordinary industrial action, this may bring the contributory fault reduction into play (*Tracey* v. *Crosville Wales Ltd* [1997] ICR 862, HL).

An employee's failure to follow the statutory grievance procedure introduced in October 2004 can lead to a reduction in compensation of up to 50 per cent (Employment Act 2002, s.31). This must be made before any reductions are made for contributory fault or redundancy (ERA 1996, s.124A). The statutory grievance procedure is to be abolished by the Employment Bill currently before Parliament, which will repeal Employment Act 2002, ss.29–33 and the schedules relating to them, probably with effect from April 2009.

Step 6: Deduct contractual redundancy pay

It will be recalled that under Step 2 (deductions), a specific exception to the rule that monies received from the employer should be deducted was contractual redundancy payments, to the extent that they exceed the statutory basic award. The excess is deducted after any reductions for *Polkey* reasons and contributory fault. Thus if an employee is entitled to a basic award of £1,000, but received a contractual redundancy payment of £2,500, the first £1,000 is offset against the basic award (so that the employee receives no basic award). The excess of £1,500 is deducted from the compensatory award after the *Polkey* and contributory fault reductions are applied. The reason for this is that under statute, the employer is entitled to have any compensation payment reduced by the full amount to which a redundancy payment exceeds the basic award (ERA 1996, s.123(7)). If the award of four weeks' wages made against the employer when an order for reinstatement was made (and the employee was treated as being unfairly dismissed as a result of the employer's subsequent failure to comply with the order), this should also be deducted at this stage (ERA 1996, s.123(8)).

Step 7: Gross up the award if it exceeds £30,000

Although an employee's losses are calculated on a net basis, the employee is liable to pay tax on any tribunal award over £30,000 (except awards for injury to feelings, discussed in the following paragraph). Accordingly, it is necessary to gross up any award in excess of this sum (Income and Corporation Taxes Act 1988, ss.148 and 188). Thus if an employee who falls into the higher rate tax bracket has net losses of £36,000, the tribunal should gross this up to £40,000 since 40 per cent tax is payable on the excess over £30,000, i.e. on £10,000 of the award, thus resulting in a charge of £4,000 by HM Revenue & Customs once the money is in the employee's hands (*Richardson (HM Inspector of Taxes)* v. *Delaney* [2001] IRLR 663; *Shove* v. *Downs Surgical plc* [1984] ICR 532).

This step was not considered in *Digital Equipment Co Ltd* v. *Clements (No.2)* [1998] ICR 258, CA because at the time of that case the maximum compensatory award was set at a level significantly below £30,000 and therefore the issue did not arise.

Where a claim for unfair dismissal is compromised, any payment made in consideration for the compromise agreement is not generally taxable as an emolument. Providing that it is less than £30,000, it will not be subject to tax under the sweeping-up provision of the Income Tax (Earnings and Pensions) Act 2003, s.401 (*Wilson (Inspector of Taxes)* v. *Clayton* [2005] IRLR 108, CA).

Step 8: Apply the statutory 'cap'

The last stage is to apply the statutory maximum for the compensatory award. This is adjusted in line with inflation each year, usually in or around February. The current maximum, for dismissals taking place on or after 1 February 2008, is £63,000 (ERA 1996, s.124).

Note, however, that if the dismissal was for health and safety reasons or because the employee was a whistleblower making a protected disclosure, then no statutory maximum is applied (ERA 1996, s.124(1A) as amended by Employment Rights (Increase of Limits) Order 2007, SI 2007/3570).

19.2.6 Interim relief

Although the High Court has powers to grant interim relief in most proceedings before it (Civil Jurisdiction and Judgments Act 1982, ss.24 and 25) 'interim relief' is an exceptional remedy in employment law cases. If an employee considers that he has been unfairly dismissed on certain specified grounds he can make an application to a tribunal for 'interim relief'. An interim relief order has the effect of ensuring that the dismissed employee continues to be paid his wages or salary pending a full tribunal hearing.

The original underlying purpose was to enable an employment tribunal to give a preliminary ruling at an emergency hearing to head off industrial trouble before it began or became too serious. Hence the relief is generally available only in cases where collective industrial action is likely to be in point. Also in order to be eligible the employee has to move quickly – there is a seven day time-limit from date of dismissal for making an interim relief application (ERA 1996, s.128(2)).

The specified grounds on which an application for interim relief can be made are set out in ERA 1996, s.128(1)(b), Employment Relations Act 1999, s.12 and TULRCA 1992, s.152. They are as follows:

- whistleblowing – dismissal for whistleblowing;
- disciplinary and grievance hearings – dismissal for seeking to exercise the right to be accompanied at (or to accompany someone else to) a disciplinary or grievance hearing;
- workers' representatives:
  - dismissal of a member of a safety committee for a reason connected with that role;
  - dismissal of a workers' representative in connection with WTR 1998;
  - dismissal of an employee-trustee of an occupational pension scheme for a reason connected with that role;
  - dismissal of an employee representative for a reason connected with that role;
- trade union related reasons – dismissal for reasons related to trade union membership or non-membership or trade union activity;
- dismissal resulting from obstruction or promotion of official recognition of a trade union.

The Northern Irish Court of Appeal ruled in 2007 that a statement in the employment law textbook *Harvey on Industrial Relations* that 'An employee unfairly selected for redundancy on union grounds may not claim interim relief . . .' is too broad (*Bombardier Aerospace-Shorts Brothers plc* v. *McConnell* [2008] IRLR 51). The Northern Irish Court of Appeal indicated that that statement is correct when the principal reason for dismissal is a true redundancy but is wrong if the reason for dismissal is what it called a 'fabricated redundancy designed to be used as a means to dismiss a trade union activist . . .'.

19.2.7 Compensation: other awards

A number of other awards exist, which can be awarded by an employment tribunal in an unfair dismissal claim. The names are confusing and are often mixed up. They are summarised only and readers are referred to the statutory provisions for more detail.

Additional award

This is an award of between 26 and 52 weeks' pay made to the employee when the employer fails to comply with an order for reinstatement or re-engagement (ERA 1996, s.117(3)(b)). This is addressed in more detail in **section 19.2.2**: 'What if the employer does not comply?'

Protective award

This is an award of up to 90 days' pay to individuals whom an employer has failed to consult properly during redundancy consultations (TULRCA 1992, s.189). There is a statutory cap on the amount payable if the employer is insolvent and the liability to pay the protective award moves to the Secretary of State (see ERA 1996, s.186).

This award is designed to provide a sanction for breach of the provisions, not damages; in other words, the award is punitive, not compensatory. It follows from the fact that the protective award is punitive that a deduction must not be made by reason of the fact that the employees concerned continued to work and to receive salary during the protected period (*Cranswick Country Foods plc v. Beall & ors* [2007] ICR 691 in which the EAT ruled that TULRCA 1992, s.190(4) should not be construed to mean the contrary).

The Court of Appeal has suggested that where there has been a complete failure to consult, the tribunal should start with the maximum period and reduce it only if there are mitigating factors. That the consultation would have made no difference anyway will not, of itself, lead to any reduction in the award (*Susie Radin Ltd v. GMB* [2004] ICR 893). On its own the fact that the redundancy consultation period was 30 days not 90 days because fewer than 100 employees were being made redundant is not a good reason for reducing the amount of protective award to below 90 days' pay (*Evans, Motture & Hutchins v. Permacell Finesse Ltd (In administration)* (unreported, EAT, 23 October 2007)). The tribunal at first instance has a wide discretion in making the protective award and the EAT will be reluctant to substitute a different one (*Amicus v. GBS Tooling Ltd* [2005] IRLR 683).

An application for protective award must be made by appropriate representatives, who will be representatives of the union if a trade union is recognised (TULRCA 1992, s.189(1) and (1B)(a)). Only employees in respect of whom the union concerned was the recognised trade union can then benefit. Other employees have to make a separate claim (*TGWU v. Brauer Coley Ltd (In Administration)* [2007] ICR 226, EAT and *Harford & ors v. DTI* (unreported, EAT, 12 February 2008)).

Award for failure to consult during TUPE transfer

Under regs.13–16 of TUPE 2006, employers are obliged to inform and consult about the implications of a TUPE transfer with any recognised trade union or if no union is recognised with specially appointed employee representatives. Where no employee representatives have been appointed, the onus is on the employer to initiate the elections of representatives. Where none have been appointed, the obligation is to consult with the employees (*Howard v. Millrise Ltd* [2005] ICR 435, EAT).

Failure to comply will result in an award of up to 13 weeks' pay for each affected employee (TUPE 2006, reg.16(3)). A week's pay for this purpose is now subject to the statutory cap set out in ERA 1996, s.227 (TUPE 2006, reg.16(4) – £330 from 1 February 2008). Compensation for failure to consult as required is punitive and is meant to be a deterrent not compensation for loss. Therefore unless there are mitigating factors the award should be the maximum 13 weeks' pay (*Sweetin v. Coral Racing* [2006] IRLR 252, EAT).

Special award

The 'special award' was abolished with effect from October 1999. It was a potentially large award (the minimum award was £14,500) made when an employer dismissed an employee for various reasons, principally trade union or health and safety connected.

19.3   DISCRIMINATION

19.3.1   Introduction

Awards for discrimination are unlimited. The concepts of 'basic' and 'compensatory' award do not exist in discrimination cases: a tribunal will adopt principles of compensation from the law of tort.

The tests for compensation under the age, sex, sexual orientation, race, religion and belief, and disability discrimination legislation are all broadly similar. Unlike liability issues, principles of compensation developed under one cause of action can generally be analogously applied in another, and thus all discrimination statutes are dealt with together in the text.

In addition to ordering compensation, tribunals have jurisdiction to make a declaration as to the parties' rights and to make recommendations as to actions to be taken within a specific period.

19.3.2   Compensation

The tribunal has power to order the payment of compensation, the damages being assessed as if the act of discrimination were a tort. In other words, ordinary tortious principles for assessing damages are adopted (SDA 1975, ss.65 and 66; RRA 1976, ss.56 and 57; DDA 1995, s.8; Employment Equality (Sexual Orientation) Regulations 2003, regs.30 and 31; Employment Equality (Religion or Belief) Regulations 2003, regs.30 and 31; Employment Equality (Age) Regulations 2006, regs.38–40).

Discrimination awards can be made jointly and severally against both the employer (who is primarily liable) and any person who has actually committed the acts of discrimination. If making a joint and several award, tribunals should apportion blame between the respondents (*Way & IntroCate Chemicals* v. *Crouch* [2005] IRLR 603).

The award normally comprises two elements: injury to feelings and loss of earnings. In addition, tribunals have jurisdiction to award damages for personal injury. Further, interest falls to be awarded on compensation awards for discrimination.

Injury to feelings

The statutory provisions governing compensation expressly state that 'for the avoidance of doubt' the compensation 'may include compensation for injury to feelings' (SDA 1975, s.66(4); RRA 1976, s.57(4); DDA 1995, s.8(4)).

It is difficult to estimate the value of awards for injury to feelings. However, the Court of Appeal set out clear guidelines in *Vento* v. *Chief Constable of West Yorkshire (No.2)* [2003] IRLR 102, namely:

1. A 'top band', normally between £15,000 and £25,000 for the most serious cases.
2. A 'middle band' of between £5,000 and £15,000 for serious cases.
3. Awards of between £500 and £5,000 for less serious or one-off cases. Awards of less than £500 should be avoided.

Inflation can play a part in assessment of the award. In 2006 the EAT noted that *Vento* was decided a few years ago and that 'whilst we do not have raging inflation which has been known in various stages of this country's history, we nevertheless do have quiet inflation which devalues monetary values' (*Miles* v. *Gilbank & anor* [2006] ICR 1297, CA). Since then, of course, inflation has mounted.

There are conflicting authorities on whether there is a minimum of £500 or £750 for injury to feelings, or whether there is no minimum at all (*Purves* v. *Joydisc Ltd* [2003] IRLR 420; *Greig* v. *Initial Security* (unreported, 19 October 2005, EAT) EAT/0036/05).

It is legitimate to treat stress and depression as part of the injury to be compensated for under the head 'injury to feelings'. If a separate award is made for psychiatric injury (see below), tribunals must ensure that they are not awarding compensation for the same loss twice (*HM Prison Service* v. *Salmon* [2001] IRLR 425, EAT). Injury to feelings is different in kind from anxiety – anxiety may be an element within injury to feelings but is not compensatable on its own (*Johnston* v. *NEI International Combustion Ltd; Rothwell* v. *Chemical & Insulating Co Ltd* [2007] ICR 1745, HL).

It has been held that the appropriate test for deciding whether an employer is liable to pay compensation for psychiatric injury suffered by an employee is not whether the injury was reasonably foreseeable but simply whether the unlawful discrimination caused the injury (see *Essa* v. *Laing Ltd* [2003] IRLR 346). However, this decision was delivered before the speeches were handed down by the House of Lords in *Simmons* v. *British Steel plc* [2004] ICR 585, where Lord Rodger of Earlsferry set out a test for determining questions of remoteness of psychiatric injury:

(1) The respondent is not liable for a consequence of a kind which is not reasonably foreseeable.
(2) While a respondent is not liable for damage that was not reasonably foreseeable, it does not follow that he is liable for all damage that was reasonably foreseeable: depending on the circumstances, the respondent may not be liable for damage caused by a *novus actus interveniens* or unreasonable conduct on the part of the pursuer, even if it was reasonably foreseeable.
(3) Subject to the qualification in (2), if the claimant's injury is of a kind that was foreseeable, the defender is liable, even if the damage is greater in extent than was foreseeable or it was caused in a way that could not have been foreseen.
(4) The respondent must take his victim as he finds him.
(5) Subject again to the qualification in (2), where personal injury to the claimant was reasonably foreseeable, the respondent is liable for any personal injury, whether physical or psychiatric, which the claimant suffers as a result of his wrongdoing.

Tribunals can also award aggravated damages as an ancillary award to the injury to feelings. This is a smaller sum, rarely exceeding £5,000, to be awarded if the employer's conduct has been exceptionally high handed, malicious or oppressive such that an ordinary injury to feelings award will not suffice. Whilst the authorities suggest that it should not be regarded as a punitive award so as to express the tribunal's disapproval of the employer's conduct, in practice, this is precisely what it is used for (*Alexander* v. *Home Office* [1988] IRLR 396, CA; *HM Prison Service* v. *Salmon* [2001] IRLR 425, EAT; *Zaiwalla & Co* v. *Walia* [2002] IRLR 697; *Leeds Rhino Club* v. *Sterling* (unreported, EAT, 9 September 2002)).

Tribunals cannot award exemplary damages (*Deane* v. *London Borough of Ealing* [1993] ICR 329, EAT).

Loss of earnings

The bulk of a tribunal's award is usually loss of earnings. Loss of earnings is assessed in the ordinary way (see **section 19.2**) and claimants have a duty to mitigate their losses. In discrimination cases, tribunals tend to be more sympathetic to employees' claims that they will have difficulty obtaining further employment – particularly if they have developed psychological problems as a result of bullying, harassment or employment-related stress – and in some cases tribunals will award a loss of earnings for many years into the future.

An employer cannot rely on a subsequent dismissal that was unfair as a break in the chain of causation between the discrimination and a future loss of earnings (*HM Prison Service* v. *Beart (No.2)* [2005] ICR 1206). Where there is an award for loss of earnings, the same deductions as would be made for an award of personal injuries must be made. Whether insurance payments to which the employer is entitled should be deducted can be problematic. It is sufficient to observe, however, that some of the difficulties surrounding deductions can be avoided if the tribunal instead recommends (e.g. under DDA 1995, s.8(2)(c)) that the employee is retained under his contract of employment until retirement age, being paid his contractual salary. Such an order can, for example, require the employee to attend medical examinations required by an insurance company. The tribunal can only make this recommendation if the employee requests it (see, generally, *Atos Origin IT Services UK Ltd* v. *Haddock* [2005] ICR 277, EAT).

Personal injury

Since compensation is assessed on a tortious basis, tribunals have jurisdiction to award damages for personal injuries as well as injury to feelings. Most claims for damages for personal injury on dismissal are for psychiatric injury, e.g. depression or stress (see **section 8.4.4**). An employee should support any claim for personal injuries with medical evidence. Note that if an employee brings a claim for discrimination in the employment tribunal, the right to bring a claim for personal injuries in the civil courts (in so far as they arise from the same facts) will be lost because of the doctrines of *estoppel, res judicata* and abuse of process (*Sheriff* v. *Klyne Tugs (Lowestoft) Ltd* [1999] IRLR 481, CA). Any psychiatric injury that is claimed, however, must have been of a general type that was reasonably foreseeable, even if the particular form of the injury was not (*Simmons* v. *British Steel plc* [2004] ICR 585).

Ancillary losses

Ancillary losses, such as loss of pension rights or expenses in seeking new employment, can also be recovered.

Interest

Tribunals have the power to order interest on compensation awards for discrimination (unlike for unfair dismissal). This accrues daily on a simple basis, from the date of discrimination (for the award for injury to feelings) or from the mid-point between the act of discrimination and the hearing (for all other heads of loss) unless 'serious injustice' would occur, in which case the tribunal may calculate interest differently (Employment Tribunals (Interest on Awards in Discrimination Cases) Regulations 1996, SI 1996/2803).

Statutory maximum

Since 1993, there has been no statutory maximum award in discrimination cases. This can lead to enormous claims. For example, in May 2008 a fund management company in the City of London lost an appeal against a finding by an employment tribunal that it had been guilty of sex discrimination and newspaper reports suggest that at a subsequent remedies hearing in June 2008, Gill Switalski was claiming as much as £19m compensation (*F & C Asset Management plc & ors* v. *Switalski* (unreported, EAT, 23 May 2008)).

19.3.3 Declaration/recommendation

In addition to ordering compensation, tribunals have the power to:

- make an order declaring the rights of the complainant and respondent in relation to the act to which the complaint relates; and/or
- make a recommendation that the respondent takes, within a specified period, action appearing to the tribunal to be practicable for the purpose of obviating or reducing the adverse effect on the complainant of any act of discrimination to which the complaint relates. Note that the word 'reasonable' is used in the disability legislation, rather than 'practicable' which is used in the other anti-discrimination legislation (SDA 1975, s.65(1); RRA 1976, s.56(1); DDA 1995, s.17A(2); Employment Equality (Sexual Orientation) Regulations 2003, reg.30; Employment Equality (Religion or Belief) Regulations 2003, reg.30; Employment Equality (Age) Regulations 2006, reg.38).

These remedies are not frequently pursued, often because the employee has left the respondent's employ by the time the claim comes to be heard. If the tribunal makes a recommendation that the employer take action, and it fails to comply, the tribunal has power to increase the level of compensation (or to order it if not previously ordered) (SDA 1975, s.65(3); RRA 1976, s.56(4); DDA 1995, s.17A(5); Employment Equality (Sexual Orientation) Regulations 2003, reg.30; Employment Equality (Religion or Belief) Regulations 2003, reg.30; Employment Equality (Age) Regulations, reg.38(3)).

A dedicated website at **www.emplaw.co.uk/lshandbook** provides links to judgments and other source material referred to in this chapter.

CHAPTER 20

Time limits, procedure and settlement

20.1 GENERAL INFORMATION

From a system which was originally set up to avoid formality and encourage swift resolution of disputes, the employment tribunal system has become one awash with formality and procedure. In 2004, substantial new procedural rules were introduced. They are considered further below (see **section 20.3**).

The Employment Appeal Tribunal rules of procedure are still essentially as introduced in 1993. They have been subject to five sets of amendments, most recently in 2005. A consolidated version of the EAT rules of procedure, incorporating all amendments, is available at **www.employmentappeals.gov.uk/ Documents/FormsLeafletsGuidance/EAT_Rules.pdf**. A revised practice direction on EAT procedure, supplementing the rules, was issued in May 2008.

A fundamentally important provision (first introduced for employment tribunals in 2001 and for the Employment Appeal Tribunal in 2004) is the 'overriding objective' derived from the Civil Procedure Rules used in the courts (see the Employment Tribunal (Constitution and Rules of Procedure) Regulations 2004, SI 2004/1861, reg.3 and the Employment Appeal Tribunal (Amendment) Rules 2004, SI 2004/2526, r.3). The 'overriding objective' requires tribunals and chairmen to deal with cases justly, specifically by ensuring that the parties are on an equal footing; dealing with the case in ways which are proportionate to the complexity or importance of the issues; ensuring that it is dealt with expeditiously and fairly; and saving expense.

This chapter deals with procedure in employment tribunals (not the EAT). It includes a section dedicated to the somewhat complex matter of time limits. In addition, compromising of claims is also considered as a separate matter.

20.2 TIME LIMITS

20.2.1 Introduction

The majority of employment claims must be presented at the tribunal within three months of the employee's dismissal, or of the act (say of discrimination) complained of. Some claims have a slightly longer limitation period, for example, six months in which to bring a claim for a statutory redundancy payment or a claim under EqPA 1970. There is discretion to extend time for some claims. Claims in the civil courts (for tort and breach of contract) attract the normal six-year limitation period set out in the Limitation Act 1980.

The claim form (known as an ET1 – copies available on **www.employment-tribunals.gov.uk/claim/claiming_responding.htm**) must be presented within the three-month (or other) period. This means it must be delivered to the tribunal (see **Appendix A** for a list of tribunal addresses).

Putting the form through the tribunal letterbox will qualify (*Swainston* v. *Hetton Victory Club Ltd* [1983] ICR 341; *Consignia plc* v. *Sealy* [2002] IRLR 624) at any time up to midnight on the last day for presentation (*Post Office* v. *Moore* [1981] ICR 621 and *Initial Electronic Security Systems Ltd* v. *Avdic* [2005] IRLR 671, EAT). Proof of postage is insufficient (*Secretary of State* v. *Banks* [1983] ICR 48, EAT) but it is not necessary that the tribunal opens or processes the originating application within that time period. Faxing the application has been held to suffice in a non-employment law context and, in practice, suffices in employment claims (*Re a Debtor nos. 2021 and 2022* (unreported, ChD, 20 November 1995)).

Claimants are able to submit their claim forms online directly to employment tribunals. Electronic submission of an ET1 does not constitute presentation for the purposes of the employment tribunal rules until it is received by the tribunal. A claimant is entitled to assume that claim forms submitted electronically will arrive within an hour or so, and will be able to rely on the 'not reasonably practicable' argument to extend time if the claim form is delayed or lost in the ether (*Initial Electronic Security Systems* v. *Avdic* [2005] IRLR 671).

The time limit is strictly imposed: in one case a claim 'submitted' on the ET website at 23:59:59 on the last day of the three-month time limit was received at 00:00:08 – 9 seconds late. The employment tribunal rejected it as out of time and the EAT upheld that decision (*Miller* v. *Community Links Trust* (unreported, EAT, 29 October 2007)). The Court of Appeal and the EAT both upheld a tribunal's decision not to accept an unfair dismissal claim that was presented 1 minute and 22 seconds late in *Beasley* v. *National Grid* [2008] EWCA Civ 742.

The Employment Act 2002 (Dispute Resolution) Regulations 2004, SI 2004/752, reg.15 provides for relevant limitation periods to be extended in order to enable employees to go through a meaningful grievance discussion before presenting their claim form. The overall effect of reg.15 is that the normal time limit for presenting a tribunal claim is automatically extended by three months provided that before expiry of the normal time limit the employee has either started the statutory grievance procedure by writing a step one grievance letter or has tried to lodge a complaint with an employment tribunal (which of course the tribunal will have rejected precisely because, by definition, the employee would not have started the statutory grievance procedure). It follows that, if the employee neither sends a stage 1 letter, nor tries to lodge an ET1 within the normal time limit, there will be no extension of time under the statutory grievance procedures.

As noted above (see **Chapter 4**) the Employment Act 2002 (Dispute Resolution) Regulations are due to be revoked in their entirety, probably from April 2009, after the Employment Bill currently before Parliament is enacted. Therefore we are not covering their effect in detail in this book.

The time limits (and, where applicable, rules relating to extension of those time limits) for each of the main causes of action are addressed in turn.

20.2.2 Unfair dismissal claims

An unfair dismissal claim must normally be presented to an employment tribunal before the end of three months, beginning with the effective date of termination (EDT). The EDT is included in calculating the three months (*Joshi* v. *Manchester City Council* (unreported, EAT, 30 January 2008)); thus if the EDT is 12 February, the claim must be presented by 11 May (ERA 1996, s.111).

The claim can be presented once notice of dismissal has been given, even before the EDT has occurred. This encourages claims to be brought as early as possible (ERA 1996, s.111(3)).

If it is unclear whether the employee has the legal right to bring a claim (for example, if guidance is being awaited in a similar case from the ECJ) and it is prudent to lodge the claim form and apply for a stay (see, for example, *Johns* v. *Solent SD Ltd* [2008] EWCA Civ 790 – an age discrimination case but similar principles apply). If the employee waits more than three months, he is unlikely to obtain an extension of time (*Biggs* v. *Somerset County Council* [1996] ICR 364, CA).

Extension of time

In addition to the automatic three-month extension noted above under Employment Act 2002 (Dispute Resolution) Regulations 2004, SI 2004/752, reg.15, likely to come to an end in April 2009, there is also an automatic extension to six months if the employee is taking part in official industrial action (or was locked out by the employer) and other employees dismissed at the same time have been offered re-engagement but the employee in question has not (TULRCA 1992, s.239(2)).

More generally, a tribunal has power to hear an unfair dismissal claim if it is presented more than three months after the EDT of the claimant's employment or such further period as the tribunal considers reasonable if 'it is satisfied that it was not reasonably practicable for the complaint to be presented before the end of that period of three months' (ERA 1996, s.111(2)). It will be seen that it is thus not strictly accurate under ERA 1996, s.111 to refer to a tribunal allowing an extension of time as under that section the task of a late applicant is to persuade a tribunal that: (i) it was not reasonably practicable for him to have presented his claim in time; and (ii) that it was eventually presented within a period which was reasonable. However, tribunal chairmen have discretionary power to grant extensions of time (under r.10 of the 2004 Employment Tribunals Rules of Procedure) and s.111 is, of course, critically important in deciding whether or not that discretion can properly be exercised.

Practicable means feasible. It is historically a strict test: that it was not practicable to lodge an application is a higher hurdle to overcome than whether it is reasonable to extend time (*Noel* v. *London Underground Ltd* [1999] IRLR 621). In recent years, the appellate courts have been interpreting this in an increasingly pro-employee manner (*Marks & Spencer* v. *Williams-Ryan* [2005] IRLR 562).

Practicability is primarily a question of fact. Thus there is normally no appeal from the employment tribunal's decision whether or not to extend time (*London International College Ltd* v. *Sen* [1993] IRLR 333). However, if the tribunal's decision is so unreasonable that it is 'perverse' then a question of law will be involved and the EAT will have jurisdiction (*Agrico UK Ltd* v. *Amanda Ireland* (unreported, EAT, 10 August 2005) in which the EAT held that it had been perverse for a tribunal to allow a claim to be filed out of time when a solicitor who had not filed the claim before he went on holiday instructed his secretary to do it – but she went off sick and failed to do so).

Lord Denning's judgment in the leading case of *Dedman* v. *British Building & Engineering Appliances Ltd* [1974] ICR 53, CA supported the proposition that a liberal interpretation in favour of the employee should be given to the words 'not practicable'. However, this judgment was delivered before the word 'reasonably' was inserted. Insertion of the word 'reasonably', after the *Dedman* decision, restricts the 'liberality' of the *Dedman* approach (*Royal Bank of Scotland plc* v. *Theobald* (unreported, EAT, 10 January 2007)).

The task of an employment tribunal has been described by the EAT as 'to carry out a thorough examination of the facts focusing on the evidence before them in order to determine whether an employee for whom it was not reasonably practicable to issue his claim in the prescribed three-month period had thereafter issued his claim "within such period as the tribunal considers reasonable" ' (*Northumberland County Council & anor.* v. *Thompson* (unreported, EAT, 14 September 2007)).

Ignorance of the three-month limit is no excuse in deciding whether presentation within the time limit was reasonably practicable (*Camarthen & Pumsaint Farmers Ltd* v. *Evans* (unreported, EAT, 12 October 2007)). However, ignorance of the right to claim unfair dismissal might be (*Biggs* v. *Somerset County Council* [1996] ICR 364, CA; *Barber* v. *Staffordshire County Council* [1996] ICR 379, CA). So also might be the fact that the claimant spoke no English (*Bleuse* v. *MBT Transport Ltd & anor* [2008] IRLR 264, EAT).

Being stressed is no excuse for not presenting a claim in time and nor is a wrong belief that a claim cannot be presented while police enquiries are continuing (*Asda Stores Ltd* v. *Kauser* (unreported, EAT, 28 September 2007)).

TIME LIMITS, PROCEDURE AND SETTLEMENT

An 'innocent' employee will not be allowed an extension of time because he relied on advisors who advised him incorrectly about time limits (*London International College Ltd* v. *Sen* [1993] IRLR 333). In general it will make no difference whether the advice came from a solicitor or someone else (*Ashcroft* v. *Haberdashers Aske's Boys School* [2008] IRLR 375, EAT; *London Borough of Islington* v. *Brown* (unreported, EAT, 24 June 2008); and *Alliance & Leicester plc* v. *Kidd* (unreported, EAT, 13 April 2007) in which a trade union representative had wrongly advised Ms Kidd that time for lodging an unfair dismissal claim ran from when her internal appeal to her employer had been rejected whereas the correct position is that time runs from the EDT). However, erroneous advice from tribunal staff or Job Centre staff might be an acceptable excuse entitling a claimant to an extension of time (*Marks & Spencer* v. *Williams-Ryan* [2005] IRLR 562).

Solicitors have a duty to check that the application has arrived if they have not received an acknowledgment from the tribunal (*Capital Foods Retail* v. *Corrigan* [1993] IRLR 430, EAT).

If a letter is sent by first-class post, it is safe to assume it will arrive on the second day after it was posted, excluding Sundays and bank holidays. If it arrives later due to postal delays, an extension of time will normally be granted (*Consignia plc* v. *Sealy* [2002] IRLR 624 – in which ironically the claimant was a postman and the employer opposing his application for extension for time was the organisation responsible for the postal delay).

If an extension of time is granted, it will only be for such further period as the tribunal considers reasonable beyond the initial three-month period (ERA 1996, s.111). Merely because it was not reasonably practicable to present the claim within three months does not give applicants the right to an indefinite period in which to present their claims. There is no absolute bar on the length of time which will be considered reasonable, although tribunals will expect employees to act swiftly once it becomes practicable to lodge a claim (*Marley (UK) Ltd* v. *Anderson* [1996] ICR 728, CA).

20.2.3 Discrimination claims

The same three-month time limit exists. The basic rule is that time starts to run when the act complained of was done. However, there are three additional points to bear in mind:

1. Where an unlawful act is attributable to a term in a contract, it is to be treated as extending throughout the duration of the contract.
2. Any act extending over a period shall be treated as done at the end of that period.
3. A deliberate omission is treated as done when the person in question decided upon it (SDA 1975, s.76; RRA 1976, s.68; DDA 1995, Sched.3, para.3; *Barclays Bank* v. *Kapur* [1991] ICR 208, HL; *Cast* v. *Croydon College* [1998] ICR 500, CA).

In *Hendricks* v. *Metropolitan Police Commissioner* [2003] IRLR 96, the Court of Appeal considered the meaning of the phrase 'any act extending over a period'. It held that ongoing acts of harassment, which evidenced a general culture of discrimination, will amount to an ongoing state of affairs which falls within RRA 1976, s.68. Accordingly, on the basis that the last act of harassment fell within the three-month period, the claimant could claim in respect of acts of harassment extending back over many years. It has sometimes been argued that there must have been a 'policy, practice or regime' of unlawful behaviour to be able to take advantage of the principle established in *Hendricks* (see, for example, *Robertson* v. *Bexley Community Centre* [2003] IRLR 434). However, the EAT has said this is wrong and that provided the employee could show, as she did in *Hendricks*, that she has a good arguable *prima facie* case then an employment tribunal should accept that it has jurisdiction to consider the matter (*Pugh* v. *National Assembly for Wales* (unreported, EAT, 26 September 2006)).

Extension of time

For reasons noted above, we are not here considering in any detail the position under the Employment Act 2002 (Dispute Resolution) Regulations 2004, reg.15 which ensure that if a claimant sends his grievance within the normal three-month period, he will benefit from an automatic extension of time of an additional three months to present his claim.

Apart from the 2004 regulations, tribunals have a greater discretion to grant an extension of time in discrimination cases than in unfair dismissal claims (*Davidson* v. *Ministry of Defence* (unreported, EAT, 17 June 1999); *Aniagwu* v. *London Borough of Hackney* [1999] IRLR 303). In discrimination cases statute provides a less rigid 'just and equitable' test rather than the 'not reasonably practicable' test (SDA 1976, s.76; RRA 1976, s.68; DDA 1995, Sched.3, para.3).

Thus a solicitor's failure to file in time can be relevant in deciding whether an extension of time should be allowed in discrimination cases (*Chohan* v. *Derby Law Centre* [2004] IRLR 685, EAT and *Anderson* v. *George S Hall Ltd* (unreported, EAT, 3 March 2006)).

In a 2006 combined race and disability discrimination case the EAT overruled an employment tribunal's refusal to allow an extension of time for submission of a claim when the failure to submit on time was the fault of the solicitors concerned. The EAT said that '... if the failings are those of the solicitor and not the claimant that is highly material. But the errors of his solicitors should not be visited on his [i.e. the claimant's] head ...'. The EAT ruled that the race discrimination claim which had been submitted just one day out of time should be allowed to proceed and that in relation to the disability discrimination claim which was three months out of time the question of whether an extension should be allowed should be remitted back to the tribunal for reconsideration (*Virdi* v. *Commissioner of Police of the Metropolis* [2007] IRLR 24, EAT).

20.2.4 Equal pay claims

Claims under EqPA 1970 must generally be brought within six months of the end of employment (s.2(4)). Until the statutory procedures are abolished (as noted above this is likely to be in April 2009) a grievance must be lodged during that time as a condition of bringing a claim and lodging the grievance triggers an automatic three-month extension for presenting the tribunal claim, making it effectively nine months.

The EAT has ruled that where employment has been under a series of short fixed-term contracts (typically a school teacher employed on a series of short contracts reflecting the terms in the academic year) the six months runs from the end of the last contract forming part of that stable employment relationship not from the end of the stable employment relationship itself if that is different (*Jeffery & ors* v. *Sec'y of State for Education & anor* [2006] ICR 1062).

The original British limitation that claims could not go back for more than two years was held to be unlawful by the ECJ (see *Preston* v. *Wolverhampton Healthcare NHS Trust* [2001] IRLR 237, HL). It was therefore changed to (normally) six years (by the Equal Pay Act 1970 (Amendment) Regulations 2003, SI 2003/1656, reg.5 inserting a new EqPA 1970, s.2ZB for England and Wales and EqPA 1970, s.2ZC for Scotland). The ECJ effectively 'blessed' this six-year period on the basis that it was 'derived from equivalence with the six year limitation period applicable to ordinary domestic claims' (see *Levez* v. *T.H. Jennings (Harlow Pools) Ltd* [2000] ICR 58, EAT).

20.2.5 Statutory redundancy claims

Claims for a statutory redundancy payment must be made within six months of the termination of employment, although there is a discretion to extend time for a further six months if it is just and equitable to do so (ERA 1996, s.164). Crown and civil servants are not eligible for statutory redundancy pay (ERA 1996, s.159). However, their terms and conditions of service usually give them equivalent or better rights – but these are contractual not statutory rights.

20.2.6 Contractual claims

A contractual claim (including a claim for contractual redundancy payments) must be brought in the employment tribunal within three months of the EDT of employment.

There is discretion to extend time if it was not reasonably practicable to present the claim within three months (see **section 20.2.2** for further discussion) (Employment Tribunals Extension of Jurisdiction (England and Wales) Order 1994, SI 1994/1623, art.7). However, an employee remains entitled to bring a contract claim in the county court or High Court, when the normal limitation period of six years will apply (Limitation Act 1980, s.5).

Contract claims in employment tribunals cannot be brought by employees during their employment. They can be brought only after employment has ended as one of the conditions for being able to bring such a claim is that it 'arises or is outstanding on the termination of the employee's employment' (Employment Tribunals Extension of Jurisdiction (England and Wales) Order 1994, SI 1994/1623, art.3(c)).

20.2.7   Time for appeals to the EAT

The time within which an appeal must be instituted depends on whether the appeal is against a judgment or against an order or decision of the employment tribunal (see para.3 of the EAT Practice Direction issued on 22 May 2008, replacing the previous 2004 Practice Direction).

If the appeal is against an order or decision, the appeal must be instituted within 42 days of the date of the order or decision. The EAT will treat a tribunal's refusal to make an order or decision as itself constituting an order or decision. The date of an order or decision is the date when the order or decision was sent to the parties.

If the appeal is against a judgment, the appeal must be instituted within 42 days from the date on which the written record of the judgment was sent to the parties.

However, in three situations the time for appealing against a judgment will be 42 days from the date when written reasons were sent to the parties. This will be the case only if:

(a) written reasons were requested orally at the hearing before the tribunal; or
(b) written reasons were requested in writing within 14 days of the date on which the written record of the judgment was sent to the parties; or
(c) the tribunal itself reserved its reasons and gave them subsequently in writing.

Time runs from the date the written reasons or written record of the judgment were sent not from the date it was received (Employment Appeal Tribunal Rules 1993, r.3(2) as amended and see *Sian* v. *Abbey National plc* [2004] ICR 55, EAT). Papers must be received by the EAT by 4 pm on the relevant day for a Notice of Appeal to be in time – any document received after 4 pm will be deemed to be lodged on the next working day (see para.1.8.2 of the 2008 EAT Practice Direction). Further detail is set out in the Employment

TIME LIMITS, PROCEDURE AND SETTLEMENT

Appeal Tribunal Rules 1993, r.3(3)(a) as substituted by SI 2001/1128 and amended by the Employment Appeal Tribunal (Amendment) Rules 2004, SI 2004/2526, r.4 and in the 2008 EAT Practice Direction.

The 42-day time limit is strictly applied. The EAT has discretion to extend time but will exercise this only in rare and exceptional cases (*United Arab Emirates* v. *Abdelghafar* [1995] ICR 65, EAT). This means it will only be in rare and exceptional cases that it will be appropriate to extend time, NOT that the case itself must be a rare and exceptional one (*Jurkowska* v. *Hlmad Ltd* [2008] EWCA Civ 231, 19 March 2008).

Certain documents (the written reasons, the claim form and the response form) must be sent with the notice of appeal or it is not valid. Thus if they are not all attached to the notice of appeal as required by the rules, the appeal will not have been properly lodged and no extension of time will ordinarily be granted (*Kanapathiar* v. *London Borough of Harrow* [2003] IRLR 571). However, there was a case in 2008 in which an employer filed the main papers for appeal in time but omitted to include an essential attachment. In the event that attachment was filed 33 minutes late. The EAT exercised its discretion to allow the employer's appeal to go ahead. It was pointed out that the EAT Rules of Procedure specifically provide that dealing with a case 'justly' is the 'overriding objective' and the decision was confirmed by the Court of Appeal (*Jurkowska* v. *Hlmad Ltd*).

20.3 TRIBUNAL PROCEDURES

Procedure of Employment Tribunals is governed by rules set out in schedules to the Employment Tribunals (Constitution and Rules of Procedure) Regulations 2004, SI 2004/1861. These replaced the previous 2001 rules on 1 October 2004, and there have been minor amendments since.

In addition to the Rules of Procedure an Employment Tribunal President can make Practice Directions. At the time of writing – late June 2008 – three Practice Directions had been made. Unlike the general Practice Directions made by the EAT, they take the form of specific orders, two of which are for particular categories of case to be stayed pending judgments by superior courts in similar cases and one for combining certain specified cases.

20.3.1 Starting a claim

A claim is commenced by a claimant presenting a claim form (known as an ET1) at any regional office of the employment tribunals. Claim forms must contain the following information:

- the name and address of the parties;
- whether the claimant was an employee of the respondent;
- the grounds of the complaint, with particulars;

EMPLOYMENT LAW HANDBOOK

- whether or not the claim includes a complaint that the respondent has dismissed the claimant or has contemplated doing so;
- whether or not the claimant has raised the subject matter of the claim with the respondent in writing at least 28 days prior to presenting the claim to an employment tribunal office and if not, why the claimant has not done so (Employment Tribunal (Constitution and Rules of Procedure) Regulations 2004, SI 2004/1861, Sched.1, r.4 (ET(CRP)R 2004)).

The claim forms must be on a prescribed form (which can be obtained from any employment tribunal office, or online at **www.employmenttribunals.gov.uk**), failing which the claim form will not be accepted. The requirements for presenting an ET1 are addressed at **section 20.2.1**.

Upon receipt of the ET1, it will be passed to the Central Office of the Employment Tribunals and entered in the register. A copy will be sent to the respondent (ET(CRP)R 2004, Sched.1, r.2(2)).

The EAT has been critical of legalistic interpretation of the 2004 rules and where possible ensures that failure to follow precisely the detail of bureaucratic requirements will not prevent a claim being made or defended (*Grimmer* v. *KLM Cityhopper* [2005] IRLR 596, *Richardson* v. *U Mole Ltd* [2005] IRLR 668 and *Butlins Skyline Ltd and Smith* v. *Beynon* [2007] ICR 121, EAT). Thus in one case a tribunal chairman rejected a claim because the claimant's solicitor's address was given on the claim form rather than the claimant's address as required by r.1(4)(b). The EAT said that this error was neither 'relevant' nor 'material' and ordered that the claim form be accepted (*Hamling* v. *Coxlease School Ltd* [2007] IRLR 8, EAT).

If a claim form is rejected it must be returned to the claimant 'with an explanation of why the claim has been rejected ...' (ET(CRP)R 2004, Sched.1, r.3(1) and *Grant* v. *In 2 Focus Sales Development Services Ltd* (unreported, EAT, 30 January 2007)).

20.3.2 The response form

The employer's defence is known as its response, or ET3. Respondents must use a prescribed form which must contain the following minimum information: the respondent's full name and address; whether or not the respondent wishes to resist the claim in whole or in part; and if the respondent wishes to so resist, the grounds upon which the respondent intends to rely (ET(CRP)R 2004, Sched.1, r.4(3)). If the prescribed form is not used, the ET3 will not be accepted and default judgment might be entered against the respondent.

If, and only if, the claimant has included a claim for breach of contract, then the respondent may include a counterclaim in its response for breach of contract by the claimant (see **Chapter 3**) (ET(CRP)R 2004, Sched.1, r.7(1)).

The ET3 must be sent to the tribunal within 28 days of the date when the employer was sent a copy of the claim. If the respondent wants extra time

TIME LIMITS, PROCEDURE AND SETTLEMENT

to present its response it must apply to the tribunal for an extension of time within the same 28-day period. If this is not done, the respondent is (according to the rules) debarred from participating in the proceedings, except for a number of limited purposes only (ET(CRP)R 2004, Sched.1, r.4). However, the EAT has held that this inflexible approach in the rules can be circumvented by the device of using the tribunal's powers of review to admit the response form out of time (*Blake Envelopes* v. *Cromie* [2005] IRLR 535).

20.3.3 Default judgments

The 2004 rules introduce a system of default judgments, similar to those used in the civil courts, under which a tribunal chairman may, in certain circumstances, determine a claim without a hearing if the respondent has failed to submit a response (or make a request for an extension of time) within the 28-day time limit, or where the response fails to meet the pre-acceptance conditions. The default judgment may decide liability alone, or liability and remedy (ET(CRP)R 2004, Sched.1, r.8).

If a default judgment is issued, an employer will have only very limited rights to take a further part in the proceedings (ET(CRP)R 2004, Sched.1, r.9). However, either the employer or the employee can apply to have a default judgment reviewed (ET(CRP)R 2004, Sched.1, r.8(5) and r.33).

In considering review a tribunal should take '... account of all relevant factors including the explanation or lack of explanation for the delay and merits of the defence, weighing and balancing them one against the other and reach a conclusion which was objectively justified on the grounds of reason and justice and, in doing so, to balance the possible prejudice to each party' (*The Pestle & Mortar* v. *Turner* (unreported, EAT, 9 December 2005)).

If the parties settle the proceedings (either by means of a compromise or through Acas) before or on the date on which a default judgment in those proceedings is issued, the default judgment has no effect (ET(CRP)R 2004, Sched.1, r.8(6)).

20.3.4 Case management

Tribunals have wide powers to manage their own procedure. In doing so, they are governed by the overriding objective to deal with cases justly, which includes – so far as practicable – ensuring the parties are on an equal footing, saving expense and dealing with the case in a cost-effective and proportionate manner (ET(CRP)R 2004, reg.3).

Tribunals can make directions either following the application of a party, or of their own volition. Most tribunals automatically issue a set of standard directions, which include requirements for exchange of documents and witness statements. Almost all tribunals require the prepared witness statements to be read aloud. A minority of tribunals will not then permit further evidence-in-chief; it is therefore important that witness statements be carefully and thoroughly prepared.

It is common for tribunals to order further and better particulars or answers to questions put by the other party if they will help clarify the issues in the proceedings. However, no order will be made unless the asking party has first given the other side an opportunity to provide the information voluntarily and the other side has failed to do so.

Tribunals can also order any person within Great Britain to attend as a witness at the hearing, or to attend in order to produce documents. It is a criminal offence to fail to do so when ordered (ET(CRP)R 2004, Sched.1, r.10).

A failure by a party to comply with directions (including orders to produce documents or provide information) gives the tribunal the power at a prehearing review or at the hearing to dismiss the claim or debar the respondent from defending (ET(CRP)R 2004, Sched.1, r.13(1)). Such power is very rarely exercised in practice, since the defaulting party will usually comply once it is required to show cause why its claim/response should not be struck out (*National Grid Co plc* v. *Virdee* [1992] IRLR 555, EAT).

Striking out orders will only be made in exceptional circumstances. The Court of Appeal specifically said in 2007 that a judge should 'consider carefully whether the sanction being imposed is appropriate to all the circumstances of the case. Of course . . . the party in default can always apply for relief, but a conditional order striking out a statement of claim or dismissing the claim or counterclaim is one of the most powerful weapons in the court's case management armoury and should not be deployed unless its consequences can be justified' (*Marcan Shipping* v. *Kefalas* [2007] EWCA Civ 463).

There is no rule that striking out must be an 'all or nothing' affair. Where appropriate only part of a claim may be struck out (*Yearwood* v. *Commissioner of Police for the Metropolis* [2004] ICR 1660, EAT and *Nagy* v. *Metropolitan Police Commissioner & anor* (unreported, EAT, 22 September 2004)).

Prehearing review

Either party may apply for a prehearing review. A tribunal chairman can also order a prehearing review to determine an interim or preliminary matter (such as employment status), issue directions, and strike out a claim.

This can also be a tactical opportunity for one side to challenge the strength of the other side's case. If the tribunal considers, having examined the ET1 and ET3 and read/heard any written or oral submissions, that one party's contentions have no reasonable prospect of success, the tribunal may make an order requiring them to pay a deposit of up to £500 as a condition of proceeding. If that deposit is not paid within 21 days (or 35 days if extended), the ET1 or ET3 will be struck out (ET(CRP)R 2004, Sched.1, r.20).

20.3.5 The hearing

The hearing will usually be conducted by a panel of three: a legally qualified employment judge (known as the chairman until December 2007) and two lay 'wing' members, one with experience from an employer's perspective and the other with experience from an employee's perspective, often a trade union official. A hearing can be conducted by an employment judge and one lay member only if both parties consent (rr.8 and 9).

Very infrequently, a case can be heard by an employment judge sitting alone: this will be where there is only an issue of law to be determined and there are no disputes of fact (*Clarke* v. *Arriva Kent Thameside Ltd* (unreported, EAT, 25 July 2001)). The government has suggested that in the near future new rules will be introduced to enable an employment judge to sit alone in determining unlawful deductions from wages claims, breach of contract claims, redundancy pay claims, holiday pay claims and national minimum wage claims (Hansard, HC, col.650W, 19 February 2008).

Despite the original aim of relative informality within tribunal proceedings, they have become increasingly formal and have a remarkably similar procedure to cases in the civil courts. Opening statements are seen only in the most complex of cases and the parties usually proceed straight to evidence: however, the pattern of examination-in-chief, cross-examination, re-examination and closing speeches mirrors that of civil courts.

The order of presenting the cases is determined by the burden of proof, with the side with the primary burden of proof presenting evidence first and making the last closing submission. Usually, the applicant has the burden of proof in discrimination cases (even though the burden later shifts to the respondent once less favourable treatment has been established). In unfair dismissal cases, the applicant goes first if dismissal is not admitted (usually in constructive dismissal cases) and the respondent goes first if dismissal is admitted.

Technically, the tribunal is not 'bound by any enactment or rule of law relating to admissibility of evidence before the courts' (ET(CRP)R 2004, Sched.1, r.14(2)). In practice the only real difference is that tribunals accept hearsay evidence. They will not permit leading questions, cross-examination of one's own witnesses, or irrelevant or scandalous questions.

The decision

Decisions are usually unanimous, although they can be by a majority (with the employment judge possessing the casting vote when just two members sit).

The tribunal will usually give oral reasons for its judgment at the end of the hearing. Either party has the right to request written reasons for the judgment, either orally at the hearing or in writing within 14 days of the date on which the judgment was sent to the parties (ET(CRP)R 2004, Sched.1, r.30(3)). Written reasons are needed before an appeal can be lodged (Employment Appeal Tribunal Rules 1993, r.3 (as amended by the Employment Appeal Tribunal (Amendment) Rules 2001 and 2004)).

Costs

There is a fundamental difference between the civil courts and tribunals in relation to costs. In the courts the general rule is that costs follow the event – in other words the general rule is that reasonable costs are awarded against the losing party. In tribunals the general rule is and remains that no costs are awarded.

However, it will be different if a party in an employment tribunal case can show that the other side has, in bringing or conducting proceedings, acted vexatiously, abusively, disruptively or otherwise unreasonably, or if the bringing or conducting of proceedings was misconceived. In any of those cases a tribunal can, and with increasing frequency does, award costs (ET(CRP)R 2004, Sched.1, r.40(3)). It does not matter in those circumstances whether the party concerned won or lost. Thus in *Wolff* v. *Kingston upon Hull City Council & anor* (unreported, EAT, 7 June 2007) an employee won a constructive unfair dismissal case but had costs awarded against him because he unreasonably demanded and persisted in demanding that a re-engagement order should be made in his favour when this was quite inappropriate.

In addition if an adjournment is caused by the default of one party the other will often have a good argument for a contribution to costs (ET(CRP)R 2004, Sched.1, r.40(1)). Indeed if the adjournment is caused because the employer has not come prepared with evidence to resist a reinstatement/re-engagement application, costs must be awarded against the employer unless exceptional circumstances apply (ET(CRP)R 2004, Sched.1, r.39).

In a change to the pre-2004 position, the tribunal may now take into account the paying party's ability to pay when deciding whether to make costs orders, and deciding how much to award (ET(CRP)R 2004, Sched.1, rr.41(2) and 45(3)). The fact that an otherwise impecunious claimant has recovered a sum of money in the proceedings, or is backed by an organisation such as a union or insurance company, can be taken into account when deciding whether (and how much) to award against that claimant (*Walker* v. *Heathrow Refuelling Services* (unreported, EAT, 6 October 2004)).

The rules distinguish between 'preparation time orders', 'costs orders' and 'wasted costs' orders

- *Preparation time orders.* Preparation time orders can only be made if the receiving party has not been legally represented. They do not extend to covering the time involved in the hearing itself. Preparation time costs cannot exceed £10,000 and are subject to a fixed hourly rate (currently £25, and increasing by £1 each year from 6 April 2006) (ET(CRP)R 2004, Sched.1, r.42 and r.45(4)).

- *Costs orders.* Costs orders can only be awarded where the receiving party is legally represented at the hearing (or, if earlier, when the proceedings are determined). The amount of the costs can be agreed or, in the absence of agreement, can be assessed by the tribunal up to a maximum of £10,000, or referred to the county court for assessment by a costs judge (ET(CRP)R 2004, Sched.1, r.38 and r.41). Much higher amounts are then possible (*Sharma* v. *Ealing Borough Council* (unreported, EAT, 5 January 2006) and *Khan* v. *Kirklees Metropolitan Borough Council* [2007] EWCA Civ 1342, where an employment tribunal had referred to Mr Khan as 'by some distance the most obdurate, recalcitrant and openly contemptuous party that any of us have ever had to deal with'. He was ordered to pay more than £80,000).
- *Wasted costs orders.* A party's representative (unless a 'not for profit' organisation such as a union or Citizens Advice Bureau) who has incurred unnecessary costs may be ordered to pay 'wasted costs', even to his own client, if he has acted improperly, unreasonably or negligently and the tribunal considers it reasonable to make such an order (ET(CRP)R 2004, Sched.1, r.48).

Rather strangely, a tribunal has no power to award costs against an employer who totally fails to take any part at all in the proceedings and who does not even put in a response to an employee's claim. Under r.38(4) costs can only be awarded in relation to any part the employer has taken in the proceedings and therefore if he has taken no part at all costs simply cannot be awarded (*Sutton* v. *The Ranch Ltd* [2006] ICR 1170, EAT).

If requested a tribunal must provide written reasons for making a costs order within 14 days of making it (ET(CRP)R 2004, Sched.1, r.38(10)). A tribunal's failure (under the previous 2001 rules) to provide clear reasons for a costs order resulted in the order being overruled by the Court of Appeal in *Lodwick* v. *London Borough of Southwark* [2004] ICR 884, CA.

The common tactic by which a party to a case suggests to his opponent, before trial, that his case is incontrovertible and that if the opponent proceeds to trial, he will make an application for costs does not amount to 'unreasonable conduct' entitling the opponent to costs if in fact he wins (*Read* v. *The Members of Llanyrafon Community* (unreported, EAT, 9 February 2006), a case concerning the EAT rules on costs, but presumably the same logic would apply in the case of a costs application in an employment tribunal). Nevertheless it can make an order for costs more likely. In a 2006 case the EAT indicated that the employers involved, having threatened to apply for costs if they won, '. . . can have little complaint at being ordered to pay the costs of this appeal' (*Sims Ltd* v. *McKee* (unreported, EAT, 16 March 2006)).

20.3.6 Reviews/appeals

Either party can seek to review or appeal the tribunal's decision.

EMPLOYMENT LAW HANDBOOK

Review

The tribunal can review its own decision on one of a number of specified grounds. These grounds concern issues relating to the fairness of the hearing, for example, if one party was not notified of the hearing date or failed to attend, or if new evidence has become available which could not have been produced at the original hearing. An application for a review must be made within 14 days of the tribunal's written decision being sent to the parties. The tribunal can also review a default judgment. On a review, the tribunal can confirm its earlier decision, vary it, or revoke the decision and order a rehearing (ET(CRP)R 2004, Sched.1, r.36).

Appeal

A disgruntled litigant can appeal a tribunal's decision. An appeal must be made to the EAT and lodged at the EAT Office, Audit House, 58 Victoria Embankment, London EC4Y 0DS, tel: 020 7233 1041 (Employment Tribunals Act 1996, s.21).

Appeals to the EAT (and the Court of Appeal) can be on points of law only. As a judge pithily put it recently 'the EAT does not do appeals on fact, it does appeals on law' (*Whitehead* v. *Governors of Corley School and Coventry City Council* (unreported, EAT, 13 March 2007)). Only in a very clear case of plain perversity or a total absence of discernible reasoning will the EAT find an error of law in an employment tribunal's assessment of the amount of compensation. Save in such a case the original tribunal's assessment will therefore invariably be upheld by the EAT (*J P Ticktum & Shranks Solicitors* v. *Bannister* (unreported, EAT, 5 July 2007)).

New points which were not raised at the original hearing will only be permitted in exceptional circumstances (*Kumchyk* v. *Derby City Council* [1978] ICR 116, EAT; *Glennie* v. *Independent Magazines (UK) Ltd* [1999] IRLR 719, CA; and *Khan* v. *Royal Mail plc* [2006] EWCA Civ 2). The same applies to points conceded at the original tribunal hearing, although the EAT does have a discretion to hear such points which it will exercise in exceptional circumstances (see, for example, *Lipscombe* v. *Forestry Commission* (unreported, EAT, 28 September 2006)). Exceptional circumstances can include new interpretation of EC law by the European Court of Justice (*Celtec Ltd* v. *Astley & ors* [2006] ICR 992, HL and *Leicestershire County Council* v. *Unison* [2006] EWCA Civ 825). New evidence will be allowed on appeal only if it could not have been obtained with reasonable diligence for the original hearing, is relevant and apparently credible and would probably have had an important influence on the original hearing (*Jones* v. *Governing Body of Burdett Coutts School* [1999] ICR 38, CA).

An appeal must be lodged by 4 pm within 42 days from the date on which written reasons of the tribunal's decision were sent to the parties (see **section 20.2.7** for more information on time limits). Sometimes, the appellant will be required to attend a preliminary hearing in order to demonstrate that there is an arguable point of law. The EAT will not take kindly to any attempt to dress up what it regards as really an appeal based on a question of fact as an appeal on a question of law. If successful, or if a full hearing is ordered following a sift of the papers, a full hearing will take place with both sides appearing. The entire process from start to finish normally takes four to nine months. Parties to an appeal must ensure that they comply with the 2008 Employment Appeal Tribunal Practice Direction (a copy of which is normally sent to the parties when an appeal is lodged).

Appeals from the EAT are to the Court of Appeal. The traditional view is that it is the original employment tribunal's, not the EAT's, decision which will then be under scrutiny (*Hennessy* v. *Craigmyle & Co Ltd* [1986] ICR 461, CA). However, the Court of Appeal has recently suggested that this is too simplistic an approach. In *Gover* v. *Property Care Ltd* [2006] ICR 1073, CA, Buxton LJ said:

> I would be less than frank if I did not express some reserve about [the guidance in *Hennessy* v. *Craigmyle*], both from the point of view of jurisdiction and from the point of view of the management of the business of this court. As to authority, this court's jurisdiction to hear this appeal, coming as it does from a statutory tribunal, is only to be found in Employment Tribunals Act 1996, s.37(1), which provides for an appeal from the EAT on a question of law only. I do not see how we can in any realistic sense be hearing an appeal from the EAT if we are only concerned with whether the ET was right. As to the business of this court, the assumption that we in effect repeat the exercise already performed by the expert EAT of reviewing the decision of the ET tends in practice to impose on this court an exercise that is inappropriate both in its nature and in its extent.

20.4 COMPROMISE OF CLAIMS

In order to prevent employees being pressured into signing away their rights, perhaps as a condition of being given employment or receiving a final salary payment, the employment legislation provides that clauses in agreements which have the effect of contracting out of, disapplying or compromising an employee's rights are void (Employment Tribunals Act 1996, s.18; ERA 1996, s.203; SDA 1975, s.77 (also covering EqPA 1970); RRA 1976, s.72; TULRCA 1992, s.288; DDA 1995, s.9; National Minimum Wage Act 1998, s.49; WTR 1998, reg.35; Employment Equality (Sexual Orientation) Regulations 2003, Sched.4, Part 1; Employment Equality (Religion or Belief) Regulations 2003, Sched.4, Part 1; Employment Equality (Age) Regulations 2006, Sched 5, Part 1).

There are three main exceptions to this:

1. Where the parties enter into a formal compromise agreement to settle a dispute.
2. Where the settlement has been concluded through Acas.
3. Settlement via the tribunal.

20.4.1 Compromise agreements

In order to compromise an employee's claims, the parties can enter into a formal compromise agreement. The requirements for the compromise agreement to be effective are:

1. It must be in writing.
2. It must relate to the particular proceedings.
3. The employee must have received advice from a relevant independent advisor as to the terms and effect of the proposed agreement and, in particular, its effect on the employee's ability to pursue a claim before an employment tribunal. A relevant independent advisor must be a qualified lawyer, a Fellow of the Institute of Legal Executives employed by a solicitors' practice, a Citizens Advice Bureau or Law Centre advisor or a trade union official certified by the union as competent to give advice.
4. The advisor must be covered by professional indemnity insurance.
5. The advisor must be identified in the agreement.
6. The agreement must state that the above requirements are satisfied.

The rules for compromise agreements are set out in ERA 1996, s.203 in relation to that Act. The anti-discrimination Acts and regulations contain similar provisions (see the section and clause references noted at the beginning of this section).

Note that a compromise agreement can only bind in respect of the particular proceedings being settled. If an employer wishes to enter into a blanket full and final settlement agreement, some commentators suggest it is safer to do so via Acas. However, doubt has been cast on the parties' abilities to enter into very wide-ranging settlements and the authors' view is that there is no real difference caused by the method of settlement: what is important is the precise words used in the agreement (*Lunt* v. *Merseyside TEC Ltd* [1999] ICR 17, EAT; *Royal National Orthopaedic Hospital Trust* v. *Howard* [2002] IRLR 849). The parties must expressly identify the particular proceedings to which the compromise agreement relates, either by generic description (i.e. 'unfair dismissal'), or by reference to the section of the relevant statute. It is not enough to use a rolled-up expression such as 'all statutory rights' nor to simply refer to the title of the statute nor that the 'particular proceedings' were identified in correspondence before the compromise agreement was concluded (*Hinton* v. *University of East London* [2005] ICR 1260, CA).

To be valid a compromise agreement must state that the conditions regulating compromise agreements set out in the relevant statute are satisfied. The absence of a clause confirming that the conditions are satisfied is fatal. The EAT has held that a compromise agreement which confirmed that the conditions in ERA 1996, s.203 had been satisfied but did not specifically confirm that the conditions in relevant discrimination statutes (SDA 1975, s.77 and RRA 1976, s.72) had been satisfied was therefore not valid to cover claims of race and sex discrimination. This was so even though the conditions had in fact been satisfied and even though for practical purposes the conditions are the same in all of them (*Palihakkara* v. *British Telecommunications Plc* (unreported, EAT, 9 October 2006)).

If a representative had neither actual nor ostensible authority to negotiate a compromise it will not be binding (*Gloystarne & Co Ltd* v. *Martin* [2001] IRLR 15, EAT).

The courts have held that a settlement of a race discrimination claim prevented the employee from bringing a personal injury claim arising out of the same facts in the county court, since damages for personal injury are available for race discrimination claims and the settlement must be taken to have settled that as well. It is highly likely that the same principle will hold true for settlements of other discrimination claims (*Sheriff* v. *Klyne Tugs (Lowestoft) Ltd* [1999] IRLR 481).

A point of considerable practical importance for employers is that it can be prudent to ensure that any compromise agreement is made subject to warranties being given by the employee to the effect that he is not in breach of any significant term of his employment contract (save as might be specified) including in particular any breach which would have entitled the employer to terminate his contract without notice or payment in lieu of notice. A clause along these lines can give valuable protection to an employer (*Collidge* v. *Freeport Plc* [2008] EWCA Civ 485, 5 March 2008). Other useful warranties might include one confirming that the employee has returned any property (e.g. computers) belonging to the employer and/or that he has not found other employment. Of course, even without specific warranties an employer will have rights if it turns out that representations by the employee on which he relied in agreeing to enter a compromise agreement were fraudulently untrue (*Crystal Palace FC (2000) Ltd* v. *Dowie* [2007] IRLR 682, QBD).

20.4.2 Settlement through Acas

Acas, the Advisory, Conciliation and Arbitration Service, is a non-departmental body governed by an independent council but funded by the government. It is best known for its involvement in attempts to settle collective disputes but it also has a statutory duty, under ETA 1996, s.18, to endeavour to promote a settlement of most disputes of a kind falling within the jurisdiction of employment tribunals 'without their being determined by an employment tribunal'. This statutory duty exists whether or not tribunal proceedings have been started. ET(CRP)R 2004 altered Acas's approach in individual rights disputes by making a distinction between complex cases where no fixed conciliation period would apply and others where there are fixed 'conciliation periods' within which the parties have to reach an Acas conciliated settlement if they are going to do so.

Although Acas still had power to provide conciliation after expiry of that period it did so only rarely. At the end of March 2008 Acas announced that, in the light of the government's intention to abolish fixed periods of conciliation along with the statutory dispute resolution procedures it would with effect from 1 April 2008 exercise its power to conciliate in all cases, irrespective of whether the fixed period for conciliation has expired (see Acas letter to National Stakeholders re Fixed Periods, March 2008).

Acas conciliation officers can be a useful go-between amongst the parties, particularly when one or more parties are unrepresented. However, conciliation officers will not simply rubber-stamp an agreement reached between the parties: Acas must have played some part in bringing that agreement about. Acas's role is likely to be considerably increased from April 2009 when the compulsory statutory dispute resolution procedures are due to be ended (see **Chapter 4**).

While Acas conciliation has been quite frequently used successfully in individual rights disputes, Acas has traditionally not been so successful in attempts at using arbitration or mediation in individual disputes. The formality of the rules governing arbitration may put off potential applicants and mediation, while not unknown, is a relatively new area of activity for Acas.

It may be that there will be much greater interest in using Acas-provided mediation once the compulsory statutory dispute resolution procedures have been ended. In the authors' view, a significant reason for the infrequent use of mediation in employment disputes generally is financial – if an employee knows that he can go to a tribunal without being liable for costs, why should he agree to contribute to the costs of a mediator? And if the employer has agreed to pay the mediator's costs, the employee may not be easily convinced that the mediator will be totally unbiased. If Acas can promote and provide mediation services without charge to the parties, this problem will be solved – and given that in February 2008 the government announced up to an extra £37 million of funding over three years for Acas 'in the shake-up to simplify the dispute resolution system' it may be that this will be a real possibility.

If the parties reach settlement through Acas 'where a conciliation officer has taken action under ETA 1996, s.18' (ERA 1996, s.203(2)(e)) it will be recorded in a document known as a COT3. Such a settlement is binding. It does not need to comply with the formalities of a compromise agreement. Acas will notify the tribunal that the parties have settled.

20.4.3 Settlement via the tribunal

Cases frequently settle at the door of the tribunal. When that occurs, there are two common methods of effecting the settlement. The first, and least desirable, is asking the tribunal to make an order by consent. This is disadvantageous to the employer, because the tribunal will record a finding against the employer (which the employer is usually keen to avoid). It is also disadvantageous to many employees because, when the tribunal makes a formal order, the recoupment regulations apply (Employment Protection (Recoupment of Jobseeker's Allowance and Income Support) Regulations 1996, SI 1996/2349). Under these regulations social security benefits paid, for example, while a dismissed employee was out of work, will be clawed back by the DWP out of the settlement monies.

The preferred method is for the parties to draft a *Tomlin* order (named after Mr Justice Tomlin, dating from *Dashwood* v. *Dashwood* [1927] WN 276). This is a short consent order providing for an application be stayed upon terms attached in a schedule to the order with the parties having permission to apply to reinstate the application. The schedule contains the terms of agreement between the parties which will usually include a provision that their liabilities to each other shall be discharged on payment of the sums agreed and/or if no application to reinstate is made within a defined period, say 28 days. If the employer fails to pay any monies under the order, the employee can apply to reinstate the claim. This has the advantage that, technically, the tribunal has not ordered payment of any monies: thus the recoupment regulations do not apply.

A dedicated website at **www.emplaw.co.uk/lshandbook** provides links to judgments and other material referred to in this chapter.

APPENDIX A
Employment tribunal addresses

Travel information, maps and e-mail addresses for each office are available at the Tribunals Service website at **www.employmenttribunals.gov.uk/index.htm**. Enquiries for Hearing Centres should be made through the relevant tribunal office.

National Enquiry Line
100 Southgate St
Bury St Edmunds
Suffolk IP33 2AQ
Tel: 0845 795 9775
Fax: 01284 766334

REGIONAL OFFICES

Aberdeen
Mezzanine Floor
Atholl House
84–88 Guild Street
Aberdeen AB11 6LT
Tel: 01224 593137
Fax: 01224 593138

Ashford
1st Floor
Ashford House
County Square Shopping Centre
Ashford
Kent TN23 1YB
Tel: 01233 621346
Fax: 01233 624423

EMPLOYMENT TRIBUNAL ADDRESSES

Bedford
8–10 Howard Street
Bedford MK40 3HS
Tel: 01234 351306
Fax: 01234 352315

Birmingham
Phoenix House
1–3 Newhall Street
Birmingham B3 3NH
Tel: 0121 236 6051
Fax: 0121 236 6029

Bristol
Ground Floor
The Crescent Centre
Temple Back
Bristol BS1 6EZ
Tel: 0117 929 8261
Fax: 0117 925 3452

Bury St Edmunds
100 Southgate Street
Bury St Edmunds
Suffolk IP33 2AQ
Tel: 01284 762171
Fax: 01284 706064

Bury St Edmunds ET has hearing centres at:

Norwich
Elliot House
130 Ber Street
Norwich
NR1 3TZ
and at:
Cambridge
1st Floor
Eastbrook
Shaftesbury Road
Cambridge
CB2 2DJ

APPENDIX A

Cardiff
2nd Floor
Caradog House
1–6 St Andrew's Place
Cardiff CF10 3BE
Tel: 029 2067 8100
Fax: 029 2022 5906

Dundee
Ground Floor
Block C
Caledonian House
Greenmarket
Dundee DD1 4QX
Tel: 0138 222 1578
Fax: 0138 222 7136

Edinburgh
54–56 Melville Street
Edinburgh EH3 7HF
Tel: 0131 226 5584
Fax: 0131 220 6847

Exeter
2nd Floor
Keble House
Southernhay Gardens
Exeter EX1 1NT
Tel: 01392 279665
Fax: 01392 430063

Glasgow
Eagle Building
215 Bothwell Street
Glasgow G2 7TS
Tel: 0141 204 0730
Fax: 0141 204 0732

Leeds
4th Floor
City Exchange
11 Albion Street
Leeds LS1 5ES
Tel: 0113 245 9741
Fax: 0113 242 8843

Leeds ET has a hearing centre at
Hull
Wilberforce Court
Alfred Gelder Street
Hull HU1 1YR

Leicester
5A New Walk
Leicester LE1 6TE
Tel: 0116 255 0099
Fax: 0116 255 6099

Liverpool
1st Floor
Cunard Building
Pier Head
Liverpool L3 1TS
Tel: 0151 236 9397
Fax: 0151 231 1484

London Central
Ground Floor
Victory House
30–34 Kingsway
London WC2B 6EX
Tel: 020 7273 8603
Fax: 020 7273 8686

Stratford East *(formerly London East)*
44 The Broadway
Stratford
London E15 1XH
Tel: 020 8221 0921
Fax: 020 8221 0398

APPENDIX A

Watford *(formerly London North)*
3rd Floor
Radius House
51 Clarendon Road
Watford
Herts WD1 1HU
Tel: 01923 281750
Fax: 01923 281781

London South
Montague Court
101 London Road
West Croydon CR0 2RF
Tel: 020 8667 9131
Fax: 020 8649 9470

Manchester
Alexandra House
14–22 The Parsonage
Manchester M3 2JA
Tel: 0161 833 6100
Fax: 0161 832 0249

Newcastle-upon-Tyne
Quayside House
110 Quayside
Newcastle-upon-Tyne NE1 3DX
Tel: 0191 260 6900
Fax: 0191 222 1680

Newcastle ET has hearing centres at
Thornaby
Part Ground Floor
Christine House
4 Sorbonne Close
Thornaby-on-Tees
Cleveland
TS17 6DA
and at:

Carlisle
1st Floor
Stocklund House
Castle Street
Carlisle
Cumbria

Nottingham
3rd Floor
Byron House
2A Maid Marian Way
Nottingham NG1 6HS
Tel: 0115 947 5701
Fax: 0115 950 7612

Nottingham ET has hearing centres at:
Boston
Boston Court House
55 Norfolk Street
Boston
Lincs
PE21 6PE
and at:
Lincoln
Lincoln Magistrates' Court
358 High Street
Lincoln
LN5 7QA

Reading
5th Floor
30–31 Friar Street
Reading RG1 1DY
Tel: 0118 959 4917
Fax: 0118 956 8066

Sheffield
14 East Parade
Sheffield S1 2ET
Tel: 0114 276 0348
Fax: 0114 276 2551

APPENDIX A

Shrewsbury
Prospect House
Belle Vue Road
Shrewsbury SY3 7AR
Tel: 01743 358341
Fax: 01743 244186

Southampton
3rd Floor
Duke's Keep
Marsh Lane
Southampton
SO14 3EX
Tel: 023 8071 6400
Fax: 023 8063 5506

Southampton ET has a hearing centre at:
Brighton
City Gate House
185 Dyke Road
Brighton
BN3 1TL

APPENDIX B
Legislative changes in progress

See also Appendix C – Bills before Parliament and Appendix D – Postscript: important developments between 1 July 2008 and 1 October 2008.

On 15 May 2008 the government published a draft legislative programme for 2008/09. This includes proposals for:

- a right to time off to train;
- enhanced flexible working;
- more rights for agency workers; and
- further welfare reform to enhance skills and get people ready for work.

On 26 June 2008 the government published a White Paper entitled 'A Framework for a Fairer Future – The Equality Bill'. This includes proposals for an Equality Bill which will be written in plain English to 'declutter what has become a thicket of legislation and guidance' (nine major pieces of discrimination legislation, around 100 statutory instruments setting out connected rules and regulations and more than 2,500 pages of guidance and statutory codes of practice) and includes proposals for:

- positive sex and race discrimination to be allowed where appropriate;
- a ban on the 'gagging clauses' which some companies use to forbid staff from discussing their remuneration;
- all public sector firms and firms with public sector contracts to be required to publish figures showing the 'gender pay gap';
- extension of use of women-only shortlists in selecting parliamentary candidates to 2030 (but there are no plans for ethnic minority shortlists);
- giving tribunals power to make wider recommendations in discrimination cases so that there are benefits for the rest of the workforce of the employer found to have discriminated;
- enabling EHRC, trade unions and other bodies (with permission of the court) to be able to bring representative discrimination law actions.

There follows below a table of items known as at 1 July 2008 to be subject to change in the near future.

APPENDIX B

Subject	Statutory or other provision	Proposed and/or likely implementation
Apprentices	Hansard, HC col.468, 29 November 2007	Not known
Dispute Resolution Procedures (proposals for abolition and/or replacement of the 2004 statutory rules)	Employment Bill	6 April 2009
Holiday entitlement	Working Time (Amendment) Regulations 2007, SI 2007/2079	1 October 2007 and 1 April 2009
Maternity and Adoption Leave and Pay (removing differences in contractual entitlements between ordinary and additional leave periods)	(Draft) Maternity and Parental Leave etc. and the Paternity and Adoption Leave (Amendment) Regulations 2008. Sex Discrimination Act 1975 (Amendment) Regulations 2008, SI 2008/656	If expected week of childbirth/adoption begins on or after 5 October 2008.
Maternity and Adoption Leave and Pay (extension to 52 weeks)	HMRC notes 'Important information relating to Additional Paternity Leave and Pay' (Oct 2007)	If expected week of childbirth/adoption begins on or after 1 April 2010.
Additional Paternity Leave and Pay (introduction of)	HMRC notes 'Important information relating to Additional Paternity Leave and Pay' (Oct 2007)	If expected week of childbirth/adoption begins on or after 1 April 2010.
National minimum wage increase	(Draft) National Minimum Wage Regulations 1999 (Amendment) Regulations 2008	1 October 2008 (and annually).
Partnership law	(Draft) Partnerships Bill (drafted by the Law Commission, Nov 2003)	Draft only – not known.
Services Directive 2006/123/EC	EC Directive 2006/123 was signed on 12 December 2006	Final date for implementation is 28 December 2009.
Statutory Sick Pay (agency workers on short fixed-term contracts to have same rights as other employees)	(Draft) Fixed-term Employees (Prevention of Less Favourable Treatment) (Amendment) Regulations 2008	27 October 2008

LEGISLATIVE CHANGES IN PROGRESS

Subject	Statutory or other provision	Proposed and/or likely implementation
Temporary/agency workers	EU political agreement on Working Time and Working Conditions for Temporary Agency Workers, 10 June 2008	Not known but probably in 'next parliamentary session'.
Working time – on-call time and 48 hr week opt-out	EU political agreement on Working Time and Working Conditions for Temporary Agency Workers, 10 June 2008	Not known but probably in 'next parliamentary session'.
Working time – doctors in training	Working Time Regulations/doctors	1 August 2007 (interim stage – 56 hrs max pw); 1 August 2009 (final stage – 48 hrs max pw).
Working time regulations – road transport	Working Time Regulations/HGV and PSV drivers	4 April 2005 (for self-employed drivers, 23 March 2009).

APPENDIX C

Main employment law related Bills before Parliament

The main employment law related Bills before Parliament as at 1 July 2008 are listed in the table below.

Title	Main employment law related provision	1st reading date
Autumn Bank Holiday Bill	To introduce a bank holiday in the Autumn.	4 March 2008 (HC)
Bank Holiday (Contribution of Polish Citizens) Bill	Establish a bank holiday to celebrate the contribution of Polish citizens to Great Britain since 1940.	4 June 2008 (HC)
Crown Employment (Nationality) Bill	Open more civil service jobs to those of any nationality.	10 December 2007
Education and Skills Bill	Raise age for leaving school or training.	28 November 2007 (HC)
Employment Bill	See notes below.	6 December 2007 (HL)
Employment Retention Bill	Rehabilitation assessments and leave for newly disabled workers.	29 January 2008 (HC)
Health and Safety (Offences) Bill	Increase to £20K maximum fine imposed by lower courts.	5 December 2007 (HC)
Human Rights Act 1998 (Meaning of Public Function) Bill	Clarifies the meaning of 'public function' in Human Rights Act 1998, s.6.	18 December 2007 (HC)
National Insurance Contributions Bill	Aims to align the upper earnings limit for NICs with the higher rate threshold.	12 November 2007

MAIN EMPLOYMENT LAW RELATED BILLS BEFORE PARLIAMENT

EMPLOYMENT BILL

The Employment Bill is quite short (22 clauses) but very significant. It is a government Bill introduced in the House of Lords on 6 December 2007. It passed all stages in the House of Lords and then had its first reading in the House of Commons on 4 June 2008.

A draft Employment Act 2008 (Commencement No.1 and Transitional and Saving Provisions) Order 2008 proposes 6 April 2009 as the date for clauses 1–7 to come into force (Annex B to the BERR Dispute Resolution Consultation published July 2008).

In outline it provides for:

- replacement of the 2004 compulsory dispute resolution procedures (clauses 1–7);
- new National Minimum Wage enforcement powers (clauses 8–14);
- strengthening the Employment Agencies Act 1973 (clauses 15–17);
- rights of unions to expel members (clause 18).

As recommended by the March 2007 Gibbons Review, the Employment Bill (clause 1) will, when enacted and brought into force, repeal ss.29–33 of, and Scheds.2–4 to, the Employment Act 2002. The statutory dispute resolution procedures introduced in October 2004 will then be removed in their entirety. Instead, the Acas Code of Practice on Disciplinary and Grievance Procedures is to be reviewed and given teeth.

The current position is that employment tribunals do little more than take note of official Codes of Practice, but new rules will provide that if an employer has failed to follow various Codes of Practice including this one there will be specific power for an employment tribunal to increase compensatory award on unfair dismissal by up to 25 per cent if it considers it just and equitable to do so (cl.3 of the Employment Bill provides for a new TULRCA 1992, s.207A to implement this proposal).

Of particular note is that cl.2 of the Employment Bill provides for repeal of ERA 1996, s.98A. This section was introduced in October 2004 to partially override the House of Lords 1998 ruling in the *Polkey* case (*Polkey* v. *AE Dayton Services Ltd* [1988] ICR 142, HL). The House of Lords had ruled that a dismissal could be unfair on procedural grounds alone, but that in such a case the tribunal should reduce or eliminate compensatory award (but not basic award) to reflect any likelihood that the dismissal would have gone ahead anyway even if correct procedures had been followed. Section 98A provided that as from October 2004 a dismissal would be automatically unfair if an employer had not completed the then new statutory procedures – but that the employer's failure to comply with other (e.g. contractual) procedures in respect of the dismissal would not be taken into account if the employment tribunal was satisfied that following them would have had no effect on the employer's decision to dismiss.

When cl.2 of the Employment Bill comes into force the position will revert to that established by the House of Lords in *Polkey*.

Clauses 5 and 6 amend provisions governing Acas conciliation in employment disputes (amendments are to be made to the Employment Tribunals Act 1996). Fixed periods of Acas conciliation will be abolished.

Clause 7 will give employment tribunals power to award compensation for any financial loss which is attributable to an unlawful deduction from wages or payments or to non-payment of statutory redundancy pay.

Clauses 8–14 provide for tightening up of National Minimum Wage enforcement processes and increased remuneration where arrears of NMW are outstanding for a long time.

Clauses 15–17 increase protection for agency workers.

Clause 18 concerns the right of a union to expel a member who belongs to a political party of which the union disapproves, following the ruling by the European Court of Human Rights in *ASLEF* v. *United Kingdom*, ECtHR, 27 February 2007. It provides for the relevant part of trade union law (TULRCA 1992, s.174) to be amended to ensure compatibility with the ECHR

It was suggested during second reading in the House of Lords on 7 January 2008 that the time has come for a new employment law consolidating Act (the most recent consolidating Act being the still current ERA 1996, which itself replaced the 1978 consolidating Act).

APPENDIX D

Postscript: important developments between 1 July 2008 and 1 October 2008

CONTENTS

- Introduction
- Employment law related statutory instruments in force from 1 October 2008
- Compromise agreements
- Compulsory school age
- Disability discrimination
- Disciplinary and grievance procedures
- Discrimination (general)
- Discrimination on grounds of religion or belief
- Equal pay and terms of employment
- Flexible working
- Maternity leave
- Minimum wages and tips
- Redundancy pay (enhanced)
- Remedies and compensation
- Trade unions
- Tribunal procedure

INTRODUCTION

The main text of this book is based on law at 1 July 2008.

There follow below notes on main British employment law developments between 1 July 2008 and 1 October 2008 not covered in the main text.

References are to pages or chapters in the main text where the most relevant main commentary can be found.

BERR policy is where possible to introduce changes made by statutory instrument on 1 April and 1 October in each year. There follows immediately below a list of the main employment law related statutory instruments which came into force on 1 October 2008

APPENDIX D

EMPLOYMENT LAW RELATED STATUTORY INSTRUMENTS IN FORCE FROM 1 OCTOBER 2008

- Armed Forces Act 2006 (Commencement No. 3) Order 2008, SI 2008/1650
- Companies Act 2006 (Commencement No. 6, Saving and Commencement Nos. 3 and 5 (Amendment)) Order 2008, SI 2008/674
- Employers' Liability (Compulsory Insurance) (Amendment) Regulations 2008, SI 2008/1765
- Mesothelioma Lump Sum Payments (Claims and Reconsiderations) Regulations 2008, SI 2008/1595
- Mesothelioma Lump Sum Payments (Conditions and Amounts) Regulations 2008, SI 2008/1963
- Metropolitan Police Authority Regulations 2008, SI 2008/631 apply in respect of appointments of members of the Metropolitan Police Authority taking effect on or after 1 October 2008
- National Minimum Wage Regulations 1999 (Amendment) Regulations 2008, SI 2008/1894
- Occupational Pension Schemes (Transfer Values) (Amendment) Regulations 2008, SI 2008/1050
- Personal and Occupational Pension Schemes (Amendment) Regulations 2008, SI 2008/1979
- Police Authority Regulations 2008, SI 2008/630 in so far as they revoke the Police Authorities (Selection Panel) Regulations 1994, SI 1994/2023
- Social Security (Miscellaneous Amendments) (No. 3) Regulations 2008, SI 2008/2365
- Social Security (Recovery of Benefits) (Lump Sum Payments) Regulations 2008, SI 2008/1596

Note also the Sex Discrimination Act 1975 (Amendment) Regulations 2008, SI 2008/656 and the Maternity and Parental Leave etc. and the Paternity and Adoption Leave (Amendment) Regulations 2008, SI 2008/1966. These did not come into force on 1 October 2008 and so are not in the list above. They came into force on 6 April 2008 and 23 July 2008 respectively but affect those whose expected week of childbirth (or adoption) begins on or after 5 October 2008 (see **section 7.3.4**).

COMPROMISE AGREEMENTS

Page 422

A BERR dispute resolution consultation document issued in July 2008 invites comments on proposals from the Chartered Institute of Personnel and Development (CIPD) to include their qualified HR Professionals within the definition of 'relevant independent advisor'.

POSTSCRIPT: IMPORTANT DEVELOPMENTS

COMPULSORY SCHOOL AGE

Pages 94, 97, 120, 130, 131, 132, 155, 325, 436

Amongst other things the Education and Skills Bill will raise the age until which young people must stay in education or training. The government's stated intention is that by 2013, all 17 year olds, and by 2015, all 18 year olds, will be participating in some form of education or training.

The Bill completed all stages in the House of Commons in May 2008 and then moved to the House of Lords. It had not been enacted by 1 October 2008.

DISABILITY DISCRIMINATION

Page 312

The European Court of Justice ruled on 17 July 2008 that discrimination against a non-disabled employee because he or she is a carer of, or is otherwise associated with, a disabled person is forbidden by the EC Equal Treatment Framework Directive, 2000/78/EC (*Coleman* v. *Attridge Law*, ECJ Case C-303/06 reported at [2008] IRLR 722).

The result will be to undermine the basis of much of the employment related part of the Disability Discrimination Act 1995. In particular it will follow that Disability Discrimination Act 1995 s.3A(5) is incompatible with EC law unless in some way its language can be given a 'purposive interpretation' to bring it into line and make it say what it apparently does not say.

DISCIPLINARY AND GRIEVANCE PROCEDURES

Page 5 (and throughout)

As noted in the main text, the compulsory statutory dispute resolution procedures introduced in 2004 have not been a success and are to be replaced with less prescriptive procedures being introduced under the current Employment Bill.

The Employment Bill had not been enacted at 1 October 2008. However the government has issued in advance a draft Employment Act 2008 (Commencement No 1 and Transitional and Saving Provisions) Order 2008 which confirms 6 April 2009 as the intended start date for the new less prescriptive procedures referred to in the main text. This draft order is annexed as a schedule to a BERR consultation document issued in July 2008.

As a separate matter, the Court of Appeal ruled in July 2008 that unreasonable delay in completing a statutory disciplinary/dismissal procedure cannot be said to be a failure to complete the procedure. It follows that delay on its own will not make a resulting dismissal automatically unfair under the 2004 dispute resolution procedures (*Selvarajan* v. *Wilmot & ors* [2008] IRLR 824 on 23 July, effectively overruling a line of EAT authorities from *Khan* v. *Home Office* (EAT, unreported, 17 November 2006), *Sovereign Business Integration Plc* v. *Trybus* (EAT, unreported, 15 June 2007) and *Yorkshire Housing Ltd* v. *Swanson* [2008] IRLR 607).

DISCRIMINATION (GENERAL)

Chapters 14–16

A BERR dispute resolution consultation document issued in July 2008 invites comments on proposals to give employment tribunals a new power, similar to one which already exists in Northern Ireland, to make recommendations in cases revealing unlawful discrimination that an employer should 'take action' to reduce the adverse effect on persons other than the complainant.

DISCRIMINATION ON GROUNDS OF RELIGION OR BELIEF

Page 339

If only because of the publicity the case received, a further example should be added to the list in the main text. In July 2008 an employment tribunal ruled that Islington Council had discriminated against one of its registrars, Lillian Ladele, who had been disciplined by the Council for refusing to conduct civil partnership ceremonies on the basis that they went against her Christian faith.

EQUAL PAY AND TERMS OF EMPLOYMENT

Page 351

The Court of Appeal handed down judgment in *Redcar & Cleveland Borough Council* v. *Bainbridge and others; Surtees and others* v. *Middlesbrough Council* [2008] EWCA Civ 885 on 29 July 2008, also reported at [2008] IRLR 776.

Main points arising from the judgment include:

1. When considering the genuine material factor (gmf) defence to an equal pay claim the start point is to consider whether the factor which the employer says was the reason for inequality of pay between men and women is in any way connected with sex. There are three possible positions: (a) that sex was the reason for the disparity – the gmf defence then

POSTSCRIPT: IMPORTANT DEVELOPMENTS

clearly fails; (b) that sex had nothing whatsoever to do with the reason for the disparity – the gmf defence then clearly succeeds; and (c) the position is somewhere in between in that the reason for the pay disparity is not directly sex-related but it is indirectly sex-related. In this third situation in order to decide whether the gmf defence can succeed the correct test to apply is the one relevant generally in indirect discrimination cases, namely whether the putative gmf was a proportionate means to achieve a legitimate aim.

2. Arrangements for phasing in pay adjustments to eliminate unlawful unequal pay can themselves breach the equal pay rules if they provide 'pay protection' for those whose pay will actually reduce but exclude those whose pay would reduce if they had been properly paid in the first place. Those whose pay would reduce if they had been properly paid in the first place may therefore bring an equal pay claim based on their exclusion from the phasing in arrangements. If they do so the question of whether the employer can successfully use the gmf defence (by claiming that he was using a proportionate means to achieve a legitimate aim) should be considered by reference to the exclusion of the claimants from the pay protection arrangements and not by reference to the pay protection arrangement as a whole. In other words, in those circumstances a narrow rather than a wide view should be taken of what constitutes the 'means' used to achieve the legitimate aim.

3. The fact that a claim under the 'work rated as equivalent' provisions of EqPA 1970, s.1(2)(b) has already been decided does not prevent the same claimants bringing a further claim under the 'work of equal value' provisions of EqPA 1970, s.1(2)(c) as the two claims are sufficiently distinct to mean that the doctrine of *res judicata* does not apply.

FLEXIBLE WORKING

Page 149

The main text notes government proposals to increase the age limit of children in respect of whom parents (and guardians) have the right to request flexible working arrangements (under current law the age limit is 6 unless the child is disabled when it is 18).

In August 2008 the government issued a consultation paper proposing:

- to increase the child's age limit from age 6 to age 16;
- to remove the current obligation on an employer (often not observed) to give written notice to an employee of agreement to flexible working arrangements (the obligation to give written notice will *not* be removed if the employer has refused a flexible working request).

APPENDIX D

MATERNITY LEAVE

Pages 99–107

As noted in the main part of this book, draft Maternity and Parental Leave etc and the Paternity and Adoption Leave (Amendment) Regulations 2008 were issued on 27 June 2008. These came into force on 23 July as the Maternity and Parental Leave etc. and the Paternity and Adoption Leave (Amendment) Regulations 2008 SI 2008/1966 (MLPAL Regs 2008). They affect those whose expected week of childbirth (or adoption) begins on or after 5 October 2008.

The basic position is, as stated in the main text, that the right to non-pay contractual terms and conditions to which women have for many years been entitled during ordinary maternity leave now continues throughout additional maternity leave.

To be clear, the law does not use the expression 'non-pay contractual terms and conditions'. Rather it refers to 'terms and conditions about remuneration' not continuing during maternity leave and specifically states that 'only sums payable by way of wages or salary are to be treated as remuneration' (ERA 1996. s.71(5)(b) as applied by Maternity and Parental Leave etc Regs 1999, reg.9 as amended by MPLPAL Regs 2008, reg.4).

Generally it is obvious whether a contractual term or condition does or does not relate to pay – the official explanatory notes to MPLPAL Regs 2008 confirm the long standing suggestion that the matters covered 'are, for example: contractual annual leave above the statutory minimum, company cars, gym membership, and mobile telephones, among others'.

However, MPLPAL Regs 2008 appear to have introduced an element of uncertainty in connection with pension fund contributions. It seems that the legal liability of an employer to pay employer pension contributions in respect of a woman who is on maternity leave and who is a member of an occupational pension scheme may cease half way through her additional maternity leave.

The basic position is, as it has been for many years, that an employer must maintain any employer pension contributions for a woman on ordinary maternity leave at the same level as if she had been at work and receiving normal pay. This is provided for by Social Security Act 1989, Sched.5, para.5.

The complication introduced by MPLPAL Regs 2008 is that the extension to additional maternity leave of rights previously reserved to ordinary maternity leave is expressly stated not to impose 'a requirement which exceeds the requirements of' Social Security Act 1989, Sched.5, para.5 (new Maternity and Parental Leave etc Regs 1999, reg.9(4) inserted by MPLPAL Regs 2008, reg.4(1)(f)).

Assuming a woman is not entitled to contractual pay during maternity leave, the relevant requirement of Social Security Act 1989, Sched.5, para.5 is for the employer to pay employer pension contributions while he is paying SMP. But of course SMP is payable for only 39 weeks – so it seems there may

POSTSCRIPT: IMPORTANT DEVELOPMENTS

be a 13 week legal lacuna if a woman is taking the full 52 weeks maternity leave to which she is now entitled.

This is so even though employer pension fund contributions for women on maternity leave have for many years had to be made during periods of ordinary maternity leave and even though the general effect of the new rules is to remove the differences between ordinary and additional maternity leave. This potential problem will, of course, evaporate if and when the government implements its stated intention to extend the period for which SMP is payable from 39 to 52 weeks

As a separate, but related, matter it should be noted that in addition to the alignment of 'non-pay' rights during ordinary and additional maternity leave, the definition of 'remuneration' for the purpose noted above has been refined by the Sex Discrimination Act 1975 (Amendment) Regulations 2008, SI 2008/656, regs.1(3) and (5). The overall effect is to ensure that a woman remains entitled to remuneration to which she is entitled as a result of being pregnant or being on maternity leave (referred to as 'maternity related remuneration'). 'Maternity related remuneration' is defined to include any increases calculated by reference to increases the woman would have received had she not been on maternity leave and also any '. . . bonus in respect of times when a woman is on compulsory maternity leave'.

Thus a woman whose expected week of childbirth begins on or after 5 October 2008 is entitled to 'maternity related remuneration' even though, as noted above, she is not entitled to normal contractual pay during maternity leave.

Finally, on 3 October 2008 the European Commission published a draft directive proposing amendments to the EC Pregnant Workers Directive 92/85/EC. The main proposal is for compulsory paid maternity leave to be increased to 18 weeks, six of which will have to be after the birth and the other 12 weeks will be available either before or after the birth

MINIMUM WAGE AND TIPS

Pages 158–159

As noted in the main text, the position under current law is essentially that if tips are collected as part of the customer's bill and then paid out by the employer to staff they count as part of wages but if they are paid direct by a satisfied customer to, for example, a waitress they do not.

There have been two recent developments:
- The government has announced proposals to 'end the practice by which employers can use gratuities and service charges processed through the payroll to "top up" staff wages to meet the National Minimum Wage'. Changes to the law are expected in 2009.

APPENDIX D

- The EAT has moved the law slightly towards the government's proposed position. Under some older forms of the 'tronc' system for sharing tips between restaurant staff the total tips would be paid regularly by the employer to an independent troncmaster who would himself run a payroll, make the payments to the employees and deduct PAYE tax. The EAT has ruled that under that type of arrangement, the troncmaster holds the money in trust for tronc members. The tronc amounts are therefore not 'money payments made by the employer to the worker' under National Minimum Wage Regulations 1999, reg.30, and so are not remuneration counting towards the NMW (*HMRC* v. *(1) Annabels (Berkeley Square) Ltd (2) George (Mount Street) Ltd (3) Harry's Bar* [2008] ICR 1076, EAT).

REDUNDANCY PAY (ENHANCED)

Page 233 and 332

The main text points out that payments of enhanced redundancy pay can be exempted from the anti-age discrimination rules – this is subject to compliance with the conditions set out in the Employment Equality (Age) Regulations 2006, reg.33 unless of course the normal 'justification' defence can be used.

Essentially the conditions are that the enhanced amount must be calculated in the same way as statutory redundancy pay is calculated but with the following relaxations:

- there is no limit on the amount of a week's pay; and
- the amount may be increased (but not reduced) by applying a multiplier either to the amount of a week's pay used in the calculation or to the result of the calculation.

We are aware of three cases since 1 July 2008 which show that that enhanced redundancy pay schemes can easily be unlawful under the Age Discrimination regulations.

In the first a tribunal held an enhanced redundancy pay scheme did not comply with reg.33, was not objectively justified and amounted to unlawful age discrimination. Under the scheme employees would receive a payment of 3 weeks gross pay for each year's service under 40 years of age and 4 weeks gross pay for each year above it (*Galt and ors* v. *National Starch and Chemical Limited* (Case 2101804/07) (ET, unreported, 14 July 2008)).

In the second case (*MacCulloch* v. *Imperial Chemical Industries Plc* (EAT, unreported, 22 July 2008)) a tribunal found that discrimination was justified but on appeal the EAT remitted the case back for reconsideration. The EAT found that the original tribunal had identified legitimate aims which the quite complicated scheme was designed to achieve but 'there had been no proper attempt to determine whether the means adopted were proportionate to those aims, having regard to the significant detriment suffered by the claimant'.

The third case was brought by a Mr Loxley who had been excluded from a voluntary redundancy scheme because he had reached the age of 60. Mr Loxley claimed that the scheme discriminated against him on grounds of age discrimination. There were tapering provisions in place between the ages of 57–60. Again a tribunal found that discrimination was justified but again on appeal the EAT remitted the matter back for reconsideration (*Loxley* v. *BAE Systems Land Systems (Munitions & Ordnance) Ltd* (EAT, unreported, 28 July 2008)).

In the latter two cases the EAT set out some general guidelines to help determine whether the age discrimination in any particular scheme can be objectively justified as a proportionate means of achieving a legitimate aim. These can be distilled as meaning that the following matters can generally be taken into account in considering justification, although none will be determinative on its own:

- creating job opportunities for younger people;
- the amount of pension to which the employee will be entitled;
- whether a trade union approved the scheme;
- preventing a substantial cash windfall shortly before retirement;
- providing extra help for older workers because they may find it more difficult to get other jobs.

REMEDIES AND COMPENSATION

Page 383

A BERR dispute resolution consultation document issued in July 2008 invites comments on proposals:

- for interest on unpaid awards to be at a variable rate of 1.5 per cent or 2 per cent above Bank of England base rate rather than at a fixed rate (currently 8 per cent);
- for interest on all unpaid tribunal awards to accrue as from the date of the award unless paid within 14 days. This is already the position in discrimination cases but, under current rules, in other cases interest is payable only on awards which are unpaid for more than 42 days (i.e. from the end of the time limit for lodging an appeal).

APPENDIX D

TRADE UNIONS (RIGHT NOT TO BE DISCRIMINATED AGAINST BY A TRADE UNION)

Page 73

The Court of Appeal has reversed the EAT decision in *GMB* v. *Mrs Allen & ors* and restored the original tribunal's decision in favour of Mrs Allen and her colleagues. It is understood that the GMB is seeking leave to appeal to the House of Lords.

Importantly, the Court of Appeal found no fault with the basic proposition that the correct test for deciding whether the defence of justification can be relied on in an indirect discrimination case is whether the alleged discriminatory actions were a 'proportionate means of achieving a legitimate aim' (*Allen & ors* v. *GMB* [2008] EWCA Civ 810 on 16 July 2008, also reported at [2008] IRLR 690).

TRIBUNAL PROCEDURE

Page 405

A BERR dispute resolution consultation document issued in July 2008 invites comments on various detailed proposals for changes to the 2004 rules of procedure for employment tribunals. The most significant is a proposal to enable certain types of cases to be determined in writing, without a hearing.

The parties would have to agree to this streamlined procedure, the employment judge would have to consider it appropriate and the eligible jurisdictions would be exclusively unlawful deductions from wages, breach of contract, redundancy pay, holiday pay and national minimum wage.

Appeal to the EAT would be allowed in the ordinary way.

The same document suggests that it will not be long before there is implementation of proposals for employment judges to be able to sit on their own in more cases. The government said in 2007 that it was considering this in respect of five jurisdictions:

- unlawful deductions from wages claims;
- breach of contract claims;
- redundancy pay claims;
- national minimum wage claims; and
- holiday pay claims.

The July 2008 consultation document suggests that the last of these (holiday pay claims) will soon be added to the list of jurisdictions where an employment judge will normally sit on his own.

Index

Administrator
  appointment 185
Adoption leave 110–3
  alternative employment on redundancy and 246–7
  automatically unfair dismissals 220
  commencing 111–2
  enforcement 113
  pay and other contractual terms during 63, 111
  problems with adoption 112
  qualification 110
  right to return to work 112–3
  small employers 63
Adoption pay 111
  small employers 63
Advertisements *see* Job advertisements
Advisory, Conciliation and Arbitration Service (Acas) 4, 5–6
  Codes of Practice 14, 54
  compromise of claims and 423–4
Age discrimination 8, 324–34
  exemptions 331–2
  justification 328–9
  recruitment and job advertisements 332–3
  redundancy and 333–4
  retirement and 330–1
  selection for redundancy and 242
  unfair dismissal law 333–4
  vicarious liability 333
  who is protected 327–8
Agencies *see* Employment agencies
Agreements
  collective *see* Collective agreements
  compromise agreements 422–3
  dismissal procedures agreements 193
  termination of employment by mutual agreement 181–2
  workforce agreements for working time regulations 96
Agriculture
  Agricultural Wages Board 13
  gangmasters' code of practice 15
Alternative employment
  ill-health 206
  incompetence of employees 203
  redundancy 245–7
  trial period 247
Ante-natal care
  time off for 99
Appeals 420–1
  redundancy 249
  time limits 412–3
Apprentices 32, 156
Arbitration 4
Asbestos 128–9
Assertion of statutory rights 220–1
Associated companies 60
Automatically unfair dismissals 218–29, 232

Bank holidays 135–6
Building sites
  Sikhs employed at 297
Bullying at work 136–7
Bumping 248

Capabilities of employees 199
  ill-health 203–6
  incompetence 200–3
Care
  exercising reasonable care 45
Carers
  minimum wages and 156–7
Case management 415–6
Casual workers 29–30

INDEX

Categories of workers 20–34
  agency workers 26–9
  apprentices 32
  casual/homeworkers 29–30
  civil servants 31–2
  company directors 33–4
  contracts of employment 23–6
  future 34
  ministers of religion 30–1
  overseas workers 32
  partners 34
  police 32–3
  reasons for importance 20–3
  statutory definitions 21–2
  zero hour contracts 30
Central Arbitration Committee (CAC) 12
Check-off 76
Children 130
  time off for dependants 115–6, 228
Cigarette smoking at work 164–6
Civil partnership 275, 344
Civil servants 31–2
  time off 123
Claims
  appeals 412–3, 420–1
  case management 415–6
  compromise 421–5
  costs 418–9
  decision 417–8
  default judgments 415
  hearing 417–9
  prehearing review 416
  response form 414–5
  reviews 420
  starting claim 413–4
Closed shops 11
Codes of Practice 13–5, 54
Collective agreements
  sexual orientation discrimination and 342
  terms in contracts and 37–9
  working time regulations workforce agreements 96
Collective bargaining 11–2
  consultation 141
Collective labour law 66
  historical outline 10–2
Communications
  interception of 15
Companies
  directors 33–4, 137–8
  insolvency *see* Insolvency
  single European companies 222
  takeover *see* Transfer of undertakings
  winding up 185
Compensation 10
  disability discrimination claims 321–2
  equal pay and terms of employment claims 362
  infringement of right not to join trade union 72
  infringement of right to join trade union 70–1
  interest on awards 364, 403
  offset 16–7
  race/sex discrimination 10, 400–4
  religious discrimination 338
  unfair dismissal 10, 16–7, 387–400
  whistleblowing 168
  wrongful dismissal 10, 16–7, 370–1, 374–8
Competition
  after employment 47
  during employment 46–7
Compromise of claims 421–5
Conciliation 6
Conditional fee agreements 354
Conduct
  dismissal and 206–12
Confidentiality
  duty of 46
  informers 57–8
  trade secrets 48
Constructive dismissal 17–8, 174–6
  cumulative acts 179–80
  employee's resignation in response to breach 180–1
  employer's breach of contract 176–9
  repudiatory breach 179–80
Consultation 138–42
  automatically unfair dismissals for seeking to exercise rights 224
  collective bargaining 141
  dismissal 139
  European Works Councils 141, 229
  health and safety 127, 141
  pension schemes 140–1
  redundancy 61–2, 139–40, 236–41, 244–5
  regulations 141–2
  selection for redundancy 244–5
  small employers 61–2
  time off for 120–1
  transfer of undertakings 140, 254–7
  variation of contract terms 51
  Works Councils 61, 229

450

Contracts 35–6
  duties of fidelity 46–7
  employer's breach of contract 176–9
  equality in *see* Equal pay and terms of employment
  express terms 37–9
  frustration 182–3
  illegal 36, 194–6
  implied terms 10, 17–9, 39–40, 40–5
  mutuality of obligations 22–3
  repudiatory breach 179–80
  restrictive covenants 47–50
  test for employment status 23–6
  time limits for claims 411–2
  transfer of undertakings and 50
  variation of terms *see* Variation of contract terms
  zero hour contracts 30
Contributory fault 395–6
Convictions
  spent 227
Costs 418–9
  employment tribunals 3–4
Covenants
  restrictive 47–50
Criticising employees 177
Customers
  restrictive covenants and 48

Damages *see* Compensation
Data protection 15, 142–3
Death
  of employee 184
  of employer 184
Declarations 404
Deductions from wages 13, 143–5
  check-off for trade union membership dues 76
  wrongful deduction from wages claim 365–6
Default judgments 415
Department for Business, Enterprise & Regulatory Reform (BERR)
  Codes of Practice 14
  company insolvency/dissolution fund 186
Dependants
  time off for 115–6, 228
Diplomatic immunity 145–6
  unfair dismissal and 192–3
Direct discrimination 271, 278–85
  age and 326
  burden of proof 283–5

  justification 285
  less favourable treatment 279–83
  religion and 336
  selecting comparator 278–9
  sexual orientation and 342
Directors of companies 33–4, 137–8
Disability 303–9
  adjustments to premises 313–6
  discrimination *see* Disability discrimination
  impairment 304–6
  long term 308–9
  normal day-to-day activities 309
  rehabilitation leave 79
  substantial 306–8
Disability discrimination 8, 270, 301–3
  adjustments to premises 313–6
  comparators 317–9
  definition 310–1
  job advertisements 154, 322–3
  justification defence 316–7
  police 33
  protections 312–3
  remedies 321–2
  selection for redundancy and 243
  small employers 62
  time limits for claim 320
  trade unions 73
  vicarious liability 320–1
  victimisation 321
  who is protected 311–2
Disciplinary procedures 54, 56–8
  employer's non-compliance 394–5
  failure to follow 222
  meetings 57–8
  reasonable exercise of duties 42–3
  reasonableness of sanctions 216–8
  right to be accompanied 55–6
  trade unions 71–2
Discrimination 7–8
  see also individual types of discrimination
Dismissal
  ambiguous 172–3
  conduct 206–12
  constructive *see* Constructive dismissal
  consultation before 139
  contravention of statutory duty 212–3
  heat of the moment 172–3
  notice periods 1, 159–60
  other substantial reason 213–6
  procedures agreements 193

INDEX

reasonableness of disciplinary sanctions 216–8
relating to capabilities or qualifications 199–206
transfer of undertakings 258–9
unfair *see* Unfair dismissal
written statement of reasons 58–9
wrongful *see* Wrongful dismissal
Dispute resolution procedures 4–5, 7
Dress codes 280

Education 130
Elections
gender qualifications 296
Employees
bullying at work 136–7
capabilities 199, 200–6
categories *see* Categories of workers
competition after employment 47
competition during employment 46–7
consent to variation of contract terms 50–1
consultation *see* Consultation
criticising 177
death 184
exercising reasonable care 45
fixed-term 7, 182, 193–4, 223, 345–6
flexible working 9, 149–50, 223
freedom of movement 150–1
guarantee payments 152
inadequate support for 178
incompetence 200–3
lay off and short time working 154–5
obeying instructions 45
obligation to work 44–5, 79
part-time *see* Part-time workers
patents and inventions 162
problems during employment 54–5
see also Disciplinary procedures; Dismissal; Grievance procedures
qualifications 200
restrictive covenants 47–50
right not to work 163
right to work 163–4
smoking at work 164–6
staff handbooks 39
swearing at 177
termination payments 50
Employers' liability insurance 62, 148–9
Employment agencies 146–8
agency workers 7, 26–9
race/sex discrimination and 273–4

Employment Appeal Tribunal 412–3, 413–4, 420–1
Employment law
outline history 1–13
Employment Lawyers Association 9
Employment tribunals 2–6, 10, 371
addresses 426–32
appeals 412–3, 420–1
case management 415–6
costs 418–9
decision 417–8
default judgments 415
hearing 417–9
prehearing review 416
procedures 362–4, 413–21
response form 414–5
reviews 420
starting claim 413–4
Equal pay and terms of employment 270, 350–2, 367
basics of equal pay 354–5
comparators 355–6
compensation 362
defences 359–60
extended meaning of 'pay' 356–8
interest on awards 364
meaning of 'like work' 361
questionnaires 364–5
recent importance of Equal Pay Act 352–4
rules of procedure 362–4
time limits for claim 353, 361–2, 411
wrongful deduction from wages as alternative claim 365–6
Equality and Human Rights Commission
Codes of Practice 14
European Union (EU)
trade union rights and 73
workers' freedom of movement 150–1
working time regulation and 80, 81–2
European Works Councils 141, 229
Express terms in contracts 37–9

Family friendly policies 6, 9
Feelings
injury to 389–90, 401–2
Fidelity duties 46–7
competition during employment 46–7
confidential information 46
Fire regulations
small employers 62
Fishermen 123
profit sharing 197

INDEX

Fixed-term employees 7, 182, 193–4, 223, 345–6
Flexible working 9, 149–50, 223
Freedom of movement 150–1
Frustration 182–3

Gender reassignment (transsexuality)
  sex discrimination and 274
Golden handshakes 50
Grievance procedures 4, 54
  reasonable exercise of duties 42–3
Guarantee payments 152

Handbooks *see* Staff handbooks
Harassment
  age discrimination and 326
  racial 291–2
  religious discrimination 336–7
  sexual 291
Health and safety 124
  asbestos 128–9
  automatically unfair dismissals 223–4
  children and young persons 130–2
  common law duties 124–5
  consultation 127, 141
  policies 126
  pregnancy 106–7, 132
  providing safe working environment 43–4
  reporting obligations 127–8
  representatives 127
  risk assessments 126–7
  small employers 62
  statutory duties 125–8
  stress 132–4
  time off for health and safety activities 116
Health and Safety Commission
  Codes of Practice 14–5
Health and Safety Executive 124
Hearings 417–9
History of employment law
  collective labour law 10–2
  individual employment rights 1–10
  wage regulation 12–3
HM Revenue and Customs (HMRC)
  codes of practice 15
Holiday rights 85–92
  bank and public holidays 135–6
  calculation problems 87–8
  holiday pay 89–91
  'rolled–up' holiday pay 91–2
  time limits for claims 92
  when holiday can be taken 89
Homeworkers 29–30, 157
Homosexuality *see* Sexual orientation discrimination
House sitters 157
Human rights
  trade unions and 67

Illegal contracts 36, 194–6
Illness *see* Sickness
Immigration control 36
Implied terms in contracts 10, 17–9, 39–40, 40–5
  disciplinary and grievance procedures 42–3
  exercising reasonable care 45
  obeying instructions 45
  obligation to work 44–5, 79
  paying wages 44
  providing safe working environment 43–4
  providing work 44–5
  references 43
  trust and confidence 17, 18–9, 40–2, 176
Incompetence of employees 200–3
  alternative employment 203
  opportunities to improve 202–3
  warnings 201–2
Independent Police Complaints Commission 33
Indirect discrimination
  age and 326
  'considerably smaller portion of one group' 287–8
  justification 289–90, 293
  nature of statutory provisions 286–7
  persons at particular disadvantage 288–9
  race discrimination 271, 285–90
  religion and 336
  sex discrimination 271, 285–90, 367
  sexual orientation and 342
Individual employment rights
  historical outline 1–10
Industrial action *see* Strikes
Industrial Cases Reports 9
Industrial Law Society 9
Industrial Relations Law Reports 9
Industrial training levies
  small employers 62–3

453

INDEX

Industrial tribunals 2–3, 6
  see also Employment tribunals
Informers 167–8
  confidentiality 57–8
Injunctions
  wrongful dismissal and 373–4
Injury to feelings
  remedies and 389–90, 401–2
Insolvency 185–6
  guarantees 152–3
  transfer of undertakings and 266–7
Institute of Occupational Safety and Health 124
Insurance
  wrongful dismissal compensation and 375
  see also Employers' liability insurance
Interception of communications 15
Interest on awards 364, 403
Interim relief
  unfair dismissal 397–8
International organisations
  unfair dismissal and 192–3
Inventions
  employees and 162

Job advertisements
  age discrimination 332–3
  disability discrimination 154, 322–3
  race/sex discrimination 153–4
Job location 177
Job share
  right to return after maternity leave 105
Judgments 417–8
  default 415
Jury service
  dismissals for carrying out 224
  time off for 121–2
Justification defence
  age discrimination 328–9
  disability discrimination 316–7
  race/sex discrimination 285, 289–90, 293

Keeping in Touch (KIT) days 103–4

Labour Party
  funding by trade unions 12
'Last in first out'
  selection for redundancy and 242–3
Lay off 154–5
Legal aid 354

Limitation periods
  holiday rights claims 92
Local government
  codes of practice 15
  equal pay claims and 353–4

Marital status
  discrimination and 275
  sexual orientation discrimination and 343–4
Maternity leave 99–106
  alternative employment on redundancy and 246–7
  automatically unfair dismissals 225
  commencement and duration 103
  enforcement 105–6
  KIT days 103–4
  other contractual terms during 102–3
  pay during 63, 101–2
  right to 99–101
  right to return to work 103–5
  small employers 63
  unfair dismissal and temporary replacements for women on leave 197–8
Maternity pay 101–2
Matrix method
  selection for redundancy 243–4
Mediation 6
Meetings
  disciplinary procedures 57–8
Merchant seamen 122
Military personnel
  time off 122, 123
  unfair dismissal exceptions 192
Minimum wages 7, 13, 155–9
  automatically unfair dismissals 225
  young workers 156
Ministers of religion 30–1
  race/sex qualification 296
Misconduct
  dismissal and 206–12
Mitigation of loss
  wrongful dismissal claims 379–82
Modern apprentices 32, 156
Mutuality of obligations 22–3

National Insurance
  company insolvency/dissolution fund 186
National insurance
  small employers and 63–4

454

Nationality
  discrimination and 8, 276
Night work 95–6
Notice periods
  dismissal 1, 159–60
  pay in lieu of notice 380

Obligations
  mutuality of 22–3
  obligation to work 44–5, 79
Offset of compensation 16–7
On call workers
  minimum wages and 156–7
Overseas workers 32, 122, 160–1
  unfair dismissal exception 198–9
Overtime 177

Parental leave 113–5
  automatically unfair dismissals 225–6
  default provisions 114
  enforcement 115
  qualification 114
  right to 113–4
  right to return to work 114–5
Partnerships 34
  death of partner 184
  race discrimination in small partnerships 64
Part-time workers 8
  automatically unfair dismissals 226
  discrimination and 288, 300, 346–9
  right to return after maternity leave 105
Patents
  employees and 162
Paternity leave 107–10
  automatically unfair dismissals 226
  commencing and duration 108
  enforcement 109–10
  pay and other contractual terms during 63, 108–9
  right to 107–8
  right to return to work 109
Paternity pay 108–9
  small employers 63
Pay *see* Wages
PAYE
  small employers 63–4
Pensions
  age discrimination and 327
  automatically unfair dismissals of trustees 226

  consultation 140–1
  equal pay and equal treatment and 357, 358
  small employers 64
  time off for pension fund trustees 119–20
  transfer of undertakings and 265–6
Perks
  equal pay and equal treatment and 357
Personal injury 10
  compensation awards 403
Piece workers
  minimum wages and 157–8
Police 32–3
  race/sex discrimination 297
  strikes 69
  time off 123
  unfair dismissal exception 196–7
Political fund contributions 72
Positive discrimination 298, 344
Pregnancy
  ante-natal care 99
  automatically unfair dismissals 225
  health and safety issues 106–7, 132
  less favourable treatment 280–3
  maternity pay 63
  suspension from work on maternity grounds 106–7
  see also Maternity leave; Paternity leave
Prehearing review 416
Prison officers
  race/sex discrimination 297
  unfair dismissal exception 196–7
Private households
  race/sex qualification in employment 295, 297
Problems during employment 54–5
  see also Disciplinary procedures; Dismissal; Grievance procedures
Profits
  profit sharing fishermen 197
  secret 47
Public duties
  time off for 119
Public holidays 135–6
Public sector
  civil servants 31–2, 123
  employment code of practice 15
  police 32–3
  transfer of undertakings and 267–9

INDEX

Qualifications of employees 200
Questionnaires
  age discrimination 327
  equal pay and terms of employment 364–5
  race/sex discrimination 292–3
  sexual orientation discrimination 342

Race discrimination 8, 270–2
  compensation 10
  defences and exemptions 285, 289–90, 293–7, 300
  direct discrimination 271, 278–85
  genuine occupational qualification defence 293, 294, 295
  harassment 291–2
  indirect discrimination 271, 285–90
  job advertisements 154
  particular types of employment exemption 296–7
  police 33
  positive discrimination 298
  qualifications for bringing claim 273–7
  questionnaires 292–3
  remedies 400–4
  selection for redundancy and 243
  small partnerships 64
  time limits 409–11
  trade unions 73
  vicarious liability 298–300
  victimisation 272–3
  who is protected 276–7
Receiver
  appointment 185
Recommendations 404
Redundancy 212, 230
  age discrimination and 333–4
  appeals 249
  bumping 248
  candidates for 241
  challenging fairness 233–4
  consultation 61–2, 139–40, 236–41, 244–5
  qualifying for statutory redundancy payment 233
  selection for 38, 226–7, 234–6, 241–5
  statutory pay 1–2
  suitable alternative employment 245–7
  time limits for claims 411
  time off for redundant workers seeking new work 121, 249
  unfair dismissal and 234, 396
  when an employee is redundant 230–2
  who argues redundancy 232
References 43
Reinstatement remedy 383–7
  continuity of employment and 386–7
  employer's non-compliance 385–6
  terms of order 384–5
  when it will be ordered 384
Religion
  ministers 30–1, 296
Religious discrimination 9, 153, 277, 334–40
  direct/indirect 336
  examples 338–9
  exceptions 337–8
  harassment 336–7
  potential conflict with other legislation 339–40
  remedies 338
  vicarious liability 337
  victimisation 336–7
Remedies
  disability discrimination 321–2
  equal pay and terms of employment claims 362
  race/sex discrimination 400–4
  reinstatement/re-engagement 383–7
  religious discrimination 338
  unfair dismissal 383–400
  wrongful dismissal 10, 16–7, 370–1, 373–8
  see also Compensation
Representatives
  accompanying to meetings 55–6, 121
  automatically unfair dismissals 221–2, 228
  health and safety 127
  time off 121
  trade disputes and 55–6
Reserve services
  time off for 122
Resident workers
  minimum wages and 157
Resignation 172
  ambiguous 173
  heat of the moment 173
  pressured 173–4
  ultimatums to resign 173–4
  see also Constructive dismissal
Rest breaks 92–4
Restrictive covenants 47–50
  extent 49

456

protection of legitimate business interests 48
specific consideration 50
standard form clauses 50
Retirement 212
age discrimination and 330–1
Reviews 420
Risk assessments
health and safety 126–7

Safety *see* Health and safety
Secret profits 47
Selection for redundancy 38, 241–5
consultation 244–5
improper 226–7, 234–6
'last in first out' 242–3
matrix method 243–4
pool of candidates 241
Self-employment
minimum wages and 158
test for employment status 24–6
Severance pay
equal pay and equal treatment and 357
Sex change (transsexuality)
sex discrimination and 274
Sex discrimination 7–8, 270–2
compensation 10
defences and exemptions 285, 289–90, 293–7, 300
direct discrimination 271, 278–85
genuine occupational qualification defence 293, 294, 295–6
harassment 291
indirect discrimination 271, 285–90, 367
job advertisements 154
particular types of employment exemption 296–7
part-time workers 288, 300
police 33
positive discrimination 298
pregnancy and 280–3
qualifications for bringing claim 273–7
questionnaires 292–3
remedies 400–4
selection for redundancy and 243
time limits 409–11
trade unions 73
vicarious liability 298–300
victimisation 272–3
who is protected 274–5
see also Equal pay and terms of employment

Sexual orientation discrimination 8, 153, 275, 276, 340–5
collective agreements 342
direct/indirect 342
examples 344–5
exemptions 343
positive discrimination 344
questionnaires 342
religious discrimination and 339–40
trade unions and 342
who is protected 342
Shop workers
Sunday trading 166–7
Short time working 154–5
Sickness
capabilities and 203–6
sick pay 98–9
time off 98–9
Single European companies 222
Small employers 60–1
consultation with employees 61–2
disability discrimination 62
employers' liability insurance 62
health and safety 62
industrial training levies 62–3
maternity and adoption leave 63
maternity/adoption/paternity pay 63
national insurance and 63–4
PAYE 63–4
race discrimination in small partnerships 64
stakeholder pensions 64
trade union recognition 64
written particulars of employment 65
Smoking at work 164–6
Spent convictions 227
Sports 297
Staff handbooks
terms in contracts and 39
Stakeholder pensions
small employers 64
Standard clauses
restrictive covenants 50
Statutes
assertion of statutory rights 220–1
definitions of workers 21–2
dismissal for contravention of statutory duty 212–3
legislative changes in progress 433–5, 436–8
purposive construction 10
statutory terms in contracts 36–7
Stress 132–4

INDEX

Strikes 68–9
  automatically unfair dismissals 224
  dismissal during 75
  unfair dismissal and 197
Study
  time off for 120
Suitable alternative employment *see* Alternative employment
Sunday trading 166–7
  automatic unfair dismissal for refusal to work on Sunday 227
Suppliers
  restrictive covenants and 48
Support
  inadequate 178
Suspension from work
  maternity grounds 106–7
  medical grounds 118
Swearing at employees 177

Takeovers *see* Transfer of undertakings
Taxation
  evasion 194–6
  PAYE and small employers 63–4
  tax credits 227
  wrongful dismissal compensation and 376
Termination of employment 171
  death 184
  frustration of contract 182–3
  insolvency/dissolution of company 185–6
  mutual agreement 181–2
  payments 50
  see also Dismissal; Redundancy; Resignation; Retirement
Terms of employment
  written particulars *see* Written particulars of employment
Test for employment status 23–6
Time limits 405–7
  appeals to EAT 412–3
  contractual claims 411–2
  discrimination claims 320, 327, 409–11
  equal pay and terms of employment claims 411
  equal pay claims 353, 361–2
  statutory redundancy claims 411
  unfair dismissal claims 407–9
  wrongful dismissal claims 378–9
Time off 98
  accompanying workers to disciplinary/grievance hearings 121

  ante-natal care 99
  for dependants 115–6, 228
  health and safety activities 116
  information and consultation 120–1
  jury service 121–2
  pension fund trustees 119–20
  public duties 119
  redundant workers seeking new work 121, 249
  rehabilitation leave 79
  reserve services 122
  sickness 98–9
  specific categories of employment 123–4
  study 120
  toilet breaks 122–3
  training 79, 120
  union duties 76, 116–8
  see also Holiday rights; Suspension from work
Tips 158–9
Tobacco smoking at work 164–6
Toilet breaks 122–3
Tort law
  trade union immunities 10–1
Trade disputes
  representation of employees 55–6
  trade union immunities 10–1
  unjustifiable discipline 71–2
  see also Strikes
Trade secrets 48
Trade unions 6, 7, 8, 66–9
  accounts 77
  check-off 76
  closed shops 11
  collective agreements 37–9
  collective bargaining 11–2
  consultation *see* Consultation
  detriment for union-related reason 73–4, 77–8
  discrimination by 72–3
  dismissal for union-related reason 74–6, 228–9
  equal pay claims 353–4, 367
  immunities 10–1, 68, 77
  Labour Party funding 12
  political fund contributions 72
  recognition 11–2, 64–5, 69, 78
  register of members 76
  right not to join 71
  rules 77
  sexual orientation discrimination and 342

small employers 64–5
time off for duties 76, 116–8
Training
  industrial training levies 62–3
  minimum wages and 156
  time off for 79, 120
Transfer of undertakings 8, 15, 50, 250–2
  automatically unfair dismissals 221
  changes to terms of employment 53, 178–9, 257–8
  compensation for failure to consult 399–400
  consultation 140
  continuity of employment 253
  coverage of regulations 259–63
  differences between 1981 and 2006 regulations 252–3
  dismissal connected with 258–9
  information and consultation 254–7
  insolvent companies 266–7
  opting out not allowed 265
  pensions and 265–6
  public sector 267–9
  rights and obligations transferred 263–4
  who can benefit 264
Transsexuality
  sex discrimination and 274
Trial periods
  alternative employment 247
Tribunals *see* Employment tribunals; Industrial tribunals
Trust and confidence
  breach 176
  implied terms in contracts 17, 18–9, 40–2
Trustees
  automatically unfair dismissals 226
  time off for 119–20

Unfair dismissal 2, 5, 6, 15–6, 187
  age discrimination and 333–4
  automatically unfair dismissals 218–29, 232
  compensation 10, 16–7, 374–8
  employment status qualification 187–8
  exceptions 190–9
  legal process 17
  reasonableness of disciplinary sanctions 216–8
  redundancy and 234
  remedies 383–400
  small employers and 60–1

time limits 407–9
for union-related reason 74–6, 228–9

Variation of contract terms 50–3
  consent of employee 50–1
  consultation 51
  following TUPE transfer 53, 178–9, 257–8
  if agreement cannot be obtained 52
  obtaining agreement 51–2
  written statement of changes 52
Vicarious liability
  age discrimination 333
  disability discrimination 320–1
  race/sex discrimination 298–300
  religious discrimination 337
Victimisation
  age discrimination and 326
  disability discrimination 321
  race/sex discrimination 272–3
  religious discrimination 336–7

Wages
  adoption pay 63, 111
  deductions *see* Deductions from wages
  employer's breach of contract 176
  guarantee payments 152
  itemised pay statements 153
  in lieu of notice 380
  loss of earnings awards 402–3
  maternity pay 63, 101–2
  minimum *see* Minimum wages
  paternity pay 63, 108–9
  payment of 44
  refusing to offer pay rise 177–8
  regulation of 12–3
  see also Equal pay and terms of employment
Wages Councils 13
Warnings
  incompetence 201–2
Whistleblowing 8, 57–8, 167–8, 229
  police 33
Winding up 185
Work
  changing patterns of 8–10
  employee's obligation to work 44–5, 79
  flexible working 9, 149–50, 223
  lay off and short time working 154–5
  providing 44–5
  rest breaks 92–4

INDEX

right not to work 163
right to work 163–4
smoking at work 164–6
time *see* Working time regulations
time off *see* Time off
Workers *see* Employees
Workforce agreements
  working time regulations 96
Working time regulations 79, 80–5
  automatically unfair dismissal and 229
  calculation of number of hours 82
  enforcement 97–8
  EU and 80, 81–2
  exclusion and special provisions 83–5
  holiday rights 85–92
  keeping records 83
  night work 95–6
  opting out 85
  what time counts 82–3
  workforce agreements 96
  young workers 92, 94–5, 130, 131–2
Works Councils 61, 229
  European 141, 229

Written particulars of employment 1, 168–70
  small employers 65
Written statement of changes in contract terms 52
Written statement of reasons for dismissal 58–9
Wrongful dismissal 15–6, 368–73
  compensation 10, 16–7, 370–1, 374–8
  legal process 17
  mitigation of loss 379–82
  remedies 10, 16–7, 370–1, 373–8
  time limits 378–9

Young workers
  health and safety issues 130–2
  minimum wages 156
  working time regulations 92, 94–5, 130, 131–2

Zero hour contracts 30